Economics U$A

SIXTH EDITION

ECONOMICS U$A

SIXTH EDITION

EDWIN MANSFIELD

UNIVERSITY OF PENNSYLVANIA

NARIMAN BEHRAVESH

STANDARD & POOR'S

W. W. NORTON AND COMPANY

NEW YORK • LONDON

Copyright © 2001, 1998, 1995, 1992, 1989, 1986 by W. W. Norton & Company, Inc.

The text of this book is composed in Zapf Book
with the display set in Gill Sans
Composition by UG / GGS Information Services, Inc.
Manufacturing by Quebecor-World
Book design by Joan Greenfield

Library of Congress Cataloging-in-Publication Data

Mansfield, Edwin.
    Economics U$A / Edwin Mansfield, Nariman Behravish.—6th ed.
      p. cm
    Includes bibliographical references and index.
    ISBN 0-393-97621-1 (pbk.)
      1. Economics.   2. United States—Economic conditions—1945-   I. Title: Economics
USA.   II. Behravish, Nariman.   III. Title.

  HB171 .M325 2001
  330—dc21

                                                                              00-046059

W. W. Norton & Company, Inc., 500 Fifth Avenue, New York, N.Y. 10110
www.wwnorton.com

W. W. Norton & Company Ltd., 10 Coptic Street, London WC1A 1PU

1 2 3 4 5 6 7 8 9 0

Contents in Brief

Contents

PART 3   MONEY, BANKING, AND STABILIZATION POLICY

PART 4   **ECONOMIC DECISION MAKING: THE FIRM, THE
                CONSUMER, AND SOCIETY**

PART 6   GROWTH, GOVERNMENT, AND INTERNATIONAL ECONOMICS

Preface

This book has been prepared to accompany the telecourse *Economics U$A*, which was developed under a grant from the Annenberg/CPB Pr0oject. The telecourse is designed to use economic events in America, present and past, to help teach the principles of economics. The elements of this telecourse include: a 28-part television series, this textbook, a telecourse study guide, a text review guide, a 28-part audio series, a faculty manual, and a test bank. The aim of this integrated approach to teaching introductory economics is to use actual economic events to motivate study of the principles of economics, and to show how these principles can help us understand the complex and dynamic American economy.

New with this Sixth Edition of the textbook, a set of on-line applications have been provided to augment the video programs with up-to-date material. These are posted on the publisher's Internet site for this textbook [www.wwnorton.com/college/econ/econusa]. Also available is the WebCT Edition, for conducting Internet-supported distance courses. The WebCT *Economics U$A* course template provides an electronic edition of the Telecourse Study Guide, one that may be customized to meet the specific needs of your course.

This text is an adaptation of Edwin Mansfield's *Economics: Principles, Problems, Decisions*. The chapters in the text follow the same sequence as the television programs, and there is much overlap in content between text and video. All chapters include case studies that focus on economic events covered in the corresponding television programs. The telecourse also includes a set of audio programs, intended especially for two-semester principles courses, that helps students review major points and explore subjects further through additional interviews. *Economics U$A* integrates text, video, and audio to an unprecedented degree in introductory economics.

Among the new features contained in this Sixth Edition are the following case studies: (1) Comparing the U.S. Savings and Loan Crisis and the Japanese Banking Crisis, (2) How Widespread Was the Productivity Boom of the Late 1990s? (3) What to Do with the Federal Budget Surplus? (4) How Much Attention Should the Fed Pay to the Stock Market? (5) Network Effects and the Case against Microsoft, (6) The Kyoto Summit, Emissions Targets, and Tradable Permits, (7) The Story of an Internet Start-Up, (8) Is Welfare Reform Working?

(9) The Euro: Europe's New Currency. In addition, the book includes six cross-chapter cases: (1) The Key Role of Saving and Investment in Raising Per Capita Income, (2) The Treasury Launches a New Type of Security, (3) Is the U.S. Business Cycle Dead? (4) What Should Be Done About Global Warming? (5) The Biggest Investment You'll Probably Ever Make, (6) Globalization: Should We Fear It or Embrace It? Further, all of the tables and figures as well as the discussion of events and relationships have been updated.

As an aid to students enrolled in the telecourse, the Southern California Consortium and James Sondgeroth of Austin Community College have prepared a Telecourse Study Guide, which includes learning objectives, key terms, overviews of text and video, questions and problems (with answers), and "Extended Learning" sections for the two-semester course. The Telecourse Study Guide will help students bridge the material in the text, the video, and the audio programs.

This book can be used as the text in a telecourse based on the entire *Economics U$A* television series, and can stand on its own as the text in a traditional lecture course. (If they like, teachers of such courses can supplement their lectures with individual television programs from the series.) The text is suitable for the one-semester survey of economics or, with the supplementary "Exploring Further" sections at the ends of chapters, for the two-semester principles course.

In courses where this book is used on its own, many students will want to use the accompanying *Text Review Guide,* revised by Deborah Paige. Each chapter of the *Text Review Guide* contains many completion questions, true-false questions, multiple-choice questions, discussion questions, and problem sets. These batteries of questions can be used by students for review, as well as for classroom discussion. All of these questions have withstood the test of widespread classroom use.

While it is difficult in many jointly authored works to assign responsibility, in this case it is relatively easy. For the first five editions Nariman Behravesh reorganized and edited the material in Mansfield's *Economics* to make it parallel the telecourse; in addition, he prepared and revised many of the case studies that appear in the book, as well as the glossary of terms. Edwin Mansfield was responsible for the text itself (other than Behravesh's case studies and glossary); also, he performed a detailed edit of the final version of the manuscript. With the untimely death of Professor Mansfield in 1998, Behravesh took over responsibility for all the updates of the sixth edition.

We are grateful to the following teachers, who commented in detail on a preliminary version of the manuscript: Robert C. Augur, Pasadena City College; Carlos Aguilar, El Paso Community College; James E. Clark, Wichita State University; Curtis Clarke, Eastfield College; Peter Dorman, University of Massachusetts; Dorsey Dyer, Davidson County Community College; Clinton Greene, College of St. Benedict; Paul Grimes, Mississippi State University; Dan Harrison, Murray State University; Bruce Herrick, Washington and Lee University; Ralph F. Lewis, Economics Research, Inc.; James Phillips, Cypress College; Victor H. Rieck, Miami-Dade Community College; David L. Schwartz, Albright College; Steve Smith, Rose State College; John Somers, Portland Community College; and Michael Vaughan, Weber State College. In addition we would like to thank Ed Parsons, Ann Marcy, Carol Loomis and Kate Barry of Norton for their efficient handling of the publishing end of the work.

Lexington, MA   N.B.

PART ONE

Introduction to Economics

Economic Problems:
A Sampler

George Bernard Shaw, the great playwright, once said, "The only time my education was interrupted was when I was in school." Fortunately, economics, if properly presented, can contribute mightily to your education—and you can learn it without leaving school. To help you understand the pervasive importance of economics, we begin by looking at a sample of the major problems economists deal with. Each of these problems could have a big effect on your life.

LABOR PRODUCTIVITY AND RISING LIVING STANDARDS

The history of the U.S. economy is for the most part a story of growth. Our output—the amount of goods and services we produce annually—has grown rapidly over the years, giving us a standard of living that could not have been imagined a century ago. For example, the output per person in the United States was about $33,000 in 1999; in 1900 it was much, much smaller. The rise in our standard of living is closely correlated with how productive we are.

Labor productivity is defined as the amount of output that can be obtained per hour of labor. All countries are interested in increasing labor productivity, since it is intimately related to a country's standard of living. Many factors, including new technologies like the Internet and biotechnology, influence the rate of increase of labor productivity. Historically, labor productivity has increased relatively rapidly in the United States.

However, beginning in the late 1960s, U.S. labor productivity rose at a slower pace. At first, it was unclear whether this slowdown was only temporary, but during the 1970s the situation got worse, not better. Between 1977 and 1980, labor productivity in the United States actually declined. (In other words, less was produced per hour of labor in 1980 than in 1977!) During the 1980s and early 1990s, productivity growth picked up, but was still below what it was in the 1960s.

In the 1970s, 1980s, and early 1990s many observers worried about the poor productivity performance of the United States rela-

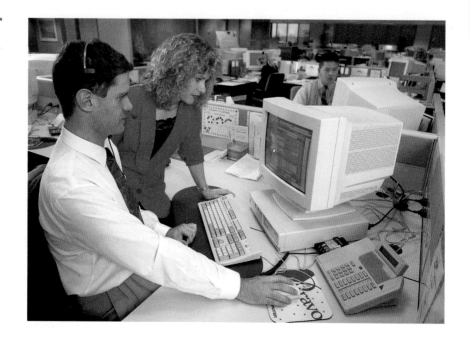

Information technologies like desktop computers have helped fuel recent increases in labor productivity.

tive to other industrialized countries, especially Japan and Germany. There was much talk of a "competitiveness problem" in the United States. However, by the late 1990s productivity growth was strong again, thanks, in part, to large investments in information technologies earlier in the decade and the explosive growth of the Internet.

Our first example of an economic problem is: *What determines the rate of increase of labor productivity? Why did productivity growth slow down in the 1970s and 1980s? Why did it accelerate in the 1990s? What can be done to sustain high growth rates of productivity?* Economics provides a considerable amount of information on this score. Not only does economics tell us a good deal about the broad factors influencing national productivity levels; it also provides rules and principles that are useful in increasing the productivity and efficiency of individual firms (and government agencies).

UNEMPLOYMENT AND INFLATION

Unfortunately, the growth of output in the United States has not been steady or uninterrupted; instead, our output has tended to fluctuate—and so has unemployment. In periods when output has fallen, thousands, even millions, of people have been thrown out of work. In the Great Depression of the 1930s, for example, over 20 percent of the labor force was unemployed (see Figure 1).

FIGURE I

Unemployment Rates, United States, 1929–99

The unemployment rate has varied substantially from year to year. In the Great Depression, it reached a high of over 24 percent. In late 1999, it was 4.1 percent.

Our second example of an economic problem is: *What determines the extent of* **unemployment** *in the U.S. economy, and what can be done to reduce it?* This problem is complicated by a related phenomenon: the level of prices may rise when we reduce the level of unemployment. In other words, inflation may occur. Thus the problem is not only to curb unemployment but to do it without producing an inflation so ruinous to the nation's economic health that the cure proves more dangerous than the ailment. Consequently, another major accompanying question is: *What determines the rate of* **inflation,** *and how can it be kept under control?* As Figure 2 shows (p. 6), we have experienced considerable inflation since 1929; the dollar has lost over four-fifths of its purchasing power during the past 70 years. Moreover, in the 1970s and early 1980s, our economy was bedeviled by "stagflation"—a combination of high unemployment and high inflation.

During the past 50 years, economists have learned a great deal about the factors that determine the extent of unemployment and inflation. As a responsible citizen, you should understand what

Unemployed laborers rally for jobs.

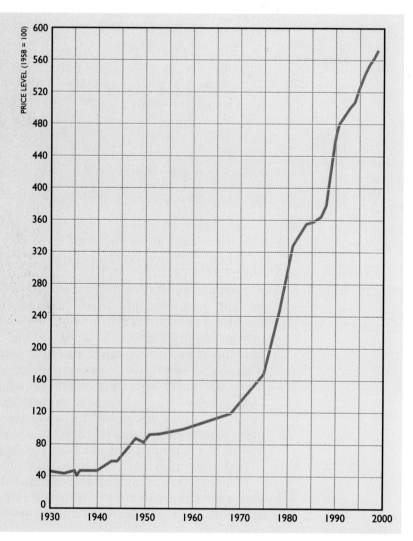

FIGURE 2

Changes in Price Level, United States, 1929–99

The price level has increased steadily since the 1930s, and is now almost six times as high as it was in 1950.

has been learned. You should also be aware of the differences of opinion among leading economists on this score. To understand many of the central political issues of the day and to vote intelligently, this knowledge is essential. Also, to understand the fallacies in many apparently simple remedies for the complex economic problems in this area, you need to know some economics.

CHALLENGES FACING EMERGING MARKET ECONOMIES

In 1900, income per capita in the United States was about 10 times greater than that of the poorest country, after adjusting for differences in purchasing power. By 1999 that gap had widened so that

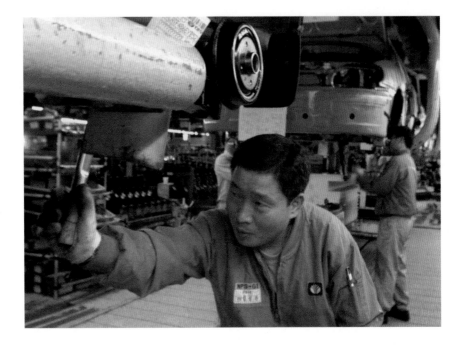

**Korean worker on
Daewoo assembly
line**

the typical American earned almost 50 times as much as the typical Ethiopian. Nevertheless, some emerging market economies, notably those in East Asia, have made significant strides in closing the gap in recent years. In 1999 South Korea's and Taiwan's per capita income levels were, respectively, 46 and 58 percent of the U.S. level. Other emerging markets, such as Chile and Mexico, have also succeeded in closing the gap in the 1980s and 1990s.

Unfortunately, even for those countries which have been successful in engineering rapid improvements in living standards, the path has been a very bumpy one. Latin America suffered through a debt crisis in the early 1980s. In 1994 and 1995 Mexico suffered through its worst recession in 50 years, triggered by a currency crisis. In 1997 and 1998 many of the East Asian economies, Russia, and Brazil were dragged down by the emerging markets crisis.

Our third example of an economic problem is: *Why do some countries grow much faster than others? Why has the growth rate in emerging markets in recent years been so volatile? What can be done to improve living standards worldwide?*

In recent years economic research has highlighted the value of high levels of educational attainment and national savings (to fund investments in productivity capacity) as key determinants of growth. Just as crucial are free trade and unencumbered access to global capital. The recent emerging market crises have also underlined the importance of stable macroeconomic policies, well-regulated banking systems, and the rule of law, especially the enforcement of property rights.

7

THE ELIMINATION OF POVERTY

As pointed out by Philip Wicksteed, a prominent twentieth-century British economist, "A man can be neither a saint, nor a lover, nor a poet, unless he has comparatively recently had something to eat." Although relatively few people in the United States lack food desperately, about 35 million—approximately 13 percent of the population—live in what is officially designated as **poverty**. These people have frequently been called invisible in a nation where the average yearly income per family is about $45,000; but the poor are invisible only to those who shut their eyes, since they exist in ghettos in the wealthiest U.S. cities like New York, Chicago, and Los Angeles, as well as near Main Street in thousands of small towns. They can also be found in areas where industry has come and gone, as in the former coal-mining towns of Pennsylvania and West Virginia and in areas where decades of farming have depleted the soil.

Table I shows the distribution of income in the United States in 1997. Clearly, income levels differ very substantially among families. Indeed, the cats and dogs of the very rich eat better than some human beings. You as a citizen and a human being need to understand the social mechanisms underlying the distribution of income, both in the United States and in other countries, and to judge how reasonable and just they are.

Our fourth example of an economic problem is: *Why does poverty exist in the world today, and what can be done to abolish it?* To help the poor effectively, we must understand the causes of poverty.

TABLE I Percentage Distribution of Households, by Annual Money Income, United States, 1997	MONEY INCOME (DOLLARS)	PERCENT OF ALL HOUSEHOLDS
	Under 5,000	4
	5,000– 9,999	8
	10,000–14,999	8
	15,000–24,999	15
	25,000–34,999	14
	35,000–49,999	17
	50,000–74,999	18
	75,000–99,999	9
	100,000 and over	8
	Total	100

Source: U.S. Bureau of the Census. Because of rounding errors, percentages do not sum to 100.

LOOKING AHEAD

Despite the problems described here, the U.S. economy is among the most prosperous in the world. The average U.S. family has plenty of food, clothing, housing, appliances, and luxuries of many kinds, and the average U.S. worker is well educated and well trained. The tremendous strength and vitality of the U.S. economy should be recognized, as well as its shortcomings. Nothing is gained by overlooking either the successes or the faults of our system.

As a first step toward understanding why we are so well-off in some respects and so lacking in others, we need to understand how our economy works. Of course, this is a big task. Indeed, you could say that this whole book is devoted to discussing the subject. So we will not try to present a detailed picture of the operation of the U.S. economy at this point. Instead, in the following chapters we will give a basic blueprint of what an economic system must do.

CHAPTER I

What Is Economics?

LEARNING OBJECTIVES

In this chapter, you should learn:

- The definition of economics, including the concepts of resources, scarcity, and choice
- The four basic tasks that must be accomplished by any economic system
- The concept of opportunity cost
- *(Exploring Further)* What a production possibilities curve shows and why the curve is important

There has been a political battle for years over the extent to which our natural resources should be commercially exploited. Why did Congress in 1980 ban the exploitation of over 100 million acres of Alaskan wilderness? One purpose of this chapter is to answer this question.

More broadly, we must now provide a definition of economics, as well as a description of the basic questions regarding any economic system that are of particular interest to economists. Furthermore, we need to understand the basic methodology of economics.

WHAT IS ECONOMICS?

According to one standard definition, *economics is concerned with the way resources are allocated among alternative uses to satisfy human wants.* This definition is fine, but it does not mean much unless we define what is meant by *human wants* and *resources.* What do these terms mean?

Human wants

Human wants are the things, services, goods, and circumstances that people desire. Wants vary greatly among individuals and over time for the same individual. Some people like sports, and others like books; some want to travel, and others want to putter in the yard. An individual's desire for a particular good during a particular period of time is not infinite, but in the aggregate, human wants seem to be insatiable. Besides the basic desires for food, shelter, and clothing, which must be fulfilled to some extent if the human organism is to maintain its existence, wants stem

Economic resources

Free resources

from cultural factors. For example, society, often helped along by advertising and other devices to modify tastes, promotes certain images of the good life, which frequently entail owning an expensive car and living in a $300,000 house in the suburbs.

Resources are the things or services used to produce goods, which then can be used to satisfy wants. **Economic resources** are scarce; **free resources**, such as air, are so abundant that they can be obtained without charge. The test of whether a resource is an economic resource or a free resource is price: economic resources command a nonzero price; free resources do not. The number of free resources is quite limited. For instance, although the earth contains a huge amount of water, it is not a free resource to typical urban or suburban homeowners, who must pay a local water authority for providing and maintaining their water supply. In a world where all resources were free, there would be no economic problems, since all wants could be satisfied.

Economic resources can be classified into three categories:

1. *Land.* A shorthand expression for natural resources, land includes minerals as well as plots of ground. Clearly, land is an important and valuable resource in both agriculture and industry. Think of the fertile soil of Iowa or Kansas, which produces such abundant crops. Or consider Manhattan island, which supports the skyscrapers, shops, and theaters in the heart of New York. In addition, land is an important part of our environment, and it provides enjoyment above and beyond its contribution to agricultural and industrial output.

2. *Labor.* Human efforts, both physical and mental, are included in the category of labor. Thus, when you study for a final examination or make out an income tax return, this is as much labor as if you were to dig a ditch. In 1999, over 133 million people were employed (or looking for work) in the United States. This vast labor supply is, of course, an extremely important resource, without which our nation could not maintain its current output level.

3. *Capital.* Buildings, equipment, inventories, and other nonhuman producible resources that contribute to the production, marketing, and distribution of goods and services all fall within the economist's definition of capital. Examples are machine tools and warehouses. But not all types of capital are big or bulky; for example, a hand calculator, or a pencil for that matter, is a type of capital. Workers in the United States have an enormous amount of capital to work with. Think of the oil refineries in New Jersey and Philadelphia, the electronics factories near Boston and San Francisco, the aircraft plants in California, and the host of additional types of capital we have and use in this country. Without this capital, the nation's output level would be a great deal less than it is.

Technology

Choice

■ TECHNOLOGY AND CHOICE

As pointed out above, economics is concerned with the way resources are allocated among alternative uses to satisfy human wants. An important determinant of the extent to which human wants can be satisfied from the amount of resources at hand is technology. **Technology** is society's pool of knowledge concerning the industrial arts. It includes the knowledge of engineers, scientists, artisans, managers, and others concerning how goods and services can be produced. For example, it includes the best existing knowledge regarding the ways in which an automobile plant or a synthetic rubber plant should be designed and operated. The level of technology sets limits on the amounts and types of goods and services that can be derived from a given amount of resources.

To see this, suppose that engineers do not know how an automobile can be produced with less than 500 hours of labor's being used in its manufacture. Clearly, this sets limits on the number of automobiles that can be produced with the available labor force. Or suppose that scientists and engineers do not know how to produce a ton of synthetic rubber with less than a certain amount of capital's being used in its manufacture. This sets limits on the amount of synthetic rubber that can be produced with the available quantity of capital.

Given the existing technology, the fact that resources are scarce means that only a limited amount of goods and services can be produced from them. In other words, the capacity to produce goods and services is limited—*far more limited than human wants*. Thus there arises the necessity for **choice**. Somehow or other, a choice must be made as to how the available resources will be used (or if they will be used at all). And somehow or other a choice must be made as to how the output produced from these resources will be distributed among the population.

Economics is concerned with how such choices are made. Economists have spent a great deal of time, energy, and talent trying to determine how such choices *are* made in various circumstances, and how they *should* be made. Indeed, as we shall see in the next section, the basic questions that economics deals with are problems of choice of this sort. Note that these problems of choice go beyond the problems of particular individuals in choosing how to allocate their resources; they are problems of social choice.

■ CENTRAL QUESTIONS IN ECONOMICS

Economists are particularly concerned with four basic questions regarding the working of any economic system—ours or any other:

1. What determines what and how much is produced?
2. What determines how it is produced?
3. What determines how the society's output is distributed among the members?
4. What determines the rate at which the society's per capita income will grow?

These questions lie at the core of economics, because they are directed at the most fundamental characteristics of economic systems. And as stressed in the previous section, they are problems of choice.

To illustrate the nature and basic importance of these questions, suppose that because of war or natural catastrophe, your town is isolated from the adjoining territory. No longer is it possible for the town's inhabitants to leave or for people or goods to enter. (Lest you regard this as fanciful, it is worthwhile to note that St. Petersburg was under siege in World War II for over two years.) In this situation, you and your fellow townspeople must somehow resolve each of these questions. You must decide what goods and services will be produced, how each will be produced, who will receive what, and how much provision there will be for increased output in the future.

In a situation of this sort, your very survival will depend on how effectively you answer these questions. If a decision is made to produce too much clothing and too little food, some of the townspeople may starve. If a decision is made to allot practically all the town's output to friends and political cronies of the mayor, those who oppose the mayor may have a very rough time. And if a decision is made to eat, drink, and be merry today and not to worry about tomorrow, life may be very meager in the days ahead.

Because we are considering a relatively small and isolated population, the importance of these questions may seem more obvious than in a huge country like the United States, which is constantly communicating, trading, and interacting with the rest of the world. But the truth is that these questions are every bit as important to the United States as to the isolated town. And for this reason, it is important that we understand how these decisions are made and whether they are being made effectively. Just as in the hypothetical case of the isolated town, your survival depends on these decisions, but in the United States the situation isn't hypothetical!

OPPORTUNITY COST: A FUNDAMENTAL CONCEPT

In previous sections, we have emphasized that economics is concerned with the way resources are allocated among alternative uses to satisfy human wants. To help determine how resources should be allocated, economists often use the concept of opportunity cost. We turn now to an introductory discussion of this concept, which should help to acquaint you with how it is used.

Since a specific case is more interesting than abstract discussion, let's return to the case of the town that is isolated from the adjoining territory because of a war or natural catastrophe. Suppose you are a member of the town council that is organized to determine how the town's resources should be utilized. To keep things simple, suppose that only two goods—food and clothing—can be produced. (This is an innocuous assumption that allows us to strip the problem to its essentials.) You must somehow figure out how much of each good should be produced. How can you go about solving this problem?

Clearly, the first step toward a solution is to list the various resources contained within the town. Using the technology available to the townspeople, each of these resources can be used to produce either food or clothing. Some of these resources are much more effective at producing one good than the other. For example, a tailor probably is better able to produce clothing than food. Nonetheless, most resources can be adapted to produce either good. For example, the tailor can be put to work on a farm, even though he or she may not be very good at farming.

After listing the various available resources and having determined how effective each is at producing food or clothing, the next step is to see how much food the town could produce per year if it produced nothing but food and how much clothing it could produce per year if it produced nothing but clothing. Also, you should determine, if various amounts of food are produced per year, the maximum amount of clothing that the town can produce per year. For example, if the town produces 100 tons of food per year, what is the maximum amount of clothing it can produce per year? If the town produces 200 tons of food per year, what is the maximum amount of clothing it can produce per year? And so on.

Having carried out this step, suppose that the results are as shown in Table 1.1. According to this table, the town can produce (at most) 200 tons of clothing per year if it produces nothing but clothing (possibility *A*). Or it can produce (at most) 400 tons of food per year if it produces nothing but food (possibility *E*). Other possible combinations (labeled *B*, *C*, and *D*) of food output and clothing output are specified in Table 1.1.

Table 1.1 puts in bold relief the basic problem of choice facing you and the other members of the town council. Because the town's resources are limited, the town can only produce limited amounts of each good. There is no way, for example, that the town can produce 200 tons of clothing per year and 200 tons of food per year. This is beyond the capacity of the town's resources. If the

TABLE 1.1 Combinations of Output of Food and Clothing That the Town Can Produce per Year	POSSIBILITY	AMOUNT OF FOOD PRODUCED PER YEAR (TONS)	AMOUNTOF CLOTHING PRODUCED PER YEAR (TONS)
	A	0	200
	B	100	180
	C	200	150
	D	300	100
	E	400	0

town wants to produce 200 tons of clothing, it can produce no food—hardly a pleasant prospect. And if the town wants to produce 200 tons of food, it can produce 150 (not 200) tons of clothing per year. Table 1.1 shows which combinations of food and clothing outputs are attainable.

■ MORE FOOD MEANS LESS CLOTHING

A very important fact illustrated by Table 1.1 is that whenever the town increases its production of one good, it must cut back its production of the other good. For example, if the town increases its production of food from 100 to 200 tons per year, it must cut back its production of clothing from 180 to 150 tons per year. Thus *the cost to the town of increasing its food output from 100 to 200 tons per year is that it must reduce its clothing output from 180 to 150 tons per year.*

Opportunity (or alternative) cost

Economists refer to this cost as **opportunity cost** (or **alternative cost**); it is one of the most fundamental concepts in economics. *The opportunity cost of using resources in a certain way is the value of what these resources could have produced if they had been used in the best alternative way.* In this case, the opportunity cost of the extra 100 tons of food per year is the 30 tons of clothing per year that must be forgone. This is what the town must give up in order to get the extra 100 tons of food.

Why is opportunity cost so important? Because for you and the other members of the town council to determine which combination of food and clothing is best, you should compare the value of increases in food output with the opportunity costs of such increases. For example, suppose that the town council is considering whether to increase food output from 100 to 200 tons per year. To decide this question, the council should compare the value of the extra 100 tons of food with the opportunity cost of the extra food (which is the 30 tons of clothing that must be given up). If the town council feels that the extra 100 tons of food are worth more to the town's welfare than the 30 tons of clothing that are given up, the extra food should be produced. Otherwise it should not be produced.

THE IMPACT OF ECONOMICS ON SOCIETY

Economics has influenced generations of political leaders, philosophers, and ordinary citizens and has played a significant role in shaping our society today. Skim through the articles in a daily newspaper. Chances are that you will find a report of an economist testifying before Congress, perhaps on the costs and benefits of a program to reduce unemployment among minority teenagers in the Bedford-Stuyvesant area of New York City or on the steps to be taken to make U.S. goods more competitive with those of Japan or Germany. Still another economist may appear on the editorial page, discussing the pros and cons of various proposals for reducing the federal deficit.

Economics and economists play a key role at the highest levels of our government. The president, whether a Democrat or a Republican, relies heavily on economic advisers in making the decisions that help to shape the future of the country. In Congress, too, economics plays a major role. Economists are frequent witnesses before congressional committees, staff members for the committees, and advisers to individual members of Congress. Many congressional committees focus largely on economic matters, and members of Congress spend large chunks of their time wrestling with budgetary and tax questions.

■ POSITIVE ECONOMICS VERSUS NORMATIVE ECONOMICS

**Positive
economics**

From the outset, it is essential that we recognize the distinction between positive economics and normative economics. **Positive economics** *contains descriptive statements, propositions, and predictions about the world.* For instance, an economic theory may predict that the price of copper will increase by 1 cent a pound if income per person in the United States rises by 10 percent; this is positive economics. Positive economics tells us only what will happen under certain circumstances. It says nothing about whether the results are good or bad, or about what we should do. **Normative economics,** *on the other hand, makes statements about what ought to be, or about what a person, organization, or nation ought to do.* For instance, a theory might say that Chile should introduce new technology more quickly in many of its copper mines; this is normative economics.

**Normative
economics**

Clearly, positive economics and normative economics must be treated differently. Positive economics is science in the ordinary sense of the word. Propositions in positive economics can be tested by comparisons with facts. In a nonexperimental science like economics, it is sometimes difficult to get the facts you need to test particular propositions. For example, if income per person in the United States does not rise by 10 percent, it may be difficult to tell what the effect of such an increase would be on the price of copper. Moreover, even if per capita income does increase by this amount, it may be difficult to separate the effect of the increase in income per person on the price of copper from the effects of other factors. But nonetheless we can, in principle, test propositions in positive economics by an appeal to the facts.

In normative economics, however, this is not the case. *In normative economics, the results you get depend on your values or preferences.* For example, if you believe that reducing unemployment is more important than maintaining the purchasing power of the dollar, you will get one answer to certain questions; if you believe that maintaining the purchasing power of the dollar is more important than reducing unemployment, you are likely to get a different answer to the same questions. This is not at all strange. After all, if people desire different things (which is another way of saying that they have different values), they may well make different decisions and advocate different policies. It would be strange if they did not.

THE METHODOLOGY OF ECONOMICS

■ MODEL BUILDING IN ECONOMICS

Models

Like other types of scientific analysis, economics is based on the formulation of **models.** *A model is a theory. It is composed of a number of assumptions from which conclusions—or predictions—are deduced.* An astronomer who wants to formulate a model of the solar system might represent each planet by a point in space and assume that each would change position in accord with certain mathematical equations. On the basis of this model, the astronomer might predict when an eclipse would occur, or estimate the probability of a planetary collision. Economists proceed along similar lines when they set forth a model of economic behavior.

There are several important points to be noted concerning models:

1. *To be useful, a model must simplify the real situation.* The assumptions made by a model need not be exact replicas of reality. If they were, the model would be too complicated to use. The basic reason for using a model is that the real world is so complex that masses of detail often obscure underlying patterns. The economist faces the familiar problem of seeing the forest as distinct from just

Land use in Alaska

In November 1980, the Alaska National Interest Lands Conservation Act declared more than 100 million acres of Alaskan wilderness off-limits to extensive mining and resource exploitation. Interior Secretary Cecil Andrus and Arizona Senator Morris Udall supported the bill, but Alaskan representatives such as Senator Mike Gravel sought to have the federally owned lands opened for development.

The bill was the culmination of the environmental battle that started when the conservationists inserted conditions for the preservation of the wilderness in the 1958 Alaska Statehood Act. Environmentalists felt that the value of the land as wilderness—the preservation of the habitat of many plant and animal species, and the use of the land by backpackers—greatly exceeded the potential value of its soil or minerals. Those who sought to postpone the act, including the majority of people in Alaska, argued that the value of the land for mining or logging should be assessed first. They argued in particular that the potential oil reserves should be estimated, in light of the then-recent doubling in the price of oil caused by the 1979 oil shortage. It would be foolhardy, they said, to reduce artificially the amount of oil available for domestic consumption when the dependence of the United States on foreign oil caused so much harm in terms of inflation and unemployment.

The vote in Congress implicitly maintained that the benefit of keeping the land as wilderness was greater than that of any alternative use. The bill President Jimmy Carter signed into law sought to "protect the resources of Alaska's crown jewels in perpetuity as national parks, wildlife refuges, forests and wild and scenic rivers." Put in the language of this chapter, the opportunity cost of keeping the land as wilderness was regarded as less than the benefits of doing so.

However, in 1991, President George Bush proposed to open for oil explorations the 1.5-million-acre coastal plain of the Arctic National Wildlife Refuge in Alaska. The proposal included many restrictions and regulations to protect animals and their environment in the refuge, but environmentalists argued that oil drilling should not occur there. Obviously, President Bush felt that the opportunity cost of keeping this land as wilderness was greater than the benefits of doing so. The environmentalists disagreed. Arguments of this sort between developers and environmentalists continue and are an important illustration of the role of opportunity costs in discussions of public policy.

the trees. Other scientists must do the same; physicists work with simplified models of atoms, just as economists work with simplified models of markets. However, this does not mean that *all* models are good or useful. A model may be so oversimplified and distorted that it is utterly useless. The trick is to construct a model so that irrelevant and unimportant considerations and variables are neglected, but the major factors—those that seriously affect the phenomena the model is designed to predict—are included.

2. *The purpose of a model is to make predictions about the real world; in many respects the most important test of a model is how well it predicts.* In this sense, a model that predicts the price of copper within plus or minus 1 cent a pound is better than a model that predicts it within plus or minus 2 cents a pound. Of course, this does not mean that a model is useless if it cannot predict very accurately. We do not always need a very accurate prediction. For example, a road map is a model that can be used to make predictions about the route a driver should take to get to a particular destination. Sometimes, a very crude map is good enough to get you where you want to go, but such a map would not, for instance, serve hikers who need to know the characteristics of the terrain through which they plan to walk. How detailed a map you need depends on where you are going and how you want to get there.

3. *If you want to predict the outcome of a particular event, you will be forced to use the model that predicts best, even if your model does not predict very well.* The choice is not between a model and no model; it is between one model and another. After all, a person who must make a forecast will use the most accurate device available, and any such device is a model of some sort. Consequently, when economists make simplifying assumptions and derive conclusions that are only approximately true, it is somewhat beside the point to complain that the assumptions are simpler than reality or that the predictions are not always accurate. This may be true, but if the predictions based on the economists' model are better than those based on other models, their model must and will be used until something better comes along. Thus if a model can predict the price of copper to within plus or minus 1 cent per pound and no other model can do better, this model will be used even if those interested in the predictions bewail the model's limitations and wish it could be improved.

■ ECONOMIC MEASUREMENT

To utilize and test their models, economists need facts of many sorts. For example, suppose that an economist constructs a model that predicts that a household's annual clothing expenditure tends to increase by $60 when its income increases by $1,000. To see whether this model is correct, the economist must gather data concerning the incomes and clothing expenditures of a large number of households and study the relationship between them. Suppose that the relationship proves to be as shown in Figure 1.1. The line represents an average relationship between household income

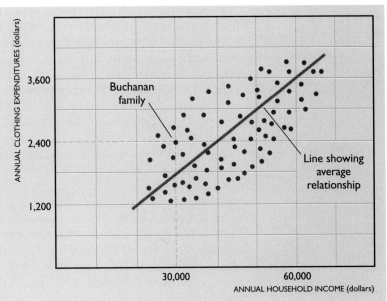

FIGURE 1.1

Relationship between Annual Clothing Expenditures and Annual Household Income

Each family is represented by a dot. The line shows the average relationship. The line does not fit all families exactly, since all the points do not fall on it. The line does, however, show average clothing expenditure for each income level.

ANNUAL CLOTHING EXPENDITURES (dollars)

3,600

2,400

1,200

Buchanan family

Line showing average relationship

30,000

60,000

ANNUAL HOUSEHOLD INCOME (dollars)

and household clothing expenditure. Judging by Figure 1.1, the model is reasonably accurate, at least for households with incomes between $30,000 and $60,000 per year.[1]

Measurements like those in Figure 1.1 enable economists to *quantify* their models; in other words, they enable them to construct models that predict *how much* effect one variable has on another. If economists did not quantify their models, they (and their models) would be much less useful. For example, the economist in the previous paragraph might have been content with a model that predicts that higher household income results in higher household clothing expenditures, but this model would not have been interesting or useful, since you do not need an economist to tell you that. A more valuable model is one that is quantitative, that predicts how much clothing expenditure will increase if household income rises by a certain amount. This is the sort of model that economists usually try to construct.

GRAPHS AND RELATIONSHIPS

To conclude our brief discussion of economic methodology, we must describe the construction and interpretation of graphs, such as Figure 1.1, which economists use to present data and relationships.

[1] It is worth noting that, although it is useful to see how well a model would have fit the historical facts, this is no substitute for seeing how well it will predict the future. According to one old saying, "It's a darned poor person who can't predict the past."

1. A graph has a horizontal axis and a vertical axis, each of which has a scale of numerical values. For example, in Figure 1.1, the horizontal axis shows a household's annual income, and the vertical axis shows the annual amount spent by the household on clothing. The intersection of the two axes is called the origin and is the point where both the variable measured along the horizontal axis and the variable measured along the vertical axis are zero. In Figure 1.1, the origin is at the lower left-hand corner of the figure, labeled 0.

2. To show the relationship between two variables, one can plot the value of one variable against the value of the other variable. Thus in Figure 1.1 each family is represented by a dot. For example, the dot for the Buchanan family is in the position shown in Figure 1.1 because its income was $30,000 and its clothing expenditure was $2,400. Clearly, the line showing the average relationship does not fit all the families exactly, since all the points do not fall on the line. This line does, however, give the average clothing expenditure for each level of income: it shows the average relationship.

3. The relationship between two variables is *direct* if, as in Figure 1.1, the line of average relationship is upward sloping. In other words, if the variable measured along the vertical axis tends to increase (decrease) in response to increases (decreases) in the variable measured along the horizontal axis, the relationship is direct. On the other hand, if the line of the average relationship is downward sloping, as in Figure 1.2, the relationship is *inverse*. In other words, if the variable measured along the vertical axis tends to decrease (increase) in response to increases (de-

FIGURE 1.2

Relationship between Quantity Demanded and Price of Tennis Balls (as Shown in Table 1.2)

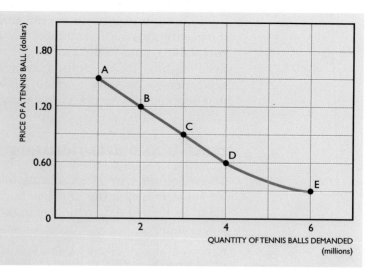

TABLE 1.2 Quantity of Tennis Balls Demanded in a Particular Market at Various Prices	PRICE OF A TENNIS BALL (DOLLARS)	QUANTITY OF TENNIS BALLS DEMANDED (MILLIONS)
	1.50	1
	1.20	2
	0.90	3
	0.60	4
	0.30	6

creases) in the variable measured along the horizontal axis, the relationship is inverse.

To illustrate how one can graph a relationship between two variables, consider Table 1.2, which shows the quantity of tennis balls demanded in a particular market at various prices. Putting price on the vertical axis and quantity demanded on the horizontal axis, one can plot each combination of price and quantity in this table as a point on a graph; and that is precisely what has been done in Figure 1.2 (points *A* to *E*).

THE TASKS OF AN ECONOMIC SYSTEM

Having discussed the nature and quantification of economic models, we conclude by describing what an economic system—*ours or any other*—must do. Basically, as we saw earlier in this chapter, there are four tasks that any economic system must perform:

1. *An economic system must determine the level and composition of society's output.* That is, it must answer questions like: To what extent should society's resources be used to produce new aircraft carriers and missiles? To what extent should they be used to produce sewage plants to reduce water pollution? To what extent should they be used to produce swimming pools for the rich? To what extent should they be used to produce low-cost housing for the poor? Pause for a moment to think about how important—and how vast—this function is. Most people simply take for granted that somehow it is decided what we as a society are going to produce, and too few people think about the social mechanisms that determine the answers to such questions.

2. *An economic system must determine how each good and service is to be produced.* Given existing technology, a society's resources can be used in various ways. Should the skilled labor in Birmingham, Alabama, be used to produce cotton or steel? Should

Eliminating brown lung disease

Textile worker in a contemporary manufacturing plant

Perhaps as many as 150,000 Americans suffer from brown lung disease. The disease is brought on by inhaling the particles of cotton dust and fiber that are a by-product of textile manufacturing. Growing public awareness of brown lung disease was a prime force behind the passage of the Occupational Safety and Health Act in 1970. But over the next decade, as competition increased and profits shrank, managers, workers, and the government wrestled with the question: how much more should we spend to protect our workforce? This is a question involving **normative economics**, and as has already been pointed out, the answer you get depends on your values or preferences.

Throughout the 1970s, the U.S. textile industry was locked in a fierce struggle against foreign competition. Asian competitors were undercutting U.S. mills. The U.S. textile industry was spending millions to protect workers' health. The Asian textile industries spent almost nothing. Faced with this competition, the U.S. industry looked for ways to cut costs. Then, along came the Occupational Safety and Health Administration (OSHA), telling business it had to spend more money, not less.

Indeed OSHA proposed tough new standards for cotton dust in the mills. The industry claimed that the new regulations would require it to spend $2 billion on new equipment and that it could achieve almost the same result by spending $1.49 per worker on dust masks. The Amalgamated Clothing and Textile Workers Union disagreed. Workers were still dying from brown lung disease, and dust masks would not eliminate the risk. The union argued fiercely for the tougher standards, but many in Washington sided with the industry.

The textile industry sued OSHA, arguing that the new regulations would impose a relatively high cost to protect a relatively small number of lives. They argued that eliminating all risk of brown lung disease would destroy the ability of the industry to survive against overseas competition and that the most effective dollars had already been spent. Late in 1980, the Supreme Court heard arguments from both sides. In June 1981, the Court agreed with the union that Congress had intended the question of worker health to be considered first, above all other considerations of cost.

By 1985, most U.S. textile companies had installed the new equipment to meet the cotton dust regulations. Brown lung disease had virtually disappeared, but so had 300,000 jobs in the textile mills. Many in the industry argued that regulations of this sort were to blame.

a particular machine tool be used to produce aircraft or automobiles? The way questions of this sort are answered will determine the way each good and service is produced. In other words, it will determine which resources are used to produce which goods and services. If this function is performed badly, society's resources are put to the wrong uses; this results in less output than if this function is performed well.

3. *An economic system must determine how the goods and services that are produced are to be distributed among the members of*

**How should this car
be produced and
for whom?**

society. In other words, how much of each type of good and service
should each person receive? Should there be a considerable
amount of income inequality, the rich's receiving much more than
the poor? Or should income be relatively equal? Take your own
case. Somehow or other, the economic system determines how
much income you will receive. In our economic system, your income depends on your skills, the property you own, how hard you
work, and prevailing prices, as we shall see in succeeding chapters. But in other economic systems, your income may depend on
quite different factors. This function of the economic system has
generated and will continue to generate heated controversy. Some
people favor a relatively egalitarian society where the amount received by one family varies little from that received by another
family of the same size. Other people favor a society where the
amount a family or person receives can vary a great deal. Few people favor a thoroughly egalitarian society, if for no other reason
than that some differences in income are required to stimulate
workers to do certain types of work.

4. *An economic system must determine the rate of growth of per
capita income.* An adequate growth rate has come to be regarded as
an important economic goal, particularly in the developing countries of Africa, Asia, and Latin America. There is very strong pressure in these countries for changes in technology, the adoption of
superior techniques, increases in the stock of capital resources,
and better and more extensive education and training of the labor
force. These are viewed as some of the major ways to promote the
growth of per capita income.

Adam Smith, father of modern economics

Adam Smith

To illustrate the importance of economic ideas, let's consider some of the precepts of Adam Smith (1723–90), the man who is often called the father of modern economics. Much of his masterpiece *The Wealth of Nations* seems trite today because it has been absorbed so thoroughly into modern thought, but it was not trite when it was written.* On the contrary, Smith's ideas were revolutionary. *He was among the first to describe how a free, competitive economy can function—without central planning or government interference—to allocate resources efficiently. He recognized the virtues of the "invisible hand" that leads the private interest of firms and individuals toward socially desirable ends, and he was properly suspicious of firms that are sheltered from competition, since he recognized the potentially undesirable effects on resource allocation.*

In addition, Smith—with the dire poverty of his times staring him in the face—was interested in the forces that determined the evolution of the economy—the forces determining the rate of growth of average income per person. Although Smith did not approve of avarice, he felt that saving was good because it enabled society to invest in machinery and other forms of capital. Accumulating more and more capital would, according to Smith, allow output to grow. In addition, he emphasized the importance of increased specialization and division of labor in producing economic progress. By specializing, people can concentrate on the tasks they do best, with the result that society's total output is raised.

All in all, Smith's views were relatively optimistic. Leave markets alone, said Smith, and beware of firms with too much economic power and of government meddling. If this is done, there is no reason why considerable economic progress cannot be achieved. Smith's work has been modified and extended in a variety of ways in the past 225 years. Some of his ideas have been challenged and, in some cases, discarded. But his influence on modern society has been enormous.

* Adam Smith, *The Wealth of Nations*. Originally published in 1776.

EXPLORING FURTHER[2]

A SIMPLE INTRODUCTORY MODEL OF THE ECONOMIC SYSTEM

▉ THE PRODUCTION POSSIBILITIES CURVE AND THE DETERMINATION OF WHAT IS PRODUCED

In a previous section, we said that economists use models to throw light on economic problems. At this point, let's try our hand at constructing a simple model to illuminate the basic functions any economic system, ours included, must perform. To keep things simple, suppose that society produces only two goods, food and

[2] Sections titled "Exploring Further" are optional.

tractors. This, of course, is unrealistic, but as we stressed in a previous section, a model does not have to be realistic to be useful. Here, by assuming that there are only two goods, we eliminate a lot of unnecessary complexity and lay bare the essentials. In addition, we suppose that society has at its disposal a certain amount of resources and that this amount is fixed for the duration of the period in question. This assumption is quite realistic. So long as the period is relatively short, the amount of a society's resources is relatively fixed (except, of course, under unusual circumstances, such as if a country annexes additional land).[3] Finally, suppose as well that society's technology is fixed. So long as the period is relatively short, this assumption too is realistic.

Under these circumstances, it is possible to figure out the various amounts of food and tractors that society can produce. Specifically, we can proceed as we did at the beginning of this chapter to determine the amounts of food and clothing that an isolated town could produce. Let's begin with how many tractors society can produce if all resources are devoted to tractor production. According to Table 1.3, the answer is 15 million tractors. Next, let's consider the opposite extreme, where society devotes all its resources to food production. According to Table 1.3, it can produce 12 million tons of food in this case. Next, let's consider cases where both products are being produced. Such cases are represented by possibilities B to F in the table. As emphasized earlier in this chapter, the more of one good that is produced, the less of the other good that can be produced. Why? Because to produce more of one good, resources must be taken away from the production of the other good; this lessens the amount of the other good produced.

TABLE 1.3 **Alternative Combinations of Outputs of Food and Tractors That Can Be Produced**	POSSIBILITY	FOOD (MILLIONS OF TONS)	TRACTORS (MILLIONS)
	A	0	15
	B	2	14
	C	4	12
	D	6	10
	E	8	7
	F	10	4
	G	12	0

[3] For example, in 1990, Iraq tried to take over Kuwait but was driven out by the United States and its allies.

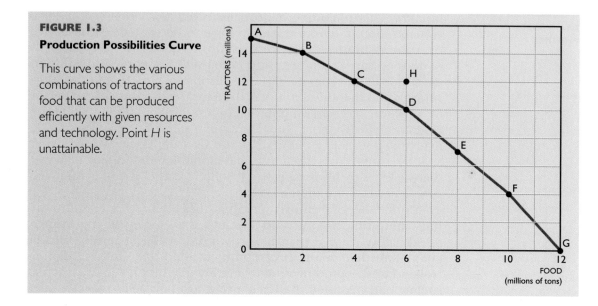

FIGURE 1.3

Production Possibilities Curve

This curve shows the various combinations of tractors and food that can be produced efficiently with given resources and technology. Point *H* is unattainable.

Figure 1.3 shows how we can use a graph to show the various production possibilities society can attain. It is merely a different way of presenting the data in Table 1.3: The output of food is plotted on the horizontal axis and the output of tractors on the vertical axis. The curve in Figure 1.3, which shows the various combinations of output of food and tractors that society can produce, is called the **production possibilities curve**.

Production possibilities curve

The production possibilities curve sheds considerable light on the economic tasks facing any society. It shows the various production possibilities open to society. In Figure 1.3, society can choose to produce 4 million tons of food and 12 million tractors (point *C*), or 6 million tons of food and 10 million tractors (point *D*), but it cannot choose to produce 6 million tons of food and 12 million tractors (point *H*). Point *H* is inaccessible with this society's resources and technology. Perhaps it will become accessible if the society's resources increase or if its technology improves, but for the present, point *H* is out of reach.

If resources are fully and efficiently utilized, *the first function of any economic system—to determine the level and composition of society's output—is really a problem of determining at which point along the production possibilities curve society should be.* Should society choose point *A, B, C, D, E, F,* or *G*? In making this choice, one thing is obvious from the production possibilities curve: *You cannot get more of one good without giving up some of the other good.* In other words, you cannot escape the problem of choice. So long as resources are limited and technology is less than magic, you must deal with the fact (emphasized earlier in this chapter) that more of one thing means less of another. The old phrase "you don't get something for nothing" is hackneyed but true, so long as resources are fully and efficiently utilized.

■ THE PRODUCTION POSSIBILITIES CURVE AND THE DETERMINATION OF HOW GOODS ARE PRODUCED

Let's turn now to the second basic function of any economic system: to determine how each good and service should be produced. In Table 1.3 we assumed implicitly that society's resources would be fully utilized and that the available technology would be applied in a way that would get the most out of the available resources. In other words, we assumed that the firms making food and tractors were as efficient as possible and that there was no unemployment of resources. But if there is widespread unemployment of people and machines, will society still be able to choose a point on the production possibilities curve? Clearly, the answer is no. Since society is not using all of its resources, it will not be able to produce as much as if it used them all. Thus *if there is less than full employment of resources, society will have to settle for points inside the production possibilities curve.* For example, the best society may be able to do under these circumstances is to attain point *K* in Figure 1.4. Point *K* is a less desirable point than *C* or *D*, but that is the price of unemployment.

Suppose, on the other hand, that there is full employment of resources but that firms are inefficient. Perhaps they promote relatives of the boss, regardless of their ability; perhaps the managers are lazy or not very interested in efficiency; or perhaps the work-

FIGURE 1.4

Production Possibilities Curve

Point *K* is less desirable than point *C* or *D*, because less output is produced at this point. But because of unemployment or inefficiency, society may wind up at point *K*.

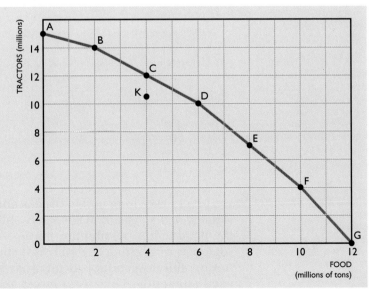

Producing both guns and butter, 1939 to 1941

Production of munitions during World War II

Throughout the 1930s, massive amounts of productive resources were wasted. In 1938, even after the economy had recovered from the worst years of the Depression, the unemployment rate was 19 percent, more than 10 million people who were willing and able to work could not find jobs, and the capacity utilization rate for the nation's plant and equipment was very low.

With the outbreak of war in Europe in 1939, the demand for U.S. goods jumped sharply. Orders flowed in, and U.S. firms put their dormant factories to work and increased their hiring. Real national output increased 7.7 percent in 1939, 7.6 percent in 1940, and 16 percent in 1941. Munitions production went from almost zero in 1938 to $3 billion by the end of 1940 and $10 billion by the end of 1941 (all figures are in 1943 dollars).

Because consumers' incomes had increased along with the recovery, the demand for consumer goods also grew. But with the diversion of so much of the labor force and factories into war-related production, what happened to consumer goods production? Consumer expenditures increased from $58 billion in 1938 to $70 billion in 1941. By putting existing resources to work, the U.S. economy was able to increase production of *both* guns *and* butter in the early years of war. Why? Because the United States had been operating at a point inside its production possibilities curve.

By the end of 1941, when the United States officially entered the war, the economy was already producing close to its potential. The unemployment rate had fallen to 4 percent, and capacity utilization had improved dramatically. Only by extending work hours and by upgrading and expanding the nation's capital stock could the economy grow. The United States continued to produce more and more every year of the war, but the gains in both guns and butter were no longer possible. Munitions production increased from $10 billion in 1941 to $64 billion by the end of the war, but there was no further growth in civilian consumption after 1941. In fact, the production of some civilian goods such as autos and appliances was halted completely, and others such as tires, sugar, and coffee were rationed. By 1942, after having taken up the slack of the Depression years, the economy had to face the classic trade-off between guns and butter.

ers like to take long coffee breaks and are unwilling to work hard. Whatever the reason, will society still be able to choose a point on the production possibilities curve? Again, the answer is no. Since society is not getting as much as it could out of its resources, it will not be able to produce as much as it would if its resources were used efficiently. Thus *if resources are used inefficiently, society will have to settle for points inside the production possibilities curve.* Perhaps in these circumstances too the best society can do may be point *K* in Figure 1.4. This less desirable position is the price of inefficiency.

At this point, it should be obvious that our model at least partially answers the question of how each good and service should be produced. The answer is to *produce each good and service in such a way that you wind up on the production possibilities curve, not on a point inside it.* Of course this is easier said than done, but at least our model indicates a couple of villains to watch out for: unemployment of resources and inefficiency. When these villains are present, we can be sure that society is not on the production possibilities curve. Also, the old phrase is wrong, and it *is* possible to "get something for nothing" when society is inside the production possibilities curve. That is, society can increase the output of one good without reducing the output of another good in such a situation.

▥ THE PRODUCTION POSSIBILITIES CURVE, INCOME DISTRIBUTION, AND GROWTH

The third basic function of any economic system is to distribute the goods and services that are produced among the members of society. Each point on the production possibilities curve in Figure 1.4 represents society's total pie, but to deal with the third function, we must know how the pie is divided among society's members. Since the production possibilities curve does not tell us this, it cannot shed light on this third function.

Fortunately, the production possibilities curve is of more use in analyzing the fourth basic function of any economic system: to determine the society's rate of growth of per capita income. Suppose that the society in Figure 1.4 invests a considerable amount of its resources in developing improved processes and products. It might establish agricultural experiment stations to improve farming techniques and industrial research laboratories to improve tractor designs. As shown in Figure 1.5, the production possibilities curve will be pushed outward. This will be the result of improved technology, enabling more food and/or more tractors to be produced from the same amount of resources. Thus one way for an economy to increase its output—and its per capita income—may be to invest in research and development.

Another way is for the economy to devote more of its resources to the production of capital goods than to the production of consumer goods. **Capital goods** consist of plant and equipment that are used to make other goods; **consumer goods** are items that consumers purchase like clothing, food, and drink. Since capital goods are themselves resources, a society that

**Capital goods
Consumer goods**

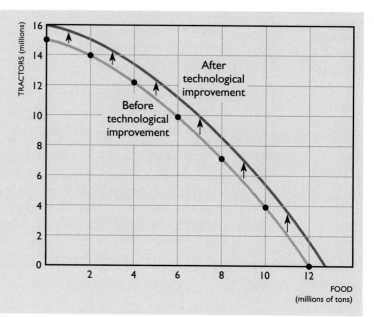

FIGURE 1.5

Effect of Improvement in Technology on the Production Possibilities Curve

An improvement in technology results in an outward shift of the production possibilities curve.

chooses to produce lots of capital goods and few consumer goods will push out its production possibilities curve much farther than a society that chooses to produce lots of consumer goods and few capital goods.

To illustrate this point, consider our simple society that produces food and tractors. The more tractors (and the less food) this society produces, the more tractors it will have in the next period, and the more tractors it has in the next period, the more of both goods—food and tractors—it will be able to produce. Thus the more tractors (and the less food) this society produces, the farther out it will push its production possibilities curve—and the greater the increase in output (and per capita income) that it will achieve in the next period. If this society chooses point *F* (shown in Figures 1.3 and 1.4), the effect will be entirely different than if it chooses point *C*. If it chooses point *F*, it produces 4 million tractors, which we assume to be the number of tractors worn out each year. Thus if it chooses point *F* it adds nothing to its stock of tractors; it merely replaces those that wear out. Since it has no more tractors in the next period than in the current period, the production possibilities curve does not shift out at all if point *F* is chosen. On the other hand, if point *C* is chosen, the society produces 12 million tractors; this means that it has 8 million additional tractors at the beginning of the next period. Thus, as shown in Figure 1.6, the production possibilities curve is pushed outward. By producing more capital goods (and fewer consumer goods), the society has increased its production possibilities and its per capita income.

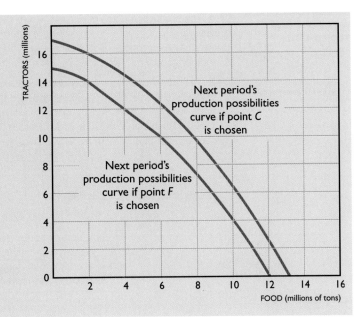

FIGURE 1.6

Effect of an Increase in Capital Goods on the Production Possibilities Curve

An increase in the amount of capital goods results in an outward shift of the production possibilities curve. The choice of point C means the production of more capital goods than the choice of point F.

(Graph labels)
TRACTORS (millions)

Next period's production possibilities curve if point C is chosen

Next period's production possibilities curve if point F is chosen

FOOD (millions of tons)

REVIEW AND PRACTICE

■ SUMMARY

1 According to one standard definition, economics is concerned with the way resources are allocated among alternative uses to satisfy human wants. Economists often classify economic resources into three categories: land, labor, and capital.

2 Since economic resources are scarce, only a limited amount of goods and services can be produced from them, and there arises the necessity for choice. The opportunity cost (or alternative cost) of using a resource to increase the production of one good is the value of what the resource could have produced had it been used in the best alternative way.

3 Economists are particularly concerned with four basic questions regarding the working of an economic system—ours or any other:

1. What determines what (and how much) is produced?
2. What determines how it is produced?
3. What determines how the society's output is distributed among its members?
4. What determines the rate at which the society's per capita income will grow?

4 Economists often distinguish between positive economics and normative economics. Positive economics contains descriptive statements, propositions, and predictions about the world; normative economics contains statements about what ought to be or about what a person, organization, or country ought to do.

5 The methodology used by economists is much the same as that used in any other kind of scientific analysis. The basic procedure is the formulation and testing of models. A model must in general simplify and abstract from the real world. Its purpose is to make predictions concerning phenomena in the real world, and in many respects the most important test of a model is how well it predicts these phenomena.

*6 The production possibilities curve, which shows the various production possibilities a society can attain, is useful in indicating the nature of the economic tasks any society faces. Society has to recognize that it cannot get more of one good without giving up some of another good if resources are fully and efficiently used.

*7 The task of determining how each good and service should be produced is, to a considerable extent, a problem of keeping society on its production possibilities curve, rather than at points inside the curve. By doing research and development or by producing capital goods (rather than consumer goods), society may push its production possibilities curve outward, and thus increase its per capita income.

PROBLEMS AND QUESTIONS

*1 Suppose that a society's production possibilities curve is as follows:

	OUTPUT (PER YEAR)	
POSSIBILITY	FOOD (MILLIONS OF TONS)	TRACTORS (MILLIONS)
A	0	30
B	4	28
C	8	24
D	12	20
E	16	14
F	20	8
G	24	0

(a) Is it possible for the society to produce 30 million tons of food per year?

(b) Can it produce 30 million tractors per year?

(c) Suppose this society produces 20 million tons of food and 6 million tractors per year. Is it operating on its production possibilities curve? If not, what factors might account for this?

*2 Plot the production possibilities curve in question 1 on a graph. At what point along the horizontal axis does the curve cut the axis? At what point along the vertical axis does the curve cut the axis?

*3 Suppose that, because of important technological improvements, the society in question 1 can double its production of tractors at each level of food production. If so, is this society on its new production possibilities curve if it produces 20 million tons of food and 16 million tractors? Plot new production possibilities curve. At which point along the horizontal axis does the new curve cut the axis? At which point along the vertical axis does it cut the axis?

4 Suppose that the quantity of corn demanded annually by U.S. consumers at each price of corn is as follows:

*The starred items refer to material covered in Exploring Further.

PRICE (DOLLARS PER BUSHEL)	QUANTITY OF CORN (MILLIONS OF BUSHELS)
1	2.0
2	1.0
3	0.5
4	0.4

How much will farmers receive for their corn crop if it is 2 million bushels? If it is 1 million bushels? If you owned all the farms producing corn, would you produce 2 million bushels? Why or why not?

5 Plot the relationship between price and quantity demanded in question 4 on a graph. Is the relationship direct or inverse? On the basis of your graph, estimate how much corn is likely to be demanded if the price is (a) $1.50, (b) $2.50, and (c) $3.50.

■ KEY TERMS

human wants	positive economics
economic resources	normative economics
free resources	models
technology	production possibilities curve
choice	capital goods
opportunity (or alternative) cost	consumer goods

■ VIEWPOINT FOR ANALYSIS

In his 1997 Economic Report, President Clinton said: "To succeed in the new global economy, our children must receive a world-class education. Every child in America should be able to read by the age of 8, log onto the Internet by the age of 12, and receive at least 14 years of quality education: 2 years of college should become as universal as high school is today. And we must make sure that every child who wants to go to college has the resources to do so."*

(a) Suppose that an economy produces only two things: food and education. What would the production possibilities curve for such an economy look like? Draw its general shape on a graph.

(b) Can this production possibilities curve tell us whether all the citizens in this economy have access to a quality education? Why or why not?

(c) Can this production possibilities curve indicate the cost of carrying out the program put forth by President Clinton? If so, how?

*Economic Report of the President (Washington, D.C.: U.S. Government Printing Office, 1997), p. 4.

CHAPTER 2

Markets and Prices

LEARNING OBJECTIVES

In this chapter, you should learn:

- What market demand and market supply curves show
- The distinction between shifts in a commodity's demand or supply curve and changes in the quantity demanded or supplied of the commodity
- The significance of equilibrium price
- How the price system accomplishes the four basic tasks of an economic system, and what general limitations the price system suffers from
- *(Exploring Further)* The effects of shifts in the demand and supply curves

Politicians, industrialists, and consumers frequently lament the fact that low-cost housing is hard to find in the United States. After World War II, a builder named William Levitt produced a lot of low-cost houses and offered them for sale. What determined whether his venture succeeded? One purpose of this chapter is to answer this question.

Capitalist economies use the price system to perform the four basic tasks any economic system must carry out. However, the U.S. economy is a mixed capitalist system, not a pure one. Both government and private decisions are important. This does not mean that the price system is unimportant. On the contrary, the price system plays a vital role in the U.S. economy, and to obtain even a minimal grasp of the workings of our economic system, one must understand how the price system operates. This chapter takes up the nature and functions of the price system, as well as some applications of our theoretical results to real-life problems.

CONSUMERS AND FIRMS

We begin by describing and discussing consumers and firms, the basic building blocks that make up the private, or nongovernmental, sector of the economy. What is a consumer? Sometimes—for example, when a person buys a beer on a warm day—the consumer is an individual. In other cases—for example, when a family buys a new car—the consumer may be an entire household. **Consumers** purchase the goods and services that are the end products of the economic system.

Consumers

Firms

There are over 10 million firms in the United States. About nine-tenths of the goods and services produced in this country are produced by firms. (The rest are provided by government and not-for-profit institutions like universities and hospitals.) A **firm** is an organization that produces a good or service for sale. In contrast to not-for-profit organizations, firms attempt to make a profit. It is obvious that our economy is centered around the activities of firms.

Like consumers, firms are extremely varied in size, age, power, and purpose. Consider two examples, Peter Amacher's drugstore on Chicago's South Side and the General Motors Corporation. The Amacher drugstore, started in 1922 by Mr. Amacher's father-in-law, is known in the retail drug trade as an independent, because it has no affiliation with a chain-store organization. Mr. Amacher and two other pharmacists keep the store open for business 13 hours a day, except on Sundays. The store sells about $150,000 worth of merchandise per year.

In contrast, General Motors is one of the giants of U.S. industry. It is the largest manufacturer of automobiles in the United States. Besides cars, it makes trucks, locomotives, aircraft engines, household appliances, and other products. It has long been a leading symbol of industrial might, but during the 1980s and early 1990s it encountered formidable competition, particularly from Japanese cars.

MARKETS

Markets

Consumers and firms come together in a market. The concept of a market is not quite as straightforward as it may seem, since most markets are not well defined geographically or physically. For example, the New York Stock Exchange is an atypical market because it is located principally in a particular building. For present purposes, *a **market** can be defined as a group of firms and individuals that are in touch with each other in order to buy or sell some good.* Of course, not every person in a market has to be in contact with every other person in the market. Persons or firms are part of a market even if they are in contact with only a subset of the other persons or firms in the market.

Markets vary enormously in their size and procedures. For some goods, like toothpaste, most people (assuming they have their own teeth and are interested in keeping them) are members of the same market; for other goods, like Picasso paintings, only a few connoisseurs (dealers, collectors, and museums in certain parts of the world) may be members of the market. And for still other goods, like lemonade sold by neighborhood children for a quarter a glass at a sidewalk stand, only people who walk by—and are brave enough to try the stuff—are members of the market. Basically, however, all markets consist primarily of buyers and sellers, although third parties like brokers and agents may be present as well.

Markets also vary in the extent to which they are dominated by a few large buyers or sellers. For example, in the United States, there was for many years only one producer of aluminum. This firm, the Aluminum Company of America, had great power in the market for aluminum. In contrast, the number of buyers and sellers in some other markets is so large that no single buyer or seller has any power over the price of the product. This is true in various agricultural markets, for example. When a market for a product contains so many buyers and sellers that none of them can influence the price, economists call the market **_perfectly competitive_**. In these introductory chapters, we make the simplifying assumption that markets are perfectly competitive. We will relax that assumption later.

THE DEMAND SIDE OF A MARKET

Market demand curve

Every market has a demand side and a supply side. _The **demand side** can be represented by a_ **market demand curve**, _which shows the amount of the commodity buyers would like to purchase at various prices._ Consider Figure 2.1, which shows the demand curve for wheat in the U.S. market during the mid-1990s.[1] The figure shows that about 2.3 billion bushels of wheat will be demanded annually if the farm price is $3.50 per bushel, about 2.4 billion bushels will be demanded annually if the farm price is $3.10 per bushel, and about 2.5 billion bushels will be demanded annually if the farm price is $2.70 per bushel. The total demand for wheat is of several types: to produce bread and other food products for domestic use, for feed use, for export purposes, and for industrial uses. The demand curve in Figure 2.1 shows the total demand—including all these components—at each price.

Take a good look at the demand curve for wheat in Figure 2.1. This simple, innocent-looking curve influences a great many people's lives. After all, wheat is the principal grain used for direct human consumption in the United States. To states like Kansas, North Dakota, Oklahoma, Montana, Washington, Nebraska, Texas, Illinois, Indiana, and Ohio, wheat is a very important cash crop. Note that the demand curve for wheat slopes downward to the right. In other words, the quantity of wheat demanded increases as the price falls. This is true of the demand curve for most com-

---

[1]Officials of the U.S. Department of Agriculture provided this information. Of course, these estimates are only approximations, but they are good enough for present purposes.

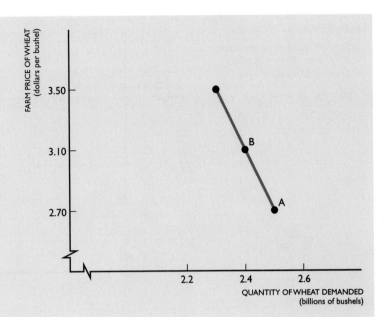

FIGURE 2.1

Market Demand Curve for Wheat, Mid-1990s

The curve shows the amount of wheat buyers would demand at various prices. At $2.70 per bushel, about 9 percent more wheat can be sold than at $3.50 per bushel.

modities: they almost always slope downward to the right. This makes sense; one would expect increases in a good's price to result in a smaller quantity demanded.

Any demand curve is based on the assumption that the tastes, incomes, and number of consumers, as well as the prices of other commodities, are held constant. Changes in any of these factors are likely to shift the position of a commodity's demand curve, as indicated below.

Consumer tastes. If consumers show an increasing preference for a product, the demand curve will shift to the right; that is, at each price, consumers will desire to buy more than previously. On the other hand, if consumers show a decreasing preference for a product, the demand curve will shift to the left, since at each price, consumers will desire to buy less than previously. Take wheat: If consumers become convinced that foods containing wheat prolong life and promote happiness, the demand curve may shift, as shown in Figure 2.2. The greater the shift in preferences, the larger the shift in the demand curve.

Income level of consumers. For some types of products, the demand curve shifts to the right if per capita income increases; for other types of commodities, the demand curve shifts to the left if per capita income increases. Economists can explain why some goods fall into one category and other goods fall into the other, but at present this need not concern us. All that is important here is

39

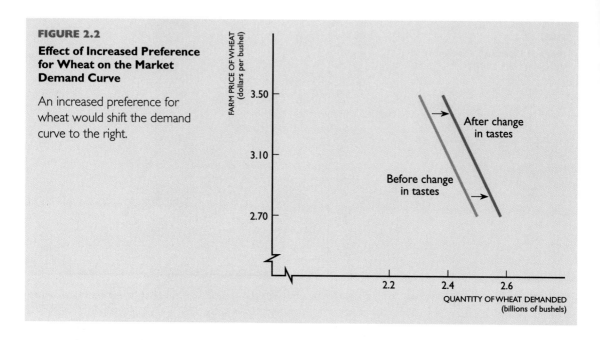

FIGURE 2.2

Effect of Increased Preference for Wheat on the Market Demand Curve

An increased preference for wheat would shift the demand curve to the right.

that changes in per capita income affect the demand curve; the size and direction of this effect vary from product to product. In the case of wheat, a 10 percent increase in per capita income would probably have a relatively small effect on the demand curve, as shown in Figure 2.3.

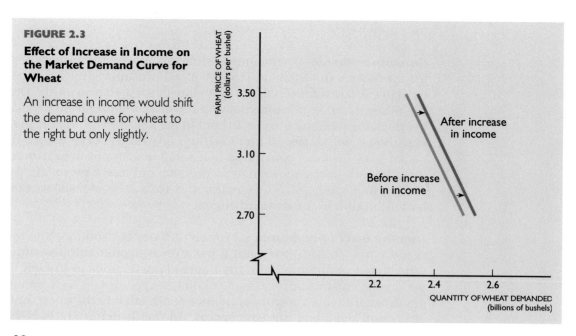

FIGURE 2.3

Effect of Increase in Income on the Market Demand Curve for Wheat

An increase in income would shift the demand curve for wheat to the right but only slightly.

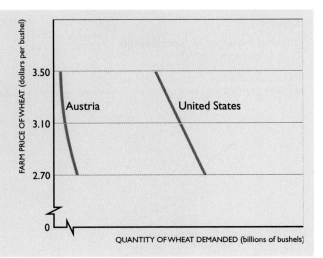

FIGURE 2.4

Market Demand Curve for Wheat, Austria and the United States

Since the United States has far more consumers than Austria, the demand curve in the United States is far to the right of Austria's.

Number of consumers in the market. Compare Austria's demand for wheat with that of the United States. Austria is a small country with a population of about 8 million; the United States is a huge country with a population of over 270 million. Clearly, at a given price of wheat, the quantity demanded by U.S. consumers will greatly exceed the quantity demanded by Austrian consumers, as shown in Figure 2.4. Even if consumer tastes, income, and other factors were held constant, this would still be true simply because the United States has so many more consumers in the relevant market.[2]

Level of other prices. A commodity's demand curve can be shifted by a change in the price of other commodities. Whether an increase in the price of good B will shift the demand curve for good A to the right or the left depends on the relationship between the two goods. If they are substitutes, such an increase will shift the demand curve for good A to the right. Consider the case of corn and wheat. If the price of corn goes up, more wheat will be demanded since it will be profitable to substitute wheat for corn. If the price of corn drops, less wheat will be demanded since it will be profitable to substitute corn for wheat. Thus, as shown in Figure 2.5, increases in the price of corn will shift the demand curve for wheat to the right, and decreases in the price of corn will shift it to the left.[3]

[2]Note that no figures are given along the horizontal axis in Figure 2.4. This is because we do not have reasonably precise estimates of the demand curve in Austria. Nonetheless, the hypothetical demand curves in Figure 2.4 are close enough to the mark for present purposes.

[3]If goods A and B are complements, an increase in the price of good B will shift the demand curve for good A to the left. Thus an increase in the price of chips is likely

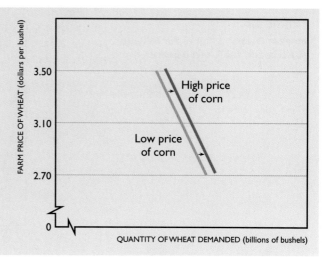

FIGURE 2.5

Effect of Price of Corn on Market Demand Curve for Wheat

Price increases for corn will shift the demand curve for wheat to the right.

■ DISTINCTION BETWEEN CHANGES IN DEMAND AND CHANGES IN THE QUANTITY DEMANDED

It is essential to distinguish between a *shift in a commodity's demand curve* and a change in the *quantity demanded of the commodity*. A shift in a commodity's demand curve is a change in the *relationship* between price and quantity demanded. Figures 2.2, 2.3, and 2.5 show cases where such a change occurs. A change in the quantity demanded of a commodity may occur even if *no* shift occurs in the commodity's demand curve. For example, in Figure 2.1, if the price of wheat increases from $2.70 to $3.10 per bushel, the quantity demanded falls from 2.5 to 2.4 billion bushels. This change in the quantity demanded is due to a *movement along* the demand curve (from point *A* to point *B* in Figure 2.1), not to a *shift* in the demand curve.

When economists refer to an *increase in demand*, they mean a *rightward shift* in the demand curve. Thus Figures 2.2, 2.3, and 2.5 show increases in demand for wheat. When economists refer to a *decrease in demand*, they mean a *leftward shift* in the demand curve. An increase in demand for a commodity is not the same as an increase in the quantity demanded of the commodity. In Figure 2.1, the quantity demanded of wheat *increases* if the price falls from $3.10 to $2.70 per bushel, but this is not due to an increase in demand, since there is no rightward shift of the demand curve. Similarly, a decrease in demand for a commodity is not the same as

to shift the demand curve for salsa to the left. Why? Because chips and salsa tend to be used together. The increase in the price of chips will reduce the quantity of chips demanded; this in turn will reduce the amount of salsa that will be demanded at each price of salsa.

a decrease in the quantity demanded of a commodity. In Figure 2.1, the quantity demanded of wheat *decreases* if the price rises from $2.70 to $3.10 per bushel, but this is not due to a decrease in demand, since there is no leftward shift of the demand curve.

THE SUPPLY SIDE OF A MARKET

Market supply curve

So much for our first look at demand. What about the other side of the market: supply? *The **supply** side of a market can be represented by a **market supply curve** that shows the amount of the commodity sellers would offer at various prices.* Let's continue with the case of wheat. Figure 2.6 shows the supply curve for wheat in the United States in the mid-1990s, based on estimates made informally by government experts.[4] According to the figure, about 2.2 billion bushels of wheat would be supplied if the farm price were $2.70 per bushel, about 2.4 billion bushels if the farm price were $3.10 per bushel, and about 2.6 billion bushels if the farm price were $3.50 per bushel.

Look carefully at the supply curve shown in Figure 2.6. Although it looks innocuous enough, it summarizes the potential behavior of thousands of U.S. wheat farmers, and their behavior plays an important role in determining the prosperity of many

FIGURE 2.6

Market Supply Curve for Wheat, Mid-1990s

The curve shows the amount that sellers would supply at various prices. At $3.50 per bushel, about 18 percent more wheat would be supplied than at $2.70 per bushel.

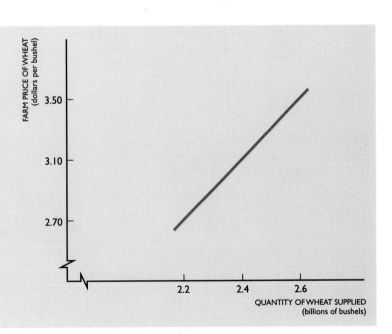

[4]Officials of the U.S. Department of Agriculture provided these estimates. Although rough approximations, they are good enough for present purposes.

states and communities. Note that the supply curve for wheat slopes upward to the right. In other words, the quantity of wheat supplied increases as the price increases. This seems plausible, since increases in price give a greater incentive for farms to produce wheat and offer it for sale. Empirical studies indicate that the supply curves for a great many commodities share this characteristic of sloping upward to the right.

Any supply curve is based on the assumption that technology and input prices are held constant. Changes in these factors are likely to shift the position of a commodity's supply curve.

Technology. Recall that technology was defined in Chapter 1 as society's pool of knowledge concerning the industrial arts. As technology progresses, it becomes possible to produce commodities more cheaply, so firms often are willing to supply a given amount at a lower price than formerly. Thus technological change often causes the supply curve to shift to the right. This certainly has occurred in the case of wheat, as shown in Figure 2.7. There have been many important technological changes in wheat production, ranging from advances in tractors to the development of improved varieties, like semidwarf wheats.

Input prices. The supply curve for a commodity is affected by the prices of the resources (labor, capital, and land) used to produce it. Decreases in the price of these inputs make it possible to produce commodities more cheaply, so that firms may be willing to supply a given amount at a lower price than they formerly would. Thus decreases in the price of inputs may cause the supply curve to shift to the right. On the other hand, increases in the price of inputs

FIGURE 2.7

Effect of a Technological Change on the Market Supply Curve for Wheat

Improvements in technology often shift the supply curve to the right.

FIGURE 2.8

Effect of an Increase in Farm Wage Rates on the Market Supply Curve for Wheat

An increase in the wage rate might shift the supply curve to the left.

may cause it to shift to the left. For example, if the wage rates of farm labor increase, the supply curve for wheat may shift to the left, as shown in Figure 2.8.

An *increase in supply* is defined to be a *rightward shift* in the supply curve; a *decrease in supply* is defined to be a *leftward shift* in the supply curve. A change in supply should be distinguished from a change in the quantity supplied. In Figure 2.6, the quantity supplied of wheat will increase from 2.2 to 2.4 billion bushels if the price increases from $2.70 to $3.10 per bushel, but this is not due to an increase in supply, since there is no rightward shift of the supply curve in Figure 2.6.

EQUILIBRIUM PRICE

The two sides of a market, demand and supply, interact to determine the price of a commodity. Prices in a capitalistic system are important determinants of what is produced, how it is produced, who receives it, and how rapidly per capita income grows. It behooves us, therefore, to look carefully at how prices are determined in a capitalist system. As a first step toward describing this process, we must define the equilibrium price of a product. At various points in this book, you will encounter the concept of an equilibrium, which is very important in economics, as in many other scientific fields.

Put briefly, *an equilibrium is a situation where there is no tendency for change;* in other words, it is a situation that can persist.

Equilibrium price   Thus an **equilibrium price** *is a price that can be maintained.* Any price that is not an equilibrium price cannot be maintained for long, since there are basic forces at work to stimulate a change in

FIGURE 2.9

Determination of the Equilibrium Price of Wheat, Mid-1990s

The equilibrium price is $3.10 per bushel, and the equilibrium quantity is 2.4 billion bushels. At a price of $3.50 per bushel, there would be an excess supply of 300 million bushels. At a price of $2.70 per bushel, there would be an excess demand of 300 million bushels.

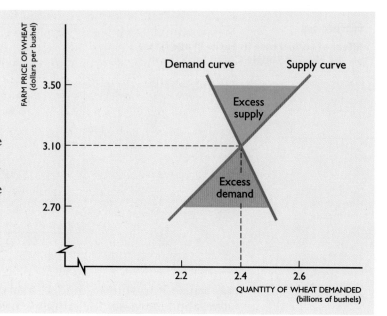

price. The best way to understand what we mean by an equilibrium price is to take a particular case, such as the wheat market. Let's put the demand curve for wheat (in Figure 2.1) and the supply curve for wheat (in Figure 2.6) together in the same diagram. The result, shown in Figure 2.9, will help us determine the equilibrium price of wheat.

We begin by seeing what would happen if various prices were established in the market. For example, if the price were $3.50 per bushel, the demand curve indicates that 2.3 billion bushels of wheat would be demanded, while the supply curve indicates that 2.6 billion bushels would be supplied. Thus if the price were $3.50 a bushel, there would be a mismatch between the quantity supplied and the quantity demanded per year, since the rate at which wheat is supplied would be greater than the rate at which it is demanded. Specifically, as shown in Figure 2.9, there would be an **Excess supply** **excess supply** of 300 million bushels. Under these circumstances, some of the wheat supplied by farmers could not be sold, and as inventories of wheat built up, suppliers would tend to cut their prices in order to get rid of unwanted inventories. Thus a price of $3.50 per bushel would not be maintained for long and for this reason $3.50 per bushel is not an equilibrium price.

If the price were $2.70 per bushel, on the other hand, the demand curve indicates that 2.5 billion bushels would be demanded, while the supply curve indicates that 2.2 billion bushels would be supplied. Again we find a mismatch between the quantity supplied and the quantity demanded per year, since the rate

Excess demand

at which wheat is supplied would be less than the rate at which it is demanded. Specifically, as shown in Figure 2.9, there would be an **excess demand** of 300 million bushels. Under these circumstances, some of the consumers who want wheat at this price would have to be turned away empty handed. There would be a shortage. And given this shortage, suppliers would find it profitable to increase the price, and competition among buyers would bid the price up. Thus a price of $2.70 per bushel could not be maintained for long, so $2.70 per bushel is not an equilibrium price.

Under these circumstances, the equilibrium price must be the price where the quantity demanded equals the quantity supplied. Obviously, this is the only price at which there is no mismatch between the quantity demanded and the quantity supplied, and consequently it is the only price that can be maintained for long. In Figure 2.9, the price at which the quantity supplied equals the quantity demanded is $3.10 per bushel, the price where the demand curve intersects the supply curve. Thus $3.10 per bushel is the equilibrium price of wheat under the circumstances visualized in Figure 2.9, and 2.4 billion bushels is the equilibrium quantity.

ACTUAL PRICE

Actual price

The price that counts in the real world, however, is the **actual price**, not the equilibrium price, and it is the actual price that we set out to explain. In general, economists simply assume that the actual price will approximate the equilibrium price; this seems reasonable enough, since the basic forces at work tend to push the actual price toward the equilibrium price. Thus if conditions remain fairly stable for a time, the actual price should move toward the equilibrium price.

So long as the actual price exceeds the equilibrium price, there will be downward pressure on price. Similarly, so long as the actual price is less than the equilibrium price, there will be upward pressure on price. Thus there is always a tendency for the actual price to move toward the equilibrium price. But it should not be assumed that this movement is always rapid. Sometimes it takes a long time for the actual price to get close to the equilibrium price. Sometimes the actual price never gets to the equilibrium price because by the time it gets close, the equilibrium price changes (because of shifts in either the demand curve or the supply curve or both). All that safely can be said is that the actual price will move toward the equilibrium price. But of course this information is of great value, both theoretically and practically. For many purposes, all that is needed is a correct prediction of the direction in which the price will move.

THE PRICE SYSTEM AND THE DETERMINATION
OF WHAT IS PRODUCED

Having described how prices are determined in free markets, we can now describe somewhat more fully how the price system goes about performing the four tasks (described in the previous chapter) that face any economic system. Let's begin by considering the determination of what society will produce: How does the price system carry out this task?

A product's demand curve is an important determinant of how much firms will produce of the product, since it indicates the amount of the product that will be demanded at each price. From the producers' point of view, the demand curve indicates the amount they can sell at each price. In a capitalist economy, firms are in business to make money: The manufacturers of any product will turn it out only if the amount of money they receive from consumers exceeds the cost of putting it on the market. Acting in accord with the profit motive, firms are led to produce what consumers desire. We saw in a previous section that if consumers' tastes shift in favor of foods containing wheat, the demand curve for wheat will shift to the right, which will increase the price of wheat. (If this is not obvious, see the section "Exploring Further" in this chapter.) Given the shift in the demand curve, it is profitable for firms to raise output. Acting in their own self-interest, they are led to make production decisions geared to the wants of the consumers.

Thus the price system uses the self-interest of the producers to get them to produce what consumers want. Consumers register what they want in the marketplace by their purchasing decisions, which can be represented by their demand curves. Producers can make more money by responding to consumer wants than by ignoring them. Consequently, they are led to produce what consumers are willing to pay for. (In addition, as we have seen above, the level of production costs as well as demand determines what will be produced.) Note that producers are not forced by anyone to do anything. They can produce air conditioners for Eskimos if they like, and if they are prepared to absorb the losses. The price system uses prices to communicate the relevant signals to producers and metes out penalties and rewards in the form of losses or profits.

THE PRICE SYSTEM AND THE DETERMINATION
OF HOW GOODS ARE PRODUCED

Next, consider how society determines how each good and service is produced. How does the price system carry out this task? The price of each resource gives producers an indication of how

How the price system determines what is produced: Low-cost homes after World War II

Suburban development after World War II in Levittown, New York

When World War II was over, millions of ex-GIs came home, fell in love, got married, and started families. And there was one thing they all needed: homes. But homes were not easy to come by. Depression and war had put home building on hold for almost twenty years.

What housing there was was beyond the means of most young vets with new jobs and new families. Young families were looking for low-cost housing. Home builders needed customers. It was demand in search of supply.

For most people the "American dream" included a house and a car. Henry Ford had made the dream come true for cars. Were there any Henry Fords in the postwar home-building business? William Levitt rose to the challenge.

Backed by the promise of VA and FHA mortgages, Levitt put his money where his judgment was. He laid out 6,000 lots on low-cost, Long Island potato fields and poured 6,000 concrete slabs. Specialized construction teams hit Levittown streets like commandos. But as with Ford's Model T, assembly-line methods could mean assembly-line sameness. In a nation dedicated to individualism, would mass production houses have mass appeal?

The houses were built. The ads were placed. The case went to the jury. The verdict was not slow in coming in. It was the unprecedented demand by World War II veterans for affordable housing that drew William Levitt and thousands of other builders into the low-cost housing market and built one of the foundations for postwar prosperity.

scarce this resource is and how valuable it is in other uses. Clearly, firms should produce goods and services at minimum cost. Suppose that there are two ways of producing tables: technique A and technique B. Technique A requires four hours of labor and $10 worth of wood per table, whereas technique B requires five hours of labor and $8 worth of wood. If the price of an hour of labor is $4, technique A should be used since a table costs $26 with this technique, as opposed to $28 with technique B.[5] In other words, technique A uses fewer resources per table.

The price system nudges producers to opt for technique A rather than technique B through profits and losses. If each table

---

[5]To obtain these figures, note that the cost with technique A is four labor-hours times $4 plus $10, or $26, while the cost with technique B is five labor-hours times $4 plus $8, or $28.

49

commands a price of $35, then by using technique A, producers make a profit of $35 − $26 = $9 per table. If they use technique B, they make a profit of $35 − $28 = $7 per table. Thus producers, if they maximize profit, will be led to adopt technique A. Their desire for profit leads them to adopt the technique that will enable society to get the most out of its resources. No one commands firms to use particular techniques. Washington officials do not order steel plants to substitute the basic oxygen process for open hearths, or petroleum refineries to substitute catalytic cracking for thermal cracking. It is all done through the impersonal marketplace.

You should not, however, get the idea that the price system operates with kid gloves. Suppose all firms producing tables used technique B until this past year, when technique A was developed: in other words, technique A is based on a new technology. Given this technological change, the supply curve for tables will shift to the right, and the price of a table will fall. (If this is not obvious, see the section "Exploring Further" in this chapter.) Suppose it drops to $27. If some firm insists on sticking with technique B, it will lose money at the rate of $1 a table; and as these losses mount, the firm's owners will become increasingly uncomfortable. The firm will either switch to technique A or go bankrupt. The price system leans awfully hard on producers who try to ignore its signals.

THE PRICE SYSTEM AND THE DETERMINATION OF WHO GETS WHAT

Let's turn now to how society's output will be distributed among the people. How does the price system carry out this task? The amount of goods and services people receive depends on their money income, which in turn is determined under the price system by the amount of various resources that they own and by the price of each resource. Thus, under the price system each person's income is determined in the marketplace: people come to the marketplace with certain resources to sell, and their income depends on how much they can get for these resources.

The question of who gets what is solved at two levels by the price system. Consider an individual product: for example, the tables discussed in the previous section. For the individual product, the question of who gets what is solved by the equality of quantity demanded and quantity supplied. If the price of these tables is at its equilibrium level, the quantity demanded will equal the quantity supplied. Consumers who are willing and able to pay the equilibrium price (or more) get the tables, while those who are unwilling or unable to pay it do not get them. It is just as simple—and as impersonal—as that. It doesn't matter whether you are a nice guy or a scoundrel, or whether you are a connoisseur of tables or someone who doesn't know good workmanship from poor. All that matters is whether you are able and willing to pay the equilibrium price.

Next, consider the question of who gets what at a somewhat more fundamental level. After all, whether consumers are able and willing to pay the equilibrium price for a good depends on their money income. As we have already seen, consumers' money income depends on the amount of resources of various kinds that they own and the price that they can get for them. Some people have lots of resources: they are endowed with skill and intelligence and industry, or they have lots of capital or land. Other people have little in the way of resources. Moreover, some people have resources that command a high price, whereas others have resources that are of little monetary value. The result is that under the price system, some consumers get a lot more of society's output than others.

THE PRICE SYSTEM AND ECONOMIC GROWTH

Let's turn now to the task of determining a country's rate of growth of per capita income. How does the price system do this? A country's rate of increase of per capita income depends on the rate of growth of its resources and the rate of increase of the efficiency with which they are used. First, consider the rate of growth of society's resources. The price system controls the amount of new capital goods produced much as it controls the amount of consumer goods produced. Similarly, the price system influences the amount society invests in educating, training, and upgrading its labor resources. To a considerable extent, the amount invested in such resource-augmenting activities is determined by the profitability of such investments, which is determined in turn by the pattern of prices.

Next, consider the rate of increase of the efficiency with which a society's resources are used. Clearly, this factor depends heavily on the rate of technological change. If technology is advancing at a rapid rate, it should be possible to get more and more out of a society's resources. But if technology is advancing rather slowly, it is likely to be difficult to get much more out of them. The price system affects the rate of technological change in a variety of ways: it influences the profitability of investing in research and development, the profitability of introducing new processes and products into commercial practice, and the profitability of accepting technological change—as well as the losses involved in spurning it.

The price system establishes strong incentives for firms to introduce new technology. Any firm that can find a cheaper way to produce an existing product or a way to produce a better product

Art auction at Sotheby's, the world-renowned auction house

will have a profitable jump on its competitors. Until its competitors can do the same thing, this firm can reap higher profits than it otherwise could. Of course, these higher profits will eventually be competed away, as other firms begin to imitate this firm's innovation. But lots of money can be made in the period during which this firm has a lead over its competitors. These profits are an important incentive for the introduction of new technology.

THE CIRCULAR FLOWS OF MONEY AND PRODUCTS

So far we have been concerned largely with the workings of a single market. But how do all of the various markets fit together? This is a very important question. Perhaps the best way to begin answering it is to distinguish between product markets and resource markets. As their names indicate, **product markets** are markets where products are bought and sold, and **resource markets** are markets where resources are bought and sold. Let's first consider product markets. As shown in Figure 2.10, firms provide products to consumers in product markets and receive money in return. The money the firms receive is their receipts; to consumers, on the other hand, it is their expenditures.

Product markets
Resource markets

Next, let's consider resource markets. Figure 2.10 shows that consumers provide resources—including labor—to firms in resource markets, and they receive money in return. The money the consumers receive is their income; to firms, on the other hand, it is their costs. Note that the flow of resources and products in Figure 2.10 is counterclockwise: *consumers provide resources to firms which in turn provide goods and services to consumers.* On the other hand, the flow of money in Figure 2.10 is clockwise: *firms pay*

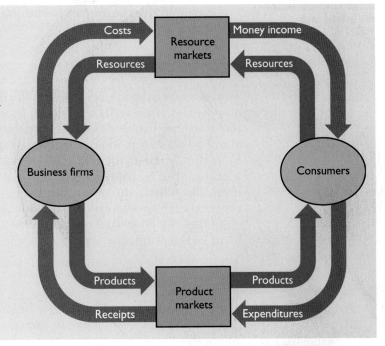

FIGURE 2.10

The Circular Flows of Money and Products

In product markets, consumers exchange money for products and firms exchange products for money. In resource markets, consumers exchange resources for money and firms exchange money for resources.

money for resources to consumers who in turn use the money to buy goods and services from the firms. Both flows—that of resources and products and that of money—go on simultaneously and repeatedly.

So long as consumers spend all their income, the flow of money income from firms to consumers is exactly equal to the flow of expenditures from consumers to firms. Thus these circular flows keep rolling along. As a first approximation, this is a perfectly good model. But capitalist economies have experienced periods of widespread unemployment and severe inflation that this model cannot explain. Also, note that our simple economy in Figure 2.10 has no government sector. In later chapters, we will bring the government into the picture. Under pure capitalism, the government would play a limited role in the economic system, but in the mixed capitalistic system we have in the United States, the government plays an important role indeed.

LIMITATIONS OF THE PRICE SYSTEM

Despite its many advantages, the price system suffers from limitations. Because these limitations are both significant and well known, no one believes that the price system, left to its own devices, can be trusted to solve all society's basic economic problems. To a considerable extent, the government's role in the economy has developed in response to the limitations of the price system, which are described below.

■ DISTRIBUTION OF INCOME

There is no reason to believe that the distribution of income generated by the price system is *fair* or, in some sense, *best*. Most people feel that the distribution of income generated by the price system should be altered to suit humanitarian needs—in particular, that help should be given to the poor. Both liberals and conservatives tend to agree on this score, although there are arguments over the extent to which the poor should be helped and the conditions under which they should be eligible for help. But the general principle that the government should step in to redistribute income in favor of the poor is generally accepted in the United States today.[6]

■ PUBLIC GOODS

Some goods and services *cannot be provided through the price system because there is no way to exclude citizens from consuming the goods whether they pay for them or not*. For example, there is no way to prevent citizens from benefiting from national expenditures on defense, whether they pay money toward defense or not. Consequently, the price system cannot be used to provide such goods; no one will pay for them since all will receive them whether they pay or not. Further, some goods, like the quality of the environment and national defense (and others cited below), *can be enjoyed by one person without depriving others of the same enjoyment*. Goods with the above characteristics are called **public goods**. Government provides many public goods. Such goods are consumed collectively or jointly, and it is inefficient to try to price them in a market. They tend to be indivisible; that is, they cannot easily be split into pieces and be bought and sold in a market.

Public goods

■ EXTERNAL ECONOMIES AND DISECONOMIES

In cases where *the production or consumption of a good by one firm or consumer has adverse or beneficial uncompensated effects on other firms or consumers, the price system will not operate effectively*. An **external economy** is said to occur when consumption or pro-

External economy

---

[6]Also, because the wealthy have more money to spend than the poor, the sorts of goods and services that society produces will reflect this fact. Thus luxuries for the rich may be produced in larger amounts, and necessities for the poor may be produced in smaller amounts than some critics regard as sensible and equitable. This is another frequently encountered criticism of the price system.

The food stamp program and the allocation of resources

Food stamps

Although the free market encourages an efficient allocation of resources, it responds only to those who have money to spend. If people are willing and able to spend money to fulfill a *need* for a good, there is an *effective demand* for that good, and the market will automatically respond to that need. Needs that are not backed up by spending power, however, will not be met by the market.

Clearly, the market system does not ensure that everyone will have money. Income is primarily dependent on one's being able to sell one's services in exchange for a wage. Those who cannot or will not sell their labor services, such as children,

the adults who must care for young children, the aged, or the disabled, will have small incomes under the market system. Their needs are not translated into effective demand, so the market will not, by itself, provide for these people.

The government has set up programs that provide varying degrees of assistance to those who have an income below the poverty level. One of the largest, the food stamp program, began as a pilot program in 1961 and was greatly expanded under the Johnson administration in the Food Stamp Act of 1964. Any low-income households meeting the basic eligibility requirements could buy food stamps at a price below

their market value. By 1969 there were 3.2 million people using food stamps at a cost to the government of $272 million.

The food stamp program was expanded in 1971 under President Richard Nixon. By the early 1980s, about one out of every eleven Americans was a food stamp recipient, and the program cost $11.3 billion. The rapid growth of the program made it a focus of controversy, and the Reagan administration sought to reduce the growth in outlays. Part of the debate concerned the perennial question of the extent of the federal government's responsibility to help the poor. Should government programs be only a safety net for the truly needy, or should the government create programs of such scope that they would have a major impact on income distribution?

In 1996, significant changes were made to the Food Stamp program as part of a major overhaul of the welfare system in the United States. The most significant change required able-bodied food stamp recipients between the ages of 18 and 50 who did not have dependents to work an average of at least 20 hours per week or participate in a state-approved work, training, or workfare program. Otherwise, they could receive no more than three months of food stamps out of every three years. This was part of an overall attempt to reduce the disincentives to work in the welfare system.

duction by one person or firm results in uncompensated benefits to another person or firm. A good example of an external economy exists where fundamental research carried out by one firm is used by another firm. (To cite one such case, there were external economies from the Bell Telephone Laboratories' invention of the transistor. Many electronics firms, such as Texas Instruments and Fairchild, benefited considerably from Bell's research.) Where external economies exist, it is generally agreed that the price system will produce too little of the good in question and that the government should supplement the amount produced by private enterprise. This is the basic rationale for much of the government's huge investment in basic science. An **external diseconomy** is said to occur when consumption or production by one person or firm results in uncompensated costs to another person or firm. A good example of an external diseconomy occurs when a firm dumps pollutants into a stream and makes the water unfit for use by firms and people downstream. Where activities result in external diseconomies, it is generally agreed that the price system will tolerate too much of the activities and that the government should curb them.

**External
diseconomy**

EXPLORING FURTHER

EFFECTS OF SHIFTS IN THE DEMAND AND SUPPLY CURVES

■ SHIFTS IN THE DEMAND CURVE

The ancient Greek philosopher Heraclitus said you cannot step in the same stream twice: everything changes, sooner or later. One need not be a disciple of Heraclitus to recognize that demand curves shift. Indeed, we have already seen that demand curves shift in response to changes in tastes, income, population, and prices of other products and that supply curves shift in response to changes in technology and input prices. Any supply-and-demand diagram like Figure 2.9 is essentially a snapshot of the situation during a particular period of time. The results in Figure 2.9 are limited to a particular period because the demand and supply curves in the figure, like any demand and supply curves, pertain only to a certain period.

What happens to the equilibrium price of a product when its demand curve changes? This is an important question because it sheds a good deal of light on how the price system works. Suppose that consumer tastes shift in favor of foods containing wheat and cause the demand curve for wheat to shift *to the right*, as shown in Figure 2.11. It is not hard to see the effect on the equilibrium price of wheat. Before the shift, the equilibrium price is *P*. But when the

FIGURE 2.11

Effect on the Equilibrium Price of a Shift to the Right of the Market Demand Curve

This shift of the demand curve to the right results in an increase in the equilibrium price from P to P_1 and an increase in the equilibrium quantity from Q to Q_1.

demand curve shifts to the right, a shortage develops at this price: that is, the quantity demanded exceeds the quantity supplied at this price.[7] Consequently, suppliers raise their prices. After some testing of market reactions and trial-and-error adjustments, the price will tend to settle at P_1, the new equilibrium price, and quantity will tend to settle at Q_1.

On the other hand, suppose that consumer demand for wheat products falls off, perhaps because of a great drop in the price of corn products. The demand for wheat now shifts *to the left*, as shown in Figure 2.12. What will be the effect on the equilibrium price of wheat? Clearly, the equilibrium price falls to P_2, where the new demand curve intersects the supply curve.

In general, *a shift to the right in the demand curve results in an increase in the equilibrium price, and a shift to the left in the demand curve results in a decrease in the equilibrium price*. This is the lesson of Figures 2.11 and 2.12. Of course, this conclusion depends on the assumption that the supply curve slopes upward to the right, but, as we noted in a previous section, this assumption is generally true.

At this point, since all this is theory, you may be wondering how well this theory works in practice. In 1972 and 1973, there was a vivid demonstration of the accuracy of this model in various agricultural markets, including wheat. Because of poor harvests

[7]This shortage is equal to $Q_i - Q$ in Figure 2.11.

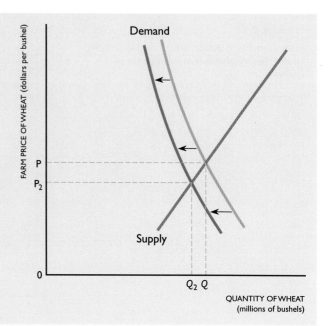

FIGURE 2.12

Effect on the Equilibrium Price of a Shift to the Left of the Market Demand Curve

This shift of the demand curve to the left results in a decrease in the equilibrium price from P to P_2 and a decrease in the equilibrium quantity from Q to Q_2.

abroad and greatly increased foreign demand for U.S. wheat, the demand curve for wheat shifted markedly to the right. What happened to the price of wheat? In accord with our model, the price increased spectacularly, from about $1.35 a bushel in the early summer of 1972 to over $4.00 a year later. Anyone who witnessed this phenomenon could not help but be impressed by the usefulness of this model.

■ SHIFTS IN THE SUPPLY CURVE

What happens to the equilibrium price of a product when its supply curve changes? For example, suppose that because of technological advances in wheat production, wheat farmers are willing and able to supply more wheat at a given price than they used to, with the result that the supply curve shifts *to the right*, as shown in Figure 2.13. What will be the effect on the equilibrium price? Clearly, it will fall from P (where the original supply curve intersects the demand curve) to P_3 (where the new supply curve intersects the demand curve).

On the other hand, suppose that the weather is poor, with the result that the supply curve shifts *to the left*, as shown in Figure 2.13. What will be the effect? The equilibrium price will increase from P (where the original supply curve intersects the demand curve) to P_4 (where the new supply curve intersects the demand curve).

FIGURE 2.13

Effects on the Equilibrium Price of Shifts in the Market Supply Curve

The shift of the supply curve to the right results in a decrease in the equilibrium price from P to P_3. The shift of the supply curve to the left increases the equilibrium price from P to P_4.

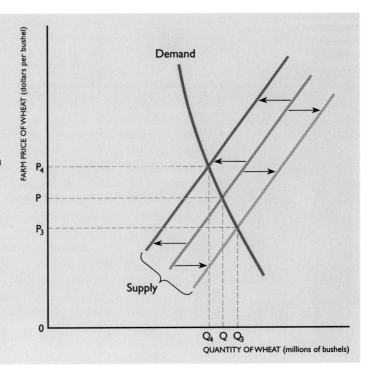

In 1993, buyers of Brazil nuts, the most popular nuts in American and British homes at Christmastime, were shown vividly what a shift to the left in the supply curve of a commodity will do. Because of droughts in Brazil, Bolivia, and Peru, the major producers of such nuts, the price of Brazil nuts shot up by 20 percent in 1993.[8]

In general, *a shift to the right in the supply curve results in a decrease in the equilibrium price, and a shift to the left in the supply curve results in an increase in the equilibrium price.* Of course, this conclusion depends on the assumption that the demand curve slopes downward to the right, but, as we noted in a previous section, this assumption is generally true.

REVIEW AND PRACTICE

■ SUMMARY

❚ Consumers and firms are the basic units composing the private sector of the economy. A market is a group of firms and individuals that are in touch with each other to buy some commodity or service.

[8]*New York Times*, December 24, 1993, p. D12.

2 There are two sides to every market: the demand side and the supply side. The demand side can be represented by the market demand curve, which almost always slopes downward to the right and the position of which depends on consumer tastes, the number and income of consumers, and the prices of other commodities.

3 The supply side of the market can be represented by the market supply curve, which generally slopes upward to the right and the position of which depends on technology and resource prices.

4 The equilibrium price and equilibrium quantity of a commodity are given by the intersection of the market demand and market supply curves.

5 To determine what goods and services society will produce, the price system sets up incentives for firms to produce what consumers want. Also, the price system sets up strong incentives for firms to produce goods at minimum cost.

6 To determine who gets what, the price system results in people's receiving an income that depends on the quantity of resources they own and the prices that these resources command. The price system also establishes incentives for activities that result in increases in a society's per capita income.

7 There are circular flows of money and products in a capitalist economy. In product markets, firms provide products to consumers and receive money in return. In resource markets, consumers provide resources to firms and receive money in return.

8 The price system, despite its many virtues, suffers from serious limitations. There is no reason to believe that the distribution of income generated by the price system is equitable or optimal. Also, there is no way for the price system to handle public goods properly, and because of external economies or diseconomies, the price system may result in too little or too much of certain goods being produced.

*9 Changes in the position and shape of the demand curve—in response to changes in consumer tastes, income, population, and prices of other commodities—result in changes in the equilibrium price and equilibrium output of a product. Similarly, changes in the position and shape of the supply curve—in response to changes in technology and resource prices, among other things—also result in changes in the equilibrium price and equilibrium output of a product.

■ PROBLEMS AND QUESTIONS

1 Assume that the market for electric toasters is competitive and that the quantity supplied per year depends as follows on the price of a toaster:

PRICE OF A TOASTER (DOLLARS)	NUMBER OF TOASTERS SUPPLIED (MILLIONS)
12	4.0
14	5.0
16	5.5
18	6.0
20	6.3

*The starred item refers to material covered in Exploring Further.

Plot the supply curve for toasters. Is this a direct or inverse relationship? Are supply curves generally direct or inverse relationships?

2 Suppose that the quantity of toasters demanded per year depends as follows on the price of a toaster:

PRICE OF A TOASTER (DOLLARS)	NUMBER OF TOASTERS DEMANDED (MILLIONS)
12	7.0
14	6.5
16	6.2
18	6.0
20	5.8

Plot the demand curve for toasters. If the price is $14, will there be an excess demand for toasters? If the price is $20, will there be an excess demand? What is the equilibrium price of a toaster? What is the equilibrium quantity? (Use the data in question 1.)

3 Suppose that the government imposes a price ceiling on toasters. In particular, suppose that it decrees that a toaster cannot sell for more than $14. Will the quantity supplied equal the quantity demanded? What sorts of devices may come into being to allocate the available supply of toasters to consumers? What problems will the government encounter in keeping the price at $14? What social purposes, if any, might such a price ceiling serve? (Use the data in questions 1 and 2.)

4 Suppose that the government imposes a price floor on toasters. In particular, suppose that it decrees that a toaster cannot sell for less than $20. Will the quantity supplied equal the quantity demanded? How will the resulting supply of toasters be taken off the market? What problems will the government encounter in keeping the price at $20? What social purposes, if any, might such a price floor serve? (Use the data above.)

■ **KEY TERMS**

consumers	excess demand
firms	actual price
markets	product markets
market demand curve	resource markets
market supply curve	public goods
equilibrium price	external economy
excess supply	external diseconomy

■ **VIEWPOINT FOR ANALYSIS**

In a speech delivered at the American Bar Association, William Brewer said, "The suggestion was put forth in a newspaper article last year that to solve the problem of the oversupply of attorneys, the government should pay lawyers $500,000 each to turn in their bar cards. It was proposed as a sort of a 'farm subsidy' solution . . . whereby the government would pay lawyers *not* to practice law. So instead of say, wheat, the uncultivated crop in the fallow north forty would be litigation."*

(a) Is there a market for lawyers? If so, what determines the location and shape of the demand curve? Of the supply curve?

(b) If the market for lawyers were perfectly competitive, could there be an oversupply in the sense that the quantity of lawyers supplied exceeded the quantity demanded? Under conditions of equilibrium, could such an oversupply exist? Why or why not?

(c) If the government were to pay lawyers $500,000 to leave their profession, would this influence the demand curve for lawyers? Would it influence the supply curve? Would it influence the wage paid lawyers? Do you favor such a policy? Why or why not?

*Vital Speeches, March 1, 1993, p. 318.

The Key Role of Saving and Investment in Raising Per Capita Income

In the first ten thousand years of human development there was almost no economic growth to speak of, and per capita income in Europe in the 1600s was barely higher than in the time of the Roman Empire. However, in the late 1700s and early 1800s something began to change. In the intervening two centuries European income per capita (after adjusting for inflation) rose almost 15-fold! What happened?

One of the most remarkable developments in human history was the Industrial Revolution. Until the middle of the eighteenth century, industry (as distinct from agriculture or commerce) played a small role in the economies of Europe or America. But during the late eighteenth and early nineteenth centuries a host of important technological innovations, such as James Watt's steam engine and Richard Arkwright's spinning jenny, made possible a very rapid growth in the output of industrial goods (like textiles

Spinning jenny

and pig iron). And accompanying this growth of industrial output was the advent of the factory—a social and economic institution which is taken for granted today but which was largely unknown prior to the Industrial Revolution.

The Industrial Revolution was characterized by major improvements in technology and by large increases in the amount of capital resources available to society. Due to the improvements in technology, the standard of living in England, as measured by per capita income (total income divided by population), grew at an unprecedented rate. As the Industrial Revolution spread, this rise in living standards occurred too on the European continent and in the United States; it remained one of the lasting effects of industrialization.

As stressed above, the Industrial Revolution was characterized by considerable increases in capital. How did England (and other countries) bring about this increase in capital? By saving and investing. In other words, the English people had to set aside some of their resources and say in effect, "These resources will *not* be used to satisfy the current needs of our population for food, clothing, and other forms of consumption. Instead, they will be used to produce capital—factories, machines, equipment, railroads, and canals—which will increase our future productive capacity." Much more will be said about this saving process in subsequent chapters. For now, the essential point is that was one of the necessary conditions for the Industrial Revolution.

Turning from the Industrial Revolution to the present, one of the reasons for Japan's remarkable increase in output during the period since World War II has been the very high Japanese savings rate. In this period during the 1960s and early 1970s when output in Japan was growing at about 10 percent per year, the Japanese were saving about 25 percent of their income. Like the English during the Industrial Revolution, the Japanese said in effect, "These resources will be used for factories, equipment, and other forms of investment, not for consumption." Thanks to the liberalization of trade and the rapid transfer of technology, the improvement in living standards in East Asian countries in recent decades was even faster than in Europe and the United States during the Industrial Revolution. In the 1800s, it took five decades for per capita output to double in Britain and in the United States. In recent years, South Korea and China accomplished the same feat in one-fifth the time! As in Japan, saving rates in East Asia were an important factor.

QUESTIONS

I Did the major improvements in technology in the late eighteenth and early nineteenth centuries, such as Watt's steam engine and Arkwright's spinning jenny, have an effect on the production possibilities curve in England? Why or why not?

2 If these inventions had an effect on the production possibilities curve in England, did they shift it to the left or to the right? Explain.

3 Why did these inventions result in an increase in the standard of living in England? Did they alone accomplish this, or were increases in the amount of capital resources important too?

4 Why couldn't the Industrial Revolution have occurred without considerable increases in capital?

5 In Japan after World War II, did the Japanese invent lots of new techniques, as the English did at the beginning of the Industrial Revolution? If not, where did they get the advanced technology required to transform their economy?

PART TWO

National Income and Output

CHAPTER 3

National Income and Product

LEARNING OBJECTIVES

In this chapter, you should learn:

■ What gross domestic product (GDP) measures and why it is important

■ The nature of a price index and how it can be used

■ Two approaches for measuring GDP

Economics is important in both war and peace. For example, in World War II, U.S. policy makers had to figure out how much our nation could produce to support the war effort. How did they make such estimates? One purpose of this chapter is to answer that question.

Gross domestic product

The **gross domestic product**, or GDP as it is often called, of the United States was about $9.3 trillion in 1999, as compared with about $6.3 trillion in 1992. Put in the simplest terms, the GDP is the value of the total amount of final goods and services produced by our economy during a particular period of time. This measure is important for its own sake and because it helps us to understand both inflation and unemployment. The federal government and the business community watch the GDP figures avidly. Government officials, from the president down, are interested because these figures indicate how prosperous we are and because they are useful in forecasting the future health of the economy. Business executives are also extremely interested in GDP figures because the sales of their firms are related to the level of the GDP, and so the figures are useful in forecasting the future health of their businesses. All in all, it is no exaggeration to say that the gross domestic product is one of the most closely watched numbers in existence. In this chapter, we discuss the measurement, uses, and limitations of the gross domestic product.

GROSS DOMESTIC PRODUCT

As noted above, the gross domestic product is a measure of how much the economy produces in a particular period of time. But the U.S. economy produces millions of types of goods and services.

How can we add together everything from lemon meringue pies to helicopters, from books to houses? The only feasible answer is to use money as a common denominator and to make the price of a good or service—the amount the buyer is willing to pay—the measure of value. In other words, we add the values in money terms of all the goods and services output by the economy during a certain period, normally a year, and the result is the gross domestic product during that period.

Although the measurement of the gross domestic product may seem straightforward (just "add the values in money terms of all the goods and services output by the economy"), this is by no means the case. Some of the more important pitfalls that must be avoided and problems that must be confronted are the following.

Avoidance of double counting. Gross domestic product does not include the values of *all* the goods and services produced; it includes only the values of the *final* goods and services produced. **Final goods and services** are goods and services destined for the ultimate user. For example, flour purchased for family consumption is a final good, but flour to be used in manufacturing bread is an **intermediate good**, not a final good. We would be double counting if we counted both the bread and the flour used to make the bread as output. Thus the output of intermediate goods—goods that are not destined for the ultimate user but are used as inputs in producing final goods and services—must not be included in the gross domestic product.

Final goods and services

Intermediate good

Valuation at cost. Some final goods and services that must be included in the gross domestic product are not bought and sold in the marketplace, so they are valued at what they cost. Consider the services performed by government: police protection, fire protection, the use of the courts, defense, and so forth. Such services are not bought and sold in any market (despite the old saying about the judge who was "the best that money could buy"). Yet they are an important part of our economy's final output. Economists and statisticians have decided to value them at what they cost the taxpayers. This is not ideal, but it is the best practical solution advanced to date.

Nonmarket transactions. For practical reasons it is necessary to omit certain types of final output from the gross domestic product. In particular, some nonmarketed goods and services, such as the services performed by homemakers, are excluded from the gross domestic product. This is not because economists fail to appreciate these services but because it is extremely difficult to get reasonably reliable estimates of the money value of a homemaker's services. At first glance, this may seem to be a very important weakness in our measure of total output, but so long as the value of these services does not change much (in relation to total output), the variation in the gross domestic product will provide a reasonably accurate picture of the variation in total output—and, for our purposes, this is all that is required.

Nonproductive transactions. Purely financial transactions are excluded from the gross domestic product because they do not reflect current production. Such financial transactions include government transfer payments, private transfer payments, and the sale and purchase of securities. ***Government transfer payments*** are payments made by the government to individuals who do not contribute to production in exchange for them. Payments to welfare recipients are a good example of government transfer payments. Since these payments are not for production, it would be incorrect to include them in the GDP. ***Private transfer payments*** are gifts or other transfers of wealth from one person or private organization to another. Again these are not payments for production, so there is no reason to include them in the GDP. The sale and purchase of securities are not payments for production, so they too are excluded from the GDP.

Secondhand goods. Sales of secondhand goods are also excluded from the gross domestic product. The reason for this is clear: when a good is produced, its value is included in the GDP. If its value is also included when it is sold on the secondhand market, it will be counted twice, and thus lead to an overstatement of the true GDP. Suppose that you buy a new bicycle and resell it a year later. The value of the new bicycle is included in the GDP when the bicycle is produced. But the resale value of the bicycle is not included in the GDP; to do so would be double counting.

ADJUSTING GDP FOR PRICE CHANGES

■ CURRENT DOLLARS VERSUS CONSTANT DOLLARS

In the Prologue, we stressed that the general price level has changed over time. (Recall the rapid inflation of the 1970s and early 1980s.) Since the gross domestic product values all goods and services at their current prices, it is bound to be affected by changes in the price level as well as by changes in total output. If all prices doubled tomorrow, this would produce a doubling of the gross domestic product. Clearly, if the gross domestic product is to be a reliable measure of changes in total output, we must correct it to eliminate the effects of such changes in the price level.

Base year
To make such a correction, economists choose some **base year** and express the value of all goods and services in terms of

71

their prices during that year. If 1999 is taken as the base year and if the price of beef was $2 per pound in 1999, beef is valued at $2 per pound in all other years. Thus, if 100 million pounds of beef were produced in 2002, this total output is valued at $200 million even though the price of beef in 2002 was actually higher than $2 per pound. In this way, distortions caused by changes in the price level are eliminated.

Gross domestic product is expressed either in current dollars or in constant dollars. Figures expressed in **current dollars** are actual dollar amounts, whereas those expressed in **constant dollars** are corrected for changes in the price level. Expressed in current dollars, the gross domestic product is affected by changes in the price level. Expressed in constant dollars, the gross domestic product is not affected by the price level because the prices of all goods are maintained at their base-year level. After being corrected for changes in the price level, the GDP is called **real GDP**.

Figure 3.1 shows the behavior of both real GDP and GDP expressed in current dollars. GDP expressed in current dollars has increased more rapidly (due to inflation) than GDP in constant dollars (real GDP).

**Current dollars
Constant dollars**

Real GDP

FIGURE 3.1

Gross Domestic Product, Expressed in Current Dollars and 1996 Dollars, United States, 1960–99

Because of inflation, GDP expressed in current dollars has increased more rapidly in recent years than GDP in constant (1996) dollars. This was particularly true in the 1970s and 1980s, reflecting the price surge then.

Understanding the new estimates of GDP

U.S. Department of Commerce

In 1995 and in 1999 the Bureau of Economic Analysis (BEA) of the U.S. Department of Commerce made major benchmark revisions to the national income and to the product accounts data. Both of these revisions made major improvements in the calculation of the impact of computers on the U.S. economy. They also corrected some of the biases that had crept into the estimates of GDP. In the 1995 revisions the BEA shifted its emphasis from fixed-weighted measures to chain-weighted measures of real output and prices. What do these terms mean and why did the government make the switch?

The government obtains its estimates of real output—the inflation-adjusted quantity of goods and

services produced—in two steps. In the first step, the current market value of spending for each detailed component of GDP is calculated from the basic source data. This is called current-dollar or nominal output. In the second step, the effects of inflation are removed by dividing the nominal output of each type of good or service by its price index. These price indexes are normalized to equal 1 (or 100) in the base year, currently 1992. The government calculates price indexes and real output for more than 1,000 different categories of goods and services. At this most-detailed level, the real output data underlying fixed-weight and chain-weight measures are identical.

The crucial question is how real output for these subcomponents of GDP should be added together to obtain broader concepts, like real GDP or real consumption. Under the fixed-weight system, the subcomponents are added together using their relative prices in the base year. Thus, if an apple cost twice as much as an orange in 1992, apples would be given twice the weight of oranges in every year, no matter what their relative prices were in other years.

As long as relative prices do not change much, this weighting system functions reasonably well, as it did with few exceptions until the late 1980s. However, the growing importance of computers, coupled with the sharp decline in their relative price, has introduced problems into this system. As a result, real fixed-weighted GDP has become less reliable as a measure of the value of economic output and as an indicator of the amount of resources necessary to produce that output.

In the chain-weighted method of aggregation, these problems are avoided because the change in real output between successive years depends only on relative prices in those years, not on relative prices in the base year. For example, to calculate the growth in real chain-weighted GDP between 1992 and 1993, one would create two fixed-weight measures of real GDP for each year, one pair using 1992 prices as weights, the other pair using 1993 prices as weights. One can then calculate two different growth rates for real GDP in 1993, one using 1992 price weights, the other using 1993 price weights. The 1993 growth rate for real chain-weighted GDP then equals the average of these two growth rates.

The new chain-weighted estimates of GDP have two disadvantages. First, they are more complex and harder to understand. Second, unlike fixed-weight estimates, chain-weighted estimates of the components of GDP (consumer spending, investments, exports, and so on) do not precisely add to total GDP. This nonadditivity introduces a distortion of its own, which, however, is much smaller on average than the bias of the fixed-weight estimates. Thus, on balance, the new approach provides a better estimate of GDP than the old.

In the 1999 revisions, the BEA made two major changes in the way it calculates the impact of software purchases and electronic transactions on the growth of productivity and real GDP. First, instead of treating software purchases as production inputs (in the same way that steel is a production input for a car), these purchases are now categorized as investments—recognizing that software is used over and over. Thus, software purchases are now added directly to the computed value of GDP.

Second, the 1999 revisions corrected a flaw in the measurement of bank-ing productivity. Previously, banking productivity was assumed to be zero, so output rose at the same rate as the number of hours worked by bank employees. The new estimates now calculate the impact of ATM and other electronic transactions on banking productivity.

As a result of these two revisions, nonfarm productivity is now estimated to have grown between 0.5 and 0.7 percent faster during the 1980s and 1990s than was previously estimated. Similarly, real GDP growth over the past twenty years is calculated to have averaged approximately 3.2 percent instead of the previously estimated 2.8 percent.

■ PRICE INDEXES

It is often useful to have some measure of how much prices have changed over a certain period of time. One way to obtain such a measure is to divide the value of a set of goods and services expressed in current dollars by the value of the same set of goods and services expressed in constant (base-year) dollars. Suppose that a set of goods and services costs $100 when valued at 2002 prices, but $70 when valued at 1999 prices. Apparently, prices have risen an average of 43 percent for this set of goods between 1999 and 2002. How do we get 43 percent? The ratio of the cost in 2002 prices to the cost in 1999 prices is 100 ÷ 70 = 1.43; thus prices must have risen on the average by 43 percent for this set of goods.

Price index

The ratio of the value of a set of goods and services in current dollars to the value of the same set of goods and services in constant (base-year) dollars is a **price index**. Thus 1.43 is the price index in the example above. An important function of a price index is to convert values expressed in current dollars into values expressed in constant dollars. This conversion, known as *deflating*, can be achieved simply by dividing values expressed in current dollars by the price index. In the illustration above, values expressed in 2002 dollars can be converted into constant (1999) dollars by dividing by 1.43. This procedure is an important one, with applications in many fields other than the measurement of the gross domestic product. For example, firms use it to compare their output in various years. To correct for price changes, they deflate their sales by a price index for their products.

In many cases, price indexes are multiplied by 100; that is, they are expressed as percentage changes. Thus, in the case described above, the price index might be expressed as 1.43 × 100, or 143, which would indicate that 2002 prices on the average were 143 percent of their 1999 level. In Chapter 7, we shall say more about price indexes that are expressed in this way. For now, we assume that the price index is not multiplied by 100.

■ APPLICATIONS OF PRICE INDEXES

To illustrate how a price index can be used to deflate some figures, suppose that we want to measure how much the output of bread rose in *real terms*—that is, in constant dollars—between 1999 and 2003. Suppose that the value of the output of bread in current dollars during each year was as shown in the first column of Table 3.1 and that the price of bread was as shown in the second column. To determine the value of the output of bread in 1999 dollars, we form a price index with 1999 as the base year, as shown in the third column. Then, dividing the figures in the first column by this price index, we get the value of the output of bread during each year in 1999 dollars, shown in the fourth column. Thus the fourth column shows how much the output of bread has grown in real terms. The real output of bread has risen by 19 percent—(1,900 − 1,600) ÷ 1,600—between 1999 and 2003.

Next, let's take up an actual case. The first column of Table 3.2 shows the gross domestic product in selected years during the 1980s and 1990s. The second column shows the relevant price index for the GDP for each of these years. (The base year is 1996.)

	(1) OUTPUT OF BREAD (CURRENT	(2) PRICE OF BREAD	(3) PRICE INDEX (PRICE ÷	(4) OUTPUT OF BREAD
YEAR	DOLLARS)	(DOLLARS)	1999 PRICE)	(1999 DOLLARS)[a]
1999	1,600 million	.50	1.00	1,600 million
2000	1,768 million	.52	1.04	1,700 million
2001	1,980 million	.55	1.10	1,800 million
2002	2,090 million	.55	1.10	1,900 million
2003	2,204 million	.58	1.16	1,900 million

TABLE 3.1

Use of the Price Index to Convert from Current to Constant Dollars

[a]This column was derived by dividing column 1 by column 3.

TABLE 3.2

Calculation of Real
Gross Domestic
Product

YEAR	GDP (BILLIONS OF CURRENT DOLLARS)	PRICE INDEX (1996 = 1.000)	REAL GDP (BILLIONS OF 1996 DOLLARS)
1982	3,259	0.663	4,919 (= 3,529 ÷ 0.663)
1995	4,213	0.737	
1988	5,108	0.802	6,368 (= 5,108 ÷ 0.802)
1991	5,986	0.897	6,676 (= 5,986 ÷ 0.897)
1996	7,813	1.0	
1999	9,254	1.046	8,847 (= 9,254 ÷ 1.046)

What was the real GDP in 1999? To answer this question, we must divide the GDP in current dollars in 1998 by the price index for 1999. Thus the answer is $9,254 billion divided by 1.046, or $8,847 billion. In other words, when expressed in constant 1996 dollars, the GDP in 1998 was $8,847 billion. What was the real GDP in 1988? Applying the same principles, the answer is $5,108 billion divided by 0.082, or $6,368 billion. In other words, when expressed in constant 1996 dollars, the GDP in 1988 was $6,368 billion. To test your understanding, see if you can figure out the value of the real GDP in 1985. (To check your answer, consult footnote 1.)[1]

[1]The real GDP in 1985 equaled $4,213 billion divided by .737, or $5,716 billion in 1998 dollars.

We have pointed out that the gross domestic product includes the value of only the final goods and services produced. Obviously, however, the output of final goods and services is not due solely to the efforts of the producers of the final goods and services. The total value of an automobile when it leaves the plant, for example, represents the work of many industries besides the automobile manufacturers. The steel, tires, glass, and many other components of the automobile were not produced by the automobile manufacturers. In reality, the automobile manufacturers only added a certain amount of value to the value of the intermediate goods—steel, tires, glass, and so forth—they purchased. This point is basic to an understanding of how the gross domestic product is calculated.

Value-added

To measure the contribution of a firm or industry to final output, we use the concept of value-added. **Value-added** means just what it says: *the amount of value added by a firm or industry to the total worth of the product.* It is a measure in money terms of the extent of production taking place in a particular firm or industry. Suppose that $160 million of bread was produced in the United States in 2002. To produce it, farmers harvested $50 million of wheat, which was used as an intermediate product by flour mills, which turned out $80 million of flour. This flour was used as an intermediate product by the bakers who produced the $160 million of bread. What is the value-added at each stage of the process? For simplicity, assume that the farmers did not have to purchase any materials from other firms in order to produce the wheat. Then the value-added by the wheat farmers is $50 million; the value-added by the flour mills is $30 million ($80 million − $50 million);

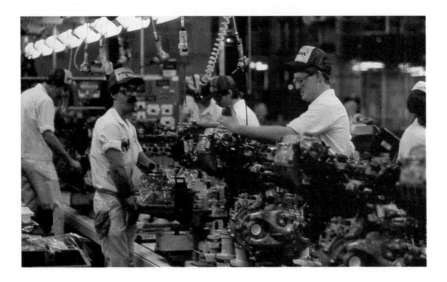

Assembly line at
Honda's Anna, Ohio,
engine plant

and the value-added by the bakers is $80 million ($160 million − $80 million). The total of the value-added at all stages of the process ($50 million + $30 million + $80 million) must equal the value of the output of final product ($160 million) because each stage's value-added is its contribution to this value.

THE LIMITATIONS OF GDP

It is essential that the limitations of the gross domestic product be understood. Although very useful, it is by no means an ideal measure of economic well-being. At least five limitations of this measure must always be borne in mind.

Population. GDP is not very meaningful unless one knows the size of the population of the country in question. For example, the fact that a particular country's GDP equals $50 billion means one thing if the country has 10 million inhabitants and quite another thing if it has 500 million inhabitants. To correct for the size of the population, GDP per capita—GDP divided by the population—is often used as a rough measure of output per person in a particular country.

Leisure. GDP does not take into account one of our most prized activities: leisure. During the past century, the average workweek in the United States has decreased substantially, from almost 70 hours in 1850 to about 40 hours today. As people have become more affluent, they have chosen to substitute leisure for increased production. Yet this increase in leisure time, which surely contributes to our well-being, does not show up in the GDP. Neither does the personal satisfaction (or displeasure and alienation) people get from their jobs.

Quality changes. GDP does not take adequate account of changes in the quality of goods. An improvement in a product is not reflected accurately in the GDP unless its price reflects the improvement. For example, if a new type of drug is put on the market at the same price as an old drug, and if the output and cost of the new drug are the same as those of the old drug, GDP will not increase, even though the new drug is twice as effective as the old one.

Value and distribution. The GDP says nothing about the social desirability of the composition and distribution of the country's output. Each good and service produced is valued at its price. If the price of a Bible is $10 and the price of a pornographic novel is $10, both are valued at $10, whatever you or I may think about their respective worth. Moreover, GDP measures only the total quantity of goods and services produced. It tells us nothing about how this output is distributed among the people. If a country's GDP is $500 billion, this is its GDP whether 90 percent of the output is consumed by a relatively few rich families or the output is distributed relatively equally among the citizens.

Social costs. GDP does not reflect some of the social costs arising from the production of goods and services. In particular, it does not reflect the environmental damage resulting from the operation of our nation's factories, offices, and farms. It is common knowledge that the atmosphere and water supplies are being polluted in various ways by firms, consumers, and governments. Yet these costs are not deducted from GDP, even though the failure to do so results in an overestimate of our true economic welfare.

TWO APPROACHES TO GDP

Suppose that we want to measure the market value of an automobile. One way to do this is to look at how much the consumer pays for the automobile. Although this is the most straightforward way to measure the car's market value, it is not the only way it can be done. Another, equally valid way is to add all the wage, interest, rental, and profit incomes generated in the car's production. As pointed out in the circular flow model in Figure 2.10, the amount that the car's producer receives for this car is equal to its profit (or loss) on the car plus the amount it pays the workers and other resource owners who contributed their resources to its production. Thus, if we add all the wage, interest, rental, and profit incomes resulting from the production of the automobile, the result is the same as if we determine how much the consumer pays for the automobile.

By the same token, there are two ways to measure the market value of the output of the economy as a whole. Or, put differently, there are two ways of looking at GDP. One is the **expenditures approach**, which regards GDP as the sum of all the expenditures on the final goods and services produced this year. The other is the **income approach**, which regards GDP as the sum of all the incomes derived from the production of this year's total output.

**Expenditures
approach**

Income approach

Since both of these approaches are valid, it follows that GDP can be viewed as either the total expenditure on this year's total output or as the total income stemming from the production of this year's total output:

Total expenditure on this year's total output

= GDP

= total income from the producton of this year's total output.

Using GDP estimates in World War II

Guided missile cruiser USS *Leyte Gulf* (CG-55)

During the Great Depression, policy-makers had little idea of what was happening to the economy. In contrast, during World War II economists did have a reasonably accurate picture of the economy's total output thanks to the new estimates of GDP, first published by the U.S. Department of Commerce in 1934. [Actually, estimates of GNP (gross *national* product), not GDP, were published in those days, but the differences between them tend to be small.] At the Commerce Department, economists were being pushed by events to come up with predictions of what the U.S. economy could produce. At home, the first mobilization committees were set up under the Victory program. And at the Commerce Department, economists went to work to see what kind of arsenal the United States could become and how quickly.

As the war intensified in Europe, the planners went to work. Experts were dispatched to London to find out what the Allies needed to survive. Specifically, the war planners began asking questions like:

Could the United States produce enough steel (for ships, guns, and tanks), aluminum (airplanes), and copper (ammunition)?

How much of the entire economy could be diverted to the war effort without jeopardizing the basic needs of the U.S. people for food, clothing, housing, and transportation?

How much money would the U.S. public be able to pay in taxes to support the war?

The effort that went into answering these questions helped to refine the national income and product accounts, and after the end of the war, the Commerce Department began to regularly produce estimates of GDP and related measurements.

This is an *identity*; the left-hand side of this equation must equal the right-hand side. (More precisely, the right-hand side should also include depreciation and indirect business taxes, as we will see below. But this refinement can be ignored at this point.)

It is important to understand both the expenditures approach and the income approach to GDP. In the following sections we describe both approaches in more detail.

THE EXPENDITURES APPROACH TO GDP

To use the expenditures approach to determine GDP, one must add all the expenditures on final goods and services. Economists distinguish among four broad categories of spending: personal consumption expenditures, gross private domestic investment, government purchases of goods and services, and net exports.

■ PERSONAL CONSUMPTION EXPENDITURES

Personal consumption expenditures include spending by households on durable goods, nondurable goods, and services. This category of spending includes your expenditures on items like food and drink, which are nondurable goods. It also includes your family's expenditures on a car or on an electric washer or dryer, which are durable goods. Further, it includes your payments to a dentist, who is providing a service (painful though it sometimes may be). Table 3.3 shows that in 1999 personal consumption accounted for about two-thirds of the total amount spent on final goods and services in the United States. Expenditures on consumer durable goods are clearly much less than expenditures on

TABLE 3.3

Expenditures on Final Goods and Services, United States, 1999

TYPE OF EXPENDITURE		AMOUNT (BILLIONS OF DOLLARS)
Personal consumption		6,257
Durable goods	758	
Nondurable goods	1,843	
Services	3,656	
Gross private domestic investment		1,623
Expenditures on plant and equipment	1,116	
Residential structures	412	
Increase in inventories	45	
Net exports		−254
Exports	998	
Imports	1,252	
Government purchases of goods and services		1,630
Federal	570	
State and local	1,060	
Gross domestic product		9,254

Source: U.S. Department of Commerce.

consumer nondurable goods, whereas expenditures on services are now larger than expenditures on either durable or nondurable goods.

■ GROSS PRIVATE DOMESTIC INVESTMENT

Gross private domestic investment consists of all investment spending by U.S. firms. As shown in Table 3.3, three broad types of expenditures are included in this category. First, *all final purchases of tools, equipment, and machinery* are included. Second, *all construction expenditures*, including expenditures on residential housing, are included. (One reason why houses are treated as investment goods is that they can be rented out.) Third, the *change in total inventories* is included. An increase in inventories is a positive investment; a decrease in inventories is a negative investment. The change in inventories must be included, because GDP measures the value of all final goods and services produced, even if they are not sold this year. Thus GDP must include the value of any increases in inventories that occur during the year. On the other hand, if a decrease occurs during the year in the value of inventories, the value of this decrease must be subtracted in calculating GDP because these goods and services were produced prior to the beginning of the year. In other words, a decline in inventories means that society has purchased more than it has produced during the year.

Gross private domestic investment is "gross" in the sense that it includes all additions to a country's stock of investment goods, whether or not they are replacements for equipment or plant that are used up in producing the current year's output. Net private domestic investment includes only the addition to the country's stock of investment goods after allowing for the replacement of used-up plant and equipment. To illustrate the distinction between gross and net private domestic investment, consider the situation in 1999. In that year, the nation produced $1,623 billion worth of investment goods; thus gross private domestic investment equaled $1,623 billion. But in producing the 1999 GDP, $1,136 billion worth of investment goods were used up. Thus net private domestic investment equaled $1,623 billion minus $1,136 billion, or $487 billion. This was the net addition to the nation's stock of investment goods.

Net private domestic investment indicates the change in a country's stock of capital goods. If it is positive, the country's productive capacity, as gauged by its capital stock, is growing. If it is negative, the country's productive capacity, as gauged by its capital stock, is declining. As pointed out in Chapter 1, the amount of goods and services that the country can produce is influenced by the size of its stock of capital goods. (Why? Because these capital goods are one important type of resource.) Thus this year's net private domestic investment is a determinant of how much the country can produce in the future.

■ GOVERNMENT PURCHASES OF GOODS AND SERVICES

This category of spending includes the expenditures of the federal, state, and local governments for the multitude of functions they perform: defense, education, police protection, and so forth. It does not include transfer payments, since they are not payments for current production. Table 3.3 shows that government spending in 1999 accounted for about one-fifth of the total amount spent on final goods and services in the United States. State and local expenditures are bigger than federal expenditures. Many of the expenditures of the federal government are on items like national defense, health, and education, whereas at the state and local levels the biggest expenditures are for items like education and highways.

■ NET EXPORTS

Net exports equal the amount spent by other countries on our goods and services less the amount we spent on other countries' goods and services. This factor must be included since some of our national output is destined for foreign markets and since we import some of the goods and services we consume. There is no reason why this component of spending cannot be negative, since imports can exceed exports. The quantity of net exports tends to be quite small. Table 3.3 shows that net exports in 1999 were equal (in absolute terms) to about 3 percent of the total amount spent on final goods and services in the United States.

■ PUTTING TOGETHER THE SPENDING COMPONENTS

Finally, because the four categories of expenditures described above include all possible types of spending on final goods and services, their sum equals the gross domestic product. In other words,

GDP = personal consumption expenditures

+ gross private domestic investment

+ government purchases of goods and services

+ net exports.

As shown in Table 3.3, the gross domestic product in 1999 equaled 6,257 + 6,123 + 1,630 − 254, or $9,254 billion.

THE INCOME APPROACH TO GDP

To use the income approach to determine GDP, one must add all the incomes from the production of this year's output. These incomes are of various types: compensation of employees, rents, interest, proprietors' income, and corporate profits. In addition, for reasons that need not concern us here, we must also include depreciation and indirect business taxes.[2] Each of these items is defined and discussed below.

■ COMPENSATION OF EMPLOYEES

This is the largest of the income categories. It includes the wages and salaries paid by firms and government agencies to suppliers of labor. In addition, it contains a variety of supplementary payments by employers for the benefit of their employees, such as payments into public and private pension and welfare funds. These supplementary payments are part of the employers' costs and are included in the total compensation of employees.

■ RENTS

In the present context, rent is defined as a payment to households for the supply of property resources. It includes house rents received by landlords. Quite different definitions of rent are used by economists in other contexts.

■ INTEREST

Interest includes payments of money by private businesses to suppliers of money capital. If you buy a bond issued by General Motors, the interest payments you receive are included. Interest payments made by the government on Treasury bills, savings bonds, and other securities are excluded on the grounds that they are not payments for current goods and services. They are regarded as transfer payments.

■ PROPRIETORS' INCOME

What we have referred to as profits are split into two parts in the national income accounts: proprietors' income and corporate

---

[2]For a detailed explanation of the reasons why depreciation and indirect business taxes must be included, see E. Mansfield, *Economics: Principles, Problems, Decisions* (7th ed.; New York: Norton, 1992).

profits. Proprietors' income consists of the net income of unincorporated businesses. In other words, it consists of the net income of proprietorships and partnerships (as well as cooperatives).

■ CORPORATE PROFITS

Corporate profits consist of the net income of corporations. This item contains three parts: (1) dividends received by the stockholders, (2) retained earnings, and (3) the amount paid by corporations as income taxes. In other words, it is equal to corporate profits before the payment of corporate income taxes.

■ DEPRECIATION

All the items discussed above—compensation of employees, rents, interest, proprietors' income, and corporate profits—are forms of income. In addition, there are two nonincome items, depreciation and indirect business taxes, that must be added to the sum of the income items to obtain GDP. Depreciation is the value of a country's plant, equipment, and structures that are worn out this year. In the national income accounts, depreciation is often called a *capital consumption allowance*, because it measures the value of the capital consumed during the year.

■ INDIRECT BUSINESS TAXES

The government imposes certain taxes, such as general sales taxes, excise taxes, and customs duties, which firms treat as costs of production. These taxes are called indirect business taxes because they are not imposed directly on the business itself, but on its products or services instead. A good example of an indirect business tax is the tax on cigarettes; another is the general sales tax. Before a firm can pay out income to its workers, suppliers, or stockholders, it must pay these indirect business taxes to the government.

■ PUTTING TOGETHER THE INCOME COMPONENTS (PLUS DEPRECIATION AND INDIRECT BUSINESS TAXES)

As we have stated repeatedly, the sum of the five types of income described above (plus depreciation and indirect business taxes) equals gross domestic product. In other words,

TABLE 3.4

Claims on Output, United States, 1999

TYPE OF CLAIM ON OUTPUT	AMOUNT OF CLAIM (BILLIONS OF DOLLARS)
Employee compensation	5,332
Rental income	146
Interest	468
Income of proprietors and professionals	659
Corporate profits	893
Indirect business taxes	716
Depreciation	1,136
Statistical discrepancy[a]	−96
Gross domestic product	9,254

[a]This also includes some minor items that need not be of concern here. See the source.
Source: U.S. Department of Commerce.

$$\begin{aligned}
\text{GDP} = \ & \text{compensation of employees} \\
& + \text{rents} \\
& + \text{interest} \\
& + \text{proprietors' income} \\
& + \text{corporate profits} \\
& + \text{depreciation} \\
& + \text{indirect business taxes.}
\end{aligned}$$

Table 3.4 shows the total amounts of various types of income paid out (or owed) during 1999. It also shows depreciation and indirect business taxes. You can see for yourself that the total of these items equals gross domestic product.

REVIEW AND PRACTICE

■ SUMMARY

1 One of the key indicators of the health of any country's economy is the gross domestic product, which measures the total value of the final goods and services the country produces in a particular period. Since gross domestic product is affected by the price level, it must be deflated by a price index to correct for price-level changes. When deflated in this way, GDP is called real GDP, or GDP in constant dollars.

2 There are many pitfalls in calculating the gross domestic product. One must avoid counting the same output more than once. Purely financial transactions that do not reflect current production must be excluded. Also, some final goods and services that must be included in GDP are not bought and sold in the marketplace, so they are valued at what they cost.

3 GDP is not an ideal measure of total economic output, let alone a satisfactory measure of economic well-being. It takes no account of a country's population, the amount of leisure time, or the distribution of income. It does not reflect many changes in the quality of goods and many social costs like pollution.

4 One approach to GDP is the expenditures approach, which regards GDP as the sum of all the expenditures that are involved in taking the total output of final goods and services off the market. To determine GDP in this way, one must add all the expenditures on final goods and services. Economists distinguish among four broad categories of spending: personal consumption expenditures, gross private domestic investment, government purchases, and net exports. GDP equals the sum of these four items.

5 Another approach to GDP is the income approach, which regards GDP as the sum of all the incomes derived from the production of this year's output (plus depreciation and indirect business taxes). To determine GDP in this way, one must add all the income from the production of this year's total output (plus depreciation and indirect business taxes). Economists identify five broad categories of income: compensation of employees, rent, interest, proprietors' income, and corporate profits. GDP equals the sum of these five items (plus depreciation and indirect business taxes).

■ PROBLEMS AND QUESTIONS

1 The table below shows the value of GDP in the nation of Puritania. The figures shown are in millions of 1980 dollars and current dollars. Fill in the blanks.

YEAR	GDP (MILLIONS OF 1980 DOLLARS)	GPD (MILLIONS OF CURRENT DOLLARS)	CURRENT PRICE LEVEL / 1980 PRICE LEVEL
1980	1,000	—	1.00
1984	—	1,440	1.20
1988	1,300	—	1.40
1992	1,500	—	1.60
1996	—	2,720	1.70
2000	1,700	—	1.80

2 If Bill Clinton wins $100,000 from Newt Gingrich in a poker game, will this increase, decrease, or have no effect on GDP? Explain.

3 If a paper mill produces $1 million worth of paper this year but adds considerably to the pollutants in a nearby river, are the social costs arising from this pollution reflected in the gross domestic product? If so, how? Should these costs be reflected in the GDP? If so, why?

4 A (small) country contains only ten firms. William Moran, the country's top statistician, calculates the country's GDP by totaling the sales of these ten firms. Do you agree with this procedure? Why or why not?

■ KEY TERMS

gross domestic product

final goods and services

intermediate goods

base year

current dollars

constant dollars

real GDP

price index

value-added

expenditures approach

income approach

■ VIEWPOINT FOR ANALYSIS

In 1993, Robert Eisner, Professor of Economics at Northwestern University and a former president of the American Economic Association, wrote: "Our GDP is running some $400 billion a year below normal. We are losing $100 billion a year of gross private domestic investment. We are losing countless billions more in public investment as states and localities across the country . . . are forced to curtail even necessary services."*

(a) Why should we care whether GDP is $400 billion a year below normal? What are the arguments in favor of increasing GDP? What are arguments against doing so?

(b) Based on Eisner's estimates, if net exports are equal to normal, can consumption expenditure be $300 billion a year below normal? Why or why not?

(c) How can anyone estimate the level of GDP that would be "normal" in a particular year? Do you think that Democrats and Republicans would agree on this score? Why or why not?

*R. Eisner, "Clinton, Deficits, and the Economy," *Challenge*, May–June 1993, p. 49.

CHAPTER 4

Business Fluctuations and Unemployment

LEARNING OBJECTIVES

In this chapter, you should learn:

- The nature of business fluctuations and their four phases
- What aggregate demand and aggregate supply curves show
- The types of unemployment and the costs they impose on society
- *(Exploring Further)* The effects of shifts in the aggregate demand and aggregate supply curves

John Maynard Keynes, unquestionably one of the most influential economists of this century, changed the way that people thought about cures for economic depression. At present, some of his ideas are widely accepted; others have been rejected. What exactly did he say? One purpose of this chapter is to answer this question; in subsequent chapters we shall consider the views of his followers and critics.

First, however, we must recognize that, while the U.S. economy has grown considerably over the past century, the ascent has not been a smooth one. The U.S. economy can be compared to a roller coaster that keeps moving higher and higher. In subsequent chapters we will discuss, at length, some of the reasons behind economic fluctuations and some of the proposed remedies. In this chapter we need to define what we mean by a business cycle. Given the economic tools that we have developed so far, we can describe in simple terms some of the fundamental forces that bring about business cycles. We also need to consider what the consequences of these fluctuations are for individuals and for the economy as a whole. In particular, we must discuss unemployment.

BUSINESS FLUCTUATIONS

To illustrate what we mean by business fluctuations—or the business cycle—let's look at how national output has grown in the United States. Figure 4.1 shows the behavior of real GDP (in con-

FIGURE 4.1

Gross Domestic Product (in 1996 dollars), United States, 1962–99

Real GDP has not grown steadily. Instead, it has tended to approach its potential level (that is, its full-employment level), then to falter and fall below this level, then to rise once more, and so on.

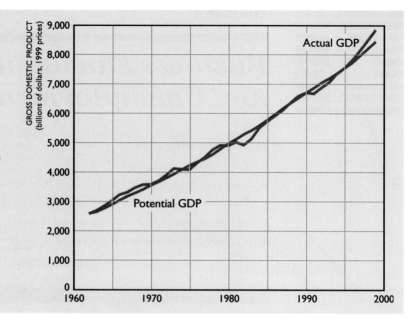

stant dollars) in the United States since 1962. It is clear that output has grown considerably during this period. Indeed, GDP is more than six times what it was forty years ago. It is also clear that this growth has not been steady. On the contrary, although the long-term trend has been upward, there have been periods—1969–70, 1973–75, January–July 1980, 1981–82, and 1990–91—when national output has declined.

Potential GDP is the total amount of goods and services that could have been produced if the economy had been operating at full capacity, or full employment. Figure 4.1 shows that national output tends to rise and approach its potential level (that is, its full-employment level) for a while, then falter and fall below this level, then rise to approach it once more, then fall below it again, and so on. For example, output (having remained close to its potential level in the prosperous 1960s) fell below this level in the 1970s and rose again to this level in the 1980s and 1990s. This movement of national output is sometimes called the **business cycle**, but it must be recognized that business cycles are far from regular or consistent. On the contrary, they are very irregular.

Each cycle can be divided into *four phases*, as shown in Figure 4.2. The **trough** is the point where national output is lowest relative to its potential level (that is, its full-employment level). **Expansion** is the subsequent phase during which national output rises. The **peak** occurs when national output is highest relative to

Business cycle

Trough
Expansion

Peak

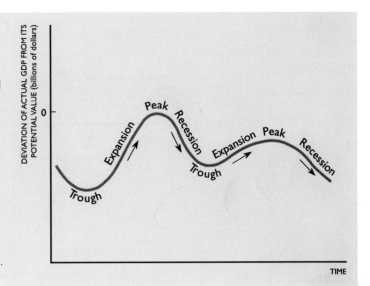

FIGURE 4.2

Four Phases of Business Cycle

Each cycle can be divided into four phases: trough, expansion, peak, and recession.

Recession

Depression

Prosperity

its potential level. Finally, **recession** is the subsequent phase during which national output falls.[1]

Two other terms are frequently used to describe stages of the business cycle. A **depression** is a period when national output is well below its potential level; it is a severe recession. Depressions are, of course, periods of excessive unemployment. **Prosperity** is a period when national output is close to its potential level (indeed, sometimes above it). If total spending is too high relative to potential output, prosperity can be a time of inflation. (Of course, in some business cycles, the peak may not be a period of prosperity because output may be below its potential level, or the trough may not be a period of depression because output may not be far below its potential level.)

From 1946 to 1999, peaks have occurred in 1948, 1953, 1957, 1960, 1969, 1973, 1980 (January), 1981, and late 1990, while troughs have occurred in 1949, 1954, 1958, 1961, 1970, 1975, 1980 (July), 1982 (November), and 1991. Relative to the great depression, none of these recessions has been very long or very deep (although the 1974–75 and 1981–82 recessions resulted in substantial unemployment).

Although business cycles have certain things in common, they are highly individualistic (see Figure 4.3). For certain classes of

---

[1]More precisely, the peak and trough are generally defined in terms of deviations from the long-term trend of national output, rather than in terms of deviations from the potential (that is, the full-employment) level of national output. Also, according to some people, a rough definition of a recession is at least two consecutive quarters of falling real GDP; it is not sufficient for output just to fall.

FIGURE 4.3

Business Fluctuations in the United States, 1860–1999

To construct this chart, a single index of economic activity was used. After fitting a trend line to it, the deviations of this index from its trend value were plotted. The

phenomena, it may be true that "if you've seen one, you've seen them all," but not for business cycles. They vary too much in length and nature. Moreover, the basic set of factors responsible for the recession and the expansion differs from cycle to cycle. This means that any theory designed to explain them must be broad enough to accommodate their idiosyncracies. In subsequent chapters, much will be said about the causes of business fluctuations; however, using aggregate demand and supply curves, we can begin to understand how some of these fluctuations can come about.

■ AGGREGATE SUPPLY AND DEMAND

In Chapter 2 we described the demand and supply curves for an individual commodity like wheat. Using these demand and supply curves, we analyzed the forces determining the price and output of a commodity in a competitive market. For example, we saw that a shift to the right in the demand curve for wheat tends to increase both the price and output of wheat.

Here, we will analyze the changes in the price level (that is, the average of all prices of goods and services) and output of the entire economy. That is, we are going to determine why the price level increases in some periods but not in others and why the gross domestic product soars in some periods and plummets in others. To understand the factors underlying inflation and unemployment,

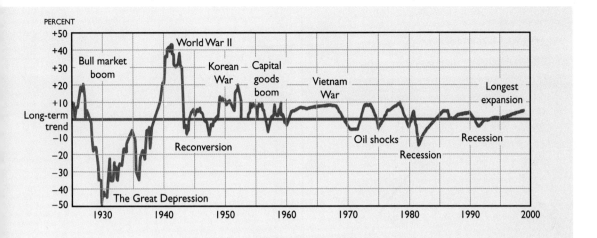

results show the fluctuations in economic activity in the United States. *Source*: Ameritrust Company. Adapted with changes.

we must know why changes occur in the price level and in national output.

Can we use demand and supply curves for the entire economy in much the same way as we did in individual markets? Are there demand and supply curves for the whole economy that are analogous to the demand and supply curves for individual products like wheat? The answer to both questions is yes. And in the next few sections of this chapter, we shall indicate the nature and usefulness of these aggregate demand and supply curves.

THE AGGREGATE DEMAND CURVE

Aggregate demand curve

To begin with, consider the aggregate demand curve. The **aggregate demand curve** shows the level of real national output that will be demanded at each price level. (Recall from Chapter 3 that real national output is measured by real gross domestic product. Thus real national output is composed of the output of food, automobiles, machine tools, ships, and the host of other final goods and services that are produced.) As can be seen in Figure 4.4, the aggregate demand curve slopes downward and to the right. In other words, when other things are held equal, the higher the price level, the smaller the total output demanded will be, and the lower the price level, the higher the total output demanded will be. This might be expected, since the demand curve for an individ-

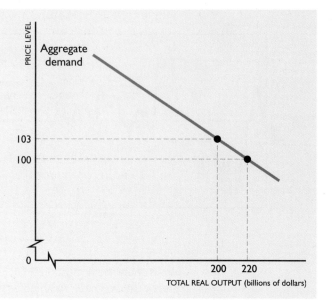

FIGURE 4.4

Aggregate Demand Curve

The aggregate demand curve shows the level of total real output that will be demanded at each price level. If the price level is 100, a total real output of $220 billion will be demanded. If the price level is 103, a total real output of $200 billion will be demanded.

ual product also slopes downward and to the right, as we saw in Chapter 2.

There are two fundamental reasons why the demand curve for an individual commodity like wheat slopes downward and to the right. (1) As the price of the commodity falls, consumers buy more of it because it is less expensive relative to other commodities, and (2) as the commodity's price falls, each consumer's money income (which is held constant) will buy a larger total amount of goods and services, so it is likely that more of this commodity will be bought.

Neither of these reasons can be used to explain the shape of the aggregate demand curve, which relates the economy's total real output to the price level. When the price level falls, the average price of all goods and services falls.[2] Unlike the demand curve for an individual commodity, there is not just a single price that falls, with the result that consumers find the relevant commodity relatively cheap and buy more of it. Since the aggregate demand curve is concerned with the economy's price level and total real output, not the price and output of a single commodity, the reasons for the downward slope of a demand curve for an individual commodity are not applicable to the aggregate demand curve.

■ REASONS FOR THE AGGREGATE DEMAND CURVE'S SHAPE

Why then does the aggregate demand curve slope downward and to the right? The basic reasoning is described in the following two

[2]Of course, this does not mean that the price of each good and service falls when the price level falls. Only the *average* falls.

steps. In later chapters, we will fill in many of the details regarding the demand for money and the effects of the supply of money on interest rates and of interest rates on total spending. For present purposes, only a rough sketch is needed.

Step 1: *Increases in the price level will push up interest rates*. In constructing the aggregate demand curve, it is assumed that the quantity of money in the economy is fixed. An increase in the price level increases the average *money* cost of each transaction because the price of each good tends to be higher. Thus, if the price level increases considerably, people will have to hold more money in their wallets and checking accounts to pay for the items they want to buy, since prices will be so much higher. Since the quantity of money is fixed, and the demand for money increases, there will be a shortage of money. In an attempt to increase their money holdings, people will borrow or will sell government securities and other financial assets. As this happens, interest rates—the prices paid for borrowing money—will be bid up. (The interest rate is the annual amount that a borrower must pay for the use of a dollar for a year. If the interest rate is 10 percent, a borrower must pay 10 cents per year for the use of a dollar for a year.)

Step 2: *Increases in interest rates will reduce total output*. When interest rates go up, firms that borrow money to invest in plant and equipment and consumers who borrow money to buy automobiles or houses tend to cut down on their spending on these items. Due to the higher interest rates, the cost of borrowing money is greater, and hence some of these investment projects and purchases no longer seem profitable or worthwhile. Because of the reduced spending on these items, the country's total real output declines.[3]

THE AGGREGATE SUPPLY CURVE

**Aggregate supply
curve**

Just as the aggregate demand curve is analogous to the demand curve for an individual product, so the aggregate supply curve is analogous to the supply curve for an individual product. The **aggregate supply curve** *shows the level of real national output that will be supplied at each price level*. Aggregate supply curves can pertain to either the short run or the long run. In the short run, the

---

[3]There are other reasons for the shape of the aggregate demand curve. For one thing, an increase in the price level reduces the real value of the currency and government bonds held by the public. (If you have $500 in cash, it represents less purchasing power if a hamburger costs $5 than if it costs $.50.) A reduction in the real value of people's wealth lessens their demand for goods and services. Also, increases in the price level tend to lower net exports because foreigners tend to respond to our price increases by cutting back their purchases from us (and we purchase more from them).

FIGURE 4.5

Short-Run Aggregate Supply Curve

The short-run aggregate supply curve shows the level of total real output that will be supplied at each price level, given that the prices of all inputs are fixed. If the price level is 100, a total real output of $190 billion will be supplied. If the price level is 103, a total real output of $200 billion will be supplied.

Short-run aggregate supply curve

prices of all inputs are assumed to be fixed; in the long run, they are permitted to adjust fully to eliminate the unemployment or shortage of inputs (like labor).[4]

As can be seen in Figure 4.5, the **short-run aggregate supply curve** slopes upward and to the right. In other words, when other things are held equal, the higher the price level, the larger the total output supplied will be, and the lower the price level, the smaller the total output supplied will be. This might be expected since the supply curve for an individual product also slopes upward and to the right, as we saw in Chapter 2.

But just as we could not derive the aggregate demand curve simply by adding the demand curves for all the individual commodities in the economy, so we cannot derive the aggregate supply curve by adding the supply curves for all the individual commodities. If we did this, we would commit a grave error because the factors held constant in constructing an individual supply curve are not held constant in constructing an aggregate supply curve. In particular, in constructing an individual supply curve, the price of only one commodity is allowed to vary, whereas in constructing an aggregate supply curve, the price level (and thus every price) is allowed to vary.

[4]These definitions of the short run and long run are different from those in Chapter 15, but there is little danger of confusion, since the contexts in which the terms are used are quite different.

WHY THE SHORT-RUN AGGREGATE SUPPLY CURVE SLOPES UPWARD TO THE RIGHT

To see why most economists believe that the short-run aggregate supply curve slopes upward to the right, let's begin by noting the obvious fact that firms are motivated to make profits. Because the profits earned by producing a unit of output equal the product's price minus the cost of producing it, increases in the product's price tend to increase the firm's profits. (Why? Because the wages of workers and the prices of raw materials are fixed in the short run.) Thus, *since increases in product prices tend to increase the profit per unit resulting from the production of the product, they tend to induce firms to produce more output.*

As an illustration, consider the Montgomery Corporation, which produces computer software that sells for $12 per unit. Suppose that it uses one hour of labor to produce one unit of software. If the wage rate is $10 per hour and if we suppose for simplicity that Montgomery has no other costs, its profit per unit of output is

$$\text{Profit per unit of output} = \text{price} - \text{cost per unit of output}$$
$$= \$12 - \$10$$
$$= \$2.$$

Now suppose that the price of its software increases from $12 to $13 per unit. If the wage rate remains constant at $10 per hour, Montgomery's profit per unit of output increases to

$$\text{Profit per unit of output} = \text{price} - \text{cost per unit of output}$$
$$= \$13 - \$10$$
$$= \$3.$$

Given that production is more profitable than before the price increase, Montgomery is likely to increase its output.

WHY THE SHORT-RUN AGGREGATE SUPPLY CURVE GETS STEEPER

According to many economists, the short-run aggregate supply curve tends to be close to horizontal at relatively low levels of output and gets steeper and steeper as output increases. To see why it tends to be close to horizontal at relatively low output levels, note that there is likely to be considerable unutilized productive capacity under these conditions. If business picks up, firms are likely to increase their output by bringing this unutilized capacity back into operation. Since their costs per unit of output will not increase appreciably as their production rises, they will not raise prices substantially. Thus the short-run aggregate supply curve will be close to horizontal.

On the other hand, at relatively high levels of output, production is pushing hard against capacity constraints, and it becomes increasingly difficult and costly for firms to increase their output further. Thus, the short-run aggregate supply curve becomes steeper as output rises. Why? Because bigger and bigger increases in the price level are required to elicit a given additional amount of output. Moving from point B to point C to point D in Figure 4.5, the price level must go up by increasing amounts to elicit an additional billion dollars of real output. Eventually the short-run aggregate supply curve may become close to vertical.

Not all economists agree that the short-run aggregate supply curve has the shape indicated in Figure 4.5. The new classical macroeconomists, discussed in Chapter 14, say that the short-run aggregate supply curve may be vertical. A discussion of their views must be postponed to Chapter 14. All that you should note at this point is that the shape of the short-run aggregate supply curve is a matter of controversy.

NATIONAL OUTPUT AND THE PRICE LEVEL

In the short run, *the equilibrium level of real national output and the equilibrium price level are given by the intersection of the aggregate demand curve and the short-run aggregate supply curve.* In Figure 4.6, the equilibrium level of real national output is $200 billion and the equilibrium price level is 103. The reasoning here is essentially the same as in Chapter 2, where we showed that the equilibrium price and output of a commodity are given by the intersection of the commodity's demand and supply curves. In the present case, an equilibrium can occur only at a price level and level of real national output where aggregate demand equals aggregate supply.

■ TWO EXAMPLES

Using aggregate demand and aggregate supply curves, we can begin to understand what has caused some of the swings in the U.S. economy. To illustrate, let's consider how aggregate demand changed in the Great Depression and World War II.

The Great Crash. Let's begin with the late 1920s. During 1928 and 1929, the U.S. economy was in the midst of prosperity, and the

FIGURE 4.6

Equilibrium Price Level and Total Real Output

The equilibrium level of total real output and the equilibrium price level are given by the intersection of the aggregate demand curve and the short-run aggregate supply curve. Here the equilibrium price level is 103 and the equilibrium level of total real output is $200 billion.

gross domestic product was approximately equal to its potential value. Unemployment was low. Among the reasons for this prosperity was a relatively strong demand for machinery and equipment to produce new products (like the automobile, radio, telephone, and electric power) and to replace old machinery and equipment that had been worn out or outmoded during World War I and its aftermath.

The picture changed dramatically in 1929. After the stock market plummeted in October of that year, the economy headed down

The New York Stock Exchange, October 1929

FIGURE 4.7

Shift of the Aggregate Demand Curve, 1929–33

A marked shift to the left in the aggregate demand curve was the principal reason for the onset of the Great Depression. (For simplicity, we assume here that the aggregate supply curve remained fixed.) Output fell drastically (from Q_1 to Q_2); the price level fell too (from P_2 to P_1).

at a staggering pace. Real GDP fell by almost one-third between 1929 and 1933. By 1933, unemployment rose to an enormous 25 percent of the labor force. One important reason was the severe contraction of gross private domestic investment. (Recall from Chapter 3 that gross private domestic investment is spending on tools, equipment, machinery, construction, and additional inventories.) Whereas gross private domestic investment was about $16 billion in 1929, it fell to about $1 billion in 1933. (The reasons for this decrease will be discussed in later chapters.) Another important factor was the decrease in the supply of money between 1929 and 1933. For reasons discussed in Chapters 9 and 13, this too tended to depress spending and output.

Put in terms of the aggregate demand and supply curves, the situation was as shown in Figure 4.7. For the reasons given in the previous paragraph, the aggregate demand curve shifted markedly to the left; and, as would be expected on the basis of Figure 4.7, total real output and the price level fell between 1929 and 1933.

World War II. The United States remained mired in the Great Depression until World War II (and the mobilization period that preceded the war). To carry out the war effort, the government spent huge amounts on military personnel and equipment. One result of this increase in spending was a substantial increase in real GDP, which rose by about 90 percent between 1939 and 1945. Another result was a marked reduction in unemployment, as the armed forces expanded and jobs opened up in defense plants and elsewhere. Still another result was the appearance of serious inflationary pressures. As the aggregate demand curve shifted to the right,

FIGURE 4.8

Shifts of the Aggregate Demand Curve in World War II

When we entered World War II, the aggregate demand curve shifted to the right as military expenditures mushroomed. Output increased (from Q_0 to Q_1 to Q_2), and inflationary pressures mounted. (For simplicity, we assume that the aggregate supply curve remained fixed.)

there was severe upward pressure on the price level as increases in spending pushed national output to its maximum (see Figure 4.8). To counter this pressure, the government instituted price controls (which mandated that firms charge no more than particular amounts) and other measures that kept a temporary lid on prices, but when these controls were lifted after the termination of the war, the price level increased dramatically. Between 1945 and 1948, prices to consumers rose by about 34 percent.

UNEMPLOYMENT

In previous sections of this chapter, we have been concerned with business fluctuations. One of the principal reasons why economists and policymakers are so interested in business fluctuations

Unemployed workers

is that the unemployment rate tends to go up during recessions and depressions. As we stressed in the Prologue, unemployment is an economic and social problem that concerns us all. The balance of this chapter is devoted to the definition, measurement, and effects of unemployment.

About a century ago, Pope Leo XIII said, "Among the purposes of a society should be to arrange for a continuous supply of work at all times and seasons."[5] The word *unemployment* can be one of the most frightening in the English language—and for good reason. Unemployed people become demoralized, lose prestige and status, and often see their families break apart. Sometimes they are pushed toward crime and drugs; often they feel terrible despair. Their children are innocent victims too. Indeed, perhaps the most devastating effects of unemployment are on children, whose education, health, and security may be ruined. After a few minutes' thought, most people would agree that in this or any other country, every citizen who is able and willing to work should be able to get a job.

We are not saying that all unemployment, whatever its cause or nature, should be eliminated. (For example, some unemployment may be voluntary.) According to the U.S. government, any person 16 years old or older who does not have a job and is actively looking for one is unemployed. Since this definition is necessarily quite broad, it is important that we distinguish among three different kinds of unemployment.

Frictional unemployment occurs because people quit jobs, because ex-students are looking for their first job, or because of seasonal workers. **Structural unemployment** occurs when new goods and new technologies call for different skills than old ones, and workers with older skills cannot find jobs. **Cyclical unemployment** occurs because of business fluctuations of the sort shown in Figure 4.3.

**Frictional
unemployment
Structural
unemployment
Cyclical
unemployment**

■ THE UNEMPLOYMENT RATE

Each month, the federal government conducts a scientific survey of the U.S. people, asking the individuals in a carefully selected sample of the population whether they have a job and, if not, whether they are looking for one. According to most experts, the resulting figures are quite reliable but subject to a number of qualifications. One is that the figures do not indicate the extent to which people are underemployed. Some people work only part-time or at jobs well below their level of education or skill, but the government figures count them as fully employed. Also, some people have given up looking for a job and are no longer listed among

[5]Pope Leo XIII, "Encyclical Letter on the Conditions of Labor," May 15, 1891.

Unemployment: The classical view

In early 1914, it was obvious that something was wrong with the U.S. economy. Unemployment was climbing, prices were falling, and factories were closing. While many were quick to blame the Wilson administration for the slump, few thought that the government should intervene to promote higher employment. The prevailing view among classical economists was that, by purchasing more goods and services to take up the slack in business investment, the government might do more harm than good.

Economists of the time saw business cycle fluctuations as temporary aberrations that the price system, left to its own devices, would automatically correct. Classical economic thought held that there could be no such thing as general overproduction. Depressions would cure themselves. If labor was unemployed, workers had only to accept lower wages, whereupon business would

TRAITÉ

D'ÉCONOMIE POLITIQUE,

OU

SIMPLE EXPOSITION

DE LA MANIÈRE DONT SE FORMENT, SE DISTRI-
BUENT, ET SE CONSOMMENT LES RICHESSES.

Par JEAN-BATISTE SAY, Membre du Tribunat.

gladly rehire them and prosperity would return.

Underlying this assumption was a doctrine called Say's law, after the nineteenth-century French economist J. B. Say. According to this law, the production of a certain amount of goods and services results in the generation of an amount of income which, if spent, is precisely sufficient to buy that output. In other words, *supply creates its own demand. The total amount paid out by the producers of the goods and services to resource owners must equal the value of the goods and services. Thus, if this amount is spent, it must be sufficient to purchase all the goods and services that are produced.*

But what if resource owners do not spend all their income but save some of it instead? How, then, will the necessary spending arise to take all the output off the market? The answer the classical economists offered is that each dollar saved will be invested. Therefore, investment (expenditures by business firms on plant, equipment, and other productive assets) will restore to the spending stream what resource owners take out through the saving process. The classical economists believed that the amount invested would automatically equal the amount saved because the interest rate—the price

paid for borrowing money—would fluctuate in such a way as to maintain equality between them.

Further, the classical economists said that the amount of goods and services firms can sell depends on the prices they charge, as well as on total spending. For example, $1 million in spending will take 100 cars off the market if the price is $10,000 per car, and 50 cars off the market if the price is $20,000 per car. Recognizing this, the classical economists argued that firms would cut prices to sell their output. Competition among firms would prod them to reduce their prices in this way, with the result that the high employment level of output would be taken off the market.

The prices of resources must also be reduced under such circumstances. Otherwise firms would incur losses because they would be getting less for their product but paying no less for resources. The classical economists believed that it was realistic to expect the prices of resources to decline in such a situation. Indeed they were quite willing to assume that the wage rate—the price of labor—would be flexible in this way. Through the processes of competition among laborers, they felt that wage rates would be bid down to the level where everyone who really wanted to work could get a job.

the unemployed, even though they would be glad to get work if any was offered. To be counted as unemployed in the government figures, one must be actively seeking employment.

To obtain the unemployment rate, the Bureau of Labor Statistics (the government agency responsible for producing the unemployment data) divides the estimated number of people who are unemployed by the estimated number of people in the labor force. To be in the labor force, a person must be either employed or unemployed. Note that the unemployment rate can rise either because people who formerly were employed are thrown out of work or because people who formerly were not in the labor force decide to look for jobs. For example, an increasing number of homemakers who return to the labor force may tend to raise the unemployment rate.

■ HOW MUCH UNEMPLOYMENT IS THERE?

To get some idea of the extent of unemployment, we can consult Figure 4.9, which shows the percentage of the labor force unemployed during each year from 1929 to 1999. Note the wide fluctuations in the unemployment rate, and the very high unemployment rates during the 1930s. Fortunately, unemployment since World War II has never approached the tragically high levels of the Great Depression of the 1930s. In 1981 and 1982 it rose to about 9.5 percent, after which it fell to about 5.2 percent in 1989. It rose again from 1990 to 1992 and then declined to about 4.1 percent in late 1999. Although many of these variations in the unemployment rate may seem small, they are by no means unimportant. With a labor force of over 140 million in the United States, a 1 percentage point

FIGURE 4.9

Unemployment Rates, United States, 1929–99

The unemployment rate has varied substantially. Fortunately, since World War II it has not approached the very high levels of the Great Depression of the 1930s. But the recession of 1981 showed that the nation is not immune to severe bouts of unemployment.

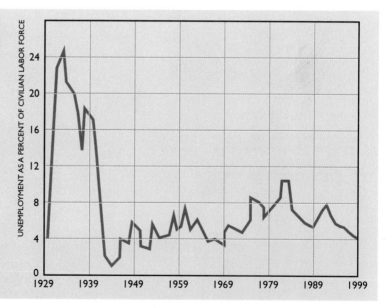

Karl Marx on unemployment

Karl Marx

World War I had been good for the U.S. labor movement. But with the armistice, the economy slowed down, the demand for labor shrank, and support for unions almost vanished. Unemployment, virtually nonexistent during the war, jumped to 14 percent in 1921. To some workers, angry at unemployment, the views of Karl Marx were appealing. While the classical economists held that depressions were temporary and self-correcting aberrations, Marx argued that economic crises were not accidents but a built-in feature of the capitalist system. A meticulous German scholar who spent much of his life in poverty-ridden circum-

stances in Britain, Marx (1818–83) wrote a huge, four-volume work on economics, *Das Kapital.** Eighteen years in the making, it remains one of the most influential books ever written.

To understand Marx, we need to know something about the times in which he lived. The period was characterized by revolutionary pressures against the ruling classes. In most of the countries of Europe, there was little democracy as we know it. The masses participated little, if at all, in the world of political affairs and very fully in the world of drudgery. For example, at one factory in Manchester, England, in 1862, people worked an average of about 80 hours per week. For these long hours of toil, the workers generally received small wages. They often could do little more than feed and clothe themselves. Given these circumstances, it is little wonder that revolutionary pressures were manifest.

Marx, viewing the economic system of his day, believed that capitalism was doomed to collapse. He believed that the workers were exploited by the capitalists—the owners of factories, mines, and other types of capital. And he believed that the capitalists, by introducing new labor-saving technology, would throw more and more workers into unemployment. This army of unem-

ployed workers, by competing for jobs, would keep wages at a subsistence level. Marx felt that as machinery was substituted for labor, profits would fall. Unemployment would become more severe. Big firms would absorb small ones. Eventually the capitalistic system was bound to collapse.

According to Marx, the inevitable successor to capitalism would be socialism, an economic system with no private property. Instead, property would be owned by society as a whole. Socialism, constituting a "dictatorship of the proletariat," would be only a transitional step to the promised land of communism. Marx did not spell out the characteristics of communism in detail. He was sure that it would be a classless society where everyone worked and no one owned capital, and he was sure that the state would "wither away," but he did not attempt to go much beyond this in his blueprint for communism. For present purposes, it is not necessary to detail the many places where Marx's theories went astray. The important point here is that although the classical view of unemployment (discussed in Case Study 4.1) was the dominant one, it did not go unchallenged, even in the nineteenth century.

*Karl Marx, *Das Kapital* (New York: Modern Library, 1906).

increase in the unemployment rate means that over 1.4 million more people are unemployed. Any administration, Democratic or Republican, watches these figures closely and tries to avoid significant increases in unemployment.

THE COSTS OF UNEMPLOYMENT

High levels of unemployment impose great costs on society. In this section, we describe these costs, which are both economic and noneconomic.

▓ ECONOMIC COSTS

The economic costs of unemployment include the goods and services that could have been produced by the unemployed. Because these people were unemployed, society had to forgo the production of the goods and services they might have produced, with the result that human wants were less effectively fulfilled than would otherwise have been the case. To determine how much society loses in this way by tolerating an unemployment rate above the minimum level resulting from frictional (and some structural) unemployment, economists estimate the **potential GDP**, which is the level of gross domestic product that can be achieved with full employment. (We first introduced the concept of potential GDP in Figure 4.1). Thus, if **full employment** is defined as a 5 percent unemployment rate, potential GDP can be estimated by multiplying 95 percent of the labor force times the normal hours of work per year times the average output per hour of work at the relevant time.

Potential GDP

Full employment

The gap between actual and potential GDP is a measure of what society loses by tolerating less than full employment. Figure 4.1 shows the estimated size of this gap from 1962 to 1999. Clearly, the economic costs of unemployment have been very substantial. Consider 1975, a recession year when unemployment was about $8\frac{1}{2}$ percent. As shown in Figure 4.1, society lost about $100 billion in that year alone. Although this estimate is very rough, it is accurate enough to suggest the social waste that accompanies large-scale unemployment.

One important problem in estimating this gap stems from the difficulty of defining full employment. For many years, a common definition of full employment was a 4 percent unemployment rate, since it was felt that frictional and structural unemployment could not be reduced below this level. During the seventies, some argued that an unemployment rate of about 5 percent was a more realistic measure of full employment than 4 percent because there were more young people, women, and minority workers in the labor force. All these groups find it relatively hard to find jobs. In the 1980s, many economists felt that 6 percent (or higher) was a more appropriate figure, but in 1999 some argued it was much lower, closer to the 4 percent of the 1960s (see Case Study 7.2).

◼ NONECONOMIC COSTS

Unemployment strikes at the social fabric of families and societies; it is not only an economic phenomenon. There are a wide variety of responses to unemployment. Some people weather it pretty well, and others sink into despair; some people have substantial savings they can draw on, and others are hard pressed; some people manage to shield their families from the blow, and others allow their misfortunes to spread to the rest of their families. But despite these variations, being without work generally deals a heavy blow to a person's feelings of worth. It hits hard at a person's self-image, indicating that he or she is not needed, cannot support a family, is not really a full and valuable member of society. The impact of widespread and persistent unemployment is most clearly visible at present among blacks and other racial minorities, where unemployment rates (28 percent among black teenagers in 1999) are much higher than among the white population. Unquestionably, the prevalence of unemployment among blacks and other racial minorities greatly influences how they view themselves, as well as the way they interact with the rest of the community.

EXPLORING FURTHER

EFFECTS OF SHIFTS IN AGGREGATE DEMAND AND SHORT-RUN AGGREGATE SUPPLY CURVES

◼ SHIFTS IN THE AGGREGATE DEMAND CURVE

In Chapter 2 we saw that shifts in the demand curve for an individual commodity result in changes in the price and output of this commodity. We now see that shifts in the aggregate demand curve result in changes in the price level and total real output.

◼ EFFECT OF A RIGHTWARD SHIFT

Suppose that consumers or investors decide to *increase* their spending, perhaps because of a change in their expectations. (They anticipate a marked improvement in economic conditions.) Since the level of total real output demanded at each price level increases, the aggregate demand curve shifts outward and to the right, as shown in Figure 4.10. What is the effect on the price level and on total output? The answer depends on where the aggregate demand curve intersected the short-run aggregate supply curve before the shift in the aggregate demand curve.

FIGURE 4.10

Effect of a Shift to the Right in the Aggregate Demand Curve

Panel A shows that, in the horizontal range of the short-run aggregate supply curve, a rightward shift of the aggregate demand curve increases output, but not the price level. Panel B shows that, in the vertical range of the short-run aggregate supply curve, a rightward shift of the aggregate demand curve increases the price level, but not output. Panel C shows that, in the positively sloped range of the short-run aggregate supply curve, a rightward shift of the aggregate demand curve increases both output and the price level.

Horizontal range of the short-run aggregate supply curve. If the intersection occurred in the horizontal range of the short-run aggregate supply curve, the rightward shift of the aggregate demand curve will increase total real output, but will not affect the price level (see panel A of Figure 4.10). As noted above, many economists argue that this is so because of considerable unemployment of resources. More output does not entail increased prices.

Vertical range of the short-run aggregate supply curve. If the intersection occurred in the vertical range of the short-run aggregate supply curve, the rightward shift of the aggregate demand curve will increase the price level but will have no impact on total real output (see panel B of Figure 4.10). As pointed out above, this is because the economy has no unutilized productive capacity. More spending bids up prices but cannot augment total real output, which is at its maximum level.

Positively sloped range of the short-run aggregate supply curve. If the intersection occurred in the positively sloped range of the short-run aggregate supply curve, the rightward shift of the aggregate demand curve will increase both the price level and

CASE STUDY 4.3

John Maynard Keynes and the Great Depression

John Maynard Keynes

The son of a British economist who was famous in his own right, John Maynard Keynes (1883–1946) was enormously successful in a variety of fields. He published a brilliant book on the theory of probability while still a relatively young man. Working for a half-hour in bed each morning, he made millions of dollars as a stock market speculator. He was a distin-

guished patron of the arts and a member of the Bloomsbury set, a group of London intellectuals who were the intellectual pacesetters for British society. He was a faculty member at Cambridge University and a key figure at the British Treasury.

Keynes was born in the year that Marx died. His world was quite different from Marx's world, and Keynes himself—polished, successful, a member of the elite—was quite different from the poverty-stricken, revolutionary Marx. But the two great economists were linked in at least one important respect. Both were preoccupied with unemployment and the future of the capitalist system. As we saw in Case Study 4.2, Marx predicted that unemployment would get worse and worse, until at last the capitalist system would collapse. In the 1930s, when Keynes was at the height of his influence, the Great Depression seemed to many people to be proving Marx right.

In 1936, while the world was still in the throes of this economic disas-

ter, Keynes published *The General Theory of Employment, Interest, and Money.** His purpose in this book was to explain how the capitalist economic system could get stalled in the sort of depressed state of equilibrium that existed in the 1930s. He also tried to indicate how governments might help to solve the problem.

Contrary to the classical economists, Keynes concluded that no automatic mechanism in a capitalist society would generate a high level of employment—or, at least, would generate it quickly enough to be relied on in practice. Instead, the equilibrium level of national output might for a long time be below the level required to achieve high employment. To push the economy toward a higher level of employment, Keynes advocated the conscious, forceful use of the government's power to spend and tax.

*John Maynard Keynes, *The General Theory of Employment, Interest, and Money* (New York: Harcourt, Brace, 1936)

total real output (see panel c of Figure 4.10). This is because increases in output can be attained in this range only if the price level increases, as we saw in a previous section.

■ EFFECT OF A LEFTWARD SHIFT

In contrast to the previous situation, suppose that consumers or investors decide to *decrease* their spending. Since the level of total real output demanded at each price level falls, the aggregate demand curve shifts inward to the left, as shown in Figure 4.11. The effect of this shift depends on where the aggregate demand curve

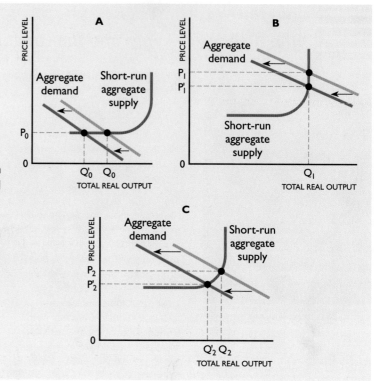

FIGURE 4.11

Effect of a Shift to the Left in the Aggregate Demand Curve

Panel A shows that, in the horizontal range of the short-run aggregate supply curve, a leftward shift of the aggregate demand curve reduces output but not the price level. Panel B shows that, in the vertical range of the short-run aggregate supply curve, a leftward shift of the aggregate demand curve reduces the price level but not output. Panel C shows that, in the positively sloped range of the short-run aggregate supply curve, a leftward shift of the aggregate demand curve reduces both output and the price level.

intersected the short-run aggregate supply curve before the shift occurred.

If the intersection occurred in the horizontal range of the short-run aggregate supply curve, the leftward shift of the aggregate demand curve will reduce total real output but will have no effect on the price level (see panel A of Figure 4.11). If the intersection occurred in the vertical range of the short-run aggregate supply curve, this shift will reduce the price level but will have no effect on total real output (see panel B of Figure 4.11). If the intersection occurred in the positively sloped range of the short-run aggregate supply curve, this shift will reduce both the price level and total real output (see panel C of Figure 4.11).

■ SHIFTS IN THE SHORT-RUN AGGREGATE SUPPLY CURVE

Shifts in the short-run aggregate supply curve, like those in the aggregate demand curve, result in changes in the price level and total real output, as indicated below.

FIGURE 4.12

**Effect of a Shift to the Right in the Short-Run Aggregate
Supply Curve**

If the short-run aggregate supply curve shifts to the right, the
result will be increased real output (Q' rather than Q) and a
lower price level (P' rather than P).

EFFECT OF A RIGHTWARD SHIFT

Suppose that, because of increases in productive capacity or
changes in technology, firms are willing and able to supply *more*
goods and services (at any given price level) than in the past. Under
these circumstances, the short-run aggregate supply curve shifts
outward to the right, as shown in Figure 4.12. What is the effect on
the price level and on total output? If prior to this shift the aggregate demand curve intersected the short-run aggregate supply
curve at a point where the latter was positively sloped, the result
will be an increase in total real output and a reduction in the price
level, as can readily be seen in Figure 4.12.

EFFECT OF A LEFTWARD SHIFT

On the other hand, suppose that firms are willing and able to supply *less* goods and services (at any given price level) than in the
past. For example, suppose that there is a worldwide shortage of
important raw materials like oil or iron ore that results in increases in their prices. In this case, a given level of total real output can be produced only at a higher price level than previously.
That is, the short-run aggregate supply curve shifts upward and to
the left, as shown in Figure 4.13. The effect will be a reduction in
total real output and an increase in the price level, as shown in
Figure 4.13.

FIGURE 4.13

Effect of a Shift to the Left in the Short-Run Aggregate Supply Curve

If the short-run aggregate supply curve shifts to the left, the result will be reduced real output (Q' rather than Q) and a higher price level (P' rather than P).

EXPLORING FURTHER

THE LONG-RUN AGGREGATE SUPPLY CURVE

As pointed out at the beginning of this chapter, whereas input prices are fixed in the short run, in the long run they can adjust fully to eliminate the unemployment or shortage of inputs (like labor). Thus, *once these adjustments have been made, full employment will occur, and real national output will be at its potential level.* If the potential output of a particular economy is 100 billion (1999) dollars, this will be the amount of output supplied regardless of the price level.

In other words, *the aggregate supply curve is vertical in the long run.* Why? Because in the long run, wages and the prices of nonlabor inputs adjust. For example, there is time for old labor contracts to expire and for new ones to be negotiated. Shortages of raw materials are resolved. Unemployed workers find jobs. In the long run, input prices change by the same proportion as product prices, with the result that there is no incentive for firms to alter their output levels. When the price of everything changes by the same proportion, the real value of everything is unchanged.

To see this, consider a firm that experiences a 10 percent increase in the price of its product. If this is due to a 10 percent increase in the general price level, this firm will in the long run pay 10 percent more for its inputs. Consequently, its profit per dollar of sales will be no different in the long run than it was before the 10 percent increase in the price level. Since this is the case, it has

FIGURE 4.14

Equilibrium Price Level and Total Real Output: Long Run

In the long run, the aggregate supply curve is vertical. The equilibrium level of total real output and the equilibrium price level are given by the intersection of the aggregate demand and supply curves. Here the equilibrium price level is *P* and the equilibrium level of total real output is *Q*.

Long-run aggregate supply curve

no incentive to produce more than it did before the increase in the price level.

Figure 4.14 shows the **long-run aggregate supply curve** for an economy with potential real GDP equal to *Q*. It is a vertical line because the total quantity of goods and services produced when all inputs are efficiently and fully utilized does not depend on the price level. If the price level were to increase from 100 to 120 (and if wages and the prices of nonlabor inputs were to increase by the same proportion), the total quantity of goods and services produced would remain equal to *Q*.

In the long run, the equilibrium level of real national output and the equilibrium price level are given by the intersection of the aggregate demand curve and the long-run aggregate supply curve. Thus, in Figure 4.14, the equilibrium value of real GDP is *Q*, and the equilibrium value of the price level is *P*. Note that *the aggregate demand curve affects only the price level, not the level of real output, in the long run. The level of output equals its potential level regardless of the price level.* In Chapter 25, which deals with economic growth, we will study the factors determining the level of potential output—or, what amounts to the same thing, the factors determining the location of the long-run aggregate supply curve.

REVIEW AND PRACTICE

■ SUMMARY

❙ National output tends to rise and approach its potential (its full-employment) level for a while, then to falter and fall below this level, then to rise to approach it once more, and so on. These ups and downs are called business fluctuations or business cycles.

2 Each cycle can be divided into four phases: trough, expansion, peak, recession. These cycles are very irregular and highly variable in length and amplitude.

3 Until the 1930s, most economists (classical economists) were convinced that the price system, left to its own devices, would ensure the maintenance of full employment. They thought it unlikely that total spending would be too small to purchase the full-employment level of output and argued that prices would be cut if any problem of this sort developed.

4 John Maynard Keynes, in the 1930s, developed a theory to explain how the capitalist economic system remained mired in the Great Depression, with its high levels of unemployment. Contrary to the classical economists, he concluded that there was no automatic mechanism in a capitalist system to generate and maintain full employment—or, at least, to generate it quickly enough to be relied on in practice.

5 The aggregate demand curve shows the level of real national output that will be demanded at each price level. It slopes downward and to the right.

6 The short-run aggregate supply curve shows the level of real national output that will be supplied at each price level if the prices of all inputs are fixed. Since increases in the price level tend to raise the profitability of firms' increasing output, the short-run aggregate supply curve tends to slope upward to the right.

7 The equilibrium level of real national output and the equilibrium price level are given by the intersection of the aggregate demand and supply curves.

8 Unemployment is of various types: frictional, structural, and cyclical. The overall unemployment rate conceals considerable differences among types of people.

9 High levels of unemployment impose great costs on society. The economic costs of unemployment include the goods and services that could have been produced (but weren't) by the unemployed. Potential GDP is the level of GDP that could have been achieved if full employment had been reached.

∗10 Whereas input prices are fixed in the short run, in the long run they can adjust fully to eliminate the unemployment or shortage of inputs (like labor). Once these adjustments have been made, full employment will occur, and real national output will be at its potential level. Thus, the long-run aggregate supply curve is vertical.

PROBLEMS AND QUESTIONS

1 What sorts of shifts in either the aggregate demand curve or the short-run aggregate supply curve (or both) would result in an increase in the price level but constant real output?

2 "One of the principal reasons why the short-run aggregate supply curve slopes upward to the right is that, as total real output increases, the quantity of money must increase as well; this means that the price level must rise, at least beyond some point." Do you agree? Why or why not?

3 Suppose that the aggregate demand curve is $P = 120 - Q$, where P is the price level and Q is real output (in billions of dollars). If the short-run aggregate supply curve (which is a horizontal line in the relevant range) shifts upward from $P = 102$ to $P = 104$, what will happen to real output?

*The starred item refers to material covered in Exploring Further.

4 The aggregate demand curve in country X shifts to the right, with the result that the price level rises. Do you think that this will affect country X's short-run aggregate supply curve? Why or why not?

5 Suppose that the Organization of Petroleum Exporting Countries raises oil prices by 50 percent in 2001. What effect will this have on the U.S. aggregate demand curve? On the U.S. short-run aggregate supply curve?

■ KEY TERMS

business cycle	aggregate supply curve
trough	short-run aggregate supply curve
expansion	frictional unemployment
peak	structural unemployment
recession	cyclical unemployment
depression	potential GDP
prosperity	full employment
aggregate demand curve	long-run aggregate supply curve

■ VIEWPOINT FOR ANALYSIS

According to testimony by Nobel laureate Robert Solow of Massachusetts Institute of Technology before the Joint Economic Committee of Congress on February 11, 1993, "If actual GDP grows by 2¼ percent during the four quarters of 1993, the gap between actual and potential [GDP] will still be 4 percent early in 1994 and the unemployment rate will remain near 7.1 percent. It would take faster growth of GDP to narrow the gap and reduce unemployment."*

(a) In dollar terms, about how great would have been the amount of forgone output in 1993 if this gap were 4 percent?

(b) Would a rightward shift of the aggregate demand curve have increased the rate of growth of GDP and narrowed this gap? Why or why not?

(c) What factors might have shifted the aggregate demand curve to the right?

(d) What might have been the disadvantage of a rightward shift of the aggregate demand curve?

*R. Solow, "Statement to Joint Economic Committee, U.S. Congress," February 11, 1993, p. 4.

The Determination of National Output and the Keynesian Multiplier

LEARNING OBJECTIVES

In this chapter, you should learn:

- The nature of the consumption function and the marginal propensity to consume
- The nature of the saving function and the marginal propensity to save
- The determinants of the level of gross investment
- The significance of equilibrium GDP and why it must equal total intended spending
- How equilibrium GDP can change and how the multiplier affects these changes
- (*Exploring Further*) The causes and effects of shifts in the consumption and saving functions

The expenditure of firms on plant, equipment, and other forms of investment can vary greatly from year to year. Spending of this sort is dependent on the expectations of industrial managers concerning the size of prospective markets, among other things. How much effect do changes in investment spending have on GDP? One purpose of this chapter is to answer this question.

In the previous chapter, we presented an introductory sketch of business fluctuations and indicated how aggregate demand and supply curves can be used to analyze these fluctuations. In this chapter, we go a step further. Rather than simply taking the position of the aggregate demand curve as given, we are concerned with why the equilibrium level of national output is what it is. Why is the aggregate demand curve positioned so as to intersect the aggregate supply curve at this (rather than some other) output? We also discuss how the economy can move from one equilibrium to another.

■ SIMPLIFYING ASSUMPTIONS

Essentially, the model presented in this chapter is the simple Keynesian model, which was put forth by John Maynard Keynes in the 1930s (recall page 109). This model assumes that the price level is constant; in other words, the short-run aggregate supply curve is assumed to be horizontal. In subsequent chapters, this assumption is relaxed.

In addition, we shall make three other simplifying assumptions:

1. We assume that there are no government expenditures and that the economy is closed (no exports or imports). Thus *total spending on final output—that is, on gross domestic product—in this simple case equals consumption expenditure plus gross investment.*[1] (Why? Because the other two components of total spending—government expenditures and net exports—are zero.)

2. We assume that there are no taxes, no transfer payments, and no undistributed corporate profits. Thus, if we define ***disposable income*** as the total amount of income that people get to keep after paying personal taxes, *GDP equals disposable income in this simple case.* Later chapters relax this and the first assumption.

3. We shall assume that the total amount of intended investment (that is, the total amount that firms and individuals intend to invest) is *independent* of the level of gross domestic product. This, of course, is only a rough simplification, since the amount firms invest will be affected by the level of national output. But this simplification is very convenient, and it is relatively easy to extend the model to eliminate this assumption.

THE CONSUMPTION FUNCTION

**Consumption
function**

An important part of the simple Keynesian theory of the determination of national output is the **consumption function**, *which is the relationship between consumption spending and disposable income. It seems clear that consumption expenditures—whether those of a single household or the total consumption expenditures in the entire economy—are influenced heavily by income.* Families with higher incomes tend to spend more on consumption than families with lower incomes. Of course, individual families vary a good deal in their behavior; some spend more than others even if their incomes are the same. But, on the average, a family's consumption expenditure is tied very closely to its income.

What is true for individual families also holds for the entire economy: total personal consumption expenditures are closely related to disposable income. This fact is shown in Figure 5.1, where personal consumption expenditure in each year (from 1929 to 1999) is plotted against disposable income in the same year (from 1929 to 1999). The points fall very near the straight line drawn in

---

[1]Since *personal consumption expenditure* and *gross private domestic investment* are cumbersome terms, we shall usually use *consumption expenditure* and *gross investment* instead in this and subsequent chapters.

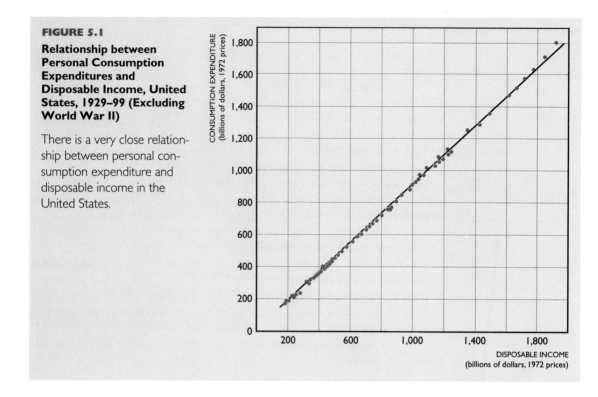

FIGURE 5.1

Relationship between Personal Consumption Expenditures and Disposable Income, United States, 1929–99 (Excluding World War II)

There is a very close relationship between personal consumption expenditure and disposable income in the United States.

Figure 5.1 but not right on it. For most practical purposes, we can regard the line drawn in Figure 5.1 as representing the relationship between personal consumption expenditure and disposable income. In other words, we can regard this line as the consumption function.

■ THE MARGINAL PROPENSITY TO CONSUME

Suppose that we know what the consumption function for a given society looks like in a particular time period. For example, suppose that it is given by the figures for disposable income and personal consumption expenditure in the first two columns of Table 5.1. On the basis of our knowledge of the consumption function, we can determine the *extra* amount families will spend on consumption if they receive an *extra* dollar of disposable income. *This amount—the fraction of an extra dollar of income that is spent on consumption—is called the* **marginal propensity to consume**.

Marginal propensity to consume

To make sure that you understand exactly what the marginal propensity to consume is, consult Table 5.1. What is the marginal

TABLE 5.1

The Consumpton Function

DISPOSABLE INCOME (BILLIONS OF DOLLARS)	PERSONAL CONSUMPTION EXPENDITURE (BILLIONS OF DOLLARS)	MARGINAL PROPENSITY TO CONSUME	AVERAGE PROPENSITY TO CONSUME
1,000	950		.95
		$\frac{30}{50} = .60$	
1,050	980		.93
		$\frac{30}{50} = .60$	
1,100	1,010		.92
		$\frac{30}{50} = .60$	
1,150	1,040		.90
		$\frac{30}{50} = .60$	
1,200	1,070		.89
		$\frac{30}{50} = .60$	
1,250	1,100		.88
		$\frac{30}{50} = .60$	
1,300	1,130		.87
		$\frac{30}{50} = .60$	

propensity to consume when disposable income is between $1,000 billion and $1,050 billion? The second column shows that when income rises from $1,000 billion to $1,050 billion, consumption expenditure rises from $950 billion to $980 billion. Consequently, the fraction of the extra $50 billion of income that is consumed is $30 billion ÷ $50 billion, or .60. Thus the marginal propensity to consume is .60. On the basis of similar calculations, the marginal propensity to consume when disposable income is between $1,050 billion and $1,100 billion is .60, the marginal propensity to consume when disposable income is between $1,100 billion and $1,150 billion is .60, and so forth.

The marginal propensity to consume can be interpreted geometrically as the slope of the consumption function. The slope of any line is the ratio of the vertical change to the horizontal change when a small movement occurs along the line. As shown in Figure 5.2, the vertical change is the change in personal consumption expenditure, and the horizontal change is the change in disposable income. Thus the ratio of the vertical change to the horizontal change must equal the marginal propensity to consume.

In general, the marginal propensity to consume can differ, depending on the level of disposable income. For example, the marginal propensity to consume may be higher at lower levels than at higher levels of disposable income. Only if the consumption func-

FIGURE 5.2

The Marginal Propensity to Consume Equals the Slope of the Consumption Function

The slope of the consumption function between points A and B equals the vertical change (which is the change in personal consumption expenditure) divided by the horizontal change (which is the change in disposable income).

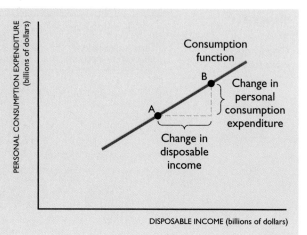

tion is a straight line, as in Figure 5.1 and Table 5.1, will the marginal propensity to consume be the same at all levels of income. For simplicity, we assume in much of the subsequent analysis that the consumption function is a straight line, but this assumption can easily be relaxed without affecting the essential aspects of our conclusions.

■ THE AVERAGE PROPENSITY TO CONSUME

Average propensity to consume

It is important to distinguish between the marginal propensity to consume and the **average propensity to consume**. The average propensity to consume equals the proportion of disposable income that is consumed. In other words, it equals

$$\frac{\text{Personal consumption expenditure}}{\text{Disposable income}}.$$

Clearly, this will not in general equal the marginal propensity to consume, which is

$$\frac{\text{Change in personal consumption expenditure}}{\text{Change in disposable income}}.$$

The point is that the marginal propensity to consume is the proportion of *extra* income consumed; this proportion is generally quite different from the proportion of *total* income consumed. For example, in Table 5.1, the average propensity to consume when

120

disposable income is $1,100 billion is .92, but the marginal propensity to consume when disposable income is between $1,050 billion and $1,100 billion is .60.

THE SAVING FUNCTION

If people don't devote their disposable income to personal consumption expenditure, what else can they do with it? They can save it. When families refrain from spending their income on consumption goods and services—that is, when they forgo present consumption to provide for larger consumption in the future—they save. Thus we can derive from the consumption function the total amount people will save at each level of disposable income. All we have to do is subtract the total personal consumption expenditure from disposable income at each level of disposable income. The difference is the total amount of saving at each level of disposable income. This difference is shown in the third column of Table 5.2. We can plot the total amount of saving against disposable income, as in Figure 5.3. The resulting relationship between total saving **Saving function** and disposable income is the **saving function**. Like the consumption function, it plays a major role in the theory of national output determination.

TABLE 5.2
The Saving Function

DISPOSABLE INCOME (BILLIONS OF DOLLARS)	PERSONAL CONSUMPTION EXPENDITURE (BILLIONS OF DOLLARS)	SAVINGS (BILLIONS OF DOLLARS)	MARGINAL PROPENSITY TO SAVE
1,000	950	50	
			$\frac{20}{50} = .40$
1,050	980	70	
			$\frac{20}{50} = .40$
1,100	1,010	90	
			$\frac{20}{50} = .40$
1,150	1,040	110	
			$\frac{20}{50} = .40$
1,200	1,070	130	
			$\frac{20}{50} = .40$
1,250	1,100	150	
			$\frac{20}{50} = .40$
1,300	1,130	170	
			$\frac{20}{50} = .40$

FIGURE 5.3

The Saving Function

The saving function describes the total amount of saving at each level of disposable income. The slope of the saving function equals the change in saving divided by the change in disposable income. Thus the slope of the saving function equals the marginal propensity to save.

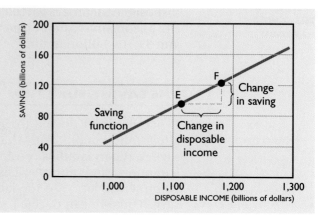

■ THE MARGINAL PROPENSITY TO SAVE

Marginal propensity to save

If we know the saving function, we can calculate the marginal propensity to save at any level of disposable income. *The* **marginal propensity to save** *is the proportion of an extra dollar of disposable income that is saved.* To see how to calculate it, consult Table 5.2. The third column shows that when income rises from $1,000 billion to $1,050 billion, savings rise from $50 billion to $70 billion. Consequently, the fraction of the extra $50 billion of income that is saved is $20 billion ÷ $50 billion, or .40. Thus the marginal propensity to save is .40. Similar calculations show that the marginal propensity to save when disposable income is between $1,050 billion and $1,100 billion is .40, the marginal propensity to save when disposable income is between $1,100 billion and $1,150 billion is .40, and so forth.

Note that *at any particular level of disposable income, the marginal propensity to save plus the marginal propensity to consume must equal 1.* By definition, the marginal propensity to save equals the proportion of an extra dollar of disposable income that is saved, and the marginal propensity to consume equals the proportion of an extra dollar of income that is consumed. The sum of these two proportions must equal 1, for, as stated above, the only things that people can do with an extra dollar of disposable income are consume it or save it. Table 5.2 shows this fact clearly.

Finally, it is worth noting that the marginal propensity to save equals the slope of the saving function, just as the marginal propensity to consume equals the slope of the consumption function. As pointed out above, the slope of a line equals the vertical distance between any two points on the line divided by the horizontal distance between them. Since (as shown in Figure 5.3) the vertical distance is the change in saving and the horizontal distance is the change in disposable income, the slope of the saving function must equal the marginal propensity to save.

DETERMINANTS OF INVESTMENT

In Chapter 3, we stressed that investment consists largely of the amount firms spend on new buildings and factories, new equipment, and increases in inventory. Investment plays a central role in the Keynesian theory of output and employment. To understand this theory, it is essential that you understand the factors determining the level of gross private domestic investment. Basically, there are two broad determinants of the level of gross private domestic investment: the expected rate of return from capital and the interest rate.

■ EXPECTED RATE OF RETURN

Expected rate of return

The **expected rate of return** from capital is the perceived rate of return that businesses believe they can obtain if they put up new buildings or factories, add new equipment, or increase their inventories. Each of these forms of investment requires the expenditure of money. The rate of return measures the profitability of such an expenditure; it shows the annual profits to be obtained per dollar invested. Thus a rate of return of 10 percent means that, for every dollar invested, an annual profit of 10 cents is obtained.

Firms hope to profit from capital investments like these office buildings.

**THE DETERMINATION
OF NATIONAL
OUTPUT AND
THE KEYNESIAN
MULTIPLIER**
CHAPTER 5

Interest rate

Clearly, the higher the expected rate of return from a particular investment, the more profitable the investment is expected to be.

■ INTEREST RATE

The **interest rate** is the cost of borrowing money. As pointed out in Chapter 4, it is the annual amount that a borrower must pay for the use of a dollar for a year. Thus, if the interest rate is 8 percent, a borrower must pay 8 cents per year for the use of a dollar. And if the interest rate is 12 percent, a borrower must pay 12 cents per year for the use of a dollar. Anyone with a savings account knows what it is to earn interest; anyone who has borrowed money from a bank knows what it is to pay interest.

THE INVESTMENT DECISION

To determine whether to invest in a particular project (a new building, piece of equipment, or other form of investment), a firm must compare the project's expected rate of return with the interest rate. If the expected rate of return is less than the interest rate, the firm will lose money if it borrows money to carry out the project. For example, if the firm invests in a project with a 10 percent rate of return and borrows the money to finance the project at 12 percent interest, it will receive profits of 10 cents per dollar invested and pay out interest of 12 cents per dollar invested. So it will lose 2 cents (12 cents minus 10 cents) per dollar invested.

Even if the firm does not borrow money to finance the project, it will be unlikely to invest in a project where the expected rate of return is less than the interest rate. Why? Because, if the firm can lend money to others at the prevailing interest rate, it can obtain a greater return from its money by doing this than by investing in the project. Thus if the interest rate is 12 percent and an investment project has an expected rate of return of 10 percent, a firm will do better, if it has a certain amount of money, to lend it out at 12 percent than to earn 10 percent from the investment project.

Since firms are likely to invest only in projects where the expected rate of return exceeds the interest rate, it is obvious that the *level of gross private domestic investment depends on the total volume of investment projects where the expected rate of return exceeds the interest rate.* For example, if the interest rate is 10 percent, the level of gross investment depends on the total volume of investment projects where the expected rate of return exceeds 10 percent. The more such projects there are, the higher will be the level of gross investment. Also, the higher the interest rate, the lower will be the level of gross investment.

THE EQUILIBRIUM LEVEL OF GROSS DOMESTIC PRODUCT

As stressed in Chapter 2, an equilibrium is a situation where there is no tendency for change; it is a situation that can persist. In Chapter 2, we studied the equilibrium value of a product's price. Here we are interested in the equilibrium value of gross domestic product. In Chapter 2, we saw that price is at its equilibrium value when the quantity demanded equals the quantity supplied. Here we shall see that GDP is at its equilibrium value when the flow of income (generated by this value of GDP) results in a level of spending that is just sufficient (not too high, not too low) to take this level of output off the market. To understand this equilibrium condition, it is essential to keep three points in mind:

1. *The production of goods and services results in a flow of income to the workers, resource owners, and managers that help to produce them.* Each level of GDP results in a certain flow of income. More specifically, under the assumptions made here, GDP equals disposable income. Thus whatever the level of GDP may be, we can be sure that the level of disposable income will be equivalent to it.

2. *The level of spending on final goods and services is dependent on the level of disposable income.* As we saw earlier in this chapter, consumption expenditure depends on the level of disposable income. (For the moment, we assume that investment is independent of the level of output in the economy.) Thus if we know the level of disposable income, we can predict what level of spending will be forthcoming.

3. *The level of production is dependent mainly on the level of spending.* If producers find that they are selling goods faster than they are producing them, their inventories will decline. If they find that they are selling goods slower than they are producing them, their inventories will rise. *If GDP is at its equilibrium value, the intended level of spending must be just equal to GDP.* Why? Because otherwise there will be an unintended increase or decrease in producers' inventories—a situation that cannot persist. Much more will be said on this score in the sections that follow.

AGGREGATE FLOWS OF INCOME AND EXPENDITURE

■ OUTPUT DETERMINES INCOME

Let's look in more detail at the process whereby national output (that is, GDP) determines the level of income, which in turn determines the level of spending. Suppose that the first column of Table 5.3 shows the various possible output levels—that is, the various

125

TABLE 5.3	(1) GROSS DOMESTIC PRODUCT (= DISPOSABLE INCOME)	(2) INTENDED CONSUMPTION EXPENDITURE	(3) INTENDED SAVING	(4) INTENDED INVESTMENT	(5) TOTAL INTENDED SPENDING (2) + (4)	(6) TENDENCY OF NATIONAL OUTPUT
Determination of Equilibrium Level of Gross Domestic Product (billions of dollars)	1,000	950	50	90	1,040	Upward
	1,050	980	70	90	1,070	Upward
	1,100	1,010	90	90	1,100	No change
	1,150	1,040	110	90	1,130	Downward
	1,200	1,070	130	90	1,160	Downward
	1,250	1,100	150	90	1,190	Downward

possible values of GDP—that the economy might produce this year. This column shows the various output levels that may be produced *if producers expect that there will be enough spending to take this much output off the market at the existing price level.* And, as stressed above, disposable income equals GDP.

■ INCOME DETERMINES SPENDING

Since disposable income equals GDP (under our current assumptions), the first column of Table 5.3 also shows the level of disposable income corresponding to each possible level of GDP. From this it should be possible to determine the level of spending corresponding to each level of GDP. Specifically, suppose that the consumption function is as shown in Table 5.1. In this case, intended consumption expenditure at each level of GDP will be as shown in column 2 of Table 5.3. For example, if GDP equals $1,000 billion, intended consumption expenditure equals $950 billion.

But consumption expenditure is not the only type of spending. What about investment? Suppose that firms want to invest $90 billion regardless of the level of GDP. Under these circumstances, total spending at each level of GDP will be as shown in column 5 of Table 5.3. (Since total intended spending equals intended consumption expenditure plus intended investment, column 5 equals column 2 plus column 4.)

■ OUTPUT MUST EQUAL SPENDING

Column 5 of Table 5.3 shows the level of total intended spending at each level of national output (and income). *If GDP is at its equilibrium value, total intended spending must equal total output.* In other

words, *if GDP is at its equilibrium value, total intended spending must
equal GDP.* The easiest way to show this is to show that if intended
spending is not equal to GDP, GDP is not at its equilibrium value.
The following discussion provides such a proof. First we show that
if intended spending is greater than GDP, GDP is not at its equilibrium level. Then we show that if intended spending is less than
GDP, GDP is not at its equilibrium level.

If intended spending is greater than GDP, what will happen?
Since the total amount that will be spent on final goods and services exceeds the total amount of final goods and services produced (the latter being, by definition, GDP), firms' inventories will
be reduced. Consequently, firms will increase their output rate to
avoid continued depletion of their inventories and to bring their
output into balance with the rate of aggregate demand. Since an increase in the output rate means an increase in GDP, it follows that
GDP will tend to increase if intended spending is greater than
GDP. GDP therefore is not at its equilibrium level.

On the other hand, what will happen if intended spending is
less than GDP? Since the total amount that will be spent on final
goods and services falls short of the total amount of final goods
and services produced (the latter being, by definition, GDP), firms'
inventories will increase. As inventories pile up unexpectedly,
firms will cut back their output to bring it into better balance with
aggregate demand. Since a reduction in output means a reduction
in GDP, it follows that GDP will tend to fall if intended spending is
less than GDP. Once again, GDP is not at its equilibrium level.

Since GDP is not at its equilibrium value when it exceeds or
falls short of intended spending, it must be at its equilibrium value
only when it equals intended spending.

■ WHY GDP MUST EQUAL INTENDED SPENDING: THREE CASES

To get a better idea of why GDP will be at its equilibrium value
only if it equals intended spending, consider three possible values
of GDP—$1,050 billion, $1,150 billion, and $1,100 billion—and see
what would happen in our simple economy (in Table 5.3) if these
values of GDP prevailed.

Case 1: GDP = $1,050 billion. What would happen if firms pro-
duced $1,050 billion of final goods and services? Given our as-
sumptions, disposable income would also equal $1,050 billion
(since disposable income equals GDP), so consumers would spend
$980 billion on consumption goods and services. (This follows
from the nature of the consumption function: see column 2 of
Table 5.3.) Since firms want to invest $90 billion, total intended
spending would be $1,070 billion ($980 billion + $90 billion, as

THE DETERMINATION
OF NATIONAL
OUTPUT AND
THE KEYNESIAN
MULTIPLIER
CHAPTER 5

shown in column 5). But the total amount spent on final goods and services under these circumstances would exceed the total value of final goods and services produced by $20 billion ($1,070 billion − $1,050 billion), so firms' inventories would be drawn down by $20 billion. Clearly, this situation could not persist for long. As firms saw their inventories becoming depleted, they would step up their production rates, so that the value of output of final goods and services—GDP—would increase.

Case 2: GDP = *$1,150 billion.* What would happen if firms produced $1,150 billion of final goods and services? Given our assumptions, disposable income would also equal $1,150 billion (since disposable income equals GDP), with the result that consumers would spend $1,040 billion on consumption goods and services. (Again, this follows from the consumption function: see column 2 of Table 5.3.) Since firms want to invest $90 billion, total spending would be $1,130 billion ($1,040 billion + $90 billion, as shown in column 5). But the total amount spent on final goods and services under these circumstances would fall short of the total value of final goods and services produced by $20 billion ($1,150 billion − $1,130 billion), so that firms' inventories would increase by $20 billion. Clearly, this situation, like the previous one, could not continue for long. When firms saw their inventories increasing, they would reduce their production rates, and this would cause the value of output of final goods and services—GDP—to decrease.

Case 3: GDP = *$1,100 billion.* What would happen if firms produced $1,100 billion of final goods and services? Disposable income would also equal $1,100 billion (since disposable income equals GDP), so consumers would spend $1,010 billion on consumption goods and services. (Once again, this follows from the consumption function: see column 2 of Table 5.3.) Since firms want to invest $90 billion, total spending would be $1,100 billion ($1,010 billion + $90 billion, as shown in column 5). Thus the total amount spent on final goods and services under these circumstances would exactly equal the total value of final goods and services produced. Consequently, there would be no reason for firms to alter their production rates. This would be an equilibrium situation—a set of circumstances where there is no tendency for GDP to change—and the equilibrium level of GDP in this situation would be $1,100 billion.

These three cases illustrate the process that pushes GDP toward its equilibrium value (and maintains it there). So long as GDP is below its equilibrium value, the situation is like that described in our first case. So long as GDP is above its equilibrium value, the situation is like that described in our second case. Whether GDP is

below or above its equilibrium value, there is a tendency for production rates to be altered so that GDP moves toward its equilibrium value. Eventually, GDP will reach its equilibrium value, and
the situation will be like that described in our third case. The important aspect of the third case—the equilibrium situation—is that
for it to occur, intended spending must equal GDP.

■ USING A GRAPH TO DETERMINE EQUILIBRIUM GDP

We can represent the same argument in a diagrammatic, rather
than tabular, analysis. Let's show again that the equilibrium level
of GDP is at the point where intended spending equals GDP, but
now using a graph. Since disposable income equals gross domestic
product in this simple case, we can plot consumption expenditure
(on the vertical axis) versus gross domestic product (on the horizontal axis), as shown in Figure 5.4. This is the consumption function. Also, we can plot the sum of consumption expenditure and
investment expenditure against GDP, as shown in Figure 5.4. This
relationship, shown by the $C + I$ line, indicates the level of total intended spending on final goods and services for various amounts
of GDP. Finally, we can plot a 45-degree line, as shown in Figure
5.4. This line contains all points where the amount on the horizontal axis equals the amount on the vertical axis. Thus since GDP is
on the horizontal axis and intended spending is on the vertical
axis, it contains all points where total intended spending equals
gross domestic product.

FIGURE 5.4

**Determination of the Equilibrium
Value of Gross Domestic Product**

The consumption function is C, and
the sum of consumption and investment expenditure is $C + I$. The equilibrium value of GDP is at the point
where the $C + I$ line intersects the 45-
degree line, here $1,100 billion.

THE DETERMINATION
OF NATIONAL
OUTPUT AND
THE KEYNESIAN
MULTIPLIER
CHAPTER 5

45-degree line

**Income-
expenditure
analysis**

The equilibrium level of gross domestic product will be at the point where total intended spending equals GDP. Consequently, the equilibrium level of GDP will be at the point on the horizontal axis where the $C + I$ line intersects the 45-degree line. In Figure 5.4, this occurs at $1,100 billion. Under the conditions assumed here, no other level of GDP can be maintained for any considerable period of time.

Why can we be sure that the point where the $C + I$ line intersects the 45-degree line is the point where intended spending equals GDP? Because a **45-degree line** is, by construction, a line that includes all points where the amount on the vertical axis equals the amount on the horizontal axis. In this case, as noted above, intended spending is on the vertical axis and GDP is on the horizontal axis. Thus at point A, the point where the $C + I$ line intersects the 45-degree line, intended spending must equal GDP, because point A is on the 45-degree line.

RECONCILING AGGREGATE DEMAND AND SUPPLY CURVES WITH INCOME-EXPENDITURE ANALYSIS

At this point, we must reconcile and integrate the income-expenditure analysis presented here with the aggregate demand-aggregate supply analysis presented in Chapter 4. According to **income-expenditure analysis**, the equilibrium level of GDP occurs at the point where the $C + I$ line intersects the 45-degree line, as shown in panel A of Figure 5.5. This analysis assumes that firms set their output levels in accord with the level of demand at current prices. If intended spending increases, firms increase their output levels; if intended spending falls, firms cut their output levels.

FIGURE 5.5

Relationship between Income-Expenditure Analysis and Aggregate Demand–Aggregate Supply Analysis

Income-expenditure analysis uses the intersection of the $C + I$ line and the 45-degree line to find the equilibrium level of GDP. Aggregate demand–aggregate supply analysis uses the intersection of the aggregate demand and supply curves to find the equilibrium level of GDP. Both types of analysis yield the same result, namely, that the equilibrium value of GDP is Y.

Income-expenditure analysis assumes that firms will produce whatever is demanded at the going price level. In other words, it assumes that the economy is situated on the horizontal range of its short-run aggregate supply curve. As shown in panel B of Figure 5.5, the aggregate demand curve intersects the short-run aggregate supply curve in this range. Put differently, income-expenditure analysis assumes that the equilibrium level of output is demand determined and that supply adjusts passively to demand.

If the economy is experiencing considerable unemployment, and the horizontal range of the short-run aggregate supply curve is the relevant one, as Keynes and his followers argued in the 1930s, income-expenditure analysis tends to be a more revealing way of looking at the determinants of national output than aggregate demand–aggregate supply analysis. It shows the nature of the changes in spending, which are the prime movers in the model.

But if the economy is operating at a point where the aggregate supply curve is upward sloping or vertical, aggregate demand–aggregate supply analysis is more relevant than income-expenditure analysis because it focuses on changes in the price level, which are not included or shown in income-expenditure analysis.

CHANGES IN EQUILIBRIUM OUTPUT

On the basis of the simple model we constructed in the previous sections, we can see that equilibrium output can be altered by changes in investment or by changes in consumption that are not due to changes in income. We conclude this chapter by discussing the volatility of investment spending and how changes in such spending have an amplified—multiplier—effect on output. In the section "Exploring Further," we show that shifts in the consumption function have similar effects on national output.

THE VOLATILITY OF INVESTMENT

As pointed out at the beginning of this chapter, investment expenditure tends to be relatively unstable (see Figure 5.6). That is, it varies from year to year by greater percentages than consumption expenditure does. There are many reasons for this.

Irregularity of innovation rate. Technological innovation occurs irregularly—in fits and starts—not at a constant rate. Thus investment, which is dependent on the rate of technological change, also tends to occur irregularly. Investment booms seem to have occurred in response to major innovations like the railroad and the automobile. The innovation wave that swept through the informa-

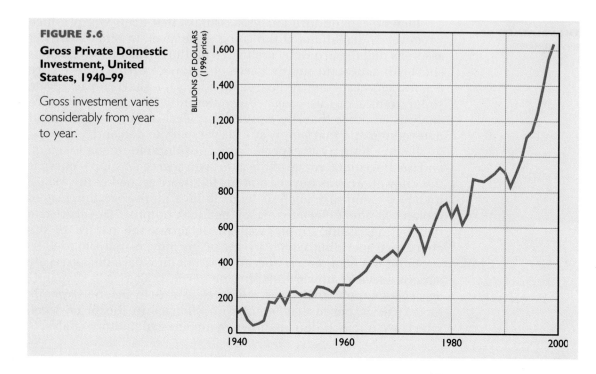

FIGURE 5.6

Gross Private Domestic Investment, United States, 1940–99

Gross investment varies considerably from year to year.

BILLIONS OF DOLLARS (1996 prices)

tion and telecommunications industries in the 1990s also brought with it a surge in new investment spending (see Figure 5.6).

Durability of capital goods. Because capital goods tend to be quite durable, firms frequently can postpone investment decisions. For example, they can postpone the replacement of a piece of equipment by using it even though it is not as reliable as it once was. Or they can postpone the construction of a new building by tolerating crowded conditions in their existing buildings. Since many investment decisions are postponable, the exact time when projects are accepted may depend on the state of business expectations and the level of firms' profits, both of which are highly variable. Also, since the optimism or pessimism of business expectations tends to be contagious, firms often tend to invest at the same time.

Capacity utilization. There are great differences from one year to the next in the extent to which existing productive capacity is being utilized. In some years, sales are so great that firms are working their plants at full capacity. In other years, sales are so slack that firms have plenty of excess capacity. In periods when the existing stock of capital goods is more than sufficient to meet current sales, the level of investment will tend to be lower than in periods when the existing stock of capital goods is only barely sufficient to

**Industrial robots assembling
washing machines**

meet current sales. Because of the year-to-year variation in the extent to which sales levels press against productive capacity, there is considerable variation in the level of investment.

EFFECTS OF CHANGES IN INTENDED INVESTMENT

Looking at the highly simplified model we constructed in previous sections to explain the level of national output, what is the effect of a change in the amount of intended investment? Specifically, if the firms increase their intended investment by $1 billion, what effect will this increase have on the equilibrium value of gross domestic product?

This is a very important question, the answer to which sheds considerable light on the reasons for changes in national output in the simple Keynesian model. In the following sections devoted to answering this question, we assume that the change in investment is autonomous, not induced. An **autonomous** change in spending is one that *is not* due to a change in income or GDP. An **induced** change in spending is one that *is* due to a change in income or GDP.

**Autonomous
spending
Induced spending**

■ THE SPENDING CHAIN: ONE STAGE AFTER ANOTHER

The effects of intended investment can be divided into a number of stages. If there is a $1 billion increase in intended investment, in the first stage firms spend an additional $1 billion on plant, equipment, or inventories. This extra $1 billion is received by workers and suppliers as extra income, which results in a second stage of extra spending on final goods and services. How much of their

133

Keynes's criticisms of the classical view

As Keynes and his followers saw it, there were at least two basic flaws in the classical model. First, in their view, *there is no assurance that total intended spending will equal GDP at a level ensuring high employment.* The people and firms who save are often not the same people and firms who invest, and they often have quite different motivations. In particular, a considerable amount of saving is done by families who want to put something aside for a rainy day or for a car or appliance. On the other hand, a considerable amount of investment is done by firms interested in increasing their profits by expanding their plants or by installing new equipment. According to Keynes, one cannot be sure that changes in the interest rate will bring about the equality of saving and investment visualized by the classical economists. Total intended spending may equal GDP at a level corresponding to considerable unemployment (or to considerable inflation). Thus the Keynesian view is that a purely capitalist economic system, in the absence of appropriate government policies, has no dependable rudder to keep it clear of the shoals of serious unemployment or serious inflation.

Second, *Keynes and his followers disputed the classical economists' assumption that prices and wages are flexible.* In their view, the modern economy contains many departures from perfect competition that are barriers to downward flexibility of prices and wages. In particular, many important industries are dominated by a few producers who try hard to avoid cutting prices. Even in the face of a considerable drop in demand, such industries have sometimes maintained extraordinarily stable prices. Moreover, the labor unions fight to avoid wage cuts. According to Keynes, it is unlikely that price and wage reductions can be depended on to maintain full employment.

extra $1 billion in income will the workers and suppliers spend? If the marginal propensity to consume is .6, they will spend .6 times $1 billion, or $.6 billion. This extra expenditure of $.6 billion is received by firms and disbursed to workers, suppliers, and owners as extra income. This brings about a third stage of extra spending on final goods and services. How much of this extra income of $.6 billion will they spend? Since the marginal propensity to consume is .6, they will spend 60 percent of this $.6 billion, or $.36 billion. This extra expenditure of $.36 billion is received by firms and disbursed to workers, suppliers, and owners as extra income, which results in a fourth stage of spending, then a fifth stage, a sixth stage, and so on.

Totaling up the stages. Table 5.4 shows the total increase in expenditure on final goods and services arising from the original $1 billion increase in intended investment. The total increase in expenditures is the increase in the first stage, plus the increase in the second stage, plus the increase in the third stage, and so on. Since there is an endless chain of stages, we cannot list all the increases. But because the successive increases in spending get smaller and smaller, we can determine their sum, which in this case is $2.5 billion. Thus the $1 billion increase in intended investment results—

TABLE 5.4	STAGE	AMOUNT OF EXTRA SPENDING (BILLIONS OF DOLLARS)
The Multiplier Process	1	1.00
	2	0.60
	3	0.36
	4	0.22
	5	0.13
	6	0.08
	7	0.05
	8	0.03
	9 and beyond	0.03
	Total	2.50

after all stages of the spending and respending process have worked themselves out—in a $2.5 billion increase in total expenditures on final goods and services. In other words, it results in a $2.5 billion increase in GDP.

THE MULTIPLIER

In general, *a $1 billion increase in intended investment results in an increase in equilibrium GDP of (1/MPS) billions of dollars, where MPS is the marginal propensity to save.* This is a famous conclusion of the simple Keynesian model. To understand more clearly what it means, let's consider a couple of numerical examples involving values of the marginal propensity to save other than .4. For instance, if the marginal propensity to save is 1/3, a $1 billion increase in intended investment will increase equilibrium GDP by $1 ÷ 1/3 billion, that is, by $3 billion. Or take a case where the marginal propensity to consume equals 3/4. What is the effect of a $1 billion increase in intended investment? Since the marginal propensity to save must equal 1 − 3/4, or 1/4, the answer must be $1 ÷ 1/4 billion. That is, equilibrium GDP will increase by $4 billion.

Multiplier

Since a dollar of extra intended investment results in 1/*MPS* dollars of extra GDP, 1/*MPS* is called the **multiplier**. If you want to estimate the effect of a given increase in intended investment on GDP, multiply the increase in intended investment by 1/*MPS*. The result will be the increase in GDP. Moreover, it is easy to show that the same multiplier holds for decreases in intended investment as

CASE STUDY 5.2

Investment and a great crash

Between 1929 and 1933, annual investment spending in the United States fell by about $100 billion (1984 dollars). To get some idea of how a great crash, such as occurred then, can take place, let's consider a simple economy with no government or foreign trade. Suppose that intended investment in this economy falls from $104 billion to $4 billion, and that the saving function is as shown below:

According to the graph, intended saving equals $4 billion when GDP is $200 billion, and it equals $104 billion when GDP is $600 billion. Thus since GDP equals disposable income under the assumed (highly simplified) conditions, the marginal propensity to save equals $(104 - 4) \div (600 - 200) = .25$. The multiplier equals the reciprocal of the marginal propensity to save, or $1/.25 = 4$ in this highly simplified case. The drop in investment ($100 billion) times the multiplier (4) is equal to the drop in GDP ($400 billion). So in this example GDP must have dropped by $400 billion.

This is an illustration of how the multiplier can be used, presuming that the assumptions underlying the simple Keynesian model hold. Knowing the marginal propensity to save (.25), we can calculate the multiplier (4), which enables us to determine the change in GDP ($400 billion).

well as for increases. That is, a dollar less of intended investment results in 1/*MPS* dollars less of GDP. Consequently, to estimate the effect of a given change in intended investment (positive or negative) on GDP, multiply the change in intended investment by 1/*MPS*.

It is important to note that since *MPS* is less than 1, *the multiplier must be greater than 1*. In other words, an increase in intended investment of $1 will result in an increase in GDP of more than $1. This means that GDP is relatively sensitive to changes in intended investment. Moreover, since the multiplier is the reciprocal of the marginal propensity to save, the smaller the marginal propensity to save, the bigger the multiplier—and the more sensitive GDP is to changes in intended investment.

EXPLORING FURTHER

NONINCOME DETERMINANTS OF CONSUMPTION

In previous sections of this chapter, we were concerned with the effects on GDP of changes in investment spending. Now we must consider the effects of changes in consumption expenditure. It is important to recognize that many other factors besides disposable income have an effect on personal consumption expenditure. Holding disposable income constant, personal consumption expenditure is likely to vary with the amount of wealth in the hands of the public, the ease and cheapness with which consumers can borrow money, consumers' expectations, the amount of durable goods on hand, the income distribution, and the size of the population. In this section we discuss the effects of these nonincome factors on consumption expenditure.

■ SHIFTS IN THE CONSUMPTION AND SAVING FUNCTIONS

Suppose that a change occurs in one of these nonincome factors. For example, suppose that there is a marked increase in the amount of wealth in the hands of the public. What effect will this have on the consumption function? Obviously, it will shift the consumption function upward, as from position 1 to position 2 in Figure 5.7A. Or suppose that it becomes more difficult and expensive for consumers to borrow money. What effect will this have on the consumption function? Obviously, it will shift the consumption function downward, as from position 1 to position 3 in Figure 5.7A.

■ SHIFTS IN FUNCTIONS VERSUS MOVEMENTS ALONG THEM

It is important to distinguish between a *shift* in the consumption function and a *movement along* a given consumption function. A shift in the consumption function means that the public wants to spend a different amount on consumption goods out of a given amount of disposable income than in the past. Thus if the consumption function shifts to position 2 in Figure 5.7A, this means that the public wants to spend more on consumption goods out of a given amount of disposable income than when the consumption function was at position 1. And if the consumption function shifts to position 3 in Figure 5.7A, this means that the public wants to spend less on consumption goods out of a given amount of dis-

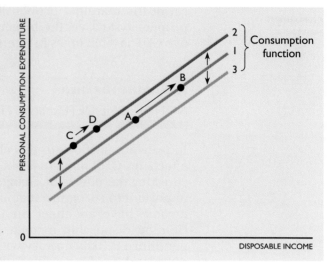

FIGURE 5.7A

A Shift versus a Movement along the Consumption Function

If the consumption function moves from position 1 to position 2 (or position 3), this is a shift in the consumption function. A movement from A to B (or from C to D) is a movement along a given consumption function.

posable income than when the consumption function was at position 1.

In contrast, a movement along a given consumption function is a change in personal consumption expenditure induced by a change in disposable income, with no change in the relationship between personal consumption expenditure and disposable income. For example, the movement from point *A* to point *B* is a movement along a consumption function (in position 1). Similarly, the movement from point *C* to point *D* is a movement along a consumption function (in position 2).

■ HOW SHIFTS IN THE CONSUMPTION FUNCTION ARE RELATED TO SHIFTS IN THE SAVING FUNCTION

Note that an *upward* shift in the consumption function must be accompanied by a *downward* shift in the saving function. If the public wants to spend *more* on consumption goods out of a given amount of disposable income, it must want to save *less* out of that amount of disposable income. (Why? Because personal consumption expenditure plus saving equals disposable income.) Thus if the consumption function shifts upward from position 1 to position 2 in Figure 5.7A, the saving function must shift downward from position 4 to position 5 in Figure 5.7B.

Also, a *downward* shift in the consumption function must be accompanied by an *upward* shift in the saving function. If the public wants to spend *less* on consumption goods out of a given amount of disposable income, it must want to save *more* out of that amount of disposable income. (Why? Because personal consumption expenditure plus saving equals disposable income.) Thus if the con-

FIGURE 5.7B

Effects of Shifts in Consumption Function on Saving Function

An upward shift in the consumption function (as from position 1 to position 2 in panel A) is accompanied by a downward shift in the saving function (from position 4 to position 5 in panel B). A downward shift in the consumption function (as from position 1 to position 3 in panel A) is accompanied by an upward shift in the saving function (from position 4 to position 6 in panel B).

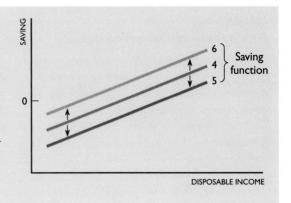

sumption function shifts downward from position 1 to position 3 in Figure 5.7A, the saving function must shift upward from position 4 to position 6 in Figure 5.7B.

▓ EFFECTS OF SHIFTS IN THE CONSUMPTION FUNCTION

Earlier in this chapter, we showed that, in the simple Keynesian model, changes in intended investment have an amplified effect on GDP, with the extent of the amplification measured by the multiplier. But it is important to note at this point that a shift in the consumption function will also have such an amplified effect on GDP. For example, in Figure 5.8, if the consumption function shifts from C_1 to C_2, this means that at each level of disposable income, consumers intend to spend $1 billion more on consumption goods and services than they did before. This $1 billion upward shift in the consumption function will have precisely the same effect on equilibrium GDP as a $1 billion increase in intended investment.

Moreover, *a $1 billion downward shift in the consumption function will have precisely the same effect on equilibrium GDP as a $1 billion decrease in intended investment.* Thus both upward and downward shifts in the consumption function—due to changes in tastes, assets, prices, population, and other things—will have a magnified effect on GDP. GDP is sensitive to shifts in the consumption function in the same way that it is sensitive to changes in intended investment. This is an important point. Finally, to prevent misunderstanding, recall from the previous sections that a *shift* in the consumption function is quite different from a *movement along* a given consumption function. (An example of the latter would be the movement from point *G* to point *H* in Figure 5.8.) We are concerned here with shifts in the consumption function, not movements along a given consumption function.

FIGURE 5.8

Shift in the Consumption Function

If the consumption function shifts from C_1 to C_2, this means at each level of disposable income, consumers intend to spend $1 billion more on consumption goods and services. Such a shift results in an increase of $1/MPS$ billion dollars in equilibrium GDP.

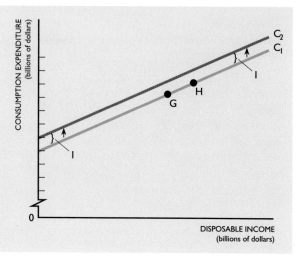

REVIEW AND PRACTICE

■ SUMMARY

1 The consumption function is the relation between personal consumption expenditure and disposable income. From the consumption function, one can determine the marginal propensity to consume, which is the proportion of an extra dollar of income that is spent on consumption. The marginal propensity to save is the proportion of an extra dollar of income that is saved.

2 The level of gross private domestic investment is determined by the expected rate of return from capital and the interest rate. The expected rate of return from capital is the rate of return that businesses expect to obtain if new buildings are put up, new equipment is added, or inventories are increased. The interest rate is the cost of borrowing money.

3 The equilibrium level of gross domestic product will be at the point where intended spending on final goods and services equals GDP. If intended spending exceeds GDP, GDP will tend to increase. If intended spending falls short of GDP, GDP will tend to fall.

4 If GDP is below its equilibrium level, the total amount spent on goods and services will exceed the total amount produced, so firms' inventories will be reduced. Firms will step up their output rates, and thus increase GDP.

5 If GDP is above its equilibrium value, the total amount spent on goods and services will fall short of the total amount produced, so firms' inventories will increase. Firms will cut their output rates, and thus reduce GDP.

6 Investment expenditure tends to vary from year to year by greater percentages than does consumption expenditure. This is due in part to the irregularity of innovation, the durability of capital goods, and the differences from year to year in the extent to which existing productive capacity is utilized.

7 A $1 billion change in intended investment will result in a change in equilibrium GDP of $1/MPS$ billion, where MPS is the marginal propensity to save. In other words, the multiplier is $1/MPS$. The multiplier can be interpreted in terms of—and derived from—the successive stages of the spending process.

*8 Holding disposable income constant, personal consumption expenditure is likely to depend on the amount of wealth in the hands of the public, the ease and cheapness with which consumers can borrow money, consumers' expectations, the amount of durable goods on hand, the income distribution, and the size of the population. Changes in these factors are likely to cause shifts in the consumption function.

*9 A shift in the consumption function will also have an amplified effect on GDP: a $1 billion shift in the consumption function will result in a $1/MPS$ billion change in GDP.

PROBLEMS AND QUESTIONS

1 Suppose that the consumption function in a particular economy is given by the following table:

DISPOSABLE INCOME (BILLIONS OF DOLLARS)	CONSUMPTION EXPENDITURE (BILLIONS OF DOLLARS)
400	300
500	360
600	410
700	440
800	470

If firms want to invest $140 billion, what is the equilibrium value of GDP? Can we be sure that this is the full-employment value of GDP? Why or why not? (The full-employment value of GDP is defined as the value of GDP that can be produced if there is full employment.)

2 Using the data in question 1, plot the consumption function and the $C + I$ line on a graph, and derive the equilibrium value of GDP graphically. Is the consumption function a straight line? If the consumption function is not a straight line, does this affect the validity of the analysis in any way?

3 Using the data in question 1, plot the saving function. Show that intended saving equals intended investment at the equilibrium level of GDP. Explain why this is true.

4 Suppose that the consumption function in a certain economy is $C = 100 + .8D$, where C is consumption expenditure and D is disposable income. If intended investment equals 10, what is the equilibrium value of GDP?

■ KEY TERMS

consumption function	interest rate
marginal propensity to consume	45-degree line
average propensity to consume	income-expenditure analysis
saving function	autonomous spending
marginal propensity to save	induced spending
expected rate of return	multiplier

*The starred items relate to material covered in Exploring Further.

**THE DETERMINATION
OF NATIONAL
OUTPUT AND
THE KEYNESIAN
MULTIPLIER**

CHAPTER 5

■ VIEWPOINT FOR ANALYSIS

On February 11, 1993, Allan Meltzer, Professor of Economics at Carnegie-Mellon University, testified before the Joint Economic Committee of Congress. He said, "Public policy has discouraged investment in several ways.... The 1986 tax act shifted taxes from consumers to owners of capital.... Taxes should be shifted from earned income to consumed income.... This change would increase saving."*

(a) What is the difference between earned income and consumed income? Would a shift in taxes from earned income to consumed income tend to increase the average propensity to save? Why or why not?

(b) Why would a shift in taxes from consumers to owners of capital discourage investment? If investment falls, what is likely to happen to GDP in the short run? In the long run? Why?

(c) Would you favor a policy of increasing investment? Why or why not? Can there be too much investment? Explain.

*A. Meltzer, "The Economy and Policy As 1993 Begins," statement prepared for the Joint Economic Committee, February 11, 1993.

CHAPTER 6

Fiscal Policy and National Output

LEARNING OBJECTIVES

In this chapter, you should learn:

- How government spending and taxation affect the level of GDP
- The objectives and methods of fiscal policy
- The problems in formulating effective fiscal policy
- The types of expenditures made and taxes collected by the federal, state, and local levels of government
- *(Exploring Further)* How to include net exports in the analysis

Most governments change tax rates—sometimes up, sometimes down. What effect do these changes have on GDP? One purpose of this chapter is to answer this question. In the period after World War II, the idea that the government's power to spend and tax should be used to stabilize the economy—that is, to reduce unemployment and fight inflation—gained acceptance throughout the world. However, time has revealed that fiscal policy (the use of government spending and taxation for stabilization purposes) is far from a panacea. This chapter presents a first look at fiscal policy, beginning with the simplest Keynesian model and then using aggregate demand and aggregate supply curves. In Chapters 12 and 14, a more sophisticated analysis of fiscal policy is presented.

GOVERNMENT EXPENDITURE AND GROSS DOMESTIC PRODUCT

In the previous chapters, we showed how the equilibrium level of gross domestic product was determined in a simplified economy without government spending or taxation. We must now extend this theory to include both government spending and taxation. As we shall see, the results form the basis for some of our nation's past and present economic policy. In this section, we incorporate government spending into the simple Keynesian model of the determination of gross domestic product. In so doing, we assume that government spending will not affect the consumption function or the level of intended investment. In other words, we assume that government spending does not reduce or increase private desires to spend out of each level of income. (Government here includes federal, state, and local.)

Suppose that the government purchases $50 billion worth of goods and services and that it purchases this amount whatever the level of GDP. (As pointed out in Chapter 3, only government purchases, not transfer payments, are included here.) Clearly, adding this public expenditure to the private expenditures on consumption and investment results in a higher total level of intended spending. In an economy with government spending (but no net exports), total intended spending on output equals consumption expenditure plus intended investment expenditure plus intended government expenditure. Since an increase in government expenditure (like increases in consumption or investment expenditure) results in an increase in total intended spending and since the equilibrium value of gross domestic product is at the point where total intended spending equals GDP, it follows that an increase in government expenditure, as well as the induced increase in private spending, brings about an increase in the equilibrium value of GDP.

To see the effects of government expenditure on the equilibrium value of GDP, we can use a graph similar to those in Chapter 5. We begin by plotting the consumption function, which shows intended consumption expenditure at each level of GDP (since GDP equals disposable income under our assumptions): the result is line C in Figure 6.1. Then we can plot the sum of intended consumption expenditure and investment expenditure at each level of

FIGURE 6.1

Determination of Gross Domestic Product, Including Government Expenditure

The consumption function is C, the sum of consumption and investment expenditures is C + I, and the sum of consumption, investment, and government expenditures is C + I + G. The equilibrium value of GDP is at the point where the C + I + G line intersects the 45-degree line, which here is $1,225 billion.

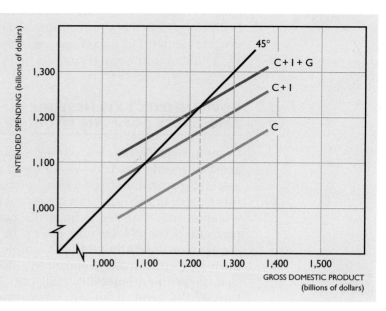

FIGURE 6.2

Effects on the Equilibrium Gross Domestic Product of a $5 Billion Increase and Decrease in Government Expenditure

A $5 billion increase raises the equilibrium value of GDP from $1,225 billion to $1,237.5 billion. A $5 billion decrease reduces the equilibrium value of GDP from $1,225 billion to $1,212.5 billion.

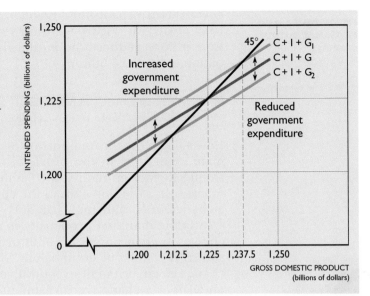

C + I + G line

GDP. The result is line $C + I$. Next, we plot the sum of intended consumption expenditure, investment expenditure, and government expenditure at each level of GDP, to get line $C + I + G$. Since the **$C + I + G$ line** shows total intended spending and since, as we stressed in Chapter 5, the equilibrium value of GDP is at the point where total intended spending equals GDP, it follows that the equilibrium value of GDP is at the point where the $C + I + G$ line intersects the 45-degree line. This is at an output of $1,225 billion.

■ EFFECT OF INCREASED GOVERNMENT EXPENDITURE

What happens to the equilibrium level of GDP if government expenditure increases? Figure 6.2 shows the results of a $5 billion increase in government spending. The increased government expenditure (G_1) will raise the $C + I + G$ line by $5 billion, as the figure shows. Since the $C + I + G_1$ line must intersect the 45-degree line at a higher level of GDP, increases in government expenditure result in increases in the equilibrium level of GDP. In Figure 6.2, the $5 billion increase in government expenditure raises the equilibrium value of GDP from $1,225 billion to $1,237.5 billion.

■ EFFECT OF DECREASED GOVERNMENT EXPENDITURE

Figure 6.2 also shows what happens when government spending goes down by $5 billion (to G_2). The new $C + I + G_2$ line is $5 billion lower than the old $C + I + G$ line. Since the new $C + I + G_2$ line intersects the 45-degree line at a lower level of GDP, decreases in

145

government expenditure result in decreases in the equilibrium level of GDP. In Figure 6.2 the $5 billion decrease in government expenditure reduces the equilibrium value of GDP from $1,225 billion to $1,212.5 billion.

■ WHAT IS THE MULTIPLIER EFFECT FOR GOVERNMENT EXPENDITURE?

How sensitive is the equilibrium level of GDP to changes in government spending? In the previous chapter, we found that, in the simple Keynesian model, a $1 billion change in intended investment—or a $1 billion shift in the consumption function—results in a change in equilibrium GDP of $(1/MPS)$ billions of dollars, where MPS is the marginal propensity to save. The effect of a $1 billion change in government expenditure is exactly the same. It will result in a change in equilibrium GDP of $(\$1/MPS)$ billion. Thus a change in government expenditure has the same multiplier effect on GDP as a change in investment or a shift in the consumption function. For example, if the marginal propensity to consume is .6, an extra $1 billion in government expenditure will increase equilibrium GDP by $2.5 billion.

TAXATION AND GROSS DOMESTIC PRODUCT

The previous section added government expenditure to the simple Keynesian model, but it did not include taxes. (Here we assume taxes to be net of transfer payments.) For simplicity, assume that all tax revenues stem from personal taxes. How do tax collections influence the equilibrium value of gross domestic product? For example, if consumers pay $16\frac{2}{3}$ percent of their income to the government in taxes, what effect does this have on GDP? Clearly, the imposition of this tax means that for each level of GDP, people have less disposable income than they would with no taxes. In particular, disposable income now equals $83\frac{1}{3}$ percent of GDP, whereas without taxes it equaled GDP. Thus *the relationship between consumption expenditure and GDP is altered by the imposition of the tax.* Before the tax was levied, the relationship was given by line C_0 in Figure 6.3; after the imposition of the tax, it is given by line C_1.

The relationship between consumption expenditure and national output changes in this way because consumption expenditure is determined by the level of disposable income. For instance, in the case in Figure 6.3, consumption expenditure equals $350 billion plus 60 percent of disposable income. Thus since the tax reduces the amount of disposable income at each level of GDP, it also reduces the amount of consumption expenditure at each level of GDP. In

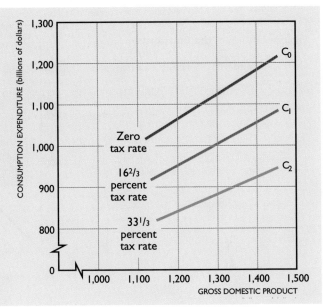

FIGURE 6.3

Relationship between Consumption Expenditure and Gross Domestic Product, Given Three Tax Rates

If taxes are zero, C_0 is the relationship between consumption expenditure and GDP. If consumers pay $16\frac{2}{3}$ percent of their income in taxes, C_1 is the relationship, and if consumers pay $33\frac{1}{3}$ percent of their income in taxes, C_2 is the relationship. Clearly, the higher the tax rate, the less consumers spend on consumption from a given GDP.

other words, since people have less after-tax income to spend at each level of GDP, they spend less on consumption goods and services at each level of GDP. This seems reasonable. It is illustrated in Figure 6.3, where at each level of GDP, consumption expenditure after tax (given by line C_1) is less than before the tax (given by line C_0).

Because the imposition of the tax influences the relationship between consumption expenditure and GDP, it also influences the equilibrium value of GDP. As we have stressed, the equilibrium value of GDP is at the point where intended spending on output equals GDP. Lines C_0 and C_1 in Figure 6.3 show intended consumption expenditure at each level of GDP, before and after the tax. Adding intended investment and government expenditure to each of these lines, we get the total intended spending before and after the tax. The results are shown in Figure 6.4, under the assumption that the sum of intended investment and government spending equals $140 billion. The $C_0 + I + G$ line shows intended spending before the tax, while the $C_1 + I + G$ line shows intended spending after the tax.

■ EFFECT OF THE TAX

The equilibrium level of GDP is appreciably lower after the imposition of the tax than before. Specifically, as shown in Figure 6.4, it is $980 billion after the imposition of the tax and $1,225 billion before. The tax reduced the equilibrium level of GDP because it lowered

147

FIGURE 6.4

Determination of the Equilibrium Value of Gross Domestic Product, with Zero and 16⅔ Percent Tax Rates

The tax rate influences the relationship between consumption expenditure and GDP. (C_0 is the relationship with a zero tax rate, while C_1 is the relationship with a 16⅔ percent tax rate. See Figure 6.3.) Consequently, the equilibrium value of GDP is $1,225 billion if the tax rate is zero, and $980 billion if it is 16⅔ percent.

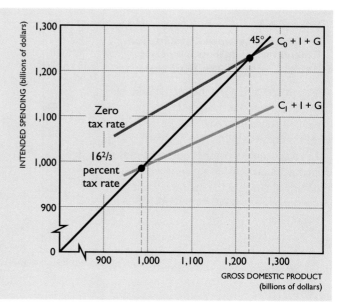

the $C + I + G$ line from $C_0 + I + G$ to $C_1 + I + G$. It did this because it reduced the amount people wanted to spend on consumption goods at each level of GDP. People still wanted to spend the same amount *from each (after-tax) income level,* but because of the tax, their spending decisions had to be based on a *reduced (after-tax) income,* so they spent less on consumption goods and services at each level of GDP.

■ EFFECT OF A TAX INCREASE

Going a step further, *the higher the tax rate, the lower the equilibrium value of GDP; and the lower the tax rate, the higher the equilibrium value of GDP.* This is a very important proposition, as we shall see in subsequent sections. To demonstrate it, let's see what will happen to the equilibrium value of GDP when the tax rate is increased from 16⅔ percent of GDP to 33⅓ percent of GDP. If the tax rate is 33⅓ percent, total intended spending at each level of GDP will be given by line $C_2 + I + G$ in Figure 6.5.

Since the equilibrium value of GDP will be at the point where the $C_2 + I + G$ line intersects the 45-degree line, the equilibrium value of GDP will be $816⅔ billion, rather than $980 billion (which was the equilibrium value when the tax rate was 16⅔ percent). Thus the increase in the tax rate will reduce the equilibrium value of GDP. By reducing the amount people want to spend on consumption at each level of GDP, the increase in the tax rate will lower the $C + I + G$ line from $C_1 + I + G$ to $C_2 + I + G$.

FIGURE 6.5

Determination of the Equilibrium Value of Gross Domestic Product, with $16\frac{2}{3}$ percent and $33\frac{1}{3}$ Percent Tax Rates

The $C_1 + I + G$ line shows total intended spending at each level of GDP if the tax rate is $16\frac{2}{3}$ percent, and the $C_2 + I + G$ line shows total intended spending at each level of GDP if the tax rate is $33\frac{1}{3}$ percent. So, the equilibrium value of GDP is \$980 billion if the tax rate is $16\frac{2}{3}$ percent and \$$816\frac{2}{3}$ billion if it is $33\frac{1}{3}$ percent.

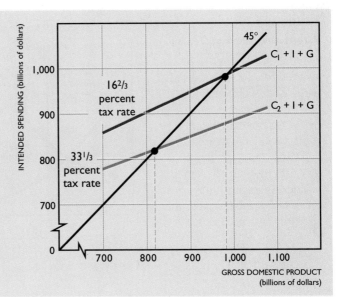

FISCAL POLICY: AGGREGATE DEMAND AND SUPPLY CURVES

In previous sections of this chapter, we have described the effects of fiscal policy in the simple Keynesian model, where the price level is constant and the short-run aggregate supply curve is horizontal. But as pointed out in Chapter 5, these assumptions often are not applicable. Our purpose in this section is to analyze the effects of fiscal policy in the situation where the price level is not constant and the short-run aggregate supply curve is not horizontal. As in previous chapters, we shall make extensive use of aggregate supply and demand curves.

■ A RECESSIONARY GAP

Recessionary gap

To begin with, suppose that the economy is suffering from excessive unemployment and that output is well below its potential level. There is a **recessionary gap**, which means that equilibrium output is less than potential output. In particular, let's assume that the situation is as shown in the top left-hand panel of Figure 6.6. As you can see, the equilibrium value of total real output is \$200 billion, which is well below \$250 billion, the economy's potential output. Given this situation, there are several ways in which output can be pushed up to its potential level, so full employment can be restored. One way is to wait for wage rates and other input prices to fall in response to the high unemployment rate, and thus shift

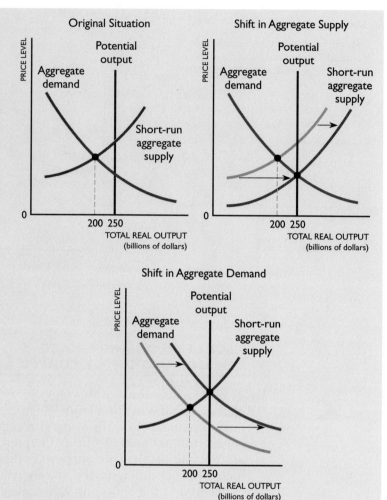

FIGURE 6.6

Alternative Ways of Dealing with a Recessionary Gap

As shown in the top left-hand panel, equilibrium output is $200 billion, which is well below the potential output of $250 billion. Thus there is a recessionary gap. One way to deal with this situation is to wait for wages and other input prices to fall, and thus push the short-run aggregate supply curve to the right, as shown in the top right-hand panel. Another way is to wait for an increase in private sector spending to push the aggregate demand curve to the right, as shown in the bottom panel. Still another way is for the government to shift the aggregate demand curve to the right (as in the bottom panel) by increasing its own spending and/or by cutting taxes.

the short-run aggregate supply curve to the right, as shown in the top right-hand panel of Figure 6.6. Although some economists believe that such a strategy is feasible, most believe that it would take too long because, in their view, wages tend to be quite sticky (recall Chapter 4). In Chapter 14, we will discuss more fully the controversies and evidence on this score.

Another way to deal with the recessionary gap in the top left-hand panel of Figure 6.6 is to wait for spending by the private sector to pick up, and thus shift the aggregate demand curve to the right, as shown in the bottom panel of Figure 6.6. Here too the problem is that it may take a painfully long time for such a shift in the aggregate demand curve to occur. As we have seen in Chapter 4, some recessions have gone on for years.

Still another strategy is for the government to increase its spending and/or to cut taxes, and thus shift the aggregate demand curve to the right. As in the case described in the previous paragraph, such a shift in the aggregate demand curve can push output up to its potential level, as shown in the bottom panel of Figure 6.6. Governments eager to restore full employment often have used fiscal policy in this way. One problem has been that the stimulus resulting from their actions has sometimes been felt when spending by the private sector has picked up, and the consequence has been inflationary pressure because the aggregate demand curve has been pushed too far to the right.

■ AN INFLATIONARY GAP

Having described how fiscal policy has been used to deal with an economy suffering from excessive unemployment, let's turn to a case where an economy is suffering from serious inflation. If the equilibrium value of real national output exceeds potential output, as shown in the top left-hand panel of Figure 6.7, economists say that there is an **inflationary gap**. In a situation of this sort, there will be substantial inflationary pressures. Why? Because labor is in short supply, and wages will be bid up, and thus increase firms' costs. There are several ways that the equilibrium value of real national output can be reduced so it no longer exceeds potential output and so price stability can be restored.

Inflationary gap

One way is to allow market forces to take their course. Since wages and other input prices will be bid up, the short-run aggregate supply curve will shift to the left. The result will be inflation, but when the price level increases to 115 in the top right-hand panel of Figure 6.7, the inflation should stop.

Another way to deal with the inflationary gap in the top left-hand panel of Figure 6.7 is to wait for spending by the private sector to recede, and thus shift the aggregate demand curve to the left, as shown in the bottom panel of Figure 6.7. Unfortunately, however, such a reduction in aggregate demand may not occur in time to prevent the inflationary process in the top right-hand panel of Figure 6.7 from taking place.

Still another strategy is for the government to cut its spending and/or raise taxes, and thus shift the aggregate demand curve to the left. As in the case described in the previous paragraph, such a shift in the aggregate demand curve can push output down to its potential level, as shown in the bottom panel of Figure 6.7. Governments, eager to cut back inflationary pressures, often have used fiscal policy in this way. One problem is that the economic restraint resulting from government's actions has sometimes been felt when spending by the private sector has receded, with the consequence

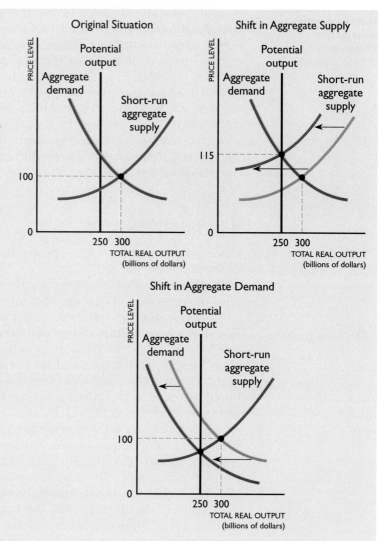

FIGURE 6.7
Alternative Ways of Dealing with an Inflationary Gap

As shown in the top left-hand panel, equilibrium output is $300 billion, which is well above the potential output of $250 billion. Thus, there is an inflationary gap. One way to deal with this situation is to allow wages and other input prices to rise, and thus push the short-run aggregate supply curve to the left, as shown in the top right-hand panel. Another way is to wait for a decrease in private sector spending to push the aggregate demand curve to the left, as shown in the bottom panel. Still another way is for the government to shift the aggregate demand curve to the left (as in the bottom panel) by cutting its own spending and/or by raising taxes.

that output has fallen below its potential level and unemployment has risen.

MAKERS OF FISCAL POLICY

When you go to a ball game, you generally get a program telling you who on each team is playing each position. To understand the formulation and implementation of fiscal policy in the United States, we need the same kind of information. Who are the people who establish our fiscal policy? Who decides that in view of the current and prospective economic situation, tax rates or government expenditures should be changed? This is not a simple question because many individuals and groups play important roles. In the Congress, the House and Senate Budget Committees, as well as the Congressional Budget Office, have been charged with important responsibilities in this area. The Appropriations Committees, the House Ways and Means Committee, and the Senate Finance Committee also have considerable influence. In addition, another congressional committee is of importance: the Joint Economic Committee of Congress. Established by the Employment Act of 1946, this committee goes over the annual *Economic Report of the President* on the state of the economy and, through its hearings, provides a major forum for review of economic issues.

In the executive branch of government, the most important person in the establishment of fiscal policy is, of course, the president. Although he must operate in the context of the tax and expenditure laws passed by Congress, he and his advisers are the country's principal analysts of the need for fiscal expansion or restraint and its leading spokespersons for legislative changes to meet these needs. Needless to say, he doesn't pore over the latest economic data and make the decisions all by himself. The Office of Management and Budget, which is part of the Executive Office of the President, is a very powerful adviser to the president on expenditure policy, as is the Treasury Department on tax policy. In addition, there is the *Council of Economic Advisers*, which is part of the Executive Office of the President. Established by the Employment Act of 1946, its job is to help the president carry out the objectives of that act. During the past 45 years, the Council of Economic Advisers, headed by a series of distinguished economists who left academic and other posts to contribute to public

Jack Lew, head of the Office of Management and Budget

CASE STUDY 6.1

The Employment Act of 1946

President Harry S. Truman signing the Employment Act of 1946

As previous chapters have indicated, the experiences of the Depression and the war convinced many Americans that the government had both the duty and the power to guarantee jobs for all its citizens. And the theoretical basis for this belief came from John Maynard Keynes. (See Case Study 4.3.) Keynes argued that an industrial economy could stabilize at high levels of unemployment, and the length and depth of the Great Depression seemed to bear him out. He argued that massive government intervention could restore prosperity to a stalled economy, and the wartime experience seemed to prove him right. When prosperity was threatened at the end of the war, a Full Employment Bill was introduced in the U.S. Senate in January 1945.

The first shot had been fired in a yearlong legislative battle. While everyone had been anxious to talk about full employment during the political campaigns of 1944, there was still plenty of resistance to the idea of this much government intervention in the economy. A year of compromises saw many changes in the language of the bill. The words *full employment* were replaced by the phrase "maximum employment, production and purchasing power." Gone were the original instructions to the president to initiate spending programs to guarantee employment. Conservatives rejoiced in a watered-down bill. Liberals denied that there was any retreat involved.

The bill that President Truman signed into law on February 20, 1946, was called the Employment Act of 1946. It instructed the federal government "to promote maximum employment, production and purchasing power." The president was instructed to form a Council of Economic Advisers to assist him in preparing economic forecasts. The idea of a right to a job, and a spending program to guarantee that right, disappeared from the final bill. By the time the Employment Act became law, the war was over, but the prosperity continued. Dire predictions of hard times and high unemployment vanished in the explosion of pent-up consumer demand. The end of the war marked the beginning of a long period of prosperity. And the Employment Act of 1946 marked the commitment of the government to use its considerable power to try to ensure a continuation of this prosperity.

policy, has become an important actor on the national economic policy stage.

AUTOMATIC STABILIZERS

Automatic stabilizers

Now that we have met some of the major players, we must point out that, in their efforts to fight serious unemployment or inflation, they get help from some **automatic stabilizers**—structural features of our economy that tend to stabilize national output. Although these economic stabilizers cannot do all that is required to keep the economy on an even keel, they help a lot. As soon as the economy turns down and unemployment mounts, they give the economy a helpful shot in the arm. As soon as the economy gets overheated and inflation breaks out, they tend to restrain it. These stabilizers are automatic because they come into play without the need for new legislation or administrative decisions.

■ TAX REVENUES

Changes in income tax revenues are an important automatic stabilizer. Our federal system relies heavily on the income tax. The amount of income tax collected by the federal government goes up with increases in GDP and goes down with decreases in GDP. This, of course, is just what we want to occur. When output falls off and unemployment mounts, tax collections fall off too, so disposable income falls less than GDP. This means less of a fall in consumption expenditure, which tends to break the fall in GDP. When output rises too fast and the economy begins to suffer from serious inflation, tax collections rise too; this tends to restrain the increase in GDP. Of course, corporate income taxes, as well as personal income taxes, play a significant role here.

■ UNEMPLOYMENT COMPENSATION AND WELFARE PAYMENTS

Unemployment compensation is paid to workers who are laid off, according to a system that has evolved over the past 70 years. When unemployed workers go back to work, they stop receiving unemployment compensation. Thus when GDP falls off and unemployment mounts, the tax collections to finance unemployment compensation go down (because of lower employment), while the amount paid out to unemployed workers goes up. On the other hand, when GDP rises too fast and the economy begins to suffer from serious inflation, the tax collections to finance unemployment compensation go up, while the amount paid out goes down because there is less unemployment. Again, this is just what we want to see happen. The fall in spending is moderated when unemployment is high, and the increase in spending is curbed when there are serious inflationary pressures. Various welfare programs have the same kind of automatic stabilizing effect on the economy.

DISCRETIONARY FISCAL POLICY

**Discretionary
fiscal policy**

The federal government frequently has changed tax rates—and to a lesser extent expenditures—in an attempt to cope with unemployment and inflation. The following kinds of measures, **discretionary fiscal policy**, can be adopted.

President Eisenhower and automatic stabilizers

President Dwight D. Eisenhower

When Dwight Eisenhower took office in 1953, he inherited a prosperity that had been bubbling along since the postwar boom. But by August 1953, there were signs that the economy was headed for a recession. By 1954 the unemployment rate was 6 percent, the highest since the Great Depression. Although Eisenhower remained outwardly confident, behind the scenes there was concern about the deepening recession and a debate about what the government should do. Because the recession reduced tax revenues, the government was running a deficit, and some people felt that taxes should be raised.

But President Eisenhower was getting other advice. In 1954 the Committee for Economic Development (composed largely of top business executives) urged the president to forget about balancing the budget and to leave the economy alone. As 1954 wore on and the Democrats and the labor unions demanded action, the economy stumbled, sputtered, and then took off in an upward direction. The first Republican recession since 1929 had come and gone, and even dedicated Democrats had to admit that the nation had survived. But we survived by doing nothing. And in hindsight, nothing turns out to have been just the thing to do.

An important factor in promoting recovery was the existence of our economy's automatic stabilizers. The concept of automatic stabilizers had been brought to the Eisenhower administration by Arthur F. Burns, who chaired the Council of Economic Advisers. Ironically, in 1952 Congress had tried to kill the council by cutting off its funding. By the end of 1954 it was clear that the council, its chairperson, and its stabilizing budget policy had passed a major test with honors.

1. The government can vary its expenditure for goods and services. If increased unemployment seems to be in the wind, the government can step up outlays on roads, urban reconstruction, and other public programs. Of course, these programs must be well thought out and socially productive. There is no sense in pushing through wasteful and foolish spending programs merely to make jobs. Or if, as in 1969, the economy is plagued by inflation, the government can (as President Nixon did) stop new federal construction programs temporarily.

2. The government can vary welfare payments and other types of transfer payments. For example, a hike in Social Security benefits may provide a shot in the arm for an economy with too much unemployment. An increase in veterans' benefits or in aid to dependent children may do the same thing. The federal government has sometimes helped the states to extend the length of time that the unemployed can receive unemployment compensation; this too was expected to have the desired effect.

3. *The government can vary tax rates.* For example, if there is considerable unemployment, the government may cut tax rates, as it did in 1975. Or if inflation is the problem, the government may increase taxes, as it did in 1968, when after considerable political maneuvering and buck-passing, Congress was finally persuaded to put through a 10 percent tax surcharge to try to moderate the inflation caused by the Vietnam War. However, temporary tax changes may have less effect than permanent ones, since consumption expenditure may be influenced less by transitory changes in income than by permanent changes.

■ PROBLEMS IN FORMULATING EFFECTIVE DISCRETIONARY FISCAL POLICIES

While governments frequently carry out discretionary fiscal policies, it is important to recognize the many types of problems that can interfere with the effectiveness of such policies. *One of the big disadvantages of public works and similar spending programs is that they take so long to get started.* Plans must be made, land must be acquired, and preliminary construction studies must be carried out. By the time the expenditures are finally made and have the desired effect, the dangers of excessive unemployment may have given way to dangers of inflation, so that the spending, coming too late, may not be the right economic medicine at all.

In recent years, there has been a widespread feeling that government expenditures should be set on the basis of their long-run desirability and productivity and not on the basis of short-term stabilization considerations. The optimal level of government expenditure is at the point where the value of the extra benefits to be derived from an extra dollar of government expenditure is at least equal to the dollar of cost. This optimal level is unlikely to change much in the short run, and it would be wasteful to spend more—or less—than this amount for stabilization purposes when tax changes could be used instead. Thus many economists believe that tax cuts or tax increases should be the primary fiscal weapons to fight unemployment or inflation.

However, *one of the big problems with tax changes is that it sometimes is difficult to get Congress to take speedy action.* There is often considerable debate over a tax bill, and sometimes it becomes a political football. Another difficulty with tax changes is that it generally is much easier to reduce taxes than it is to get them back up again. To politicians, lower taxes are attractive because they are popular, and higher taxes are dangerous because they may hurt a politician's chances of reelection. In discussing fiscal policy (or most other aspects of government operations for that matter), to ignore politics is to risk losing touch with reality.

157

President Kennedy and the tax cut of 1964

President John F. Kennedy and Walter Heller

When the Kennedy administration took office in 1961, it was confronted with a relatively high unemployment rate—about 7 percent in mid-1961. By 1962, although unemployment was somewhat lower (about 6 percent), the president's advisers, led by Walter W. Heller, chairperson of the Council of Economic Advisers, pushed for a tax cut to reduce unemployment further.

The president, after considerable discussion of the effects of such a tax cut, announced in June 1962 that he would propose such a measure to the Congress, and in January 1963, the bill was finally sent to Congress.

The proposed tax bill was a victory for Heller and the Council of Economic Advisers. Even though it would mean a deliberately large deficit, the president had been persuaded to cut taxes to push the economy closer to full employment. But the Congress was not so easily convinced. Many members of Congress labeled the proposal irresponsible and reckless. Others wanted to couple tax reform with tax reduction. It was not until 1964, after President Kennedy's death, that the tax bill was enacted. It took a year from the time the bill was sent to Congress for it to be passed, and during this interval, there was a continuous debate in the executive branch and the Congress. The secretary of the Treasury, Douglas Dillon; the chairperson of the Federal Reserve Board, William M. Martin; and numerous

congressional representatives—all powerful and all initially cool to the proposal—were eventually won over. The result was a tax reduction of about $10 billion per year.

The effects of the tax cut are by no means easy to measure, in part because the rate of growth of the money supply increased at the same time and this should also affect GDP. But in line with the theory presented in earlier sections, consumption expenditure did increase sharply during 1964. Moreover, the additional consumption expenditure undoubtedly induced additional investment. According to some estimates, the tax cut resulted in an increase in GDP of about $24 billion in 1965 and more in subsequent years. The unemployment rate, which had been about 5½ to 6 percent during 1962 and 1963, fell to 5 percent during 1964 and to 4.7 percent in the spring of 1965. It is fair to say that most economists were extremely pleased with themselves in 1965. Fiscal policy based on their theories seemed to work very well indeed!

Further, economists warn that, to the extent that discretionary fiscal policy involves reacting to short-term economic developments with little consideration of longer-term consequences, the result may be more harm than good. This problem is discussed at length in Chapter 14. The point is that changes in taxes and government spending aimed at stabilizing the economy in the short run may not be most effective in promoting the long-term health of the economy.

SIZE AND NATURE OF GOVERNMENT ACTIVITIES

■ HOW BIG IS THE GOVERNMENT?

Up to this point, we have been concerned primarily with fiscal policy and the role of the government in trying to stabilize the economy. We have made no attempt to describe the size and nature of the functions of the U.S. government in quantitative terms. It is time now to turn to some of the relevant facts.

To begin with, government expenditures are a much larger percentage of our national output than was true 75 or 100 years ago. There are many reasons why government expenditures have grown so much faster than total output. Three of these are particularly important. First, *the United States did not maintain anything like the kind of military force in pre–World War II days that it does now.* In earlier days, when weapons were relatively simple and cheap, and when we viewed our military and political responsibilities much more narrowly than we do now, our military budget was relatively small. The cost of being a superpower in the days of nuclear weaponry is high by any standards. Second, *there has been a long-term increase in the demand for the services provided by government*, like more and better schooling, more extensive highways, more complete police and fire protection, and so forth. As incomes rise, people want more of these services. Third, **government transfer payments**—*payments in return for no products or services—have grown very substantially.* For example, various types of welfare payments have risen, and Social Security payments have increased greatly.

Government transfer payments

■ HOW THE FEDERAL, STATE, AND LOCAL GOVERNMENTS SPEND MONEY

There are three levels of government in the United States: federal, state, and local. The state governments spend the least, while the federal government spends the most. This was not always the case. Before World War I, local governments spent more than the federal government. In those days, the federal government did not maintain the large military establishment it does now, nor did it engage in the many programs in health, education, welfare, and other areas that it currently does.

Table 6.1 shows how the federal government spends its money. *Over one-half goes for Social Security, Medicare, welfare (and other income security) programs, health, and education. About one-fifth goes for defense and other items connected with international relations and national security. The rest goes to support farm, transportation, housing, and other such programs, as well as to pay interest on the federal debt and to run Congress, the courts, and the executive branch of the federal government.*

159

TABLE 6.1

Federal Expenditures, Fiscal 2001

PURPOSE	AMOUNT (BILLIONS OF DOLLARS)	PERCENT OF TOTAL
National defense	291	16
International affairs	20	1
Energy	−1	b
Veterans' benefits	46	2
General science, space, and technology	19	1
Agriculture	22	1
Education, training, employment, and social services	67	4
Health	167	9
Natural resources and environment	25	1
Commerce and housing credit	3	b
Transportation	50	3
Community and regional development	10	1
Interest	208	11
General government	15	1
Income security	256	14
Administration of justice	31	2
Medicare	220	12
Social Security	426	23
Offsetting receipts	−47	−2
Total[a]	1,835	100

[a]Because of rounding errors, the figures may not sum to totals.
[b]Less than half of 1 percent.
Source: Economic Report of the President (Washington D.C.: Government Printing Office, 2000). These are estimates made in 1999.

What about local and state governments? On what do they spend their money? Table 6.2 shows that *the biggest expenditure of state and local governments is on schooling.* Traditionally, schools in the United States have been a responsibility of local governments—cities and towns. *State governments spend most of their money on education, on welfare, old age, and unemployment benefits, and on highways.* (Besides supporting education directly, they help localities to cover the costs of schooling.) In addition, local and state governments support hospitals, redevelopment programs, courts, and police and fire departments.

■ WHAT THE FEDERAL, STATE, AND LOCAL
GOVERNMENTS RECEIVE IN TAXES

To get the money to cover most of the expenditures discussed in previous sections, governments collect taxes from individuals and firms. As Table 6.3 shows, *at the federal level the personal income tax*

TABLE 6.2

Expenditures of State and Local Governments, United States, 1995–96

TYPE OF EXPENDITURE	AMOUNT (BILLIONS OF DOLLARS)	PERCENT OF TOTAL
Education	399	33
Highways	79	7
Public welfare	197	17
Other	517	43
Total[a]	1,193	100

[a]Because of rounding errors, the figures may not sum to totals.
Source: Economic Report of the President, 2000.

is the biggest single money raiser. It brings in almost one-half of the tax revenue collected by the federal government. The next most important taxes at the federal level are the Social Security, payroll, and employment taxes. Other important taxes are the corporation income taxes, excise taxes—levied on the sale of tobacco, liquor, imports, and certain other items—and death and gift taxes. (Even when the Grim Reaper shows up, the Tax Man is not far behind.)

As shown in Table 6.4, *at the local level, on the other hand, the most important form of taxation and source of revenue is the property tax.* This is a tax levied primarily on real estate. Other important local taxes—although dwarfed in importance by the property tax— are local sales taxes and local income taxes. Many cities—for example, New York City—levy a sales tax, equal to a certain percent—nearly 8 percent in New York City—of the value of each retail sale. The tax is simply added on to the amount charged the customer. Also, many cities—for example, Philadelphia and Pitts-

TABLE 6.3

Federal Receipts by Tax, Fiscal 2001

TYPE OF TAX	AMOUNT (BILLIONS OF DOLLARS)	PERCENT OF TOTAL
Personal income tax	972	48
Corporation income tax	195	10
Social insurance taxes	682	34
Excise taxes	77	4
Estate and gift taxes	32	2
Other revenues	61	3
Total[a]	2,019	100

[a]Because of rounding errors, figures may not sum to totals.
Source: Economic Report of the President, 2000. These are estimates made in 1999.

TABLE 6.4

State and Local Tax Revenues, by Source, 1995–96

SOURCE	REVENUES (BILLIONS OF DOLLARS)	PERCENT OF TOTAL
General sales tax	248	20
Property tax	209	17
Personal income tax	146	1.2
Corporate income tax	32	3
Other taxes	586	48
Total[a]	1,222	100

[a]Because of rounding errors, the figures may not sum to the totals.
Source: *Economic Report of the President,* 2000.

burgh—levy an income (or wage) tax on their residents and even on people who work in the city but live outside it. *At the state level, sales (and excise) taxes are the biggest money raiser,* followed by income taxes and highway-user taxes. The latter include taxes on gasoline and license fees for vehicles and drivers. Often they exceed the amount spent on roads, and the balance is used for a variety of nonhighway uses.

EXPLORING FURTHER

INCLUDING NET EXPORTS IN THE SIMPLE KEYNESIAN MODEL

We began this chapter by describing the effects of government spending and taxation in the simple Keynesian model. To keep matters as simple as possible, we assumed that net exports were zero. Now we relax that assumption. Recall from Chapter 3 that gross domestic product = consumption expenditure + gross investment + government spending + net exports, where net exports equal exports minus imports. In other words, $Y = C + I + G + (X - M_I)$, where Y is GDP, C is consumption expenditure, I is investment, G is government spending, X is exports, and M_I is imports. Recall too that *the equilibrium level of GDP will be at the point where intended spending on GDP equals GDP.*

Thus in Figure 6.8 the equilibrium level of GDP must be $500 billion, since this is the level at which the **$C + I + G + (X - M_I)$ line** intersects the 45-degree line. To see this, note that we are merely carrying out a straightforward extension of the analysis in Figure 6.1, where we assumed that net exports were zero. Once this assumption is relaxed, intended net exports must be

$C + I + G + (X - M_I)$ line

FIGURE 6.8

Effects of Foreign Trade on Gross Domestic Product

The equilibrium level of GDP is at the point where the $C + I + G + (X - M_I)$ line intersects the 45-degree line, in this case, $500 billion.

added to the $C + I + G$ line to get total intended spending, and the equilibrium level of GDP is at the point where the resulting total-intended-spending line, $C + I + G + (X - M_I)$, intersects the 45-degree line.

Note that increases in spending on net exports result in increases in GDP. If intended spending on net exports increases from $20 billion to $40 billion, as shown in Figure 6.9, the equilibrium level of GDP increases from $500 billion to $550 billion. *Increases in spending on net exports have a multiplier effect,* which is like the multiplier effect for investment or government spending. Thus a $1 increase in intended spending on net exports results in more than a $1 increase in GDP.[1] Since governments during the 1930s wanted desperately to increase their GDP to reduce unemployment, it is clear why they tried to increase their net exports. (However, all that resulted was a reduction in international trade, because of retaliatory measures.)

---

[1] If we assume that exports, government expenditures, and tax receipts are the same at all levels of GDP, then a $1 increase in intended spending on net exports will result in an increase in equilibrium GDP of $1 ÷ (*MPS* + *MPI*), where *MPS* is the marginal propensity to save and *MPI* is the marginal propensity to import. (The *marginal propensity to import* is the proportion of an extra dollar of income that is spent on imports.) Note that the multiplier is smaller now than in the case of a closed economy (where *MPI* equals zero).

FIGURE 6.9

Effect of Increase in Net Exports on Gross Domestic Product

If net exports increase from $20 billion to $40 billion, the equilibrium level of GDP increases from $500 billion to $550 billion.

REVIEW AND PRACTICE

■ SUMMARY

1 Assuming that net exports are zero, the equilibrium level of gross domestic product is the level where intended consumption plus intended investment plus intended government spending equal gross domestic product.

2 An increase in the tax rate shifts the relationship between consumption expenditure and GDP downward, and thus reduces the equilibrium value of GDP. A decrease in the tax rate shifts the relationship upward, and thus increases the equilibrium value of GDP.

3 If GDP is below its potential value, there is a recessionary gap. Under these circumstances, governments frequently try to push the aggregate demand curve to the right. Fiscal policy is often used for this purpose.

4 If GDP exceeds its potential value, there is an inflationary gap. Under these circumstances, the government is likely to try to use fiscal policy to induce a leftward shift of the aggregate demand curve, and thus cause the price level to be lower than it otherwise would be.

5 Policymakers receive a lot of help in stabilizing the economy from our automatic stabilizers—automatic changes in tax revenues, unemployment compensation, and welfare payments. However, the automatic stabilizers can only cut down on variations in unemployment and inflation, not eliminate them.

6 Discretionary programs are often used to supplement the effects of these automatic stabilizers. Such discretionary actions include changing tax rates, changing government expenditure on public works and other programs, and changing welfare payments and other such transfers.

7 In the past 70 years, government spending has increased considerably both in absolute terms and as a proportion of total output. It is now about one-third of our total output.

8 To get the money to cover most of these expenditures, governments collect taxes from individuals and firms. At the federal level, the most important form of taxation is the personal income tax; at the local level, the property tax is very important; and at the state level, sales (and excise) taxes are the biggest money raiser.

*9 If net exports are not zero, the equilibrium level of GDP is where intended spending on GDP—which equals intended consumption expenditure plus intended investment plus government spending plus intended net exports—equals GDP.

■ PROBLEMS AND QUESTIONS

1 Suppose that the consumption function in a particular economy is given by the following table:

DISPOSABLE INCOME (BILLIONS OF DOLLARS)	CONSUMPTION EXPENDITURE (BILLIONS OF DOLLARS)
400	350
500	425
600	500
700	575
800	650

Assuming that no taxes are imposed (and that net exports are zero), what is the equilibrium value of GDP if government expenditures are $50 billion and intended investment is $50 billion?

2 Based on the data in question 1, plot the $C + I + G$ line in a graph. Using a graph of this sort, estimate the effect on the equilibrium level of GDP of a $10 billion increase in government spending.

3 Suppose that taxes are 20 percent of GDP. Using the data in question 1, fill in the blanks below.

GDP (BILLIONS OF DOLLARS)	CONSUMPTION EXPENDITURE (BILLIONS OF DOLLARS)
—	350
—	425
—	500
—	575
—	650

4 Using the data in question 3, what is the equilibrium value of GDP if government expenditures are $50 billion and intended investment is $50 billion? How does this result compare with that in question 1? Explain the difference between these two results.

*The starred item refers to material covered in Exploring Further.

5 Using the data in question 3, is the government's budget balanced at the equilibrium level of GDP if government expenditures are $50 billion and intended investment is $50 billion? If not, how big is the surplus or deficit?

■ KEY TERMS

$C + I + G$ line

recessionary gap

inflationary gap

automatic stabilizers

discretionary fiscal policy

government transfer payments

$C + I + G + (X - M_i)$ line

■ VIEWPOINT FOR ANALYSIS

James Tobin, Sterling Professor Emeritus of Economics at Yale University, has written: "Recoveries from almost every previous postwar recession have had the help of fiscal stimulus. The much touted 1983–88 recovery was driven by fiscal demand stimulus massively greater than any previous peacetime fiscal expansion. It took two main forms: consumption by affluent taxpayers enjoying lower tax rates and a rapid buildup of defense spending."*

(a) Explain why a rapid buildup of defense spending constitutes fiscal stimulus. Is such a buildup likely to push the economy out of a recession? Why or why not?

(b) Would lower income tax rates be expected to shift the consumption function? Would such a shift be likely to push the economy out of a recession? Why or why not?

(c) Can there be too much fiscal stimulus? Under what circumstances can an expansionary fiscal policy be a mistake?

*J. Tobin, "Thinking Straight About Fiscal Stimulus and Deficit Reduction," *Challenge*, March–April 1993, p. 18.

CHAPTER 7

Inflation

LEARNING OBJECTIVES

In this chapter, you should learn:

- The nature and effects of inflation
- How inflation is measured
- The difference between demand-side and supply-side inflation
- The nature and instability of the Phillips curve

In 1999, the rate of inflation in the United States was about 2.1 percent, which was better than in the United Kingdom, but not as good as in France, Germany, Canada, and Japan. However, as both Democrats and Republicans pointed out, this was far better than during the inflation-ridden 1970s and early 1980s. How is inflation measured, and why are people so concerned about it? One purpose of this chapter is to answer this question.

At the very beginning of this book, we stressed that unemployment and inflation are two major economic evils. Up to this point, we have devoted much more attention to unemployment than to inflation. According to most economists, inflation and unemployment are not unrelated. Unfortunately, the linkage between them is a complex one and has consequently been the subject of much debate among economists. Inflation, its costs, and its causes cannot be covered in one chapter alone. This chapter contains part of the relevant discussion; the rest is in Chapter 10.

INFLATION

Inflation

It is hard to find anyone these days who does not know the meaning of inflation firsthand. Try to think of goods you regularly purchase that cost less now than they did several years ago. Chances are that you can come up with precious few. **Inflation** is a general upward movement of prices. In other words, inflation means that goods and services that currently cost $10 may soon be priced at $11 or even $12, and that wages and other input prices will increase as well. It is essential to distinguish between the movements of individual prices and the movement of the entire price level. As we saw in Chapter 2, the price of an individual commodity can move up or down with the shifts in the commodity's demand or

167

Runaway inflation
Creeping inflation

supply curve. If the price of a particular good—corn, say—goes up, this need not be a sign of inflation: if the prices of other goods are going down at the same time, the overall price level—the general average level of prices—remains much the same. Inflation occurs only if the prices for most goods and services in a society move upward—that is, if the average level of prices increases.

In periods of inflation, the value of money is reduced. A dollar is worth what it will buy, and what it will buy is determined by the price level. Thus a dollar was more valuable in 1940, when the price of a Hershey chocolate bar was 5 cents, than in 1999, when it was about 50 cents. But it is important to recognize that inflations may vary in severity. **Runaway inflation** wipes out the value of money quickly and thoroughly, while **creeping inflation** erodes its value gradually and slowly. The following examples indicate the important differences between runaway inflation and creeping inflation.

■ RUNAWAY INFLATION

The case of Germany after World War I is a good example of runaway inflation. Germany was required to pay large reparations to the victorious Allies after the war. Rather than attempting to tax its people to pay these amounts, the German government merely printed additional quantities of paper money. This new money increased total spending in Germany, and this in turn resulted in higher prices because the war-devastated economy could not increase output substantially. As more and more money was printed, prices rose higher and higher, until they reached utterly fantastic levels. By 1923, it took a *trillion* marks (the unit of German currency) to buy what one mark would buy before the war began in 1914.

The effect of this runaway inflation was to disrupt the economy. Prices had to be adjusted from day to day. People rushed to the stores to spend the money they received as soon as possible, since very soon it would buy much less. Speculation was rampant. This inflation was a terrible blow to Germany. The middle class was wiped out; its savings became completely worthless. It is no wonder that Germany has in recent years been more sensitive than many other countries to the evils of inflation.

■ CREEPING INFLATION

For the past fifty years, the price level in the United States has tended to go one way only—up. Since 1950, there hasn't been a single year when the price level has fallen. Certainly, this has not been a runaway inflation, but it has resulted in a very substantial erosion in the value of the dollar. Like a beach slowly worn away by ocean waves, the dollar has gradually lost a considerable portion of its value. Specifically, prices now tend to be six times what they were about fifty years ago. Thus the dollar now is worth about a sixth of what it was worth then. Although a creeping inflation of this sort is much less harmful than a runaway inflation, it has a number of unfortunate social consequences, which are described in detail in subsequent sections of this chapter.

THE MEASUREMENT OF INFLATION

Consumer Price Index

The most widely quoted measure of inflation in the United States is the **Consumer Price Index**, published monthly by the Bureau of Labor Statistics. Until 1978, the purpose of this index was to measure changes in the prices of goods and services purchased by urban wage earners and clerical workers and their families. In 1978, the index was expanded to include all urban consumers (although the narrower index was not discontinued). The first step in calculating the index is to find out how much it costs in a particular month to buy a market basket of goods and services that is representative of the buying patterns of these consumers. This amount is then expressed as a ratio of what it would have cost to buy the same market basket of goods and services in the base period (1982–84), and this ratio is multiplied by 100. This (like most commonly used indexes) shows the *percentage,* not the proportional, change in the price level. For example, the Consumer Price Index equaled 168.3 in December 1999; this meant that it cost 68.3 percent more to buy this market basket in December 1999 than in 1982–84. To obtain results based on Chapter 3's definition of a price index, all we have to do is divide this index by 100.

The market basket of goods and services that is included in the Consumer Price Index is chosen with great care and is the result of an extensive survey of people's buying patterns. Among the items that are included are food, automobiles, clothing, homes, furniture, home supplies, drugs, fuel, doctors' fees, legal fees, rent, repairs, transportation fares, recreational goods, and so forth. Prices, as defined in the index, include sales and excise taxes. Also, real estate taxes, but not income or personal property taxes, are included in the index. Besides the overall index, a separate price index is computed for various types of goods or services, such as food, rent, new cars, medical services, and a variety of other items. Also, a separate index is computed for each of 28 metropolitan areas, as well as for the entire urban population.

FIGURE 7.1

Consumer Price Index 1946–99

Inflation has been a continual problem in the United States, particularly in the late 1970s and early 1980s.

The Consumer Price Index is widely used by industry and government. Labor agreements often stipulate that, to offset inflation, wages must increase in accord with changes in the index. Similarly, pensions, welfare payments, royalties, and even alimony payments are sometimes related to the index. However, this does not mean that it is an ideal, all-purpose measure of inflation. For one thing, it does not include the prices of industrial machinery or raw materials. For another thing, it is not confined to currently produced goods and services.

Figure 7.1 shows the behavior of the Consumer Price Index since 1946. As pointed out in the previous section, the price level has increased considerably in the United States in the past 55 years. Substantial inflation followed World War II: the price level increased by about 24 percent between 1946 and 1948. Bursts of inflation recurred during the Korean War and then during the Vietnam War. The 1970s were a period of particularly high inflation; between 1969 and 1979 the price level doubled. The 1980s began with double-digit inflation, but there was a reduction in the inflation rate in 1982 to 1999. How long this respite will continue is not clear.

IMPACT OF INFLATION

Citizens and policymakers generally agree that inflation, like unemployment, should be minimized. For example, in 1981, the Council of Economic Advisers identified inflation as the chief economic problem confronting the United States. Why is inflation so widely feared? What are its effects? Inflation affects the distribution of income and wealth, as well as the level of output, as we will see in the following discussion.

■ REDISTRIBUTIVE EFFECTS

Because all money incomes do not go up at the same rate as prices, inflation results in an arbitrary redistribution of income. People with relatively fixed incomes, lenders, and savers tend to be hurt by it, and major inflations tend to cripple total output as well. To understand the redistributive effects of inflation, it is necessary to distinguish between **money income** and **real income**. A family's money income is its income measured in current dollars, whereas its real income is adjusted for changes in the price level. During periods of inflation, a family with a relatively fixed money income will experience a declining real income.

Money income
Real income

Suppose that the Murphy family earns $41,000 this year and $40,000 last year and that the price level is 10 percent higher this year than last year. Under these circumstances, the Murphy family's money income has increased by $1,000, but its real income has fallen (because its money income has risen by a smaller percentage than the price level). This is the sort of effect that inflation has on people with relatively fixed incomes, lenders, and savers—three groups that tend to be hit hard by inflation.

Fixed money incomes. Inflation may seem no more than a petty annoyance; after all, most people care about relative, not absolute, prices. For example, if the Howe family's money income increases at the same rate as the price level, the Howe family may be no better or worse off under inflation than if its money income remained constant and no inflation occurred. But not all people are as fortunate as the Howes. Some people cannot increase their wages to compensate for price increases because they work under long-term contracts, among other reasons. These people take a considerable beating from inflation. One group that sometimes is particularly hard hit by inflation is the elderly, since old people often must live on pensions and other relatively fixed forms of income. Thus inflation sometimes has a substantial, inequitable, and unwelcome impact on our older citizens.

Elderly citizen hurt by inflation

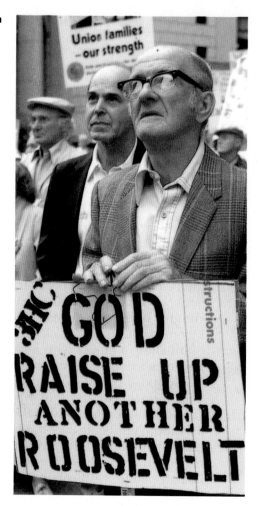

Lenders. Inflation hurts lenders and benefits borrowers, since it results in the depreciation of money. A dollar is worth what it will buy, and what it will buy is determined by the price level. If the price level increases, a dollar is worth less than it was worth before. Consequently, if you lend Bill Dvorak $100 in 2001 and he pays you $100 in 2006—when a dollar will buy less than in 2001— you are losing on the deal. In terms of what the money will buy, he is paying you less than what he borrowed. Of course, if you antici-pate considerable inflation, you may be able to recoup by charging him a high enough interest rate to offset the depreciation of the dollar, but it is not so easy to forecast the rate of inflation and pro-tect yourself.

Savers. Inflation can have a devastating and inequitable effect on savers. The family that works hard and saves for retirement (and a rainy day) finds that its savings are worth far less, when it finally spends them, than the amount it saved. Consider the well-meaning souls who invested $1,000 of their savings in U.S. savings bonds in 1939. By 1949, these bonds were worth only about $800 in 1939 dollars, including the interest received in the ten-year period. Thus these people had $200 taken away from them, in just as real a sense as if someone had picked their pockets.[1]

■ EFFECTS OF ANTICIPATED AND UNANTICIPATED INFLATION

**Anticipated
inflation
Unanticipated
inflation**

Economists are fond of pointing out that the effects of **anticipated inflation** tend to be less severe than those of **unanticipated inflation**. To see why this is the case, suppose that everyone anticipates (correctly) that the price level will be 6 percent higher next year than this year. In such a situation, everyone will build this amount of inflation into his or her decisions. Workers will realize that their money wage rates must be 6 percent higher next year just to avoid a cut in their real wage rates. The Murphy family, which earns $41,000 this year, will realize that it must earn 1.06 × $41,000, or $43,460, next year if it is to avoid a reduction in its real earnings. And people who are thinking of lending money for a year will recognize that they must charge 6 percent interest just to break even. Why? Because when the money is repaid next year, $1.06 will be worth no more in real terms than $1.00 is now.

Because people build the anticipated rate of inflation into their calculations, the effects of anticipated inflation are likely to be less pronounced than those of unanticipated inflation. However, in the real world in which we all live, this frequently is of small comfort, since it is very difficult to anticipate the rate of inflation correctly. Even the most sophisticated econometric models have not had a very distinguished record in forecasting the rate of inflation. Thus it seems foolish to believe that the typical citizen (like those who invested in U.S. savings bonds in 1939) can anticipate inflation well enough to protect himself or herself against its consequences.

■ AN ARBITRARY "TAX"

While inflation hurts some people, it benefits others. Those who are lucky enough to invest in goods, land, equipment, and other items that experience particularly rapid increases in price may make a killing. For this reason, speculation tends to be rampant during severe inflations. However, it is important to recognize that

---

[1]However, it is important to recognize that the form of the savings matters. If one can put his or her savings in a form where its monetary value increases as rapidly as the price level, the saver is not harmed by inflation. But this isn't always easy to do.

173

the rewards and penalties resulting from inflation are meted out with little or no regard for society's values or goals. As the late Arthur Okun, a former chairperson of the Council of Economic Advisers, put it, "'sharpies' . . . make sophisticated choices and often reap gains on inflation which do not seem to reflect any real contribution to economic growth. On the other hand, the unsophisticated saver who is merely preparing for the proverbial rainy day becomes a sucker." This is one of the most undesirable features of inflation, and it helps to account for inflation's sometimes being called an arbitrary "tax."

■ EFFECTS ON OUTPUT

Creeping inflation, unlike unemployment, does not seem to reduce national output; in the short run, output may increase, for reasons taken up in subsequent chapters. But, although a mild upward creep of prices at the rate of a few percentage points per year is not likely to reduce output, a major inflation can have adverse effects on production. For one thing, it encourages speculation rather than the productive use of savings. People find it more profitable to invest in gold, diamonds, real estate, and art (all of which tend to rise in monetary value during inflations) than in many kinds of productive activity. Also, businesspeople tend to be discouraged from carrying out long-range projects because of the difficulty of forecasting what future prices will be. If the rate of inflation reaches the catastrophic heights that prevailed in Germany after World War I, the monetary system may break down. People may be unwilling to accept money. They may insist on trading goods or services directly for other goods and services. The result is likely to be considerable inefficiency and substantially reduced output.

DEMAND-SIDE AND SUPPLY-SIDE INFLATION

Inflation is often triggered by rightward shifts of the aggregate demand curve (see the left-hand panel of Figure 7.2). This kind of inflation stems from the demand or spending behavior of the country's consumers, firms, and government. We have had many inflations of this kind. The major inflations during the Revolutionary War and Civil War were basically caused by demand-side factors; and so, much more recently, was the inflation arising from the Vietnam War.

In those extreme cases where resources are fully utilized, the rise in the price level that occurs in **demand-side inflation** can be viewed as a matter of arithmetic: since national output is fixed, the rise in the price level must be proportional to the increase in

Demand-side inflation

FIGURE 7.2

Demand-Side and Supply-Side Inflation

In the left-hand panel, the price level increases from 100 to 110 because of a rightward shift of the aggregate demand curve. This is a case of demand-side inflation. In the right-hand panel, the price level increases from 100 to 108 because of a leftward shift of the aggregate supply curve. This is a case of supply-side inflation.

total spending. For example, take the very simple case where a country produces only one good, corn. Suppose that the amount of money spent on this country's corn crop doubles while the size of the corn crop is fixed. What will happen to the price of corn? It will double.

Besides demand-side inflation, which is due to rightward shifts of the aggregate demand curve, there is also **supply-side inflation**, which results from leftward shifts of the aggregate supply curve (see the right-hand panel of Figure 7.2). For example, when the oil-producing countries increased the price of crude oil in 1974 and 1979, this resulted in price increases in a wide variety of products that are made (directly or indirectly) from petroleum. Because these price increases were not offset by price reductions elsewhere in the economy, the overall price level increased (and at a very rapid rate) in 1974 and 1979. Of course, the price hike for crude oil (and other materials) was not the sole reason for the inflation during the 1970s, but unquestionably it did play a noteworthy role in shifting the aggregate supply curve upward and to the left, as shown in the right-hand panel of Figure 7.2. This was an example of supply-side inflation.

Supply-side inflation

THE PHILLIPS CURVE

During the 1960s, economists placed a great deal of emphasis on the Phillips curve, named after A. W. Phillips of the London School of Economics, who first called attention to it. The **Phillips curve** shows the relationship between the annual rate of change of the price level in an economy and the unemployment rate in that

Phillips curve

175

Demand-side inflation and the tax surcharge of 1968

President Lyndon B. Johnson with economic adviser Walter Heller

The economic policies carried out under Presidents Kennedy and Johnson seemed successful in stimulating growth in demand; business was thriving, plants were operating close to capacity, and there were plenty of jobs. But many felt that by mid-1965, the economy showed signs of overheating.

Besides the boost to private demand, government spending was beginning to grow rapidly. President Johnson had succeeded in getting many of his programs to reduce domestic poverty passed. In addition, military spending rose as dark war clouds began to gather in Southeast Asia. In late July 1965, President Johnson announced that the United States would send 50,000 more troops to Vietnam. From fiscal 1965 to fiscal 1966, defense expenditures rose from $50 billion to $60 billion—a large increase in government expenditure and one that took place at a time of relatively full employment. Such an increase in government expenditure could be expected to cause inflationary pressures. The Council of Economic Advisers recognized this danger and recommended in late 1965 that the president urge Congress to increase taxes. Johnson was reluctant. Inflationary pressures mounted during 1966, and little was done by fiscal policymakers to quell them.

Even in 1967, Congress was unwilling to raise taxes. The case for fiscal restraint was, it felt, not clear enough. As for the president, he said, "It is not a popular thing for a president to do . . . to ask for a penny out of a dollar to pay for a war that is not popular either." Finally, in mid-1968, a 10 percent surcharge on income taxes, together with some restraint in government spending, was enacted. This increase in taxes was obviously the right medicine, but it was at least two years too late, and its effects were delayed and insufficient. In the meantime, the rate of inflation had risen from 2 percent in 1965 to 6 percent in 1969.

economy.[2] For example, if the relationship is like that plotted in Figure 7.3, the inflation rate is inversely related to the unemployment rate. If the unemployment rate is 6 percent, the inflation rate will be 5 percent per year. To reduce the inflation rate to 2 percent, the unemployment rate must be increased to 9 percent.

If the Phillips curve in Figure 7.3 remains fixed, the government is faced with a fundamental choice. It can reduce unemployment only if it is willing to accept a higher rate of inflation, and it can reduce the rate of inflation only if it is willing to accept a higher rate of unemployment. For example, in Figure 7.3, if the un-

[2]Originally, Phillips plotted data showing the relationship between the unemployment rate and the rate of change of wages, not prices. Thus the Phillips curve sometimes is defined as the relationship between the rate of change of the wage level (not the price level) and the unemployment rate. But for present purposes, it is more convenient to adopt the definition in the text, which is often used by economists.

FIGURE 7.3

The Phillips Curve

If all inflation is demand-side inflation, one might expect the inflation rate to be inversely related to the unemployment rate. (Expected inflation is assumed to be constant.)

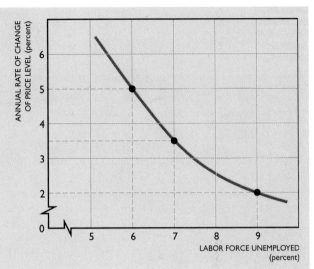

employment rate is 7 percent and the inflation rate is 3.5 percent, the government would like to reduce unemployment, but if it reduces it to 6 percent, the inflation rate will jump to 5 percent. It would also like to reduce inflation, but if it cuts it to 2 percent, the unemployment rate will jump to 9 percent. This poses a problem for the government (and for society as a whole), since it would be desirable to reduce both inflation and unemployment.

Why should the Phillips curve be downward-sloping to the right? In other words, why should the inflation rate be inversely related to the unemployment rate? If all inflation is demand-side inflation, some economists have explained such an inverse relationship in the following way. Suppose that the economy is in equilibrium at point A in Figure 7.4. If the aggregate demand curve shifts to the right from D_0 to D_1, total real output will increase from $100 billion to $110 billion, and the price level will increase from 100 to 105. On the other hand, suppose that the aggregate demand curve shifts farther to the right—from D_0 to D_2. Then total real output will increase from $100 billion to $120 billion (rather than $110 billion), and the price level will increase from 100 to 110 (rather than 105).

Clearly, the greater rightward shift of the aggregate demand curve (to D_2 rather than D_1) results in a bigger increase in output (to $120 billion rather than $110 billion); this means that the unemployment rate will be lower than if the aggregate demand curve shifted only to D_1. At the same time, the greater rightward shift of the aggregate demand curve results in a 10 percent inflation rate rather than a 5 percent inflation rate. (Recall that the price level increases from 100 to 110 if the aggregate demand curve shifts to D_2, whereas it increases from 100 to 105 if the aggregate demand

177

What is the NAIRU?

Unemployed workers line up to file claims at their local union.

The unemployment rate influences inflation through its impact on the relative bargaining position of businesses and their workers. A low unemployment rate increases businesses' willingness to give pay increases to their workers, because finding replacements is more difficult and because the existing workers can find alternative employment more easily. On the other hand, a high unemployment rate puts downward pressure on wages because potential replacements are more plentiful and existing workers have fewer viable alternatives. Because labor costs ultimately account for almost two-thirds of the cost of production, a low unemployment rate translates into rising price inflation, while a high unemployment rate reduces inflation.

Economists define the NAIRU—the non-accelerating inflation rate of unemployment—as the unemployment rate at which the labor market is exerting no upward or downward

pressure on inflation. Inflation will accelerate if the unemployment rate remains below the NAIRU and will decelerate if the unemployment rate remains above the NAIRU. The degree of acceleration or deceleration is proportional to the difference between the unemployment rate and the NAIRU. Economists often refer to the NAIRU as the natural rate of unemployment or the full-employment rate.

Although the unemployment rate primarily reflects the looseness or tightness of the labor market, it also reflects the age distribution of the labor force. In particular, unemployment rates fall as age increases, so the aggregate unemployment rate will be higher the higher the percentage of teenagers and 20–24-year-olds in the working-age population. The entrance of the baby boomers into the labor force added more than one-half of a percentage point to the NAIRU between the early

1960s and the late 1970s, while the aging of this generation and a gradual downtrend in women's unemployment rates have subtracted more than one-half of a percentage point since then.

Changes in productivity growth, however, have produced much more dramatic movements in the NAIRU. During most of the 1960s, when productivity growth averaged almost 3 percent per year, the NAIRU was below 5 percent. As productivity growth slowed, the NAIRU rose to around 6 percent in the late 1960s and early 1970s and then surged to roughly 7.5 percent after the first OEPC shock, much higher than was realized at the time. As productivity growth picked up again in the late 1980s and 1990s, the NAIRU fell back to about 5 percent.

A surge in productivity is also part of the explanation for the remarkable performance of the U.S. economy in the late 1990s and beginning 2000s. During this period the unemployment rate hovered just above 4 percent—a thirty-year low—while inflation remained quiescent. Part of this was due to good luck. The emerging markets crisis in 1997 and 1998 triggered a collapse of commodity prices and a drop in world inflation. However, an improvement in productivity growth, thanks to high-tech investments and the Internet, also played a crucial role. Recent estimates suggest that productivity growth in the late 1990s was around 2.5 percent compared to 1.5 percent in the 1980s. This led some analysts to speculate that the NAIRU may be closer to 4 percent!

FIGURE 7.4

Effects of Rightward Shifts of the Aggregate Demand Curve (from D_0 to D_1 or D_2) on the Total Real Output and the Price Level

If the aggregate demand curve shifts from D_0 to D_2, there will be a greater increase in total real output and a greater increase in the price level than if the aggregate demand curve shifts from D_0 to D_1. Specifically, total real output increases from $100 billion to $120 billion if the aggregate demand curve shifts from D_0 to D_2, but it increases only from $100 billion to $110 billion if the curve shifts from D_0 to D_1. The price level increases from 100 to 110 if the aggregate demand curve shifts from D_0 to D_2, but it increases only from 100 to 105 if the curve shifts from D_0 to D_1.

curve shifts to D_1.) Hence, a lower unemployment rate is associated with a higher inflation rate.

As we shall see in Chapter 10, the Phillips curve in Figure 7.3 has not remained fixed. Instead, during the 1970s and early 1980s, the curve in Figure 7.3 shifted upward and to the right. High unemployment coexisted with high inflation. In recent years, more and more economists seem to have become persuaded that the reductions in unemployment due to increased inflation are only transitory and that increases in inflation bring little or nothing in the way of reduced unemployment in the long run. Much more will be said on this score in Chapter 10.

REVIEW AND PRACTICE

■ SUMMARY

1 Inflation is a general upward movement of prices. Runaway inflation occurs when the price level increases very rapidly, as in Germany after World War I. Creeping inflation occurs when the price level rises a few percentage points per year, as in the United States during the 1950s and 1960s.

2 High rates of inflation produce considerable redistributions of income and wealth. People with relatively fixed incomes, such as the elderly, tend to take a beating from inflation. Inflation hurts lenders and benefits borrowers, since it results in the depreciation of money. Inflation can also have a devastating effect on savers. The penalties (and rewards) resulting from inflation are meted out arbitrarily, with no regard for society's values or goals. Substantial rates of inflation may also reduce efficiency and total output.

3 Inflation caused by rightward shifts of the aggregate demand curve is called demand-side inflation. Inflation caused by leftward shifts of the aggregate supply curve is called supply-side inflation.

4 The Phillips curve shows the relationship between the rate of increase of the price level and the level of unemployment. If the Phillips curve remains fixed, it poses an awkward dilemma for policymakers. If they reduce unemployment, inflation increases; if they reduce inflation, unemployment increases.

5 During the 1970s and early 1980s, the Phillips curve shifted upward and to the right. High unemployment and high inflation occurred simultaneously.

■ PROBLEMS AND QUESTIONS

1 "The Employment Act of 1946 should be amended to include the goal of stabilizing the purchasing power of the dollar as well as the goal of maintaining high-level employment." Comment and evaluate.

2 "Inflation is a necessary cost of economic progress." Comment and evaluate.

3 Suppose that a family's money income remains constant at $40,000 and that the price level increases 10 percent per year. How many years will it take for the family's real income to be cut in half?

4 If you believe that the United States is about to suffer severe inflation, would you be better off to invest money in land or in government bonds? Explain your answer.

5 "The inflations arising from the Revolutionary, Civil, and Vietnam wars were largely supply-side." Comment and evaluate.

6 Suppose that the relationship between the annual rate of increase of the price level and the percent of the labor force unemployed is as shown in the table below:

RATE OF INCREASE OF PRICE LEVEL (PERCENT PER YEAR)	UNEMPLOYMENT RATE (PERCENT)
5	8
6	7
7	6
8	5

Plot the Phillips curve on a graph.

■ KEY TERMS

inflation	anticipated inflation
runaway inflation	unanticipated inflation
creeping inflation	demand-side inflation
Consumer Price Index	supply-side inflation
money income	Phillips curve
real income	

■ VIEWPOINT FOR ANALYSIS

On July 20, 1993, Alan Greenspan, chairperson of the Board of Governors of the Federal Reserve System, testified before a congressional committee. He said, "The role of expectations in the inflation process is crucial. Even expectations not validated by economic fundamentals can themselves add appreciably to wage and price pressures for a considerable period, potentially derailing the economy from its growth path."*

(a) If workers are convinced that inflation is about to increase greatly, what effect will this have on their wage demands? Will their wage demands fuel further inflation?

(b) If the managers of firms are convinced that inflation is about to increase greatly, what effect will this have on their pricing decisions? Will their pricing decisions fuel further inflation?

(c) How can inflation derail the economy from its growth path? Cite cases in the past where inflation derailed the U.S. economy from its growth path. Be specific.

*A. Greenspan, testimony before the Committee on Banking, Finance, and Urban Affairs of the U.S. House of Representatives on July 20, 1993.

The Treasury Launches a New Type of Security

In late 1996, the U.S. Treasury announced that it would issue inflation-indexed bonds. The value of an inflation-indexed bond is protected from inflation because it is adjusted periodically in accord with changes in the Consumer Price Index. As in the case of ordinary bonds, the investor lends the government a certain amount of money (say $10,000), receives interest (say 3.25 percent) on the loan, and is promised by the government that he or she will be repaid in a fixed amount of time (say 10 years). The new wrinkle is that the government adjusts the size of the loan to keep pace with inflation. Thus, if inflation during a particular year is 4 percent, the amount owed by the Treasury to a bondholder goes up by 4 percent.

In early 1997, the first U.S. inflation-indexed securities were issued. The United States is not the first country to issue such securities; for example, Australia, Canada, New Zealand, and Sweden have already done so. The country with the biggest amount of such debt is the United Kingdom, where it totals about $60 billion. The biggest demand for such bonds in Britain occurred in 1981, when they were first issued. Inflation was considered a serious problem, and people were frightened. It seemed sensible to purchase protection from inflation. More recently, as inflation (both actual and expected) has fallen, higher returns on these bonds have been required to attract buyers.

According to the Council of Economic Advisers, the U.S. Treasury "will issue indexed securities once each quarter. . . . Indexed securities are available in denominations as small as $1,000, to encourage demand from small savers. . . . One recent study concluded that investor concerns about inflation risk might add as much as .5 to 1 percent point to the required yield on some Treasury securities. Thus, by issuing indexed securities, the Treasury may be able to reduce average borrowing costs."*

Ironically, soon after the inflation-indexed bonds were issued, the demand for them slackened. Low inflation in 1997 through 1999 was an important factor behind the lack of interest. Equally

*Economic Report of the President, 1997, pp. 62, 64.

**Secretary of the
Treasury, Lawrence
Summers**

important was the surge in equity prices that occurred during those same years. Most investors were more interested in the high returns offered by the stock market than in protecting their investments against inflation. However, should there be a correction in stock prices and should inflation become a problem once again, the attractiveness of inflation-indexed bonds will undoubtedly increase.

■ QUESTIONS

1 What do investors get from this new type of government bonds that they did not get from older types?

2 According to the Council of Economic Advisers, a shift from conventional government bonds to these new bonds should reduce the Treasury's average borrowing costs. Why?

3 An executive at a Chicago investment firm expressed some skepticism regarding these new bonds. He said, "In the 1970s, inflation-indexed bonds would have been a great investment, but I think we have learned our lesson very well. . . ."* In his view, high inflation is no longer a threat. Do you agree? Why or why not?

4 Some observers worry that, if a large amount of such securities were issued, there might be less political pressure on the government to keep inflation low. Does this seem reasonable? Why or why not?

Philadelphia Inquirer, September 26, 1996.

PART THREE

Money, Banking, and Stabilization Policy

CHAPTER 8

Money and the Banking System

LEARNING OBJECTIVES

In this chapter, you should learn:

- The nature and functions of money
- What the money supply is and how it is measured
- How commercial banks operate, including the concept of fractional reserve banking
- How banks can increase or decrease the money supply

The Bank of America does not have enough cash to pay off all its depositors if they decide to withdraw all the funds in their accounts; neither does Chase, Citibank, . . . , or your own bank. Is this dangerous, and if not, why not? One purpose of this chapter is to answer this question.

In this chapter, we are concerned with the nature of money and the key economic role played by banks and the banking system. Banking is often viewed as a colorless, dull profession whose practitioners are knee-deep in deposit slips and canceled checks. Yet despite these notions, most people recognize the importance of the banks in our economy, perhaps because banks deal in such an important and fascinating commodity: money. One purpose of this chapter is to introduce you to the operations of the banking system, which is neither as colorless nor as mysterious as is sometimes assumed.

WHAT IS MONEY?

Money

We begin by defining **money**. At first, it may seem natural to define it by its physical characteristics, and to say that money consists of bills of a certain size and color with certain words and symbols printed on them, as well as coins of a certain type. But this definition would be too restrictive, since money in other societies has consisted of whale teeth, wampum, and a variety of other things. Thus it seems better to define money by its functions than by its physical characteristics. Like beauty, money is as money does.

■ MEDIUM OF EXCHANGE

Money acts as a *medium of exchange*. People exchange their goods and services for something called money, and then use this money to buy the goods and services they want. To see how important money is as a medium of exchange, let's suppose that it did not exist. To exchange the goods and services they produce for the goods and services they want to consume, people would resort to *barter,* or direct exchange. If you were a wheat farmer, you would have to contact the people who produce the meat, clothes, and other goods and services you want and swap some of your wheat for each of these goods and services. Of course this would be a very cumbersome procedure, since it would take lots of time and effort to locate and make individual bargains with each of these people. To get some idea of the extent to which money greases the process of exchange in any highly developed economy, consider all the purchases your family made last year: cheese from Wisconsin and France, automobiles from Detroit or Japan, oil from Texas and the Middle East, books from New York, and thousands of other items from all over the world. Imagine how few of these exchanges would have been feasible without money.

■ STANDARD OF VALUE, STORE OF VALUE

Money acts as a *standard of value*. It is the unit in which the prices of goods and services are measured. How do we express the price of coffee or tea or shirts or suits? In dollars and cents. Thus money prices tell us the rates at which goods and services can be exchanged. If the money price of a shirt is $30 and the money price of a tie is $15, a shirt will exchange for two ties. Put differently, a shirt will be "worth" twice as much as a tie.

Money acts as a *store of value*. A person can hold onto money and use it to buy things later. You often hear stories about people who hoard a lot of money under their mattresses or bury it in their backyards. These people have an overdeveloped appreciation of the role of money as a store of value. But even those of us who are less miserly use this function of money when we carry some money with us or keep some in the bank to make future purchases.

Finally, it should be recognized that money is a social invention. It is easy to assume that money has always existed, but this is not the case. Someone had to get the idea, and people had to come to accept it. Nor has money always had the characteristics it has today. In ancient Greece and Rome, money consisted of gold and silver coins. By the end of the seventeenth century, paper money was established in England, but this paper currency, unlike today's currency, could be exchanged for a stipulated amount of gold. Only recently has the transition been made to money that is not convertible into a fixed amount of gold or silver. But regardless of its form or characteristics, anything that is a medium of exchange, a standard of value, and a store of value is money.

THE MONEY SUPPLY, NARROWLY DEFINED

In practice, it is not easy to draw a hard-and-fast line between what is money and what is not money, for reasons discussed below. But everyone agrees that coins, currency, demand deposits (that is, checking accounts), and other checkable deposits are money. And the sum total of coins, currency, demand deposits, and other checkable deposits is called the money supply narrowly defined.[1]

■ COINS AND CURRENCY

Coins

Coins are a small proportion of the total quantity of money in the United States. This is mainly because coins come in such small denominations. It takes a small mountain of pennies, nickels, dimes, quarters, and half-dollars to make a billion dollars. Of course, the metal in each of these coins is worth less than the face value of the

[1]In addition, traveler's checks are included in the money supply, narrowly defined, since one can pay for goods and services about as easily with traveler's checks as with cash. As indicated in Table 8.1, traveler's checks are only about 1 percent of the money supply narrowly defined. Since they are so small a percentage of the money supply, we ignore them in the following discussion.

TABLE 8.1
Money Supply,
March 2000

	AMOUNT (BILLIONS OF DOLLARS)
Demand deposits	343
Currency and coins[a]	517
Other checkable deposits[b]	243
Traveler's checks[c]	8
Total	1,111

[a]Only currency and coins outside bank vaults (and the Treasury and Federal Reserve) are included.
[b]Includes ATS and NOW balances at all institutions, credit union, share draft, and other minor items.
[c]See footnote 1.

coin; otherwise people would melt them down and make money by selling the metal. In the 1960s, when silver prices rose, the government stopped using silver in dimes and quarters to prevent coins from meeting this fate.

Currency

Currency—paper money like the five- and ten-dollar bills everyone likes to have on hand—constitutes a second and far larger share of the total money supply. Together, currency and coins outstanding totaled about $517 billion in early 2000, as shown in Table 8.1. The Federal Reserve System, described in detail in the next chapter, issues practically all our currency in the form of Federal Reserve notes. Before 1933, it was possible to exchange currency for a stipulated amount of gold, but this is no longer the case. (The price of gold on the free market varies; thus the amount of gold one can buy for a dollar varies too.) All U.S. currency (and coin) is presently *fiat* money: it is money because the government says so, and because the people accept it. There is no metallic backing of the currency anymore. But this does not mean that we should be suspicious of the soundness of our currency, since gold backing is not what gives money its value. (In fact, to some extent, cause and effect work the other way. The use of gold to back currencies has in the past increased the value of gold.) Basically, the value of currency depends on its acceptability by people. And the government, to ensure its acceptability, must limit its quantity.

■ DEMAND DEPOSITS AND OTHER CHECKABLE DEPOSITS

Demand deposits

Demand deposits—bank deposits subject to payment on demand—are another part of the narrowly defined money supply. They are a larger part than currency and coins, as shown in Table 8.1. At first you may question whether these demand deposits—or checking accounts, as they are commonly called—are money at all. In everyday speech, they often are not considered money. But economists include demand deposits as part of the money supply, and for good reason. After all, you can pay for goods and services just as easily by check as with cash. Indeed, the public pays for more things by check than with cash. This means that checking accounts are just as much a medium of exchange—and just as much a standard of value and a store of value—as cash. Thus, since they perform all the functions of money, they should be included as money.

Other checkable deposits include negotiable order of withdrawal (NOW) accounts and other accounts that are very close to being demand deposits. A *NOW account* is essentially an interest-bearing checking account available at banks, savings banks, and other thrift institutions. First created in 1972 by a Massachusetts savings bank, such accounts became available in more and more states, particularly in the Northeast. In 1980, Congress passed a financial reform act that permitted federally chartered thrift institutions to have NOW accounts. Banking innovations like NOW accounts have blurred the distinction between checking and savings accounts. Since many savings and loan associations, mutual savings banks, and credit unions are now providing accounts against which checks can be drawn, it would make no sense to include as money only demand deposits in commercial banks. Instead, all such checkable deposits are included.

In the past fifty years the quantity of money has generally increased from one year to the next and the increase has been at an average rate of about 5 to 10 percent per year. However, the rate of increase of the quantity of money has not been constant. In some years, like 1990, the quantity of money increased by about 4 percent; in others, like 1986, it increased by over 10 percent. A great deal will be said later about the importance and determinants of changes in the quantity of money.

THE MONEY SUPPLY, BROADLY DEFINED

The narrowly defined money supply (which includes coins, currency, demand deposits, and other checkable deposits) is not the only definition of the money supply that is used by economists. There is also the broadly defined money supply, which includes savings and small time deposits (under $100,000), money market mutual fund balances and money market deposit accounts, as well as coins, currency, demand deposits, and other checkable deposits. The money supply narrowly defined is often called **M1**, whereas the money supply broadly defined is often called **M2**.

M1
M2

The traditional reason for excluding time and savings deposits from the narrow definition of money has been that, in most instances, you could not pay for anything with them. For example, suppose that you had a savings account at a commercial bank. You could not draw a check against it, as you could with a demand deposit. And to withdraw your money from the account, you might have to give the bank a certain amount of notice (although in practice this right might be waived and the bank would ordinarily let you withdraw your money when you desired). Nonetheless, since this savings account could so readily be transformed into cash, it was almost like a checking account—not quite, but almost.

Besides time and savings accounts, many other assets can be transformed into cash without much difficulty—though not quite as easily as time and savings deposits. There is no way to draw a hard-and-fast dividing line between money and nonmoney, since many assets have some of the characteristics of money. Consequently, there are still other definitions of the money supply that are more inclusive than M2. Any dividing line between money and nonmoney must be arbitrary. In this book, we shall use the narrow definition, M1, when we refer to the money supply.

COMMERCIAL BANKS IN THE UNITED STATES

There are thousands of commercial banks in the United States. This testifies to the fact that in contrast to countries like England, where a few banks with many branches dominate the banking scene, the United States has promoted the growth of a great many local banks. In part, this has stemmed from a traditional suspicion in this country of "big bankers."

Commercial banks have two primary functions. First, *banks hold demand deposits and permit checks to be drawn on these deposits.* This function is familiar to practically everyone. Most people have a checking account in some commercial bank and draw checks on this account. Second, *banks lend money to industrialists, merchants, homeowners, and other individuals and firms.* At one time or another, you will probably apply for a loan to finance some project for business, home, or education.

Commercial banks are not the only kind of financial institution. Mutual savings banks and savings and loan associations hold savings and time deposits and various forms of checkable deposits, "consumer finance" companies lend money to individuals, insurance companies lend money to firms and governments, "factors" provide firms with working capital, and investment bankers help firms sell their securities to the public. All these types of financial institutions play an important role in the U.S. economy. In general, they all act as intermediaries between savers and investors; that is, they all turn over to investors money that they receive from savers. This process of converting savings into investment is very important in determining gross domestic product.

HOW BANKS OPERATE

Although it is difficult to generalize about the operation of commercial banks because they vary so much, certain principles and propositions generally hold.

1. *Banks generally make loans to both firms and individuals, and invest in securities, including the bonds (which are essentially IOUs) of state and local governments, as well as federal government bonds.* The relationship between a business firm and its bank is often a close and continuing one. The firm keeps a reasonably large deposit with the bank for long periods of time, and the bank provides the firm with needed and prudent loans. The relationship between individuals and their banks is much more casual, but banks like consumer loans because they tend to be relatively profitable. Besides lending to firms and individuals, banks buy large quantities of government bonds.

2. *Banks, like other firms, operate to make a profit.* They don't do it by producing and selling a good, like automobiles or steel. Instead, they perform various services, including lending money, making investments, clearing checks, keeping records, and so on. They manage to make a profit from these activities by lending money and making investments that yield a higher rate of interest than they must pay their depositors. For example, the Bank of America, one of the nation's largest banks, may be able to get 12 percent interest on the loans it makes, whereas it must pay only 6

percent interest to its depositors. (Commercial banks pay interest on some but not all deposits.) If so, it receives the difference of 6 percent, which goes to meet its expenses—and to provide it with some profits.

3. Banks must constantly balance their desire for high returns from their loans and investments against the requirement that these loans and investments be safe and easily turned into cash. Since a bank's profits increase if it makes loans or investments that yield a high interest rate, it is clear why a bank favors high returns from its loans and investments. But those that yield a high interest rate often are relatively risky, which means that they may not be repaid in full. Because a bank lends out its depositors' money, it must be careful to limit the riskiness of the loans and investments it makes. Otherwise it may fail.

Until about seventy years ago, banks used to fail in large numbers during recessions and cause depositors to lose their money. Even during the prosperous 1920s, over 500 banks failed per year. It is no wonder that the public viewed the banks with less than complete confidence. Since the mid-1930s, bank failures have been far fewer, in part because of tighter standards of regulation by federal and state authorities. For example, bank examiners audit the books and practices of the banks. In addition, confidence in the banks was strengthened by the creation in 1934 of the Federal Deposit Insurance Corporation (FDIC), which insures over 99 percent of all commercial bank depositors. At present, each deposit is insured up to $100,000. Nonetheless, as we shall see, there was much more concern over the safety of the banks during the early 1990s than during the previous half-century.

THE BALANCE SHEET OF AN INDIVIDUAL BANK

A good way to understand how a bank operates is to look at its balance sheet. A firm's balance sheet shows the nature of its assets, tangible and intangible, at a certain point in time. Suppose that Table 8.2 shows the balance sheet of a particular bank, as of the end of 2000.

The left-hand side. The left-hand side shows that the total assets of this bank were $187 billion and that these assets were made up as follows: $13 billion in cash, $32 billion in bonds and other securities, $123 billion in loans, and $19 billion in other assets. In particular, note that the loans included among the assets of this bank are the loans it made to firms and individuals. As we have emphasized, lending money is one of the major functions of a commercial bank.

TABLE 8.2

Balance Sheet, Hypothetical Bank, December 31, 2000 (billions of dollars)

ASSETS		LIABILITIES AND NET WORTH	
Cash	13	Deposits	142
Securities	32	Other liabilities	28
Loans	123	Net worth	17
Other assets	19		
Total	187	Total	187

The right-hand side. The right-hand side of the balance sheet says that the total *liabilities*—or debts—of this bank were $170 billion and that these liabilities were made up of $142 billion in deposits (both demand and time) and $28 billion in other liabilities. Note that the deposits at this bank are included among its liabilities, since this bank owes the depositors the amount of money in their deposits. You will recall from the previous sections that maintaining these deposits is one of the major functions of a commercial bank. The difference between the bank's total assets and its total liabilities—$17 billion—is its net worth. (A firm's *net worth* is the value of its owners' claims against its assets.)

California headquarters of the Bank of America, a major commercial bank

■ CASH LESS THAN DEPOSITS

One noteworthy characteristic of any bank's balance sheet is the fact that *a very large percentage of its liabilities must be paid on demand*. For example, if all the depositors of the bank in Table 8.2 tried to withdraw their demand deposits, a substantial proportion of its liabilities would be due on demand. Of course, the chance of all depositors' wanting to draw out their money at once is infinitesimally small. Instead, on a given day some depositors withdraw some money, while others make deposits, and most neither withdraw nor deposit money. Consequently, any bank can get along with an amount of cash to cover withdrawals that is much smaller than the total amount of its deposits.[2]

Isn't it dangerous for a bank to hold an amount of cash much less than the amount it owes its depositors? The answer is no. *All banks hold much less cash than the amount they owe their depositors.* This is a perfectly sound banking practice, as we shall see.

FRACTIONAL-RESERVE BANKING

Fractional-reserve banking

To understand the crucial significance of **fractional-reserve banking**, as this practice is called, let's compare two situations: one where a bank's reserves must equal the amount the bank owes its depositors, and another where its reserves need not match that amount. In the first case, the bank's balance sheet might be as shown in Table 8.3 if demand deposits equal $2 million and net worth equals $500,000. The bank's loans and investments in this case are made entirely with funds put up by the owners of the bank. To see this, note that loans and investments equal $500,000 and that the bank's net worth also equals $500,000. Thus, if some of these loans are not repaid or if some of these investments lose

TABLE 8.3
Bank Balance Sheet: Case Where Reserves Equal Demand Deposits (millions of dollars)

ASSETS		LIABILITIES AND NET WORTH	
Reserves	2.0	Demand deposits	2.0
Loans and investments	0.5	Net worth	0.5
Total	2.5	Total	2.5

[2]Note that "cash" here includes the bank's deposit with the Federal Reserve and its deposits with other banks, as well as cash in its vault. The Federal Reserve is our nation's central bank, and will be described below and in subsequent chapters.

TABLE 8.4	ASSETS		LIABILITIES AND NET WORTH	
Bank Balance Sheet: Fractional Reserves (millions of dollars)	Reserves	0.4	Demand deposits	2.0
	Loans and investments	2.1	Net worth	0.5
	Total	2.5	Total	2.5

money, the losses are borne entirely by the bank's stockholders. The depositors are protected completely because every cent of their deposits is covered by the bank's reserves.

Now let's turn to the case of fractional-reserve banking. In this case, the bank's balance sheet might be as shown in Table 8.4 if deposits equal $2 million and net worth equals $500,000. Some of the loans and investments made by the bank are made not with funds put up by the owners of the bank but with funds deposited in the bank by depositors. Thus though depositors deposited $2 million in the bank, the reserves are only $400,000. What happened to the remaining $1.6 million? Since the bank (in this simple case) has only two kinds of assets, loans (and investments) and reserves, the bank must have lent out (or invested) the remaining $1.6 million.

■ ORIGINS OF FRACTIONAL-RESERVE BANKING

The early history of banking is the story of an evolution from the first to the second situation. The earliest banks held reserves equal to the amounts they owed depositors and were simply places where people stored their gold. But as time went on, banks began to practice fractional-reserve banking. It is easy to see how this evolution could take place. Suppose that you owned a bank of the first type. You would almost certainly be struck by the fact that most of the gold entrusted to you was not demanded on any given day. Sooner or later, you might be tempted to lend out some of the gold and obtain some interest. Eventually, as experience indicated that this procedure did not inconvenience your depositors, you and other bankers might make this practice common knowledge.

You might use several arguments to defend this practice. First, you would probably point out that none of the depositors had lost any money. (To the depositors, this would be a rather important argument.) Second, you could show that the interest you earned on the loans made it possible for you to charge depositors less for storing their gold. Consequently, you would argue that it was to the depositors' advantage (because of the savings that accrued to them) for you to lend out some of the gold. Third, you would probably argue that putting the money to work benefited the community and the economy. After all, in many cases firms can make highly productive investments only if they can borrow the money, and by lending out your depositors' gold, you would enable such investments to be made.

◼ LEGAL RESERVE REQUIREMENTS

Arguments of this sort have led society to permit fractional-reserve banking. In other words, banks are allowed to hold less in reserves than the amount they owe their depositors. But what determines how much banks hold in reserves? For example, the bank in Table 8.2 held cash equal to about 9 percent of its total deposits. It probably could have gotten away with holding much less in reserves, so long as there was no panic among depositors and it made sound loans and investments. But *the Federal Reserve System requires every commercial bank (whether or not it is a member of the system) to hold a certain percentage of its deposits as reserves.*

Federal Reserve System (Fed)

What is the **Federal Reserve System** (commonly called the **Fed**)? It is our nation's central bank, and its most important functions are to help control the quantity of money, provide facilities for the collection of checks, supply the public with currency, and supervise the operation of commercial banks.

According to the 1980 Financial Reform Act, the Fed can set the percentage of deposits that a bank must hold as reserves between the limits of 8 and 14 percent for checkable deposits (that is, deposits subject to direct or indirect transfer by check).[3] Also, on the affirmative action of five of the seven members of the Fed's board of governors, it can impose an additional reserve requirement of up to 4 percent. And in extraordinary circumstances the Fed can for 180 days set the percentage at any level it deems necessary.

Legal reserve requirements

These are **legal reserve requirements**; they also exist for time deposits (of businesses and nonprofit institutions), but are lower than for checkable deposits.

Most of these reserves are held in the form of deposits by banks at the Federal Reserve. In addition, some of any bank's reserves are held in cash on the bank's premises. However, its legal reserves are less than the "cash" entry on its balance sheet since its deposits with other banks do not count as legal reserves.

---

[3]For up to $25 million in checkable deposits, this percentage is 3 percent. Note too that the 1980 law also applies these reserve requirements to deposits in other thrift institutions (savings and loan associations, mutual savings banks, and credit unions), not just banks.

The most obvious reason why the Fed imposes these legal reserve requirements would seem to be to keep the banks safe, but in this case the obvious answer isn't the right one. Instead, *the most important reason for legal reserve requirements is to control the money supply.* It will take some more discussion before this becomes clear.

THE SAFETY OF THE BANKS

We have just argued that the reserve requirements imposed by the Federal Reserve System exceed what would be required under normal circumstances to ensure the safety of the banks. To support our argument, we might cite some authorities who claim that a bank would be quite safe if it had reserves equal only to about 2 percent of its deposits. Under these circumstances it still would be able to meet its depositors' everyday demands for cash. Obviously this level of reserves is much lower than the legally required level.

■ THE ROLE OF BANK MANAGEMENT

But high reserve requirements will not by themselves ensure bank safety. For example, suppose that a bank lends money to every budding inventor with a scheme for producing perpetual-motion machines and that it grants particularly large loans to those who propose to market these machines in the suburbs of Missoula, Montana. This bank is going to fail eventually, even if it holds reserves equal to 20 percent—or 50 percent, for that matter—of its demand deposits. It will fail simply because the loans it makes will not be repaid, and eventually these losses will accumulate to more than the bank's net worth. In other words, if the bank is sufficiently inept in making loans and investments, it will lose all the owners' money and some of the depositors' money besides.

The well-managed bank must make sensible loans and investments. In addition, it must protect itself against short-term withdrawals of large amounts of money. Although much larger than usual withdrawals are not very likely to occur, the bank must be prepared to meet a temporary upswing in withdrawals. One way is to invest in securities that can readily be turned into cash. For example, the bank may invest in short-term government securities that can readily be sold at a price that varies only moderately from day to day. Such securities are often referred to as *secondary reserves*.

■ THE ROLE OF GOVERNMENT

Banks tend to be safer today than they were one hundred years ago. The reason is that the government has put its power squarely

The failure of the Knickerbocker Trust in 1907

The Knickerbocker Trust in New York City was a successful bank at the turn of the century. The Knickerbocker Trust's main branch was at a fashionable Fifth Avenue address, where many well-to-do people (including the writer Mark Twain) kept their accounts. At its downtown office near Wall Street, the Knickerbocker Trust held some of the deposits of large corporations like General Electric and the Pennsylvania Railroad. In turn, the bank made loans to numerous growing businesses. Under its dynamic president, Charles T. Barney, the Knickerbocker held city bonds and invested in the development of the transit system, in new hotels along Fifth Avenue, and in elegant apartment buildings on the Upper West Side. Not all of the bank's loans paid off. But most did, and the bank prospered.

An opportunity then came along for Charles Barney to make a lot of

KNICKERBOCKER WILL NOT OPEN

Conference of Bankers Deems it Unwise to Aid the Trust Company Further To-day.

EIGHT MILLIONS WITHDRAWN

money if he was willing to take some major risks. Barney had connections with a speculator named Charles Morse. Morse and his partner, Frederick Heinze, formulated a scheme to manipulate the price of copper stock on Wall Street in 1907. The extent of Barney's involvement is debatable, but many believed he made behind-the-scenes arrangements for the Morse–Heinze combine, which, on October 15, 1907, tried and failed to squeeze the copper market, whereupon the syndicate went under. There was no evidence that Barney had overcommitted loans to Morse, but there were rumors to this effect, and Barney, like any banker of the day, realized that gossip could lead to the death of his bank before any facts were proven. He knew that as the word spread that the Knickerbocker was in trouble, the depositors would start a run of withdrawals. Like any banker caught in that situation, Barney also knew that, if he could temporarily pull enough cash together, he might be able to calm his customers. If they were made to believe that the bank could make its payouts, his bank might be saved.

On Sunday, October 20, Charles Barney left his home on Park Avenue to try to borrow the cash he needed. He went to appeal to the only person who could save him: J. P.

Morgan. Morgan had helped tide over banks in trouble before, and he was one of the few men who had the reputation and resources to do it. Morgan had been friendly with Barney and owned some Knickerbocker stock. But Morgan refused even to see him. For Barney, disaster was inescapable. Trying to forestall the rumors, the bank's board of directors on Monday forced Barney's resignation. It didn't help. The run on the Knickerbocker began. On Tuesday morning, bank officials announced they had $8 million cash in their vaults, but most of it was gone before the end of the day. The Knickerbocker closed its doors. Those customers who hadn't withdrawn their money were out of luck for an unforeseeable future. The failure of the Knickerbocker Trust led to doubts about other banks and snowballed into the Panic of 1907. Realizing that the ensuing bank failures could endanger the entire system—including his own holdings—J. P. Morgan subsequently stepped in, and under his leadership, a large reserve fund was pooled together. But by the time the panic was over, 246 banks had closed, and a disgraced, distraught Charles Barney had killed himself. Ironically, the Knickerbocker Trust was not all that bad a bank; it reopened five months later, and depositors got most of their money back.

behind the banking system. It used to be that runs were made on the banks: depositors, afraid that their banks would fail and that they would lose some of their money, would line up at the teller's windows and withdraw as much money as they could. Faced with runs of this sort, banks were sometimes forced to close because they could not satisfy all the demands for withdrawals. Needless to say, no fractional reserve banking system can satisfy demands for the total withdrawal of funds.

Runs on banks are rare now, for several reasons. One is that the government—including the Federal Deposit Insurance Corporation, the Federal Reserve, and other public agencies—has made it clear that it will not stand by and tolerate the panics that used to occur periodically in this country. The FDIC insures the accounts of depositors in practically all banks so that even if a bank fails, depositors will get their money back—up to $100,000. Another reason is that the banks themselves tend to be better managed and regulated. For example, bank examiners are sent out to look over the bankers' shoulders and determine whether they are solvent.

■ PROBLEMS DURING THE NINETIES

Nonetheless, this does not mean that bank regulation has been all that it might be or that the health of the banking industry has been robust. On the contrary, in early 1991, there were persistent rumors and reports that many huge New York banks, as well as a variety of smaller banks elsewhere, were in serious financial troubles because many of their real estate loans went sour when the real estate market did not live up to expectations. These banks were hurt when, beginning in the 1960s, they started to lose the business of many large firms that began to get funds from foreign banks or from the securities markets because interest rates were lower. Also, some banks had made risky investments in high-yield bonds ("junk bonds") and had made risky loans to developing countries like Argentina and Brazil. While these problems did not mean that your bank deposit was not insured (up to $100,000), it did mean that your bank might fail, with attendant losses to its owners, among others. However, as it turned out, the banks dodged the bullet. Their earnings rose substantially, and by 1994 there was no talk of widespread financial problems among the banks.

HOW BANKS CAN CREATE MONEY

Genesis tells us that God created heaven and earth. Economists tell us that banks create money. To many people, the latter process is as mysterious as the former.

To see how banks can create money, imagine the following scenario. First, suppose that someone deposits $10,000 of newly printed money in a particular bank, which we'll call bank A. Second, suppose that bank A lends Ms. Smith $8,333 and that Ms. Smith uses this money to purchase some equipment from Mr. Jones, who deposits Ms. Smith's check in his account at bank B. Third, bank B buys a bond for $6,944 from Ms. Stone, who uses the money to pay Mr. Green for some furniture. Mr. Green deposits the check to his account at bank C. We assume that the legal reserve requirements are that $1 in reserves must be held for every $6 in demand deposits.

■ MONEY CREATION AT BANK A

The first step in our drama occurs when someone deposits $10,000 in newly printed money in bank A. The effect of this deposit is shown in the first three rows of Table 8.5: Bank A's demand deposits and its reserves both go up by $10,000. Now, bank A can make a loan of $8,333, since this is the amount of its **Excess reserves** **excess reserves** (those in excess of legal requirements). Because of the $10,000 increase in its deposits, its legally required reserves increase by $10,000/6, or $1,667 (recall that $1 in reserves must be held for every $6 in deposits). Thus, if it had no excess reserves before, *it now has excess reserves of $10,000 − $1,667, or $8,333.* When Ms. Smith asks one of the loan officers of the bank for a loan to purchase equipment, the loan officer ap-

TABLE 8.5		ASSETS		LIABILITIES AND NET WORTH	
Changes in Bank A's Balance Sheet (dollars)					
Bank receives deposit	Reserves	+10,000	Demand deposits	+10,000	
	Loans & investments	No change	Net worth	No change	
	Total	+10,000	Total	+10,000	
Bank makes loan	Reserves	No change	Deposit deposits	+8,333	
	Loans & investments	+8,333	Net worth	No change	
	Total	+8,333	Total	+8,333	
Ms. Smith spends $8,333	Reserves	−8,333	Demand deposits	−8,333	
	Loans & investments	No change	Net worth	No change	
	Total	−8,333	Total	−8,333	
Total effect	Reserves	+1,667	Demand deposits	+10,000	
	Loans & investments	+8,333	Net worth	No change	
	Total	+10,000	Total	+10,000	

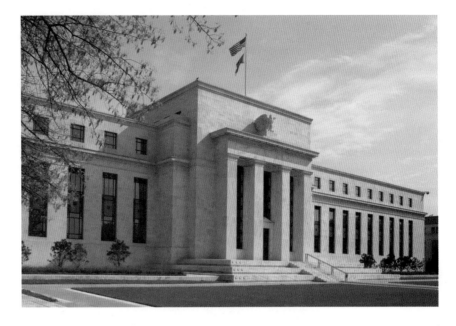

**The Federal Reserve
in Washington, D.C.**

proves a loan of $8,333. Ms. Smith is given a checking account of $8,333 at bank A.

How can bank A get away with this loan of $8,333 without winding up with less than the legally required reserves? The answer is given in the rest of Table 8.5. Rows four through six of this table show what happens to bank A's balance sheet when bank A makes the $8,333 loan and creates a new demand deposit of $8,333. Obviously, both demand deposits and loans go up by $8,333. Next, look at rows seven through nine of Table 8.5, which show what happens when Ms. Smith spends the $8,333 on equipment. As pointed out above, she purchases this equipment from Mr. Jones. Mr. Jones deposits Ms. Smith's check in his account in bank B, which presents the check to bank A for payment. After bank A pays bank B (through the Federal Reserve System), the result—as shown in rows seven through nine—is that bank A's deposits go down by $8,333, since Ms. Smith no longer has the deposit. Bank A's reserves also go down by $8,333, since bank A has to transfer these reserves to bank B to pay the amount of the check.

As shown in the last three rows of Table 8.5, the total effect on bank A is to increase its deposits by the $10,000 that was deposited originally and to increase its reserves by $10,000 minus $8,333, or $1,667. In other words, reserves have increased by one-sixth as much as demand deposits. This means that bank A will meet its legal reserve requirements.

It is important to recognize that bank A *has now created $8,333 in new money*. To see this, note that Mr. Jones winds up with a demand deposit of this amount that he didn't have before; this is a net addition to the money supply, since the person who originally deposited the $10,000 in currency still has his or her $10,000, although it is in the form of a demand deposit rather than currency.

■ MONEY CREATION AT BANK B

The effects of the $10,000 deposit at bank A are not limited to bank A. Instead, as we shall see, other banks can also create new money as a consequence of the original $10,000 deposit at bank A. Let's begin with bank B. Recall from the previous section that the $8,333 check made out by Ms. Smith to Mr. Jones is deposited by the latter in his account at bank B. This is a new deposit of funds at bank B. As pointed out in the previous section, bank B gets $8,333 in reserves from bank A when bank A pays bank B to get back the check. Thus the effect on bank B's balance sheet, as shown in the first panel of Table 8.6, is to increase both demand deposits and reserves by $8,333.

Bank B is in much the same position as bank A was when the latter received the original deposit of $10,000. Bank B can make loans or investments equal to its excess reserves, which are $6,944.[4] Specifically, it decides to buy a bond for $6,944 from Ms.

TABLE 8.6

Changes in Bank B's Balance Sheet (dollars)

		ASSETS		LIABILITIES AND NET WORTH	
Bank receives deposit	Reserves	+8,333	Demand deposits	+8,333	
	Loans & investments	No change	Net worth	No change	
	Total	+8,333	Total	+8,333	
Bank buys bond	Reserves	No change	Demand deposits	+6,944	
	Loans & investments	+6,944	Net worth	No change	
	Total	+6,944	Total	+6,944	
Mr. Green deposits money in Bank C	Reserves	−6,944	Demand deposits	−6,944	
	Loans & investments	No change	Net worth	No change	
	Total	−6,944	Total	−6,944	
Total effect	Reserves	+1,389	Demand deposits	+8,333	
	Loans & investments	+6,944	Net worth	No change	
	Total	+8,333	Total	+8,333	

[4]Since bank B's deposits increase by $8,333, its legally required reserves increase by $8,333/6, or $1,389. Thus $1,389 of its increase in reserves is legally required, and the rest ($8,333 − $1,389 = $6,944) is excess reserves.

Stone and credits her checking account at bank B for this amount. Thus, as shown in the second panel of Table 8.6, the effect of this transaction is to increase bank B's investments by $6,944 and to increase its demand deposits by $6,944. Ms. Stone writes a check for $6,944 to Mr. Green to pay for some furniture. Mr. Green deposits the check in bank C. Bank B's demand deposits and its reserves are decreased by $6,944 when it transfers this amount of reserves to bank C to pay for the check. When the total effects of the transaction are summed up, bank B, like bank A, continues to meet its legal reserve requirements, since, as shown in the bottom panel of Table 8.6, the increase in reserves ($1,389) equals one-sixth of its increase in demand deposits ($8,333).

Bank B has also created some money—$6,944, to be exact. Mr. Green has $6,944 in demand deposits that he didn't have before; this is a net addition to the money supply, since the person who originally deposited the currency in bank A still has his or her $10,000, and Mr. Jones still has the $8,333 he deposited in bank B.

■ THE TOTAL EFFECT OF THE ORIGINAL $8,333 IN EXCESS RESERVES

How big an increase in the money supply can the entire banking system support as a consequence of the original $8,333 of excess reserves arising from the $10,000 deposit in bank A? Clearly, the effects of the original injection of excess reserves into the banking system spread from one bank to another, since each bank handed new reserves (and deposits) to another bank, which in turn handed them to another bank. For example, bank C now has $6,944 more in deposits and reserves and so can create $5,787 in new money by making a loan or investment of this amount.[5] This process goes on indefinitely, and it would be impossible to describe each of the multitude of steps involved. Fortunately, it isn't necessary to do so. We can figure out the total amount of new money the entire banking system can support as a consequence of the original excess reserves at bank A without going through all these steps. *When the process works itself out, the entire banking system can support $50,000 in new money as a consequence of the original injection of $8,333 of excess reserves.*[6]

---

[5]Why $5,787? Because it must hold $6,944/6 = $1,157 as reserves to support the new demand deposit of $6,944. Thus it has excess reserves of $5,787, and it can create another new demand deposit of this amount.

[6]The proof of this is as follows. The total amount of new money supported by the $8,333 in excess reserves is $8,333 + $6,944 + $5,787 + $\cdots$, which equals $8,333 + 5/6 \times \$8,333 + (5/6)^2 \times \$8,333 + (5/6)^3 \times \$8,333 + \cdots$, which equals $8,333 $\times (1 + 5/6 + (5/6)^2 + (5/6)^3 + \cdots) = \$8,333 \times 1/(1 - 5/6) = \$50,000$, since $1 + 5/6 + (5/6)^2 + (5/6)^3 + \cdots = 1/(1 - 5/6)$.

Comparing the U.S. savings and loan crisis and the Japanese banking crisis

In the late 1980s the United States suffered through one of its worst banking crises in the postwar period. At the epicenter of the crisis was the savings and loan (S & L) industry. What brought on this debacle? The responsibility for the crisis lay with many different institutions and resulted from a number of trends, some of which had little to do with the S & L industry. One of the foundations of the crisis was laid in the late 1970s and early 1980s when the Federal Reserve drove up interest rates to rid the United States of double-digit inflation (see Case Study 14.2). This meant that the S & Ls had to pay higher interest rates on their deposits or risk losing them to other financial institutions.

At the same time, a wave of deregulation hit U.S. financial institutions. While the federal government led the way, state governments eagerly followed. The result was that S & Ls were allowed to make more risky (and higher-yielding) investments in real estate and junk bonds. This, combined with a rather lax attitude on the part of many regulators, provided a strong temptation for these thrift institutions to pursue high-risk strategies.

In the mid-1980s the energy price collapse unmasked the bad investments of many Texas S & Ls. Likewise, the bursting of the real estate bubble in New England and California in the late 1980s exposed the shakiness of the S & Ls in those regions as well. Finally, partisan politics and the inability of Congress to quickly enact an S & L bailout plan compounded the problem and raised the price tag of the eventual rescue package.

By 1990 it was estimated that the problems of the S & L industry had cost U.S. taxpayers roughly $200 billion (or 3.5 percent of GDP). Hundreds of insolvent S & Ls were closed, and since the federal government insured their deposits, taxpayers were stuck with the bill.

In the late 1980s the makings of a much larger banking crisis were brewing in Japan. Under pressure from the Japanese Ministry of Finance, the Bank of Japan held down interest rates in order to help boost domestic demand and imports, and, in so doing, cut Japan's trade surplus with the United States. As a result, credit was cheap and financial liquidity was plentiful. This led to pervasive speculation in the property and stock markets, financed primarily with bank lending. Between 1986 and 1989 equity and land prices more than doubled. Meanwhile, companies and households borrowed heavily on the basis of the rise in asset values.

On Christmas day 1989, the Bank of Japan burst the Japanese asset bubble by raising interest rates. This led to a 60 percent drop in the Japanese stock market and a 70 percent drop in Japanese property prices over the next four years. Banks that had loaned money on the basis of inflated asset values saw this collateral wiped out and were left with a huge volume of nonperforming (dud) loans. By some estimates, the size of the bad-loan problem in Japan was six to ten times as big as in the U.S. S & L crisis.

Unfortunately, the Bank of Japan and the Ministry of Finance exacerbated the problem. The central bank was too slow to ease monetary policy after the bubble burst. The Ministry of Finance badly mishandled the banking crisis by underestimating the magnitude of the problem and then moving very slowly to solve it. It was not until 1998—nine years after the crisis began—that Japan put in place a financial restructuring program that

EXPLORING FURTHER

A GENERAL PROPOSITION CONCERNING THE EFFECT OF EXCESS RESERVES

In general, *if a certain amount of excess reserves is made available to the banking system, the banking system as a whole can increase the money supply by an amount equal to the amount of excess reserves multiplied by the reciprocal of the required ratio of reserves to deposits.* In other words, to obtain the total increase in the money supply that can be achieved from a certain amount of excess reserves, multiply the amount of excess reserves by the reciprocal of the required ratio of reserves to deposits—or, what amounts to the same thing, *divide the amount of excess reserves by the legally required ratio of reserves to deposits.*

Let's apply this proposition to a couple of specific cases. Suppose that the banking system gains excess reserves of $10,000 and that the required ratio of reserves to deposits is 1/6. To determine how much the banking system can increase the money supply, we must divide the amount of the excess reserves, $10,000, by the required ratio of reserves to deposits, 1/6, to get the answer: $60,000. Now suppose that the required ratio of reserves to deposits is 1/10. By how much can the banking system increase the money supply? Dividing $10,000 by 1/10, we get the answer: $100,000. Note that the higher the required ratio of reserves to deposits, the smaller the amount by which the banking system can increase the money supply on the basis of a given amount of excess reserves.

In reality, an increase in reserves generally affects a great many banks at about the same time. For expository purposes, it is useful to trace through the effect of an increase in the reserves of a single bank—Bank A in our previous case. But usually this is not what happens. Instead, lots of banks experience an increase in reserves at about the same time. Thus they all have excess reserves at about the same time, and they all make loans or investments at about the same time. The result is that when the people who borrow money spend it, each bank tends both to gain and to lose reserves. On balance, each bank need not lose reserves. In real life the amount of bank money often *expands simultaneously* throughout the banking system until the legally required ratio of deposits to reserves is approached.

■ THE EFFECT OF A DECREASE IN RESERVES

Up to this point, we have been talking only about the effect of an increase in reserves. What happens to the quantity of money if reserves decrease?

In general, if the banking system has a deficiency of reserves of a certain amount, the banking system as a whole will reduce demand deposits by an amount equal to the deficiency in reserves multiplied by the reciprocal of the required ratio of reserves to deposits.

In other words, to obtain the total decrease in demand deposits resulting from a deficiency in reserves, *divide the deficiency by the legally required ratio of reserves to deposits.* Although there is often a simultaneous contraction of money on the part of many banks (just as there is often a simultaneous expansion), this doesn't affect the result.

Let's apply this proposition to a particular case. Suppose that the banking system experiences a deficiency in reserves of $8,333 and that the required ratio of reserves to deposits is 1/6. Applying this rule, we must divide the deficiency in reserves, $8,333, by the required ratio of reserves to deposits, 1/6, to get the answer, which is a $50,000 reduction in demand deposits. Note that the effect of a $1 deficiency in reserves is equal in absolute terms to the effect of $1 in excess reserves.[7]

REVIEW AND PRACTICE

■ SUMMARY

1 Money performs several basic functions. It serves as a medium of exchange, a standard of value, and a store of value. The money supply narrowly defined is composed of coins, currency, demand deposits, and other checkable deposits. Economists include demand (and other checkable) deposits as part of the money supply because you can pay for goods and services about as easily by check as with cash.

2 Besides this narrow definition of money, broader definitions include savings and time deposits (and money market mutual fund shares and money market deposit accounts). It is not easy to draw a line between money and nonmoney, since many assets have some of the characteristics of money.

---

[7]The results set forth in this chapter are based on a number of simplifying assumptions. We assume that when excess reserves are made available to the banking system, there is no withdrawal of part of them in the form of currency and that when deficiencies in reserves occur, no currency is deposited in banks. If such changes in the amount of currency take place, the change in demand deposits will equal the excess reserves left permanently with the banking system divided by the legally required ratio of reserves to deposits. Also, we assume that banks want to hold no excess reserves. Clearly, an injection of excess reserves or a deficiency of reserves will not have their full, or maximum, effect on demand deposits if the banks do not lend and invest as much as possible.

3 Commercial banks have two primary functions. First, they hold demand (and other checkable) deposits and permit checks to be drawn on them. Second, they lend money to firms and individuals. Most of our money supply is not coin and paper currency but bank money—demand (and other checkable) deposits. This money can be created by banks.

4 The Federal Reserve System requires every commercial bank (and other thrift institutions with checkable deposits) to hold a certain percentage of its deposits as reserves. The major purpose of these legal reserve requirements is to control the money supply.

5 Banks tend to be safer than they were one hundred years ago, in part because of better management and regulation, as well as because of the government's stated willingness to insure and stand behind their deposits. However, bank failures still occur, and bank regulation has not been as stringent as it might be.

∗6 The banking system as a whole can increase its demand deposits by an amount equal to its excess reserves divided by the legally required ratio of reserves to deposits. Thus, if excess reserves in the banking system equal a certain amount, the banking system as a whole can increase demand deposits by the amount of the excess reserves divided by the legally required ratio of reserves to deposits.

7 If there is a deficiency in reserves in the banking system, the system as a whole must decrease demand deposits by the amount of this deficiency divided by the legally required ratio of reserves to deposits.

■ PROBLEMS AND QUESTIONS

1 "Banks do not create money. After all, they can only lend out money that they receive from depositors." Comment and evaluate.

2 Suppose that the legally required ratio of reserves to deposits is 1/5 and that banks have no excess reserves. If the banking system's reserves shrink by $50 million, by how much will the money supply change?

3 "Demand deposits are increased by banks when they call in loans and sell investments." Comment and evaluate.

4 "Money, in and of itself, has no value whatsoever. It is valuable only because of what it can buy." Comment and evaluate.

5 Suppose that the legally required ratio of reserves to deposits is 1/10. If $100 million in excess reserves are made available to the banking system, by how much can the banking system increase the money supply? What is the answer if the legally required ratio of reserves to deposits is 1/6 rather than 1/10?

6 Explain in detail why the following items are not money:

(a) Government bonds   (c) Gold

(b) General Motors stock   (d) Uranium

7 Give some reasons why savings accounts should be regarded as money. Give some reasons why they should not. Which side of the argument do you find more convincing?

*The starred items refer to material in Exploring Further.

■ KEY TERMS

money	M2
coins	fractional-reserve banking
currency	Federal Reserve System (Fed)
demand deposits	legal reserve requirements
MI	excess reserves

■ VIEWPOINT FOR ANALYSIS

According to Gerard Baker, columnist for the London *Financial Times,* November 23, 1999, "In the United States, banks are, by whichever measure chosen, in unusually good shape for this stage of an expansion. There are few signs of emerging excesses that even undermined America's own banking system at the end of the 1980s. . . . Again, of course, a significant fall in asset prices would harm balance sheets, but not do anything like the scale in post-bubble Japan."*

(a) What problems beset U.S. banks at the end of the 1980s?

(b) How did these problems compare with those in Japan?

(c) How does a fall in asset (stock or property) prices hurt banks?

Financial Times, November 23, 1999.

CHAPTER 9

The Federal Reserve and Monetary Policy

LEARNING OBJECTIVES

In this chapter, you should learn:

■ The aims and nature of monetary policy

■ The groups empowered to make monetary policy

■ The workings and importance of the Federal Reserve System

■ The pros and cons of monetary policy

■ *(Exploring Further)* The effects of monetary policy on the aggregate demand curve

Like fiscal policy, monetary policy is no panacea, but it is a very important tool for stabilizing the economy. In recent years, monetary policy has been the subject of considerable controversy. For example, during the spring of 1997 when people were worried that inflation would heat up, many observers contended that the Federal Reserve should tighten the money supply and raise interest rates in order to rein in aggregate demand. Others felt that such a move would be wrong because the constraint on aggregate demand would lower the growth of GDP. Without doubt, such controversies will continue in the future, since one thing is certain: Economists of all persuasions agree that monetary policy has a major impact on the economy.

THE AIMS OF MONETARY POLICY

Monetary policy

Monetary policy is the exercise of the central bank's control over the quantity of money and interest rates to promote the objectives of national economic policy. (In the United States, the central bank is the Federal Reserve, as we saw in the previous chapter.) The money supply affects gross domestic product and the price level. Increases in the money supply tend to push up real GDP and the price level, whereas decreases in the money supply tend to push them down. The extent to which the effect is on the price level rather than real GDP depends on the steepness of the short-run aggregate supply curve. The steeper it is, the greater the effect on the

211

price level and the smaller the effect on real GDP. In the long run, increases in the money supply raise only the price level, not real GDP, and decreases in the money supply lower the price level, not real GDP.

When a recession seems imminent and business is soft, the central bank often increases the money supply and pushes down interest rates. That is, it "eases credit" or "eases money," as the newspapers put it. On the other hand, when the economy is in danger of overheating and serious inflation threatens, the central bank often reins in the money supply and pushes up interest rates. That is, in newspaper terms, it "tightens credit" or "tightens money."

In formulating monetary policy, the government's objectives generally are to attain or maintain reasonably full employment without excessive inflation. As we shall see, not all economists agree that the sorts of discretionary policies described in the previous paragraph are most likely to achieve these objectives, but we shall postpone a discussion of this controversy. Regardless of how you think the central bank should behave, it is important that you understand the ways in which it can increase or decrease the money supply.

A country's monetary authorities can influence the money supply by managing the reserves of the banking system. Suppose that the monetary authorities want to increase the money supply more rapidly. How can they realize this objective? By providing the banks with plenty of excess reserves. As we saw in the previous chapter, excess reserves enable the banks to increase the money supply. Indeed, we learned that the banks could increase the money supply by $6 for every $1 of excess reserves.[1] Thus, the $8,333 of excess reserves at bank A enabled the banking system as a whole to increase the money supply by $50,000.

On the other hand, suppose that the Federal Reserve decides to cut back on the rate of increase of the money supply. To do so, it can slow down the rate of increase of bank reserves. As we saw in Exploring Further in the previous chapter, this will force the banks to curtail the rate of growth of their demand deposits by easing off on the rate of growth of their loans and investments. Indeed, if the Federal Reserve goes so far as to reduce the reserves of the banking system, this will tend to reduce the money supply. Under the assumptions made in the previous chapter, the banks

---

[1]This assumes that the legal reserve requirement is $16\frac{2}{3}$ percent. If the legal reserve requirement were 10 percent, a $10 increase in the money supply could be supported by $1 of excess reserves. As more-advanced texts explain, a much smaller increase in the money supply may result from a dollar of reserves if banks want to hold excess reserves and if currency is withdrawn.

must cut back the money supply by $6 for every $1 deficiency in reserves.

MAKERS OF MONETARY POLICY

Who establishes our monetary policy? Who decides that, in view of the current and prospective economic situations, the money supply should be increased (or decreased) at a certain rate? As in the case of fiscal policy, this is not a simple question to answer; many individuals and groups play an important role. Certainly, however, *the leading role is played by the Federal Reserve Board and the Federal Open Market Committee,* both of which are described in detail in subsequent sections. The chairperson of the Federal Reserve Board is the chief spokesperson for the Federal Reserve System. The recent chairpeople—Alan Greenspan, Paul A. Volcker, G. William Miller, and Arthur F. Burns—undoubtedly have had considerable influence over monetary policy.

Although the Federal Reserve is responsible to Congress, Congress has established no clear guidelines for its behavior. Thus the Federal Reserve has wide discretionary powers over monetary policy. But the Federal Reserve System is a huge organization, and it is not easy to figure out exactly who influences whom and who decides what. Formal actions can be taken by a majority of the board and of the Federal Open Market Committee. However, this tells only part of the story.

To get a more complete picture, it is essential to note too that many agencies and groups other than the Fed have an effect on monetary policy, although it is difficult to measure their respective influences. The Treasury Department frequently has an important voice in the formulation of monetary policy. The Fed must take into account the problems of the Treasury, which is faced with the task of selling huge amounts of government securities (that is, government IOUs) each year. Also, congressional committees hold hearings and issue reports on monetary policy and the operations of the Federal Reserve. These hearings and reports cannot fail to have some effect on Fed policy. In addition, since 1975 Congress has stipulated that the Fed must publish its long-term targets for growth in the money supply—the purpose being to establish somewhat more control over monetary policy. Finally, the president may attempt to influence the Federal Reserve Board. To keep the board as free as possible from political pressure, members are appointed for long terms—14 years—and a term expires every 2 years. But since members frequently do not serve out their full terms, a president may be able to name more than two members during each of his terms in office.

THE FEDERAL RESERVE SYSTEM

In this and the previous chapter, we have referred repeatedly to the Federal Reserve, and stressed its importance. Now we must look in some detail at its organization and functions. After a severe financial panic in 1907, when many banks failed (recall Case Study 8.1), there was strong public pressure to do something to strengthen our banking system. At the same time, many people feared the centralized domination of the nation's banks. The result—after six years of negotiation and discussion—was the establishment by Congress of the **Federal Reserve System** in 1913.

Federal Reserve System

■ COMMERCIAL BANKS

As shown in Figure 9.1, the organization of the Federal Reserve System can be viewed as a triangle. At the base are the commercial banks. In 1980, Congress gave the Federal Reserve very substantial powers over all banks and over nonbank depository institutions, even those that did not belong to the Federal Reserve System.

■ FEDERAL RESERVE BANKS

In the middle of the triangle in Figure 9.1 are the 12 Federal Reserve Banks, each located in its own Federal Reserve district. The entire nation is divided into 12 Federal Reserve districts, with Federal Reserve Banks in New York, Chicago, Philadelphia, San Francisco, Boston, Cleveland, St. Louis, Kansas City, Atlanta, Richmond, Minneapolis, and Dallas. Though each of these banks is a corporation owned by the commercial banks, the commercial banks do not in any sense act as owners of the Federal Reserve Bank in their district. Instead, each Federal Reserve Bank is a public agency. These Federal Reserve Banks act as bankers' banks; they perform

FIGURE 9.1

Organization of the Federal Reserve System

The Federal Reserve System contains commercial banks, the 12 regional Federal Reserve Banks, and the Board of Governors, as well as the Federal Open Market Committee and various advisory councils and committees.

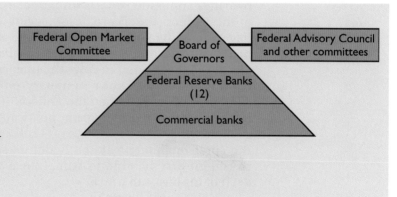

much the same sorts of functions for commercial banks that commercial banks perform for the public. That is, they hold the deposits of banks and make loans to them. In addition, the Federal Reserve Banks perform a function no commercial bank can perform: They issue Federal Reserve notes, which are the nation's currency.

■ THE BOARD OF GOVERNORS

Federal Reserve Board

At the top of the triangle in Figure 9.1 is the Board of Governors of the Federal Reserve System. Located in Washington, this board—generally called the **Federal Reserve Board**—has seven members appointed by the president for 14-year terms. The board, which coordinates the activities of the Federal Reserve System, is supposed to be independent of partisan politics and to act to promote the nation's general economic welfare. It is responsible for supervising the operation of the money and banking system of the United States. The board is assisted by the **Federal Open Market Committee**, which establishes policy concerning the purchase and sale of government securities. The Federal Open Market Committee is composed of the board plus the presidents of five Federal Reserve Banks. The board is also assisted by the Federal Advisory Council, a group of 12 commercial bankers that advises the board on banking policy.

Federal Open Market Committee

FUNCTIONS OF THE FEDERAL RESERVE

Central banks

As pointed out in the previous chapter, the Federal Reserve Board, with the 12 Federal Reserve Banks, is the central bank of the United States. Every major country has a central bank. England has the Bank of England, and France has the Bank of France. **Central banks** are very important organizations, and their most important function is to help control the quantity of money. But this is not their only function. A central bank also handles the government's financial transactions, and coordinates and controls the country's commercial banks. Specifically, the Federal Reserve System is charged with the following responsibilities.

Bank reserves. The Federal Reserve Banks hold deposits, or reserves, of the commercial banks. As we have seen, these reserves play an important role in the process whereby the Fed controls the quantity of money.

Check collection. The Federal Reserve System provides facilities for check collection. In other words, it enables a bank to collect funds for checks drawn on other banks.

215

Currency. The Federal Reserve Banks supply the public with currency by issuing Federal Reserve notes.

Government fiscal agent. The Federal Reserve Banks act as fiscal agents for the federal government. They hold some of the checking accounts of the U.S. Treasury and aid in the purchase and sale of government securities.

Bank supervision. Federal Reserve Banks supervise the operation of the commercial banks. Recall our discussion of the nature of bank supervision and regulation in the previous chapter.

THE FEDERAL RESERVE BANKS: THEIR CONSOLIDATED BALANCE SHEET

We know that the Federal Reserve controls the money supply largely by controlling the quantity of bank reserves. To understand how the Federal Reserve can control the quantity of bank reserves, we must begin by examining the consolidated balance sheet of the 12 regional Federal Reserve Banks. Such a consolidated balance sheet is shown in Table 9.1. It pertains to April 19, 2000.

As shown in Table 9.1, included among the assets of the Federal Reserve Banks are gold certificates, securities, and loans to commercial banks.

1. *Gold certificates* are warehouse receipts issued by the Treasury for gold bullion. For present purposes, this item is less important than securities or loans to commercial banks.

2. The *securities* listed on the Federal Reserve Banks' balance sheet are U.S. government bonds, notes, and bills (bonds are long-term IOUs, notes are medium-term IOUs, and bills are short-term

TABLE 9.1

Consolidated Balance Sheet of the 12 Federal Reserve Banks, April 19, 2000 (billions of dollars)

ASSETS		LIABILITIES AND NET WORTH	
Gold certificates	11	Reserves of banks	22
Securities	508	Treasury deposits	6
Loans to commercial banks and other assets	74	Outstanding Federal Reserve notes	537
		Other liabilities and net worth	28
Total	593	Total	593

Source: *Federal Reserve Bulletin,* 2000.

IOUs). By buying and selling these securities, the Federal Reserve exercises considerable leverage on the quantity of bank reserves.

3. The *loans to commercial banks* listed on the Federal Reserve Banks' balance sheet are loans of reserves that the Fed has made to commercial banks. The Fed can make such loans if it wants to. The interest rate charged for such loans—the discount rate—is discussed below.

According to the right-hand side of the balance sheet in Table 9.1, the liabilities of the Federal Reserve Banks are largely of three kinds: outstanding Federal Reserve notes, Treasury deposits, and reserves of banks.

1. The *outstanding Federal Reserve notes* are the paper currency that we use. Since these notes are debts of the Federal Reserve Banks, they are included among the banks' liabilities.

2. *Treasury deposits* are the deposits that the U.S. Treasury maintains at the Federal Reserve Banks. The Treasury draws checks on these deposits to pay its bills.

3. The *reserves of banks* were discussed in some detail in the previous chapter. Although these reserves are assets from the point of view of the commercial banks, they are liabilities from the point of view of the Federal Reserve Banks.

OPEN MARKET OPERATIONS

Table 9.1 shows that government securities constitute about 80 percent of the assets held by the Federal Reserve Banks. The market for government securities is huge and well developed. The Federal Reserve is part of this market. Sometimes it buys government securities; sometimes it sells them. Whether it is buying or selling—and how much—can have a heavy impact on the quantity of bank reserves. Indeed, the most important means the Federal Reserve has to control the quantity of bank reserves (and thus the quantity of excess reserves) are **open market operations**, which is the name given to the purchase and sale by the Federal Reserve of U.S. government securities in the open market.

Open market operations

■ BUYING SECURITIES

Suppose that the Federal Reserve buys $1 million worth of government securities in the open market and that the seller of these securities is General Motors.[2] To determine the effect of this transaction on the quantity of bank reserves, let's look at the effect on the balance sheet of the Fed and on the balance sheet of the

[2]Large corporations often hold quantities of government securities.

TABLE 9.2

Effect of Fed's Purchasing $1 Million of Government Securities (millions of dollars)

A. Effect on Fed's balance sheet

ASSETS		LIABILITIES AND NET WORTH	
Government securities	+1	Member bank reserves	+1

B. Effect on balance sheet of the Chase Bank

ASSETS		LIABILITIES AND NET WORTH	
Reserves	+1	Demand deposits	+1

Chase Bank, General Motors' bank.[3] In this transaction, the Fed receives $1 million in government securities and gives General Motors a check for $1 million. When General Motors deposits this check to its account at the Chase Bank, the bank's demand deposits and reserves increase by $1 million.

Thus, as shown in Table 9.2, the left-hand side of the Fed's balance sheet shows a $1 million increase in government securities, and the right-hand side shows a $1 million increase in bank reserves. The left-hand side of the Chase Bank's balance sheet shows a $1 million increase in reserves, and the right-hand side shows a $1 million increase in demand deposits. Clearly, *the Fed has added $1 million to the banks' reserves*. The situation is somewhat analogous to the $10,000 deposit at bank A in the previous chapter.

■ SELLING SECURITIES

Suppose that the Federal Reserve sells $1 million worth of government securities in the open market. They are bought by Merrill Lynch, Pierce, Fenner, and Smith, a huge brokerage firm. What effect does this transaction have on the quantity of bank reserves? To find out, let's look at the balance sheet of the Fed and the balance sheet of Merrill Lynch's bank, which we again assume to be Chase Bank. When Merrill Lynch buys the government securities from the Fed, the Fed gives Merrill Lynch the securities in ex-

[3]For simplicity, we assume that General Motors has only one bank, the Chase Bank. This may not be the case, but it makes no difference to the point we are making here. We make a similar assumption regarding the investment firm of Merrill Lynch in the next section.

TABLE 9.3	A. Effect on Fed's balance sheet			
Effect of Fed's Selling $1 Million of Government Securities (millions of dollars)	**ASSETS**		**LIABILITIES AND NET WORTH**	
	Government securities	−1	Member bank reserves	−1
	B. Effect on balance sheet of the Chase Bank			
	ASSETS		**LIABILITIES AND NET WORTH**	
	Reserves	−1	Demand deposits	−1

change for Merrill Lynch's check for $1 million. When the Fed presents this check to the Chase Bank for payment, Chase's demand deposits and reserves decrease by $1 million.

Thus, as shown in Table 9.3, the left-hand side of the Fed's balance sheet shows a $1 million decrease in government securities, and the right-hand side shows a $1 million decrease in reserves. The left-hand side of the Chase Bank's balance sheet shows a $1 million decrease in reserves, and the right-hand side shows a $1 million decrease in demand deposits. Clearly, *the Fed has reduced the reserves of the banks by $1 million.*

■ THE FEDERAL OPEN MARKET COMMITTEE

As indicated above, open market operations are the Fed's most important method for controlling the money supply. The Federal Reserve adds to bank reserves when it buys government securities and reduces bank reserves when it sells them. Obviously, the extent to which the Federal Reserve increases or reduces bank reserves depends in an important way on the amount of government securities it buys or sells. The greater the amount, the greater the increase or decrease in bank reserves.

The power to decide on the amount of government securities the Fed should buy or sell at any given moment rests with the *Federal Open Market Committee*. This group wields an extremely powerful influence over bank reserves and the nation's money supply. Every three or four weeks, the Federal Open Market Committee meets to discuss the current situation and trends and gives instructions to the manager of the Open Market Account at the Federal Reserve Bank of New York, who actually buys and sells the government securities.

TABLE 9.4

Legal Reserve Requirements of Depository Institutions, 2000

TYPE AND SIZE OF DEPOSITS	RESERVE REQUIREMENTS (PERCENT OF DEPOSITS)
Net transaction accounts	
Up to $47.8 million	3
Over $47.8 million	10
Nonpersonal time deposits	0

Source: *Federal Reserve Bulletin*, 2000

CHANGES IN LEGAL RESERVE REQUIREMENTS

Legal reserve requirements

Open market operations are not the only means the Federal Reserve has to influence the money supply. Another way is to change the **legal reserve requirements**. In other words, *the Federal Reserve Board can change the amount of reserves banks must hold for every dollar of demand deposits*. In 1934, Congress gave the Federal Reserve Board the power to set—within certain broad limits—the legally required ratio of reserves to deposits for both demand and time deposits. From time to time, the Fed uses this power to change legal reserve requirements. For example, in 1958 it cut the legally required ratio of reserves to deposits in big city banks from $17\frac{1}{2}$ to $16\frac{1}{2}$ percent; the ratio remained at $16\frac{1}{2}$ percent until 1968, when it was raised to 17 percent. Table 9.4 shows the legal reserve requirements in 2000.

■ EFFECT OF AN INCREASE IN RESERVE REQUIREMENTS

The effect of an increase in the legally required ratio of reserves to deposits is that banks must hold larger reserves to support the existing amount of demand deposits. This in turn means that banks with little or no excess reserves will have to sell securities, refuse to renew loans, and reduce their demand deposits to meet the new reserve requirements. For example, suppose that a bank has $1 million in reserves and $6 million in demand deposits. If the legal reserve requirement is 16 percent, it has excess reserves of $1 million minus $960,000 (0.16 × $6 million), or $40,000. It is in good shape. If the legal reserve requirement is increased to 20 percent, this bank now needs $1.2 million (0.20 × $6 million) in reserves. Since it only has $1 million in reserves, it must sell securities or refuse to renew loans.

Consider now what happens to the banking system as a whole. Clearly, an increase in the legally required ratio of re-

TABLE 9.5

Consolidated Balance Sheet of All Banks, before and after an Increase (from 16 to 20 Percent) in the Legal Reserve Requirement (billions of dollars)

A. Before the increase in the legal reserve requirement

ASSETS		LIABILITIES	
Reserves	1.00	Demand deposits	6.25
Loans and investments	7.25	Net worth	2.00
Total	8.25	Total	8.25

B. After the increase in the legal reserve requirements

ASSETS		LIABILITIES	
Reserves	1.00	Demand deposits	5.00
Loans and investments	6.00	Net worth	2.00
Total	7.00	Total	7.00

serves to deposits means that with a given amount of reserves, the banking system can maintain less demand deposits than before. For example, if the banking system has $1 billion in total reserves, it can support $1 billion/0.16, or $6.25 billion, in demand deposits when the legal reserve requirement is 16 percent. But it can support only $1 billion/0.20, or $5 billion, in demand deposits when the legal reserve requirement is 20 percent (see Table 9.5).[4] Thus *increases in the legal reserve requirement tend to reduce the amount of demand deposits—bank money—the banking system can support.*

■ EFFECT OF A DECREASE IN RESERVE REQUIREMENTS

What is the effect of a decrease in the legally required ratio of reserves to deposits? It means that banks must hold smaller reserves to support the existing amount of demand deposits; this in turn means that banks will suddenly find themselves with excess reserves. If the banking system has $1 billion in reserves and $5 billion in demand deposits, there are no excess reserves when the legal reserve requirement is 20 percent. But suppose the Federal Reserve lowers the legal reserve requirement to 16 percent. Now

---

[4]We assume arbitrarily in Table 9.5 that the total net worth of the banks is $2 billion. Obviously, this assumption concerning the amount of total net worth makes no difference to the point we are making here. Also, for simplicity, here and below we ignore checkable deposits other than demand deposits.

The independence of the Federal Reserve

Alan Greenspan

During World War II, the Federal Reserve was called on to buy up Treasury securities to aid the Treasury in financing the war. Buying bonds pumped lots of money into circulation; this could have caused inflation, had not the high employment of the war effort, combined with wage and price controls, offset the inflationary pressure. When the war ended, the Treasury insisted on continuing this arrangement with the Fed. In effect, the Fed lost control of the money supply, and Marriner Eccles, Fed chairperson in the late 1940s, called the agreement an "engine of inflation."

In 1951, the Fed and the Treasury worked out an accord that gave the Fed a freer hand in conducting monetary policy: The Fed would temporarily support long-term government securities but would thereafter be free to follow a more flexible policy consistent with noninflationary growth. Nevertheless, the independence of the Fed has been and will continue to be the subject of much debate.

Some say the Fed is responsible to Congress. Its enabling legislation was passed by Congress in 1913, and it could presumably be reorganized should it sufficiently rouse Congress' wrath. But Congress moves with nothing if not deliberate speed, and it seldom has sought to influence the Federal Reserve through major new legislation. The president fills vacancies on the Board of Governors, but since terms on the board run for 14 years, presidents may have to wait until their second term to appoint a majority of the board.

In fact, as knowledgeable observers often agree, there are two groups that, without appearing prominently on the organization chart, exercise considerable influence over the policies of the Fed. One is the business community—a group with a definite interest in preserving the value of a dollar. The other is the board's professional staff of senior economists. Administrations come and go, but staff economists remain, and their uniquely detailed knowledge of the workings of the Fed assure them a hearing at 20th and Constitution.

All chairpeople of the Fed—such as Alan Greenspan, Paul Volcker, G. William Miller, and Arthur Burns in recent years—have been sensitive to the ultimate vulnerability of the Fed's independence, and so have been reluctant to buck administration policy too dramatically. Whether the Federal Reserve's current procedures can survive a general call for more accountability is an open question. In early 1975, Congress passed a resolution that the Federal Reserve must publish its targets for growth in the money supply. But the extent to which this really has tied the Fed's hands is by no means clear.

the amount of legally required reserves is $800 million ($5 billion × 0.16), so the banks have $200 million in excess reserves; this means that they can increase the amount of their demand deposits. Thus *decreases in the legal reserve requirements tend to increase the amount of demand deposits—bank money—the banking system can support.*

Changes in legal reserve requirements are a rather drastic way to influence the money supply; they are to open market operations as a cleaver is to a scalpel, and so are made infrequently. For example, for about ten years—from April 1958 to January 1968—no change at all was made in legal reserve requirements for demand deposits in city banks. Nonetheless, the Fed can change legal reserve requirements if it wants to. And there can be no doubt about the potential impact of such changes. Large changes in reserve requirements can rapidly alter bank reserves and the money supply. When the Fed eased credit in December 1990, it eliminated the 3 percent reserve requirement on certificates of deposit held by corporations with maturities of less than 18 months—and quickly added billions of dollars to bank reserves.

CHANGES IN THE DISCOUNT RATE

Discount rate

Still another way that the Federal Reserve can influence the money supply is through changes in the discount rate. As shown by the balance sheet of the Federal Reserve Banks (in Table 9.1), commercial banks can borrow from the Federal Reserve when their reserves are low (if the Fed is willing). This is one of the functions of the Federal Reserve. The interest rate the Fed charges the banks for loans is called the **discount rate**, and the Fed can increase or decrease the discount rate whenever it chooses. Increases in the discount rate discourage borrowing from the Fed, while decreases in the discount rate encourage it.

The discount rate can change substantially and fairly often (Table 9.6). For instance, the discount rate was increased from 12 to 13 percent in early 1980, then reduced to 12 percent in May, 11 percent in June, and 10 percent in July, after which it was raised back to 13 percent by December 1980. When the Fed increases the discount rate (relative to other interest rates), it makes it more expensive for banks to augment their reserves by borrowing from the Fed; hence it tightens up a bit on the money supply. On the other hand, when the Fed decreases the discount rate, it is cheaper for banks to augment their reserves in this way; hence the money supply eases up a bit. Thus, from 1990 to 1993, the Fed, trying to stimulate a weak economy, reduced the discount rate from 7 to 3 percent. Between 1994 and 1995 the Fed raised the discount rate to above 5 percent to cool down the economy. During the merging markets crisis (1997 to 1998) the Fed reversed course and cut interest rates. However, in 1999 and 2000, as the crisis dissipated and the U.S. economy began to show signs of overheating, the Fed began raising rates once again.

The Fed is largely passive in these relations with the banks. It cannot make the banks borrow. It can only set the discount rate

TABLE 9.6

Average Discount Rate, 1963–99

YEAR	DISCOUNT RATE (PERCENTAGE)	YEAR	DISCOUNT RATE (PERCENT)
1963	3.23	1982	11.02
1964	3.55	1983	8.50
1965	4.04	1984	8.80
1966	4.50	1985	7.69
1967	4.19	1986	6.33
1968	5.17	1987	5.66
1969	5.87	1988	6.20
1970	5.95	1989	6.93
1971	4.88	1990	6.98
1972	4.50	1991	5.45
1973	6.45	1992	3.25
1974	7.83	1993	3.00
1975	6.25	1994	3.60
1976	5.50	1995	5.21
1977	5.46	1996	5.02
1978	7.46	1997	5.00
1979	10.28	1998	4.92
1980	11.77	1999	4.62
1981	13.41		

Source: Economic Report of the President, 2000

and see how many banks show up at the "discount window" to borrow. Also, the Fed will not allow banks to borrow on a permanent or long-term basis. They are expected to use this privilege only to tide themselves over for short periods, not in order to relend at a profit. To discourage banks from excessive use of the borrowing privilege, the discount rate is kept relatively close to short-term market interest rates.

Most economists agree that changes in the discount rate have relatively little direct impact and that the Fed's open market operations can and do offset easily the amount the banks borrow. Certainly changes in the discount rate cannot have anything like the direct effect on bank reserves of open market operations or changes in legal reserve requirements. *The principal importance of changes in the discount rate lies in their effects on people's expectations.* When the Fed increases the discount rate, this is generally interpreted as a sign that the Fed will tighten credit and the money supply. A cut in the discount rate is generally interpreted as a sign of easier money and lower interest rates.

EXPLORING FURTHER

MORE ON THE EFFECTS OF MONETARY POLICY

In this section we describe how monetary policy influences the aggregate demand curve. We discuss the view that changes in the money supply were an important cause of the Great Depression, and we present some evidence concerning the lags in the effects of monetary policy.

■ MONETARY POLICY AND THE AGGREGATE DEMAND CURVE

Monetary policy has an important effect on the aggregate demand curve. As you will recall from Chapter 4, the aggregate demand curve is drawn on the assumption that the money supply is fixed. An increase in the money supply shifts the aggregate demand curve to the right. A decrease in the money supply shifts the aggregate demand curve to the left. Because an increase in the money supply lowers interest rates and increases investment, it raises aggregate demand (when the price level is held constant).

Suppose that the economy is experiencing inflationary pressures. Specifically, assume that the price level is P and the aggregate demand curve is AD_1, as shown in Figure 9.2. If the money supply remains fixed, the price level will increase to P_1, at which point aggregate demand and short-run aggregate supply will be equal.

Suppose that the Fed increases the money supply to such an extent that the aggregate demand curve shifts from AD_1 to AD_2. When the price level increases from P to P_1, there still are inflationary pressures. The price level must increase from P_1 to P_2, at which point aggregate demand and short-run supply will be equal. Thus inflation does not abate after the increase in the price level to P_1. (And so long as the Fed continues to increase the money supply at a relatively rapid rate, it will not abate.)

FIGURE 9.2

Effect of Increase in the Money Supply

If the Fed increases the money supply so that the aggregate demand curve shifts from AD_1 to AD_2, the price level will increase from P_1 to P_2.

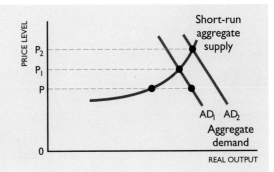

Crisis management by the Fed

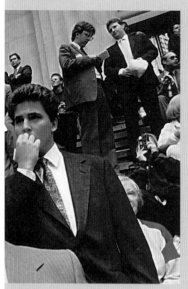

Wall Street in the midst of the 1987 crash

There is almost universal agreement that the Fed was at least partly to blame for the depth of the Great Depression, and some economists have given it a failing grade for crisis management in the 1930s (see "What Caused the Great Depression?" in this chapter). However, the Fed has received much higher grades for crisis management during the last couple of decades. Both in 1987 and 1998 the central bank moved quickly to prevent financial panics from turning into anything worse

On Monday October 19, 1987— since dubbed Black Monday—the Dow Jones Industrial Average plummeted over 500 points (a 35 percent drop in the market). The panic that ensued brought financial markets to a virtual standstill, and there was a serious threat of one or more large

securities firms' collapsing, as investors fled the stock market. Concerned about a financial meltdown, the Fed moved quickly. Before markets opened on Tuesday, October 20, Chairperson Alan Greenspan announced the Fed's "readiness to serve as a source of liquidity to support the economic and financial system." In addition to this unprecedented announcement, the Fed made it clear that it would provide discount loans to any bank that would make loans to the securities industry. The stock market recovered and a recession was averted. However, later some analysts blamed the Fed for being too generous and setting the stage for higher inflation in 1989 and 1990.

On August 17, 1998, a little more than a year and a month after the beginning of the Asian financial crisis, Russia defaulted on its short-term domestic debt and devalued its currency, allowing the ruble to fall 35 percent in one day. Western investors had poured money into the Russian government bond markets believing (foolishly, in retrospect) that the Russian government would neither default on its obligations nor devalue. In the panic that followed, investors not only fled from Russian markets but also from other emerging markets, creating a severe liquidity crunch in global financial markets.

Many banks and mutual funds felt the squeeze and one large hedge fund, Long-Term Capital Management (LTCM), almost went under. Hedge funds typically invest in high-risk-high-

reward financial instruments (such as Russian government bonds) and, in so doing, provide liquidity in many markets. More often than not, their bets pay off and they make a lot of money for their investors. However, when such bets fail in the spectacular way they did in the summer of 1998, then highly leveraged funds, such as LTCM, can fail. It is no small irony that two of the principles of LTCM, Myron Scholes and Robert Merton, had won the Nobel Prize in economics a year earlier for their pioneering work in options-pricing theory.

The near collapse of LTCM sent shock waves through the United States and global financial markets. The Dow Jones Industrial Average fell almost 20 percent from August to October. The Fed began to worry that the problems of LTCM would spill over into the banking sector. It engineered a swift rescue of the hedge fund, by persuading a consortium of large banks to keep lending money to LTCM. It also pumped liquidity into the U.S. financial system and cut the federal funds rate by 75 basis points. The liquidity crunch was eased and the financial panic dissipated. Thanks to the Fed, and also interest rate cuts by the European Central Bank, a global recession was avoided.

After the fact, some analysts again criticized the Fed for being overly generous with liquidity. Nevertheless, there is little doubt that the Fed did a much better job of crisis management in the 1980s and 1990s than in the 1930s.

■ WHAT CAUSED THE GREAT DEPRESSION?

There has been much disagreement over the causes of the Great
Depression of the 1930s. According to Nobel laureate Milton Friedman and Anna Schwartz, the Great Depression was due in large
measure to changes in the money supply, indicated below.

| YEAR | MONEY SUPPLY (BILLIONS OF DOLLARS) | |
	M1	M2
1929	26.6	46.6
1930	25.8	45.7
1931	24.1	42.7
1932	21.1	36.0
1933	19.9	32.2
1934	21.9	34.4

In response to the substantial drop in GDP after 1929, the Fed,
according to Friedman and Schwartz, did not undertake large-
scale open market purchases until 1932. Friedman and Schwartz,
among others, argue that this was an incorrect policy and that the
Fed should have adopted a more expansionary policy in the early
1930s. The Friedman-Schwartz interpretation of the Great Depression has been challenged by MIT's Peter Temin, who argues that
the decline in the money supply in 1929 to 1933 was due to a reduction in the demand for money. A drop in investment or a
downward shift in the consumption function might have reduced
GDP. The reduction in GDP would have reduced the demand for
money. The result: a decrease in interest rates, which could reduce the money supply. For example, banks might have been induced to hold more excess reserves.

■ HOW QUICKLY DOES MONETARY POLICY WORK?

An enormous amount of statistical and econometric research has
been carried out to determine how quickly an unanticipated recession can be combated by monetary policy. According to Robert
Gordon of Northwestern University, the total lag between the oc-
currence of such an unanticipated slowdown in economic activity
and the impact of monetary policy is about 14 months. In other
words, it takes about 14 months for the Federal Reserve to become
aware of the slowdown, to take the appropriate actions, and to
have these actions affect real GDP. According to Gordon, the lags
are approximately as follows:

LAG	MONTHS
From slowdown to reflection in economic data	2
From reflection in economic data to change in money supply	3
From change in money supply to effect on real GDP	9
Total	14

By the time the effects of the expansionary monetary policy are felt, the economy may not need additional stimulus. Suppose you were driving a car in which the wheels responded to turns of the steering wheel with a substantial lag. The problems would be analogous to those confronting the Fed.

REVIEW AND PRACTICE

■ SUMMARY

1 The Federal Reserve System is responsible for regulating and controlling the money supply. Established in 1913, the Federal Reserve System is composed of commercial banks, 12 regional Federal Reserve Banks, and the Federal Reserve Board, which coordinates the activities of the system. The Federal Reserve is the central bank of the United States.

2 Monetary policy is concerned with the money supply and interest rates. Its purpose is to attain and maintain full employment without inflation.

3 When a recession seems imminent, the monetary authorities are likely to increase the money supply and reduce interest rates. On the other hand, when the economy is in danger of overheating and inflation threatens, the monetary authorities are likely to rein in the money supply and push up interest rates.

4 Although monetary policy is influenced by Congress, the Treasury, and other segments of the government and the public at large, the chief responsibility for the formulation of monetary policy lies with the Federal Reserve Board and the Federal Open Market Committee. To a very large extent, monetary policy operates by changing the quantity of bank reserves.

5 The most important tool of monetary policy is open market operations, which involve the buying and selling of government securities in the open market by the Federal Reserve. When the Fed buys government securities, this increases bank reserves. When the Fed sells government securities, this reduces bank reserves.

6 The Fed can also tighten or ease the money supply by increasing or decreasing legal reserve requirements or by increasing or decreasing the discount rate.

*7 Monetary policy influences the aggregate demand curve. Increases in the money supply tend to push the aggregate demand curve to the right. Decreases in the money supply tend to push the aggregate demand curve to the left.

*The starred item refers to material covered in Exploring Further.

■ PROBLEMS AND QUESTIONS

I Suppose that the Federal Reserve buys $5 million worth of government securities from General Motors. Insert the effects in the blanks below.
Effects on Fed's balance sheet:

Securities _____ Member bank reserves _____

Effects on balance sheet of General Motors' bank:

Reserves _____ Demand deposits _____

2 Suppose that the Federal Reserve sells $5 million worth of government securities to General Motors. What is the effect on the quantity of bank reserves?

3 "When the Fed increases legal reserve requirements, it loosens credit, because the banks have more reserves." Comment and evaluate.

4 If the Federal Reserve buys $500 million worth of government securities, will this tend to shift the aggregate demand curve to the right? To the left? Explain.

5 Suppose that you have $5,000 to invest. At a restaurant you overhear someone saying that the Fed is almost certain to increase the discount rate dramatically. If this rumor is correct, do you think that you should invest now or wait until after the increase in the discount rate? Or doesn't it matter? Be sure to explain the reasons for your preference (or lack of it) in this regard.

■ KEY TERMS

monetary policy

open market operations

legal reserve requirements

discount rate

■ VIEWPOINT FOR ANALYSIS

In testimony before the Joint Economic Committee of Congress, W. Lee Hoskins, CEO of the Huntington National Bank, said, "Try as we will, people cannot accurately forecast short-term movements in business activity, and even if we could, monetary policy cannot be used reliably to influence these fluctuations. . . . [T]he role that monetary authorities can play in achieving maximum sustainable growth is to provide a stable purchasing power for the nation's currency, that is, a stable price level."*

(a) If the aggregate supply curve is upward sloping to the right, can the Federal Reserve use monetary policy to get the economy out of a recession and at the same time maintain a stable price level?

(b) If forecasts of short-term movements in business activity are subject to very large errors, should the monetary authorities try to use monetary policy to dampen short-term business fluctuations?

(c) Do you agree that monetary policy cannot be used reliably to influence short-term business fluctuations? Why or why not?

*Vital Speeches, March 1, 1993, p. 290.

CHAPTER 10

Supply Shocks and Inflation

LEARNING OBJECTIVES

In this chapter, you should learn:

■ How supply shocks affect inflation

■ The relationship between supply-side and demand-side inflation

■ The nature of stagflation

■ The disadvantage of wage and price controls

■ *(Exploring Further)* How the Fed may accommodate supply-side inflation

Supply shocks—a spike in oil prices or a bumper crop that pushes down food prices—can push up or push down the rate of inflation. In the 1970s and early 1980s successive oil shocks dramatically raised the rate of inflation in the United States and other industrialized economies. During the late 1990s the emerging markets financial crisis triggered a collapse in commodity prices and lowered inflation in most of the world. Thus, in the 1970s and 1980s the United States had high unemployment and inflation (stagflation), and in the late 1990s low unemployment and inflation. This contradicts the logic of the Phillips curve (introduced in Chapter 7) and means that the task of policymakers, especially the Fed, is far more complicated. In this chapter we will continue our discussion of inflation and anti-inflationary measures. We will explore the topic of supply shocks further in Chapter 14.

During the supply shocks of the 1970s—and previously during wartime—the United States and other countries have adopted price and wage controls to combat inflation. But few economists or policymakers believe that such controls are either effective in the long run or an appropriate anti-inflationary tool. This chapter also looks at the case for and against such controls.

SUPPLY-SIDE INFLATION

Supply-side inflation

As we saw in Chapter 7, demand-side inflation is not the only kind of inflation. There is another kind: **supply-side inflation**. According to some observers, strong labor unions can sometimes play a role in supply-side inflation. By pushing up wages, unions may increase firms' costs; then, in an attempt to protect their profit

FIGURE 10.1

Increase in the Price Level Due to a Shift in the Short-Run Aggregate Supply Curve

According to many economists, the inflation of the middle and late 1970s was due in considerable part to shifts upward and to the left in the aggregate supply curve because of shortages and price increases in oil and other materials. Such a shift results in an increase in the price level from P to P'.

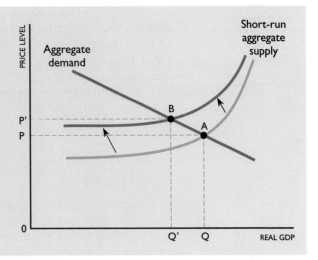

margins, firms push up the prices of their goods and services. These price increases affect the costs of other firms and the consumer's cost of living. As the cost of living goes up, labor feels entitled to, and obtains, higher wages to offset the higher living costs. Firms again pass on the cost increase to the consumer in the form of a price increase. This so-called **wage-price spiral** can be important in supply-side inflation.

Wage-price spiral

Also, increases in the prices of materials may play a major role in supply-side inflation. When the oil-producing countries like Saudi Arabia and Iraq raised the price of crude oil in 1974 and 1979, this resulted in price increases in a host of products made directly or indirectly from petroleum and helped to shift the aggregate supply curve upward and to the left, as shown in Figure 10.1. The result, as we know from Chapter 7, was substantial inflation in 1974 and 1979.

DIFFICULTIES IN DISTINGUISHING SUPPLY-SIDE FROM DEMAND-SIDE INFLATION

Generally, it is difficult, if not impossible, to sort out supply-side inflation from demand-side inflation. For example, an increase in aggregate demand may raise firms' demand for labor and cause workers to demand higher wages; this in turn may lead firms to raise their prices. In such a case, the inflation may be demand side in the sense that the ultimate cause was an increase in aggregate demand, but it is supply side in the sense that the proximate cause of the increase in the price level was an increase in wages.

Also, it is important to note that a supply-side inflation of the sort shown in Figure 10.1 is unlikely to continue for a long period of time unless the Fed "accommodates" or "validates" it by following policies that shift the aggregate demand curve to the right. If the aggregate demand curve does not shift, the inflation will die out. (In Figure 10.1, once the economy moves from point *A* to point *B*, the inflation will be over. There will be no further increases in the price level.) For further discussion, see page 244.

THE INSTABILITY OF THE PHILLIPS CURVE

In Chapter 7 we introduced the Phillips curve and discussed the trade-off between inflation and unemployment that it implied. During the 1960s economists came to believe that the Phillips curve was a stable, predictable relationship. Panel A of Figure 10.2 shows the relationship between the inflation rate and the unemployment rate in the United States between 1955 and 1969. As you can see, there was a fairly close relationship between them in this period. Economists relied heavily on these data to buttress their belief that the Phillips curve really existed and that it had the hypothesized shape. It is no exaggeration to say that the Phillips curve in Figure 10.2 (the heavy line) had a major influence on both economic analysis and economic policy in the sixties.

But then something unforeseen (by most economists) occurred. *The inflation and unemployment rates in the seventies and eighties did not conform at all closely to the relationship that prevailed in the sixties.* As shown in panel B of Figure 10.2, the points for 1970 to 1990 lie far above and to the right of the relationship that prevailed earlier. In other words, holding constant the unemployment rate, the inflation rate tended to be much higher in the seventies and eighties than in the sixties. Or, holding the inflation rate constant, the unemployment rate tended to be much higher in the seventies and eighties than in the sixties. Whichever way you look at it, this departure from the earlier relationship between inflation and unemployment was bad news.

Why did this departure from the earlier relationship occur? In part, it occurred because the inflation of the 1970s was to a considerable extent of the supply-side, not the demand-side, variety. Recall that, when we explained in Chapter 7 why the Phillips curve might exist, we assumed that all inflation was demand-side inflation. Clearly, this was not true during the 1970s. On the contrary, there was a shift to the left in the aggregate supply curve due to price hikes in oil, agricultural products, and other raw materials. Because of this shift, both the inflation rate and the unemployment rate increased. And the rapid inflation of the seventies helped to bring on higher levels of unemployment. The oil price

FIGURE 10.2

Relationship between the Inflation Rate and Unemployment Rate

Source: Economic Report of the President, 1979, 1991, and 2000.

hikes acted like an excise tax levied on the consumer; they reduced the amount that consumers could spend on other things. The general inflation raised people's money incomes, and thus pushed them into higher income tax brackets and increased the amount they had to pay in taxes. (Similarly, the inflation swelled the paper profits of many firms and increased their tax bills.) Be-

233

Stagflation

A meeting of the OPEC oil ministers

The 1970s and early 1980s were characterized by a combination of high unemployment and high infla-tion: **stagflation.** (The term *stagflation* was coined by combining *stagnation* and *inflation*.) What caused this turn of events? According to many economists, it was because the short-run aggregate supply curve shifted upward and to the left, as shown in Figure 10.1. Since a reduction in national output means high unemployment, and an increase in the price level means inflation, it is easy to see that such a shift in the short-run aggregate supply curve might result in stagflation.

But why did the short-run aggregate supply curve shift upward and to the left during the seventies? The follow-ing reasons are among those fre-quently cited:

1. Food prices shot up, beginning in late 1972, because of bad crops around the world (and the disap-pearance of Peruvian anchovies, which caused a drop in the fish catch off the South American coast).
2. Many other raw material prices increased rapidly because of worldwide shortages.
3. As pointed out in a previous sec-tion, the price of crude oil in-creased greatly in 1974, 1979, and other years, because of the ac-tions of Arab and other oil-producing countries.

Because of these factors, a given level of GDP could be produced only at a higher price level than was previously the case. That is, the short-run aggregate supply curve shifted upward and to the left.

cause of the oil price increases and the effective increase in taxes, as well as other factors, like the decline in the stock market, con-sumers cut back on their spending. Thus, the equilibrium value of GDP fell.

In the mid- to late-1990s the Phillips curve shifted once again—this time to the left. The cluster of data points was again very reminiscent of the 1960s—unemployment rates of 4 percent and inflation rates between 2 and 3 percent. There were at least two reasons for this fortuitous turn of events. First, the emerging markets crisis, which started in Asia in the summer of 1997 and subsequently spread to Russia and Latin America, brought about a sharp decline in commodity prices and a drop in the rate of in-flation. This had the same effect as a tax cut and resulted in a boom in consumer spending in 1998 and 1999. The second trend that shifted the Phillips curve back was much stronger pro-ductivity growth in the late 1990s (see Chapter 11). Both these trends pushed the supply curve in Figure 10.1 down and to the right.

THE TRANSITORY NATURE OF THE TRADE-OFF BETWEEN INFLATION AND UNEMPLOYMENT

Another reason for the collapse of the Phillips curve was that policy-makers (and some economists) misinterpreted this curve and attempted to establish combinations of inflation and unemployment that were unsustainable. As we have seen in earlier chapters, the economy, left to its own devices, will tend to eliminate gaps between actual and potential output. By doing so, it will make certain points on the Phillips curve unsustainable. That is, if the government pushes the economy to any of these points, the economy will not stay there.

Leading economists like Milton Friedman and Edmund Phelps pointed out that the Phillips curve in Figure 7.3 (page 175) is only a short-run relationship. They were not surprised that, holding constant the unemployment rate, the rate of inflation was higher in the 1970s than in the 1960s. In their view, expansionary monetary and fiscal policies that resulted in inflation would only reduce unemployment temporarily, with the result that the rate of inflation would tend to accelerate.

Their basic point was that *the Phillips curve in the long run is vertical*. That is, the unemployment rate in the long run will be the same, regardless of the inflation rate. There is a certain natural (or full-employment) rate of unemployment, which is determined by how long workers search before taking a new job. The more reluctant they are to take unattractive or low-paying jobs, the higher the natural rate of unemployment. Economists who stress the importance of structural unemployment argue that the natural rate of unemployment depends too on the rates at which changes in technology and tastes occur and the speed with which workers in declining industries can be retrained for jobs in expanding industries.

THE IMPORTANCE OF EXPECTATIONS

Expectations

Why will expansionary monetary and fiscal policies aimed at pushing the unemployment rate below its natural (or full-employment) level produce only temporary reductions in unemployment (but accelerate inflation)? To answer this question, it is essential to recognize that the short-run Phillips curve reflects people's **expectations** concerning the future rate of inflation. If people have come to expect a higher rate of inflation than in the past, this will shift the Phillips curve upward and to the right. To illustrate, let's compare two situations, one where workers and firms expect that prices will increase by 10 percent per year in the immediate future, the other where they expect no inflation at all. In the former

Is inflation dead?

Physician making a virtual house call using time-saving technology

After two bouts of double-digit inflation in the mid-1970s and early 1980s, the United States has seen a trend decline in its inflation rate to under 2.5 percent in 1999—a process sometimes referred to as disinflation. Much of the credit for this improvement goes to the Fed, which started taking a tougher stance against inflation in the early 1980s and has been vigilant ever since. The Fed's job has been made easier by a shift in popular opinion and political consensus against inflation. The absence of supply shocks in the past decade has also helped.

In the mid-1990s, a small but vocal group of analysts began asserting that inflation was dead, because of structural changes in the U.S. and global economies. They based this conclusion on three trends: (1) labor-saving technologies that raise productivity and help to keep down price pressures; (2) a decline in the membership and power of unions which has kept a lid on wage growth; and (3) increased competition both in the United States (because of deregulation and privatization) and from abroad (because of fierce competition from low-wage countries).

While there is agreement among economists that technology and globalization have allowed the United States and other economies to grow somewhat faster than in the past before inflation takes off, this is a far cry from saying that inflation is dead. Moreover, the three trends cited as causes of inflation's demise have not only been part of the U.S. economic landscape for some time, but their influence may be overstated by those who believe that inflation is no longer a problem. The United States still is not a very open economy; exports and imports each account for only about 14 percent of GDP. Thus, foreign competition only has a limited impact on the economy. Also, the service sectors of the economy, which account for over 75 percent of jobs, generally do not compete in the global marketplace. Thus, while the structural changes in the global economy may have helped to reduce inflationary pressures, they were not the principal cause of disinflation. The lower inflation we enjoy today is, in large measure, due to more sensible macroeconomic policies.

There is a sense in which global financial markets may be doing a better job of acting as watchdogs than they did twenty or twenty-five years ago (see Case Study 28.1). International bond markets and foreign exchange markets react more quickly these days to poor policy decisions by the Fed and other central banks. Thus, one can make a plausible argument that this structural change has reduced the likelihood that inflation will rise because of excessively stimulative macroeconomic policies. But this too does not mean that inflation is dead; rather, it has been in check.

case, unions will not be content to obtain less than a 10 percent increase in money wages, since a smaller increase would mean a cut in real wages. In the latter case, unions can afford to settle for a much more moderate increase in money wages, since none of the money wage increase is expected to be offset by inflation. Thus the rate of increase of wages is likely to be greater in the former than the latter case if the unemployment rate is the same.

In summary, *the more inflation people expect, the further upward and out from the origin the short-run Phillips curve is likely to be. And the less inflation people expect, the further downward and close to the origin the short-run Phillips curve will be.*

HOW THE PHILLIPS CURVE SELF-DESTRUCTS: AN EXAMPLE

Having stressed the importance of people's expectations concerning the inflation rate, we can turn to the following example. Suppose that the natural rate of unemployment is $5\frac{1}{2}$ percent and that the government, not realizing that it is this high, uses expansionary monetary and fiscal policies to reduce unemployment to 4 percent. Because of the resulting increase in aggregate demand, the price level rises, *and if the level of money wages remains relatively constant,* firms' profits go up. Higher profits lead to expanded output and more employment. Thus the economy moves from point *C* (where it was before the government's expansionary policies) to point *D* in Figure 10.3. This movement is entirely in accord with

FIGURE 10.3

A Vertical Long-Run Phillips Curve

Expansionary monetary and fiscal policy results in a temporary reduction in the unemployment rate from $5\frac{1}{2}$ to 4 percent (a movement from point *C* to point *D*). But the increase in the inflation rate (from 4 to 6 percent) results in a higher expected rate of inflation, which shifts the short-run relationship from curve 1 to curve 2. If the government persists in trying to reduce the unemployment rate below the natural rate of $5\frac{1}{2}$ percent, all that it will achieve is a higher and higher rate of inflation. In the long run, the unemployment rate returns to the natural rate ($5\frac{1}{2}$ percent in this case). Thus the long-run relationship between the unemployment rate and inflation rate is vertical.

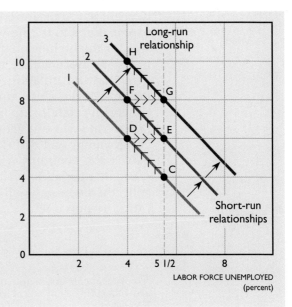

the concept of the Phillips curve: a reduction in unemployment is gained at the expense of more inflation (6 percent rather than 4 percent).[1]

However, this movement is only temporary because workers adjust their expectations concerning inflation. Before the government's expansionary monetary and fiscal policies were adopted, the inflation rate was 4 percent, and this was (more or less) what workers expected. The movement from point C to point D means an increase in the inflation rate to 6 percent, which the workers do not expect. Although they are fooled at first, people *adapt* their expectations; that is, the rate of inflation they expect is adjusted upward toward the new 6 percent rate. As pointed out in the previous section, this increase in the expected amount of inflation will shift the short-run Phillips curve upward and out from the origin. The short-run relationship between the unemployment rate and the inflation rate will shift from curve 1 to curve 2 in Figure 10.3, and unemployment will return to $5\frac{1}{2}$ percent, the natural rate. In other words, the economy will move from point D to point E. Faced with this new short-run curve, the government will raise the inflation rate to 8 percent if it persists in trying to maintain the unemployment rate at 4 percent. That is, it will have to move to point F in Figure 10.3.

■ A SECOND TRY

Suppose that the government continues to try to maintain a 4 percent unemployment rate. Since the inflation rate increases to 8 percent as a consequence, people once more begin to adapt their expectations to the new inflation rate. Workers, trying to compensate for the higher inflation rate, ask for bigger wage increases, and firms are more willing to grant such increases because they recognize that the inflation rate has risen. Once again, the short-run Phillips curve shifts upward and outward from the origin. The short-run relationship between the unemployment rate and the inflation rate will shift from curve 2 to curve 3 in Figure 10.3 and unemployment will return to $5\frac{1}{2}$ percent, the natural rate. In other words, the economy will move from point F to point G. If the government persists in trying to keep the unemployment rate at 4 percent, the economy will move next to point H, where the inflation rate is 10 percent.

[1]To prevent confusion, note that we are not assuming that the Phillips curve in Figure 10.3 is the same as in Figure 7.3. Figure 10.3 pertains to one situation; Figure 7.3 pertains to another situation (perhaps another country or time period).

■ THE LONG-RUN RELATIONSHIP

If the government keeps trying to reduce the unemployment rate below the natural rate of $5\frac{1}{2}$ percent, it will continually fail to do so. All that it will achieve is a higher and higher rate of inflation. Thus, the downward-sloping Phillips curve really does not exist, except in the short run, and governments that believe in its existence can cause considerable mischief. It is not possible for the economy to remain permanently at any point on the short-run curves in Figure 10.3 other than at the natural rate of unemployment ($5\frac{1}{2}$ percent in this case). Thus the long-run relationship between the unemployment rate and the inflation rate is a vertical line, as shown in Figure 10.3.

WAGE AND PRICE CONTROLS

Wage and price controls

One aim of government policy is to lower the inflation rate corresponding to a given unemployment rate—or to lower the unemployment rate corresponding to a given inflation rate. One way that the government can try to do this is by adopting **wage and price controls**. During 1971 to 1974 (as well as during various wartime emergencies), the government imposed controls of this sort. The government intervened directly in the marketplace to make sure that wages and prices did not increase by more than a certain amount. The economics profession has little enthusiasm for direct controls of wages and prices, for several reasons.

1. *Such controls are likely to result in a distorted allocation of resources.* Wage and price controls do not permit prices to perform their functions in allocating resources, and the result is inefficiency and waste.

2. *Such controls are likely to be expensive to administer.* For example, during the Korean War, the Economic Stabilization Agency had 16,000 employees; even so, it was difficult to prevent violation or evasion of the controls.

3. *There is widespread opposition to detailed government regulation and control of this sort, on the grounds that it impairs our economic freedom.* The Council of Economic Advisers undoubtedly spoke for most of the economics profession when it said in 1968:

> The most obvious—and least desirable—way of attempting to stabilize prices is to impose mandatory controls on prices and wages. While such controls may be necessary under conditions of an all-out war, it would be folly to consider them as a solution to the inflationary pressures that accompany high employment under any other circumstance.... Although such controls may be unfortunately popular when they are not in effect, the appeal quickly disappears once people live under them.

INCOMES POLICIES

As we have stressed, the 1970s and early 1980s were a period of uncomfortably high inflation. For example, in 1980, the price level in the United States was increasing by more than 10 percent per year. Such high rates of inflation spurred considerable interest, both here and abroad, in using incomes policies to help curb inflation without cutting back on aggregate demand. According to one common definition, an **incomes policy** contains three elements:

Incomes policy

1. *Targets for wages (and other forms of income) and prices for the economy as a whole.* For example, the target may be to stabilize the price level, to permit the Consumer Price Index to increase by less than 2 percent per year, or to allow wage increases not exceeding a certain percentage.

2. *Giving particular firms and industries more detailed guides for decision making on wages (and other forms of income and prices).* These guides are set in such a way that the overall targets for the entire economy will be fulfilled. For example, if the aim is price stability, these guides tell firms and unions what kinds of decisions are compatible with this target. To be useful, the guides must be specific and understandable enough to be applied in particular cases. There obviously is little point in telling firms and unions to avoid inflationary wage and price decisions if they don't know whether a particular decision is inflationary.

3. *Mechanisms to get firms and unions to follow its guidelines.* An incomes policy differs from wage and price controls in that it seeks to induce firms and unions to follow its guidelines voluntarily. But if it is to have any effect, clearly the government must be prepared to use certain forms of persuasion beyond appeals to patriotism. In fact, governments sometimes have publicly condemned decisions by firms and unions that were regarded as violating the guidelines. Government stockpiles of materials and government purchasing policies have also been used to penalize or reward particular firms and industries. Other pressures too have been brought to bear in an attempt to induce firms to follow the established guidelines. Thus the difference between an incomes policy and wage and price controls is one of degree and emphasis, not a clear-cut difference in kind.

An example of an incomes policy in the United States was the so-called Kennedy-Johnson guidelines. Although earlier administrations (for example, the Eisenhower and Truman administrations) had often appealed to business and labor to limit wage and price increases, the first systematic attempt at a fairly specific incomes policy in the United States occurred during the Kennedy administration. In 1961, President Kennedy's Council of Economic Advisers issued the following wage-price guidelines:

The general guide for noninflationary wage behavior is that the rate of increase in wage rates (including fringe benefits) in each industry be equal to the trend rate of *overall productivity advance.* General acceptance of this guide would maintain stability of labor cost per unit of output for the economy as a whole—though not of course for individual industries. The general guide for noninflationary price behavior calls for price reduction if the industry's rate of productivity increase exceeds the overall rate—for this would mean declining unit labor costs; it calls for an appropriate increase in price if the opposite relationship prevails; and it calls for stable prices if the two rates of productivity increase are equal.

Productivity here means output per hour of labor. (*Labor productivity* is another term meaning the same thing.) To see what these guidelines mean, let's consider prices and wages in the auto industry. Suppose that labor productivity in the economy as a whole was increasing at 3.2 percent per year. Then according to the guidelines, *wages in the automobile industry should increase by 3.2 percent per year.* If labor productivity in the auto industry increased by 4.2 percent per year, then, if the automakers applied this guideline, the labor cost of producing a unit of output would decrease by 1 percent per year in the auto industry (since the 3.2 percent rate of increase of wages minus the 4.2 percent rate of increase of labor productivity equals −1 percent). Thus the guidelines specified that *prices in the auto industry should decrease,* perhaps by about 1 percent per year.

■ THE STEEL PRICE INCREASE: INCOMES POLICY IN ACTION

To conform to our definition of an incomes policy, the Kennedy-Johnson wage-price policy had to have an overall target, more-detailed guidelines for wage and price decisions, and a mechanism to get firms and unions to observe these guidelines. The overall target was the stabilization of prices, and the more-detailed guidelines for wage and price decisions were described in the previous section. But what about the mechanisms to induce acceptance of these guidelines? How did the government get industry and labor to go along?

The famous confrontation in 1962 between President Kennedy and the steel industry is an interesting case study of how pressure was brought to bear. Before the wage-price guidelines were issued, President Kennedy asked the major steel companies to avoid raising prices, and no price increases occurred. Then, after the issuance of the guidelines, he asked the steel union for restraint in the wage negotiations coming up in March 1962. Arthur Goldberg, Kennedy's secretary of labor, played an important role in persuading the union to accept a 2.5 percent increase in compensation, which was clearly noninflationary. At this point, government and the press felt quite optimistic about the apparent success of the president's program.

In the week following the wage agreement, however, the United States Steel Corporation (now USX Corporation) increased all its prices by 3.5 percent, and most of the major steel companies followed suit. The price increase was clearly a violation of the president's guidelines. It almost seemed as if the steel companies were trying to demonstrate once and for all that pricing was up to them, and them alone. Their action elicited a wrathful speech by the president publicly denouncing them. Roger M. Blough, chairperson of U.S. Steel, tried to rebut the president's arguments by claiming that U.S. Steel's profits were too low to attract new capital.

Three of the major steel producers—Armco, Inland, and Kaiser—did not follow U.S. Steel's lead in the day or so after its price increase. Government officials, noting this fact as well as prior public arguments against price increases by Inland officials, quickly began to apply pressure on these three producers to hold their prices constant. Government officials who knew executives of these firms called them and tried to persuade them to do so. The firms were also informed that government contracts would be directed to firms that held their prices constant. Apparently, the government's campaign succeeded. Inland and Kaiser made public statements that they would not raise prices. Faced with this fact, the other steel companies had no choice but to rescind the price increase.

This is an example of how presidential pressure can induce firms to go along with wage and price guidelines. Often Kennedy's Council of Economic Advisers tried to head off price increases before they were announced. The council would learn of an impending price increase, sometimes from the companies themselves, and then ask the firms to meet to discuss the situation. In these meetings, the council would explain the importance of price stability and both parties would discuss the proposed increase. It is difficult, of course, to measure the impact of such discussions, but according to the council, they sometimes resulted in the postponement or reduction of planned price increases.

■ THE KENNEDY-JOHNSON GUIDELINES: CRITICISM AND EXPERIENCE

Soon after the announcement of the Kennedy-Johnson wage-price guidelines, critics began to point out the following problems with them:

Inefficiency. Some observers feared that the guidelines would result in inefficiency and waste. In a free-enterprise economy, we rely on price changes to direct resources into the most productive uses and to signal shortages or surpluses in various markets. If the guidelines were accepted by industry and labor, prices would not be free to perform this function. Of course, the guidelines specified that modifications of the general rules could be made in case of shortages, but critics of the guidelines felt that this escape hatch was too vague to be very useful.

Freedom. Many observers were concerned about the reduction in economic freedom. Of course, the guidelines were presented in the hope that they would be observed voluntarily. But a time was sure to come when they would be in serious contradiction with the interests of firms and unions. In such a situation, what would happen if the firms or unions decided not to follow them? To the extent that the government applied pressure on the firms or unions, there would certainly be a reduction in economic freedom, and to some observers, it seemed likely that the next step might well be direct government controls. Moreover, the nonlegislated character of the guidelines and the government's freedom to choose whom to pursue raised important political questions.

Feasibility. Many people felt that the guidelines really were not workable. Even if the public went along with them, they felt that in many cases they would be impossible to apply, because accurate and relevant data on changes in labor productivity in particular industries were often unobtainable, and the situations where exceptions were allowed were so vaguely specified.

Symptoms. Some economists felt that reliance on the guidelines was dangerous because it focused attention on the symptoms rather than the causes of inflation. In their view, inflation was largely the result of improper monetary and fiscal policies. In other words, the basic causes had to be laid at the government's door. But by setting up guidelines, the government seemed to be saying that the fault lay with industry and labor. Thus some critics felt that the guidelines tended to cloud the real issues and so let the government escape responsibility for its actions.

From 1962 to 1964 the government claimed that the guidelines were working well. Their success during this period may have resulted from the considerable slack the economy still had and from the noninflationary expectations of firms and individuals engendered by several years of relative price stability. By 1965, as labor markets tightened and prices rose in response to the Vietnam buildup, it became much more difficult to use the guidelines. Union leaders fought them tooth and nail, mainly because consumer prices were rising. In various important labor negotiations, unions demanded and got higher wage increases than the guidelines called for. The airline machinists, for example, got a 4.9 per-cent increase in 1966. By 1968, the guidelines were dead. No one was paying any attention to them.

What effect did the guidelines have? Some people claim that they had no real effect at all, whereas others claim that they reduced supply-side inflation in the early 1960s by a considerable amount. Since it is difficult to separate the effects of the guidelines from the effects of other factors, there is considerable dispute over the question. Considering the level of unemployment in the early 1960s, wages increased less rapidly then than in earlier or later periods. Prices, too, increased less rapidly during that period—holding unemployment constant—than earlier or later. But whether these developments were due to the guidelines, to noninflationary expectations, or to some other factors is hard to say.

The guidelines broke down largely because they could not deal with the strong demand-side inflation of the late 1960s. Even the strongest defenders of the guidelines are quick to point out that they are no substitute for proper monetary and fiscal policy. *If fiscal or monetary policy is generating strong inflationary pressures, such as existed in the late 1960s, it is foolish to think that guidelines can save the situation.* Perhaps they can cut down on the rate of inflation for a while, but in the long run, the dike is sure to burst. If the guidelines are voluntary, firms and unions will ignore them, and the government will find it difficult, if not impossible, to do anything. *Even wage and price controls won't contain the strong inflationary pressures generated by an overly expansive fiscal or monetary policy. Such controls may temporarily suppress the symptoms of inflation, but over the long haul these inflationary pressures will have their effect.*

EXPLORING FURTHER

THE FED AND SUPPLY-SIDE INFLATION

Suppose that labor unions suddenly demand that their wage rate (in money, not real terms) be doubled. Since firms must increase prices if they are to be willing to produce the same output as before, the short-run aggregate supply curve will shift upward and to the left, as shown in Figure 10.4.

If the Federal Reserve holds the money supply at its initial level, as shown in Figure 10.4, the economy will move from point A to point B. Thus real output will fall from Q_0 to Q_1 and the decrease in real output will increase unemployment. Because the price level at point B is higher than at point A, although the money wage has doubled, the real wage has less than doubled.

By increasing the money supply, the Fed can push the aggre-

FIGURE 10.4

Accommodation of Supply-Side Inflation by the Fed

By increasing the money supply, the Fed can maintain real output at Q_0, but the price level will increase greatly.

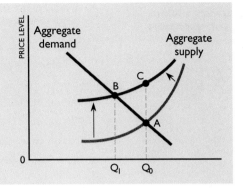

gate demand curve to the right. If it pushes it far enough to the right, it can make it intersect the new aggregate supply curve at point C, where real GDP is at its original level Q_0. The price level will rise considerably. As shown in the diagram, the price level at point C is much higher than at point A. The Fed, by enabling the action of the unions to increase the price level without resulting in additional unemployment, is said to have *accommodated* the supply-side inflation.

REVIEW AND PRACTICE

■ SUMMARY

1 The Phillips curve shows the relationship between the rate of increase of the price level and the level of unemployment. If the Phillips curve remains fixed, it poses an awkward dilemma for policymakers. If they reduce unemployment, inflation increases; if they reduce inflation, unemployment increases.

2 During 1955 to 1969, there was a fairly close relationship between the inflation rate and the unemployment rate. But then something unforeseen by most economists occurred. The inflation and unemployment rates in the 1970s and 1980s did not conform at all closely to the relationship that prevailed in the 1960s. Both the unemployment rate and the inflation rate tended to be much higher in the 1970s and 1980s than in the 1960s. However, by the late 1990s both the unemployment and the inflation rate had returned to their 1960s levels.

3 The accelerationists, led by Milton Friedman, believe that the downward-sloping Phillips curve is only a short-run relationship. They believe that in the long run, it is vertical. In their view, expansionary policies that result in inflation will reduce unemployment only temporarily, with the result that the government, if it sets out to reduce unemployment to below its natural level, will have to permit higher and higher rates of inflation.

4 To reduce the inflation rate (at a given unemployment rate), governments have tried wage and price controls. Although a few economists favor such controls during peacetime, most do not. Such controls are likely to distort the allocation of resources, to be difficult to administer, and to run counter to our desire for economic freedom.

5 Many countries have experimented with various kinds of incomes policies. An incomes policy contains targets for wages and prices for the economy as a whole, more-detailed guidelines for wage and price decisions in particular industries, and some mechanisms to get firms and unions to follow these guidelines. Although guidelines of this sort have a short-term effect on the price level, how much effect they have in the long run is hard to say.

■ PROBLEMS AND QUESTIONS

1 According to Milton Friedman, "It is far better that inflation be open than that it be suppressed [by price guidelines]." Do you agree? Why or why not?

2 "The Kennedy-Johnson guidelines for noninflationary price behavior called for price reduction if an industry's rate of productivity increase exceeded the overall rate. It is unrealistic to expect price cuts of this sort." Do you agree? Why or why not?

3 "Reliance on incomes policies is dangerous because it looks at symptoms, not the basic causes of our problems." Comment and evaluate.

4 According to former President Ronald Reagan, wage and price controls "didn't work when Hammurabi tried them in Babylon. They didn't work when Diocletian tried them in Rome." In this context, what does *work* mean? Why do you think they didn't "work"?

■ KEY TERMS

stagflation

expectations

wage and price controls

incomes policy

■ VIEWPOINT FOR ANALYSIS

According to the 1993 Annual Report to Congress of President Bush's Council of Economic Advisers, "The costs of high and variable inflation are considerable but more subtle than the costs of recessions. In a market economy, prices provide essential information about the relative scarcity of goods and services. High and volatile inflation obscures this information and distorts the allocation of resources."*

(a) Do you agree that inflation obscures this information and distorts the allocation of resources? If so, why does this occur?

(b) Do both supply-side and demand-side inflation have these effects? Or do neither have such effects?

(c) A U.S. senator argues that, if wage and price controls are adopted, these costs of inflation can be reduced greatly, if not eliminated. Do you agree? Why or why not?

(d) A Treasury official claims that, if the Phillips curve were stable, inflation would not have these effects. Do you agree? Why or why not?

*Economic Report of the President, 1993, p. 79.

CHAPTER II

Productivity, Growth, and Technology Policy

LEARNING OBJECTIVES

In this chapter, you should learn:

■ The importance of productivity and what causes it to increase or decrease

■ The nature of the productivity slowdown in the United States in the 1970s and 1980s and its effects on the economy

■ The sorts of public policies that can be used to stimulate productivity

■ *(Exploring Further)* The effects of supply-side government policies

A few years ago, McKinsey and Company, a leading consulting firm, published a study indicating that output per hour of labor was higher in the United States than in Germany or Japan in the production of computers, soap, beer, and food. But in the production of autos, steel, and consumer electronics, the United States and Germany lagged behind Japan. Why do some countries trail behind others in productivity? One purpose of this chapter is to answer this question.

In the 1970s and 1980s the rate of increase of output per hour in the United States declined dramatically, causing enormous concern in Washington and elsewhere. However, by the late 1990s productivity growth had picked up again and was almost at the rate of the 1960s. Another purpose of this chapter is to describe and analyze these productivity swings.

GROWTH OF PER CAPITA OUTPUT IN THE UNITED STATES

Let's begin by looking at the salient facts about the rate at which per capita output in the U.S. economy has grown in the past. Soon after its emergence as an independent nation, the United States achieved a relatively high level of economic development. By 1840, it ranked fourth in per capita output, behind England, France, and Germany. During the next thirty years, the United States experienced relatively rapid economic growth. By 1870, it ranked second only to England in per capita output. Over the next forty years, the U.S. economy continued to grow rapidly. National product per person employed grew by about 2.2 percent per year between 1871 and 1913. This growth rate was higher than for practically any other major industrialized nation; and well before the turn of the century, output per capita was greater in the United States than in any other country in the world.

Between 1913 and 1959, the U.S. growth rate was somewhat lower than in previous years. National product per person employed grew by about 1.8 percent per year. Nonetheless, although we grew less rapidly than in earlier years, we pulled further ahead of most other industrialized countries, because we continued to grow faster than they did. Of course, our rate of economic growth varied from decade to decade (by *rate of economic growth* we mean the rate of growth of real GDP per capita). Economic growth does not proceed at a steady rate. In some decades (like the 1920s), our economy grew very rapidly, while in others (like the 1930s), it grew little if at all. During periods of recovery and prosperity, the growth rate was high; during depressions, it was low.

Table 11.1 shows the annual rates of growth of per capita real GDP in the United States and other major Western industrialized countries up to 1970. You can see that, for the period as a whole, per capita real GDP in the United States grew at an average rate of about 2 percent per year. Compared to Germany, France, Italy, Canada, or the United Kingdom, our growth rate was impressive. In recent years, however, many industrialized countries have shown growth rates larger than or equal to ours. And many observers have been concerned about the slowdown of our rate of productivity increase.

TABLE 11.1

Average Annual Growth Rates of Per Capita Real GDP, Selected Western Industrialized Countries

COUNTRY	1870–1964 (PERCENT)	1929–70 (PERCENT)
United States	1.9	1.9
Canada	1.7	2.1
France	1.5	2.0
Germany	1.7	3.0
Italy	1.4	2.5
United Kingdom	1.3	1.7

Source: U.S. Department of Commerce, *Long-term Economic Growth,* 1966, and *Statistical Abstract of the United States.*

TABLE 11.2

Estimated Sources of Growth in Real National Income in the United States, 1909–73

SOURCE	1909–29	1929–57	1969–73
	(PERCENT OF TOTAL GROWTH)		
Increase in quantity of labor	39	27	33
Increase in quantity of capital	26	15	16
Improved education and training	13	27	20
Advance of knowledge	12	20	48
Other factors	10	11	−17
Total	100	100	100

Source: E. Denison, *The Sources of Economic Growth in the United States* (New York: Committee for Economic Development, 1962), and his *Accounting for Slower Economic Growth*, (Washington, D.C.: Brookings Institution, 1979). The 1969–73 figures pertain to nonresidential business output.

■ TECHNOLOGICAL CHANGE

Technological change

Technological change takes the form of new methods of producing existing products, new designs that make it possible to create new products, and new techniques for organization, marketing, and management. Economic growth in the United States has been due in very considerable part to technological change. Table 11.2 shows that according to Edward Denison of the Brookings Institution, the advance of knowledge contributed about one-eighth of the growth in real output during 1909 to 1929, about one-fifth during 1929 to 1957, and even a larger share in 1969 to 1973. (However, in 1973 to 1976, this factor seemed to contribute little or nothing to economic growth.) Such estimates are rough but useful. It is very difficult to separate the effects of technological change on economic growth from those of investment in physical capital, since in order to be used, new technology often must be embodied in physical capital, such as new machines and equipment. For example, to apply thin-slab casting technology, Nucor built a new plant in Crawfordsville, Indiana. Nor can the effects of technological change easily be separated from those of education. After all, the returns from increased education are enhanced by technological change, and the rate of technological change is influenced by the extent and nature of a society's investment in education. Nonetheless, the estimates in Table 11.2 are useful.

In interpreting U.S. economic growth, we must recognize that the United States has long been a technological leader. Even be-

249

A NASA communications satellite

fore 1850, scattered evidence gives the impression that the United States was ahead of other countries in many technological areas. And after 1850, the available evidence indicates that productivity was higher in the United States than in Europe, that the United States had a strong position in technically progressive industries, and that Europeans tended to imitate U.S. techniques. Needless to say, the United States did not lead in all fields, but it appears to have held a technological lead in many important aspects of manufacturing. This was in contrast to pure science where, until World War II, the United States was not a leader.

Research and development

Recent decades have witnessed tremendous growth in the amount spent on **research and development** (R & D). In the United States in 1993 R & D expenditures were over twenty times what they were in 1945. Although the bulk of these expenditures go for rather minor improvements rather than major advances, this vast increase in research and development has generated much economic growth. As shown in Table 11.3, the federal government is the source of over one-third of all R & D funds, which are heavily concentrated on defense and space technology. In the eyes of many economists, this vast investment in R & D would probably have had a bigger impact on the rate of economic growth if more of it had been directed at civilian rather than military and political objectives.

TABLE 11.3

Transfers of Funds for Research and Development, United States, 1995 (billions of 1987 dollars)

SOURCES OF FUNDS	PERFORMERS					
	FEDERAL GOVERNMENT	INDUSTRY	UNIVERSITIES AND COLLEGES	FFRDCs[a]	OTHER NONPROFIT INSTITUTIONS	TOTAL[b]
Federal government	13	16	11[c]	6	2	48
Industry	—	77	1	—	1	79
Universities and colleges	—	—	3	—	—	3
Other nonprofit institutions	—	—	1	—	1	3
Total[b]	17	110	21	6	4	132

[a]Federally Funded Research and Development Centers. These are organizations exclusively or substantially financed by the federal government to meet a particular requirement or to provide major facilities for research and training purposes. Those that are administered by industry (such as Oak Ridge National Laboratory or Sandia Laboratory) or nonprofit institutions (such as the RAND Corporation) are included in the respective totals for industry or nonprofit institutions.

[b]Because of rounding errors, items do not always sum to total.

[c]Includes nonfederal government.

Source: Science and Engineering Indicators (Washington, D.C.: National Science Foundation, 1996).

THE PRODUCTIVITY SLOWDOWN AND ITS CONSEQUENCES

During the 1970s and 1980s, the decreasing rate of growth of output per hour of labor was a cause of concern among U.S. policymakers. According to the Bureau of Labor Statistics, output per hour of labor (in the business sector) grew at an average annual rate of about 3.4 percent from 1950 to 1966 but at an average annual rate of about 2.3 percent from 1966 to 1977. In 1977 to 1995, the annual growth rate of productivity fell further, to about 1.5 percent (see Table 11.4). However, between 1996 and 1999 productivity growth rose to an average 2.7 percent.

The slowdown in the rate of productivity increase worried policymakers for at least two reasons. First, *to the extent that it reflected a decrease in the rate of technological change, it spelled trouble for our rate of economic growth, since the latter is dependent on our rate of technological change. Second, since higher productivity can offset the effect of higher wages on average cost, the slowdown in productivity increase was likely to contribute to a higher rate of inflation.*

Besides being concerned about the slowdown in our rate of increase of productivity, many observers were concerned about the apparent reduction of the U.S. technological lead over other coun-

TABLE 11.4

Output per Hour of Labor, United States, Percent Change from Previous Year, 1950–99

YEAR	PERCENT CHANGE	YEAR	PERCENT CHANGE	YEAR	PERCENT CHANGE	YEAR	PERCENT CHANGE
1952	3.2	1964	4.6	1976	3.2	1988	1.2
1953	3.8	1965	3.5	1977	1.5	1989	−0.9
1954	1.5	1966	4.1	1978	1.5	1990	1.3
1955	3.1	1967	2.1	1979	−0.2	1991	1.5
1956	1.4	1968	3.5	1980	−0.1	1992	4.3
1957	2.7	1969	0.5	1981	2.0	1993	0.1
1958	2.9	1970	2.0	1982	−0.2	1994	1.3
1959	3.3	1971	4.0	1983	3.4	1995	0.7
1960	1.9	1972	3.1	1984	2.8	1996	2.9
1961	3.6	1973	3.0	1985	2.0	1997	2.2
1962	4.9	1974	−1.3	1986	3.0	1998	2.8
1963	3.9	1975	3.6	1987	0.6	1999[a]	2.8

[a](January through September)

Source: *Economic Report of the President*, various years.

tries and about the slow rate of productivity growth in the United States relative to other major countries. During 1960 to 1995, the percentage gain in output per worker was smaller in the United States than in France, Germany, Japan, or the United Kingdom. However, by the late 1990s U.S. productivity was growing faster than in these countries.

CAUSES OF PRODUCTIVITY SWINGS

What factors were responsible for this significant slackening of U.S. productivity growth in the 1970s and 1980s and the subsequent rebound in the 1990s? To begin with, let's consider the following factors that have been frequently cited.

Changes in the composition of the labor force. Output per hour of labor tends to be relatively low among women and among new entrants into the labor force, in part because of their limited experience and training and the sort of work they get. During the late 1960s, women and new entrants increased as a proportion of the labor force. On the basis of calculations by the Bureau of Labor Statistics, this change in labor force composition may have been responsible for a 0.2 to 0.3 percentage point of the difference between the average rate of productivity increase in 1947 to 1966 and that in 1966 to 1973. With the maturation of the baby boom generation these trends have likely reversed somewhat.

The rate of growth of the capital-labor ratio. During 1948 to 1973, relatively high rates of private investment resulted in a growth of the capital-labor ratio of almost 3 percent per year. After 1973, relatively low rates of investment resulted in the growth of the capital-labor ratio by only about 1.75 percent per year. According to the Council of Economic Advisers, this reduction in the rate of growth of the capital-labor ratio may have reduced the rate of productivity increase by up to a 0.5 percentage point per year. An investment boom in the 1990s also reversed this trend.

Government regulation. A variety of new environmental, health, and safety regulations were adopted in the 1970s. Because reduced pollution, enhanced safety, and better health are generally not included in measured output, the use of more of society's resources to meet these regulations is likely to result in a reduction in measured productivity growth. Also, the litigation and uncertainty associated with new regulations may discourage investment and efficiency, and the form of the regulations sometimes may inhibit socially desirable adaptations by firms. According to the Council of Economic Advisers, the direct costs of compliance with environmental, health, and safety regulations may have reduced the growth of productivity by about a 0.4 percentage point per year during the 1970s.

Shift of national output toward services and away from goods. There has been considerable disagreement over whether the shift in the composition of national output toward services and away from goods is responsible for much of the productivity slowdown. For example, some economists argue that it is more difficult to increase productivity in service industries than in manufacturing industries. Others feel that this factor is of relatively little importance. However, recent revisions to the national income and product accounts show much higher productivity growth in some services over the past couple of decades (see Case Study 3.1).

PRODUCTIVITY,
GROWTH, AND
TECHNOLOGY
POLICY
CHAPTER 11

Innovation

HAS THERE BEEN A DECLINE IN THE U.S. INNOVATION RATE?

In recent years, some observers have asserted that the productivity slowdown was due in part to a decline in the rate of **innovation** in the United States. In their opinion, the rate of introduction of new products and processes has fallen. This hypothesis is difficult to test and should be viewed with caution. In many parts of the economy, such as microelectronics, the rate of innovation seems to be hale and hearty. Recent advances in microprocessors and microcomputers are regarded by experts as extremely important, and should have widespread effects on many areas of the economy. Computers have become cheaper, smaller, and smarter. Another potentially important area is biotechnology, where many major advances are expected. For instance, new biological techniques may allow the development of new plants.

■ THE DIMINISHING U.S. TECHNOLOGICAL LEAD

It is important to distinguish between a reduction in the rate of technological change in the United States and a reduction in the ***U.S. technological lead*** over other countries. Obviously, the United States no longer has the commanding technological lead it enjoyed during the 1950s and 1960s. As countries like Japan and Germany completed their recoveries from World War II and devoted much more attention to transferring, adapting, and extending technology, they narrowed the technological gap considerably and in some areas surpassed the United States. But this does not mean that the U.S. rate of innovation declined. Even in microelectronics, where there is little or no evidence of a decline in the U.S.

A microchip manufactured by IBM

VARIOUS
MECHANISMS
FOR ADDITIONAL
FEDERAL SUPPORT
OF CIVILIAN
TECHNOLOGY

rate of innovation, the gap between the United States and Japan has been reduced considerably, because, according to many experts, the Japanese rate of advance (from a lower level) has exceeded our own.

VARIOUS MECHANISMS FOR ADDITIONAL FEDERAL SUPPORT OF CIVILIAN TECHNOLOGY

There are various means by which the federal government can encourage investment in civilian technology.

■ R & D TAX CREDITS

In 1981 Congress passed an incremental tax credit (extended through 2004) to encourage industrial R & D. Such an R & D tax credit reduces the after-tax cost of R & D, and thus encourages R & D. Perhaps the most important advantages of this mechanism are that it requires less direct government control than some of the other mechanisms and that in some respects it is relatively easy to administer. Its most important disadvantages are that it rewards firms for doing R & D that they would have done anyhow and that it does not help firms that have no profits. Moreover, any program of this sort is likely to run into difficulties in defining R & D, since firms have an incentive to use as wide a definition as possible. Studies of such tax credits, both in the United States and in other countries (like Canada and Sweden), seem to indicate that they have had only a modest effect on industrial R & D expenditures.

■ FEDERAL GRANTS AND CONTRACTS

The federal government can also make grants and contracts in support of civilian technology. This, of course, is the route taken by the Department of Defense and the National Aeronautics and Space Administration in much of their work. It has the advantage of being direct and selective, but it can involve political problems in the choice of contractors, as well as problems relative to the disposition of patents resulting from such contracts and grants. Still another, more fundamental difficulty with this mechanism for supporting private sector R & D is that it is so difficult to predict the social costs and benefits of a proposed R & D project and that government agencies may not be very adept at making what are essentially commercial development decisions.

The Clinton administration has spent considerable amounts in support of civilian technology. For example, the Advanced Technology Program awards matching funds to industry to conduct research on processes and products.

255

Asian growth: miraculous or not?

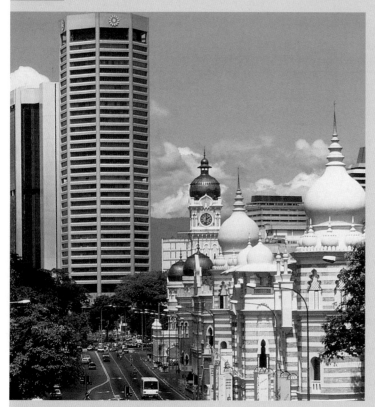

Malaysia's capital, Kuala Lumpur

In the years immediately preceding the Asian financial crisis in 1997 and 1998 a noisy argument erupted between a group of U.S. academic economists and a number of Asian policymakers. The subject of this vocal debate was the sustainability of the Asian "miracle." Key policy analysts in Asia, especially in Singapore and Malaysia, had been arguing that high Asian growth rates were not only sustainable but the logical result of a combination of thrift, educational emphasis, and cultural values. The U.S. challenge to this view was led by Professors Alwyn Young of Boston University and Paul Krugman of MIT. They pointed out that most of the growth in Asia was the result of factor accumulation (for example, high levels of investment in human and physical capital), not special cultural advantages. The analyses of Krugman, Young, and others showed that growth in Asian productivity was not any higher than in the OECD countries or, for that matter, in Latin America and other developing regions.* Moreover, they asserted that, as the returns to factor accumulation

diminished, growth rates in Asia would also fall.

More specifically, the critique of the Asian "miracle" suggested that four key trends accounted for most of the growth in Asia.

1. Rising labor force participation rates, especially among women, accounted for as much as 1 to 1.5 percentage points of the growth rates in the region.
2. Rapid rises in educational attainment improved the quality of the labor force. In 1960 only one-quarter of the labor force in countries like Korea and Taiwan had a secondary or higher education. By the 1990s this proportion had risen to almost 70 percent.
3. High and rising investment rates accounted for 40 to 70 percent of the high growth rates. In Singapore and Korea the investment-to-GDP ratio quadrupled from 1960 to 1990.
4. The movement of workers from agriculture to manufacturing also played a critical role in success. Employment in manufacturing rose 1.5 to 2.5 times faster than population growth during the last 35 years.

Proponents of the Asian "miracle" pointed out that the large number of regional success stories suggested that there were common attributes shared by these countries: high rates of investment in human and physical capital; macroeconomic stability; and relatively low levels of trade, price,

*Alwyn Young, "Lessons From the East Asian NICS: a Contrarian View," National Bureau of Economic Research, Working Paper No. 4482.

and exchange rate distortions. Most important, they claimed that the outward orientation of these economies and their integration into the global economy had been the key to continued high rates of return on investment. In the open economies of Asia, returns from investment were likely to stay high longer because they were servicing worldwide demand.

Nevertheless, some of the more thoughtful proponents of Asian growth conceded that little of the growth in Singapore, Malaysia, and Indonesia was a result of innovation and that these countries faced an "innovation challenge." Still, they maintained that, while growth was likely to slow down, in the worst-

case scenario it would only decelerate by a couple of percentage points.

The Asian financial crisis resulted in deep recessions in many of the fast-growing East Asian economies, including Thailand, Malaysia, South Korea, Indonesia, and Hong Kong. Critics of the Asian "miracle" saw this as a vindication of their point of view. However, this may be unfair. The crisis was triggered by a combination of poor macroeconomic policies, volatile capital flows, poorly regulated banks, and crony capitalism that led to a surge in speculative investments during the early 1990s. It is true that the high rates of investment during the late stages of the "miracle" years were either

wasted—on stock market or property speculation—or used inefficiently—to add capacity in industries where there was already a global capacity glut. Nevertheless, the other building blocks of Asia's success (higher educational attainment, greater labor force participation, and so on) were not causes of the crisis and in fact helped to set the stage for a return to rapid growth in 1999 and 2000.

Asia's growth was not miraculous. However, the Asian economies did many of the things that economic theory suggests will boost growth. The challenge for Asia over the next few decades is to build on its successes and learn from its failures.

■ EXPANDED RESPONSIBILITY OF FEDERAL LABORATORIES

The federal government could support additional civilian R & D by initiating and expanding relevant work in its own laboratories. While this approach has the advantage of being direct and selective, there are great problems when R & D is conducted by organizations that are not in close touch with the production and marketing of the product. It is very important that there be unimpeded flows of information and good coordination of R & D on the one hand, and production and marketing on the other.

IMPORTANCE OF INVESTMENT IN PLANT AND EQUIPMENT

Since investment in plant and equipment accounts for a relatively large proportion of the cost of many innovations, measures which encourage investment are likely to encourage innovation. And since the profitability of R & D is dependent on the profitability of the entire business venture of which the R & D is a part, measures that reduce the after-tax costs to the firm of plant and equipment are likely to increase the profitability of R&D.

Encouragement of investment in plant and equipment also is likely to increase the rate of diffusion of new techniques, and

257

How widespread was the productivity boom of the late 1990s?

Information technology stimulated productivity growth in the late 1990s.

Starting in 1990 there was an acceleration in the trend rate of growth of investment in equipment. From 1960 to 1990 spending on this type of investment grew at a steady 6 percent a year. In the 1990s that growth rate doubled to 12 percent a year. Most of this faster growth was due to the spread of PCs and the Internet.

The impact of this acceleration in investment on productivity was felt with a lag. In the first half of the 1990s, productivity growth was 1.75 percent annually, unchanged from the rate in the 1970s and 1980s. However, in the second half of the 1990s, productivity growth accelerated to 2.3 percent, and the rate in 1998 and 1999 was an even higher 2.8 percent.

The pervasiveness and sustainability of this productivity boom became hotly debated topics. On the one hand were the proponents of the "new economy" and "new paradigms," who believed that the U.S. economy was in the midst of a technological revolution with far-reaching and long-lasting ramifications for productivity growth and living standards.

On the other hand there were skeptics. Chief among these was Robert Gordon, professor of economics at Northwestern University. In a study released in 1999, he showed that all of the surge in productivity was due to gains in the high-tech sectors. Thus, computer hardware and software manufacturers and related businesses had achieved productivity gains of more than 40 percent. However, in the rest of the economy, productivity growth was no higher than the rate in the 1970s and 1980s—1.75 percent.

Most mainstream economists found themselves somewhere in between these two extreme views. While not disputing Gordon's methodology, they questioned the overall quality of the productivity data, especially in the services sector. Most economists believed that the acceleration of productivity was reasonably widespread among a large number of industries (in fact research at the Federal Reserve confirmed this) but were quick to point out that there was no guarantee that the productivity boom would last. Some even raised an intriguing prospect. If Professor Gordon's estimates were correct, then the potential for higher and more pervasive productivity gains throughout the U.S. economy were high and the productivity boom still had a long way to go before it ran out of steam.

thus increase the rate of growth of productivity. Many new techniques cannot be employed unless new plant or equipment is constructed and utilized. Thus public policies that encourage investment are likely to encourage both innovation and the diffusion of new technology.

Recent studies suggest that the amount that a country invests in machinery has an important influence on its rate of growth of per capita output. During 1965 to 1980, countries that invested relatively heavily in equipment (like Japan) tended to expand output per capita more rapidly than countries (like Argentina) that invested relatively little in equipment. Investments in structures seem to have had far less effect on a country's rate of productivity growth than investments in equipment. One reason why countries with high productivity growth rates tend to invest more in equipment than countries with low productivity growth rates is that the former countries have lower equipment prices than do the latter countries. Some economists believe that one key to raising a country's productivity growth rate is to increase its investment in equipment.

Relative to countries like Japan and Germany, the United States has tended to devote a low percentage of its output to plant and equipment. For example, in the 1970s, the United States devoted about 15 percent of its output to plant and equipment, whereas Germany devoted about 20 percent and Japan devoted about 25 percent. This factor is often cited as a reason why the rate of growth of per capita output has been lower in the United States than in Japan and Germany. However, recent evidence suggests that at least in the 1990s the United States used its plant and equipment more efficiently than Germany or Japan. In other words, the productivity of its capital was higher than any other country.

IMPORTANCE OF THE GENERAL ECONOMIC CLIMATE

Broad economic policies can have a major impact on innovation. One of the strongest influences on technological innovation is the general economic climate; measures that encourage economic growth, saving and investment, and price stability are quite likely to enhance our technological position. Indeed, improvements in our general economic climate may have more impact on the state of U.S. technology than many of the specific measures that have been proposed to stimulate technological change.

As an illustration, consider the effects of the high rate of inflation in the United States during the late 1970s and early 1980s. Inflation that is high on the average tends to be very variable in its rate; this reduces the efficiency of the price system as a mechanism for coordinating economic activity. In particular, economists, both liberals and conservatives, worry about the effect of high rates of inflation on investment. Thus Washington consultant Robert Nathan has stated: "There are many serious consequences of an economic, social, and political nature flowing from high rates of inflation. Perhaps its most clearly identifiable negative impact has to do with investment. High interest rates, . . . the tendency of government policies to fight inflation with recessions, the drop in the value of the dollar, all relate to inflation and all serve to discourage new investment."

Supply-side economics and the tax cut of 1981

In the late 1970s and early 1980s, some economists advocated tax reductions in order to stimulate national output. Their views came to be known as **supply-side economics,** and they came to be known as supply siders. Their views received considerable attention when some of them received high-level posts in the Reagan administration. The supply siders played an important role in formulating and helping to push through the very large tax cut passed in August 1981.

They advocated cuts in taxes on labor income on the grounds that people would then work longer and harder. Many economists are skeptical of this proposition. The available evidence seems to indicate that the hours worked by prime-age males would not be affected much by tax changes. But the amount of work done by married women seems more responsive to changes in tax rates. (If the marginal tax rate—the proportion of an extra dollar of income paid in taxes—is high, some women feel it is not worthwhile to work outside the home.)

The supplysiders also advocated reductions in taxes on capital income. For example, they called for cuts in taxes on dividends, interest income, and capital gains (capital gains are increases in the value of assets). In their view, such cuts would encourage additional saving. Although economists agree that saving and investment tend to promote the growth of an economy, there is considerable controversy over the extent to which saving is influenced by tax cuts. Early studies of consumption and saving found saving behavior to be relatively insensitive to changes in the rate of return that savers receive. (That is, if people can obtain a 10 percent annual return from their savings in banks and elsewhere, they may not save much more than if they can obtain only 5 percent.) More recent studies challenge this conclusion, but critics respond that the 1981 tax cut did not increase the percent of total income devoted to saving.

Some supplysiders argued that the tax burden had been so high that further increases in the marginal tax rate would result in lower, not higher, total tax revenue. To explain why they believed this to be true, they used the **Laffer curve,** which relates the amount of income tax revenue collected by the government to the marginal tax rate. According to Arthur Laffer (after whom the curve was named), tax revenues will be zero if the tax rate is zero. This is indisputable. Also, he points out that tax revenues will be zero if the marginal tax rate is 100 percent.

Why? Because if the government takes all the income in taxes, an individual has no incentive to earn taxable income.

According to the Laffer curve (shown below), the maximum tax revenue is reached when the tax rate is at some intermediate level between 0 and 100 percent. This level is *a*. According to Laffer, U.S. tax rates already had reached or exceeded this level. Many other economists denied this. Although they admitted that a reduction in tax rates could reduce the incentive to cheat on taxes and to find tax loopholes (as well as encourage people to work harder and save more), they felt that Laffer's evidence was too weak to support his conclusions. It seems fair to say that there is considerable uncertainty about the shape of the Laffer curve and where the United States is located on it. Even the existence and usefulness of such a curve is a matter of dispute.

Despite academic skepticism, supply-side tax cuts have continued to be a

Of course, very high unemployment rates, as well as very high inflation rates, will tend to discourage innovation. When sales are depressed and the future looks grim, the climate for innovation is not bright. Neither severe and prolonged recession nor double-digit inflation constitutes a benign climate for industrial innovation. The long expansion, low inflation, and low unemployment rate in the 1990s helped to boost investment and productivity.

EXPLORING FURTHER

SUPPLY-SIDE GOVERNMENT POLICIES AND THE AGGREGATE SUPPLY CURVE

It is clear that rightward shifts of the aggregate supply curve are likely to result in more output and a quelling of inflationary pressures (see Figure 11.1). Since these are desirable goals, it is not surprising that government policies have often emphasized measures designed to push the aggregate supply curve outward and to the

FIGURE 11.1

Effect of a Shift to the Right in the Aggregate Supply Curve

If the short-run aggregate supply curve shifts to the right, the result will be increased real output (Q' rather than Q) and a lower price level (P' rather than P). In the early 1980s, there was much discussion of supply-side policies to achieve such a shift in the aggregate supply curve. Of course, the emphasis was on shifting the long-run aggregate supply curve as well as the short-run aggregate supply curve.

261

right. This emphasis on the aggregate supply curve is not new; in fact, in 1776 Adam Smith recognized the importance of such shifts in the aggregate supply curve, although he did not couch his discussion in those terms. But in the late 1970s and early 1980s, much more talk was heard about the supply side—that is, shifts in the short-run (and long-run) aggregate supply curve—than in previous decades (see Case Study 11.3).

When the Reagan administration took office, it pushed through Congress a number of measures that it felt would help to shift the aggregate supply curve to the right. In particular, the 25 percent cut in the personal income tax and the accelerated depreciation of plant and equipment (both included in the 1981 tax bill) were supposed to further this aim. According to the administration, the important thing was to encourage people and firms to work, invest, and take prudent risks. There has been considerable controversy inside and outside the economics profession as to the effectiveness and side effects of some of these tax changes. All that we want to emphasize here is that the Reagan administration promoted measures to shift the aggregate supply curve.

REVIEW AND PRACTICE

■ SUMMARY

1 Compared to other major industrial countries, the U.S. rate of growth of per capita output generally has been impressive over the past century, because of rapid technological change, increases in education and training, investment in plant and equipment, plentiful natural resources, and our social and entrepreneurial climate.

2 Since the late 1960s, the United States has experienced a notable slowdown in its rate of increase of output per hour of labor. Among the factors cited in the 1970s as being responsible for the slowdown were:

1. The increase in the proportion of youths and women in the labor force
2. The reduction in the rate of growth of the capital-labor ratio
3. Increased government regulation
4. The reduction in the proportion of GDP devoted to research and development

The reversal of some of these trends in the 1990s helped to boost productivity growth in the second half of the decade.

3 In recent years, some observers have asserted that the productivity slowdown is due in part to a decline in the rate of innovation in the United States. The R & D tax credits, federal R & D grants and contracts, and expanded work by federal laboratories are among the measures that have been adopted or proposed to help deal with whatever underinvestment in R & D exists.

4 Investment in plant and equipment is an important factor that can raise productivity substantially. In the United States, investment in plant and equipment (as a percentage of output) has been considerably lower than in other major industrialized countries, such as Germany and Japan.

5 One of the strongest influences on the rate of innovation is the general economic climate. Measures that encourage economic growth, saving and investment, and price stability are likely to enhance our technological position.

＊6 The Reagan administration pushed through Congress some very large tax cuts in 1981; the intention was to shift the aggregate supply curve to the right. This was part of the emphasis at that time on supply-side economics.

■ PROBLEMS AND QUESTIONS

1 According to the available evidence, Japanese firms devote a larger percentage of their R & D expenditures to new processes (rather than new products) than U.S. firms do. What advantages accrue to firms that do considerable research into their own productive processes, rather than leave this work to equipment manufacturers and input suppliers?

2 Did the United States have a technological lead over many other industrialized countries in the nineteenth century? In the twentieth century? If so, what were some of the factors that were responsible?

3 One of the most important determinants of the extent of the economic impact of a new technique like the industrial robot is its rate of diffusion. Why is the rate of diffusion of a new technique so important? What influences the rate of diffusion?

4 Must increases in the rate of technological change result in increases in aggregate unemployment? Why or why not?

5 "There is a role for government policy in financing technological progress because the full benefits of research are rarely captured solely by the firm or individual undertaking the research. Rather, additional benefits accrue to society as a whole."† Why does this imply that the government should support research and development?

■ KEY TERMS

technological change

research and development

innovation

supply-side economics

Laffer curve

■ VIEWPOINT FOR ANALYSIS

On December 9, 1992, Daniel Goldin, head of the National Aeronautics and Space Administration, gave a speech in Arlington, Virginia, in which he said: "Our failure to embrace new technology is killing us. Technology is a perishable product. If technology is invented but not used, it's like it doesn't really exist. It's like the tree that fell in the forest that no one heard. Except our competitors have been listening, and are integrating new technology faster than we are."‡

(a) Should firms have sole responsibility for deciding which new technologies are to be commercialized and when? Why or why not? At present, do firms have sole responsibility of this sort in the United States?

---

*The starred item refers to material covered in Exploring Further.

†*Economic Report of the President,* 1990, p. 112.

‡*Vital Speeches,* January 15, 1993, p. 203.

(b) What sorts of programs can the federal and state governments adopt to encourage the application and commercialization of new technologies? What are the potential pitfalls of such programs? What are the potential benefits?

(c) Did the Clinton administration's approach to technology policy differ from that of the Bush administration? If so, in what ways, and which approach do you favor?

CHAPTER 12

Surpluses, Deficits, Public Debt, and the Federal Budget

LEARNING OBJECTIVES

In this chapter, you should learn:

■ The issues concerning a balanced federal budget

■ The significance of the structural deficit

■ The nature and effects of the national debt

■ The fiscal policies employed in the United States in recent decades

Budget deficit

Budget surplus

Regardless of who occupies the White House, there are controversies over the federal budget. Every candidate, Democrat or Republican, seems to be concerned. A perennial question that arises is: Should the federal government balance its budget? One purpose of this chapter is to answer this question.

In the mid-1990s the **budget deficit**—that is, the difference between federal expenditures and federal revenue—was huge. (In 1996, it was about $174 billion.) During the 1980s, there was a sharp increase in both the deficit and the national debt (the amount owed by the federal government). The rise in both the deficit and the debt rekindled the controversy about how government spending should be financed and whether the federal budget should be balanced. In the late 1990s, with the economy booming, the deficits had turned into surpluses. A **budget surplus** occurs when revenues are larger than expenditures. There were new arguments about what to do with these surpluses. In this chapter we consider under what circumstances the government's budget should or should not be balanced and how the deficit or surplus should be measured. We also discuss how deficits can be financed, the impact of the national debt, and how surpluses should be used.

HOW BIG ARE U.S. BUDGET SURPLUSES OR DEFICITS?

To begin with, it is important to be clear regarding the size of the surplus or deficit. Obviously, the size of the deficit or surplus must be related to the size of the economy. A $175 billion surplus or deficit means one thing if a country's GDP is $100 billion and quite

265

FIGURE 12.1

Federal Deficit and Surplus as a Percentage of GDP, 1960–99

The federal deficit increased from about 1 percent of GDP in the 1960s to about 2 percent in the 1970s to about 4 or 5 percent in the 1980s and early 1990s. However, by the late 1990s the budget was in surplus.

another thing if its GDP is $10 trillion. Thus a surplus or deficit that would be huge for a tiny country like Monaco would be insignificant for a large country like the United States.

One way to relate the size of the deficit to GDP is to express the deficit as a percentage of GDP. Figure 12.1 shows that the deficit increased from about 1 percent of GDP in the 1960s to about 2 percent in the 1970s to about 4 or 5 percent in the 1980s and early 1990s. Clearly, there was a substantial increase in the deficit, relative to GDP.[1] By 1999, however, the budget had a surplus of about 1.5 percent of GDP.

CONTROVERSIES OVER DEFICITS

Are budget deficits really such a bad thing? This question has been raised repeatedly. In 1984, there was a public fracas within the Reagan administration over the need to reduce the deficit. According to Martin Feldstein, then chairperson of President Ronald Reagan's Council of Economic Advisers, the deficits of the early 1980s were very dangerous to the long-term health of the economy. If they were allowed to continue, they would push up interest rates and result in a crowding-out of private investment in plant and

---

[1] However, not all economists believed that these measurements were correct. The late Robert Eisner of Northwestern University argued that, when adjusted for inflation, the budget deficit was smaller than it appeared when stated in nominal terms. For these and other reasons, he believed that fiscal policy was not as effective as it could be. For example, in his view, the reported deficit in 1980 of $61 billion was actually an adjusted surplus of almost $8 billion. However, Eisner's views were controversial and failed to comfort the many people who were concerned about the size and persistence of recent federal budget deficits.

equipment. Also, U.S. exports would be hurt because high U.S. interest rates would push up the value of the dollar relative to other currencies, and thus make our exports more expensive to foreign purchasers. For these and other reasons, Feldstein (and many other economists) were extremely worried about the deficit.

In contrast, Donald Regan, who in 1984 was secretary of the Treasury, played down the importance of the deficit. In his view, deficits do not push up interest rates and result in an overvaluation of the dollar relative to other currencies. In part, his arguments seemed to be based on studies carried out by some supply-side economists (see Case Study 11.3), including members of the Treasury staff. But most economists did not buy these arguments. If the government increases its demands for credit because of the very large deficits, the interest rate (which is the price of borrowing money) will rise.

ARE BUDGET DEFICITS INFLATIONARY?

One reason why the public is concerned about deficits is that they are often thought to cause inflation. Whether this is the case depends on how the deficits are financed. One way the government can finance a deficit is to print new money. In other words, the Fed can increase the money supply, and thus enable the government to use the additional money to pay for the portion of its expenditures not covered by tax revenues. If deficits are financed in this way and if the consequent increases in the money supply are substantial, the result may be inflation. This follows from the fact, stressed repeatedly in previous chapters, that substantial increases in the money supply may cause inflation.

But recent deficits in the United States have been financed largely by government borrowing. Every so often, the Treasury sells a few billion dollars worth of IOUs (bonds, notes, or bills). To sell its securities, the Treasury must offer potential buyers a high enough rate of return to make them an attractive investment. Suppose that the Treasury issues today $1 billion of one-year securities to cover a deficit of $1 billion. If the rate of interest is 10 percent, it must pay the $1 billion plus interest of $100 million at the end of one year. To pay this $1.1 billion to the holders of these securities, it must borrow $1.1 billion a year from now. If it again has to pay 10 percent interest, it will owe $1.21 billion (the principal of $1.1 billion plus $.11 billion in interest) a year hence. Thus, the amount that the government has to borrow to finance a $1 billion deficit today grows over time.

However, so long as the government does not create new money to finance the deficit, the result need not be inflationary. But what if the government sells its securities to the Federal Reserve, rather than to households and firms? In this case, when the Fed purchases the securities from the government, it creates new money to buy them. (Recall from Chapter 9 that the Fed increases bank reserves when it buys government securities. But unlike the case considered on page 217, the Fed purchases the securities from the government, not from General Motors.) This increase in the money supply results in an increase in aggregate demand, which eventually pushes up the price level.

Going a step further, Thomas Sargent of Stanford University and Neil Wallace of the University of Minnesota have pointed out that, even if deficits are not financed right away by the creation of new money, they may have inflationary consequences. As pointed out in the paragraph before last, the interest payments resulting from a growing national debt can become very large. Suppose that investors become convinced that at some point in the reasonably near future the level of government debt will have become so big that the interest payments will constitute a disturbingly large proportion of the government's budget. If they think that the government will resort to the creation of new money at that time to finance all or part of the deficit, they are likely to fear that there will be substantial inflation then.

Faced with this prospect, investors may insist on a relatively high interest rate on government securities to compensate them for the anticipated inflation, and they may try to hold less money, since the value of money is expected to fall. At the same time, they may increase their demand for goods, thus pushing up the price level now. The result is that, even though the deficit is not financed right away by the creation of new money, there may be inflation.

But if the deficit is kept within reasonable bounds, this situation need not occur. So long as the deficit is small enough so that investors remain convinced that the government is willing and able to keep the money supply under proper control, there need not be a problem of this sort. Even if the deficit is very large, it need not occur if people believe that deficits of this magnitude are only temporary and that in a relatively short time the budget will be brought into closer balance.

DO BUDGET DEFICITS CROWD OUT PRIVATE INVESTMENT?

Another reason why people are concerned about large budget deficits is that they fear that the government's deficit spending may result in a substantial cut in investment spending by the private sector. In other words, they fear that government budget deficits may crowd out private investment. Why may this occur? Because large government borrowing may push up the interest rate, which in turn may cut private investment.

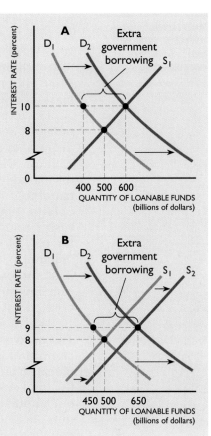

FIGURE 12.2

How Government Borrowing Can Crowd Out Private Investment

If the government enters the market for loanable funds to finance its $200 billion deficit, the demand curve for loanable funds shifts to the right from D_1 to D_2, with the result that the interest rate rises from 8 to 10 percent and the quantity of funds borrowed by the private sector drops from $500 billion to $400 billion, as shown in panel A. If the extra government expenditure increases national output (and disposable income), the amount of saving may increase, thus pushing the supply curve to the right from S_1 to S_2, as shown in panel B. The result is that the interest rate rises only to 9 percent and the quantity of funds borrowed by the private sector falls only to $450 billion, not $400 billion.

Crowding-out effect

To illustrate how the **crowding-out effect** can occur, consider panel A of Figure 12.2, which shows the private sector's demand and supply curves for loanable funds. The demand curve for loanable funds, D_1, shows the total quantity of loanable funds demanded by firms and households at each interest rate. (Recall from Chapter 5 that the interest rate is the price paid for the use of loanable funds.) The supply curve for loanable funds, S_1, shows the total quantity of loanable funds supplied by households, firms, and others at each interest rate. The equilibrium level of the interest rate, where the quantity of loanable funds demanded equals the quantity supplied, is 8 percent, and the equilibrium amount of funds borrowed for all purposes is $500 billion.

Now suppose that the government, which formerly did not have to borrow, increases its spending by $200 billion and that the spending increase is financed entirely by borrowing. The result, as shown in panel A of Figure 12.2, is that the demand curve for loanable funds shifts to the right (from D_1 to D_2); this reflects the government's demand for the additional $200 billion of funds. Because of this shift of the demand curve, the equilibrium interest rate rises to 10 percent, and the quantity of funds borrowed increases to $600 billion. But $200 billion of these funds go to the government, which means that the private sector borrows only $400 billion. Thus the private sector borrows, and hence invests, $100 billion less than it did before the government entered the market for loanable funds to finance its $200 billion deficit.

However, this analysis may be incomplete. If the extra $200 billion of government expenditure increases national output (and disposable income), the amount of saving may increase (in accord with our discussion on page 121). Consequently, the supply curve for loanable funds may shift to the right (from S_1 to S_2) as shown in panel B of Figure 12.2, with the result that the interest rate rises only to 9 percent, and the private sector borrows, and hence invests, $450 billion (rather than the $400 billion in panel A). Thus the private sector invests $50 billion (rather than the $100 billion in panel A) less than it did before the government set out to borrow $200 billion. Under these circumstances, a smaller amount of private investment is crowded out than in panel A, where the increased government expenditure did not increase national output.

Why does it matter if some private investment is crowded out? The answer is that, if private investment is crowded out, the total amount of capital in the economy will be smaller than otherwise. (Recall from Chapter 3 that net investment equals the change in the total amount of capital.) And a smaller capital stock means that our population will have fewer and poorer tools to work with, and thus less output. Consequently, large and persistent budget deficits really can harm future generations because they may result in a smaller total amount of capital's being passed on to our descendants.

In fact, however, private investment in the United States has not fallen substantially in the face of the large deficits of the 1980s, because foreigners have provided much of the funds. For example, the Japanese have purchased large amounts of our government securities. But what this means is that future generations of Americans, while they will have a capital stock that is not much reduced, will owe a substantial amount to foreigners. Obviously, when the government borrows from abroad, purchasing power is transferred from foreigners to us when the borrowing occurs but from us to foreigners when we pay interest on the debt and repay the principal.

Another effect of the high interest rates induced by large deficits has been an increase in the value of the dollar relative to other currencies. This is because foreign investors have had to buy dollars in order to purchase U.S. securities, which (because of our high interest rates) have been attractive to them. Due to the swollen demand for dollars, the value of a dollar (relative to the Japanese yen or German mark) has tended to rise. One consequence of this has been that U.S. exports have tended to fall (because U.S. goods have become more expensive relative to foreign goods) and U.S. imports have tended to rise (because foreign goods have become cheaper relative to U.S. goods). Thus large deficits have tended to depress our net exports.

Finally, under certain circumstances, some economists believe that deficits can increase, not decrease, investment. This is known

Crowding-in effect

as the **crowding-in effect**. The idea is that if the economy is experiencing considerable unemployment, the government's deficit spending may increase national output, and this in turn may increase investment. Of course, the magnitude of this effect depends on how sensitive real GDP is to the extra government spending and on how sensitive investment by the private sector is to whatever increase occurs (on this account) in real GDP. If the economy is at or close to full employment, it is unlikely that this effect will occur, but if the economy is at the pit of a depression, this effect, according to some economists, may overwhelm the crowding-out effect.

THE STRUCTURAL DEFICIT

To see whether fiscal policy is *expansionary* (increasing aggregate demand) or *contractionary* (reducing aggregate demand), people often look at the size of the budget deficit. A large deficit often is viewed as more expansionary than a small one (or a surplus). However, this can be quite misleading since budget deficits can occur because the economy is at less than full employment (that is, the lowest sustainable unemployment rate compatible with reason-

Structural deficit

able price stability). A better measure is the **structural deficit**, which shows the difference between government expenditures and tax revenues that would result if gross domestic product were at its potential, not its actual, level.

For example, consider the situation in 1958 when the Eisenhower administration ran a deficit of over $10 billion. Basically, the reason for this deficit was that, with the unemployment rate at about 7 percent, there was a substantial gap between actual and potential output. Gross domestic product fell from 1957 to 1958, and, as a result, incomes and federal tax collections fell, and the government ran a deficit. But this $10 billion deficit was entirely due to the high level of unemployment the country was experiencing.

Had gross domestic product been at its potential level, there would have been a surplus of about $5 billion in 1958. Incomes and federal tax receipts would all have been higher. Government spending and the tax rates in 1958 were not such as to produce a deficit if output had been at its potential level. On the contrary, if gross domestic product had been at its potential level, tax receipts

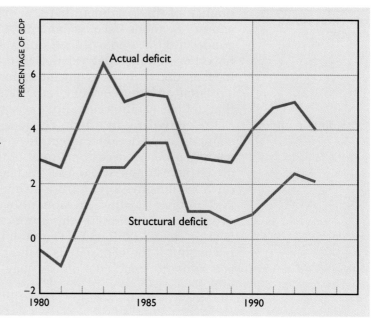

FIGURE 12.3

Structural and Actual Budget Deficits, 1980–93[a]

The structural deficit shows the difference between government expenditure and tax revenue that would result if gross domestic product were at its potential level.

[a]The structural budget deficits have been adjusted for inflation. See source.

Source: Economic Report of the President, 1994.

would have increased so that federal revenues would have exceeded expenditure by about $5 billion.

It is important to distinguish between the structural deficit and the actual deficit. If the actual budget deficit is growing but the structural budget deficit is falling, most economists would feel that fiscal policy is not becoming more expansionary. As you can see in Figure 12.3, the structural deficit can differ substantially from the actual deficit. To understand whether fiscal policy is becoming more expansionary or contractionary, you must understand the difference.

THE NATIONAL DEBT: SIZE AND GROWTH

National debt

As we have seen, when the federal government incurs a deficit, it generally borrows money to cover the difference. The **national debt**—composed of bonds, notes, and other government IOUs of various kinds—is the result of such borrowing. These IOUs are held by individuals, firms, banks, and public agencies. There is a large and very important market for government securities, which are relatively riskless and highly liquid. If you look at the *New York Times* or *Wall Street Journal,* for example, you can find each day the prices at which each of a large number of issues of these bonds, notes, and bills are quoted.

How large is the national debt? In 1999, as shown in Figure

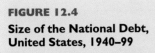

FIGURE 12.4

Size of the National Debt, United States, 1940–99

The national debt, about $5.6 trillion in 1999, grew rapidly in the 1980s and 1990s due to huge government deficits.

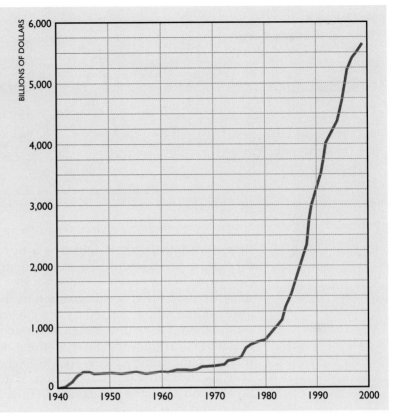

12.4, it was about $5.6 trillion. Without question, this is a huge amount, but it is important to relate the size of the national debt to the size of our national output. After all, a $5.6 trillion debt means one thing if our annual output is $9 trillion, and another thing if our annual output is $900 billion. As a percent of output, the national debt was not much larger in 1999 than in 1939. In 1999, the debt was about 61 percent of output; in 1939, it was about 53 percent of output. The debt—expressed as a percentage of output—is shown in Figure 12.5. Although the figures do not seem to provide any cause for immediate alarm, many economists have warned that there are problems in incurring large deficits of the kind that were responsible for the rapid rate of increase in the debt during the 1980s and early 1990s.[2]

A burden on future generations. Why have people been so agitated about the debt's size? One important reason has been that

[2]Note too that much of the public debt is in the hands of government agencies, not held by the public. For example, in 1999 only about 3.2 trillion dollars was held by the public.

FIGURE 12.5

National Debt as a Percent of National Output, United States, 1929–99

As a percent of national output, the national debt declined steadily from World War II to about 1980. During the 1980s and early 1990s, it increased. Since then, it has begun to fall.

they have felt that the debt was a burden that was being thrust on future generations. To evaluate this idea it is important to recognize that a public debt is not like your debt or mine, which must be paid off at a certain time in the future. In practice, new government debt is issued by the government to pay off maturing public debt. There never comes a time when we must collectively reach into our pockets to pay off the debt. And even if we did pay it off, the same generation would collect as the one that paid. However, as stressed above, the deficits that create the debt can put a burden on future generations if they crowd out private investment, and thus reduce the amount of capital turned over to future generations.

Effects of externally held debt. To the extent that the debt is held by foreigners, we must send goods and services overseas to pay the interest on it. This means that less goods and services are available for our citizens. Thus, if we finance a particular government activity by borrowing from foreigners, the costs may be transferred to future generations, since they must pay the interest. But from the point of view of the world as a whole, the current generation sacrifices goods and services, since the lending country forgoes current goods and services. Also, it must be recognized that if the debt is incurred to purchase capital goods, they may produce enough extra output to cover the interest payments.

Redistribution of income and effects on incentives. Taxes must be collected from the public at large to pay interest to the holders of government bonds, notes, and other obligations. To the extent that the bondholders receiving the interest are wealthier than the public as a whole, there is some redistribution of income from the poor to the rich. To the extent that the taxes needed to obtain the money to pay interest on the debt reduce incentives, the result also may be a smaller national output.

A final word. A postscript should be added regarding the idea that the national debt imposes a burden on future generations. *The principal way in which one generation can impose such a burden on another is by using up some of the country's productive capacity or by failing to add a normal increment in this capacity.* This, of course, is quite different from incurring debt. For example, World War II would have imposed a burden on subsequent generations whether or not the national debt was increased. However it was financed, the war would have meant that our resources had to be used for tanks and war planes rather than for keeping up and expanding our productive capacity during 1941 to 1945. And this imposed a real burden on Americans living after 1945—as well, of course, as those living during the war.

THE POLITICAL ECONOMY OF BUDGET DEFICITS

One reason why it has been so difficult to reduce the government's large budget deficits is that politicians have been extremely reluctant to favor tax hikes, which seldom are popular with voters. Another reason is that Congress and the president have found it difficult to agree on the sorts of government expenditures that should be cut.

The Reagan administration was opposed to tax increases and in favor of spending reductions but not cuts in defense spending. In 1987 and 1988, Democrats tried to pin the responsibility for the huge deficit on President Reagan, in particular because of his unwillingness to raise taxes or cut defense spending. Republicans in turn tried to pin the responsibility on congressional Democrats who resisted cuts in spending on domestic programs.

In late 1990, President Bush, abandoning his opposition to new taxes, engaged in a long series of negotiations with Congress to try to reduce the deficit. The result was an increase in the income tax rate for highest-income families from 28 to 31 percent, a hike in taxes on cigarettes, beer, and wine, and other tax increases, as well as statements that spending cuts would occur. However, government forecasts indicated that the budget deficit was likely to be over $300 billion in 1991, due in part to the recession.

When President Clinton took office in 1993, one of his first steps was to increase taxes. Income taxes on the well-to-do increased substantially, with the top income tax rate going up to about 40 percent. However, while this measure, which only narrowly passed in Congress, cut the deficit, it by no means eliminated it. In 1995 the deficit was still $200 billion. However, sustained strong economic growth in the late 1990s accomplished what the Reagan, Bush, and early Clinton administrations had failed to do—balance the budget.

ALTERNATIVE PHILOSOPHIES REGARDING THE FEDERAL BUDGET

■ SHOULD THE BUDGET BE BALANCED ANNUALLY?

At least three philosophies concerning the government budget are worthy of detailed examination. The first says that *the government's budget should be balanced each and every year.* This is the philosophy that generally prevailed, here and abroad, until a few decades ago. Superficially, it seems reasonable. After all, won't a family or firm go bankrupt if it continues to spend more than it takes in? Why should the government be any different? However, the truth is that the government has economic capabilities, powers, and responsibilities that are entirely different from those of any family or firm, and it is misleading—sometimes even pernicious—to assume that what is sensible for a family or firm is also sensible for the government.

If this policy of balancing the budget is accepted, the government cannot use fiscal policy as a tool to stabilize the economy. Indeed, if the government attempts to balance its budget each year, it may make unemployment or inflation worse rather than better. For example, suppose that severe unemployment occurs because of a drop in national output. Since incomes drop, tax receipts drop as well. Thus, if the government attempts to balance its budget, it must cut its spending and/or increase tax rates, both of which may tend to lower, not raise, national output. On the other hand, suppose that inflation occurs because spending increases too rapidly. Since incomes increase, tax receipts increase too. Thus, for the government to balance its budget, it must increase its spending and/or decrease tax rates, either of which may tend to raise, not lower, spending.

Despite these considerations, there has been a considerable amount of political support for a constitutional amendment to mandate a balanced federal budget. No doubt, the federal government, through inappropriate fiscal or monetary policies, has frequently been responsible for excessive inflation or unemployment. Some economists go so far as to say that the real problem is how to prevent the government from creating disturbances, rather than how to use the government budget (and monetary policy) to offset disturbances arising from the private sector. But for the reasons discussed above, most economists would not go so far as to conclude that the government should balance its budget each year.

■ SHOULD THE BUDGET BE BALANCED OVER THE BUSINESS CYCLE?

A second budgetary philosophy says that *the government's budget should be balanced over the course of each business cycle.* As we have seen in previous chapters, the rate of growth of national output tends to behave cyclically. It tends to increase for a while, then drop, increase, then drop, and so on. Unemployment also tends to ebb and flow in a similar cyclical fashion. According to this second budgetary policy, the government is not expected to balance its budget each year but is expected to run a big enough surplus during periods of high employment to offset the deficit it runs during the ensuing period of excessive unemployment. This policy seems to give the government enough flexibility to run the deficits or surpluses that, according to many economists, may be needed to stabilize the economy, while at the same time allaying any public fear of a chronically unbalanced budget. It certainly seems to be a neat way to reconcile the government's use of fiscal policy to promote noninflationary full employment with the public's uneasiness over chronically unbalanced budgets.

Unfortunately, however, it does contain one fundamental flaw. There is no reason to believe that the size of the deficits required to eliminate excessive unemployment will equal the size of the surpluses required to moderate the subsequent inflation. Suppose that national output falls sharply and causes severe and prolonged unemployment, then regains its full-employment level only briefly, and then falls again. In such a case, the deficits incurred to get the economy back to full employment are likely to exceed by far the surpluses run during the brief period of full employment. Thus there would be no way to stabilize the economy without running an unbalanced budget over the course of this business cycle. If this policy were adopted and the government attempted to balance the budget over the course of each business cycle, it might interfere with an effective fiscal policy designed to promote full employment with stable prices.

■ SHOULD THE BUDGET BE BALANCED AT ALL?

Finally, a third budgetary philosophy says that *the government's budget should be set so as to promote whatever attainable combination of unemployment and inflation seems socially optimal,* even if this means that the budget is unbalanced over considerable periods of time. Proponents of this policy argue that, although it may mean a continual growth in the public debt, the problems caused

Should Eisenhower have tried to balance the budget?

Richard M. Nixon

1958 was a recession year in the United States. Tax revenues declined. Unemployment compensation payments rose. The budget deficit for the year approached $10 billion.

The large deficit helped to get the recovery going, but when the recession was over, President Dwight Eisenhower set out to recoup his losses by balancing the budget. As the president forged ahead with his plan for a budget surplus, voices were raised in warning. Some of these warnings came from a group of top business executives, the Committee for Economic Development. Another person urging caution in the drive for a big surplus was Vice President Richard Nixon. During the recession of 1958, Nixon had urged a tax cut to stimulate the economy. His advice was not heeded. Now, as he prepared to run for president in 1960, he urged a more expansionary budget policy. Again his advice was rejected because the administration was more concerned about fighting inflation. Eisenhower in his last year in office was willing to take the politi-

cal risk of pinching off growth. He assumed that the next administration would be able to carry on with the expansionary policy—a next administration that was expected to be Republican.

By the summer of 1960, the recovery had ground to a halt, stopping well short of the goal of full employment. As the ranks of the jobless increased, Democratic presidential candidate John Kennedy was helped politically, while Richard Nixon watched the economy slide back into recession and victory slip through his fingers. Historians still argue whether it was the budget surplus and the unexpected recession that cost him the victory; but most economists agree that a budget deficit in 1960 would have generated more jobs and more growth in the economy.

by a moderate growth in the public debt are small when compared to the social costs of unemployment and inflation.

CHANGES IN PUBLIC ATTITUDES

Certainly, the history of the past fifty years has been characterized by enormous changes in the nation's attitude toward the government budget. Fifty years ago, the prevailing attitude was that the government's budget should be balanced. The emergence of the Keynesian theory of the determination of national output and employment shook this attitude, at least to the point where it became respectable to advocate a balanced budget over the business cycle, rather than in each year. In many circles, persistent deficits of moderate size were viewed with no alarm.

In the late 1970s and early 1980s, there was some movement back toward earlier views favoring balanced budgets. Conservatives emphasized the usefulness of the balanced budget as a device to limit government spending, which they regarded as excessive. The public tended to blame very high rates of inflation on large deficits. Although neither political party was prepared (even remotely) to renounce deficits, considerable lip service was paid to the desirability of a balanced budget. For example, in August 1982, the Senate approved a constitutional amendment requiring a balanced budget, while at the same time the government was running a deficit of over $100 billion! In the late 1990s with the budget in surplus, the debate shifted and the big fiscal policy question became what to do with the surplus: cut taxes, raise spending, or pay down the national debt (see Case Study 12.2).

■ THE FEDERAL BUDGETARY PROCESS

Federal budget

Determining how much the federal government should spend is a mammoth undertaking, involving literally thousands of people and hundreds of thousands of hours of labor. Decisions on expenditures are part of the budgetary process. The **federal budget** is a statement of the government's anticipated expenditures and revenues. The federal budget is for a fiscal year, from October 1 to September 30.

About 15 months before the beginning of a particular fiscal year, the various agencies of the federal government begin to prepare their program proposals for that year. Then they make detailed budget requests which the president, with his Office of Management and Budget, goes over. Since the agencies generally want more than the president wants to spend, he usually cuts down their requests.

In January (preceding the beginning of the fiscal year), the president submits his budget to Congress. Congress then spends many months in intensive deliberation and negotiation. Congressional committees concerned with particular areas like defense or education recommend changes in the president's budget. The Congressional Budget Office, headed in 2000 by Dan Crippen, makes various economic analyses to help senators and representatives evaluate alternative programs.

■ THE FEDERAL TAX LEGISLATIVE PROCESS

It is one thing for the federal government to decide how much to spend and on what; it is another to raise the money to underwrite these programs. This section describes how the federal government decides how much to tax. Of course, this problem is not solved from scratch every year. Instead, the government takes the existing tax structure and changes it from time to time as desirable.

What should be done with the federal budget surplus?

The National Debt Clock on Forty-second Street in Manhattan

After years of wrangling over how to distribute the pain of deficit cutting (raising taxes or slashing spending), in recent years the president and Congress have had to deal with an easier choice—at least in theory. In reality, the arguments over how to spend the surplus have been at least as contentious as debates about how to cut the deficit.

There are three basic choices about the surplus: (1) spend the money on education, health care, defense, and so on; (2) give the surplus back to the taxpayers in the form of tax cuts; or (3) pay down the national debt and, in effect, use the surplus to replenish the trust funds of the Social Security system.

In the late 1990s and the early 2000s, the pressure to cut taxes and increase spending was muted, in large measure because of the booming economy. In the summer of 1999 the *Wall Street Journal* conducted a survey that asked: "After setting aside two-thirds of the projected surpluses for Social Security and Medicare, what should be done with the rest?* Approximately 33 percent of the respondents voted for a tax cut and 55 percent voted for spending increases. During the presidential primaries in early 2000 the debate focused primarily on the choice between cutting taxes and cutting the national debt, even though the support for the former was limited.

The case for giving the surplus back to taxpayers was argued by supply siders (see Case Study 11.3). They used two types of reasoning. The first was the classic supply-side argument that tax rate reductions will increase incentives to work and save, thereby increasing economic growth. The second was a taxpayer fairness argument that the revenue belongs to the taxpayer and, if the government has no need for it, the government should return it.

Those opposed to tax cuts countered that in light of the booming economy and stock market, it was hard to argue that tax rates in the United States were depressing economic growth. As for the taxpayer fairness argument, giving back the surplus now would only leave a large debt burden for future generations. The issue was really fairness to taxpayers of this generation versus fairness to taxpayers of future generations. Finally, opponents argued that cutting taxes during an economic boom ran the risk of triggering higher inflation. Why not save the option to cut taxes for the next time the economy really needs it—during the next recession?

The case for paying off the debt relied first and foremost on classical fiscal theory, which says that running surpluses and reducing debt adds to national saving, which, in turn, spurs investment and economic growth. Second, proponents of debt repayment reasoned that, given the uncertainties of the business cycle, the surpluses could turn into deficits again in the near future; therefore, why take chances with tax cuts or spending increases?

The opposition to the debt reduction plans came from both sides of the political spectrum. Supply siders argued that raising economic growth (using tax cuts) was a much better way of reducing the debt burden than saving the surplus. Liberal Democrats maintained that accumulating budget surpluses would depress growth and increase unemployment.

In the end, the consensus seemed to coalesce around the public's priorities, namely, modest tax cuts and spending increases, with most of the money's being saved.

*Wall Street Journal, July 29, 1999; p. 1.

Frequently the major initiative leading to a change in the tax laws comes from the president, who requests tax changes in his State of the Union message, his budget message, or a special tax message. Much of the spadework underlying his proposals will have been carried out by the Treasury Department, which includes the Internal Revenue Service.

The proposal of a major tax change generally brings about considerable public debate. Representatives of labor, industry, agriculture, and other economic and social groups present their opinions. Newspaper articles, radio shows, and television commentators analyze the issues. By the time Congress begins to look seriously at the proposal, the battle lines between those who favor the change and those who oppose it are generally clearly drawn. The tax bill incorporating the change is first considered by the Ways and Means Committee of the House of Representatives, a very powerful committee composed of members drawn from both political parties. After public hearings, the committee goes into executive session and reviews each proposed change with its staff and with the Treasury staff. After careful study, the committee arrives at a bill it recommends—though this bill may or may not conform to what the president asked for. Then the bill is referred to the entire House of Representatives for approval. Only rarely is a major tax bill recommended by the committee turned down by the House.

Next, the bill is sent to the Senate. There it is referred to the Finance Committee, which is organized like the House Ways and Means Committee. The Finance Committee also holds hearings, discusses the bill at length, makes changes in it, and sends its version of the bill to the entire Senate, where there frequently is considerable debate. Ultimately, it is brought to a vote. If it does not pass, that ends the process. If it does pass (and if it differs from the House version of the bill, which is generally the case), then a conference committee must be formed to iron out the differences between the House and Senate versions. Finally, when this compromise is worked out, the result must be passed by both houses and sent to the president. The president rarely vetoes a tax bill, although it has occasionally been done.

RECENT U.S. EXPERIENCE WITH FISCAL POLICY AND DEFICITS

It should be evident by now that more is known today about the impact of deficits—and of fiscal policy generally—than at the time when the economy was staggered by the Great Depression. But this does not mean that economists have all (or nearly all) the answers. Enough is known to keep the economy from careening off a bumpy road; avoiding the potholes (some of which are very large) is another matter.

■ THE CARTER YEARS

The hard choices faced by economists in the top councils of government can be demonstrated by a close inspection of attempts in the past twenty years to give the economy a smoother ride. Let's begin with the situation in the Carter years. When Jimmy Carter became president in 1977, the unemployment rate was 6.9 percent and the inflation rate was 6.7 percent. In the face of heightened inflation, fiscal policy did not attempt to rein in the economy very much. The deficit in 1978 was about $30 billion; the structural budget deficit was over $10 billion. Some observers were not sure that the inflation rate could be reduced substantially without a recession. In 1979, there was a continuing debate within the administration and in public over this question. In 1980, there was a very brief recession, but it did little to cool off inflation. As in previous years, the federal government ran a structural budget deficit.

■ THE REAGAN YEARS

When the Reagan administration took office in 1981, it was committed to cut both government expenditures and taxes. In August 1981, the administration pushed through Congress a huge tax cut for both individuals and businesses. At the same time, it reduced federal expenditures (relative to the level that former president Carter had proposed). However, the tax cuts were far in excess of the spending cuts, particularly since reductions in GDP in late 1981 also tended to reduce tax receipts. Thus the administration was faced with record deficits of over $100 billion in fiscal 1982 and $150 billion in fiscal 1983. In early 1982, President Reagan said he would try to cut spending further in an attempt to soak up some of the red ink. But the economy was in a recession (with an unemployment rate of 9 percent) and there was little sympathy on Capitol Hill for further spending cuts. Since inflation had fallen to well under double digits, unemployment once again seemed to be Public Enemy Number One.

In November 1982, the economy pulled out of the recession, and the expansion began. Economists of all schools, but particularly supply-side economists (recall Chapter 11), gave the 1981 tax cut considerable credit for increasing real GDP and reducing unemployment. During 1983 and 1984, both years of healthy expansion, the federal government ran huge deficits of about $200 billion. President Reagan vowed that he would not raise taxes, and proposed cuts in nonmilitary government expenditures. In 1986,

Congress passed a major tax reform bill that lowered tax rates and broadened the tax base by reducing loopholes. In late 1987, after the sharp stock market decline, President Reagan and congressional leaders met to try to find a mutually agreeable way to cut the huge deficits, but limited progress was made.

▨ THE BUSH YEARS

In November 1988, George Bush, then vice president, was elected to the presidency on a platform of "no new taxes." Many critics, here and abroad, doubted that the federal deficit could be reduced without additional tax revenue. During 1989 and 1990, the deficit continued to be about $200 billion. In late 1990, Congress and President Bush agreed to a fiscal package that would reduce the deficit but by no means eliminate it. There were additional taxes, including increased tax rates for high-income families and bigger taxes on cigarettes, beer, and wine. After an expansion of record length, the U.S. economy entered a recession in late 1990, and some observers questioned whether it was a good time to raise taxes.

▨ THE CLINTON YEARS

Bill Clinton, in his campaign for the presidency, promised a tax cut for the middle class and substantial tax increases for the wealthy. After his election, he abandoned the idea of a middle-class tax cut but pressed for an upper-income tax increase. After intricate negotiations with congressional Democrats, he managed to get his plan accepted in 1993 by the narrowest of margins. Also included in his plan was a reduction in government expenditures, but Republicans (none of whom voted for the Clinton plan) argued that these spending cuts were too small (and in some cases, too uncertain). The effect of his plan was to reduce the deficit, which both Democrats and Republicans (as well as supporters of Ross Perot) seemed to favor. In Clinton's second term in office, thanks to the longest U.S. expansion, the budget deficit was eliminated and the United States had a budget surplus for the first time in over 25 years.

REVIEW AND PRACTICE

▨ SUMMARY

I The budget deficit or surplus is the difference between government expenditures and receipts. Many, but not all, economists are concerned about the size and persistence of the deficit.

2 One reason why the public is concerned about deficits is that they are thought to cause inflation. If the government finances the deficit by increasing the money supply, this may well be the case.

3 Many economists believe that the government's deficit spending may result in a significant cut in investment spending by the private sector. In other words, they fear that government budget deficits may crowd out private investment because government borrowing may push up the interest rate and this in turn may reduce private investment.

4 A large deficit is often viewed as being more expansionary than a small one (or a surplus). But this can be misleading because budget deficits may occur because the economy is at less than full employment. A better measure is the structural deficit, which is the difference between government expenditures and tax revenues that would result if gross domestic product were at its potential, not its actual, level.

5 The national debt is the result of the federal government's borrowings to finance deficits. To the extent that the debt is held by foreigners, we must send goods and services overseas to pay the interest on it (as well, of course, as the principal).

6 The spending decisions of the federal government take place in the context of the budgetary process. The president submits his budget, which is a statement of anticipated expenditures and revenues, to Congress, which votes appropriations.

■ PROBLEMS AND QUESTIONS

1 Explain how large budget deficits can discourage investment and inhibit the growth of the nation's stock of capital.

2 "An important advantage of public works as a tool of fiscal policy is that they can be started quickly. An important advantage of tax rate changes is that they almost never get embroiled in partisan politics." Comment and evaluate.

3 "The structural deficit is just a lot of hocum to persuade the public that big deficits are smaller and less inflationary than they really are." Comment and evaluate.

4 According to the 1990 *Economic Report of the President,* "research and experience have demonstrated the great advantages of establishing a credible commitment to a policy plan. Improved credibility, which is enhanced by achieving stated policy goals and consistently following stated principles, can favorably affect expectations."* Does this mean that the federal government should have acted in accord with its professed desire to reduce the budget deficit?

5 In February 1994, President Clinton said, "On August 10, 1993, I signed the historic budget plan that passed several days earlier; it will reduce federal deficits by more than $500 billion."† What difference does it make whether the deficit was cut or not? What are the advantages in cutting it?

■ KEY TERMS

budget deficit	structural deficit
budget surplus	national debt
crowding-out effect	federal budget
crowding-in effect	

Economic Report of the President, 1990, p. 22.

†*Economic Report of the President,* 1994, p. 3.

■ VIEWPOINT FOR ANALYSIS

In the year 63 B.C., the famous Roman orator Cicero said, "The budget should be balanced, the treasury should be refilled, public debt should be reduced, the arrogance of officialdom should be tempered and controlled, and the assistance to foreign lands should be curtailed lest we become bankrupt."*

(a) Would most modern economists agree with Cicero? Why or why not?

(b) Some observers fear that substantial budget deficits will lead inexorably to inflation. Do you agree? Why or why not? Deficits are also thought to result in a crowding-out of private investment. Do you agree? Why or why not?

(c) Why is it important to distinguish between the structural deficit and the actual deficit? Can the former show a surplus while the latter shows a deficit? If so, can you cite a case where this occurred?

*Vital Speeches, July 1, 1993, p. 566.

CHAPTER 13

Monetary Policy, Interest Rates, and Economic Activity

LEARNING OBJECTIVES

In this chapter, you should learn:

■ How the quantity of money affects national output

■ The relationship between the interest rate and the quantity of money

■ The importance and the limitations of the crude quantity theory

■ The Fed's performance in managing the money supply

Just as physicians differ in their treatment of arthritis or cancer, so economists do not see eye to eye on many aspects of monetary policy. In early 2000, the Federal Reserve pushed interest rates up, to the consternation of some economists and to the applause of others. Who cares what the level of interest rates is? Why all the commotion in the press and on television? One purpose of this chapter is to answer this question.

In previous chapters we discussed in general terms the impact of money on the economy. In this chapter we give a more detailed picture of how changes in the quantity of money affect interest rates and economic activity. We also consider how effective monetary policy has been in recent years. To begin with, we consider questions like: What determines the value of money? What factors influence the demand for money, and what factors influence its quantity? What is the relationship between the quantity of money and the price level? What is the relationship between the quantity of money and the level of gross domestic product? To more fully understand the workings of our economy and the nature of our government's economic policies, you must be able to answer these questions.

THE VALUE OF MONEY

Let's go back to one very important point that was mentioned briefly in Chapter 8: There is no gold backing for our money. In other words, there is no way that you can exchange a $10 bill for so many ounces of gold. (If you look at a $10 bill, you will see that it says nothing about what the government will give you in exchange for it.) Currency and demand (and other checkable) deposits are really just debts or IOUs. Currency is the debt of the government, whereas demand deposits are the debts of the banks. Intrinsically, neither currency nor a deposit has any real value. A $10 bill is merely a small piece of paper, and a deposit is merely an entry in a bank's accounts. And, as we have seen, even coins are worth far less as metal than their monetary value.

All this may make you feel a bit uncomfortable. After all, if our coins, currency, demand deposits, and other checkable deposits have little or no intrinsic value, doesn't this mean that they can easily become worthless? To answer this question, we must realize that basically, *money has value because people will accept it in payment for goods and services.* If your college will accept your check in payment for your tuition, and your grocer will accept a $20 bill in payment for your groceries, your demand deposit and your currency have value. You can exchange them for goods and services you want. And your college and your grocer accept this money only because they have confidence that they can spend it for goods and services they want.

■ MONEY'S VALUE DEPENDS ON THE PRICE LEVEL

Thus money is valuable because it will buy things. But how valuable is it? For example, how valuable is $1? Clearly, *the value of a dollar is equivalent to what a dollar will buy. And what a dollar will buy depends on the price level.* If all prices doubled, the value of a dollar would be cut in half, because a dollar would be able to buy only half as many goods and services as it formerly could. On the other hand, if all prices were reduced by 50 percent, the value of a dollar would double, because a dollar would be able to buy twice as many goods and services as it formerly could. You often hear people say that today's dollar is worth only 50 cents. What they mean is that it will buy only half of what a dollar could buy at some specified date in the past.

It is interesting and important to see how the value of the dollar, as measured by its purchasing power, has varied over time. Figure 13.1 shows how an index of the price level in the United States has changed since 1779. Over time, prices have fluctuated sharply, and some of the greatest fluctuations have resulted from wars. For example, the price level fell sharply after the Revolutionary War, and our next war—the War of 1812—sent prices skyrocketing, after which there was another postwar drop in prices. The period from about 1820 to about 1860 was marked by relative price stability, but the Civil War resulted in an upward burst followed by a postwar drop in prices. After a period of relative price stability from 1875 to 1915, there was a doubling of prices during

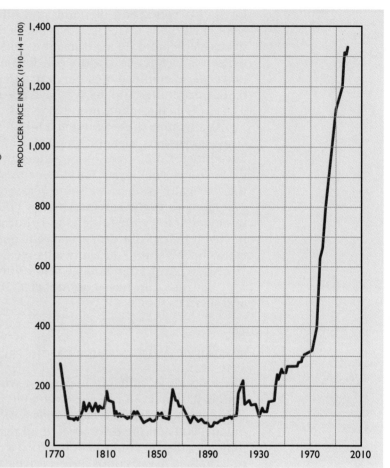

FIGURE 13.1

Index of Wholesale Prices, United States, 1779–1999 (1910–14 = 100)

The price level has fluctuated considerably; sharp increases generally occurred during wars. Since World War II, the price level has generally tended to go only one way—up. In the past thirty years, the price level has more than tripled.

World War I and the usual postwar drop. World War II saw a price increase of about 40 percent, but there was no postwar drop in prices. Instead there has been continual inflation; during the past thirty years, the price level has more than tripled.

The value of money is inversely related to the price level. In inflationary times, the value of money decreases; the opposite is true when the price level falls (an infrequent phenomenon in the past four decades). Thus the wartime periods when the price level rose greatly were periods when the value of the dollar decreased greatly. The doubling of prices during World War I meant that the value of the dollar was chopped in half. Similarly, the postwar periods when the price level fell greatly were periods when the value of the dollar increased. The 50 percent decline in prices after the Civil War meant a doubling in the value of the dollar. Given the extent of the variation of the price level shown in Figure 13.1, it is clear that the value of the dollar has varied enormously during our history.

INFLATION AND THE QUANTITY OF MONEY

If the value of money is reduced in periods of inflation, its value can be largely wiped out in periods of runaway inflation, as in Germany after World War I (recall Chapter 7). Our own country suffered from runaway inflations during the Revolutionary War and the Civil War. You may have heard the expression that something is "not worth a continental." It comes from the fact that the inflated dollars in use during the Revolutionary War were called continentals.

Generally, such severe inflations have occurred because the government increased the money supply at an enormously rapid rate. It is not hard to see why a tremendous increase in the quantity of money will result in a runaway inflation. Other things held constant, increases in the quantity of money will result in increases in total intended spending, and once full employment is achieved, such increases in intended spending will cause more and more inflation.

Eventually, when the inflation is severe enough, households and businesses may refuse to accept money for goods and services because they fear that it will depreciate significantly before they have a chance to spend it. Instead, they may insist on being paid in merchandise or services. Thus the economy will turn to barter, with the accompanying inconveniences and inefficiency.

To prevent such an economic catastrophe, the government must manage the money supply responsibly. If the value of money depends basically on the public's willingness to accept it, then the public's willingness to accept it depends on money's being reasonably stable in value. If the government increases the quantity of money at a rapid rate, and thus causes a severe inflation and an accompanying precipitous fall in the value of money, public confidence in money will be shaken, and the value of money will be destroyed. The moral is clear: *The government must restrict the quantity of money and conduct its economic policies so as to maintain a reasonably stable value of money.*

UNEMPLOYMENT AND THE QUANTITY OF MONEY

In the previous section, we were concerned primarily with what happens when the quantity of money grows too rapidly. The result is inflation. But this is only part of the story. The quantity of money also can grow too slowly. When this happens the result, according to most economists, is increased unemployment. If the money supply grows very slowly or decreases, there will be a tendency for total intended spending to grow very slowly or decrease. This in turn will cause national output to grow very slowly or decrease, and thus cause unemployment to increase. (Of course, a cut in national output is particularly likely to push up unemployment.)

According to many economists, the recession of 1974–75 was due partly to an inadequate growth of the money supply. The Federal Reserve, trying to stem the inflationary tide in 1974, cut back on the rate of increase of the money supply. Looking back over past business fluctuations, it appears that an inadequate rate of increase in the quantity of money was responsible, at least in part, for many recessions.

DETERMINANTS OF THE QUANTITY OF MONEY

Judging from our discussion thus far, it is clear that, to avoid excessive unemployment or excessive inflation, the quantity of money must not grow too slowly or too quickly. But what determines the quantity of money? To a considerable extent, it is determined by the Federal Reserve, which, as we have noted before, is our nation's central bank. Within limits, the Federal Reserve can and does control the quantity of money. But to some extent the private sector of the economy also determines the quantity of money. For example, the nation's commercial banks, through their lending (and other) decisions, can influence the money supply.[1] In the remainder of this chapter, we shall make the simplifying assumption that the money supply is governed solely by the Federal Reserve.

THE DEMAND FOR MONEY

We have discussed in general terms how changes in the quantity of money affect the tempo of economic activity. Now let's look in detail at how changes in the quantity of money affect gross domestic product. The first step in doing this is to discuss the demand for money. Why does a family or firm want to hold money? Certainly, a family can be wealthy without holding much money. We all know stories about very rich people who hold very little money, since virtually all their wealth is tied up in factories, farms, and other nonmonetary assets. Unlike assets that yield profits or interest, money produces no direct return; so why do people and firms want to hold money rather than other kinds of assets? Two of the most important reasons are the following.

**Transactions
demand for
money**

1. **Transactions demand for money**. To carry out most transactions, money is required. Thus people and firms have to

[1]Of course, banks do not create money all by themselves. The public's preferences and actions, as well as bank behavior, influence the amount of demand deposits.

keep some money on their persons and in their checking accounts to buy things. The higher a person's income—in real terms—the more goods and services that person probably will want to purchase, and hence the more money he or she will want to hold for transaction purposes. For example, in 2001, when a doctor makes about $150,000 a year, the average physician will want to keep more money on hand now for transactions purposes than many years ago when a doctor made perhaps $10,000 a year. Because the quantity of money demanded by a household or firm increases with its income, it follows that the total quantity of money demanded for transactions purposes in the economy as a whole is directly related to real gross domestic product. That is, the higher (lower) the level of real GDP, the greater (less) the quantity of money demanded for transactions purposes.

In addition, the total quantity of money demanded for transactions purposes is directly related to the price level. That is, the higher (lower) the price level, the greater (less) the quantity of money demanded for transactions purposes. Obviously, if the price level were to double tomorrow, you would want to keep more money on hand for transactions purposes. In order to purchase the same goods and services as before, you would need more money.

Precautionary demand for money

2. **Precautionary demand for money**. Besides the transactions motive, households and firms like to hold money because they are uncertain concerning the timing and size of future disbursements and receipts. Unpredictable events often require money. People get sick, and houses need repairs. Also, receipts frequently do not come in exactly when expected. To meet such contingencies, people and firms like to put a certain amount of their wealth into money and near-money. In the economy as a whole, the total quantity of money demanded for precautionary purposes (like the quantity demanded for transactions purposes) is likely to vary directly with real GDP and the price level. If GDP goes up, households and firms will want to hold more money for precautionary purposes, because their incomes and sales will be higher than before the increase in GDP. If the price level goes up, they will want to hold more money to offset the reduced purchasing power of the dollar.[2]

---

[2]Still another motive for holding money is the speculative motive. People like to hold some of their assets in a form in which they can be sure of its monetary value and can take advantage of future price reductions. The amount of money individuals and firms will keep on hand for speculative reasons will vary with their expectations concerning future price movements. In particular, if people feel that the prices of bonds and stocks are about to drop soon, they are likely to demand a great deal of money for speculative reasons. By holding money, they can obtain such securities at lower prices than at present.

■ THE INTEREST RATE AND THE DEMAND CURVE FOR MONEY

Up to this point, we have discussed why individuals and firms want to hold money. But there are disadvantages, as well as advantages, in holding money. One is that the real value of money will fall if inflation occurs. Another is that an important cost of holding money is the interest or profit one loses, since instead of holding money, one might have invested it in assets that would have yielded interest or profit. For example, the annual cost of holding $5,000 in money if one can obtain 6 percent on existing investments is $300, the amount of interest or profit forgone.[3]

With GDP constant, the amount of money demanded by individuals and firms is *inversely* related to the interest rate. *The higher the interest rate, the smaller the amount of money demanded. The lower the interest rate, the greater the amount of money demanded.* This is because the cost of holding money increases as the interest rate or yield on existing investments increases. For example, if the interest rate were 7 rather than 6 percent, the cost of holding $5,000 in money for one year would be $350 rather than $300. Thus, as the interest rate or profit rate increases, people try harder to minimize the amount of money they hold. So do firms. Big corporations like IBM or General Motors are very conscious of the cost of holding cash balances.

Figure 13.2 summarizes three important conclusions of our discussion in this and the previous section. Panel A of Figure 13.2 shows that, *holding the interest rate and the price level constant, the quantity of money demanded is directly related to real GDP.* As we explained in the previous section, the higher (lower) the level of real GDP, the greater (less) the quantity of money demanded. Panel B of Figure 13.2 shows that, *with the interest rate and real GDP constant, the quantity of money demanded is directly related to the price level.* In other words, the higher (lower) the price level, the greater (less) the quantity of money demanded. Panel C of Figure 13.2 shows that, *with real GDP and the price level constant, the quantity of money demanded is inversely related to the interest rate.*[4] This latter relationship, described in this section, is called the **demand curve for money**.

**Demand curve
for money**

---

[3]For simplicity, we assume here that money yields no interest or profit. This is not true because, as we saw earlier, the money supply includes some interest-bearing checkable deposits. But this makes no real difference to our argument. Even if money yields some interest, it yields a much smaller return than alternative investments like bonds. Thus, there is a cost involved in holding money.

[4]However, the relationship between the quantity of money and the interest rate is only short run. In the long run, increases in the money supply, if they result in increased inflation, may *raise* interest rates, because lenders will require a greater return to offset the greater rate of depreciation of the real value of the dollar. Still, however, the real rate of interest—the rate of interest adjusted for inflation—may decline.

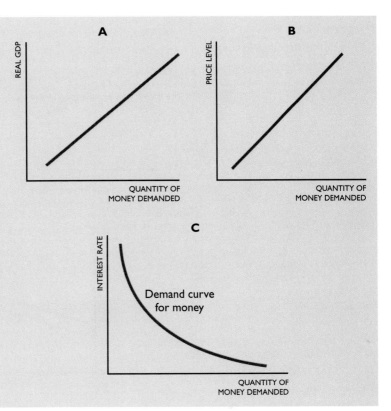

FIGURE 13.2

The Demand for Money

Holding the interest rate and the price level constant, the quantity of money demanded is *directly* related to real GDP, as shown in panel A. Holding the interest rate and real GDP constant, the quantity of money demanded is *directly* related to the price level, as shown in panel B. Holding real GDP and the price level constant, the quantity of money demanded is *inversely* related to the interest rate, as shown in panel C. This last relationship is known as the demand curve for money.

CHANGES IN THE MONEY SUPPLY AND NATIONAL OUTPUT

■ EFFECTS OF A CHANGE IN THE MONEY SUPPLY: THE SIMPLE KEYNESIAN MODEL

Now that we have investigated the demand for money, we are ready to show how changes in the quantity of money influence the value of GDP. To begin with, let's see how the money supply can be inserted into the simple Keynesian model (discussed in Chapters 5 and 6) aimed at explaining the level of GDP.

To begin with, let's trace the effects of an increase in the money supply from $200 billion to $250 billion. If the demand curve for money is as shown in panel A of Figure 13.3, the result will be a *decrease in the interest rate* from 8 to 6 percent. Why? Because, if the interest rate is 8 percent, people will demand only $200 billion of money, not the $250 billion that is supplied. Having more money on hand than they want, they will invest the excess in bonds,

FIGURE 13.3

Effect of an Increase in the Money Supply

If the money supply increases from \$200 billion to \$250 billion, the interest rate drops from 8 to 6 percent (panel A). Because of the decrease in the interest rate, the investment function shifts upward (panel B), and the equilibrium level of GDP increases from *D* to *E* (panel C).

A. Demand curve for money

B. Shift in investment function

C. Change in gross domestic product

stocks, and other financial assets, with the result that the price of bonds, stocks, and other financial assets will rise.[5]

Such a rise in the price of bonds is equivalent to a fall in the rate of interest. (To see why, suppose that a very long-term bond pays interest of \$300 per year. If the price of the bond is \$3,000, the interest rate on the bond is 10 percent. If the price of the bond rises to \$4,000, the interest rate on the bond falls to $7\frac{1}{2}$ percent. Thus the increase in price amounts to a reduction in the interest rate.) When the interest rate has fallen to 6 percent, people will be willing to hold the \$250 billion in money. At this interest rate, the quantity of money demanded will equal the quantity of money supplied.

The decrease in the interest rate from 8 to 6 percent affects the investment function.[6] Recall from Chapter 5 that the level of invest-

---

[5]For simplicity, we assume that when people have excess money balances, they use the money to buy financial assets. (Also, we assume that when people have smaller money balances than they want, they sell financial assets to get more money.) A more complete analysis is provided in E. Mansfield, *Economics: Principles, Problems, Decisions,* 7th ed. The results are essentially the same as those provided here.

[6]Changes in the money supply, interest rates, and credit availability affect the consumption function, government spending, and net exports as well as the investment

ment is inversely related to the interest rate. Because it is less costly to invest—and because credit is more readily available—*the investment function will shift upward,* as shown in panel B of Figure 13.3.[7] This occurs because at each level of gross domestic product, firms will want to invest more, since investment is more profitable (because of the cut in the interest rate) and funds are more readily available.[8]

This shift in the investment function then affects the equilibrium level of gross domestic product. As shown in panel C of Figure 13.3, *the equilibrium level of gross domestic product will increase from D to E,* in accord with the principles discussed in Chapters 5 and 6 (recall that the equilibrium value of GDP is at the point where the $C + I + G + (X - M_l)$ line intersects the 45-degree line). Thus *the effect of the increase in the money supply is to increase gross domestic product.*

This, in simplified fashion, is how an increase in the money supply affects GDP, according to the simple Keynesian model.[9] To summarize, *the increase in the money supply results in a reduction in the interest rate, which results in an increase in investment, which results in an increase in* GDP. Of course, a decrease in the money supply has just the opposite effect: *a decrease in the money supply results in an increase in the interest rate, which results in a decrease in investment, which results in a decrease in GDP.*[10]

---

function. For example, *increases (decreases) in interest rates shift the consumption function downward (upward).* These factors augment the effect of monetary policy described in the text. We focus attention on the investment function in Figure 13.3 merely because this simplifies the exposition.

[7]Note that it is not just a matter of interest rates. Availability of credit is also important. In times when money is tight, some potential borrowers may find that they cannot get a loan, regardless of what interest rate they are prepared to pay. In times when money is easy, people who otherwise might find it difficult to get a loan may be granted one by the banks. To repeat, both availability and interest rates are important.

[8]Many firms depend to a considerable extent on retained earnings to finance their investment projects. Thus, since they do not borrow externally, the effect on their investment plans of changes in interest rates and credit availability may be reduced. However, since changes in the interest rate reflect changes in the opportunity cost of using funds to finance investment projects, they still may have an appreciable effect on the investment function.

[9]The alert reader will recognize that the increase in GDP in panel C will shift the demand curve for money in panel A of Figure 13.3. For simplicity, we ignore this feedback. It is included in the more complete model presented in Mansfield, *Economics: Principles, Problems, Decisions,* 7th ed.

[10]Harking back to Chapter 4, we are in a better position to understand now why the aggregate demand curve slopes downward and to the right. An increase in the price level increases the transactions demand for money because the average money cost of each transaction tends to go up. Thus the demand curve for money shifts to the right, with the result that the interest rate increases. As indicated in this section, the higher interest rate results in reduced spending on output. Thus there is an inverse relationship between the price level and aggregate demand.

FIGURE 13.4

Effect of an Increase in the Money Supply on Real GDP and the Price Level

An increase in the money supply pushes the aggregate demand curve to the right, and thus increases real GDP from Q_0 to Q_1 and raises the price level from P_0 to P_1.

EFFECTS OF A CHANGE IN THE MONEY SUPPLY: NO ASSUMPTION OF A CONSTANT PRICE LEVEL

As pointed out in earlier chapters, the simple Keynesian model discussed in the previous section assumes that the price level is fixed. If we relax this assumption, we must use the aggregate supply and demand curves described in Chapter 4. As in the previous section, suppose that the money supply increases from $200 billion to $250 billion, with the result that the interest rate falls from 8 to 6 percent and the investment function shifts upward.[11] As indicated in Figure 13.4, the increase in investment spending pushes the aggregate demand curve to the right. This makes sense, since the quantity of total real output demanded (at the existing price level) goes up.

What will be the effect of this increase in the money supply? The answer depends heavily on the shape of the short-run aggregate supply curve. If the economy is fully employed and the short-run aggregate supply curve is vertical (or close to it), increases in the money supply will result in inflation but little or no extra real output. However, if the intersection of the aggregate demand and short-run aggregate supply curves prior to the increase in the money supply occurred in the upward-sloping range of the short-run aggregate supply curve, as in Figure 13.4, the effect is an increase in real GDP from Q_0 to Q_1 and an increase in the price level from P_0 to P_1. Thus, the increase in the money supply raises both total real output and the price level. (Of course, if the intersection

---

[11]Recall that for simplicity we assume in this and the previous section that changes in the money supply, interest rates, and credit availability influence only the investment function, not consumption expenditure, government spending, or net exports. See footnote 6.

occurred in the horizontal range of the short-run aggregate supply curve, the situation would be like that discussed in the previous section, since the price level would be constant.)

Just as an increase in the money supply pushes the aggregate demand curve to the right, so a decrease in the money supply pushes it to the left. As pointed out in the previous section, a decrease in the money supply results in an increase in the interest rate, which results in a decrease in investment. Since the quantity of total real output demanded (at each price level) goes down, the aggregate demand curve shifts to the left. If the short-run aggregate supply curve is vertical (or close to it), the result will be a reduction in the price level but little or no cut in real output. But if the economy is operating in the upward-sloping range of the short-run aggregate supply curve, the result will be a reduction in both the price level and real output. And if the short-run aggregate supply curve is close to horizontal, the result will be a reduction in real output but little or no fall in the price level.

CLOSING A RECESSIONARY GAP

In recent decades, governments throughout the world have tried to manipulate the money supply in order to close (or at least reduce) recessionary and inflationary gaps. Suppose that the economy is in the short-run equilibrium position shown in Figure 13.5. There is a recessionary gap, as evidenced by the fact that the equilibrium level of real national output, Q_1, is less than its potential level, Q_0. (Recall that potential output is the amount of output that would be produced if there were full employment.) One way to

FIGURE 13.5

Increasing the Money Supply to Close a Recessionary Gap

Initially there is a recessionary gap, since the equilibrium level of output, Q_1, is less than the potential level, Q_0. One way to close this gap may be to increase the money supply, and thus shift the aggregate demand curve from position D_1 to position D_0. Although this increases output to its potential level, there are inflationary consequences: the price level increases from P_1 to P_0.

deal with this situation is to leave things alone. As we know from previous chapters, a recessionary gap of this sort will eventually cure itself. As wages and prices eventually fall, the short-run aggregate supply curve will shift to the right, and the equilibrium level of real output will rise toward the potential level, Q_0. Eventually the economy will move to point A, where the aggregate demand curve intersects the long-run aggregate supply curve, which is the vertical line at Q_0. (If you are somewhat hazy concerning this process, review the top right-hand panel of Figure 6.6.)

But as Keynes and his followers pointed out, this process may take a long time to work itself out—and the pain inflicted on the unemployed and others may be substantial. Thus, many economists have recommended that governments increase the money supply to help close a recessionary gap. For example, in Figure 13.5, the government might increase the money supply so as to push the aggregate demand curve from its initial position (D_1) rightward to D_0, with the result that total real output will be raised from Q_1 to its potential level, Q_0. In this way, the recessionary gap will be closed.

However, one undesirable side effect is that the increase in the money supply raises the price level from P_1 to P_0. In other words, there are inflationary consequences. As pointed out in the previous section, the extent of the inflationary consequences depends on the steepness of the short-run aggregate supply curve. If the short-run aggregate supply curve is close to vertical, the inflationary consequences may be very great; but if the short-run aggregate supply curve is close to horizontal, they may be quite moderate.

CLOSING AN INFLATIONARY GAP

Turning from a recessionary gap to an inflationary gap, suppose that the economy is in the short-run equilibrium position shown in Figure 13.6. There is an inflationary gap, as indicated by the fact that the equilibrium level of real national output, Q_2, is greater than the potential level, Q_0. Here, as in the case of a recessionary gap, one way to deal with the situation is to leave things alone. As we know from previous chapters, an inflationary gap of this sort will eventually cure itself. As wages and prices are bid up, the short-run aggregate supply curve shifts to the left. Eventually the economy will move to point B, where the aggregate demand curve intersects the long-run aggregate supply curve, and the equilibrium level of real national output equals the potential level, Q_0. (For a review of this process, see the top right-hand panel of Figure 6.7.)

However, this leftward shift of the short-run aggregate supply curve will result in inflation until the price level rises to P_3 in Figure 13.6. Given the many undesirable consequences of such infla-

FIGURE 13.6

Reducing the Money Supply to Close an Inflationary Gap

Initially there is an inflationary gap, since the equilibrium level of output, Q_2, exceeds the potential level, Q_0. One way to close this gap may be to reduce the money supply, and thus shift the aggregate demand curve from position D_2 to position D_0. This will result in the price level's equaling P_0, which is lower than P_3, which it would have equaled without the shift in the aggregate demand curve.

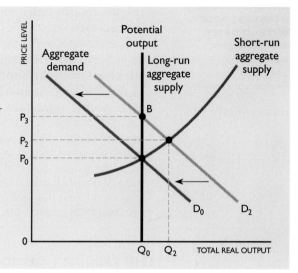

tion (detailed in Chapter 7), many economists have recommended that governments cut back on the money supply to help close an inflationary gap. For example, in Figure 13.6, the government might reduce the money supply to push the aggregate demand curve from its initial position, D_2, leftward to D_0, with the result that the price level will be P_0, rather than P_3. In this way, the government closes the inflationary gap.

Unfortunately, one side effect may be that unemployment will increase. Although this increase in unemployment will be temporary, many economists believe that it can be substantial and prolonged.

THE MONETARISTS

Monetarists

Some prominent economists, led by Milton Friedman of Stanford University's Hoover Institution, share a point of view known as *monetarism;* hence, they are called **monetarists.** During the 1950s and 1960s (and to a lesser extent during the 1970s and 1980s), there was a continuing (and sometimes bitter) controversy between the monetarists and the Keynesians. The monetarists regard the rate of growth of the money supply as the principal determinant of nominal GDP. (*Nominal GDP* means GDP in money, not real terms. In other words, nominal GDP is GDP measured in current, not constant, dollars.) At heart, the argument between the monetarists and the Keynesians was over what determines the level of output, employment, and prices. The Keynesians put more emphasis on the federal budget than did the monetarists; the monetarists put more emphasis on the money supply than did the Keynesians.

The monetarists have had a great impact on economic thought since World War II, even though theirs has been a minority view. Professor Friedman's most severe critics admit that his research in this area (which helped win him a Nobel prize) has been path-breaking and important. According to his findings,

> the rate of change of the money supply shows well-marked cycles that match closely those in economic activity in general and precede the latter by a long interval. On the average, the rate of change of the money supply has reached its peak nearly 16 months before the peak in general business and has reached its trough over 12 months before the trough in general business.[12]

THE VELOCITY OF MONEY

The monetarists revived interest in the so-called quantity theory of money, which was developed many years ago by such titans of economics as Alfred Marshall of Cambridge University and Irving Fisher of Yale University. To understand this theory, it is useful to begin by defining a new term: the *velocity of circulation of money*.

Velocity of money

The **velocity of circulation of money** is the rate at which the money supply is used to make transactions for final goods and services. It equals the average number of times per year that a dollar is used to buy the final goods and services produced by the economy. In other words,

$$V = GDP/M, \tag{13.1}$$

where V is velocity, GDP is the nominal gross domestic product, and M is the money supply. For example, if our nominal gross domestic product is $1 trillion and our money supply is $200 billion, the velocity of circulation of money is 5, which means that, on the average, each dollar of our money generates $5 worth of purchases of gross domestic product.

Nominal gross domestic product can be expressed as the product of real gross domestic product and the price level. In other words,

$$GDP = P \times Q, \tag{13.2}$$

where P is the price level—the average price at which final goods and services are sold—and Q is gross domestic product in real

---

[12]Milton Friedman, "The Relationship of Prices to Economic Stability and Growth," testimony before the Joint Economic Committee, 85th Congress, 2d session.

terms. For example, suppose that national output in real terms consists of 200 tons of steel. If the price of a ton of steel is $100, then nominal GDP equals $P \times Q$, or 100×200, or $20,000.[13]

If we substitute $P \times Q$ for GDP in equation 13.1, we have

$$V = P \times Q/M. \tag{13.3}$$

That is, velocity equals the price level (P) times real GDP (Q) divided by the money supply (M). This is another way to define the velocity of circulation of money—a way that will prove very useful.

THE EQUATION OF EXCHANGE

Equation of exchange

Now that we have a definition of the velocity of circulation of money, our next step is to present the so-called equation of exchange. The **equation of exchange** is nothing more than a restatement, in somewhat different form, of our definition of the velocity of circulation of money. To obtain the equation of exchange, all we have to do is multiply both sides of equation 13.3 by M. The result is

$$MV = PQ. \tag{13.4}$$

To understand exactly what this equation means, let's look more closely at each side. *The right-hand side equals the amount received for final goods and services during the period,* because Q is the output of final goods and services during the period and P is their average price. Thus the product of P and Q must equal the total amount received for final goods and services during the period: nominal GDP. For example, if national output in real terms equals 200 tons of steel and the price of a ton of steel is $100, then 100×200—$P \times Q$—must equal the total amount received for final goods and services during the period.

The left-hand side of equation 13.4 equals the total amount spent on final goods and services during the period. Why? Because the left-hand side equals the money supply M times the average number of times V during the period that a dollar was spent on final goods and services. Consequently, $M \times V$ must equal the amount spent on final goods and services during the period. For example, if the money supply equals $10,000 and velocity equals 2, the total amount spent on final goods and services during the period must equal $10,000 \times 2$, or $20,000.

---

[13]Since real GDP is measured here in physical units (tons), P is the price level. If real GDP had been measured in constant dollars, P would have been a price index. In either event, our conclusions would be basically the same.

Thus, since the *amount received for* final goods and services during the period must equal the *amount spent on* final goods and services during the period, the left-hand side must equal the right-hand side.

The equation of exchange—equation 13.4—holds by definition. Yet it is not useless. On the contrary, economists regard the equation of exchange as very valuable, because it sets forth some of the fundamental factors that influence GDP and the price level. This equation has been used by economists for many years. It is the basis for the crude quantity theory of money used by the classical economists, as well as the theories put forth by the monetarists.

THE CRUDE QUANTITY THEORY OF MONEY AND PRICES

The classical economists discussed in Chapter 4 assumed that both V and Q were constant. They believed that V was constant because it was determined by the population's stable habits of holding money, and they believed that Q would remain constant at its full-employment value.[14] On the basis of these assumptions, they pro-

Crude quantity theory

pounded the **crude quantity theory** of money and prices, a theory that received a great deal of attention and exerted considerable influence in its day.

If these assumptions hold, it follows from the equation of exchange—$MV = PQ$—that the price level (P) must be proportional to the money supply (M), because V and Q have been assumed to be constant. [In the short run, the full-employment level of real gross domestic product (Q) will not change much.] Thus we can rewrite equation 13.4 as

$$P = (V/Q)M, \qquad (13.5)$$

where V/Q is a constant. So P must be proportional to M if these assumptions hold.

The conclusion reached by the crude quantity theorists—*that the price level will be proportional to the money supply*—is very important if true. To see how they came to this conclusion, one must recognize that they stressed the transactions motive for holding money. Recall that, on the basis of this motive, one would expect the quantity of money demanded to be directly related to the level of nominal GDP. Further, the demand for money was assumed to be stable, and little or no attention was paid to the effect of the interest rate on the demand for money. Indeed, the crude quantity

---

[14]In some cases, they did not really assume continual full employment. Instead, they were concerned with the long-run changes in the economy and compared the peaks of the business cycle, where full employment frequently occurs.

theorists went so far as to assume that the quantity of money demanded was *proportional* to the level of nominal GDP. This amounted to assuming that velocity was constant.

Suppose there is a 10 percent increase in the quantity of money. Why would the crude quantity theorists predict a 10 percent increase in the price level? To begin with, they would assert that, since the quantity of money has increased relative to the value of nominal GDP, households and firms now hold more money than they want to hold. Further, they would argue that households and firms will spend their excess money balances on commodities and services and that the resulting increase in total intended spending will increase the nominal value but not the real value of GDP (since full employment is assumed). In other words, the increase in aggregate demand will bid up prices. More specifically, they would argue that prices will continue to be bid up until they have increased by 10 percent, since only then will the nominal value of GDP be big enough so that households and firms will be content to hold the new quantity of money.

EVALUATION OF THE CRUDE QUANTITY THEORY

The crude quantity theory is true to its name: it is only a crude approximation to reality. One important weakness is its assumption that velocity is constant. Another is its assumption that the economy is always at full employment, which we know from previous chapters to be far from true. (For a version of the quantity theory that relaxes this assumption, see Exploring Further in this chapter.) But despite its limitations, the crude quantity theory points to a very important truth. If the government finances its expenditures by an enormous increase in the money supply, the result will be drastic inflation. For example, if the money supply is increased tenfold, there will be a marked increase in the price level. If we take the crude quantity theory at face value, we would expect a tenfold increase in the price level; but that is a case of spurious accuracy. Perhaps the price level will go up only eightfold. Perhaps it will go up twelvefold. The important thing is that it will go up a lot.

There is a great deal of evidence to show that the crude quantity theory is a useful predictor during periods of runaway inflation, such as in Germany after World War I. The German inflation occurred because the German government printed and spent large bundles of additional money. You sometimes hear people warn of the dangers in this country of the government's "resorting to the printing presses" and flooding the country with a vast increase in the money supply. It is a danger in any country. And one great value of the crude quantity theory is that it predicts correctly what will occur as a consequence: rapid inflation.

The velocity of money and the Fed's 1975 decision

Arthur Burns

In view of the weakness of the economy at the end of 1974, the Federal Reserve and the Ford administration decided that stimulative measures were necessary. The administration asked for and quickly got a large retroactive tax cut in March 1975, and the Fed set a goal for a higher money growth rate. The inflation rate had been in the double digits in 1974 and was expected to be about 7 to 8 percent in 1975, but the Fed was targeting money supply growth at only 5 to 7 percent. Why did the Fed set such a low target? How could a 5 to 7 percent growth in the money supply finance an expansion of 3 to 4 percent real growth with 7 to 8 percent inflation? Many economists agreed that the Fed was embarking on a very restrictive policy and that the expansion would be choked off.

Federal Reserve Chairperson Arthur Burns argued that a dollar typically finances more transactions (and therefore supports a higher nominal income) during a business recovery than during a recession. "We knew from a careful reading of history," he said, "that the turnover of money balances tends to rise rapidly in the early stages of economic upswing. Consequently, we resisted the advice of those who wanted to open the tap and let money flow out in greater abundance." It turned out that Burns was correct. From the second quarter of 1975 to the first quarter of 1976, the velocity of money increased even more rapidly than the Fed had predicted, and the relatively low rate of monetary growth was sufficient to accommodate a growth rate of more than 14 percent for nominal GDP—6 percent in real terms.

There is also considerable evidence that the crude quantity theory works reasonably well in predicting long-term trends in the price level. For example, during the sixteenth and seventeenth centuries, gold and silver were imported by the Spanish from the New World; this resulted in a great increase in Europe's money supply. The crude quantity theory would predict a great increase in the price level, and this is what occurred. Or consider the period during the nineteenth century, when the discovery of gold in the United States, South Africa, and Canada brought about a large increase in the money supply. As the crude quantity theory would lead us to expect, the price level rose considerably as a consequence.

WHEN IS MONETARY POLICY TIGHT OR EASY?

In previous sections of this chapter, we have focused on the ways in which the money supply affects economic activity. Now we must look in more detail at the difficulties faced by the Federal Reserve in conducting monetary policy in the United States. Given what we have learned in previous sections of this chapter, we can understand these difficulties more clearly.

Everyone daydreams about being powerful and important. It is a safe bet, however, that few people daydream about being members of the Federal Reserve Board or the Federal Open Market Committee. Yet the truth is that the members of the board and the committee are among the most powerful people in the nation. Suppose you were appointed to the Federal Reserve Board. As a member, you would have to decide—month by month, year by year—exactly how many government securities the Fed should buy or sell, as well as whether and when changes should be made in the discount rate, legal reserve requirements, and other instruments of Federal Reserve policy. How would you go about making your choices?

Obviously you would need lots of data. Fortunately, the Fed has a very large and able research staff to provide you with plenty of the latest information about what is going on in the economy. But what sorts of data should you look at? One thing you would want is some information on the extent to which monetary policy is inflationary or deflationary, that is, the extent to which it is *easy* or *tight*. This is not simple to measure, but there is general agreement that the members of the Federal Reserve Board—and other members of the financial and academic communities—look closely at short-term interest rates and the rate of increase of the money supply.

■ THE LEVEL OF SHORT-TERM INTEREST RATES

As indicated earlier, Keynesians have tended to believe that changes in the quantity of money affect aggregate demand via their effects on the interest rate. High interest rates tend to reduce investment, and this in turn reduces GDP. Low interest rates tend to increase investment, and this in turn increases GDP. Because of their emphasis on these relationships, Keynesians tend to view monetary tightness or ease in terms of the behavior of interest rates. High interest rates are interpreted as meaning that monetary policy is tight. Low interest rates are interpreted as meaning that monetary policy is easy.

Real interest rate

According to many economists, the *real interest rate*, not the *nominal interest rate*, is what counts in this context. The **real interest rate** is the percentage increase in *real* purchasing power that the lender receives from the borrower in return for making the loan. The *nominal* interest rate is the percentage increase in *money* that the lender receives from the borrower in return for making the loan. The crucial difference between the real rate of interest and the nominal rate of interest is that the former is *adjusted for inflation* whereas the latter is not.

Suppose that a firm borrows $1,000 for a year at 12 percent interest and that the rate of inflation is 9 percent. When the firm repays the lender $1,120 at the end of the year, this amount of money is worth only $1,120 ÷ 1.09, or about $1,030 when corrected for inflation. Thus the real rate of interest on this loan is 3 percent, not 12 percent (the nominal rate). Why? Because the lender receives $30 in constant dollars (which is 3 percent of the amount lent) in return for making the loan. The real rate of interest is of importance in investment decisions because it measures the real cost of borrowing money.[15]

■ THE RATE OF INCREASE OF THE MONEY SUPPLY

As indicated earlier, monetarists have tended to link changes in the quantity of money directly to changes in GDP. Consequently, they have tended to view monetary tightness or ease in terms of the behavior of the money supply. When the money supply is growing at a relatively slow rate (much less than 4 or 5 percent per year), this is interpreted as meaning that monetary policy is tight. A relatively rapid rate of growth in the money supply (much more than 4 or 5 percent per year) is taken to mean that monetary policy is easy.

Monetary base

Another measure stressed by the monetarists is the **monetary base**, which by definition equals bank reserves plus currency outside banks. The monetary base is important because the total money supply is dependent on, and made from, it. A relatively slow rate of growth in the monetary base (much less than 4 or 5 percent per year) is interpreted as a sign of tight money. A relatively rapid rate of growth (much more than 4 or 5 percent per year) is taken to mean that monetary policy is easy.

SHOULD THE FED PAY MORE ATTENTION TO INTEREST RATES OR THE MONEY SUPPLY?

We have just seen that the level of interest rates and the rate of growth of the money supply are two principal indicators of monetary tightness or ease. Unfortunately, the Fed may not be able to control them both. To see this, suppose that the existing money supply equals $300 billion and that the public's demand curve for money shifts upward and to the right, as shown in Figure 13.7. At

---

[15]Expressed as an equation, $i_r = i_n - p$, where i_r is the real rate of interest, i_n is the nominal rate of interest, and p is the rate of inflation. In the example in the text, $i_n = 12$ percent and $p = 9$ percent; thus $i_r = 3$ percent.

FIGURE 13.7

Effect of a Shift in the Demand Curve for Money

If the demand curve for money shifts upward and to the right, as shown here, the equilibrium value of the interest rate will increase from 12 to 14 percent if the quantity of money supplied remains $300 billion. If the Fed wants to push the equilibrium level of the interest rate back to 12 percent, it must increase the quantity of money supplied to $330 billion.

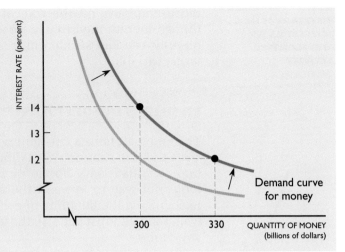

each level of the rate of interest, the public demands a greater amount of money than before. If the interest rate remains at 12 percent, the quantity of money demanded by the public will exceed $300 billion, the existing quantity supplied. Thus the level of interest rates will rise from 12 to 14 percent, as shown in Figure 13.7. Economists who favor the use of interest rates as an indicator are likely to warn that unless interest rates are reduced, a recession will ensue.

The Fed can push the level of interest rates back down by increasing the quantity of money. The equilibrium value of the interest rate is the one where the quantity of money demanded equals the quantity of money supplied. If the demand curve for money remains fixed at its new higher level, the Fed can push the interest rate back down to 12 percent by increasing the quantity of money to $330 billion. With this quantity of money, the equilibrium interest rate is 12 percent, as shown in Figure 13.7. However, by doing so, the Fed no longer is increasing the money supply in accord with its previous objectives. Economists who favor the use of the rate of growth of the money supply as an indicator are likely to warn that the Fed is increasing the money supply at too rapid a rate.

Thus the Fed is faced with a dilemma. If it does not push interest rates back down to their former level, some economists will claim it is promoting recession. If it does do so, other economists will claim it is promoting inflation. Unfortunately, it is very difficult for the Fed (or anyone else) to tell exactly how much weight should be attached to each of these indicators. In the 1950s and 1960s, the Fed paid much more attention to interest rates than to the rate of increase of the money supply. In the 1970s and early 1980s, because of the growing influence of the monetarists, the Fed put more emphasis on the rate of growth of the money supply, although it continued to pay close attention to interest rates. Subsequently, the Fed seemed more inclined to use nominal GDP as a target variable.

PROBLEMS IN FORMULATING MONETARY POLICY

The Fed maintains a constant watch on the economy; it checks for signs that the economy is sliding into a recession, being propelled into an inflationary boom, or growing satisfactorily. There is no foolproof way to forecast the economy's short-term movements. Recognizing the fallibility of existing forecasting techniques all too well, the Fed must still use these techniques as best it can to guide its actions.

Having come to some tentative conclusion about the direction in which the economy is heading, the Fed decides to what extent it should tighten or ease money. The answer depends on the Fed's estimates of when monetary changes will take effect and the magnitude of their impact, as well as on its forecasts of the economy's future direction. Also, the answer depends on the Fed's evaluation of the relative importance of full employment and price stability as national goals. If it regards full employment as much more important than price stability, it will probably want to err in the direction of easy money. On the other hand, if it thinks price stability is at least as important as full employment, it may want to err in the direction of tight money.

Once the Fed has decided what it wants to do, it must figure out how to do it. Should open market operations do the whole job? If so, how big must be the purchase or sale of government securities? Should a change be made in the discount rate or in legal reserve requirements? How big a change? These are the operational questions the Fed must answer.

In answering these questions, the Fed must reckon with two very inconvenient facts, both of which make life difficult.

1. *There is often a long lag between an action by the Fed and its effect on the economy.* Although the available evidence indicates that monetary policy affects some types of expenditures more rapidly than others, it is not uncommon for the bulk of the total effects to occur a year or more after the change in monetary policy.[16] Thus the Fed may act to head off an imminent recession but find that some of the consequences of its action are not felt until later, when inflation, not recession, is the problem. Conversely, the Fed may

---

[16]Robert Gordon of Northwestern University has estimated that it takes about nine months for a change in the money supply to affect real GDP (see Exploring Further in Chapter 9).

How much attention should the Fed pay to the stock market?

How do we know when irrational exuberance has unduly escalated asset values, which then become subject to unexpected and prolonged corrections?

Fed Chairperson Alan Greenspan asked this question on December 5, 1996. At that time, the Dow Jones Industrial Average was around 6,500. It subsequently rose 75 percent over the next three years, reaching 11,500 in January 2000. The Fed was clearly worried about the stock market's being overvalued in 1996. However, instead of trying to bring the market back down to earth by raising interest rates, the Fed tried to "talk" the market down. It did not work, and many analysts blamed the Fed for letting the market get out of control.

The Fed's mandate is to target goods inflation, not asset inflation. Nevertheless, the Fed and other central banks have many reasons to worry about bubbles in the stock and property markets.

- To begin with, asset price inflation can be a leading indicator of higher goods inflation, as measured by the Consumer Price Index (CPI) or the GDP deflator. Rising asset prices increase household wealth, encouraging consumers to splurge. Similarly, a booming stock market can reduce the cost of capital for companies, leading to a surge in investment spending. Thus, an asset bubble can lead to excess demand and higher inflation.
- Ideally, an effective measure of inflation should include not only the prices of goods consumed today but also the prices of goods consumed tomorrow. For example, a rise in housing prices today will increase the costs of repairs in future years. Thus, some economists have argued that the Fed should pay some attention to asset prices. Unfortunately, this is easier said than done because asset prices are generally more volatile than goods prices.
- Surges in asset prices can distort price signals and create misallocation of resources. A booming stock market may tempt companies to overinvest. In fact, during the 1980s Japanese bubble, there was ample evidence that companies overindulged in capacity expansion and helped to set the stage for the recession that followed. Similarly, some analysts were concerned that there was an investment bubble in the United States in the late 1990s.
- Finally, the bursting of an asset bubble is often followed by a recession or worse. The bursting of the U.S. bubble in 1929 and of the Japanese bubble in 1989 led to protracted downturns. Rising asset prices encourage households and companies to borrow heavily, leaving them heavily exposed to a fall in asset prices. When the markets do crash, borrowers often cannot repay their debts. In turn, this can lead to a banking crisis. This downward spiral has been labeled debt deflation.

As compelling as the arguments are for central banks to pay attention to asset prices, there are equally compelling arguments for proceeding with great caution.

- It is often very difficult to be sure that a rise in asset prices represents a speculative bubble. In the late 1990s there was much talk of a significant improvement in fundamentals brought on by the new technologies of the PC and the Internet. Many analysts believed that the rise in the stock market was simply a reflection of this improvement.
- The Fed only has blunt instruments (interest rates) with which to deflate asset bubbles. Too small of a rise in interest rates and the bubble persists (the United States in the 1990s). Too big of a rise in interest rates and the economy goes into a tailspin (Japan in the 1990s).
- Last but not least, the Fed and other central banks do not have the mandate to burst bubbles.

Thus, the unfortunate history of bubbles in the twentieth century has been one in which central banks have typically waited too long and done too much too late.

act to curb an imminent inflation but find that the consequences of its action are not felt until some time later, when recession, not inflation, has become the problem. In either case, the Fed can wind up doing more harm than good (recall Exploring Further in Chapter 9).

2. Experts disagree about which of the available measures—such as interest rates, the rate of increase of the money supply, or the rate of increase of the monetary base—is the best measure of how tight or easy monetary policy is. Fortunately, these measures often point in the same direction, but when they point in different directions, the Fed can be misled. During 1967–68, the Fed wanted to tighten money. Using interest rates as the primary measure of the tightness of monetary policy, it increased interest rates. However, at the same time, it permitted a substantial rate of increase in the money supply and the monetary base. By doing so, the Fed, in the eyes of many experts, really eased rather than tightened money.

SHOULD THE FED BE GOVERNED BY A RULE?

Some monetarists, led by Milton Friedman, go so far as to say that the Fed's attempts to "lean against the wind"—by easing money when the economy begins to dip and tightening money when the economy begins to overheat—do more harm than good. (The new classical economists, discussed in Chapter 14, say much the same thing.) In their view, the Fed intensifies business fluctuations by changing the rate of growth of the money supply. Why? Partly because the Fed sometimes pays too much attention to measures other than the money supply. But more fundamentally, because the Fed tends to overreact to ephemeral changes and because the effects of changes in the money supply on the economy occur with a long and highly variable lag. In the view of these monetarists, this lag is so unpredictable that the Fed—no matter how laudatory its intent—tends to intensify business fluctuations.

According to Professor Friedman and his followers, the Fed should abandon its attempts to lean against the wind. *The Fed should conform to a rule that the money supply should increase at some fixed, agreed-on rate, such as 4 or 5 percent per year. The Fed's job would be simply to see that the money supply grows at approximately this rate.* The monetarists do not claim that a rule of this sort would prevent all business fluctuations, but they do claim that it would work better than the existing system. In particular, they feel that it would prevent the sorts of major depressions and inflations we have experienced in the past. Without major decreases in the money supply (such as occurred during the crash of 1929 to 1933), major depressions could not occur. Without major increases in the money supply (such as occurred during World War II), major inflations could not occur. Of course, it would be nice if monetary policy could iron out minor business fluctuations as well, but in their view this simply cannot be done at present.

This proposal has received considerable attention from both economists and politicians. A number of studies have been carried out to try to estimate what would have happened if Friedman's rule had been used in the past. The results, although by no means free of criticism, seem to indicate that such a rule might have done better than discretionary action did in preventing the Great Depression of the 1930s and the inflation during World War II. But in the period since World War II, the evidence in favor of such a rule is less persuasive. Most economists believe that it would be a mistake to handcuff the Fed to a simple rule of this sort. The debate over rules versus discretionary action goes on, and the issues are still very much alive.

EXPLORING FURTHER:

MORE ON THE VELOCITY OF MONEY

The crude quantity theory was based on two simplifying assumptions, both of which are questionable. One assumption was that real gross domestic product (Q) remains fixed at its full-employment level. The other was that the velocity of circulation of money (V) remains constant. A more sophisticated version of the quantity theory can be derived by relaxing the first assumption. This version of the quantity theory recognizes that the economy is often at less than full employment and consequently that real gross domestic product (Q) may vary a good deal.

So long as the velocity of money remains constant, the equation of exchange, $MV = PQ$, can be used to determine the relationship between gross domestic product in current dollars and M, even if Q is allowed to vary. On the basis of the equation of exchange, it is obvious that $P \times Q$ should be proportional to M if the velocity of circulation of money (V) remains constant. Since $P \times Q$ is nominal gross domestic product, it follows that, if this assumption holds, *nominal gross domestic product should be proportional to the money supply.* In other words,

$$GDP = aM, \tag{13.6}$$

where GDP is nominal gross domestic product and V is assumed to equal a constant: a. Thus, if the money supply increases by 10 percent, the nominal value of GDP should increase by 10 percent. If the money supply increases by 20 percent, the nominal value of GDP should increase by 20 percent. And so forth.

FIGURE 13.8

Velocity of Circulation of
Money, United States,
1920–99

The velocity of circulation
of money has generally
been between 2.5 and 8.0,
except during World War II.

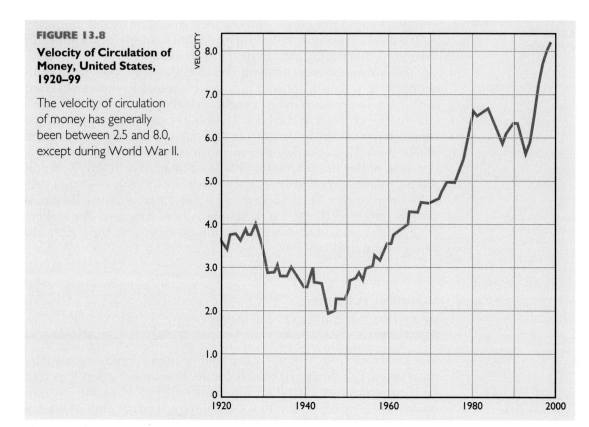

If the velocity of money is constant, this version of the quantity theory should enable us to predict nominal gross domestic product if we know the money supply. Also, if the velocity of money is constant, this version of the quantity theory should enable us to control nominal gross domestic product by controlling the money supply. Clearly, if the velocity of money is constant, equation 13.6 is an extremely important economic relationship, one that will go a long way toward helping to forecast and control GDP. But is the velocity of money constant? Since equation 13.6 is based on this assumption, we must find out.

Figure 13.8 shows how the velocity of circulation of money has behaved since 1920. Obviously, the velocity of money has not been constant. But on the other hand, it has not varied enormously. Excluding World War II, it has generally been between 2.5 and 6.5 in the United States. It has changed rather slowly, although it has varied a good deal over the business cycle. The velocity of money tends to decrease during depressions and increase during booms. *One must conclude from Figure 13.8 that although the velocity of money has not varied enormously, it is not so stable that equation 13.6*

FIGURE 13.9

Relationship between the Money Supply and Nominal GDP, United States, 1960–99

There has been a reasonably close relationship between the money supply and the money value of national product. As one goes up, the other tends to go up too.

alone can be used in any precise way to forecast or control gross domestic product.[17]

However, this does not mean that equation 13.6 is useless or that the more sophisticated quantity theory is without value. On the contrary, this version of the quantity theory points out a very important truth, which is that *the money supply has an important effect on gross domestic product (in money terms). Increases in the quantity of money are likely to increase nominal GDP; decreases in the quantity of money are likely to decrease nominal GDP.* Because velocity is not constant, the relationship between the money supply and gross domestic product is not as neat and simple as that predicted by equation 13.6, but there is a relationship, as shown in Figure 13.9.

Going a step further, sophisticated monetarists often relax the assumption that V is constant and assert that it is possible to predict V as a function of other variables, like the frequency with which people are paid, the level of business confidence, and the cost of holding money (the interest rate). According to some economists, one of Friedman's major contributions was to replace the

---

[17]It is important to note that the velocity of money figures in Figure 13.8 are based on the narrow definition of the money supply, M1. If M2 is used instead, the velocity of money has been more nearly constant. For example, between 1960 and 1976, the velocity of money based on M2 varied within a very narrow range.

constancy of V with its predictability. Other economists feel that changes in V reflect, rather than cause, changes in GDP.

In recent years, V seems to have become less predictable than in the past. This development has caused some consternation in the monetarist camp. Moreover, Federal Reserve officials have lamented that the relationship between the money supply and GDP has become less reliable because of financial deregulation and the recent tendency of people to move their money into mutual funds that are not considered part of the money supply. Obviously, this makes it more difficult for the Fed to devise an effective monetary policy.

REVIEW AND PRACTICE

■ SUMMARY

1 The United States has seen many sharp fluctuations in the price level. Some of the greatest fluctuations have resulted from wars.

2 According to the simple Keynesian model, increases in the quantity of money result in lower interest rates, which result in increased investment (and other types of spending), which results in a higher GDP. Conversely, decreases in the quantity of money result in a lower GDP.

3 An increase in the money supply tends to push the aggregate demand curve to the right; a decrease in the money supply tends to push it to the left. Governments often increase the money supply in an attempt to eliminate a recessionary gap and cut back on the money supply in an attempt to eliminate an inflationary gap.

4 The monetarists, led by Milton Friedman, have emphasized the equation of exchange: $MV = PQ$, where M is the money supply, V is velocity, P is the price level, and Q is gross domestic product in real terms.

5 If the velocity of circulation of money remains constant and real gross domestic product is fixed at its full-employment level, the price level will be proportional to the money supply. This is the crude quantity theory, which is a reasonably good approximation during periods of runaway inflation and works reasonably well in predicting long-term trends in the price level.

6 As indicators of how tight or easy monetary policy is, the Fed has looked at the level of short-term interest rates, the rate of growth of the money supply, and the rate of growth of the monetary base.

7 The job of the Federal Reserve is complicated by the fact that there is often a long—and highly variable—lag between an action by the Fed and its effect on the economy. There is also considerable disagreement over the best way to measure how tight or easy monetary policy is.

8 Some monetarists, led by Milton Friedman, believe that monetary policy would be improved if discretionary policy were replaced by a rule that the Fed should increase the money supply at some fixed, agreed-on rate, such as 4 or 5 percent per year.

*9 If the velocity of money remains constant, gross domestic product in money terms should be proportional to the money supply. In fact, however, the velocity of money has by no means remained constant over time. Nonetheless, nominal GDP has been fairly closely related to the money supply.

■ PROBLEMS AND QUESTIONS

1 If the value of GDP (in money terms) increases 10 percent and the money supply remains fixed, does the velocity of money increase? Why or why not? What are some of the factors that might cause an increase in the velocity of money?

2 "The history of the United States is an account of one inflation after another. The currency is being debased further and further. Soon we may experience a runaway inflation." Comment and evaluate.

3 Describe how the quantity of money influences nominal and real GDP according to:
(a) The Keynesian model
(b) The crude quantity theory
(c) The analysis (based on aggregate demand and supply curves) in Figure 13.4

4 Suppose that a bond pays annual interest of $100 forever. What is the interest rate if its price is (a) $1,000, (b) $2,000, and (c) $3,000?

5 Why is the interest rate regarded as the price of holding money? What factors will shift the demand curve for money to the right? To the left?

■ KEY TERMS

transactions demand for money   equation of exchange

precautionary demand for money   crude quantity theory

demand curve for money   real interest rate

monetarists   monetary base

velocity of money

■ VIEWPOINT FOR ANALYSIS

According to the *Economist* magazine in September 1999, "Mr. Greenspan's confidence that he can use monetary policy to prevent a deep recession if share prices crash exposes an awkward asymmetry in the way central banks respond to asset prices. They are reluctant to raise interest rates to prevent a bubble, but they are quick to cut rates if financial markets tremble. . . . The Fed has inadvertently created a sort of moral hazard. If investors believe that monetary policy will underpin share prices, they will take bigger risks."†

(a) Should the Fed be as quick to prevent stock market booms as it seems to have been to prevent stock market crashes (see Case Study 9.2)?

(b) What is the problem with moral hazard in this context?

(c) If you were a member of the Federal Reserve's Federal Open Market Committee, what would you consider before raising interest rates to deflate an asset bubble (see Case Study 13.2)?

*The starred item refers to material covered in Exploring Further.

†"The World Economy Survey," *Economist*, September 25, 1999, p. 25.

CHAPTER 14

Controversies over Stabilization Policy

LEARNING OBJECTIVES

In this chapter, you should learn:

- The disagreements between the new classical macroeconomists and new Keynesians (as well as among the monetarists, Keynesians, and supply-side economists) over business fluctuations, the stability of the economy, and the use of a monetary rule
- The pros and cons of policy activism
- The differences among rigid policy rules, feedback policy rules, and discretionary policy

No longer are the debates over monetary and fiscal policy dominated by the Keynesians and monetarists; there now are supply-side economists, new classical macroeconomists, and new Keynesians. How do their views differ? One purpose of this chapter is to answer this question.

During the past several decades, there have been many controversies among economists over the effects of monetary and fiscal policies on output and employment, as well as over the kinds of public policies that the government should adopt. These controversies have engaged the attention of many leading economists and have had a strong influence on the thinking of policymakers in both the public and private sectors of the economy. In previous chapters, we have discussed particular aspects of these controversies. Now we look at them in more detail.

MONETARISTS VERSUS KEYNESIANS: THE CENTRAL DEBATE OF THE 1960S AND 1970S

As stressed in the previous chapter, the principal debate of the 1960s and 1970s was between the monetarists and the Keynesians. This debate was not limited to the classroom and scholarly gatherings. It spilled over onto the pages of daily newspapers and aroused considerable interest in Congress and other parts of the government. At heart, the argument was over what determines the level of output, employment, and prices. The Keynesians put more emphasis on the federal budget than the monetarists did; the monetarists put more emphasis on the money supply than the Keynesians did. To understand this debate, we need to know something about the development of economic thought. Until the Great Depression of the 1930s, the prevailing theory was that GDP, expressed in real terms, would tend automatically to its full-employment level. (Recall from Chapter 4 the classical economists' reasons for clinging to this belief.) Moreover, the prevailing view was that the price level could be explained by the crude quantity theory of money. In other words, the price level (P) was assumed to be proportional to the quantity of money (M) because $MV = PQ$, and both Q (real GDP) and V (the velocity of money) were thought to be essentially constant.

During the Great Depression of the 1930s, this theory appeared inadequate to many economists. GDP seemed not to be tending automatically toward its full-employment level. And the crude quantity theory seemed to have little value. In contrast, Keynes's ideas appeared to offer the theoretical guidance and policy prescriptions that were needed. Keynesians did not neglect the use of monetary policy entirely, but they felt that it should play a subsidiary role. Particularly in depressions, monetary policy seemed to be of relatively little value, since you can't push on a string. In other words, monetary policy can make money available but cannot ensure that it will be spent. To Keynesians, fiscal policy was of central importance.

During the 1940s, 1950s, and early 1960s, the Keynesian view was definitely predominant, here and abroad. But by the mid-1960s, it was being challenged seriously by the monetarists, led by Milton Friedman and his supporters. The monetarist view harked back to the pre-Keynesian doctrine in many respects. In particular, it emphasized the importance of the equation of exchange as an analytical device and the importance of the quantity of money as a tool of economic policy. The monetarist view gained adherents in the late 1960s, partly because of the long delay in passing the federal tax increase of 1968. The reluctance of the Johnson administration to propose and the reluctance of Congress to enact this tax increase vividly illustrated some of the difficulties in using fiscal policy for stabilization. Even more important was the fact that the tax increase, when finally enacted, failed to have the restrictive effect on GDP (in the face of expansionary monetary policy) that some Keynesians had predicted.

During the 1970s, as more and more evidence accumulated, many of the differences between the monetarists and Keynesians seemed to wane in importance. Most monetarists conceded that fiscal policy can affect output and the price level; most Keynesians conceded the same regarding monetary policy. Although it would be incorrect to say that no differences remained on this score, there seemed to be a growing recognition that the differences had narrowed considerably. Thus Milton Friedman, the leading monetarist,

317

was quoted as saying, "We are all Keynesians now." And 1985 Nobel laureate Franco Modigliani, a leading Keynesian, responded in his 1976 presidential address to the American Economic Association by saying, "We are all monetarists now."

SUPPLY-SIDE ECONOMISTS

While the differences between the monetarists and Keynesians were narrowing, a new group of economists, known as supply-side economists, entered the fray. Since we have already discussed supply-side economics at length in Chapter 11 (pages 260–62), there is no need for a long discussion here. As you will recall, supply-side economists, who rose to prominence in the late 1970s and 1980s, are concerned primarily with influencing aggregate supply, particularly through the use of various financial incentives such as tax reductions. Supply-side economics really is not new. Major economists of the eighteenth and nineteenth (as well as twentieth) centuries were concerned with the stimulation of aggregate supply. In the early 1980s, supply-side economists were very influential in the Reagan administration (for further discussion, see Case Study 14.1).

THE NEW CLASSICAL MACROECONOMISTS

New classical macroeconomists

Another group that emerged in the 1970s were the **new classical macroeconomists**, led by Nobel laureate Robert Lucas of the University of Chicago, Thomas Sargent of Stanford University, and Neil Wallace of the University of Minnesota. They formulated a theory of macroeconomics based on three assumptions. First, they assumed that markets cleared; in other words, prices of inputs and outputs varied so as to equate the quantity supplied to the quantity demanded. Second, they assumed that people and firms have imperfect information. Third, they assumed that the expectations of people and firms conform to the theory of rational expectations.

RATIONAL EXPECTATIONS

Rational expectations

The theory of **rational expectations**, formulated initially by Indiana University's John Muth, has had a substantial impact on economic analysis and policy. Put briefly, *a person's expectations (or forecast) of a particular economic variable are rational if the person makes the best possible use of whatever information is available.* This does not mean that the person's forecast is necessarily very accurate. What it does mean is that the person does his or her home-

More on the tax cut of 1981

Internal Revenue Service

As indicated in previous chapters, supply-side economists played an important role in formulating and arguing for the huge tax cut in 1981. Individual income taxes were cut 25 percent across the board over three years. Corporate taxes were reduced as a consequence of an increase in the pace at which depreciation could be charged against current income. Other tax reductions were enacted as well.

The first phase of the tax cut occurred in 1981 and was discounted by the administration, because it was only 5 percent and did not prevent the recession of 1981–82. Economic policymakers in the Reagan administration, therefore, counted on the large tax cut of 10 percent in 1982 to stimulate the economy. They argued that the Reagan Economic Recovery Program could only be judged after the successive 10 percent tax cuts in 1982 and 1983 had occurred. They were banking on the success of the successive 10 percent tax cuts to show up in a strong recovery.

In fact, there was a strong recovery in 1983 and 1984; particularly at the beginning of 1984, the supply siders were often more accurate than other economists in forecasting how strong it would be. However, according to critics of supply-side economics, this substantial increase in real GDP should have been expected on the basis of the Keynesian model described in Chapters 5 and 6. To them, the strong recovery of 1983 and 1984 was testimony to the continued usefulness of the Keynesian model, highly simplified though it is.

Also, critics of supply-side economics pointed out that some supply siders claimed that the 1981 tax cut would increase output so dramatically that there would be no substantial increase in the federal deficit because output would rise sufficiently to offset the cut in tax rates. Instead, the deficit for fiscal 1985 was about $200 billion. In response to such criticisms, the supply siders blamed the Fed's tight-money policies for the fact that output did not grow as much as they expected.

work and does not make stupid mistakes. For example, if information is available concerning the size of the wage increases granted by the auto industry and if this information is relevant in making forecasts of what the inflation rate will be, a person is assumed to obtain and take proper account of this information in making forecasts of the inflation rate. If the person does not do so, his or her expectations are not rational, according to the economist's definition.

On the basis of the theory of rational expectations, *individuals and firms do not make systematic errors in forecasting the future.* For example, suppose that a person uses a model to forecast the inflation rate and that experience indicates that this model always underestimates the actual inflation rate. If this person's expectations are rational, one would expect him or her to recognize this downward bias and to compensate for it by adding an amount to forecasts based on this model. *On the average, forecasts, if they are rational, are correct.* To repeat, this does not mean that forecasters are always accurate. Instead, it means that, if we look at the results of a very large number of forecasts, we will find that the *average* forecasting error is zero. Unlike the forecasting model which always underestimated the inflation rate, there is no downward or upward bias. The forecasting errors are random.

UNEMPLOYMENT AND BUSINESS FLUCTUATIONS

According to the new classical macroeconomists, high rates of unemployment are not evidence of a gap between actual and potential output that can be reduced; instead, output fluctuations result from random errors. Markets are assumed to work efficiently; and firms, acting to maximize their profits, are assumed to make the best possible decisions. According to Robert Lucas, since unemployed workers have the option of accepting pay cuts to get jobs, excess unemployment is essentially voluntary.

Fluctuations in aggregate demand are due principally to erratic and unpredictable government policy, in Lucas's view. Changes in the quantity of money induce cyclical fluctuations in the economy. But the power of policy changes to affect real GDP is limited. People come to learn the way in which policy is made, and only unanticipated government policy changes can have a substantial impact on output or employment. Once firms and individuals learn of any systematic rule for adjusting government policy to events, the rule will have no effect.

■ CAN STABILIZATION POLICIES WORK?

On the basis of their theories, the new classical macroeconomists conclude that the *government cannot use monetary and fiscal policies to close recessionary and inflationary gaps in the way described in Chapters 6, 12, and 13, because the models presented in those chapters do not recognize that the expectations of firms and individuals concerning their incomes, job prospects, sales, and other relevant variables are influenced by government policies.* If firms and individuals formulate their expectations rationally, they will tend to frustrate the government's attempts to use activist stabilization policies.

To illustrate what these economists are saying, suppose that the economy is in a recession and that the government, trying to close the recessionary gap in the ways described in Chapters 6, 12, and 13, increases the amount that it spends on goods and services and increases the money supply. Because prices tend to move up while wages do not, profits tend to rise and firms find it profitable to expand. But this model is based on the supposition that labor is not smart enough to foresee that prices are going to go up and that labor's real wage is going to diminish. If labor does foresee this (that is, if its expectations are rational), it will insist on an increase in its money wage, which will mean that firms will not find it profitable to expand, and the government's antirecession policy will not work as expected.

REACTIONS PRO AND CON

These views have received considerable attention in academic and policy circles. For example, in one of its annual reports, the Federal Reserve Bank of Minneapolis stated that:

> The [new classical] view conjectures that some amount of cyclical swing in production and employment is inherent in the micro-level processes of the economy that no government macro policies can, or should attempt to, smooth out. Expected additions to money growth certainly won't smooth out cycles, if the arguments in this paper are correct. Surprise additions to money growth have the potential to make matters worse.... One strategy that seems consistent with the significant, though largely negative, findings of [the new classical macroeconomists] would have monetary policy focus its attention on inflation and announce, and stick to, a policy that would bring the rate of increase in the general price level to some specified low figure.[1]

Given the fact that the new classical macroeconomists have challenged the core of the theory underlying discretionary stabilization policies, it is not surprising that many economists, particularly liberals, have attacked their conclusions. Franco Modigliani, for instance, has claimed that their model is inconsistent "with the evidence; if it were valid, deviations of unemployment from the natural rate would be small and transitory—in which case [Keynes's] *General Theory* would not have been written."[2] Since Lucas's theory makes excess unemployment the result of purely unexpected events, one would think that unemployment would

---

[1]Federal Reserve Bank of Minneapolis, *Rational Expectations—Fresh Ideas that Challenge Some Established Views of Policy Making* (Minneapolis, 1977), pp. 12–13.

[2]F. Modigliani, "The Monetarist Controversy, or, Should We Forsake Stabilization Policies," *American Economic Review,* March 1977, p. 6.

Recession as a means to stop inflation in 1982

President Ronald Reagan presenting his tax package

When President Reagan came into office in 1981, the inflation rate was 11 percent. The combination of President Carter's efforts to stimulate the economy in 1977–78 and the oil price shock of 1979 had apparently created an underlying inflation rate of about 8 percent. In his campaign, Reagan had promised to reduce inflation by encouraging the Federal Reserve to reduce the rate of growth of the money supply and by creating greater incentives for the economy to produce more goods. He would therefore attack the traditional causes of inflation, "too much money chasing too few goods," from both sides.

By the 1980s, most economists believed that people's expectations about the possible effects of future government policies could affect how well the policies worked. For example, if the government tried to stimulate the economy by increasing the rate of growth of the money supply, its policy would fail if firms and labor unions simply raised prices and wages in expectation of higher inflation. The additional money supplied to the economy would go into higher prices rather than toward stimulating more production.

One group of economists felt that it would take a long time to get business and labor to reduce their expectations of future inflation. In addition, wage increases tended to be set in advance, by multiyear contracts, so wage gains could not be easily reduced even if expectations of future inflation fell. Because of this, the only way to reduce price increases and wage demands quickly, this group argued, would be to create a large increase in unemployment.

In contrast, another group of economists felt that inflation could be reduced without a large increase in unemployment if the government's resolve to stick to inflation-fighting policies was credible. These economists argued that the problem with the government's anti-inflation efforts in the past was that they were not steady enough. At the first sign of a recession, the Fed would back off and rekindle inflation with an easy money policy.

In fact the Fed did adhere to a tight money policy long after the recession of 1982 became quite severe. Fed Chairperson Paul Volcker had tightened up on the money supply in the summer of 1981. Interest rates rose, and the economy slid into recession. In early 1982, the unemployment rate was over 9 percent, but Volcker still maintained a tight policy. It was not until October 1982 that the Fed eased up.

By that time, the rate of inflation had fallen from the 11 percent level of early 1981 to 3.5 percent. But the cost of reducing inflation had been a severe downturn in business activity. According to many observers, the Fed had no choice but to take a strong stand against inflation. Nonetheless, the results suggested that, once inflation becomes embedded, it is difficult to reduce it because expectations of continued inflation can be halted only by deep recession.

fluctuate randomly around its equilibrium level if this theory is true. Critics point out that recessions sometimes last quite a long time.

Critics also claim that the new classical macroeconomics neglects the inertia in wages and prices. Contracts are written for long periods of time. Workers stick with firms for considerable periods. Consequently, wages and prices do not adjust as rapidly as is assumed by the new classical macroeconomists. According to the critics, most empirical analysis does not support the view that wages and prices adjust rapidly. On the contrary, wage and price movements show only slow and adaptive changes.

One of the most serious criticisms has centered on the new classical macroeconomists' contention that business fluctuations would be eliminated if firms and consumers had accurate current information about the aggregate price level. Given that the Consumer Price Index is widely disseminated with a relatively short lag, this does not seem very plausible. As Northwestern's Robert Gordon put it, "With monthly and even weekly data on the money supply available, people could make expectational errors about monetary changes lasting for only a few weeks, not nearly enough to explain business cycles lasting an average of four and one-half years in the postwar era, and twelve years for the period of high unemployment between 1929 and 1941."[3]

REAL BUSINESS CYCLE MODELS

In contrast to the models described in the previous section, some new classical macroeconomists, such as Edward Prescott of the University of Minnesota, argue that business fluctuations are due predominantly to real rather than monetary factors. These economists, whose influence within the new classical camp has grown substantially in recent years, are called **real business cycle theorists**. In their view, business fluctuations are the natural (indeed *efficient*) response of the economy to changes in technology and the availability of resources. Thus, business fluctuations are due predominantly to shifts in the aggregate supply curve, not the aggregate demand curve.

**Real business
cycle theorists**

To illustrate what they have in mind, consider Figure 14.1. Suppose that technological change shifts the long-run aggregate supply curve to the right, with the result that real GDP increases from Y_0 to Y_1 (in panel A). Then suppose that OPEC cuts back on the supply of oil, and so causes a shift of the aggregate supply curve to the left, with the result that real GDP falls from Y_1 to Y_2 (in panel B). These output fluctuations are due to shifts in the aggregate supply curve, not the aggregate demand curve. According to real business cycle models, this is the way that business fluctuations in the real world tend to occur.

What are the factors that shift the aggregate supply curve, and thus cause business fluctuations? Among the most important are

[3]R. Gordon, *Macroeconomics* (5th ed.; Glenview, Ill.: Scott Foresman, 1990), p. 202.

FIGURE 14.1

Favorable and Unfavorable Supply Shocks

In panel A, a favorable supply shock (technological advance) shifts the aggregate supply curve to the right and increases real GDP from Y_0 to Y_1. In panel B, an unfavorable supply shock (oil cutback) shifts the aggregate supply curve to the left and decreases real GDP from Y_1 to Y_2.

A

Favorable supply shock

B

Unfavorable supply shock

new products, new methods of production, new sources of raw materials, changes in the price of raw materials, and good or bad weather (recall Chapter 4). These factors are sometimes called **supply shocks** (a concept first introduced in Chapter 10). The effects of a *favorable* supply shock (one that pushes the aggregate supply curve to the right) may persist for several years, after which an *unfavorable* supply shock (one that pushes the aggregate supply curve to the left) may be felt. For example, in Figure 14.1, the technological advance that increases real GDP from Y_0 to Y_1 is a favorable supply shock, which is succeeded by an unfavorable supply shock—the cutback of oil from OPEC—which reduces real GDP from Y_1 to Y_2.

Supply shocks

As in the other new classical models discussed earlier in this chapter, real business cycle models assume that equilibrium is achieved in all markets. In other words, markets clear. Each firm produces the amount of output it desires, and hires the quantity of labor it wants. Workers get as much work as they want; there is no involuntary unemployment. Prices and wages respond flexibly to changing economic conditions. This is in contrast to the new Keynesian models, taken up in succeeding sections, which assume that there are many factors that prevent markets from clearing. It is also in contrast to the original Keynesian model, which assumed that wages were inflexible.

THE EFFECT OF A SUPPLY SHOCK

To illustrate in more detail how supply shocks can cause business fluctuations, suppose that there is a temporary decline in agricultural productivity due to bad weather and that this productivity decline reduces real income in agriculture. As Chapter 5 would lead us to expect, this cut in real income leads farmers to decrease their consumption of goods and services, but they do not decrease their consumption levels all at once. Instead, they spread the reduction of consumption over time. Thus, a supply shock of this sort would be expected to spread from one sector of the economy to another. As farmers cut back their consumption levels, nonagricultural industries—like clothing and automobiles—may feel the pinch. Also, the effects of such a supply shock would be expected to persist for some time. Since farmers cut back their consumption spending gradually, the adverse effects on the sales of other industries—like clothing and automobiles—are likely to continue for some time.

An unfavorable supply shock—such as this decline in agricultural productivity—leads firms to want fewer workers at the prevailing wage. Thus, according to real business cycle models, real wages will fall as the demand curves for labor shift to the left. The fact that these models predict that real wages will tend to fall when real GDP falls—and that real wages will tend to rise when real GDP rises—is in accord with past experience, according to some observers but not according to others.[4]

RESPONSES TO THE MODELS

According to proponents of real business cycle models, these models can explain the recent history of the U.S. economy reasonably well. If this is true, it is a remarkable achievement, given that so little attention is given to shifts in the aggregate demand curve. But many economists are skeptical, particularly because they are very uncomfortable with a theory that provides such a small role for monetary policy. As stressed in Chapter 13, there is a significant direct relationship between the money supply and real GDP. How do the proponents of real business cycle models explain this relationship? In their view, changes in real GDP cause changes in the money supply, rather than the other way around. As output goes up or down during a business cycle, the volume of transactions does the same; and the demand for money tends to go up or down too.

ENTHUSIASM AND SKEPTICISM

Proponents of real business cycle models say that these models enable economists to take a more integrated approach to business fluctuations and economic growth. At present, business

[4]Gordon, *Macroeconomics;* and C. Walsh, "New Views of the Business Cycle," *Business Review of the Federal Reserve Bank of Philadelphia,* January–February 1986.

fluctuations—the relatively short-term ups and downs of the economy—are often studied separately from economic growth—the relatively long-term, generally upward movement of the economy. According to real business cycle models, both business fluctuations and economic growth stem from factors that shift the long-run aggregate supply curve. Because some factors have only temporary effects, they result in business fluctuations, whereas other factors leave more permanent effects, and thus result in economic growth.

However, there is considerable skepticism that supply shocks of this sort are big enough to cause the business fluctuations we have experienced. As Robert Gordon of Northwestern University has put it:

> Skeptics doubt that any conceivable supply shock could explain why output fell one-third in the Great Depression of the 1930s. Only the oil price shocks of the 1970s . . . qualify as a supply shock severe enough to explain the recessions that occurred in 1974–75 and 1980–82. Proponents of the real business cycle approach have failed to identify particular events in particular sectors that could be labeled supply shocks in earlier episodes like the Great Depression and postwar recessions before 1974. At an industry level, one would expect technology shocks to occur randomly. Highly distinctive technologies are used in different industries; for instance, an innovation that increases the speed of a Macintosh desktop computer has little effect on the productivity of coal miners. Favorable shocks in some industries would cancel out adverse shocks in other industries, which deepens the skepticism that (except for the oil shocks of the 1970s) the *average* effect of all the separate industry shocks could be large enough to explain actual booms and recessions.[5]

THE NEW KEYNESIANS

New Keynesians

Just as there is a new classical macroeconomics, so there is a new Keynesianism. Like the original Keynesians, the **new Keynesians** do not believe that markets clear continuously; in other words, they do not believe that the quantity demanded of a good or input always equals the quantity supplied. Instead, they believe that if there is a sudden shift in the demand or supply curve, prices will fail to adjust quickly enough to equate the quantity demanded to the quantity supplied. In their view, the economy can stay in a state of disequilibrium for years if prices adjust slowly enough.

As we know from previous sections, this is a quite different view from that held by the new classical macroeconomists, who assume that markets clear continuously because prices adjust

[5]Gordon, *Macroeconomics*, pp. 205–6.

quickly. The new Keynesians, like the old Keynesians, say that their view is the more realistic one. They argue that it is unrealistic to assume that workers who are unemployed during recessions are voluntarily unemployed. Ask such a worker, they say, whether he or she would refuse a job offer at the prevailing wage. In their view, it is very likely that he or she would not refuse the offer, thus shedding doubt on whether the labor market actually clears. Turning to product markets, they ask whether a firm in a recession is selling all that it would desire. In their view, such a firm would be likely to say it was not, thus shedding doubt on whether the product market actually clears.

Like the new classical economists, the new Keynesians have adopted the theory of rational expectations. For example, MIT's Stanley Fisher has shown that if the public has rational expectations, systematic monetary policy can stabilize the economy. But his theory assumes that wages are inflexible, whereas the new classical macroeconomists assume that they are flexible. This is a fundamental difference.

HOW DO NEW KEYNESIANS DIFFER FROM OLD KEYNESIANS?

Both old and new Keynesians assume that prices or wages or both tend to adjust slowly in the short run, with the result that the quantity of output, more than price, tends to adjust to changes in aggregate demand. But whereas old Keynesians merely assumed that wages tend to be rigid and that prices are sticky, new Keynesians have developed theories that help to explain why such wage and price stability can be expected, given the rational behavior of individuals and firms. In other words, new Keynesians have tried to construct a microeconomic foundation for Keynesianism that old Keynesians failed to provide.

MENU COSTS AND STICKY PRICES

To explain why prices adjust slowly, the new Keynesians assume that markets are not perfectly competitive. In other words, firms are assumed to have some control over the prices of their products. For many products, like computers, oil, or beer, this is a reasonable assumption. Going a step further, they also assume that a firm incurs costs when it changes its price. Such costs are called **menu costs**. Why? Because they are the same sort of costs as a restaurant incurs when it changes its prices, and thus must print new menus.

Menu costs

TABLE 14.1 Jefferson Company's Profit If It Raises or Does Not Raise Its Prices, Original Situation		PRICES ARE RAISED	PRICES ARE NOT RAISED
	Sales	$1,095,000	$1,070,000
	Costs	840,000	850,000
	Profit	$ 255,000	$ 220,000

As an illustration, consider the Jefferson Company, a producer of a wide variety of hand tools. If it changes its price schedule, it must print new catalogs, spend a considerable amount to inform its customers of the price changes, change many aspects of its billing system, and so forth. Its accountants may figure that it costs Jefferson $40,000 every time it changes its price schedule.

Suppose that there is an upward shift in the demand curve for Jefferson's product. Given this increase in demand, Jefferson's president suspects that it may be wise to raise the firm's prices. According to the firm's accountants, the firm's sales, costs, and profits will be as shown in Table 14.1 if it raises or does not raise its prices. Clearly, the president is right; Jefferson would make higher profits if it increased its prices. However, the figures in Table 14.1 do not take into account the $40,000 cost of changing prices. When these menu costs are taken into account, it is not profitable for Jefferson to increase its prices.

In the next few months, the upward shift in the demand curve for Jefferson's product continues, and its president wonders once again whether the firm should raise its prices. The firm's accountants estimate that its sales, costs, and profits will be as shown in Table 14.2 if it now raises or does not raise its prices. At this point, is it profitable for Jefferson to change its price schedule? The answer is yes, because Table 14.2 shows that the increase in profit ($260,000 − $210,000 = $50,000) is more than sufficient to cover the menu costs of $40,000.

TABLE 14.2 Jefferson Company's Profit If It Raises or Does Not Raise Its Prices, Subsequent Situation		PRICES ARE RAISED	PRICES ARE NOT RAISED[a]
	Sales	$1,120,000	$1,080,000
	Costs	860,000	870,000
	Profit	$ 260,000	$ 210,000

[a]Note that, if prices are not raised, sales and costs differ from what they would have been in Table 14.1 if prices had not been raised. This is because Table 14.2 pertains to a later situation than Table 14.1 does.

The point here is that, according to the new Keynesians, prices can be sticky because of the existence of menu costs. This is one way that they explain why prices adjust slowly and why markets do not clear continually.

LONG-TERM LABOR CONTRACTS AND STICKY WAGES

Like prices, wages can be sticky, according to the new Keynesians, and this is due in part to long-term labor contracts. In the United States, formal labor contracts prevail in heavily unionized industries like steel, automobiles, rubber, and electrical machinery. Those contracts influence the level of wages in other industries, since they tend to be imitated elsewhere. Many contracts extend for three years; the contract calls for specified increases in wage rates each year plus (in some instances) extra wage increases that offset whatever changes occur in the Consumer Price Index.

Not all contracts come up for renewal at the same time. Instead, as shown in Figure 14.2, some contracts come up for renewal each year. Assuming for simplicity that all contracts are negotiated at the beginning of the year and that all last for three years, the contracts negotiated in 1997 cover 1997, 1998, and 1999; those negotiated in 1998 cover 1998, 1999, and 2000; and so on. One important consequence of these multiyear labor contracts is that wages adjust slowly, and with a substantial lag, to changes in aggregate demand.

Given that long-term contracts tend to slow the rate of adjustment of wages, it is interesting to ask why workers and firms prefer to enter into such agreements. One reason is that each wage negotiation costs both workers and firms a considerable amount of time and money, since each side must prepare its case thoroughly. Thus both sides are happy if these negotiations only take place every few years. Also, if labor and management do not come to an

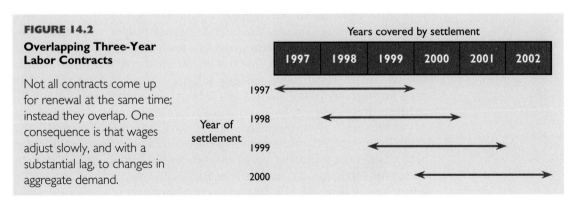

FIGURE 14.2

Overlapping Three-Year Labor Contracts

Not all contracts come up for renewal at the same time; instead they overlap. One consequence is that wages adjust slowly, and with a substantial lag, to changes in aggregate demand.

agreement, a strike may occur, with substantial potential losses to both sides. Neither side really wants a strike (except in very unusual circumstances), and if there are wide time intervals between negotiations, there also are likely to be wide time intervals between strikes.

IMPLICIT CONTRACTS

Implicit contracts

Another theory used by the new Keynesians to explain wage rigidity focuses on **implicit contracts**, which are agreements between workers and firms that are not found in any formal, written contracts. Rather, they are informal or implicit. Workers and firms have many understandings that are not formalized in any written agreement. Indeed, it would be impossible to write down all the understandings that grow up between labor and management.

According to this theory, workers are more inclined to shun risk than their employers; this seems reasonable given that the owners of firms have been willing to assume the risks of operating a business. In particular, workers are reluctant to assume the risks involved in allowing wage rates to adjust quickly to clear the labor markets, because this would mean that wage rates would vary considerably during business fluctuations. Under these circumstances, all workers would run the risk that their wages would vary over the business cycle.

Instead, according to implicit contract theory, wages are set on the basis of long-term considerations and do not go up and down during business fluctuations. Thus wages do not behave so as to clear markets, and employment will vary considerably. Firms in effect provide insurance for workers, who do not want their wages to vary over the business cycle. Responding to their workers' preferences, firms maintain relatively rigid wages but at a level that allows them to increase their profits.

In particular, firms often lay off workers with the least seniority when it is necessary to lay off anyone. This means that workers with considerable seniority have a relatively good "insurance policy" against being laid off. Most workers may prefer a system of this sort (whereby relatively few workers with little seniority are laid off when times get tough but the wages of those that are not laid off are quite rigid) to a system where wages are permitted to vary enough over the business cycle so that labor markets clear continually.

Critics note that if workers are not willing to be bound by the prevailing implicit contracts, they may refuse unemployment after being laid off by finding work elsewhere. Similarly, when the demand for labor grows, and so results in the rigid prevailing wages' being lower than what other firms may be willing to pay for their services, workers may leave the firm and take jobs elsewhere. Further, it should be recognized that according to this theory, unemployment really is voluntary since all workers enter freely into the relevant implicit contracts recognizing that they are accepting the risk of unemployment.[6]

POLICY ACTIVISM: PRO AND CON

Much of the debate between the new Keynesians and the new classical macroeconomists is really over policy activism. The new Keynesians—like the old Keynesians—tend to be policy activists; they believe that discretionary monetary and fiscal policies are required to keep the economy on a reasonably even keel. The new classical macroeconomists tend to be very skeptical about how much stabilization policies of this sort can achieve. The debate over the pros and cons of policy activism has been going on for decades. While it is hazardous to try to summarize the views of each side (since there is considerable disagreement within each camp), the disagreements tend to be along the following lines.

Stability of private spending. Many opponents of policy activism tend to believe that if the government's economic policies did not destabilize the economy, private spending would be quite stable. Policy activists, on the other hand, believe that business and consumer spending represent a substantial source of economic instability that should be offset by monetary and fiscal policies.

Flexibility of prices. Even if intended private spending is not entirely stable, flexible prices tend to stabilize it, according to the nonactivists. The policy activists reply that prices are relatively inflexible downward; in their view, the length of time that would be required for the economy to get itself out of a severe recession would be intolerably long. Their opponents seem more inclined than policy activists to believe that high unemployment will cause wages and input prices to fall, and shift the short-run aggregate supply curve to the right and increase output in a reasonable period of time.

Rules versus activism. Opponents of policy activism tend to believe that, even if intended private spending is not entirely stable, and if prices are not entirely flexible, activist monetary and fiscal policies to stabilize the economy are likely to do more damage than good. As pointed out in Chapter 13, they sometimes favor a

---

[6]For a more complete discussion of the new Keynesians, see Mansfield, *Economics: Principles, Problems, Decisions*, 7th ed.

rule stipulating that the money supply should grow steadily at a constant rate, because of the difficulties in forecasting the future state of the economy and because of the long and variable time lags in the effects of changes in the quantity of money on output and prices. The policy activists, while admitting that monetary and fiscal policies have sometimes been destabilizing, are much more optimistic about the efficacy of such policies in the future.

POLICY RULES AND TIME INCONSISTENCY

The new classical macroeconomists have stressed repeatedly the importance of the public's expectations regarding future policy. For this reason they think that one should distinguish between *rigid policy rules, feedback policy rules*, and *discretionary policy. A* **rigid policy rule** *specifies completely the behavior of the variable governed by the policy rule.* For example, Milton Friedman's suggestion that the money supply be set so that it grows at a fixed, agreed-on percentage rate is a rigid policy rule. Once the government establishes the percentage growth rate, the behavior of the money supply is completely specified. Regardless of what happens, the money supply must grow at this particular rate so long as this policy rule is in force.

Rigid policy rule

In contrast, a **feedback policy rule** *allows the behavior of the variable governed by the policy rule to change, depending on future circumstances.* For example, the government might specify that if the unemployment rate exceeds 7 percent, the rate of increase of the money supply will be set at 6 percent, whereas if the unemployment rate does not exceed 7 percent, it will be set at 5 percent. In this case, the government does not specify the behavior of the money supply completely, since one cannot predict whether at a given time in the future the unemployment rate will be above 7 percent or not. But it does issue a well-defined formula indicating how the money supply will behave, depending on future circumstances.

Feedback policy rule

The new classical macroeconomists argue that feedback policy rules cannot affect real GDP. If the public knows the feedback rule in advance, any change in the money supply specified by the rule will be anticipated by the public. Thus Robert Lucas and his coworkers believe that such a rule will not be effective. Why? Because, according to Lucas, only unexpected changes in the price level will result in changes in aggregate supply (recall page 320). Consequently, Lucas and his coworkers feel that a rigid policy rule of the sort proposed by monetarists like Milton Friedman is best. In their view, the adoption of such a rule would promote the credibility of monetary policy. In other words, the public would be convinced that the money supply really would grow in accord with this rigid policy rule.

Discretionary policy, *as we know from previous discussions, is policy that is formulated at the discretion of the policymakers.* According to the new classical macroeconomists, one of the big problems arising from discretionary policy is **time inconsistency**. Suppose, for example, that the government is trying to reduce the rate of inflation. Once it convinces the public that the inflation rate is going to go down—once it makes its disinflationary policy credible—policymakers may feel that it is in their interest to depart from their announced policy. For example, suppose that an election is coming up. If they nudge the rate of increase of the money supply up a bit, the resulting unexpected increase in the price level is likely to raise real GDP and reduce the unemployment rate, thus increasing their chances of victory in the election. Of course, as the people become more and more used to being double-crossed in this way, it becomes harder and harder for the government to convince them that any of its announced policies will really be carried out.[7]

Discretionary policy

Time inconsistency

THE NEW KEYNESIAN RESPONSE

The new Keynesians take a quite different tack. They believe that changes in the attitudes and expectations of firms and consumers can cause substantial economic instability that should be offset by government stabilization policy. In contrast to the new classical macroeconomists, they do not favor rigid policy rules. For example, they point out that the increase in the velocity of money in the United States since 1982 has been very erratic (recall page 312); this would seem to suggest that the growth rate of nominal GDP would have fluctuated considerably if a rigid rule calling for a constant growth of the money supply had been applied. As we have seen, the new Keynesians put a great deal of emphasis on the fact that long-term wage and price contracts exist. Consequently, they are less concerned than the new classical macroeconomists with the credibility of the government's policies. Because wages and prices tend to be sticky, total real output tends to be affected by the actual behavior of the money supply and the price level, not just by unanticipated changes in the price level.

In recent years, activists have recognized more fully and more openly the many difficulties in formulating an effective economic stabilization policy. In the 1960s, there was considerable talk among activists about fine-tuning the economy; such optimism is

[7]For some relevant discussion, see N. G. Mankiw, "A Quick Refresher Course in Macroeconomics," *Journal of Economic Literature*, December 1990.

long gone. Activists readily admit that there may be a long and variable lag between the time when a policy change occurs and when its effects are felt. Also, they recognize that it is very difficult to forecast what the state of the economy may be when the effects of a policy change occur. Nonetheless, activists have not abandoned the attempt to formulate effective discretionary stabilization policies. On the contrary, they continue to press for changes in monetary and fiscal policies that, in their eyes, would keep the economy on a more even keel. But they also tend to be cautious, certainly more cautious than forty years ago, in their claims for what discretionary stabilization policies can achieve.

DIVERGENT POLITICAL BELIEFS

One final and very important point: While economics is a science, not a mere reflection of the economist's political beliefs, it nonetheless is impossible to divorce an economist's views of the economy from his or her political feelings where policy issues are involved. To a considerable extent, the differences between the policy activists and their opponents stem from divergent political beliefs. The policy activists tend to be optimistic concerning the extent to which the government can be trusted to formulate and carry out a responsible set of monetary and fiscal policies. They recognize that some politicians are willing to win votes in the next election by destabilizing the economy, but they nonetheless believe that discretionary action by elected officials will generally be more effective than automatic rules. Opponents of policy activism, on the other hand, are skeptical of the willingness of politicians to do what is required to stabilize the economy, rather than what is politically expedient. Since this aspect of the debate is difficult to resolve (in any scientific way), a complete resolution of this controversy is not likely any time soon.

REVIEW AND PRACTICE

▥ SUMMARY

1 The principal debate of the 1960s and 1970s was between Keynesians and monetarists. The Keynesians put more emphasis than the monetarists did on the federal budget; the monetarists put more emphasis than the Keynesians did on the money supply.

2 In the late 1970s, supply-side economists came to prominence; their emphasis is on the aggregate supply curve. To stimulate rightward shifts in the aggregate supply curve, supply siders favor the use of various financial incentives, particularly tax cuts.

3 The new classical macroeconomists like Robert Lucas also came to prominence in the 1970s. On the basis of their assumptions, the new classical macroeconomists conclude that the government cannot use monetary and fiscal policies to close recessionary and inflationary gaps in the ways described in Chapters 6, 12, and 13. One central assumption they make is that prices and wages are completely flexible.

4 According to real business cycle models, business fluctuations are due predominantly to shifts in the aggregate supply curve, not the aggregate demand curve. Among the most important factors shifting the aggregate supply curve are new products, new methods of production, new sources of raw materials, and good or bad weather.

5 The new Keynesians, like the old Keynesians, believe that prices and wages tend to be rigid in the short run, with the result that the quantity of output, more than price, tends to adjust to changes in aggregate demand.

6 According to the new Keynesians, prices tend to be sticky because of menu costs (costs incurred by firms when they change prices), and wages tend to be sticky because of long-term labor contracts. On the basis of the theory of implicit contracts, they conclude that wages are set according to long-term considerations. (Responding to workers' aversion to risk, firms maintain relatively rigid wages.)

7 The debate over the pros and cons of policy activism continues. Opponents of policy activism tend to believe that activist monetary and fiscal policies to stabilize the economy are likely to do more damage than good. Policy activists, while admitting that discretionary monetary and fiscal policies have sometimes been destabilizing, are much more optimistic about the efficacy of such policies in the future.

■ PROBLEMS AND QUESTIONS

1 "New Keynesians are liberal activists who want to push our society in the direction of socialism. Their emphasis on policy activism is a reflection of their desire to have the government purchase more of the national output." Comment and evaluate.

2 "New classical macroeconomists are archconservatives with a strong laissez faire orientation. They prefer monetary policy over fiscal policy because it involves less direct interference by government in the marketplace." Comment and evaluate.

3 "The Keynesian model can easily be translated into monetarist terms, and the monetarist model can easily be translated into Keynesian terms. Thus there really is no basic difference between the Keynesians and the monetarists." Do you agree? Why or why not?

4 After the cyclical trough of 1982, the velocity of money fell substantially below its postwar growth path. Does this mean that monetarism is useless? Explain.

5 What are rational expectations? Do you agree with the new classical macroeconomists that much unemployment is voluntary? Explain.

6 (a) "Working hours are fixed by custom at about 40 hours per week. Cutting taxes won't affect them." Do you agree? Why or why not?
(b) "Business executives are working about as hard as they can to keep their heads above water. Cutting taxes won't affect how hard they work." Do you agree? Why or why not?

■ KEY TERMS

new classical macroeconomists	new Keynesians	feedback policy rule
rational expectations	menu costs	discretionary policy
real business cycle theorists	implicit contracts	time inconsistency
supply shocks	rigid policy rule	

■ VIEWPOINT FOR ANALYSIS

In the spring of 1994, the Federal Reserve nudged interest rates upward. According to *Business Week*, "At its heart, the Fed's thinking is simple: Move now or risk an acceleration of inflation next year. Fed officials first became seriously concerned last December, when the economy showed unmistakable signs of a boom as the expansion neared the end of its second year."*

(a) Would monetarists like Milton Friedman feel that this is the optimal way to conduct monetary policy? If not, what sort of policy would they prefer?

(b) Would new classical macroeconomists like Robert Lucas feel that discretionary monetary policy of this sort is optimal? Why or why not?

(c) Would real business cycle theorists like Edward Prescott feel that business fluctuations can be eliminated by monetary policies of this sort? Why or why not?

(d) Would new Keynesians tend to feel that discretionary policies of this sort can be effective and useful?

(e) Many liberal members of Congress opposed the Fed's actions; conservatives tended to be less critical of the Fed. Why?

Business Week, May 2, 1994, p. 25.

Is the U.S. Business Cycle Dead?

At the end of each long expansion in the United States, there has been brave talk about the end of the business cycle. The longest U.S. expansion, which started in 1991 and reached record longevity in February 2000, was no exception. Unfortunately, earlier long expansions (in the 1960s and 1980s) did end in recessions. The U.S. economy went through a significant transformation in the 1990s. However, was this enough (and of the kind) to guarantee that the business cycle is, once and for all, a thing of the past?

Better macroeconomic policies. At least some of the credit for the longevity of the 1990s expansion should go the Fed. Most economists would agree that the Fed has done a good job of keeping inflation under control without precipitating a recession. Some analysts have even suggested that without the Gulf War there would have been no recession in 1990 and 1991. However, most expansions in the postwar period have been brought to end by the Fed either by design or by accident. To assume that this can never happen again stretches credulity.

Inventory control. Most business cycles in the past have been amplified by large swings in inventories. During expansions, inventory accumulation has added to growth, and during contractions inventory decumulation has subtracted from growth. However, thanks to the revolution in computing, just-in-time inventory control methods have become pervasive over the last decade, reducing inventory swings. Nevertheless, this does not mean that inventory cycles have been eliminated, only that they are now less pronounced.

Growth of services. The service sector now dominates the U.S. economy, accounting for over three-quarters of the jobs. The demand for services is typically more stable than the demand for goods (for example, in hard times, we will postpone a new car purchase but not a haircut). Here again, it seems plausible that downturns may be more muted, but the growth of the service sector is a longer-term trend that has not eliminated cycles.

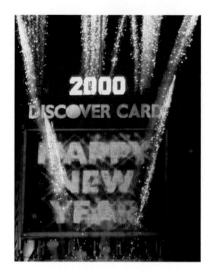

At the turn of the new century, the U.S. economy was in its longest expansion.

Technology. Much of the higher growth in the late 1990s was due to the impact of the PC and Internet technologies on productivity. Some analysts saw this as evidence of a new paradigm in which business cycles were abolished. However, while the higher productivity growth of the 1990s was probably evidence of the economy's being on the higher growth trajectory, it said nothing about how stable or cyclical growth would be.

In the final analysis, a case can be made for more subdued downturns in the U.S. economy. However, there is little evidence that the business cycle is dead. Postwar expansions in the United States have not died of old age. They typically have been killed off either by a supply shock (for example, an oil crisis) or by a policy mistake—usually by the Fed. Until and unless we are willing to bet that both these expansion killers will never haunt us again, we need to prepare for the eventuality of another downturn.

■ QUESTIONS

1 Do you think the deregulation of banks and other financial services has increased or decreased the volatility of economic growth in the United States?

2 Some have argued that increased globalization (greater global interdependence) reduces the likelihood of recessions since it diminishes the dependence of the U.S. market on domestic demand and also eases inflationary pressures. Do you agree with this? How could globalization make business cycles more pronounced?

3 Starting in the late 1990s the Untied States began running budget surpluses. If the United States did suffer a downturn in economic growth, could these surpluses be used to cushion the blow? How?

4 If you were on the Federal Reserve's Open Market Committee, what would you do if inflation started to rise? How would you balance the need to keep inflation under control without precipitating a recession?

PART FOUR

Economic Decision Making: The Firm, The Consumer, and Society

The Business Firm: Organization, Motivation, and Optimal Input Decisions

LEARNING OBJECTIVES

In this chapter, you should learn:

- The pros and cons of various types of business organizations (proprietorships, partnerships, corporations)
- What a production function is
- The law of diminishing marginal returns
- How firms should make input decisions if they want to maximize profit

David Rothermel is the manager of a large firm that produces corn in Illinois. Among other things, he must decide how much of various inputs—like fertilizer, land, labor, and capital—he should use to produce his corn. How can he solve this problem? One purpose of this chapter is to answer this question.

It is hard to overstate the importance of business firms in the U.S. economy. They produce the bulk of our goods and services, hire most of the nation's workers, and issue stocks and bonds that represent a large percentage of the nation's wealth. Judged by any yardstick—even less complimentary ones like the responsibility for environmental pollution—business firms are an extremely important part of the U.S. economy.

In this chapter, we will take a close look at the decision-making process within the firm. We begin by discussing the organization, motivation, and technology of the firm, and then focus particular attention on the following central question: If a firm attempts to maximize profits, what production technique—that is, what combination of inputs—should it choose to produce a particular quantity of output? Two points should be noted at the outset. First, when finding the optimal input combination, we take as given the quantity of output that the firm will produce. In subsequent chapters, we shall discuss how the firm should choose this output quantity. Second, an important purpose of this chapter and Chapters 16 and 18 is to show how a product's supply curve can be derived. In this chapter, we present some of the concepts and findings required for this purpose.

THE BUSINESS FIRM:
ORGANIZATION,
MOTIVATION, AND
OPTIMAL INPUT
DECISIONS
CHAPTER 15

GENERAL MOTORS: A STUDY

In Chapter 2, when we first discussed the role of the business firm in the U.S. economy, we cited two examples of business firms: Peter Amacher's drugstore and the General Motors Corporation. Now that we are considering the operations of the business firm in more detail, let's look more closely at the General Motors Corporation.

■ THE EARLY YEARS

General Motors was formed in 1908 by William C. Durant, an energetic and imaginative entrepreneur who made over a million dollars in the carriage business before he was 40. After taking over the bankrupt Buick Motor Company in 1904, Durant built it into a very successful operation. Then, in 1908, he gained control of a number of small automobile companies (including Cadillac and Oldsmobile), several truck firms, and ten parts and accessory firms. The resulting amalgamation was General Motors.

In 1910, General Motors's sales fell and Durant lacked the funds to pay his workforce and suppliers. To get the money he needed, he went to a banking syndicate, which lent him $15 million but required him to turn over the management of the company to them. By 1915, Durant had acquired another auto producer, Chevrolet, and had picked up formidable financial allies in the Du Ponts, the owners of the famous chemical firm. Using both these levers, Durant regained full control of General Motors in 1916, and between 1916 and 1920, he concentrated on expanding the productive capacity of the General Motors Corporation. A man of extraordinary vision, he recognized, as few of his contem-

Once an independent firm, by 1915 Chevrolet had become part of General Motors.

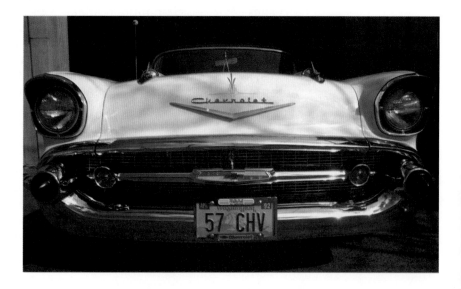

poraries did, a great potential demand for moderately priced cars, and he devoted his energy to putting General Motors in a position to satisfy this demand.

▇ REORGANIZATION OF THE FIRM

Although Durant was a man of great vision, he was not the sort of administrator who created a tidy organizational structure. The General Motors Corporation under Durant was a large agglomeration of companies in a variety of product lines, with somewhat tangled lines of communication and diffuse control. When automobile sales did not come up to expectations in 1920, the firm suffered a reduction in profits. The resulting crisis led to Durant's retirement as president of General Motors and the firm's adoption of a new organizational plan created by Alfred Sloan, a young M.I.T.-trained engineer, who soon became president.

This plan divided General Motors into a number of divisions: the Buick division, the Chevrolet division, the accessory division, and so forth. Each division was given considerable freedom, but greater attention was devoted to central control and coordination than under Durant's more anarchic organization. Sloan's organizational plan, an important innovation in its day, remained in effect with little change for many years.

▇ PROSPERITY AND NEW CHALLENGES

During the 1920s General Motors prospered. Its sales rose from $600 million in 1920 to $1.5 billion in 1929, and its profits rose from about $38 million in 1920 to about $248 million in 1929. The next decade was different. The 1930s were the years of the Great Depression, when sales and profits of most firms, including General Motors, were hard hit. But during the 1940s General Motors entered another period of prosperity and growth. Its sales rose from about $1.8 billion in 1940 to about $5.7 billion in 1949, and its profits rose from about $196 million in 1940 to about $656 million in 1949. The 1950s and 1960s saw the prosperity of General Motors continue. Of course there were short intervals when sales and profits fell, but the trend was upward, in part because of population growth and in part because higher incomes meant bigger sales of automobiles. The firm experienced no prolonged period of low profits or considerable excess capacity, as was the case in the 1930s.

However, in the 1970s trouble began to appear in the form of imported Japanese cars. By 1981, the trouble was serious, as evidenced by General Motors's third-quarter loss of about $500 million. Quotas on Japanese imported cars helped the firm to get back

343

Studebaker and the low-volume trap

Studebaker roadster, 1931

In this case study, we turn from General Motors to another major auto producer, Studebaker, which, after having had its ups and downs before World War II, started off the postwar period in good shape. Flush with cash, Studebaker capitalized on the pent-up demand of the war years by being the first to come out with a new model—a streamlined car of the future. The firm prospered in the late 1940s and early 1950s, and in 1952 it had its best year ever.

As the seller's market of the early postwar years disappeared, however, serious weaknesses in Studebaker's position became obvious. The auto industry was very competitive in the mid-1950s. There were eight major manufacturers (today's Big Three and Studebaker, plus Nash, Hudson, Packard, and Willys). Studebaker suffered from bad management and high-cost labor, but one of its major problems could not have been easily solved by either management or labor—its inability to capture the cost savings that result from a large scale of production.

General Motors and the other large manufacturers had begun to introduce new models every year. While these firms could spread the costs of new model development (about $30 million) over the 1 to 2 million units they produced each year, Studebaker was selling fewer than 300,000 cars a year. The company could not reach the minimum cost per car that was possible through large volume. In 1953, it scheduled production of 350,000 cars but built only 186,000. By 1954, Studebaker had set its break-even point at 108,000 per year and was trying to reduce the figure still further.

In 1963, Studebaker's sales dipped to 66,000 as the temporary success of the Lark slowed when the Big Three brought out compacts of their own. If the company had plowed its profits back into expansion in the late 1940s, it might have been able to reach a scale of production that would have enabled it to compete with the larger manufacturers. But its small size made it impossible for Studebaker to weather its other problems, and the company was forced to close in 1964.

into the black, and in 1984 the firm seemed healthier than it had been. But in 1987 its profits were less than Ford's, its smaller rival, and from 1990 to 1992 it racked up a total of almost $10 billion in losses. In 1999, it reported a $5.6 billion profit, but for the foreseeable future, General Motors will have to work hard to compete successfully against both its domestic rivals and the Japanese imports. The stakes are large, since the somewhat jumbled organization William Durant assembled in 1908 is now one of the biggest industrial companies in the United States.

U.S. FIRMS, LARGE AND SMALL

General Motors is an economic colossus, a huge organization with just under 400,000 employees. Of course it is not typical of U.S. business firms. If we broaden our focus to take in the entire population of business firms in the United States, the first thing we note is their tremendous number: according to government statistics, there are about 25 million. The vast majority of these firms, as one would expect, are very small. There are lots of grocery stores, gas stations, auto dealers, drugstores (like Mr. Amacher's), clothing shops, restaurants, and so on. You see hundreds of them as you walk along practically any downtown city street. But these small firms, although numerous, do not control the bulk of the nation's productive capacity. The several hundred largest firms have great economic power, measured by their sales, assets, employment, or other such indexes. The small firms tend to be weak and short lived. Although some prosper, many small firms go out of business after only a few years of existence.

Firms, large or small, can be classified into three types: proprietorships, partnerships, or corporations. What do these terms mean?

PROPRIETORSHIPS

Proprietorship

A proprietorship is a legal form of business organization—the most common form and also the simplest. Specifically, a **proprietorship** is a firm owned by a single individual. A great many of the nation's small businesses are proprietorships. For example, the corner drugstore may well be one. If so, it has a single owner, say, Donald Smith. He hires the people he needs to wait on customers, deliver orders, do the bookkeeping, and so forth. He borrows, if he can, whatever money he feels he needs. He reaps the profits, or incurs the losses. All his personal assets—his house, his furniture, his car—can be taken by creditors to meet the drugstore's bills; he has unlimited liability for the debts of the business.

Pros. What President Lincoln said about common men and women applies as well to proprietorships: God must love them, or He wouldn't have created so many of them. If proprietorships didn't have advantages over other legal forms of business organization under many sorts of circumstances, there wouldn't be so many of them. What are these advantages? First, *owners of proprietorships have complete control over their businesses*. They don't have to negotiate with partners or other co-owners. They are the boss—and the only boss. Anyone who has been in a position of complete authority knows the joy it can bring. Many proprietors treasure this feeling of independence. Second, *a proprietorship is easy and inexpensive to establish:* all you have to do is hang out your shingle and announce you are in business. This too is a great advantage.

THE BUSINESS FIRM:
ORGANIZATION,
MOTIVATION, AND
OPTIMAL INPUT
DECISIONS
CHAPTER 15

Cons. But proprietorships have important disadvantages as well, and for this reason they are seldom found in many important industries. One disadvantage is that *it is difficult for a proprietor to put together enough financial resources to enter industries like automobiles or steel.* No one in the world has enough money to establish, by himself or herself, a firm of General Motors's present size. Another disadvantage is that *proprietors are liable for all of the debts of the firm.* If their business fails, their personal assets can be taken by their creditors, and they can be completely wiped out.

PARTNERSHIPS

Partnership

A **partnership** is more complicated than a proprietorship. As its name implies, it is a form of business organization where two or more people agree to own and conduct a business. Each partner agrees to contribute some proportion of the capital and labor used by the business and to receive some proportion of the profits or losses. There are many types of partnerships. In some cases, one or more of the partners may be "silent partners" who put up some of the money but have little or nothing to do with the operations of the firm. The partnership is a common form of business organization in some industries and professions, such as the law. But partnerships are found less frequently than proprietorships or corporations in the United States.

Pros. A partnership has certain advantages. Like a proprietorship, *it can be established without great expense or legal red tape.* (However, if you ever go into a partnership with someone, you would be well advised to have a good lawyer draw up a written agreement establishing such things as the salaries of each partner and how profits are to be shared.) In addition, a partnership can avoid some of the problems involved in a proprietorship. *It can usually put together more financial resources and specialized know-how than a proprietorship,* and this can be an important advantage.

Cons. But the partnership also has certain drawbacks. First, *each partner is liable without limit for the bills of the firm.* For example, even if one partner of a law firm has only a 30 percent share of the firm, he or she may be called on to pay all the firm's debts if the other partners cannot do so. Second, *there is some red tape in keeping a partnership in existence.* Whenever a partner dies or withdraws or whenever a new partner is admitted, a new partnership must be established. Third, though preferable to a proprietorship, *the partnership is still not a very effective way to obtain the large amounts of capital required for some modern industries.* A modern automobile plant may cost $500 million, and not many partnerships could assemble that much capital. For these reasons, as well as for others discussed in the next section, the corporation has become the dominant form of business organization in the United States.

CORPORATIONS

Corporation

A far more complicated form of business organization than either the proprietorship or partnership, the **corporation** is a fictitious legal person, separate and distinct from its owners. A corporation is formed by having lawyers draw up the necessary papers stating (in general terms) what sorts of activities the owners of the corporation intend to engage in. The owners of the corporation are the stockholders. Stock, pieces of paper signifying ownership of the corporation, is issued to the owners, generally in exchange for their cash. The corporation's board of directors, which is responsible for setting overall policy for the firm, is elected by the stockholders. Ordinarily, each share of stock gives its owner one vote. The firm's owners can, if they are dissatisfied with the company's policies or think they have better opportunities elsewhere, sell their stock to someone else, assuming, of course, that they can find a buyer.

Pros. The corporation has many advantages over the partnership or proprietorship. In particular, *each of the corporation's owners has limited, not unlimited, liability.* If I decide to become one of the owners of General Motors and if a share of General Motors stock sells for $70, I can buy ten shares of General Motors stock for $700. And I can be sure that if General Motors falls on hard times, I cannot lose more than the $700 I paid for the stock. There is no way that I can be assessed beyond this. Moreover, *the corporation, unlike the partnership or proprietorship, has unlimited life.* If several stockholders want to withdraw from the firm, they simply sell their stock. The corporation goes on, although the identity of the owners changes. For these reasons, *the corporation is clearly a better device for raising large sums of money than the partnership or proprietorship.* This is an enormous advantage of the corporation, particularly in such industries as automobiles and steel, which could not otherwise finance their operations.

Cons. Without question, the corporation is a very important social invention. It permits people to assemble the large quantities of capital required for efficient production in many industries. Without limited liability and the other advantages of the corporation, it is doubtful that the opportunities and benefits of large-scale production could have been reaped. This does not mean that the corporate

347

form will work for all firms. If a firm requires only a modest amount of capital, there is no reason to go to the extra trouble and expense of establishing a corporation. Moreover, one disadvantage of the corporation is double taxation of income, since corporations themselves pay income taxes. Thus every dollar earned by a corporation and distributed to stockholders is taxed twice by the federal government—once when it is counted as income by the corporation and once when the remainder is counted as income by the stockholders.

MOTIVATION OF THE FIRM

Profit maximization

What determines the behavior of the business firm? As a first approximation, *economists generally assume that firms are motivated by a desire for* **profit maximization**. Profits are defined as the difference between the firm's revenue and its costs. In other words, economists generally assume that firms try to make as much money as possible. This assumption does not seem unreasonable; most businesses appear to be interested in making money. Nonetheless, the assumption of profit maximization oversimplifies the situation. Although businesses certainly want profits, they are interested in other things as well. Some firms claim that they want to promote better cultural activities or better racial relations in their community. At a less lofty level, other firms say that their aim is to increase their share of the market. Whether or not one takes these self-proclaimed goals very seriously, it is clear that firms are not interested only in making money.

TECHNOLOGY, INPUTS, AND THE PRODUCTION FUNCTION

The decisions a firm should make in order to maximize its profits are determined by the current state of technology.

■ TECHNOLOGY

Technology is the sum total of society's knowledge concerning the industrial arts. Just as consumers are limited by their income, firms are limited by the current state of technology. If the current state of technology is such that we do not know how to produce more than 40 bushels of corn per year from 1 acre of land and 2 units of labor, then this is as much as the firm can produce from this combination of land and labor. In making its decisions, the firm must take this into account.

What are the inputs in this production process?

■ INPUTS

In constructing a model of the profit-maximizing firm, economists must somehow represent the state of technology and include it in their model. As a first step toward this end, we must define an

Input

input. Perhaps the simplest definition of an **input** is that it is anything the firm uses in its production process. Some of the inputs of a farm producing corn might be seed, land, labor, water, fertilizer, and various types of machinery, as well as the time of the people managing the farm.

■ PRODUCTION FUNCTION

Having defined an input, we can now describe how economists represent the state of technology. The basic concept economists use for this purpose is the production function.

Production function

For any commodity, *the **production function** is the relationship between the quantities of various inputs used per period of time and the maximum quantity of the commodity that can be produced per period of time.* More specifically, the production function is a table, a graph, or an equation showing the maximum output rate that can be achieved from any specified set of usage rates of inputs. The production function summarizes the characteristics of existing technology at a given point in time. It reflects the technological constraints the firm must reckon with.

To see more clearly what we mean by a production function, consider the Milwaukee Machine Company, a hypothetical machine shop that produces a simple metal part. Suppose we are

349

TABLE 15.1	QUANTITY OF LABOR USED PER MONTH (NUMBER OF WORKERS EMPLOYED	OUTPUT PER MONTH (NUMBER OF PARTS)
Production Function, Milwaukee Machine Company	0	0
	1	100
	2	210
	3	315
	4	415
	5	500

considering a period of time that is so short that the firm's basic plant and equipment cannot be altered. For simplicity, suppose that the only input whose quantity can be altered in this period is the amount of labor used by the machine shop. Suppose that the firm collects data showing the relationship between the quantity of its output and the quantity of labor it uses. This relationship, given in Table 15.1, is the firm's production function. It shows that when 1 worker is employed, 100 parts are produced per month; when 2 workers are employed, 210 parts are produced per month; and so on. Information concerning a firm's production function is often obtained from the firm's engineers, as well as its artisans and technicians.

TYPES OF INPUTS

In analyzing production processes, we suppose that all inputs can be classified into two categories: fixed and variable inputs.

Fixed input

A **fixed input** *is one whose quantity cannot change during the period of time under consideration.* This period will vary. It may be six months in one case, six years in another case. Among the most important inputs often included as fixed are the firm's plant and equipment—its factory and office buildings, its machinery, its tooling, and its transportation facilities. In the simple example of the wheat farm in Table 15.2 on the next page, land is a fixed input since its quantity is assumed to be fixed at 1 acre.

Variable input

A **variable input** *is one whose quantity can be changed during the relevant period.* It is generally possible to increase or decrease the number of workers engaged in a particular activity (although this is not always the case, since they may have long-term contracts). Similarly, it frequently is possible to alter the amount of

TABLE 15.2	NUMBER OF UNITS OF LABOR	BUSHELS OF WHEAT PRODUCED PER YEAR
Relationship between Labor Input and Output on a 1-Acre Wheat Farm	0	0
	1	30
	2	70
	3	100
	4	125
	5	145

raw material that is used. In the case of the wheat farm in Table 15.2, labor clearly is a variable input since its quantity can be varied from 0 to 5 units.

THE SHORT RUN AND THE LONG RUN

Whether an input is considered variable or fixed depends on the length of the period under consideration. The longer the period, the more inputs are variable, not fixed. Although the length of the period varies from case to case, economists have found it very useful to focus special attention on two time periods: the short run and the long run. *The **short run** is defined as the period of time in which at least one of the firm's inputs is fixed.* More specifically, since the firm's plant and equipment are among the most difficult inputs to change quickly, *the short run is generally understood to mean the length of time during which the firm's plant and equipment are fixed.* On the other hand, *the **long run** is that period of time in which all inputs are variable.* In the long run, the firm can make a complete adjustment to any change in its environment.

Short run

Long run

To illustrate the distinction between the short run and the long run, let's consider General Motors. Any period of time during which GM's plant and equipment cannot be altered freely is the short run. A period of one year is certainly a case of the short run, because in a year GM could not vary the quantity of its plant and equipment. It takes longer than a year to construct an automotive plant or to alter an existing plant to produce a new kind of automobile. Also, because some of its existing contracts with suppliers and workers extend for more than a year, GM cannot vary all its inputs in a year without violating these contracts. On the other hand, any period of time during which GM can vary the quantity of all inputs is the long run. A period of 50 years is certainly a case of the long run. Whether a shorter period of time—10 years, say—is a long-run situation depends on the problem at hand. If all the relevant inputs can be varied, it is a long-run situation; if not, it is a short-run situation.

A useful way to look at the long run is to consider it a planning horizon. While operating in the short run, the firm must continually be planning ahead and deciding its strategy for the long run. Its decisions concerning the long run determine the sort of short-run position the firm will occupy in the future. Before a firm makes the decision to add a new type of product to its line, the firm is in a long-run situation (with regard to the new product), since it can choose among a wide variety of types and sizes of equipment to produce the new product. But once the investment is made, the firm is confronted with a short-run situation, since the type and size of equipment is, to a considerable extent, frozen.

AVERAGE PRODUCT OF AN INPUT

Average product

In order to determine which production technique—that is, which combination of inputs—a firm should use, it is necessary to define the average product and marginal product of an input. *The **average product** of an input is the firm's total output divided by the amount of input used to produce this amount of output.* The average product of an input can be calculated from the production function. Consider the wheat farm in Table 15.2. The average product of labor is 30 bushels per unit of labor when 1 unit of labor is used, 35 bushels per unit of labor when 2 units are used, $33\frac{1}{3}$ bushels per unit of labor when 3 units are used, and so forth.

MARGINAL PRODUCT OF AN INPUT

As the amount of labor used on the farm increases, so does the farm's output; but the amount of extra output from the addition of an extra unit of labor varies depending on how much labor is already being used. The extra output from the addition of the first unit of labor is $30 - 0 = 30$ bushels per unit of labor. The extra output due to the addition of the second unit of labor is $70 - 30 = 40$ bushels per unit of labor. And the extra output from the addition of the fifth unit of labor is $145 - 125 = 20$ bushels per unit of labor. **Marginal product** *The **marginal product** of an input is the addition to total output due to the addition of the last unit of input, the quantity of other inputs used being held constant.* Thus the marginal product of labor is 30 bushels when between 0 and 1 units of labor are used, 40 bushels when between 1 and 2 units of labor are used, and so on.

TABLE 15.3

Average and Marginal Products of Labor on a 1-Acre Wheat Farm

NUMBER OF UNITS OF LABOR	TOTAL OUTPUT (BUSHELS PER YEAR)	MARGINAL PRODUCT (BUSHELS PER UNIT OF LABOR)	AVERAGE PRODUCT (BUSHELS PER UNIT OF LABOR)
0	0		—
		30	
1	30		30
		40	
2	70		35
		30	
3	100		33⅓
		25	
4	125		31¼
		20	
5	145		29

Table 15.3 shows the average and marginal products of labor at various levels of utilization of labor; Figure 15.1 shows the same thing graphically. The data in both Table 15.3 and Figure 15.1 concerning the average and marginal products of labor are derived from the production function. Given the production function, shown in Table 15.2 and reproduced in Table 15.3, the average and marginal products at each level of utilization of labor can be determined in the way we have indicated.

FIGURE 15.1

Average and Marginal Products of Labor on a 1-Acre Wheat Farm

The marginal product of the first unit of labor (which, according to Table 15.3, equals 30 bushels per unit) is plotted at the midpoint between 0 and 1 units of labor. The marginal product of the second unit of labor is plotted at the midpoint between 1 and 2 units of labor. The marginal product curve connects these and other points showing the marginal product of various amounts of labor.

353

**THE BUSINESS FIRM:
ORGANIZATION,
MOTIVATION, AND
OPTIMAL INPUT
DECISIONS**
CHAPTER 15

In Figure 15.1, as in the case of most production processes, the average product of the variable input (labor in this case) rises, reaches a maximum, and then falls. The marginal product of labor also rises, reaches a maximum, and falls. This too is typical of many production processes. Why do average and marginal products behave in this way? Because of the law of diminishing marginal returns, to which we now turn.

THE LAW OF DIMINISHING MARGINAL RETURNS

**Law of
diminishing
marginal returns**

Perhaps the best-known, and certainly one of the least-understood, laws of economics is the so-called **law of diminishing marginal returns**. Put in a single sentence, this law states that *if equal increments of an input are added, the quantities of other inputs being held constant, the resulting increments of product will decrease beyond some point;* that is, the marginal product of the input will diminish.

Suppose that a small factory that manufactures a metal automobile component has eight machine tools. If this firm hires only one or two workers, total output and output per worker will be quite low. These workers will have a number of quite different tasks to perform, and the advantages of specialization will be sacrificed. Workers will spend considerable time switching from one machine to another, and many of the eight machine tools will be idle much of the time. What happens as the firm increases its workforce? As more and more workers are added, the marginal product (that is, the extra product) of each will tend to rise, as the workforce grows to the point where it can operate the fixed amount of equipment effectively. However, if the firm continues to increase the number of workers, the marginal product of a worker will eventually begin to decrease. Why? Because workers will have to wait in line to use the fixed number of machine tools and because the extra workers will have to be assigned to less and less important tasks. Eventually, if enough workers are hired (and utilized within the plant), they may get in each other's way to such an extent that production may grind to a halt.

Returning to the wheat farm discussed in the previous section, Table 15.3 shows that the law of diminishing marginal returns applies in this case too. The third column of this table indicates that beyond two units of labor, the marginal product of labor falls. Certainly, it seems entirely reasonable that as more and more of a variable input (in this case labor) is combined with a fixed amount of another input (in this case land), the additional output to be derived from an additional unit of the variable input will eventually decrease. In the case of a 1-acre wheat farm, one would expect that as more and more labor is added, the extra workers' functions eventually would become less and less important and productive.

The Coca-Cola company and input costs

In 1985 the Coca-Cola company made a well-publicized change in its formula for Coke. The company touted the change with a huge marketing campaign. In fact, the formula for Coke had been quietly changed six years earlier.

Because of worldwide shortages, the price of beet and cane sugar jumped from 19 cents per pound in Septem-

ber 1978 to 26 cents per pound in January 1979. While such a price hike does not dramatically affect most sugar buyers, for Coke it was catastrophic. A change of 1 cent per pound in sugar prices can cause a 20 million dollar swing in Coke's operating profits. The bottling empire is the United States's largest sugar buyer, taking a million tons per year, or about 10 percent of all the sugar sold in the United States.

Because of the efficiencies of corn production in this country, a sweetener made by refining corn into sugar makes high-fructose corn sweeteners about 10 percent cheaper than beet and cane sugar when prices are normal. By using a 55 percent fructose sweetener, Coca-Cola can realize substantial cost savings, particularly when sugar

prices are abnormally high. Coke publicly announced the switch to corn sweeteners in January 1979, but other than sugar producers and traders, no one seemed to notice. Eight months later, 7-Up followed suit and decided to increase its use of corn sweeteners, and Pepsi also considered such a move.

The response of the soft drink companies to the increased price of sugar is typical of any firm faced with a price hike for an input. Firms try to reduce the use of inputs whose prices rise in order to maintain profits or to avoid having to raise the price of their products (and risk losing sales to competitors). The greater the increase in the price of an input, the more incentive there is for a profit-maximizing firm to conserve on its use of that input.

The law of diminishing marginal returns plays a major part in determining the firm's optimal input combination and the shape of the firm's cost functions, as we shall see in this and the next chapter. To prevent misunderstanding and confusion, several points about this law should be stressed. First, *it is assumed that technology remains fixed.* If technology changes, the law of diminishing marginal returns cannot predict the effect of an additional unit of input. Second, *at least one input must be fixed in quantity,* since the law of diminishing marginal returns is not applicable to cases where there is a proportional increase in all inputs. Third, *it must be possible to vary the proportions in which the various inputs are utilized.* This is generally possible in industry and agriculture.

THE OPTIMAL INPUT DECISION

Now we are in a position to answer the question posed at the beginning of this chapter: Given that a firm is going to produce a particular quantity of output, which production technique—which

**THE BUSINESS FIRM:
ORGANIZATION,
MOTIVATION, AND
OPTIMAL INPUT
DECISIONS**
CHAPTER 15

combination of inputs—should it choose to maximize profits? Note first that if the firm is to maximize its profits it must minimize the cost of producing this quantity of output. This seems obvious enough. But which combination of inputs (that will produce the required quantity of output) will minimize the firm's costs? The answer can be stated like this: *The firm will minimize cost by combining inputs in such a way that the marginal product of a dollar's worth of any one input equals the marginal product of a dollar's worth of any other input used.*

Another way to say the same thing is: *The firm will minimize cost by combining inputs in such a way that, for every input used, the marginal product of the input is proportional to its price.* Why does this say the same thing? Because the marginal product of a dollar's worth of an input equals the marginal product of the input divided by its price. If the marginal product of a unit of labor is 40 units of output and if the price of labor is $4,000 per unit, the marginal product of a dollar's worth of labor is 40 ÷ $4,000 = 0.01 unit of output. Thus, if the firm is satisfying the rule for cost minimization in the previous paragraph—if it is combining inputs so that the marginal product of a dollar's worth of any one input equals the marginal product of a dollar's worth of any other input used—it must at the same time be combining inputs so that for every input used, the marginal product of the input is proportional to its price.

■ THE WHEAT FARM: A NUMERICAL EXAMPLE

To illustrate the application of this rule, let's take a numerical example from the wheat farm cited above. Suppose that the farm can vary the amount of labor and land it uses. Table 15.4 shows the marginal product of each input when various combinations of inputs (all combinations being able to produce the specified quantity of output) are used. Suppose that the price of labor is $4,000 per unit and that the annual price of using land is $1,000 per acre. (We assume that the firm takes the prices of inputs as given and that it can buy all it wants of the inputs at these prices.) For each combination of inputs, Table 15.4 shows the marginal product of each input divided by its price. Based on our rule, the optimal input combination is 4.1 acres of land and 1 unit of labor, since this is the only combination (capable of producing the required output) where the marginal product of labor divided by the price of labor equals the marginal product of land divided by the price of land.

Is this rule correct? Does it really result in a least-cost combination of inputs? Let's look at the cost of the various input combinations in Table 15.4. The first combination (0.5 unit of labor and 7 acres of land) costs $9,000; the second combination (1.0 unit of

TABLE 15.4

Determination
of Optimal Input
Combination

AMOUNT OF INPUT USED		MARGINAL PRODUCT		MARGINAL PRODUCT ÷ PRICE OF INPUT		
LABOR (UNITS)	LAND (ACRES)	LABOR (UNITS)	LAND (ACRES)	LABOR (UNITS)	LAND (ACRES)	TOTAL COST (DOLLARS)
0.5	7.0	50	5	50 ÷ 4,000	5 ÷ 1,000	9,000
1.0	4.1	40	10	40 ÷ 4,000 = 10 ÷ 1,000		8,100
1.5	3.0	30	30	30 ÷ 4,000	30 ÷ 1,000	9,000
2.5	2.0	20	50	20 ÷ 4,000	50 ÷ 1,000	12,000

labor and 4.1 acres of land) costs $8,100; and so on. An examination of the total cost of each input combination shows that the input combination chosen by our rule (1.0 unit of labor and 4.1 acres of land) is indeed the least-cost input combination, the one for the profit-maximizing firm to use.

EXPLORING FURTHER

HOW TO PRODUCE KANSAS CORN

To illustrate the practical payoff from the sort of analysis discussed in this chapter, let's consider how a distinguished agricultural economist, Earl Heady of Iowa State University, used these methods to help farmers make better production decisions. Table 15.5 shows the various amounts of land and fertilizer that will produce

TABLE 15.5

Combinations
of Fertilizer and
Land Required to
Produce 82.6
Bushels of Corn,
and the Ratio of
Marginal Products
at Each Such
Combination

AMOUNT OF INPUT USED		MARGINAL PRODUCT OF FERTILIZER ÷ MARGINAL PRODUCT OF LAND
FERTILIZER (POUNDS)	LAND (ACRES)	
0	1.19	0.0045
20	1.11	0.0038
40	1.04	0.0030
60	0.99	0.0019
80	0.96	0.0010
100	0.95	0.0003

**THE BUSINESS FIRM:
ORGANIZATION,
MOTIVATION, AND
OPTIMAL INPUT
DECISIONS**

CHAPTER 15

82.6 bushels of corn on Kansas Verdigras soil. As you can see, this amount of corn can be produced if 1.19 acres of land and no fertilizer are used, or if 1.11 acres of land and 20 pounds of fertilizer are used, or if 0.99 acre of land and 60 pounds of fertilizer are used, and so forth.

The third column of Table 15.5 shows the ratio of the marginal product of a pound of fertilizer to the marginal product of an acre of land, when each of these input combinations is used. For example, when 1.19 acres of land and no fertilizer are used, this ratio equals 0.0045. On the basis of the rule discussed in previous sections, a firm, if it minimizes costs, must set this ratio equal to the ratio of the price of a pound of fertilizer to the price of an acre of land. Why? Because the rule discussed above stipulates that the firm should choose an input combination so that

$$\frac{\text{Marginal product of fertilizer}}{\text{Price of fertilizer}} = \frac{\text{marginal product of land}}{\text{price of land}}.$$

So, if we multiply both sides of this equation by the price of fertilizer and divide both sides by the marginal product of land, we get

$$\frac{\text{Marginal product of fertilizer}}{\text{Marginal product of land}} = \frac{\text{price of fertilizer}}{\text{price of land}}.$$

Thus to minimize costs, a firm should set the ratio in the third column of this table equal to the ratio of the price of fertilizer to the price of land.

Heady and his coworkers, having obtained the results in the above table, used this technique to determine the optimal input combination farmers should use to minimize their costs.[1] The optimal input combination depends on the price of land and the price of fertilizer. Suppose that a pound of fertilizer costs 0.003 times as much as an acre of land. Under these circumstances, the minimum-cost input combination would be 40 pounds of fertilizer and 1.04 acres of land, since, as shown in the table, this is the input combination where the ratio of the marginal product of fertilizer to the marginal product of land is 0.003. No matter what the ratio of the price of fertilizer to the price of land may be, the least-cost input combination can be derived this way.

Such results are of considerable practical value to farmers. Moreover, the same kind of analysis can be used by organizations in other sectors of the economy, not just agriculture. Studies of

---

[1]E. Heady and L. Tweeten, *Resource Demand and Structure of the Agricultural Industry* (Ames: Iowa State University Press, 1963). It is assumed that a certain amount of labor is used; this amount is proportional to the number of acres of land.

how the Defense Department can reduce its costs have utilized concepts and techniques of essentially this sort. In a more peaceful vein, this same kind of analysis has been used by various manufacturing firms. For example, steel firms have made many such studies to determine least-cost ways to produce steel, and auto firms have made similar studies to reduce their costs.

REVIEW AND PRACTICE

■ SUMMARY

1 There are three principal types of business firms: proprietorships, partnerships, and corporations. Some advantages of the corporation are limited liability, unlimited life, and greater ability to raise large sums of money.

2 As a first approximation, economists generally assume that firms attempt to maximize profits. In large part, this is because it is a close enough approximation to reality for many of the most important purposes of economics. Also, economists are interested in the theory of the profit-maximizing firm because it provides rules of behavior for firms that do want to maximize profits.

3 To summarize the characteristics of existing technology at a given point in time, economists use the concept of the production function, which shows the maximum output rate of a given commodity that can be achieved from any specified set of usage rates of inputs.

4 Inputs can be classified into two categories: fixed and variable. A fixed input is one whose quantity cannot be changed during the period of time under consideration. A variable input is one whose quantity can be changed during the relevant period.

5 Whether an input is considered variable or fixed depends on the length of the period under consideration. The longer the period, the more inputs are variable, not fixed. The short run is defined as the period of time in which some of the firm's inputs (generally its plant and equipment) are fixed. The long run is the period of time in which all inputs are variable.

6 The average product of an input is the firm's total output divided by the amount of input used to produce this amount of output. The marginal product of an input is the addition to total output due to the addition of the last unit of input, the quantity of other inputs used being held constant.

7 The law of diminishing marginal returns states that if equal increments of an input are added (and the quantities of other inputs are held constant) the resulting increments of product will decrease beyond some point; the marginal product of the input will diminish.

8 To minimize its costs, a firm must choose its input combination so that the marginal product of a dollar's worth of any one input equals the marginal product of a dollar's worth of any other input used. Put differently, the firm should combine inputs so that for every input used, the marginal product of the input is proportional to its price.

■ PROBLEMS AND QUESTIONS

1 Suppose that a cost-minimizing firm in a perfectly competitive market uses two inputs: labor and capital. If the marginal product of capital is twice the marginal product of labor and if the price of a unit of labor is $4, what must be the price of a unit of capital?

2 In Figure 15.1 the marginal product of labor equals its average product when the latter is a maximum. Do you think that this is generally the case? Why or why not? (*Hint:* If the marginal product of an extra amount of labor exceeds the average product, will the average product increase? If it is less than the average product, will the average product decrease?)

3 A firm uses two inputs: capital and labor. The firm's chief engineer says that its output depends on the amount of labor and capital it uses in the following way:

$$Q = 3L + 4C,$$

where Q is the number of units of output produced per day, L is the number of units of labor used per day, and C is the amount of capital used per day. Does this relationship seem sensible? Why or why not?

4 In the previous problem, suppose that the price of using a unit of labor per day is $50 and the price of using a unit of capital per day is $100. What is the optimal input combination for the firm if the relationship in the previous problem is valid? Does this seem reasonable? Why or why not?

■ KEY TERMS

proprietorship	variable input
partnership	short run
corporation	long run
profit maximization	average product
input	marginal product
production function	law of diminishing marginal returns
fixed input	

■ VIEWPOINT FOR ANALYSIS

Dexter Baker, head of Air Products and Chemicals, Inc., gave a speech at Hilton Head Island, in which he said: "I believe we in the business community as stewards of our nation's wealth-creating processes have a special responsibility to ensure that the value systems upon which our business operates are based upon the highest ethical standards we can conceive. . . . Furthermore, [adherence to] sound ethical standards is not just a pious way to conduct one's affairs, it is also the most remunerative in the long run."*

(a) Does the goal of profit maximization ever conflict with high ethical standards? If so, give some examples.

(b) When economists assume that a firm maximizes profit, do you think that they make the tacit assumption that profit maximization occurs given the constraint that the firm observes reasonably high ethical and legal standards? For example, do you think they assume that the firm stays within federal and state laws?

(c) Are high ethical standards more likely to be remunerative in the long run than in the short run? If so, why?

*Vital Speeches, January 15, 1993, pp. 211-12.

CHAPTER 16

Getting behind the Demand and Supply Curves

LEARNING OBJECTIVES

In this chapter, you should learn:

■ How economists explain consumer behavior

■ The concept of marginal utility

■ The relation between an individual's demand curve and the market demand curve

■ The nature of the cost curves that underlie firms' decisions on supply

Droughts have been a recurring problem in California. In 1991, after five consecutive dry years, residents of Los Angeles were required by city ordinance to reduce water usage by 15 percent. What sorts of principles should be applied to determine which kinds of water use should be cut back most severely? One purpose of this chapter is to answer this question.

In a market economy, consumers decide how much to buy based on their income, their tastes, and market prices; firms decide how much to produce on the basis of their costs and what they can charge for their products. In this chapter we look behind the individual's demand curve and the firm's supply curve by outlining, first, the basic model of consumer demand and, second, the role that costs play in firms' decisions of how much to produce and, therefore, to supply. In Chapters 17 and 18 we will expand our discussions of supply and demand and consider what determines the characteristics of market demand and supply.

THE DEMAND CURVE

To a considerable extent, consumers, voting with their pocketbooks, are the masters of our economic system. No wonder, then, that economists spend much of their time describing and analyzing how consumers act. In addition, economists are interested in determining how consumers, as well as other decision-making units, should go about making rational choices. In this chapter, we present the basic model economists use to analyze consumer behavior.

CONSUMER EXPENDITURES

■ THE MARTINS OF JACKSONVILLE

Since we are concerned here with consumer behavior, let's begin by looking at the behavior of a particular consumer. It is hard to find any consumer who is "typical." There are hundreds of millions of consumers in the United States, and their behavior varies enormously. But how does one particular U.S. family—the Martins of Jacksonville, Florida[1]—spend its money? Janet and Mike Martin are about 40 years old, are both married for the second time, and have three children (by his first marriage). They own their own home, and both work. Mike is a computer programmer, and Janet is a product manager. Together the Martins make about $90,000 a year.

How do the Martins spend their money? For most consumers, we cannot answer this question with any accuracy, because people usually do not tell anyone what they do with their money. But because the Martins and their buying habits were scrutinized in a series of articles in a national magazine, it is possible to describe quite accurately where their money goes. As shown in Table 16.1, the Martins, who own their own home, spend about $1,350 a month—about 18 percent of their income—on housing. They spend about $375 a month—about 5 percent of their income—on food and

TABLE 16.1

Monthly Spending Pattern of Janet and Mike Martin of Jacksonville, Florida

ITEM	AMOUNT (DOLLARS)	PERCENT OF INCOME
Housing	1,335	18
Food and drink	375	5
Child support and education	965	13
Entertainment and clothing	965	13
Medical, dental, and insurance expenses	295	4
Transportation	295	4
Other expenditures	1,115	15
Taxes and savings	2,155	29
Monthly income	7,500	100[a]

[a]Because of rounding errors, the percentages do not sum to 100.

[1]For obvious reasons, we have changed the name and residence of the family in question. Otherwise, however, the facts given in the following paragraphs are as they were stated in a series of articles in a national magazine. To correct for inflation, we have increased the figures in the articles by the (approximate) percentage by which the price level has risen since the article appeared.

drink. About $965 a month—about 13 percent of their income—goes for child support and education.

In addition, the Martins spend about $965 a month—about 13 percent of their income—on entertainment and clothing. Medical, dental, and insurance expenses consume about $295 a month—about 4 percent of their income; another $295 a month—again, about 4 percent of their income—is spent on transportation. Finally, the Martins allocate about $1,115 a month—about 15 percent of their income—to other expenditures and about $2,155 a month—about 29 percent of their income—to taxes and savings.

This, in a nutshell, is how the Martins spend their money. The Martins exchange their resources (mostly labor) in the resource markets for $90,000 a year. They take this money into the product markets and spend about three-fourths of it for the goods and services described above. The remaining one-fourth of their income goes for taxes and savings. The Martins, like practically every family, keep a watchful eye on where their money goes and what they are getting in exchange for their labor and other resources.

■ AGGREGATE DATA FOR THE UNITED STATES

How does the way that the Martins spend their money compare with consumer behavior in general? In Table 16.2, we provide data on how all consumers allocated their aggregate income. These data tell us much more about the typical behavior of U.S. consumers than our case study of the Martins. Note first of all that U.S. households paid about 15 percent of their income in taxes. This, of course, is the price of government services. In addition, U.S. households saved about 2 percent of their income. In other words, they refrained from spending 2 percent of their income on goods and services; instead, they put this amount into stocks, bonds, bank accounts, or other such channels for saving. Also, about 3 percent of their income went for interest payments to banks and other institutions from which they had borrowed money.

They spent the remaining 80 percent of their income on goods and services. Table 16.2 makes it clear that U.S. consumers allocated much of their expenditures to housing, food and drink, and transportation. Spending on housing, household operations, and furniture and other durable household equipment accounted for about 19 percent of U.S. consumers' total income. Spending on food and beverages accounted for about 12 percent of their total income. Spending on automobiles and parts, gasoline and oil, and other transportation accounted for about 10 percent of their total income. Thus taxes, savings, housing, food and drink, and transportation accounted for about two-thirds of the total income of all households in the United States.

TABLE 16.2

Allocation of Income by U.S. Households, 1999

ITEM	PERCENT OF TOTAL
Personal taxes	15
Personal savings	2
Interest payments	3
Consumption expenditures	
Autos and parts	4
Furniture and household equipment	4
Other durable goods	2
Food and drink	12
Clothing and shoes	4
Gasoline and oil	2
Other nondurable goods	6
Housing	12
Household operations	5
Transportation	3
Medical care	12
Recreation	3
Other services	12
Total income	100[a]

[a]Because of rounding errors, the percentages do not sum to 100.
Source: Survey of Current Business.

The data in Table 16.2 make it obvious that the Martin family is not very typical of U.S. consumers. For example, it spends a much larger percentage of its income on entertainment and education than consumers as a whole do. To a large extent, this reflects the fact that people want different things. Looking around you, you see considerable diversity in the way consumers spend their money. Take your own family as an example. It is a good bet that your family spends its money quite differently from the nation as a whole. If you like to live in a big house, your family may spend much more than the average on housing. Or if you like to go to sports events, your expenditures on such entertainment may be much higher than average.

A MODEL OF CONSUMER BEHAVIOR

Why do consumers spend their money the way they do? The economist answers this question with the aid of a **model of consumer**

behavior, which is useful both for analysis and for decision making. To construct this model, the economist obviously must consider the consumer's tastes, which certainly influence how much the consumer purchases of a particular commodity. Some people like beef; others like pork. Some people like the opera; others would trade a ticket to hear Luciano Pavarotti for a ticket to a Dallas Cowboys game any day of the week.

In Chapter 1, we pointed out that, to be useful, a model must omit many unimportant factors, concentrate on the basic factors at work, and simplify in order to illuminate. To focus on the important factors at work here, let's assume that there are only two goods, food and clothing. This is an innocuous assumption, since the results we shall obtain can be generalized to include cases where any number of goods exist. For simplicity, food is measured in pounds, and clothing is measured in number of pieces of clothing.

Consider Janet Martin, making choices for her family. Undoubtedly, she regards certain market baskets—that is, certain combinations of food and clothing (the only commodities)—to be more desirable than others. She certainly regards 2 pounds of food and 1 piece of clothing to be more desirable than 1 pound of food and 1 piece of clothing. For simplicity, suppose that it is possible to measure the amount of satisfaction that she gets from each

Utility

market basket by its utility. *A* **utility** *is a number that represents the level of satisfaction that the consumer derives from a particular market basket.* For example, the utility attached to the market basket containing 2 pounds of food and 1 piece of clothing may be 10 utils, and the utility attached to the market basket containing 1 pound of food and 1 piece of clothing may be 6 utils. (A **util** is the traditional unit in which utility is expressed.)

■ MARGINAL UTILITY

It is important to distinguish between *total utility* and *marginal utility*. The total utility of a market basket is the number described in

Marginal utility

the previous paragraph; *the* **marginal utility** *measures the additional satisfaction derived from an additional unit of a commodity.* To see how marginal utility is obtained, let's take a close look at Table 16.3. The total utility the Martin family derives from the consumption of various amounts of food is given in the middle column of this table. (For simplicity, we assume for the moment that the Martins consume only food.) The marginal utility, shown in the right-hand column, is the extra utility derived from each amount of food over and above the utility derived from 1 less pound of food. Thus it equals the difference between the total utility of a certain amount of food and the total utility of 1 less pound of food.

POUNDS OF FOOD	TOTAL UTILITY	MARGINAL UTILITY
0	0	
		3(= 3 − 0)
1	3	
		4(= 7 − 3)
2	7	
		2(= 9 − 7)
3	9	
		1(= 10 − 9)
4	10	

[a]This table assumes that no clothing is consumed. If a nonzero amount of clothing is consumed, the figures in this table will probably be altered since the marginal utility of a certain amount of food is likely to depend on the amount of clothing consumed.

For example, as shown in Table 16.3, the *total* utility of 3 pounds of food is 9 utils, which is a measure of the total amount of satisfaction that the Martins get from this much food. In contrast, the *marginal* utility of 3 pounds of food is the extra utility obtained from the third pound of food, that is, the total utility of 3 pounds of food less the total utility of 2 pounds of food. Specifically, as shown in Table 16.3, it is 2 utils. Similarly, the *total* utility of 2 pounds of food is 7 utils, which is a measure of the total amount of satisfaction that the Martins get from this much food. In contrast, the *marginal* utility of 2 pounds of food is the extra utility obtained from the second pound of food, that is, the total utility of 2 pounds of food less the total utility of 1 pound of food. As shown in Table 16.3, it is 4 utils.

THE LAW OF DIMINISHING MARGINAL UTILITY

Economists generally assume that, as a person consumes more and more of a particular commodity, there is, beyond some point, a decline in the extra satisfaction derived from the last unit of the commodity consumed. For example, if the Martins consume 2 pounds of food in a particular period of time, it may be just enough to meet their basic physical needs. If they consume 3 pounds of food in the same period of time, the third pound of food is likely to yield less satisfaction than the second. If they consume 4 pounds of food in the same period of time, the fourth pound of food is likely to yield less satisfaction than the third. And so on.

Law of diminishing marginal utility

This assumption or hypothesis is often called the **law of diminishing marginal utility**. This law states that, *as a person consumes more and more of a given commodity (the consumption of other commodities being held constant), the marginal utility of the*

FIGURE 16.1

Total and Marginal Utility from Food Consumption, Martin Family

The marginal utility of the first pound of food (which, according to Table 16.3, equals 3 utils) is plotted at the midpoint between 0 and 1 pounds of food. The marginal utility of the second pound of food (which, according to Table 16.3, equals 4 utils) is plotted at the midpoint between 1 and 2 pounds of food. The marginal utility curve connects these and other points showing the marginal utility of various amounts of food consumed.

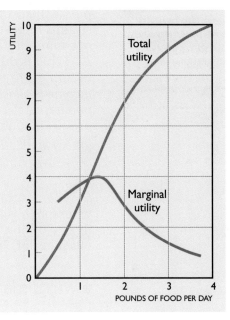

commodity eventually will tend to decline. The figures concerning the Martin family in Table 16.3 are in accord with this law, as shown in Figure 16.1, which plots the marginal utility of food against the amount consumed. Once the daily consumption of food exceeds about 1.5 pounds, the marginal utility of food declines.

THE EQUILIBRIUM MARKET BASKET

Preferences alone do not determine consumers' actions. *Besides knowing consumers' preferences, we must also know their income and the prices of commodities to predict which market basket they will buy.* Consumers' money income is the amount of money they can spend per unit of time, and this amount constrains consumers' choice of a market basket. For example, although Mike Martin may regard an Austin Reed as his favorite suit, he may not buy it because he may not have sufficient income. The prices of commodities also influence the consumer's choice of a market basket. If the Austin Reed suit were offered by a discount store at $300, rather than at its list price of $800, Mike might purchase it after all.

Given consumers' tastes, economists assume that they attempt to maximize utility. In other words, *consumers are assumed to be rational in the sense that they choose the market basket—or more generally, the course of action—that is most to their liking.* As previously noted, consumers cannot choose whatever market basket they please. Instead, they must maximize their utility subject to the constraints imposed by the size of their money income and the nature of commodity prices.

What is the optimal market basket, the one that maximizes utility subject to these constraints? It is the one where *the consumer's income is allocated among commodities so that, for every commodity purchased, the marginal utility of the commodity is proportional to its price*. Thus, in the case of the Martin family, the optimal market basket is the one where

$$MU_F/P_F = MU_C/P_C, \qquad (16.1)$$

where MU_F is the marginal utility of food, MU_C is the marginal utility of clothing, P_F is the price of a pound of food, and P_C is the price of a piece of clothing.

■ WHY IS THIS RULE CORRECT?

To understand why the rule in equation 16.1 is correct, it is convenient to begin by pointing out that MU_F/P_F is the marginal utility of the *last dollar's worth* of food and that MU_C/P_C is the marginal utility of the *last dollar's worth* of clothing. To see why this is so, take the case of food. Since MU_F is the extra utility of the *last pound* of food bought, and P_F is the price of this *last pound*, the extra utility of the *last dollar's worth* of food must be MU_F/P_F. For example, if the last pound of food results in an extra utility of 4 utils and this pound costs $2, then the extra utility from the last dollar's worth of food must be 4/2, or 2 utils. In other words, the marginal utility of the last dollar's worth of food is 2 utils.

Since MU_F/P_F is the marginal utility of the last dollar's worth of food, and MU_C/P_C is the marginal utility of the last dollar's worth of clothing, what equation 16.1 really says is that *the rational consumer will choose a market basket where the marginal utility of the last dollar spent on all commodities purchased is the same*. To see why this must be so, consider the numerical example in Table 16.4, which shows the marginal utility the Martins derive from various amounts of food and clothing. Rather than measuring food and clothing in physical units, we measure them in Table 16.4 in terms of the amount of money spent on them.

Given the information in Table 16.4, how much of each commodity should Janet Martin buy if her money income is only $4 (a ridiculous assumption but one that will help to make our point)? Clearly, the first dollar she spends should be on food since it will yield her a marginal utility of 20. The second dollar she spends should also be on food since a second dollar's worth of food has a marginal utility of 16. (Thus the total utility derived from the $2 of

TABLE 16.4		MARGINAL UTILITY (UTILS) PER DOLLARS' WORTH				
Marginal Utility Derived by the Martins from Various Quantities of Food and Clothing	COMMODITY	1	2	3	4	5
	Food	20	16	12	10	7
	Clothing	12	10	7	5	3

expenditure is 20 + 16 = 36.)[2] The marginal utility of the third dollar is 12 if it is spent on more food, and 12 too if it is spent on clothing (since it would be the first dollar spent on clothing). Suppose that she chooses more food. (The total utility derived from the $3 of expenditure is 20 + 16 + 12 = 48.) What about the final dollar? Its marginal utility is 10 if it is spent on more food, and 12 if it is spent on clothing; thus she will spend it on clothing. (The total utility derived from all $4 of expenditure is then 20 + 16 + 12 + 12 = 60.)

Equilibrium market basket

Thus Janet Martin, if she is rational, will allocate $3 of her income to food and $1 to clothing. This is the **equilibrium market basket**, the market basket that maximizes consumer satisfaction. The important thing to note is that this market basket demonstrates the principle set forth earlier in equation 16.1. As shown in Table 16.4, the marginal utility derived from the last dollar spent on food is equal to the marginal utility derived from the last dollar spent on clothing (both are 12). Thus this market basket has the characteristic described above: the marginal utility of the last dollar spent on all commodities purchased is the same.

THE CONSUMER'S DEMAND CURVE

Individual demand curve

In analyzing consumer behavior, economists often use the concept of an **individual demand curve**. Like the market demand curve, the individual demand curve is the relationship between the quantity demanded of a good and the good's price. But whereas the market demand curve shows the quantity demanded in the *entire market* at various prices, the individual demand curve shows the quantity demanded by a *particular consumer* at various prices. Applying the theory of consumer behavior presented earlier in this chapter, we can derive a particular consumer's demand curve for

[2]Since the marginal utility is the extra utility obtained from each dollar spent, the total utility from the total expenditure must be the sum of the marginal utilities of the individual dollars of expenditure.

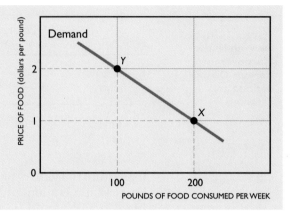

FIGURE 16.2

Janet Martin's Individual Demand Curve for Food

The consumer's individual demand curve for a commodity shows the amount of the commodity the consumer will buy at various prices.

a particular good. To see this, let's return to Janet Martin and show how we can derive the relationship between the price of food and the amount of food she will buy per month.

Assuming that food and clothing are the only goods, that Janet's weekly income is $400, and that the price of clothing is $40 per piece of clothing, we confront her with a variety of prices of food. First, we confront her with a price of $1 per pound of food. How much food will she buy? Next, we confront her with a price of $2 per pound of food. How much food will she buy? The theory of consumer behavior shows how, under each of these sets of circumstances, she will allocate her income between food and clothing. From equation 16.1, we know that she will choose an allocation where the marginal utility of the last dollar spent on food will equal the marginal utility of the last dollar spent on clothing. Suppose that she will buy 200 pounds of food when the price is $1 per pound, and 100 pounds of food when the price is $2 per pound. These are two points on Janet's individual demand curve for food—those corresponding to prices of $1 and $2 per pound. Figure 16.2 shows these two points, X and Y.

It is no trick to obtain more points on her individual demand curve for food. All we have to do is confront her with other prices of food and see how much food she buys at each price. Plotting the amount of food she buys against the price, we obtain new points on her individual demand curve for food. Connecting all these points, we get her complete individual demand curve for food, shown in Figure 16.2.

DERIVING THE MARKET DEMAND CURVE

In the previous section we described how a consumer's individual demand curve for a commodity can be derived, given the con-

| | | INDIVIDUAL DEMAND | | | MARKET DEMAND |
| PRICE OF FOOD (DOLLARS PER POUND) | JONES | KLEIN | DINARDI | MARTIN | |
	(HUNDREDS OF POUNDS PER MONTH)				
1.00	50.0	45.0	5.0	2.0	102
1.20	43.0	44.0	4.2	1.8	93
1.40	36.0	43.0	3.4	1.6	84
1.60	30.0	42.0	2.6	1.4	76
1.80	25.0	41.4	2.4	1.2	70
2.00	20.0	41.0	2.0	1.0	64

TABLE 16.5

Individual Demand Curves and the Market Demand Curve for Food

sumer's tastes and income, as well as the prices of other commodities. Suppose that we have obtained the individual demand curve for each of the consumers in the market. How can these individual demand curves be used to derive the market demand curve? The answer is simple. *To derive the market demand curve, we obtain the horizontal sum of all the individual demand curves.* In other words, to find the total quantity demanded in the market at a certain price, we add up the quantities demanded by the individual consumers at that price.

Table 16.5 shows the individual demand curves for food of four families: the Martins, Joneses, DiNardis, and Kleins. For simplicity, suppose that these four families constitute the entire market for food. (This assumption can easily be relaxed; it just makes things simple.) Then the market demand curve for food is shown in the last column of Table 16.5. Figure 16.3 shows the families' individual demand curves for food, as well as the resulting market

FIGURE 16.3

Individual Demand Curves and the Market Demand Curve for Food

The market demand curve is the horizontal sum of all the individual demand curves.

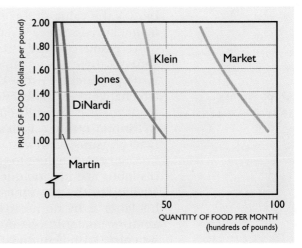

demand curve. To illustrate how the market demand curve is derived from the individual demand curves, suppose that the price of food is $1 per pound. The total quantity demanded in the market is 102 hundreds of pounds per month, since this is the sum of the quantities demanded at this price by the four families. (As shown in Table 16.5, this sum equals 50 + 45 + 5 + 2, or 102.)

Since individual demand curves for a commodity almost always slope downward to the right, it follows that *market demand curves too almost always slope downward to the right.* (Why? Because, as stressed above, the market demand curve is the horizontal sum of all the individual demand curves.) However, the shape and location of the market demand curve vary greatly from commodity to commodity and from market to market. Market demand curves, like people, do not look alike.

THE SUPPLY CURVE

We turn now from the demand to the supply curve. When we look behind the supply curve, it is obvious that a firm's decision about how much to produce is dependent on its costs. In the rest of this chapter, we shall analyze a firm's costs in some detail. Then in Chapter 18 we will show how the results enable us to derive the market supply curve.

WHAT ARE COSTS?

Cost

What do we mean by cost? Although this question may seem foolishly simple, it is in fact tricky. *Fundamentally, the **cost** of a certain course of action is the value of the best alternative course of action that could have been adopted instead.* The cost of producing automobiles is the value of the goods and services that could be obtained from the resources used currently in automobile production if those resources were no longer used to produce automobiles. In general, the costs of a firm's inputs—that is, anything the firm uses in its production process—are their values in their most valuable alternative uses. This is the **opportunity** (or **alternative**) **cost** doctrine (recall our discussion of opportunity cost in Chapter 1).

**Opportunity
(alternative) cost**

Suppose that a firm's owner devotes 50 hours a week to the firm's business and that, because he is the owner, he pays himself no salary. According to the usual rules of accounting, the costs of his labor are not included in the firm's income statement. But according to the economist's opportunity cost doctrine, the cost of his labor is by no means zero. Instead, this cost equals whatever amount he could obtain if he worked 50 hours a week for someone else. Both economists and accountants agree that opportunity costs are the relevant costs for many types of problems and that failure to use the proper concept of cost can result in serious mistakes.

Costs for the individual firm are the necessary payments to the owners of resources to get them to provide these resources to the firm. To obtain these resources as inputs, the firm must bid them away from alternative uses. The payments made to the owners of these resources may be either explicit or implicit costs. If a payment is made to a supplier, laborer, or some other resource owner besides the firm's owner, this is an ***explicit cost,*** which is paid for in an explicit way. But if a resource is owned by the firm's owner, there may be no explicit payment for it, as in the case of the labor of the owner who paid himself no salary. The *costs of such owner-supplied resources are called* **implicit costs.** As we stressed above, such implicit costs equal what these resources could bring if they were used in their most valuable alternative ways. And the firm's profits (or losses), as defined by economists, are the difference between the firm's revenues and its total costs, both explicit and implicit.

SHORT-RUN COST FUNCTIONS

In order to maximize its profits, a firm must determine the least-cost combination of inputs to produce any quantity of output. The previous chapter showed how this least-cost input combination can be found; with this information, it is easy to determine the minimum cost of producing each quantity of output. *Knowing the (minimum) cost of producing each quantity of output, we can define and measure the firm's* **cost functions**, which show how various types of costs are related to the firm's output.

Cost functions

A firm's cost functions will vary, depending on whether they are based on the short or long run. As we saw from the previous chapter, *the* **short run** *is defined as the period of time in which at least one of the firm's inputs is fixed.* On the other hand, *the* **long run** *is that period of time in which all inputs are variable.* In the long run, the firm can make a complete adjustment to any change in its environment.

In the following sections, we will concentrate on the short run, where the firm cannot vary the quantities of plant and equipment it uses. These are the firm's fixed inputs, and they determine the scale of its operations.

■ TOTAL FIXED COST

Total fixed cost

Three kinds of costs are important in the short run: total fixed cost, total variable cost, and total cost. **Total fixed cost** *is the total*

Conserving water in a California drought

From 1975 to 1977, California suffered a series of droughts. Many communities embarked on water conservation programs. Washing cars and watering lawns were forbidden. Farmers were notified that there might be a cutback of 25 percent in water allotment for the spring and that they should reduce planting. Marin County, a wealthy community just north of San Francisco, was one of the hardest-hit California communities. By the second year of the drought, residents were rationed to 46 gallons per day, one-third of their normal usage.

To maintain rationing quotas, stiff new water rates were imposed. The basic rate was doubled; anyone who used twice the quota paid more than 8 times the old rate, and usage beyond that amount cost 40 times the predrought rate. People reduced their water consumption by 25 percent in the first year and by 65 percent in the second. Water was saved for its most-valued uses. Low-volume shower heads and other apparatus were installed to reduce water usage in toilets and sinks.

Torrential rains in the final days of 1977 marked the end of this drought, but its legacy lingered on. Several conservation measures were written into law, and the people of Marin County continued to pay—and willingly pay—more for water than they had before the drought. Total water usage stayed well below the predrought levels for years, both because the higher price of water reduced the quantity demanded and because the demand curve for water had shifted to the left.

The California drought is a good illustration of marginal utility. As water became scarce, its marginal utility to the average consumer rose. People cut back on uses of water that added little to their satisfaction, such as washing cars and watering lawns, and the available water was used in ways that had a high marginal utility: drinking, cooking, and bathing.

expenditure by the firm per period of time for fixed inputs. Since the quantity of the fixed inputs is unvarying (by definition), the total fixed cost will be the same whatever the firm's level of output. Among the firm's fixed costs in the short run are property taxes and interest on bonds issued in the past. If the firm has contracts with suppliers and workers that cannot be renegotiated (without dire consequences) in the short run, the expenses involved in meeting these contracts are also fixed costs.

Consider a hypothetical firm, the Bugsbane Music Box Company. This firm produces a high-priced line of music boxes that, when opened, play your favorite rock song, show tune, or hymn and emit a deadly gas that kills all insects, rodents, or pests within a 50-foot radius. Table 16.6 shows that Bugsbane's fixed costs are $300 per day; the firm's total fixed cost function is shown in Figure 16.4.

TABLE 16.6

Fixed, Variable, and Total Costs, Bugsbane Music Box Company

NUMBER OF MUSIC BOXES PRODUCED PER DAY	TOTAL FIXED COST	TOTAL VARIABLE COST	TOTAL COST
		(DOLLARS)	
0	300	0	300
1	300	60	360
2	300	110	410
3	300	160	460
4	300	200	500
5	300	260	560
6	300	360	660
7	300	510	810
8	300	710	1,010
9	300	1,060	1,360

FIGURE 16.4

Total Fixed Cost, Bugsbane Music Box Company

The total fixed cost function is always a horizontal line, since fixed costs do not vary with output.

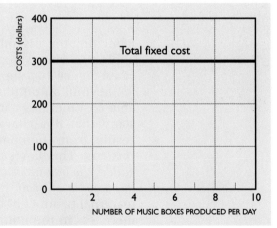

TOTAL VARIABLE COST

Total variable cost

Total variable cost is the firm's total expenditure on variable inputs per period of time. Since by definition a firm cannot vary its fixed inputs in the short run, it will have to increase its variable inputs if it wants to increase its output. And since higher output rates require greater utilization of variable inputs, they mean a higher total variable cost. Thus if Bugsbane increases its daily production of music boxes, it must increase the amount it spends per day on metal (for the components), wood (for the outside of the boxes),

FIGURE 16.5

Total Variable Cost, Bugsbane Music Box Company

Total variable cost is the total expenditure per period of time on variable inputs. Due to the law of diminishing marginal returns, total variable cost increases first at a decreasing rate and then at an increasing rate.

labor (for the assembly of the boxes), and other variable inputs. Table 16.6 shows Bugsbane's total variable costs at various output rates; Figure 16.5 shows the firm's total variable cost function.

Beyond an output rate of four music boxes per day, total variable cost increases at an increasing rate. It is important to understand that this characteristic of the total variable cost function results from the operation of the **law of diminishing marginal returns**. This law states that, *if equal increments of an input are added, the quantities of other inputs being held constant, the resulting increments of product will decrease beyond some point; that is, the marginal product of the input will diminish.* At small output rates, increases in the utilization of variable inputs may bring about increases in their productivity and cause total variable cost to increase with output but at a decreasing rate. Beyond a point, however, there are diminishing marginal returns from the variable input, with the result that total variable costs increase at an increasing rate.

■ TOTAL COST

Total cost

Total cost *is the sum of total fixed cost and total variable cost.* Thus to obtain the Bugsbane Company's total cost at a given output, we need only add its total fixed cost and its total variable cost at that output. The result is shown in Table 16.6, and the corresponding total cost function is shown in Figure 16.6. Since the total cost function and the total variable cost function differ by only a constant

Oil price increases and drilling activity

An oil recovery unit in Long Beach, California

amount of drilling activity increased in response to higher oil prices, which acted both as signals and as incentives for such resource reallocation.

The marginal cost of extracting additional barrels of oil rises steeply after a point. Drillers have to resort to more expensive techniques for secondary and tertiary recovery, that is, recovering the oil from a given well that is hard to reach. As the price of oil rose, these more expensive techniques became more affordable. Similarly, the drilling of new, deeper, and more expensive wells could be justified because the higher costs could be covered by the higher price of oil.

In the decade prior to 1973, independent domestic oil producers were finding it increasingly difficult to compete with OPEC's low world oil prices. Domestic oil production had leveled off, and many suppliers had left the industry. In the wake of the 1973–74 oil embargo and the quadrupling of oil prices, many producers were spurred to jump into the oil patch; new companies, speculative investors, and existing companies expanded their drilling. The new price and profit potential were the main motivating factors for this expansion. The lust for undiscovered "new" oil was greater than ever.

In 1979 the Carter administration announced the gradual phaseout of

control on domestic oil prices. The new high price for oil and government decontrol were the financial carrots needed to lure new suppliers back into domestic oil production. The number of active rigs had gone from under 1,000 in 1971 to over 4,000 in 1981. Over 16,500 wildcat wells were drilled in 1982, as opposed to 7,000 in 1971. As one producer put it, "Just about anywhere you went in that period, you stumbled over someone behind a bush, drilling." In the decade following the first oil crisis in 1973, oil exploration almost doubled. Independent companies, "wildcatters," accounted for roughly 90 percent of the drillings. In accord with the basic economic models presented in this text, the

What goes up must come down— and go up and come down again. In late 1985, the price of oil fell rapidly because of overproduction and weak demand. Drilling came to a virtual standstill, and many existing wells were closed. Production in the United States fell and import dependence rose again. In 1990, when the price of oil rose after Iraq invaded Kuwait, there were signs of renewed interest in drilling in the United States. After the Gulf War, drilling activity dipped a little and then remained steady until the end of the 1990s. In 1998 oil prices collapsed in the wake of the Asian Crisis. Again drilling activity dried up. By 2000 oil prices had recovered, and with them the interest in drilling for new wells. The cycle was repeating itself.

FIGURE 16.6

Total Cost, Bugsbane Music Box Company

Total cost is the sum of total fixed cost and total variable cost. It has the same shape as the total variable cost curve, since they differ by only a constant amount (equal to total fixed cost).

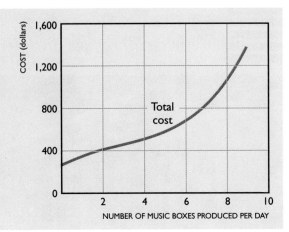

FIGURE 16.7

Fixed, Variable, and Total Costs, Bugsbane Music Box Company

All three cost functions, presented in Figures 16.4 to 16.6, are brought back for a curtain call.

amount (equal to total fixed cost), they have the same shape, as shown in Figure 16.7, which brings together all three of the total cost functions (or *cost curves,* as they are often called).

AVERAGE COSTS IN THE SHORT RUN

The president of Bugsbane unquestionably cares about the average cost of a music box as well as the total cost incurred; so do

TABLE 16.7	NUMBER OF BOXES PRODUCED PER DAY	AVERAGE FIXED COST	AVERAGE VARIABLE COST	AVERAGE TOTAL COST
Average Fixed Cost, Average Variable Cost, and Average Total Cost, Bugasbane Music Box Company		(DOLLARS)		
	1	300(= 300 ÷ 1)	60(= 60 ÷ 1)	360(= 360 ÷ 1)
	2	150(= 300 ÷ 2)	55(= 110 ÷ 2)	205(= 410 ÷ 2)
	3	100(= 300 ÷ 3)	53(= 160 ÷ 3)	153(= 460 ÷ 3)
	4	75(= 300 ÷ 4)	50(= 200 ÷ 4)	125(= 500 ÷ 4)
	5	60(= 300 ÷ 5)	52(= 260 ÷ 5)	112(= 560 ÷ 5)
	6	50(= 300 ÷ 6)	60(= 360 ÷ 6)	110(= 660 ÷ 6)
	7	43(= 300 ÷ 7)	73(= 510 ÷ 7)	116(= 810 ÷ 7)
	8	38(= 300 ÷ 8)	89(= 710 ÷ 8)	126(= 1,010 ÷ 8)
	9	33(= 300 ÷ 9)	118(=1,060 ÷ 9)	151(= 1,360 ÷ 9)

economists. *Average cost tells how much a product costs per unit of output.* There are three average cost functions, one corresponding to each of the three total cost functions.

■ AVERAGE FIXED COST

Average fixed cost

Let's begin with **average fixed cost**, *which is simply the total fixed cost divided by the firm's output.* Table 16.7 and Figure 16.8 show the average fixed cost function for the Bugsbane Music Box Company. Average fixed cost must decline with increases in output, since it equals a constant—total fixed cost—divided by the output rate.

FIGURE 16.8

Average Fixed Cost, Bugsbane Music Box Company

Average fixed cost is total fixed cost divided by the firm's output. Since it equals a constant (total fixed cost) divided by the output rate, it must decline with increases in output.

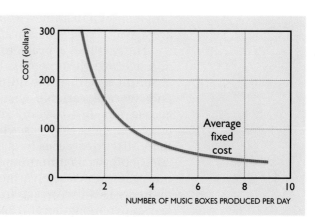

FIGURE 16.9

Average Variable Cost, Bugsbane Music Box Company

Average variable cost is total variable cost divided by the firm's output. Beyond a point (in this case, about 4 music boxes per day), average variable cost rises with increases in output because of the law of diminishing marginal returns.

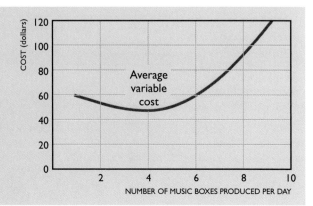

■ AVERAGE VARIABLE COST

Average variable cost

The next type of average cost is **average variable cost**, *which is total variable cost divided by output.* For Bugsbane, the average variable cost function is shown in Table 16.7 and Figure 16.9. At first, increases in the output rate result in decreases in average variable cost, but beyond a point they result in higher average variable cost. This is because the law of diminishing marginal returns is in operation. As more and more of the variable inputs are utilized, the extra output they produce declines beyond some point, so that the amount spent on variable inputs per unit of output tends to increase.

■ AVERAGE TOTAL COST

Average total cost

The third type of average cost is **average total cost**, which is total cost divided by output. For Bugsbane, the average total cost function is shown in Table 16.7 and Figure 16.10. At any level of output, *average total cost equals average fixed cost plus average variable cost.*

The fact that average total cost is the sum of average fixed cost and average variable cost helps explain the shape of the average cost function. If, as the output rate goes up, both average fixed cost and average variable cost decrease, average total cost must decrease too. But beyond some point average total cost must increase, because increases in average variable cost eventually more than offset decreases in average fixed cost. However, average total cost achieves its minimum after average variable cost, because the increases in average variable cost are for a time more than offset by decreases in average fixed cost. (All the average cost functions are shown in Figure 16.12.)

FIGURE 16.10

Average Total Cost, Bugsbane Music Box Company

Average total cost is total cost divided by output. It equals average fixed cost plus average variable cost.

MARGINAL COST IN THE SHORT RUN

Marginal cost

No one can really understand the operations of a business firm without understanding the concept of **marginal cost**, *the addition to total cost resulting from the addition of the last unit of output*. To see how marginal cost is calculated, look at Table 16.8, which

TABLE 16.8

Calculation of Marginal Cost, Bugsbane Music Box Company

NUMBER OF MUSIC BOXES PRODUCED PER DAY	TOTAL COST (DOLLARS)	MARGINAL COST (DOLLARS)
0	300	
		60(= 360 − 300)
1	360	
		50(= 410 − 360)
2	410	
		50(= 460 − 410)
3	460	
		40(= 500 − 460)
4	500	
		60(= 560 − 500)
5	560	
		100(= 660 − 560)
6	660	
		150(= 810 − 660)
7	810	
		200(= 1,010 − 810)
8	1,010	
		350(= 1,360 − 1,010)
9	1,360	

FIGURE 16.11

Marginal Cost, Bugsbane Music Box Company

The marginal cost of the first unit of output (which, according to Table 16.8, is $60) is plotted at the midpoint between 0 and 1 units of output. The marginal cost of the second unit of output is plotted at the midpoint between 1 and 2 units of output. The marginal cost function connects these and other points showing the marginal cost of various amounts of output.

shows the total cost function of the Bugsbane Music Box Company. When output is between 0 and 1 music boxes per day, the firm's marginal cost is $60, since this is the *extra cost* of producing the first music box per day. In other words, $60 equals marginal cost in this situation, because it is the difference between the total cost of producing 1 music box per day ($360) and the total cost of producing 0 music boxes per day ($300, which is the firm's total fixed cost).

In general, marginal cost will vary depending on the firm's output level. Thus Table 16.8 shows that at Bugsbane marginal cost is $50 when the firm produces between 1 and 2 music boxes per day, $100 when the firm produces between 5 and 6 music boxes per day, and $350 when the firm produces between 8 and 9 music boxes per day. Table 16.8 (and Figure 16.11, which shows the marginal cost function graphically) indicates that marginal cost, after decreasing with increases in output at low output levels, increases with further increases in output. In other words, *beyond some point it becomes more and more costly for the firm to produce yet another unit of output.*

▦ INCREASING MARGINAL COST AND DIMINISHING RETURNS

The reason why marginal cost increases beyond some output level is to be found in the law of *diminishing marginal returns. If (beyond some point) increases in variable inputs result in less and less extra output, it follows that a larger and larger quantity of variable inputs must be added to produce an extra unit of output. Thus the cost of producing an extra unit of output must increase.*

FIGURE 16.12

Average Fixed Cost, Average Variable Cost, Average Total Cost, and Marginal Cost, Bugsbane Music Box Company

All of the curves presented in Figures 16.8 to 16.11 are brought together for review. Note that the marginal cost curve intersects both the average variable cost curve and the average total cost curve at their minimum points.

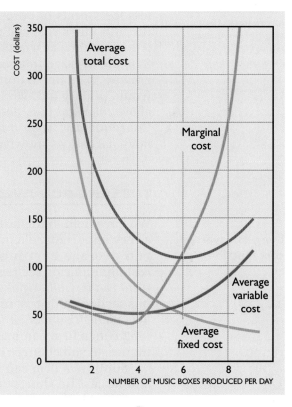

RELATIONSHIP BETWEEN MARGINAL COST AND AVERAGE COST FUNCTIONS

The relationship between the marginal cost function and the average cost functions must be noted. Figure 16.12 shows the marginal cost curve together with the three average cost curves. *The marginal cost curve intersects both the average variable cost curve and the average total cost curve at their minimum points.* The reason for this is simple. If the extra cost of a unit of output is greater (less) than the average cost of the units of output already produced, the addition of the extra unit of output clearly must raise (lower) the average cost of production. Thus if marginal cost is greater (less) than average cost, average cost must be rising (falling). And if this is so, average cost can be a minimum only when it equals marginal cost. (The same reasoning holds for both average total cost and average variable cost and for the short and long runs.)

To make sure that you understand this point, consider the following numerical example. Suppose that the average total cost of producing 4 units of output is $10 and that the marginal cost of the fifth unit of output is less than $10. Will the average total cost be less for 5 units of output than for 4 units? It will be less, because the fifth unit's cost will pull down the average. On the other hand, if the marginal cost of the fifth unit of output had been greater than $10, the average total cost for 5 units of output would have been greater than for 4 units of output, because the fifth unit's cost would pull up the average. Thus *average total cost will fall when it is above marginal cost, and it will rise when it is below marginal cost.* Consequently, *when it is a minimum, average total cost must equal marginal cost,* as shown in Figure 16.12.

THE LONG-RUN AVERAGE COST FUNCTION

Long-run average cost function

We have held to the last additional kind of cost function that plays a very important role in economic analysis. This is the firm's **long-run average cost function,** *which shows the minimum average cost of producing each output level when any desired type or scale of plant can be built.* Unlike the cost functions discussed in the previous sections, this cost function pertains to the long run—*to a period long enough so that all inputs are variable and none is fixed.* In the long run, a firm can make any adjustments in its production techniques, to suit changes in its environment.

Suppose a firm can build plants of three sizes: small, medium, and large. The short-run average total cost functions corresponding to these plants are AA', BB', and DD' in Figure 16.13. If the firm is still in the planning stage of plant construction, it can choose whichever plant has the lowest costs. Consequently, the firm will choose the small plant if it believes that its output rate will be smaller than Q_1, the medium plant if it believes that its output rate will be above Q_1 but below Q_2, and the large plant if it believes that its output rate will be above Q_2. Thus the long-run average cost

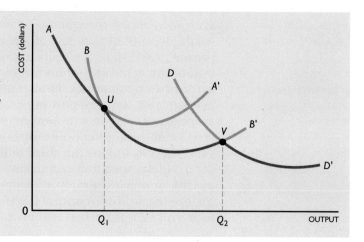

FIGURE 16.13

Short-Run Average Cost Curves and Long-Run Average Cost Curve

The short-run average total cost functions for three plants—small, medium, and large—are AA', BB', and DD'. The long-run average cost function is $AUVD'$ if these are the only three types of plants that can be built.

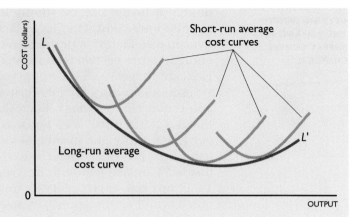

FIGURE 16.14

Long-Run Average Cost Curve

If many types of plants can be built, the long-run average cost function is *LL'*.

curve is *AUVD'*. And if, as is generally the case, there are many possible types of plants, the long-run average cost curve looks like *LL'* in Figure 16.14. (Only a few of the short-run average cost curves are shown in Figure 16.14.)

RETURNS TO SCALE

What determines the shape of the long-run average cost function in a particular industry? Its shape must depend on the characteristics of the **production function,** which shows the most output that existing technology permits the firm to extract from each quantity of inputs. Specifically, the shape of the long-run average cost function depends in part on whether there are *increasing, decreasing,* or *constant* returns to scale. To understand what these terms mean, consider a long-run situation and suppose that the firm increases the amount of all inputs by the same proportion. What will happen to output? *If output increases by a larger proportion than each of the inputs, this is a case of* **increasing returns to scale**. If output increases by a smaller proportion than each of the inputs, this is a case of **decreasing returns to scale**. *If output increases by the same proportion as each of the inputs, this is a case of* **constant returns to scale**.

Increasing returns to scale
Decreasing returns to scale
Constant returns to scale

At first glance it may seem that constant returns to scale must always prevail. After all, if two factories are built with the same equipment and use the same type and number of workers, it would seem obvious that they can produce twice as much output as one such factory. But things are not that simple. If a firm doubles its scale, it may be able to use techniques that could not be used at the smaller scale. Some inputs are not available in small units; for example, we cannot install half a robot. Because of indivisibilities of this sort, increasing returns to scale may occur. Thus, although one could double a firm's size by simply building two small factories, this may be inefficient. One large factory may be more efficient than two smaller factories of the same total capacity because it is large enough to use certain techniques and inputs that the smaller factories cannot use.

Another reason for increasing returns to scale stems from certain *geometrical relations*. For example, since the volume of a box that is 3 × 3 × 3 feet is 27 times as great as the volume of a box that is 1 × 1 × 1 foot, the former box can carry 27 times as much as the latter box. But since the area of the six sides of the 3- × 3- × 3-foot box is 54 square feet and the area of the six sides of the 1- × 1- × 1-foot box is 6 square feet, the former box only requires 9 times as much wood as the latter. Greater *specialization* also can result in increasing returns to scale. As more workers and machines are used, it is possible to subdivide tasks and allow various inputs to specialize.

Decreasing returns to scale can also occur; the most frequently cited reason is *the difficulty of coordinating a large enterprise*. It can be difficult even in a small firm to obtain the information required to make important decisions; in a large firm, the difficulties tend to be greater. It can be difficult even in a small firm to be certain that management's wishes are being carried out; in a larger firm these difficulties too tend to be greater. Although the advantages of a large organization seem to have captured the public fancy, there are often very great disadvantages as well.

Whether there are increasing, decreasing, or constant returns to scale in a particular situation must be settled case by case. Moreover, the answer is likely to depend on the particular range of output considered. There frequently are increasing returns to scale up to some level of output, then perhaps constant returns to scale up to a higher level of output, beyond which there may be decreasing returns to scale. This pattern is responsible in part for the U-shaped long-run average cost function in Figure 16.14. At relatively small output levels, there are increasing returns to scale, and long-run average cost decreases as output rises. At relatively high output levels, there are decreasing returns to scale, and long-run average cost increases as output rises.

The U-shaped pattern is not found in all industries. Within the range covered by the available data, there is little or no evidence in many industries that long-run average cost increases as output rises. But this may be because the data do not cover a wide enough range. Eventually, one would expect long-run average cost to rise because of problems of coordination, increased red tape, and reduced flexibility. Firms as large as General Motors or Exxon are continually bedeviled by the very real difficulties of enormous size.

▦ SUMMARY

1 Utility is a number that represents the level of satisfaction derived by the consumer from a particular market basket. Market baskets with higher utilities are preferred over market baskets with lower utilities.

2 The model of consumer behavior recognizes that preferences alone do not determine the consumer's actions. Choices are dictated by the size of the consumer's money income and the nature of commodity prices. These factors, as well as the consumer's preferences, determine choice.

3 If consumers maximize utility, their income is allocated among commodities so that, for every commodity purchased, the marginal utility of the commodity is proportional to its price. In other words, the marginal utility of the last dollar spent on each commodity is made equal for all commodities purchased.

4 The individual demand curve shows the quantity of a good demanded by a particular consumer at various prices of the good. The individual demand curve for practically all goods slopes downward and to the right. Its location depends on the consumer's income and tastes and the prices of other goods.

5 To derive the market demand curve, we obtain the horizontal sum of all the individual demand curves of the people in the market. Since individual demand curves for a commodity almost always slope downward to the right, it follows that market demand curves too almost always slope downward to the right.

6 The cost of a certain course of action is the value of the best alternative course of action that could have been pursued instead. This is the doctrine of opportunity cost, or alternative cost.

7 Three kinds of total cost functions are important in the short run: total fixed cost, total variable cost, and total cost. In addition, there are three kinds of average cost functions (corresponding to each of the total cost functions): average fixed cost, average variable cost, and average total cost.

8 Marginal cost—the addition to total cost due to the addition of the last unit of output—is of enormous significance in the firm's decision-making process. Because of the law of diminishing marginal returns, marginal cost tends to rise beyond some output level.

9 The firm's long-run average cost curve shows the minimum average cost of producing each output level when any desired type or scale of plant can be built. The shape of the long-run average cost curve is determined in part by whether there are increasing, decreasing, or constant returns to scale.

10 Suppose that a firm increases the amount of all inputs by the same percentage. If output increases by more than this percentage, this is a case of increasing returns to scale. If output increases by less than this percentage, this is a case of decreasing returns to scale. If output increases by this same percentage, this is a case of constant returns to scale.

▦ PROBLEMS AND QUESTIONS

1 Suppose that the total utility attached by Elaine Johnson to various quantities of hamburgers consumed (per day) is as follows:

NUMBERS OF HAMBURGERS	TOTAL UTILITY (UTILS)
0	0
1	5
2	12
3	15
4	17
5	18

Between 3 and 4 hamburgers, what is the marginal utility of a hamburger? Between 4 and 5 hamburgers? Do these results conform to the law of diminishing marginal utility?

2 If Elaine is maximizing her satisfaction and if the marginal utility of a hot dog is twice that of a bottle of beer, what must the price of a hot dog be if
(a) the price of a bottle of beer is $.75.
(b) the price of a bottle of beer is $1.
(Assume that Elaine consumes both beer and hot dogs.)

3 Suppose that a firm's short-run total cost function is as follows:

OUTPUT (NUMBER OF UNITS PER YEAR)	TOTAL COST PER YEAR (DOLLARS)
0	20,000
1	20,100
2	20,200
3	20,300
4	20,500
5	20,800

What are the firm's total fixed costs? What are its total variable costs when it produces 4 units per year?

4 In question 3, what is the firm's marginal cost when between 4 and 5 units are produced per year? Does marginal cost increase beyond some output level?

5 In question 3, what is the firm's average cost when it produces 1 unit per year? 2 units per year? 3 units per year? 4 units per year? 5 units per year?

■ **KEY TERMS**

model of consumer behavior
utility
marginal utility
law of diminishing marginal utility
equilibrium market basket
individual demand curve
cost opportunity (or alternative) cost
cost functions
total fixed cost

total variable cost
total cost
average fixed cost
average variable cost
average total cost
marginal cost
long-run average cost function
increasing returns to scale
decreasing returns to scale
constant returns to scale

■ VIEWPOINT FOR ANALYSIS

According to a study of cable television commissioned by the city of Monroe, Georgia, "A cable operator must invest in headend equipment, satellite dishes, towers, antenna, and cable distribution facilities before providing service to a single customer.... Because this large initial investment is invariant with respect to the number of customers served, the average unit (per customer) cost will decline in inverse proportion to the total number of customers served. Under these conditions ..., construction of duplicate fixed facilities will be wasteful and economically inefficient."*

(a) Does it seem reasonable that there are substantial economies of scale in cable TV? That is, does it seem likely that the average cost per subscriber will tend to fall as the number of subscribers increases?

(b) If there are substantial economies of scale, is it likely that only one cable operator will exist in most markets?

(c) On February 9, 1994, the *New York Times* reported that "government price surveys indicate that cable systems that compete against a rival have rates about 30 percent lower than the others."† Doesn't this indicate that economies of scale are not very substantial? Why or why not?

---

*J. Gomez-Ibanez and J. Kalt, *Cases in Microeconomics* (Englewood Cliffs, N.J.: Prentice-Hall, 1990), p. 41.

†*New York Times*, February 9, 1994, p. D18.

CHAPTER 17

Market Demand and Price Elasticity

LEARNING OBJECTIVES

In this chapter, you should learn:

- What the price elasticity of demand is and what it means for the demand for a good to be price elastic or price inelastic
- The nature of the income elasticity of demand
- What product substitutes and complements are
- (Exploring Further) The market conditions that present perennial problems for farmers

Airlines like American or United and aircraft producers like Boeing or Airbus must forecast the demand for air tickets 5 or 10 years ahead. An important factor influencing the quantity of air tickets demanded is the price of a ticket. If this price falls by 15 percent, what will be the effect on the quantity of tickets demanded? One purpose of this chapter is to indicate how the price elasticity of demand can be used to answer this question.

In a free market economy, market demand is a fundamental determinant of what is produced and how. The market demand curve for a commodity plays an important role in the decision-making process within each firm that produces the commodity, as well as in the economy as a whole. It is no exaggeration to say that firms spend enormous time and effort trying to cater to, estimate, and influence market demand.

MARKET DEMAND CURVES

Let's review what a **market demand curve** is. You will recall from Chapters 2 and 16 that a commodity's market demand curve shows how much of the commodity will be purchased during a particular period of time at various prices. Figure 17.1 ought to be familiar; it is the market demand curve for wheat in the mid-1990s, which figured prominently in our discussion of the price system in Chapter 2. Among other things, it shows that during the mid-1990s about 2.5 billion bushels of U.S. wheat would have been purchased per year if the price were $2.70 per bushel, that about 2.4 billion bushels would have been purchased per year if the price were

FIGURE 17.1

Market Demand Curve for Wheat, Mid-1990s

This curve shows how much wheat would be purchased per year at various prices.

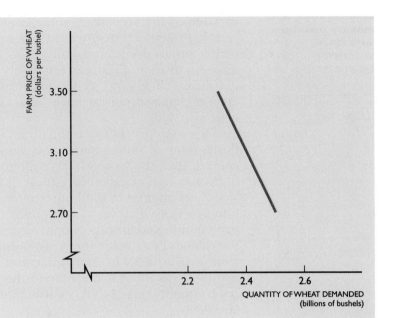

$3.10 per bushel, and that about 2.3 billion bushels would have been purchased if the price were $3.50 per bushel.

Since the market demand curve reflects what consumers want and are willing to pay for, when the market demand curve for wheat shifts upward to the right, this indicates that consumers want more wheat at the existing price. On the other hand, when the curve shifts downward to the left, this indicates that consumers want less wheat at the existing price. Such shifts in the market demand curve for a commodity trigger changes in the behavior of the commodity's producers. When the market demand curve shifts upward to the right, the price of wheat will tend to rise, and thus induce farmers to produce more wheat, because they will find that, given the price increase, their profits will increase if they raise their output levels. The same process occurs in other parts of the economy. Shifts in the demand curve reflecting the fact that consumers want more (less) of a commodity set in motion a sequence of events leading to more (less) production of the commodity.

▓ MEASURING MARKET DEMAND CURVES

To be of practical use, market demand curves must be based on careful measurements. Let's look briefly at some of the techniques used to estimate the market demand curve for particular commodities. At first glance, a quick and easy way to estimate the demand curve might seem to be interviewing consumers about their buying habits and intentions. However, although more subtle variants of this approach sometimes may pay off, simply asking people how much they would buy of a certain commodity at particular prices does not usually seem very useful, since off-the-cuff answers to such questions are rarely very accurate. Thus marketing researchers and econometricians interested in measuring market demand curves have been forced to use more complex procedures.

One such procedure is the direct market experiment. Although the designs of such experiments vary greatly and are often quite complicated, the basic idea is simple: see the effects on the quantity demanded of actual variations in the price of the product. (Researchers attempt to hold other market factors constant or to take into account whatever changes may occur.) The Parker Pen company conducted an experiment a number of years ago to estimate the demand curve for their ink, Quink. They increased the price from $.15 to $.25 in four cities and found that the quantity demanded was quite insensitive to the price. Experiments like this are frequently made to try to estimate a product's market demand curve.

Still another technique is to use statistical methods to estimate demand curves from historical data on price and quantity purchased of the commodity. For example, one might plot the price of slingshots in various periods in the past against the quantity sold, as shown in Figure 17.2. Judging from the results, curve D in Figure 17.2 seems a reasonable approximation to the demand curve. Although this simple analysis provides some insight into how statistical methods are used to estimate demand curves from historical data, it is a vast oversimplification. For one thing, the market demand curve may have shifted over time, so that curve D is not a proper estimate. Fortunately, modern statistical techniques recog-

FIGURE 17.2

Estimated Demand Curve for Slingshots

One very crude way to estimate the market demand curve is to plot the amount sold of a commodity in each year against its price in that year and draw a curve, like D, that seems to fit the points reasonably well. However, this technique is generally too crude to be reliable.

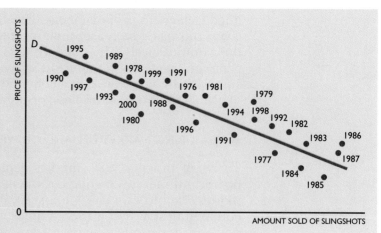

nize this possibility and allow us to estimate the position and shape
of this curve (at each point in time) in spite of it.

THE PRICE ELASTICITY OF DEMAND

The quantity demanded of some commodities, like beef in Figure
17.3, is fairly sensitive to changes in the commodity's price. That is,
changes in price result in significant changes in quantity demanded. On the other hand, the quantity demanded of other commodities, like cotton in Figure 17.3, is very insensitive to changes
in the price. Large changes in price result in small changes in the
quantity demanded.

To discuss this subject more rigorously, we must have some
measure of the sensitivity of quantity demanded to changes in
Price elasticity of
demand
price. The measure customarily used for this purpose is the **price**
elasticity of demand, defined as the percentage change in quantity demanded resulting from a 1 percent change in price.[1] For
example, suppose that a 1 percent reduction in the price of
slingshots results in a 2 percent increase in quantity demanded.
Then, using this definition, the price elasticity of demand for slingshots is 2. (Convention dictates that we give the elasticity a positive
sign even though the change in price is negative and the change in

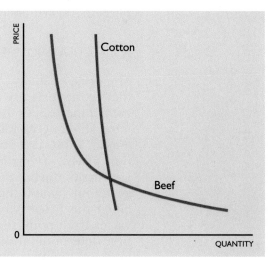

FIGURE 17.3

Market Demand Curves, Beef and Cotton

The quantity demanded of beef is much more
sensitive to price than is the quantity demanded of
cotton.

---

[1]What if price does not change by 1 percent? Then the price elasticity of demand is
defined as the *percentage change in quantity demanded divided by the percentage*
change in price. This definition will be used in the next section. Put in terms of symbols, the price elasticity of demand equals $(-\Delta Q/\Delta P) \times (P/Q)$, where P is price, ΔP is
the change in price, Q is quantity demanded, and ΔQ is the change in the quantity
demanded.

quantity demanded is positive.) The price elasticity of demand is likely to vary from one point to another on the market demand curve. For example, the price elasticity of demand for slingshots may be higher when a slingshot costs $1 than when it costs $.25.

Note that the price elasticity of demand is expressed in terms of *relative*—that is, proportional or percentage—changes in price and quantity demanded, not *absolute* changes in price and quantity demanded. Thus, in studying the slingshot market, we look at the *percentage* change in quantity demanded resulting from a 1 *percent* change in price. This is because absolute changes depend on the units in which price and quantity are measured. Suppose that a reduction in the price of good Y from $100 to $99 results in an increase in the quantity demanded from 200 to 210 pounds per month. If price is measured in dollars, the quantity demanded of good Y seems quite sensitive to price changes, since a decrease in price of 1 results in an increase in quantity demanded of 10. On the other hand, if price is measured in cents, the quantity demanded of good Y seems quite insensitive to price changes, since a decrease in price of 100 results in an increase in quantity demanded of 10. By using relative changes, we avoid this problem. Relative changes do not depend on the units of measurement. Thus the percentage reduction in the price of good Y is 1 percent, regardless of whether price is measured in dollars or cents. And the percentage increase in the quantity demanded of good Y is 5 percent, regardless of whether it is measured in pounds or tons.

■ CALCULATING THE PRICE ELASTICITY OF DEMAND

The price elasticity of demand is a very important concept and one that economists use often, so it is worthwhile to spend some time explaining exactly how it is computed. Suppose that you have a table showing various points on a market demand curve. For example, Table 17.1 shows the quantity of wheat demanded at various prices, as estimated by Professor Karl Fox of Iowa State University during the early 1960s.[2] Given these data, how do you go about computing the price elasticity of demand for wheat? Since the price elasticity of demand for any product generally varies from point to point on its market demand curve, you must first determine at what point on the demand curve you want to measure the price elasticity of demand.

Let us assume that you want to estimate the price elasticity of demand for wheat when the price of wheat is between $2.00 and $2.20 per bushel. To do this, you can use

[2]Note that Table 17.1 pertains to the early 1960s, whereas Figure 17.1 pertains to the mid-1990s. Consequently, the demand curves are quite different, as you can see.

TABLE 17.1	FARM PRICE OF WHEAT (DOLLARS PER BUSHEL)	QUANTITY OF WHEAT DEMANDED (MILLIONS OF BUSHELS)
Market Demand for Wheat, Early 1960s	1.00	1,500
	1.20	1,300
	1.40	1,100
	1.60	900
	1.80	800
	2.00	700
	2.20	6.75

Source: K. Fox, V. Ruttan, and L. Witt, *Farming, Farmers, and Markets for Farm Goods* (New York: Committee for Economic Development, 1962).

$$\text{Price elasticity} = \text{percentage change in quantity demanded} \div \text{percentage change in price}$$

$$= \frac{\text{change in quantity demanded}}{\text{original quantity demanded}} \div \frac{\text{change in price}}{\text{original price}}.$$

Table 17.1 shows that the quantity demanded equals 700 million bushels when the price is $2.00 and that it equals 675 million bushels when the price is $2.20. But should we use $2.00 and 700 million bushels as the original price and quantity? Or should we use $2.20 and 675 million bushels as the original price and quantity? If we choose the former,

$$\text{Price elasticity} = -\frac{(675 - 700)}{700} \div \frac{(2.20 - 2.00)}{2.00} = 0.36.$$

The price elasticity of demand is estimated to be 0.36. (The minus sign at the beginning of the right side of this equation is due to the fact, noted above, that convention dictates that the elasticity be given a positive sign.)

But we could just as well have used $2.20 and 675 million bushels as the original price and quantity. If this had been our choice, the answer would be

$$\text{Price elasticity} = -\frac{(700 - 675)}{675} \div \frac{(2.00 - 2.20)}{2.20} = 0.41.$$

which is somewhat different from the answer we got in the previous paragraph.

To get around this difficulty, the generally accepted procedure is to use the average values of price and quantity as the original price and quantity. In other words, we use

$$\text{Price elasticity} = \frac{\text{change in quantity demanded}}{\text{sum of quantities}/2}$$
$$\div \frac{\text{change in price}}{\text{sum of prices}/2}.$$

**Arc elasticity of
demand**

This is the **arc elasticity of demand**. In the specific case we are considering, the arc elasticity is

$$\text{Price elasticity} = -\frac{(675 - 700)}{(675 + 700)/2} \div \frac{(2.20 - 2.00)}{(2.20 + 2.00)/2} = 0.38.$$

This is the answer to our problem.

DETERMINANTS OF THE PRICE ELASTICITY OF DEMAND

Many studies have been made of the price elasticity of demand for particular commodities. Table 17.2 reproduces the results of some of them. Note the substantial differences among products. For example, the estimated price elasticity of demand for women's hats is about 3.00, whereas for cotton it is only about 0.12. Think for a few minutes about these results, and try to figure out why these differences exist. If you rack your brains for a while, chances are that you will agree that the following factors are important determinants of whether a commodity's price elasticity of demand is high or low.

Number and closeness of available substitutes. *If a commodity has many close substitutes, its demand is likely to be highly elastic;* that is, the price elasticity is likely to be high. If the price of the product increases, a large proportion of its buyers will turn to the close substitutes that are available. If its price decreases, a great many buyers of substitutes will switch to this product. Naturally, the closeness of the substitutes depends on how narrowly the commodity is defined. In general, one would expect that, as the definition of the product becomes narrower and more specific, the product has more close substitutes and its price elasticity of demand is higher. Thus the demand for a particular brand of motor oil is more price elastic than the overall demand for oil, and the demand for oil is more price elastic than the demand for fuel as a whole. If a commodity is defined so that it has perfect substitutes, its price elasticity of demand approaches infinity. Thus if one farmer's wheat is exactly like that grown by other farmers and if

COMMODITY	PRICE ELASTICITY
Women's hats	3.00
Gasoline	0.30
Sugar	0.31
Corn	0.49
Cotton	0.12
Hay	0.43
Potatoes	0.31
Oats	0.56
Barley	0.39
Buckwheat	0.99
Refrigerators	1.40
Airline travel	2.40
Radio and TV sets	1.20
Legal services	0.50
Pleasure boats	1.30
Canned tomatoes	2.50
Newspapers	0.10
Tires	0.60
Beef	0.92
Shoes	0.40

the farmer raises the price slightly (to a point above the market level), the farmer's sales will be reduced to nothing.

Importance in consumers' budgets. It is often asserted that the price elasticity of demand for a commodity is likely to depend on the importance of the commodity in consumers' budgets. The elasticity of demand for commodities like pepper and salt may be quite low. Typical consumers spend a very small portion of their income on pepper and salt, and the quantity they demand may not be influenced much by changes in price within a reasonable range. However, although a tendency of this sort is often hypothesized, there is no guarantee that it always exists.

Length of the period. Every market demand curve pertains, you will recall, to a certain time interval. In general, *demand is likely to be more sensitive to price over a long period than over a short one.* The longer the period, the easier it is for consumers and business firms to substitute one good for another. If, for example, the price of oil should decline relative to other fuels, oil consumption in the month after the price decline would probably increase very little. But over a period of several years, people would have an opportunity to take account of the price decline in choosing the type of fuel to be used in new and renovated houses and businesses. In the longer period of several years, the price decline would have a greater effect on the consumption of oil than in the shorter period of one month.[3]

PRICE ELASTICITY AND TOTAL MONEY EXPENDITURE

Many important decisions hinge on the price elasticity of demand for a commodity. One reason why this is so is that the price elasticity of demand determines whether a given change in price will increase or decrease the amount of money spent on a commodity— often a matter of basic importance to firms and government agencies. Let's look more closely at how the price elasticity of demand determines the effect of a price change on the total amount spent on a commodity.

Price elastic

Price inelastic
Unitary elastic

As a first step, we must define three terms: *price elastic, price inelastic,* and *unitary elastic.* The demand for a commodity is **price elastic** if the price elasticity of demand is *greater than 1*. The demand for a commodity is **price inelastic** if the price elasticity of demand is *less than 1*. And the demand for a commodity is **unitary elastic** if the price elasticity of demand *equals 1*. As we will see, the effect of a price change on the total amount spent on a commodity depends on whether the demand for the commodity is price elastic, price inelastic, or unitary elastic. Let's consider each case.

▓ CASE 1: DEMAND IS PRICE ELASTIC

In this case, if the price of the commodity is *reduced,* the total amount spent on the commodity will *increase.* To see why, suppose that the price elasticity of demand for television sets is 2 and that the price of the television sets is reduced by 1 percent. Because the price elasticity of demand is 2, the 1 percent reduction in price results in a 2 percent increase in the quantity of television sets demanded. Since the total amount spent on television sets equals the quantity demanded times the price, the 1 percent reduction in price will be more than offset by the 2 percent increase in quantity demanded. The result of the price cut will be an increase in the total amount spent on television sets.

[3]For durable goods like automobiles, the price elasticity of demand may be smaller over a long period than over a short one. If the price of autos increases, the quantity demanded is likely to fall substantially because many people will postpone buying a new car. But as time goes on, the quantity of autos demanded will tend to rise as old autos wear out.

Instability of farm prices and the price elasticity of demand

Between the summer of 1997 and the end of 1998 the price of soybeans fell a staggering 50 percent. This was the result of deep recessions in Asia, Russia, and Latin America. While the demand for other products, such as automobiles, fell as well, the prices of these products did not decline anywhere near as much. What explains the volatility in agricultural prices?

One of the most difficult problems for farmers is that, in a free market, farm incomes vary enormously between good times and bad, much

more than nonfarm incomes. This is so because, although farm prices vary a great deal between good times and bad, farm output is much more stable than industrial output. Why is agriculture like this?

The answer lies in considerable part with the price elasticity of demand for farm products. Food is a necessity with few good substitutes. Thus we would expect the demand for farm products to be price inelastic. And as Table 17.2 suggests, this expectation is borne out by the facts. Given that the demand curve for farm products

is price inelastic—and that the quantity supplied of farm products is also relatively insensitive to price—it follows that relatively small shifts in either the supply curve or the demand curve result in big changes in price. This is why farm prices are so unstable. Panel A of the figure below shows a market where the demand curve is much more inelastic than in panel B. As you can see, a small shift to the left in the demand curve results in a much larger drop in price in panel A than in panel B.

On the other hand, if the price of the commodity is *increased,* the total amount spent on the commodity will *fall.* For example, if the price of television sets is raised by 1 percent, this will reduce the quantity demanded by 2 percent. The 2 percent reduction in the quantity demanded will more than offset the 1 percent increase in price and result in a decrease in the total amount spent on television sets.

▓ CASE 2: DEMAND IS PRICE INELASTIC

In this case, if the price is *reduced,* the total amount spent on the commodity will *decrease.* To see why, suppose that the price elasticity of demand for corn is 0.5 and the price of corn is reduced by 1 percent. Because the price elasticity of demand is 0.5, the 1 percent price reduction results in a 0.5 percent increase in the quantity demanded of corn. Since the total amount spent on corn equals the quantity demanded times the price, the 0.5 percent increase in the quantity demanded will be more than offset by the 1 percent reduction in price. The result of the price cut will be a decrease in the total amount spent on corn.

On the other hand, if the price of the commodity is *increased,* the total amount spent on the commodity will *increase.* For example, if the price of corn is raised by 1 percent, this will reduce quantity demanded by 0.5 percent. The 1 percent price increase will more than offset the 0.5 percent reduction in quantity demanded and result in an increase in the total amount spent on corn.

▓ CASE 3: DEMAND IS UNITARY ELASTIC

In this case, a price increase or decrease results in no difference in the total amount spent on the commodity. Why? Because a price decrease (increase) of a certain percentage always results in a quantity increase (decrease) of the same percentage, so that the product of the price and quantity is unaffected.

Table 17.3 summarizes the results of this section. It should help you review our findings.

		EFFECT ON TOTAL EXPENDITURE OF:	
COMMODITY'S PRICE ELASTICITY OF DEMAND		**PRICE DECREASE**	**PRICE INCREASE**
Price elastic (elasticity is greater than 1)		Increase	Decrease
Price inelastic (elasticity is less than 1)		Decrease	Increase
Unitary elastic (elasticity equals 1)		No change	No change

TABLE 17.3

Effect of an Increase or Decrease in the Price of a Commodity on the Total Expenditure on the Commodity

INDUSTRY AND FIRM DEMAND CURVES

Up to this point, we have been dealing with the market demand curve for a commodity. *The market demand curve for a commodity is not the same as the market demand curve for the output of a single firm that produces the commodity, unless, of course, the industry is composed of only a single firm.* If the industry is composed of more than one firm, as is usually the case, the demand curve for the output of each firm producing the commodity will usually be quite different from the demand curve for the commodity. The demand curve for the output of Farmer Brown's wheat is quite different from the market demand curve for wheat.

In particular, the demand curve for the output of a particular firm is generally more price elastic than the market demand curve for the commodity, because the products of other firms in the industry are close substitutes for the product of this firm. As pointed out earlier, products with many close substitutes have relatively high price elasticities of demand.

If there are many firms selling a homogeneous product, the individual firm's demand curve becomes *horizontal,* or essentially so. To see this, suppose that 100,000 firms sell a particular commodity and that all these firms are of equal size. If any one of these firms were to triple its output and sales, the total industry output would change by only 0.002 percent—too small a change to have any perceptible effect on the price of the commodity. Consequently, each firm can act as if variations in its output—within the range of its capabilities—will have no real impact on market price. In other words, the demand curve facing the individual firm is horizontal, as in Figure 17.4.

FIGURE 17.4

Demand Curve for Output of an Individual Firm: The Case of a Great Many Sellers of a Homogeneous Commodity

If there are many firms selling a homogeneous product, the demand curve facing an individual firm is horizontal.

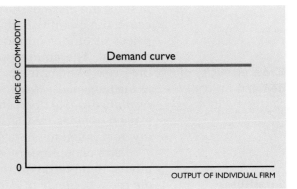

CHAPTER 17

INCOME ELASTICITY OF DEMAND

So far this chapter has dealt almost exclusively with the effect of a commodity's price on the quantity demanded of it in the market. But price is not, of course, the only factor that influences the quantity demanded of the commodity. Another important factor is the level of money income among the consumers in the market. The sensitivity of the quantity demanded to the total money income of all of the consumers in the market is measured by the **income elasticity of demand**, *defined as the percentage change in the quantity demanded resulting from a 1 percent increase in total money income (all prices being held constant).*

Income elasticity of demand

A commodity's income elasticity of demand may be positive or negative. For many commodities, increases in income result in increases in the amount demanded. Such commodities, like steak or caviar, have positive income elasticities of demand. For other commodities, increases in income result in decreases in the amount demanded. These commodities, like poor grades of vegetables, have negative income elasticities of demand. However, be careful to note that the income elasticity of demand of a commodity is likely to vary with the level of income under consideration. For example, if only families at the lowest income levels are considered, the income elasticity of demand for poor grades of vegetables may be positive.

Luxury items tend to have higher income elasticities of demand than necessities. Indeed, one way to define luxuries and necessities is to say that luxuries are commodities with high income elasticities of demand, and necessities are commodities with low income elasticities of demand.

CROSS ELASTICITY OF DEMAND

Besides the price of the commodity and the level of total money income, the quantity demanded of a commodity also depends on the prices of other commodities. Suppose the price of butter is held constant. The amount of butter demanded will be influenced by the price of margarine. The **cross elasticity of demand**, *defined as the percentage change in the quantity demanded of one commodity resulting from a 1 percent change in the price of another commodity,* is used to measure the sensitivity of the former commodity's quantity demanded to changes in the latter commodity's price.

Cross elasticity of demand

Pairs of commodities can be classified as substitutes or complements, depending on the sign of the cross elasticity of demand. *If the cross elasticity of demand is positive, two commodities are* **sub-**

Substitutes

stitutes. Butter and margarine are substitutes because a decrease in the price of butter will result in a decrease in the quantity demanded of margarine. *On the other hand, if the cross elasticity of demand is negative, two commodities are* **complements**. For example, gin and tonic may be complements since a decrease in the price of gin may increase the quantity demanded of tonic. The reduction in the price of gin will increase the quantity demanded of gin, and thus increase the quantity demanded of tonic, since gin and tonic tend to be used together.

Many studies have been made of the cross elasticity of demand for various pairs of commodities. After all, it frequently is very important to know how a change in the price of one commodity will affect the sale of another commodity. For example, what would be the effect of a 1 percent increase in the price of pork on the quantity demanded of beef? According to estimates by the late Herman Wold, a distinguished Swedish economist, the effect would be a 0.28 percent increase in the quantity demanded of beef, since he estimates that the cross elasticity of demand for these two commodities is 0.28. What effect would a 1 percent increase in the price of butter have on the quantity demanded of margarine? According to Wold, the effect would be a 0.81 percent increase in the quantity demanded of margarine, since he estimates that the cross elasticity of demand for these two commodities is 0.81.

EXPLORING FURTHER

THE FARM PROBLEM

Agriculture is an enormously important sector of the U.S. economy. Even though its size has been decreasing steadily for many decades, agriculture still employs about 3 million Americans. Its importance, moreover, cannot be measured entirely by its size. You need only think about how difficult it would be to get along without food to see the strategic role agriculture plays in our economic life. Also, agriculture is one of the most technologically progressive parts of the U.S. economy. The efficiency of U.S. agriculture is admired throughout the world.

Nonetheless, U.S. farmers have had serious problems. Historically, the clearest indication of these problems has emerged from a comparison of U.S. farmers' per capita income with per capita income among the rest of the population. Frequently, the average income of farm families has been 20 percent or more below the average income of nonfarm families. Moreover, a large proportion of the rural population has been poor. Thus the National Advisory Commission on Rural Poverty found in 1967 that "rural poverty is

**Wisconsin farmers dumping milk
during the Depression**

so widespread, and so acute, as to be a national disgrace."[4] Of
course, this does not mean that all farmers are poor; on the contrary, many do very well indeed. But a substantial percentage of
the nation's farmers have been poor by any standard.

This farm problem is nothing new. Farmers did enjoy relatively high prices and high incomes during the first two decades of
the twentieth century. But in 1920 the country experienced a
sharp depression that jolted agriculture as well as the rest of the
economy. Whereas the Roaring Twenties saw a recovery and
boom in the nonfarm sector of the economy, agriculture did not
recover as completely, and the 1930s were dreadful years; the
Great Depression resulted in a devastating decline in farm prices
and farm incomes. World War II brought prosperity to agriculture,
but in the postwar period, farm incomes have often been well
below nonfarm incomes. From 1973 to 1975, prosperity returned
to the farms, but the late 1970s and 1980s saw renewed complaints
by farmers about prices and incomes. All in all, agriculture has
been experiencing difficulties for decades.

■ CHARACTERISTICS OF DEMAND AND
SUPPLY CURVES FOR FARM PRODUCTS

Let's start with the market demand curve for farm products. This
market demand curve must have two important characteristics.
First, *its shape must reflect the fact that food is a necessity and that the
quantity demanded will not vary much with the price of food; in other
words, the demand curve is price inelastic.* Second, *the market demand curve for food is unlikely to shift to the right very much as per
capita income rises,* because consumption of food per capita faces
natural biological and other limitations. In other words, consumption of food is income inelastic as well.

[4]National Advisory Committee on Rural Poverty, *The People Left Behind* (Washington, D.C., 1967).

Next, consider the market supply curve for farm products. Again, you should be aware of two important characteristics of this market supply curve. First, *the quantity of farm products supplied tends to be relatively insensitive to price* (price inelastic) because the farmers have only limited control over their output. (Weather, floods, insects, and other factors are important.) Second, because of rapid technological change, *the market supply curve has been shifting markedly and rapidly to the right.*

■ DECLINE IN RELATIVE PRICE OF FOOD PRODUCTS

If you understand these simple characteristics of the market demand curve and market supply curve for farm products, it is no trick to understand why we have had the sort of farm problem just described. Figure 17.5 shows the market demand and market supply curves for farm products at various points in time. As you would expect, the market demand curve for farm products shifts rather slowly to the right as incomes (and population) grow over time. Specifically, the market demand curve shifted from D in the first period to D_1 in the second period to D_2 in the third period. On the other hand, the market supply curve for farm products shifted rapidly to the right as technology improved over time. It shifted from S in the first period to S_1 in the second period to S_2 in the third period.

FIGURE 17.5

Shifts over Time in the Market Demand and Supply Curves for Farm Products

The market demand curve has shifted rather slowly to the right (from D to D_1 to D_2), whereas the market supply curve has shifted rapidly to the right (from S to S_1 to S_2), with the result that the equilibrium price has declined (from P to P_1 to P_2).

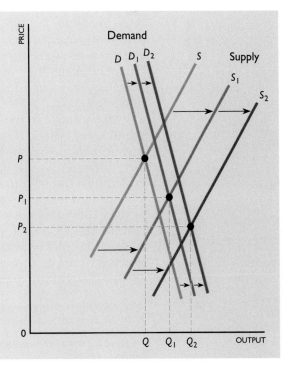

What was the consequence of these shifts in the market demand and supply curves for food products? Clearly, *the equilibrium price of food products fell (relative to other products).* Specifically, the equilibrium price fell from P to P_1 to P_2 in Figure 17.5. This price decrease was, of course, a large part of the farm problem. If we correct for changes in the general level of prices (which have tended to rise over time), there was, in general, a declining trend in farm prices. Agricultural prices generally fell, relative to other prices, in the last seventy years. Moreover, *given this fall in farm prices, farm incomes tended to fall, because, although lower prices were associated with greater amounts sold, the reduction in price was much greater than the increase in quantity sold,* as we can see in Figure 17.5.[5]

Thus the simple model of market behavior described in previous chapters makes it possible to explain the fact that farm prices and farm incomes have tended to fall in the United States. Certainly there is nothing mysterious about these trends. Given the nature and characteristics of the market demand curve and market supply curve for farm products, our simple model shows that these trends are as much to be expected as parades on the Fourth of July.

■ SLOW EXIT OF RESOURCES

However, one additional fact must be noted to understand the farm problem: *people and nonhuman resources have been relatively slow to move out of agriculture in response to these trends.* The price system uses such trends—lower prices and lower incomes—to signal producers that they should use their resources elsewhere. Farmers have been loath to move out of agriculture (even though they often could make more money elsewhere), and this has been a primary cause of the farm problem that has existed over most of the past fifty years. If more people and resources had left farming, agricultural prices and incomes would have risen, and ultimately farm incomes would have come closer to nonfarm incomes. (Poor education was, of course, one significant barrier to migration.)

Nonetheless, even though farmers have been slow to move out of agriculture, history shows that they have done so in the long run. In 1930 the farm population was about 30 million, or 25 percent of the total population; in 1950, it was about 23 million, or 15 percent of the total population; and in 1999, it was about 3 million, or 1 percent of the total population. Thus the price system has had

---

[5]The amount farmers receive is the amount they sell times the price. Thus, in Figure 17.5, the amount farmers receive in income is $P \times Q$ in the first period, $P_1 \times Q_1$ in the second period, and $P_2 \times Q_2$ in the third period. Clearly, since the price is decreasing much more rapidly than the quantity is increasing, farm incomes are falling.

its way. Resources have been moving out of agriculture in response to the signals and pressures of the price system. This movement of people and nonhuman resources unquestionably has contributed to greater efficiency and production for the nation as a whole. But during most of the past 40 years, we have continued to have a "surplus" of farmers, and this has been the root of the farm problem.

■ GOVERNMENT AID TO AGRICULTURE

Traditionally, farmers have had a disproportionately large influence in Congress. When faced with declining economic fortunes, they have appealed to the government for help. They have extolled the virtues of rural life, emphasized that agriculture is a competitive industry, and claimed that it was unfair for their prices to fall relative to the prices they have had to pay. In addition, they have pointed out that the movement of resources out of agriculture has entailed large human costs, since this movement, although beneficial to the nation as a whole, has been traumatic for the farm population. For reasons of this sort, they have argued that the government should help farmers, and in particular, the government should act to bolster farm prices and farm incomes.

■ THE CONCEPT OF PARITY

Their voices were heard. In the Agricultural Adjustment Act of 1933, the Congress announced the concept of parity as the major objective of U.S. farm policy. This concept acquired great importance, and must be clearly understood. Put in its simplest terms, the concept of **parity** holds that a farmer should be able currently to exchange a given quantity of his or her output for as much in

An abandoned farm in Oregon

the way of nonfarm goods and services as he or she could at some time in the past. For example, if a farmer could take a bushel of wheat to market in 1912 and get enough money to buy a pair of gloves, today he or she should be able to get enough money for a bushel of wheat to buy a pair of gloves.

To see what the concept of parity implies for farm prices, suppose that the price of gloves triples. Obviously, if parity is to be maintained, the price of wheat must triple too. Thus the concept of parity implies that farm prices must increase at the same rate as the prices of the goods and services farmers buy. Of course, farmers buy lots of things besides gloves, so in practice the parity price of wheat or other farm products is determined by the changes over time in the average price of all the goods and services farmers buy.

Two major points should be noted about parity. First, to use this concept, one must agree on some base period, such as 1912 in the example above, during which the relationship of farm to non-farm prices is regarded as equitable. Obviously, the higher farm prices were relative to nonfarm prices in the base period, the higher farm prices will be in subsequent periods if parity is maintained. It is significant that 1910 to 1914 was used for many years as the base period. Since this was a period of relatively high farm prices and of agricultural prosperity, the farm bloc must have wielded considerable political clout on this issue. Second, note that the concept of parity is an ethical, not a scientific, proposition. It states what the relative economic position of a bushel of wheat ought to be, or more precisely, it states one particular view of what the relative economic position of a bushel of wheat should be. On the basis of purely scientific considerations, there is no way to prove (or disprove) this proposition, since it is based on one's values and political preferences. Using the terminology in Chapter 1, it is a proposition in normative, not positive, economics.

■ PRICE SUPPORTS AND SURPLUS CONTROLS

During the four decades up to the 1970s, the concept of parity was the cornerstone of a system of government price supports. It is true that the government did not support all farm prices at a full 100 percent of parity. For example, Congress sometimes enacted bills saying that the secretary of agriculture could establish a price of wheat, corn, cotton, or some other product within a certain range, say between 65 and 90 percent of parity. But whatever the exact level of farm price supports, the idea behind them was perfectly simple: to maintain farm prices above the level that would exist in a free market.

Using the simple supply-and-demand model, we can see more clearly the effects of these price supports. The situation is shown

FIGURE 17.6

Effects of the Farm Price Support Program

The support price P' is above the equilibrium price P, so the public buys Q_2, farmers supply Q_1 units of output, and the government buys the difference $(Q_1 - Q_2)$.

in Figure 17.6. A support price P' was set by the government. Since this support price was above the equilibrium price P, the public bought *less* of farm products (Q_2 rather than Q) and paid a *higher* price for them. Farmers gained from the price supports, since the amount they received for their crop under the price support was equal to $P' \times Q_1$, a greater amount than what they would have received in a free market, which was $P \times Q$.

Note, however, that since the support price exceeded the equilibrium price, the quantity supplied Q_1 of the farm product exceeded the quantity demanded Q_2. That is, *there was a surplus of the farm product in question,* which the government had to purchase, since no one else would. These surpluses were an embarrassment, both economically and politically. They showed that society's scarce resources were being utilized to produce products consumers simply did not want at existing prices. Moreover, the cost of storing these surpluses was very large indeed: in some years, these storage costs alone hit the $1 billion mark.

■ POLICIES TO CUT SURPLUSES

To help reduce these surpluses, the government followed two basic strategies. First, *it tried to restrict the output of farm products.* In particular, the government established an acreage allotment program, which said that farmers had to limit the number of acres they planted in order to get price supports on their crops. The Department of Agriculture estimated how much of each product would be demanded by buyers (other than the government) at the

FIGURE 17.7

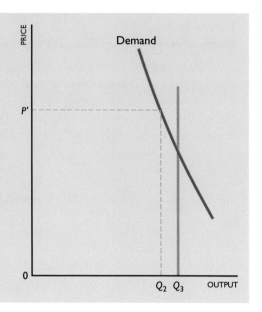

Effects of Price Supports and Output Restrictions

The government restricts output to Q_3, with the result that it buys (Q_3-Q_2) units of output.

support price and tried to cut back the total acreage planted with this crop to the point where the quantity supplied equaled the quantity demanded. These output restrictions did not eliminate the surpluses, because farmers managed to increase the yields from acreage they were allowed to plant, but undoubtedly they reduced the surpluses. Under these restrictions, the situation was as shown in Figure 17.7, where Q_3 was the total output that could be grown on the acreage that could be planted with the crop. Because of the imposition of this output control, the surplus—which the government had to purchase—was reduced from $(Q_1 - Q_2)$ in Figure 17.6 to $(Q_3 - Q_2)$ in Figure 17.7. Farmers continued to benefit from price supports because the amount they received for their crop, $P' \times Q_3$, was still greater than they would have received in a free market, because the amount demanded of farm products was not very sensitive to their price.

Second, *the government tried to shift the demand curve for farm products to the right.* An effort was made to find new uses for various farm products. Also, various antipoverty programs, such as the food stamp program, used our farm surpluses to help the poor. In addition, the government tried to expand the export markets for U.S. farm products. Western Europe and Japan increased their demand for food, and the communist countries purchased our farm products to offset their own agricultural deficiencies. Moreover, the developing countries were permitted by Public Law 480 to buy our farm products with their own currencies, rather than dollars. The result was a reduction in farm surpluses, as shown in Figure 17.8. Since the market demand curve for farm products shifted to

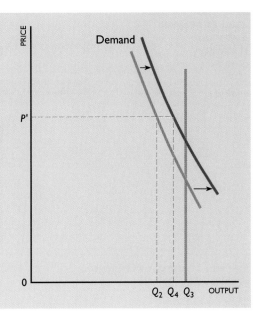

FIGURE 17.8

Effects of Price Supports, Output Restrictions, and a Shift to the Right in the Demand Curve for Farm Products

By shifting the demand curve to the right, the government reduced the surplus from $(Q_3 - Q_2)$ to $(Q_3 - Q_4)$ units of output.

the right, the surplus was reduced from $(Q_3 - Q_2)$ to $(Q_3 - Q_4)$. Because of these demand-augmenting and output-restricting measures, surpluses during the late 1960s and early 1970s were considerably smaller than they were during the late 1950s and early 1960s.

■ FARM POLICY: THE PAST THIRTY YEARS

In 1973, farm prices increased markedly, due partly to very great increases in foreign demand for U.S. agricultural products. This increase in foreign demand was due partly to poor harvests in the Soviet Union, Australia, Argentina, and elsewhere, as well as to devaluations of the dollar. (In 1972–73, the Soviet Union alone bought over $1 billion of grain, on terms that provoked considerable controversy in the United States.) As a result, farm incomes reached very high levels, farm surpluses disappeared, and for the first time in 30 years the government was trying to stimulate farm production rather than restrict it.

Taking advantage of this new climate, Congress passed a new farm bill which ended price supports. This bill, the Agriculture and Consumer Protection Act of 1973, aimed at reducing government involvement in agriculture and at a return to freer markets. Specifically, agricultural prices were allowed to fluctuate freely in accord with supply and demand. However, the government made cash payments to farmers if prices fell below certain "target" levels established by the law. These target levels were above the prices that generally prevailed in the past, but they were below the high

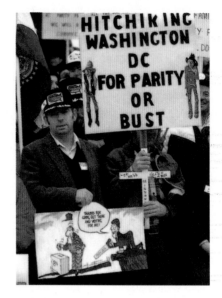

**Farmers protest in Washington
against falling prices.**

levels of prices prevailing in 1973. A program of this kind was originally proposed in 1949 by Charles F. Brannan, who was secretary
of agriculture under President Harry Truman.

By 1975, it appeared to many knowledgeable observers that
the farm sector no longer was suffering from overcapacity and
that, in this respect at least, an equilibrium had been achieved.
However, this attitude did not last long. During 1976 and 1977, U.S.
farmers harvested bumper crops, with the result that prices fell
considerably. The price of wheat, which had been about $3.50 per
bushel in 1975, fell to about $2.30 per bushel in 1977. Farmers
protested and exerted political pressure for increased government
price and income supports.

The early 1980s were a time of recession, and farmers (with
large debts incurred for expansion in the 1970s) were battered by
low farm prices and higher costs. Target prices were raised by
Congress in the 1981 farm bill. Due in part to the increased value
of the dollar relative to other currencies in the early 1980s, which
pushed up the price to foreigners of U.S. farm products, our exports of farm products were hurt. In 1984, the price of wheat fell
to about $3.50 a bushel, which was about a dollar below the target
price. More and more farmers began to default on loans and to go
bankrupt.

The Reagan administration, while originally opposed to large-
scale government intervention in agriculture, responded with aid.
In 1985, Congress passed a farm bill that lowered the price of U.S.
farm products in export markets. Government stocks of farm products were given to exporters to be provided free (as bonuses) to
foreigners who bought our farm products. Also, target prices were

reduced, but farm incomes were supported by deficiency payments (that are based on the discrepancy between the target price and the market price). During the late 1980s, the situation on the nation's farms improved, although 1988 saw a drought in the Corn Belt (and the summer of 1989 was dry in some winter-wheat states).

By the early 1990s, optimism began to spread throughout many parts of U.S. agriculture. According to Gary Benjamin of the Federal Reserve Bank of Chicago, "Land values have recovered, and farm debts have declined 30 percent from the peak of 1983." But many observers were concerned about the government's large role in agriculture. As Mark Drabenstott of the Federal Reserve Bank of Kansas City put it in 1990, "What is very bothersome is that after three years of a strong recovery, agriculture is still so dependent on government payments." (In 1988 alone, the government spent over $50 billion on agriculture.)

During the mid-1990s the Clinton administration tried to further reduce government intervention in agriculture markets. According to the February 1999 *Economic Report of the President*, "The 1994 Crop Insurance Reform Act and the Federal Agriculture Improvement and Reform (FAIR) Act of 1996 sought to replace the farm income safety net, based on government-managed price and income supports, with a system in which farmers manage their own risk through crop diversification, transactions in futures markets, and government-subsidized crop and revenue insurance."[6]

Net farm income rose to record $53.4 billion in 1996 thanks to rising commodity prices and booming exports. However, a sharp drop in world agricultural prices in 1997 and 1998, triggered by the financial crisis in Asia, resulted in a drop in farm income to $50 billion in 1997 and $48 billion in 1998. The Clinton administration put together a farm aid package of $6 billion. This episode highlights one of the dilemmas of current agricultural policy, which is market oriented but at the same time seeks to provide an adequate safety net for this important sector.

REVIEW AND PRACTICE

■ SUMMARY

1 The market demand curve is the relationship between the price of a commodity and the amount of the commodity demanded in the market. The shape and position of a product's market demand curve depend on consumers' tastes, consumers' incomes, the price of other goods, and the number of consumers in the market.

2 The price elasticity of demand, defined as the percentage change in quantity demanded resulting from a 1 percent change in price, measures the sensitivity of the amount de-

[6]*Economic Report of the President*, 1999, p. 38.

manded to changes in price. Whether a price increase results in an increase or decrease in the total amount spent on a commodity depends on the price elasticity of demand.

3 The market demand curve for a commodity is not the same as the demand curve for the output of a single firm that produces the commodity, unless the industry is composed of only one firm. In general, the demand curve for the output of a single firm will be more elastic than the market demand curve for the commodity. Indeed, if there are many firms selling a homogeneous commodity, the individual firm's demand curve becomes horizontal.

4 The income elasticity of demand, defined as the percentage change in quantity demanded resulting from a 1 percent increase in total money income, measures the sensitivity of the amount demanded to changes in total income. A commodity's income elasticity of demand may be positive or negative. Luxury items are generally assumed to have higher income elasticities of demand than necessities.

*5 The cross elasticity of demand, defined as the percentage change in the quantity demanded resulting from a 1 percent change in the price of another commodity, measures the sensitivity of the amount demanded to changes in the price of another commodity. If the cross elasticity of demand is positive, two commodities are substitutes; if it is negative, they are complements.

*6 The demand for farm products grew slowly, while rapid technological change meant that the people and resources currently in agriculture could supply more and more farm products. Because people and resources did not move out of agriculture as rapidly as the price system dictated, farm incomes in the United States often tended to be relatively low.

7 In response to political pressures from the farm blocs, the government instituted price supports to keep farm prices above their equilibrium level. But since the support prices exceeded the equilibrium prices, there was a surplus of the commodities that the government had to purchase and store. To help reduce these surpluses, the government tried to restrict the output of farm products and expand the demand for them.

*8 By the early 1990s, optimism began to spread throughout many parts of U.S. agriculture. However, many observers were concerned about the government's large role in agriculture.

■ PROBLEMS AND QUESTIONS

1 Professor Kenneth Warner of the University of Michigan has estimated that a 10 percent increase in the price of cigarettes results in a 4 percent decline in the quantity of cigarettes consumed. For teenagers, he estimated that a 10 percent price increase results in a 14 percent decline in cigarette consumption. Based on his estimates, what is the price elasticity of demand for cigarettes? Among teenagers, what is the price elasticity of demand? Why is the price elasticity different for teenagers than for the public as a whole?

2 Suppose that each of the four corners of an intersection contains a gas station and that the gasoline is essentially the same. Do you think that the price elasticity of demand for each station's gasoline is above or below 1? Why? Do you think that it is less than or greater than the price elasticity of demand for all gasoline in the United States?

3 The Bugsbane Music Box Company is convinced that an increase in its price will reduce the total amount of money spent on its product. If the company is correct, can you tell from this whether the demand for its product is price elastic or price inelastic?

4 Suppose that the relationship between the price of aluminum and the quantity of aluminum demanded is as follows:

*The starred items refer to material covered in Exploring Further.

PRICE (DOLLARS)	QUANTITY
1	8
2	7
3	6
4	5
5	4

What is the arc elasticity of demand when price is between $1 and $2? Between $4 and $5?

5 Is each of the following statements true, partly true, or false? Explain.

(a) If a good's income elasticity of demand is less than 1, an increase in the price of the good will increase the amount spent on it.

(b) The income elasticity of demand will have the same sign regardless of the level of income at which it is measured.

(c) If Mr. Miller spends all his income on steak (regardless of his income or the price of steak), Mr. Miller's cross elasticity of demand between steak and any other good is zero.

6 What is the sign of the cross elasticity of demand for each of the following pairs of commodities:

(a) Tea and coffee

(b) Tennis rackets and tennis balls

(c) Whiskey and gin

(d) Fishing licenses and fishing poles

(e) Nylon rugs and wool rugs

■ KEY TERMS

price elasticity of demand
arc elasticity of demand
price elastic
price inelastic
unitary elastic

income elasticity of demand
cross elasticity of demand
substitutes
complements

■ VIEWPOINT FOR ANALYSIS

According to Henry Ford, "it is better to sell a large number of cars at a reasonably small margin than to sell fewer cars at a larger margin of profit. Bear in mind that when you reduce the price of the car without reducing the quality you increase the possible number of purchases."*

(a) In 1909, Ford introduced the Model T at a price of $900; sales were 58,000 cars. In 1914, the price was $440; about 470,000 cars were sold. If the demand curve for the Model T remained constant during 1909 to 1914, what was the price elasticity of demand?

(b) Do you think that the demand curve remained constant during 1909 to 1914? If not, do you think that it shifted to the right or to the left? Why?

(c) Do price reductions always result in higher profits? For example, if the demand for a firm's product is price inelastic, will the firm increase its profits by cutting its price? Explain.

*John B. Rae, ed., *Henry Ford* (Englewood Cliffs, N.J.: Prentice-Hall, 1969), p. 112.

Economic Efficiency, Market Supply, and Perfect Competition

LEARNING OBJECTIVES

In this chapter, you should learn:

■ The conditions that define a perfectly competitive market structure

■ The Golden Rule of Output Determination for a perfectly competitive firm

■ The concept of economic profits

■ The long-run equilibrium position for a perfectly competitive firm

The 1990s saw the disintegration of the communist governments of central and eastern Europe and a movement from government economic planning toward the price system. Competition is to be encouraged and relied on, according to many of the new governments. What do economists mean by competition, and how does it work? One purpose of this chapter is to answer this question.

One of the important determinants of how a society's resources are used is how its markets are organized. If the market for wheat contained few sellers rather than many, it would use resources quite differently. Or if 20 firms provided telephone service in Chicago, resources would be used differently. Economists do not have any simple formulas that will eliminate all social waste. But on the basis of existing models and evidence, some forms of market organization tend to minimize social waste whereas other forms seem to promote it.

Perfect competition

In this chapter, we examine the way resources are allocated and prices are set under **perfect competition**. This type of market organization—or market structure, as it is often called—is a polar case that seldom, if ever, occurs in a pure form in the real world. But it is an extremely useful model that sheds much light on a market structure's effects on resource allocation. Anyone who wants to understand how markets work in a capitalistic economy or why our public policies toward business are what they are must understand perfect competition, as well as the other market structures we take up later.

TABLE 18.1

Types of Market Structure

MARKET STRUCTURE	EXAMPLES	NUMBER OF PRODUCERS	TYPE OF PRODUCT	POWER OF FIRM OVER PRICE	BARRIERS TO ENTRY	NONPRICE COMPETITION
Perfect competition	Parts of agriculture are reasonably close	Many	Standardized	None	Low	None
Monopolistic competition	Retail trade	Many	Differentiated	Some	Low	Advertising and product differentiation
Oligopoly	Autos, steel, machinery	Few	Standard or differentiated	Some	High	Advertising and product differentiation
Monopoly	Public utilities	One	Unique product	Considerable	Very high	Advertising

[Handwritten annotations: "→ Firm = P-Taker" near the Perfect competition row; "→ Firm = P-Maker" near the Monopoly row; circles around "POWER OF FIRM OVER PRICE" header and bracket around the Nonprice Competition column]

MARKET STRUCTURE AND ECONOMIC PERFORMANCE

On the basis of their studies of the workings of markets, many economists have come to the conclusion that, from society's point of view, certain kinds of market organization are better than others. This is a much stronger statement than merely saying, as we did in the previous section, that market structure influences market behavior. This statement is based on some set of values and preferences, explicit or implicit, and on certain economic models that predict that "better" behavior is more likely if markets are organized in certain ways. Although there is considerable controversy on this score, many economists believe that, from society's point of view, market structures should be as close as possible to perfect competition.

Economists have generally found it useful to classify markets into four broad types: ***perfect competition, monopoly, monopolistic competition,*** and ***oligopoly.*** Each of these terms describes a particular type of market structure or organization. Table 18.1 provides a capsule description of each of these types. Before looking in detail at each of them, let's go over this table to see how these market structures differ.

■ NUMBER OF FIRMS

The economist's classification of market structures is based to an important extent on the number of firms in the industry that supplies the product. In perfect competition and monopolistic competition,

417

ECONOMIC
EFFICIENCY,
MARKET SUPPLY,
AND PERFECT
COMPETITION
CHAPTER 18

there are *many* sellers, each of which produces only a small part of the industry's output. In monopoly, on the other hand, the industry consists of only a *single* seller. Oligopoly is an intermediate case where there are a *few* sellers. For example, Consolidated Edison, if it is the only supplier of electricity in New York City, is a monopoly. And since there are only a small number of computer manufacturers, the market for computers is an oligopoly.

■ CONTROL OVER PRICE

Market structures differ considerably in the extent to which an individual firm has control over price. A firm under perfect competition has no control over price. For example, a wheat farm (which is close to being a perfectly competitive firm) has no control over the price of wheat. On the other hand, a monopolist is likely to have *considerable control* over price. Thus, in the absence of public regulation, Consolidated Edison would have considerable control over the price of electricity in New York City. A firm under monopolistic competition or oligopoly is likely to have *more* control over price than a perfectly competitive firm and *less* control over price than a monopolist.

■ TYPE OF PRODUCT

These market structures also differ in the extent to which the firms in an industry produce standardized (identical) products. Firms in a perfectly competitive market all produce *identical* products. Thus Farmer Brown's corn is essentially the same as Farmer Smith's. In a monopolistic competitive industry like dress manufacturing, firms produce *somewhat different* products. One firm's dresses differ in style and quality from another firm's dresses. In an oligopolistic industry, firms *sometimes,* but not always, produce identical products. And in a monopolistic industry, there can be *no difference* among firms in their products, since there is only one firm.

■ BARRIERS TO ENTRY

Barriers to entry

The ease with which firms can enter the industry differs from one market structure to another. In perfect competition, **barriers to entry** are *low.* Thus only a small investment is required to enter many parts of agriculture. Similarly, there are *low* barriers to entry in monopolistic competition. But in oligopolies such as autos and steel, there tend to be *very considerable* barriers to entry because, among other reasons, it is so expensive to build an auto or steel plant. In monopoly, entry is blocked; once another firm enters, the monopolist is an ex-monopolist.

▓ NONPRICE COMPETITION

These market structures also differ in the extent to which firms compete on the basis of advertising and differences in product characteristics, rather than price. In perfect competition, there is *no* nonprice competition. In monopolistic competition, there is *considerable emphasis* on nonprice competition. Dress manufacturers compete by trying to develop better styles and by advertising their product lines. Oligopolies also tend to rely *heavily* on nonprice competition. For example, auto firms try to increase their sales by building better and more attractive cars and by advertising. Monopolists also engage in advertising to increase their profits, although this advertising is not directed at reducing the sales of other firms in the industry, since no other firms exist.

PERFECT COMPETITION

When business executives speak of a highly competitive market, they often mean one in which each firm is keenly aware of its rivalry with a few others and in which advertising, styling, packaging, and other such commercial weapons are used to attract business away from them. In contrast, the basic feature of the economist's definition of perfect competition is its *impersonality.* Because there are so many firms in the industry, no firm views another as a competitor, any more than one small tobacco farmer views another small tobacco farmer as a competitor. A market is perfectly competitive if it satisfies the following three conditions.

Homogeneity of product. The first condition is that *the product of any one seller must be the same as the product of any other seller.* This condition ensures that buyers do not care from which seller they purchase the goods, so long as the price is the same. This condition is met in many markets. As pointed out in the previous section, Farmer Brown's corn is likely to be essentially the same as Farmer Smith's.

Many buyers and sellers. The second condition is that there must be a large number of buyers and sellers. *Each participant in the market, whether buyer or seller, must be so small in relation to the entire market that he or she cannot affect the product's price.* All buyers and sellers must be "price takers," not "price makers." A firm under perfect competition faces a *horizontal demand curve,* since variations in its output—within the range of its capabilities—will have no effect on market price.

Mobility of resources. The third condition is that *all resources must be able to switch readily from one use to another, and consumers,*

**ECONOMIC
EFFICIENCY,
MARKET SUPPLY,
AND PERFECT
COMPETITION**
CHAPTER 18

firms, and resource owners must have complete knowledge of all relevant economic and technological data.

No industry in the real world, now or in the past, satisfies all these conditions completely; thus no industry is perfectly competitive. Some agricultural markets may be reasonably close, but even they do not meet all the requirements. But this does not mean that it is useless to study the behavior of a perfectly competitive market. The conclusions derived from the model of perfect competition have proved very helpful in explaining and predicting behavior in the real world. Indeed, as we shall see, they have permitted a reasonably accurate view of resource allocation in many important segments of our economy.

THE OUTPUT OF THE FIRM

What determines the output rate in the short run of a perfectly competitive firm? Since the firm is perfectly competitive, it cannot affect the price of its product, and it can sell any amount it wants at this price. Since we are concerned with the short run, the firm can expand or contract its output rate by increasing or decreasing its utilization of its variable, but not its fixed, inputs. (The situation in the long run will be considered in a later section.)

■ WHAT IS THE PROFIT AT EACH OUTPUT RATE?

To see how a firm determines its output rate, suppose that your aunt dies and leaves you her business, the Allegro Piano Company. Once you take over the business, your first problem is to decide how many pianos (each of which has a price of $1,000) the firm should produce per week. Having a good deal of economic intuition, you instruct your accountants to estimate the company's *total revenue* (defined as price times output) and total costs (as well as, separately, fixed and variable costs) at various output levels. They estimate the firm's total revenue at various output rates and its total cost function (as well as its total fixed cost function and total variable cost function), with the results shown in Table 18.2. Subtracting the total cost at a given output rate from the total revenue at this output rate, you obtain the total profit at each output rate, which is shown in the last column of Table 18.2.

■ FINDING THE MAXIMUM-PROFIT OUTPUT RATE

As the output rate increases from zero to four pianos per week, the total profit *rises*. As the output rate increases from five to eight pi-

TABLE 18.2

**Costs and Revenues,
Allegro Piano
Company**

OUTPUT PER WEEK (PIANOS)	PRICE	TOTAL REVENUE (PRICE × OUTPUT)	TOTAL FIXED COST	TOTAL VARIABLE COST	TOTAL COST	TOTAL PROFIT
			(DOLLARS)			
0	1,000	0	1,000	0	1,000	−1,000
1	1,000	1,000	1,000	200	1,200	−200
2	1,000	2,000	1,000	300	1,300	700
3	1,000	3,000	1,000	500	1,500	1,500
4	1,000	4,000	1,000	1,000	2,000	2,000
5	1,000	5,000	1,000	2,000	3,000	2,000
6	1,000	6,000	1,000	3,200	4,200	1,800
7	1,000	7,000	1,000	4,500	5,500	1,500
8	1,000	8,000	1,000	7,200	8,200	−200

anos per week, the total profit *falls*. Thus the *maximum* profit is achieved at an output rate between four and five pianos per week.[1] (Without more detailed data, one cannot tell precisely where the maximum occurs, but this is close enough for present purposes.) Since the maximum profit is obtained at an output of between four and five pianos per week, this is the output rate you choose.

Figure 18.1 gives a more vivid picture of the firm's situation by plotting the relationship between total revenue and total cost on the one hand and output on the other. At each output rate, the vertical distance between the total revenue curve and the total cost curve is the amount of profit the firm earns. Below an output rate of about one piano per week and above a rate of about eight pianos per week, the total revenue curve lies *below* the total cost curve, indicating that profits are negative; that is, there are losses. Both Table 18.2 and Figure 18.1 show that the output rate that will maximize the firm's profits is between four and five pianos per week. At this output rate, the firm will make a profit of over $2,000 per week, which is more than it can make at any other output rate.

There is an alternative way to analyze the firm's situation. Rather than looking at total revenue and total cost, let's look at price and marginal cost. Table 18.3 and Figure 18.2 show the product price and marginal cost at each output rate. It turns out that the maximum profit is achieved at the output rate where price equals marginal cost. In other words, both Table 18.3 and Figure 18.2

[1]This assumes that the output rate can be varied continuously and that there is a single maximum. These are innocuous assumptions.

FIGURE 18.1

Costs, Revenue, and Profit, Allegro Piano Company

Profit equals the vertical distance between the total revenue curve and the total cost curve. This distance is maximized when the output rate is between 4 and 5 pianos per week. At this output rate, profit (measured by the vertical distance) is somewhat more than $2,000.

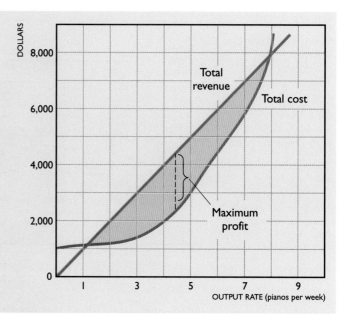

TABLE 18.3

Marginal Cost and Price, Allegro Piano Company

OUTPUT PER WEEK (PIANOS)	MARGINAL COST (DOLLARS)	PRICE (DOLLARS)
0		1,000
	200	
1		1,000
	100	
2		1,000
	200	
3		1,000
	500	
4		1,000
	1,000	
5		1,000
	1,200	
6		1,000
	1,300	
7		1,000
	2,700	
8		1,000

FIGURE 18.2

Marginal Cost and Price, Allegro Piano Company

At the profit-maximizing output rate of between four and five pianos per week, marginal cost (which is $1,000 when the output rate is between four and five) equals price ($1,000). Recall from Figure 16.11 that marginal cost is plotted at the midpoint of the range of output to which it pertains.

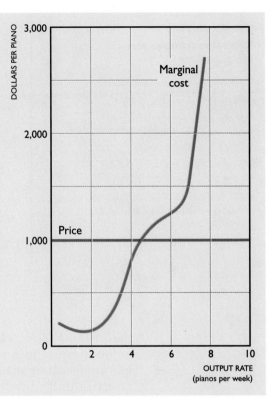

indicate that price equals marginal cost at the profit-maximizing output rate of between four and five pianos per week. This raises a question: Will price usually equal marginal cost at the profit-maximizing output rate, or is this merely a coincidence?

■ THE GOLDEN RULE OF OUTPUT DETERMINATION

Readers familiar with television scripts and detective stories will have recognized that the question just posed can only be answered in one way without ruining the plot. The equality of marginal cost and price at the profit-maximizing output rate is no mere coincidence. It will usually be true if the firm takes the price of its product as given. Indeed, the Golden Rule of Output Determination for a perfectly competitive firm is: *Choose the output rate at which marginal cost is equal to price.*

To prove that this rule maximizes profits, consider Figure 18.3, which shows a typical short-run marginal cost function. Suppose that the price is P_1. At any output rate less than Q_1, price is greater than marginal cost. This means that increases in output will increase the firm's profits since they will add more to total revenue

423

FIGURE 18.3

Short-Run Average and Marginal Cost Curves

If price is P_1, the profit-maximizing output rate is Q_1. If price is P_2, the profit-maximizing output rate is Q_2, even though the firm will incur a loss. If the price is below P_3, the firm will discontinue production. (Note that, regardless of what the price is, the demand curve facing the firm is a horizontal line at this price.)

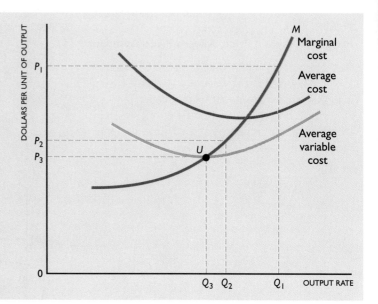

than to total cost. Why? Because an extra unit of output adds an amount equal to price to total revenue and an amount equal to marginal cost to total cost. Thus, since price exceeds marginal cost, an extra unit of output adds more to total revenue than to total cost. This is the case for the Allegro Piano Company when it is producing three pianos per week. As shown in Table 18.3, the extra cost of producing a fourth piano is $500, while the revenue brought in by producing and selling it is $1,000. Consequently, it pays the Allegro Piano Company to produce more than three pianos per week.

At any output rate above Q_1, price is less than marginal cost. This means that decreases in output will increase the firm's profits since they will subtract more from total costs than from total revenue. This happens because one less unit of output subtracts an amount equal to price from total revenue and an amount equal to marginal cost from total cost. Thus since price is less than marginal cost, one less unit of output subtracts more from total cost than from total revenue. Such a case occurs when the Allegro Piano Company is producing seven pianos per week. As shown in Table 18.3, the extra cost of producing the seventh piano is $1,300, while the extra revenue it brings in is $1,000. So it pays the Allegro Piano Company to produce less than seven pianos per week.

Since increases in output will increase profits if output is less than Q_1 and decreases in output will increase profits if output is greater than Q_1, it follows that profits must be maximized at Q_1, the output rate at which price equals marginal cost. After all, if increases in output up to this output (Q_1) result in increases in profit and further increases in output result in decreases in profit, Q_1 must be the profit-maximizing output rate. For the Allegro Piano Company, this output rate is between four and five pianos per week, as we saw above.

■ DOES IT PAY TO BE A DROPOUT?

All rules have exceptions, even the Golden Rule we just mentioned. Under some circumstances, the perfectly competitive firm will not maximize its profits if it sets marginal cost equal to price. Instead, it will maximize its profits only if it becomes an economic dropout by discontinuing production. Let's demonstrate that this is indeed a fact. The first important point is that, even if the firm is doing the best it can, it may not be able to earn a profit. If the price is P_2 in Figure 18.3, short-run average cost exceeds the price P_2 at all possible output rates. Thus the firm cannot earn a profit whatever output it produces. Since the short run is too short for the firm to alter the scale of its plant, it cannot liquidate its plant in the short run. Its only choice is to produce at a loss or discontinue production.

Under what conditions will the firm produce at a loss, and under what conditions will it discontinue production? *If there is an output rate where price exceeds average variable costs, it will pay the firm to produce, even though price does not cover average total cost. If there is no such output rate, the firm is better off to produce nothing at all.* This is true because even if the firm produces nothing it must pay its fixed cost. If the loss resulting from production is less than the firm's fixed cost, the firm is better off producing than not producing. On the other hand, if the loss resulting from production is greater than the firm's fixed cost, the firm is better off not to produce.

■ DROPPING OUT: ILLUSTRATIVE CASES

To illustrate the conditions under which it pays a firm to drop out, suppose that the cost functions of the Allegro Piano Company are as shown in Table 18.4. In this case, there exists no output rate such that average variable cost is less than price, which, you will recall, is $1,000 per piano. Thus, according to the results of the last paragraphs, the Allegro Piano Company should discontinue production under these conditions. The wisdom of this course of action is shown by the last column of Table 18.4, which demonstrates that the profit-maximizing—or, what amounts to the same thing, the loss-minimizing—output rate is zero.

Sometimes, as in the present case, the best thing to produce is nothing. The situation is analogous to the common experience of

TABLE 18.4

Costs and Revenues,
Allegro Piano
Company

OUTPUT PER WEEK (PIANOS)	PRICE	TOTAL REVENUE	TOTAL FIXED COST	TOTAL VARIABLE COST	AVERAGE VARIABLE COST	TOTAL COST	TOTAL PROFIT
				(DOLLARS)			
0	1,000	0	1,000	0	—	1,000	−1,000
1	1,000	1,000	1,000	1,200	1,200	2,200	−1,200
2	1,000	2,000	1,000	2,600	1,300	3,600	−1,600
3	1,000	3,000	1,000	4,200	1,400	5,200	−2,200
4	1,000	4,000	1,000	6,000	1,500	7,000	−3,000
5	1,000	5,000	1,000	8,000	1,600	9,000	−4,000
6	1,000	6,000	1,000	10,200	1,700	11,200	−5,200
7	1,000	7,000	1,000	12,600	1,800	13,600	−6,600
8	1,000	8,000	1,000	15,200	1,900	16,200	−8,200

leaving a movie after finding in the first ten minutes that it is not going to be a good one. One ignores the fixed costs (the nonrefundable admission price), and finding that the variable cost (the pleasure gained from activities that would be forgone by seeing the rest of the show) is going to exceed the benefits of staying, one leaves.

In 1973, many meat-processing plants discontinued production for essentially this reason. The federal government, in an attempt to control inflation, froze the price of their product but allowed the prices of the inputs they used to go up. The result was that their average variable cost exceeded price at all possible output levels. The consequence, as our theory would predict, was that many plants closed down. In Chicago, the American Meat Institute announced that 16 plants closed down in the second quarter of 1973. As the president of Detroit's Crown Packing Company put it, "Frankly, we closed down so that we would lose less money."

THE MARKET SUPPLY CURVE

In Chapters 2 and 16 we described some of the factors underlying a commodity's market supply curve, but we could not go into much detail. Now we can, because our Golden Rule of Output Determination underlies the market supply curve. As a first step, let's derive the **firm's supply curve**, which shows how much the firm will want to produce at each price.

■ THE FIRM'S SUPPLY CURVE

Since the firm takes the price of its product as given (and can sell all it wants at that price), we know from the previous sections that the firm will choose the output level at which price equals marginal cost. Or if the price is below the firm's average variable cost curve at every output level, the firm will produce nothing. These results are all we need to determine the firm's supply curve.

Suppose that the firm's short-run cost curves are as shown in Figure 18.3. The marginal cost curve must intersect the average variable cost curve at the latter's minimum point U. If the price of the product is less than P_3, the firm will produce nothing, because there is no output level where price exceeds average variable cost. If the price of the product exceeds P_3, the firm will set its output rate at the point where price equals marginal cost. If the price is P_1, the firm will produce Q_1; if the price is P_2, the firm will produce Q_2; and so forth. Consequently, *the firm's supply curve is exactly the same as the firm's marginal cost curve for prices above the minimum value of average variable cost* (P_3). For prices at or below the minimum value of average variable cost, the firm's supply curve corresponds to the price axis, where the desire to supply at these prices is uniformly zero. Thus the firm's supply curve is P_3UM.

■ DERIVING THE MARKET SUPPLY CURVE

Our next step is to derive the market supply curve from the supply curves of the individual firms. If one assumption (which we will consider shortly) holds, the **market supply curve** can be regarded *as the horizontal summation of the supply curves of all the firms producing the product.* If there were three firms in the industry and their supply curves were as shown in Figure 18.4, the market supply curve would be the horizontal summation of their three supply curves. Since these three supply curves show that firm 1 would supply 25 units of output at a price of $2 per unit, that firm 2 would supply 40 units at this price, and that firm 3 would supply 55 units at this price, the market supply curve shows that 120 units of output will be supplied if the price is $2 per unit. Why? Because the market supply curve shows the *total* amount of the product that all the firms together would supply at this price: 25 + 40 + 55 = 120. If there were only three firms, the market would not be perfectly competitive, but we can ignore this inconsistency. Figure 18.4 is designed to illustrate the fact that the market supply curve is the horizontal summation of the firms' supply curves, at least under one important assumption.

The assumption underlying this construction of the short-run market supply curve is that *increases or decreases in output by all*

FIGURE 18.4

Horizontal Summation of Short-Run Supply Curves of Firms

If each of the three firms' supply curves are as shown here (and if each firm supplies nothing if the price is below H), the market supply curve is the horizontal summation of the firms' supply curves, assuming that input prices are not influenced by the output of the industry.

firms simultaneously do not affect input prices. This is a convenient simplification, but it is not always true. Although changes in the output of one firm alone often cannot affect input prices, the simultaneous expansion or contraction of output by all firms may well alter input prices, so that the individual firm's cost curves—and supply curve—will shift. For instance, an expansion of the whole industry may bid up the price of certain inputs, with the result that the cost curves of the individual firms will be pushed upward. A sudden expansion of the aerospace industry, for instance, might well increase the price of such inputs as the services of aerospace scientists and engineers.

If, contrary to the assumption underlying Figure 18.4, input prices *are* increased by the expansion of the industry, one can still derive the short-run market supply curve by seeing how much the industry will supply in the short run at each price of the product. But it is then incorrect to assume that the market supply curve is the horizontal summation of the firms' supply curves.

PRICE AND OUTPUT: THE SHORT RUN

How much of a particular product will be produced if the market is perfectly competitive, and what will the price be? The answers depend on the length of the time period being considered. To begin with, let's consider the short run, the period during which each firm's plant and equipment are fixed. What determines the price and output of a good in a perfectly competitive market in the short run? The answer is the market demand and market supply curves. As we know from Chapter 2, the equilibrium price and output are at the point where the demand and supply curves inter-

FIGURE 18.5

Short-Run Competitive Equilibrium

In the short run, the equilibrium price is *P*, and the equilibrium output of the industry is *Q*, since (as shown in panel B) the industry demand and supply curves intersect at this price and output.

sect. Thus, in panel B of Figure 18.5, the equilibrium price and output in the short run are *P* and *Q*.

Panel A of Figure 18.5 shows the behavior of an individual firm in short-run equilibrium. Since *P* is the price, the demand curve facing the firm is a horizontal line at *P*, as shown in panel A. To maximize profit, the firm produces an output of *q*, because price equals marginal cost at this output. In short-run equilibrium, firms may be making either profits or losses. In the particular case described in panel A, the firm earns a profit equal to the shaded area shown there. Since the profit per unit of output equals *CP*, total profit equals *CP* multiplied by *q*, which is this shaded area.

Taken together, the two panels of Figure 18.5 bring out the following important point. To the *individual* firm, the price of the product is taken as given. If the price is *P*, the firm in panel A reacts to this price by setting an output rate of *q* units. It cannot alter the price; it can only react to it. But the reactions of the firms *as a group* are a major determinant of the price of the product. The supply curve in panel B shows the total amount that the entire group of firms will supply at each price. It summarizes the reactions of the firms to various levels of the price. Put briefly, the equilibrium price is viewed by the individual firm as being beyond its control; yet the supply decisions of all firms taken as a group are a basic determinant of the equilibrium price.

PRICE AND OUTPUT: THE LONG RUN

In the long run, what determines the output and price of a good in a perfectly competitive market? In the long run, a firm can change its plant size, which means that established firms may *leave* an industry if it has below-average profits or that new firms may *enter*

**ECONOMIC
EFFICIENCY,
MARKET SUPPLY,
AND PERFECT
COMPETITION**
CHAPTER 18

an industry with above-average profits. Suppose that textile firms can earn up to (but not more than) a 15 percent rate of return by investing their resources in other industries. If they can earn only 12 percent by keeping these resources invested in the textile industry, they will leave the textile industry. On the other hand, if a rate of return of 18 percent can be earned by investing in the textile industry, firms in other industries, attracted by this relatively high return, will enter the textile industry.

■ EQUILIBRIUM: ZERO ECONOMIC PROFIT

Equilibrium is achieved in the long run when enough firms—no more, no less—are in the industry so that *economic profits*— defined as the excess of a firm's profits over what it could make in other industries—are zero. This condition is necessary for long-run equilibrium because, as we have seen, new firms will enter the industry if there are economic profits, and existing firms will leave if there are economic losses. This process of entry and exit is the key to long-run equilibrium.

Note that the existence of economic profits or losses in an industry brings about a shift in the industry's short-run supply curve. If there are economic profits, new firms will enter the industry and shift the short-run supply curve to the right. On the other hand, if there are economic losses in the industry (if the industry's profits are less than could be obtained elsewhere), existing firms will leave the industry and cause the short-run supply curve to shift to the left. Only if economic profits are zero will the number of firms in the industry—and the industry's short-run supply curve—be stable. Putting this equilibrium condition another way, *the long-run equilibrium position of the firm is at the point at which its long-run average cost equals price.* If price exceeds average total cost, economic profits are being earned; if price is less than average total cost, economic losses are being incurred.

■ EQUILIBRIUM: MAXIMUM ECONOMIC PROFIT

Going a step further, *long-run equilibrium requires that price equal the lowest value of long-run average total cost.* In other words, firms must be producing at the *minimum point* on their long-run average cost curves, because to maximize their profits, as we have seen, they must operate where price equals long-run marginal cost; at the same time they also have to operate where price equals long-run average cost. But if both these conditions are satisfied, long-run marginal cost must equal long-run average cost, since both equal price. And we know from Chapter 16 that long-run marginal cost equals long-run average cost only at the point at which long-

FIGURE 18.6

Long-Run Equilibrium of a Perfectly Competitive Firm

In long-run equilibrium, output is q and the firm's plant corresponds to the short-run average and marginal cost curves shown here.

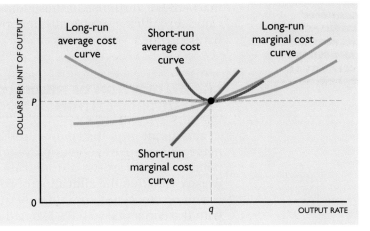

run average cost is a minimum.[2] Consequently, if long-run marginal cost equals long-run average cost, the firm must be producing at the minimum point on the long-run average cost curve.

This equilibrium position is illustrated in Figure 18.6. When all adjustments are made, price equals P. The equilibrium output of the firm is q, and its plant corresponds to the short-run average and marginal cost curves in Figure 18.6. At this output and with this plant, long-run marginal cost equals short-run marginal cost equals price. This ensures that the firm is maximizing profit. Also, long-run average cost equals short-run average cost equals price. This ensures that economic profits are zero. Since long-run marginal cost and long-run average cost must be equal, the firm is producing at the minimum point on its long-run average cost curve.

To illustrate the process of entry and exit in an industry that has approximated perfect competition, let's consider the pre–World War II bituminous coal industry. Entry into this industry was relatively easy, but exit was relatively difficult, for at least two reasons. First, it is costly to shut down a mine and reopen it later. Second, because of corrosion and water damage, it is hard to shut down a mine for longer than two years unless it is to be abandoned entirely. For these reasons, mines have tended to stay open and produce even though short-term losses have been incurred. In the period before World War II, the demand for coal fell substantially, but although the industry suffered substantial losses, mines were slow to close down. Nonetheless, the competitive process had its way. Slowly but surely, the number of mines fell

---

[2]The previous discussion of this point concerned short-run cost functions, but the argument applies just as well to long-run cost functions.

ECONOMIC
EFFICIENCY,
MARKET SUPPLY,
AND PERFECT
COMPETITION

CHAPTER 18

markedly in response to these losses. Thus, despite the barriers to rapid exit, firms eventually left the industry, just as the model would predict.

THE ALLOCATION OF RESOURCES UNDER PERFECT COMPETITION: A MORE-DETAILED VIEW

At this point, it is instructive to describe the process by which a perfectly competitive economy—one composed of perfectly competitive industries—would allocate resources. In earlier chapters we stressed that the allocation of resources among alternative uses is one of the major functions of any economic system. Equipped with the concepts we have learned since, we can now go much further in describing how a perfectly competitive economy shifts resources in accord with changes in tastes, technology, and other factors.

■ CONSUMERS TURN FROM CORN TO WHEAT

To be specific, suppose that a change occurs in tastes. Consumers become more favorably disposed toward wheat and less favorably disposed toward corn than in the past.[3] In the short run, the increase in the demand for wheat increases the price of wheat and results in some increase in the output of wheat. However, the output cannot be increased very substantially because the industry's capacity cannot be expanded in the short run. Similarly, the fall in the demand for corn reduces the price of corn and results in some reduction in output. But the output will not be curtailed greatly because firms will continue to produce as long as they can cover variable costs.

■ PRICES SIGNAL RESOURCE REALLOCATION

The change in the relative prices of wheat and corn tells producers that a reallocation of resources is called for. Because of the increase in the price of wheat and the decrease in the price of corn, wheat producers are earning economic profits and corn producers are showing economic losses. This will trigger a new deployment of resources. If some variable inputs in corn production can be used as effectively in the production of wheat, they may be switched from corn production to wheat production. Even if no variable inputs are used in both wheat and corn production, adjustments can be made in various interrelated markets, with the

---

[3]Since we assume here that the markets for wheat and corn are perfectly competitive, it is also assumed that there is no government intervention in these markets.

Price ceilings and price supports

Sugar rationing during World War II

During national emergencies, the government sometimes puts a lid on prices, **price ceilings,** not allowing them to reach their equilibrium levels. For example, during World War II, the government did not allow the prices of various foodstuffs to rise to their equilibrium levels, because it felt that this would have been inequitable (and highly unpopular). Thus the quantity demanded of a product exceeds the quantity supplied.

Since the price system is not allowed to perform its rationing function, some formal system of rationing or allocating the available supply of the product may be required. Thus in World War II families were issued ration coupons that determined how much they could buy of various commodities. And in 1979, when the Organization of Petroleum Exporting Countries cut back oil production and reduced exports of oil to the United States, there was serious talk that gasoline and oil might be rationed in a similar way. Such rationing schemes may be justified in emergencies (of reasonably short duration), but they can result eventually in serious distortions, since prices are not allowed to do the job normally expected of them.

Government authorities may also impose **price floors**—or **price supports,** as they are often called. These floors are generally defended on the ground that they enable the producers of the good in question to make a better living. For example, the federal government has imposed price supports on a wide range of agricultural commodities to increase farm incomes. The result, as we saw in Exploring Further in Chapter 17, is that the quantity supplied exceeds the quantity demanded at the support price. Thus there is a surplus of the commodity, and in the case of agricultural commodities, the government has had to buy up and store these surpluses. As in the case of a price ceiling, the result is that the price system is not allowed to do the job expected of it.

Whether price ceilings or floors are socially desirable depends on whether the loss in social efficiency resulting from them is exceeded by the gain in equity they achieve. Their purpose is to help or to protect parts of the population that would be treated inequitably by the unfettered price system.

result that wheat production gains resources and corn production loses resources. (For example, some resources may move from corn production to manufacturing, and others may move from manufacturing to wheat production.) When short-run equilibrium is attained in both the wheat and corn industries, the reallocation of resources is not yet complete, since there has not been enough

433

Starting from scratch: The transition from communism to capitalism

The Berlin Wall, after it fell in November 1989

The political revolutions that swept eastern Europe in 1989 and 1990 were the easy part. Much more difficult was the task of transforming these centrally planned economies into market economies. The microeconomic problems facing these countries were the result of: (1) centralized decision making, (2) rigid price structure, (3) lack of private ownership, and (4) lack of currency convertibility. The vast and entrenched bureaucracies in the centrally planned economies were not only highly inefficient, they also saw reform as a threat and tried to slow it down in every way possible. Thus an essential first step in microeconomic reform was the dismantling, or at least the neutralization, of the central planning apparatus.

Price reform was also essential, given the distortions caused by price controls and subsidies. For example, many of these countries deliberately kept the price of bread low to appease consumers. The predictable result of this was an excess demand for bread—and long lines of consumers at stores. When price reforms were enacted in Poland and Hungary, the long lines disappeared and goods were again in plentiful supply; however, consumer budgets were also squeezed. In addition, while ideologically a giant stumbling block for countries that until recently espoused communism, private ownership of assets is an essential element of a market economy. The challenge facing these economies in the early 1990s was to sell off (privatize) state-owned assets without turning public monopolies into private monopolies.

Finally, full currency convertibility (the ability to exchange the domestic currency for any other country's currency at prevailing market rates) is also a *sine qua non* of a market economy. Without it, the centrally planned economies could not become integrated into the world economy and reap the benefits of international trade.

The political dilemma facing many of the embryonic democracies in eastern Europe in the early 1990s was that the initial impact of all these reforms was quite painful. The payoff would come much later. It was inevitable, therefore, that many were tempted to delay the pain as long as possible. Countries that moved rapidly to reform their economies experienced a sharp but relatively short decline in output and by the mid-1990s were in full recovery. At the head of the pack was Poland whose real GDP in 1999 was 20 percent higher than in 1989, the beginning of the transition. Slovenia, Slovakia, and Hungary had also bounced back. On the other hand, the slow reformers suffered through longer periods of decline that lasted throughout the decade. Chief among these countries was Russia, whose real GDP in 1999 was still about 50 percent lower than its pretransition level. In the end, the accumulated losses for the slow reformers were considerably higher than for the fast reformers.

One of the single biggest factors that determined whether a country became a fast or slow reformer was time for producers to build new capacity or liquidate old capacity. In particular, neither industry is operating at minimum average cost. The wheat producers are operating at greater than the output level where average cost is a minimum, and the corn producers are operating at less than this level.

■ EFFECTS IN THE LONG RUN

What will happen in the long run? The shift in consumer demand from corn to wheat will result in greater adjustments in production and smaller adjustments in price than in the short run. In the long run, existing firms can leave corn production and new firms can enter wheat production. Because of short-run economic losses in corn production, some corn land and related equipment will be allowed to run down, and some firms engaged in corn production will be liquidated. As firms leave corn production, the supply curve shifts to the left and causes the price to rise above its short-run level. The transfer of resources out of corn production will stop when price has increased and costs have decreased to the point where losses are avoided.

While corn production is losing resources, wheat production is gaining them. The prospect of positive economic profits in wheat production will cause new firms to enter the industry. The increased demand for inputs will raise input prices and cost curves in wheat production, and the price of wheat will be depressed by the movement to the right of the supply curve because of the entry of new firms. Entry ceases when economic profits are no longer being earned. At this point, when long-run equilibrium is achieved, more resources will be used in the industry than in the short run. (Note that if corn land and equipment can be converted to the production of wheat, some of the entry may occur through existing farmers' shifting their crop mix toward wheat and away from corn.)

Finally, long-run equilibrium is established in both industries, and the reallocation of resources is complete. It is important to note that this reallocation can affect industries other than wheat and corn. If corn land and equipment can be easily adapted to the production of wheat, corn producers can simply change to wheat production. If not, the resources used in corn production are converted

435

ECONOMIC
EFFICIENCY,
MARKET SUPPLY,
AND PERFECT
COMPETITION
CHAPTER 18

to some use other than wheat, and the resources that enter wheat production come from some use other than corn production.

REVIEW AND PRACTICE

■ SUMMARY

1 Economists generally classify markets into four types: perfect competition, monopoly, monopolistic competition, and oligopoly. Perfect competition requires that the product of any seller be the same as the product of any other seller, that no buyer or seller be able to influence the price of the product, and that resources be able to switch readily from one use to another.

2 If it maximizes profit, a perfectly competitive firm should set its output rate in the short run at the level where marginal cost equals price, so long as price exceeds average variable cost. If there is no output rate at which price exceeds average variable cost, the firm should discontinue production.

3 The firm's supply curve coincides with its marginal cost curve for prices exceeding the minimum value of average variable cost. For prices that are less than or equal to the minimum value of average variable cost, the firm's supply curve coincides with the price axis.

4 As a first approximation, the market supply curve can be viewed as the horizontal summation of the supply curves of all the firms producing the product. This assumes that increases or decreases in output by all firms simultaneously do not affect input prices.

5 Price and output under perfect competition are determined by the intersection of the market supply and demand curves.

6 In the long run, equilibrium is achieved under perfect competition when enough firms—no more, no less—are in the industry so that economic profits are eliminated. In other words, the long-run equilibrium position of the firm is at the point where its long-run average cost equals price. But since price must also equal marginal cost (to maximize profit), it follows that the firm must be operating at the minimum point on the long-run average cost curve.

7 In a perfectly competitive economy, prices are the signals that are used to guide the reallocation of resources in response to changes in consumer tastes, technology, and other factors.

■ PROBLEMS AND QUESTIONS

1 Suppose that the total costs of a perfectly competitive firm are as follows:

OUTPUT RATE	TOTAL COST (DOLLARS)
0	40
1	60
2	90
3	130
4	180
5	240

If the price of the product is $50, what output rate should the firm choose?

2 Suppose that the firm in question 1 experienced an increase of $30 in its fixed costs. Plot its new total cost function. What effect will this increase in its fixed costs have on the output it will choose?

3 After the increase in fixed costs described in question 2, what does the firm's marginal cost curve look like? Plot it on a graph. Does it differ from what it was before the increase in fixed costs? Why or why not?

4 After the increase in fixed costs described in question 2, what output rate would the firm choose if the price of its product were $40? $50? $60?

■ KEY TERMS

perfect competition	price ceilings
barriers to entry	price floors (price supports)

■ VIEWPOINT FOR ANALYSIS

According to the *New York Times*, June 22, 1993, to New York's politicians, "rent control and rent stabilization are articles of faith. They say their opposition [to ending rent control in New York City] is based on the need to protect tenants from skyrocketing rent increases. But they must know better. Rent regulations inflate the cost of housing, rob the city of tax revenues, discourage new construction, and speed deterioration of older housing. Nonetheless, few city politicians of either party are willing to take on the powerful tenants lobby, certainly not in a mayoral election year."*

(a) Do you agree rent controls tend to discourage new construction of housing? Why or why not?

(b) Do you agree rent controls speed the deterioration of older housing? Why or why not?

(c) Do rent controls result in a loss of economic efficiency? If so, how?

(d) Do rent controls bring about a gain in equity? If so, how?

*New York Times, June 22, 1993, p. A22.

CHAPTER 19

Monopoly and Its Regulation

LEARNING OBJECTIVES

In this chapter, you should learn:

■ The conditions that define a monopolistic market structure and their causes

■ The Golden Rule of Output Determination for a monopolistic firm

■ How the prices and outputs set under monopoly compare with those set under perfect competition

■ The case against monopolies, and how they can be regulated

■ *(Exploring Further)* How monopoly power has been defended

At the opposite extreme from perfect competition is monopoly, which may well characterize the market for electricity, gas, or water in your area. Under a monopolistic market structure, what types of behavior can we expect? How much of the product will be produced, and at what level will its price be set? What are the social disadvantages of monopoly? In what ways have government commissions attempted to regulate industries whose market structures approximate monopoly? These are some of the major questions dealt with in this chapter.

Monopoly

To begin with, recall what is meant by **monopoly**: *a market where there exists one, and only one, seller.* Monopoly, like perfect competition, seldom corresponds more than approximately to conditions in real industries, but it is a very useful model. In several respects, monopoly and perfect competition stand as polar opposites. The firm in a perfectly competitive market has so many rivals that competition becomes entirely impersonal. The firm is a price taker, an inconspicuous seller in a sea of inconspicuous sellers. Under monopoly, on the other hand, the firm has no direct competitors at all; it is the sole supplier.

However, even the monopolist is affected by certain indirect and potential forms of competition. Suppose a firm managed to obtain a monopoly on wheat production. It would have to worry about competition from corn and other agricultural commodities that could be substituted for wheat. Moreover, the wheat monopolist would also have to take into account the possibility that new firms might arise to challenge its monopoly if it attempted to extract conspicuously high profits. Thus even the monopolist is subject to some restraint imposed by competitive forces.

CAUSES OF MONOPOLY

There are many reasons why monopolies, or market structures that closely approximate monopoly, may arise.

■ PATENTS

Patents

A firm may acquire a monopoly over the production of a good by having **patents** on the product or on certain basic processes used in its production. The patent laws of the United States give an inventor the exclusive right to make a certain product or to use a certain process for 20 years (from initial filing). The purpose of the patent system is to encourage invention and innovation and to discourage industrial secrecy. Many firms with monopoly power achieved it in considerable part through patents. For example, the United Shoe Machinery Company became the sole supplier of important shoemaking equipment through the control of basic patents.

■ CONTROL OF INPUTS

A firm may become a monopolist by obtaining control over the entire supply of a basic input required to manufacture a product. The International Nickel Company of Canada controls about nine-tenths of the proven nickel reserves in the world—obviously, a strong monopoly position. Similarly, the Aluminum Company of America (Alcoa) kept its dominant position for a long time by controlling practically all the sources of bauxite, the ore used to make aluminum. However, Alcoa's monopoly was broken in 1945 when the Supreme Court decided that Alcoa's control of practically all the industry's output violated the antitrust laws.

■ GOVERNMENT ACTION

A firm may become a monopolist because it is awarded a market franchise by a government agency. The government may give a particular firm the franchise to sell a particular product in a public facility. Or it may give a particular company the right to provide a service, such as electrification, to people in a particular area. In exchange for this right, the firm agrees to allow the government to regulate certain aspects of its operations. The form of regulation does not matter here; the important point is that the monopoly is created by the government.

■ DECLINING COST OF PRODUCTION

A firm may become a monopolist because the average costs of producing the product reach a minimum at an output rate that is large enough to satisfy the entire market (at a price that is profitable). In a case like this, a firm obviously has an incentive to expand until it produces all the market wants of the good. (Its costs fall as it continues to expand.) Thus competition cannot be maintained in this case. If there are a number of firms in the industry, the result is likely to be economic warfare and the survival of a single victor, the monopolist.

Cases where costs behave like this are called **_natural monopolies_**. When an industry is a natural monopoly, the public often insists that its behavior be regulated by the government. For example, electric power is an industry where there seem to be great economies of scale, and thus decreasing average costs. Fuel consumed per kilowatt-hour is lower in larger power generating units, and there are economies in combining generating units at a single site. Because of these factors, there has been little attempt to force competition in the industry, since it has been regarded as wasteful. Instead, the market for electric power in a particular area has been a regulated monopoly.[1]

■ NETWORK EFFECTS

Network effects

A firm may become a monopolist because of **network effects**. For many information technologies, consumers benefit from using a common format or operating system. When the value of a product to one user increases with the number of other users, this is called a network externality or network effect. Telephones, e-mail, Internet access, fax machines, and modems are all products with strong network externalities. Technologies subject to strong network effects tend to exhibit long lead times followed by explosive growth. As the installed base of users grows, more and more users find adoption worthwhile. Companies whose standards or systems are adopted can become monopolists.

---

[1]But technological change, deregulation, and other factors are changing the economics of electric power production, and competition is likely to become more important in the future.

DEMAND CURVE AND MARGINAL REVENUE UNDER MONOPOLY

Before we can make any statements about the behavior of a monopolistic market, we must point out certain important characteristics of the demand curve facing the monopolist. Since the monopolist is the only seller of the commodity, the demand curve it faces is the market demand curve for the product. Since the market demand curve is almost always downward-sloping to the right, the monopolist's demand curve must also be downward-sloping to the right. This is quite different from perfect competition, where the firm's demand curve is horizontal. To illustrate the situation faced by a monopolist, consider the hypothetical case in Table 19.1. The price at which each quantity (shown in column 1) can be sold by the monopolist is shown in column 2. The firm's **total revenue**—its total dollar sales volume—is shown in column 3. Obviously, column 3 is the product of the first two columns. Column 4 contains the firm's **marginal revenue**, *defined as the addition to total revenue attributable to the addition of one unit to sales.* Thus if $R(q)$ is total revenue when q units are sold and $R(q - 1)$ is total revenue when $(q - 1)$ units are sold, the marginal revenue between q units and $(q - 1)$ units is $R(q) - R(q - 1)$.

Total revenue

Marginal revenue

Marginal revenue is very important to the monopolist. We can estimate it from the figures in the first three columns of Table 19.1. The marginal revenue between one and two units of output per day is $180 - \$100$, or $80; the marginal revenue between two and three units of output per day is $240 - \$180$, or $60; the marginal revenue between three and four units of output per day is $280 - \$240$, or $40; and so on. The results are shown in column 4 of the table (and are plotted in Figure 19.1). Note that marginal revenue is analogous to marginal cost (and marginal utility and marginal product, for that matter). Recall that marginal cost is the extra cost resulting from an extra unit of production. Substitute *revenue* for *cost* and *sales* for *production* in the previous sentence, and what do you get? A perfectly acceptable definition of marginal revenue.

Marginal revenue will always be less than price if the firm's demand curve is downward-sloping (as it is under monopoly and other market structures that are not perfectly competitive). In Table 19.1, the extra revenue from the second unit of output is $80 whereas the price of this unit is $90. *The basic reason is that the firm must reduce the price of all units of output, not just the extra unit, in order to sell the extra unit.* Thus in Table 19.1 the extra revenue from the second unit of output is $80 because, while the price of the second unit is $90, the price of the first unit must be reduced by $10 in order to sell the second unit. Thus the extra revenue (marginal revenue) from selling the second unit of output is $90 - \$10$, or $80, which is less than the price of the second unit.

441

TABLE 19.1

Demand and Revenue of a Monopolist

QUANTITY	PRICE	TOTAL REVENUE	MARGINAL REVENUE
		(DOLLARS)	
1	100	100	
			80
2	90	180	
			60
3	80	240	
			40
4	70	280	
			20
5	60	300	
			0
6	50	300	
			−20
7	40	280	
			−40
8	30	240	

FIGURE 19.1

Marginal Revenue and Demand Curves

The demand curve comes from Table 19.1. Each value of marginal revenue is plotted at the midpoint of the range of output to which it pertains. Since the demand curve is downward-sloping, marginal revenue is always less than price, for reasons discussed in the text.

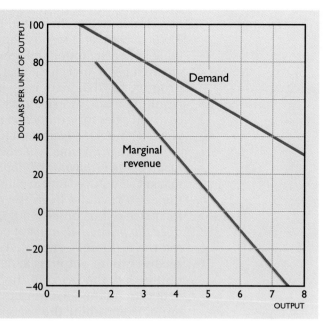

Similarly, the marginal revenue from selling the third unit of output ($60, according to Table 19.1) is less than the price at which the third unit can be sold ($80, according to Table 19.1). Why? Because to sell the third unit of output, the price of the first two units of output must be reduced by $10 each (from $90 to $80). Thus the extra revenue (marginal revenue) from selling the third unit is not $80, but $80 less the $20 reduction in the amount received for the first two units.

PRICE AND OUTPUT: THE SHORT RUN

We are now in a position to determine how output and price behave under monopoly. If the monopolist is free to maximize its profits, it will choose the price and output rate at which the difference between total revenue and total cost is greatest. Suppose that the firm's costs are as shown in Table 19.2 and that the demand curve it faces is as shown in Table 19.1. On the basis of the data in these two tables, the firm can calculate the profit that it will make at each output rate. To do so, it subtracts its total cost

TABLE 19.2 Costs of a Monopolist	TOTAL VARIABLE COST	TOTAL FIXED COST	TOTAL COSTS	MARGINAL COST
QUANTITY		(DOLLARS)		
0	0	100	100	
				40
1	40	100	140	
				30
2	70	100	170	
				40
3	110	100	210	
				40
4	150	100	250	
				50
5	200	100	300	
				60
6	260	100	360	
				90
7	350	100	450	
				100
8	450	100	550	

		TOTAL REVENUE	TOTAL COST	TOTAL PROFIT
TABLE 19.3 Profit of a Monopolist	QUANTITY		(DOLLARS)	
	1	100	140	−40
	2	180	170	10
	3	240	210	30
	4	280	250	30
	5	300	300	0
	6	300	360	−60
	7	280	450	−170
	8	240	550	−310

from its total revenue, as shown in Table 19.3. What output rate will maximize the firm's profit? According to Table 19.3, profit *rises* as its output rate increases from one to three units per day, and profit *falls* as its output rate increases from four to eight units per day. Thus the *maximum* profit is achieved at an output rate between three and four units per day.[2] (Without more-detailed data, one cannot tell precisely where the maximum occurs, but this is close enough for present purposes.) Figure 19.2 shows the same thing graphically.

What price will the monopolist charge? To maximize its profit, it must charge the price that results in its selling the profit-maximizing output, which in this case is between three and four units per day. Thus, according to Table 19.1, it must charge between $70 and $80 per unit. Why? Because if it charges $70, it will sell four units per day and, if it charges $80, it will sell three units per day. Consequently, to sell the profit-maximizing output of between three and four units per day, it must charge a price of between $70 and $80 per unit.

■ THE GOLDEN RULE OF OUTPUT DETERMINATION

In Chapter 18, we set forth the Golden Rule of Output Determination for a perfectly competitive firm. We can now formulate a Golden Rule of Output Determination for a monopolist: *Set the output rate at the point where marginal revenue equals marginal cost.* Table 19.4 and Figure 19.3 show that this rule results in a maxi-

---

[2]This assumes that the output rate can vary continuously and that there is a single maximum. These are innocuous assumptions.

FIGURE 19.2

Total Revenue, Cost, and Profit of Monopolist

The output rate that will maximize the firm's profit is between three and four units per day. At this output rate, profit (which equals the vertical distance between the total revenue and total cost curves) is over $30 per day. On the basis of the demand curve for its product (shown in Table 19.1), the firm must set a price of between $70 and $80 to sell between three and four units per day.

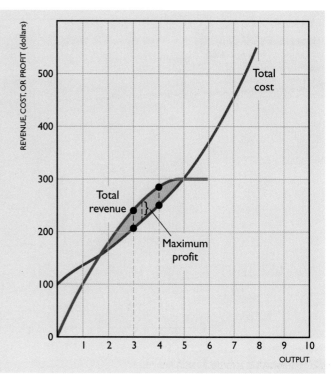

mum profit in this example. It is evident from Table 19.4 that marginal revenue equals marginal cost at the profit-maximizing output of between three and four units per day. Figure 19.3 shows the same thing graphically.

Why is this rule generally a necessary condition for profit maximization? At any output rate at which marginal revenue *exceeds* marginal cost, profit can be increased by *increasing* output, since the extra revenue will exceed the extra cost. At any output rate at which marginal revenue is *less* than marginal cost, profit can be increased by *reducing* output, since the decrease in cost will exceed the decrease in revenue. Thus since profit will *not* be a maximum when marginal revenue exceeds marginal cost or falls short of marginal cost, *it must be a maximum only when marginal revenue equals marginal cost.*

■ **THE MONOPOLIST'S EQUILIBRIUM POSITION**

Figure 19.4 shows the equilibrium position of a monopolist in the short run. Short-run equilibrium will occur at the output Q, where the marginal cost curve intersects the marginal revenue curve (the curve that shows the firm's marginal revenue at each output level).

445

TABLE 19.4

Marginal Cost and Marginal Revenue of a Monopolist

QUANTITY	TOTAL PROFIT	MARGINAL COST	MARGINAL REVENUE
	(DOLLARS)		
1	−40		
		30	80
2	10		
		40	60
3	30		
		40	40
4	30		
		50	20
5	0		
		60	0
6	−60		
		90	−20
7	−170		
		100	−40
8	−310		

FIGURE 19.3

Marginal Cost and Marginal Revenue of a Monopolist

At the profit-maximizing output rate of between three and four units per day, marginal cost (which is $40 between an output rate of three and four units per day) equals marginal revenue (which also is $40 between an output rate of three and four units per day). Both marginal cost and marginal revenue are plotted at the midpoints of the ranges of output to which they pertain.

And if the monopolist is to sell Q units per period of time, the demand curve shows that it must set a price of P. Thus the equilibrium output and price are Q and P, respectively.

It is interesting to compare the Golden Rule of Output Determination for a monopolist (set the output rate at the point where mar-

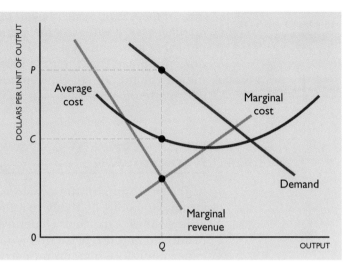

FIGURE 19.4

Equilibrium Position of a Monopolist

A monopolist sets its output rate at Q where the marginal revenue curve intersects the marginal cost curve. At this output, price must be P. And profit per unit of output equals CP, since average cost equals C.

ginal revenue equals marginal cost) with that for a perfectly competitive firm (set the output rate at the point where price equals marginal cost). The latter is really the same as the former because, *for a perfectly competitive firm, price equals marginal revenue.* Since the perfectly competitive firm can sell all it wants at the market price, each additional unit sold increases the firm's total revenue by the amount of the price. Thus *for both the monopolist and the perfectly competitive firm, profits are maximized by setting the output rate at the point where marginal revenue equals marginal cost.*

PRICE AND OUTPUT: THE LONG RUN

In contrast to the situation under perfect competition, the long-run equilibrium of a monopolistic industry may not be marked by the absence of economic profits. If a monopolist earns a short-run economic profit, it will not be confronted in the long run with competitors unless the industry ceases to be a monopoly. The entrance of additional firms into the industry is incompatible with the existence of monopoly. So the long-run equilibrium of an industry under monopoly may be characterized by economic profits.

On the other hand, if the monopolist incurs a short-run economic loss, it will be forced to look for other, more profitable uses for its resources. One possibility is that the firm's existing plant is not optimal and that it can earn economic profits by appropriate alterations to its scale and characteristics. If so, the firm will make these alterations in the long run and remain in the industry. How-

447

ever, *if there is no scale of plant that will enable the firm to avoid economic losses, it will leave the industry in the long run.* The mere fact of having a monopoly over the production of a certain commodity does not mean that the firm must be profitable. A monopoly over the production of cut-glass spittoons would be unlikely to catapult a firm into financial glory—or even allow it to avoid losses.

PERFECT COMPETITION AND MONOPOLY: A COMPARISON

At the beginning of the previous chapter, we said that a market's structure would be likely to affect the behavior of the market; in other words, a market's structure would influence how much was produced and the price that would be set. If we could perform an experiment in which an industry was operated first under conditions of perfect competition and then under conditions of monopoly (assuming that the demand for the industry's product and the industry's cost functions would be the same in either case[3]), we would find that the equilibrium price and output would differ under the two sets of conditions.

■ HIGHER PRICE AND LESS OUTPUT UNDER MONOPOLY

Specifically, if the product demand curve and the industry's cost functions are the same, *the output of a perfectly competitive industry tends to be greater and the price tends to be lower than under monopoly.* We see this in Figure 19.5, which shows the industry's demand and supply curves if it is perfectly competitive. Since price and output under perfect competition are given by the intersection of the demand and supply curves, Q_C is the industry output and P_C is the price. But what if all the competitive firms are bought by a single firm, which operates as a pure monopolist? Under these conditions, what formerly was the industry's supply curve is now the monopolist's marginal cost curve.[4] And what formerly was the industry's demand curve is now the monopolist's demand curve.

---

[3]However, the cost and demand curves need not be the same. For example, the monopolist may spend money on advertising, and thus shift the demand curve. It should be recognized that the assumption that they are the same is more significant than it appears at first glance.

[4]The monopolist will operate the various plants that would be independent under perfect competition as branches of a single firm. The marginal cost curve of a multiplant monopoly is the horizontal sum of the marginal cost curves of the individual plants. [To see why, suppose that a monopoly has two plants, A and B. The total amount that the monopoly can produce at a particular marginal cost is the sum of (1) the amount plant A can produce at this marginal cost and (2) the amount plant B can produce at this marginal cost.] This is also the supply curve of the industry if the plants are operated as separate firms under perfect competition.

FIGURE 19.5

Comparison of Long-Run Equilibria: Perfect Competition and Monopoly

Under perfect competition, Q_C is the industry output and P_C is the price. Under monopoly, Q_M is the industry output and P_M is the price. Clearly, output is higher and price is lower under perfect competition than under monopoly.

Since the monopolist chooses the output where marginal cost equals marginal revenue, the industry output will be Q_M and the price will be P_M. Clearly, Q_M is less than Q_C, and P_M is greater than P_C—which is what we set out to prove.

Of course, all this is theory. But there is plenty of evidence that monopolists restrict output and charge higher prices than firms under competition. Take the case of tungsten carbide, which sold for $50 per pound until a monopoly was established in 1927 by General Electric. Then the price went to between $225 and $453 per pound, until the monopoly was broken by the antitrust laws in 1945. The price then dropped back to between $27 and $45 per pound.[5] This case was extreme but by no means unique. Indeed, for centuries people have observed that when monopolies are formed, output tends to be restricted and price tends to be driven up.

■ MONOPOLY AND RESOURCE ALLOCATION

It has long been felt that the allocation of resources under perfect competition is socially more desirable than under monopoly. Society might be better off if more resources were devoted to producing the monopolized good in Figure 19.5 and if the competitive, not the monopolistic, output were produced. For example, in *The Wealth of Nations*, published about 200 years ago, Adam Smith stressed that when competitive forces are thwarted by "the great engine . . . of monopoly," the tendency for resources to be used "as

[5]W. Adams, *The Structure of American Industry* (5th ed.; New York: Macmillan Co., 1977), p. 485.

nearly as possible in the proportion which is most agreeable to the interest of the whole society" is thwarted as well.

Why do many economists believe that the allocation of resources under perfect competition is more socially desirable than under monopoly? This is not a simple question, and like most hard questions it can be answered at various levels of sophistication. Put most simply, many economists believe that firms under perfect competition are induced to produce quantities of goods that are more in line with consumer desires and that firms under perfect competition are induced to use the least costly methods of production. In the following section, we will indicate in detail why economists believe that these things are true.

THE CASE AGAINST MONOPOLY

Many people oppose monopolies on the grounds that they gouge the consumers by charging a higher price than would otherwise exist—a price that can be sustained only because monopolists artificially limit the supply. In other words, these people claim that monopolists reap higher profits than would be possible under perfect competition and that these profits come at the expense of consumers, who pay higher prices than under perfect competition. Is their claim accurate? As we have just seen, a monopolist will reap higher profits than under perfect competition and consumers will pay higher prices under monopoly than under perfect competition. But is this bad?

To the extent that the monopolist is rich and the consumers are poor, we are likely to answer yes. Also, to the extent that the monopolist is less deserving than the consumers, we are likely to answer the same thing. But suppose the monopolist is a selfless philanthropist who gives to the poor. Is monopoly still socially undesirable? The answer remains yes, because *monopoly imposes a burden on society by misallocating resources. In the presence of monopoly, the price system cannot be relied on to direct the allocation of resources to their most efficient use.*

■ THE MISALLOCATION OF RESOURCES

To see more precisely how monopoly interferes with the proper functioning of the price system, suppose that all industries other than the shoe industry are perfectly competitive. The shoe industry, however, has been monopolized. How does this cause a misallocation of resources? Under fairly general circumstances, a good's price can be taken as a measure of the social value of an extra unit of the good. Thus if the price of a pair of socks is $1, the value to the consumer of an extra pair of socks can be taken to be

John D. Rockefeller and Standard Oil of Ohio

The offices of Standard Oil in the 1900s

In the mid-nineteenth century, the nascent oil industry was characterized by competition. With thousands of small-scale prospectors, drillers, and refiners competing, the supply of oil was plentiful. Prices were low, but so were profits. This was the oil in-dustry John D. Rockefeller saw after the Civil War. He was doing well as a produce wholesaler, but he thought he could do better in oil. Not searching for it or drilling for it, but refining it.

By 1865 Rockefeller had built two refineries. He borrowed all he could, paid any interest, and invested it all in expanding his refineries' capacity. By 1869 he had the largest refinery in the country, and a year later Standard Oil of Ohio was born. A firestorm of competition in oil refining during the 1870s made prices erratic and squeezed profit margins. Rockefeller responded by squeezing the competition. Willing competitors were bought. Unwilling competitors were liable to find railroads and pipelines closed to their oil shipments or their credit cut off. The more completely Rockefeller dominated the industry, the higher his profits and the more pressure he could bring to bear on would-be competitors.

By 1879 Rockefeller and Standard Oil controlled, directly and indirectly, 90 to 95 percent of the nation's crude oil supplies, refining capacity, and oil product sales. Under Rockefeller's "guidance," the industry quickly became less crowded. As competition dropped and then disappeared, Rockefeller set prices where he thought they should be, for the good of Standard and, in his opinion, the good of the industry and the nation. He became a price maker. More than twenty years and four presidents were to pass before Standard Oil was broken up under the Sherman Antitrust Act of 1890.

$1. Moreover, under fairly general circumstances, a good's marginal cost can be taken as a measure of the cost to society of an extra unit of the good. Thus, if the marginal cost of a pair of shoes is $30, the cost to society of producing an extra pair of shoes can be taken to be $30.

In perfectly competitive industries, price is set equal to marginal cost, as we saw in Chapter 18. Thus each of the competitive industries produces up to the point where the social value of an extra unit of the good (which equals price) is set equal to the cost to society of producing an extra unit of the good (which equals marginal cost). This is the amount each of these industries should produce—the output rate that will result in an optimal allocation of resources.

■ WHY IS THE COMPETITIVE OUTPUT OPTIMAL?

To see that the competitive output rate is the optimal one, consider what happens when an industry produces up to the point where the social value of an extra unit of the good is *more* than the cost to

451

society of producing an extra unit. This isn't the socially optimal output rate because a one-unit increase in the output rate will increase the social value of output by more than the social cost of production; this means that it will increase social welfare. Thus since a one-unit increase in the output rate will increase social welfare, the existing output rate cannot be optimal.

Next, consider what happens when an industry produces up to the point where the social value of an extra unit of the good is *less* than the cost to society of producing the extra unit. This isn't the socially optimal output rate because a one-unit decrease in the output rate will decrease the social value of output by less than the social cost of production; this means that it will increase social welfare. Thus since a one-unit decrease in the output rate will increase social welfare, the existing output rate cannot be optimal.

Putting together the results of the previous two paragraphs, it follows that the socially optimal output rate must be at the point where the social value of an extra unit of the good *equals* the social cost of producing an extra unit of the good. Why? Because if the output rate is not optimal when the social value of an extra unit of the good exceeds or falls short of the cost to society of producing the extra unit, it must be optimal only when the two are equal.

■ THE MONOPOLIST PRODUCES TOO LITTLE

Now let's return to the monopolistic shoe industry. Is the shoe industry producing the optimal amount of shoes? The answer is no. Like any monopolist, it produces at the point where marginal revenue equals marginal cost. And since marginal revenue is *less* than price (as was proved above), the monopolist produces at a point where price is *greater* than marginal cost. Consequently, *the monopolistic industry produces at a point where the social value of an extra unit of the good (which equals price) is greater than the cost to society of producing the extra unit (which equals marginal cost).* As we saw, this means that the monopolist's output rate is too small. A one-unit increase in the output of shoes will increase the social value of output by more than the social cost of production.

Here lies the economist's principal complaint against monopoly: it results in a misallocation of resources. Too little is produced of the monopolized good. Society is less well off, in terms of its own tastes and potentialities, than it could be. The price system, which would not lead to or tolerate such waste if all industries were perfectly competitive, is not allowed to perform as it should.

■ INCOME DISTRIBUTION

Misallocation of resources is only part of the economist's case against monopoly. As we have already pointed out, *monopoly redis-*

tributes income in favor of the monopolists. In other words, monopolists can fatten their own purse by restricting their output and raising their price. Admittedly, there is no scientific way to prove that monopolists are less deserving than the rest of the population, but it is also pretty difficult to see why they are more deserving.

■ EFFICIENCY

Since monopolists do not have to face direct competition, they are likely to be less diligent in controlling costs and in using resources efficiently. As Nobel laureate Sir John Hicks put it, "The best of all monopoly profits is a quiet life." Certainly we all dream at times of being able to take life easy. It would be strange if monopolists, having succeeded in insulating themselves from direct competition, did not take advantage of the opportunity—not open to firms in perfectly competitive markets—to relax a bit and worry less about pinching pennies. For this reason, many economists believe that, to use Adam Smith's pungent statement, "Monopoly . . . is a great enemy to good management."

■ TECHNOLOGICAL CHANGE

Further, *it is often claimed that monopolists are slow to innovate and adopt new techniques and products.* This lethargy stems from the monopolist's freedom from direct competition. Innovation tends to be disruptive, whereas old ways, like old shoes, tend to be comfortable. The monopolist may be inclined, therefore, to stick with "time-honored" practices. Without question, competition is an important spur to innovation and to the rapid diffusion of innovations. But there are well-known arguments on the other side as well. Some economists argue (see Exploring Further in this chapter) that substantial monopoly power promotes innovation and technological change.

PUBLIC REGULATION OF MONOPOLY

Public regulation

One way that society has attempted to reduce the harmful effects of monopoly is through **public regulation**. Suppose that the long-run cost curve in a particular industry is such that competition is not feasible. In such a case, society may permit a monopoly to be established. But a commission or some other public body is also established to regulate the monopoly's behavior. Among the many such regulatory commissions in the United States are the Federal Energy Regulatory Commission, the Federal Communications Commission, and the Interstate Commerce Commission. They regulate the behavior of firms with monopoly power in the electric

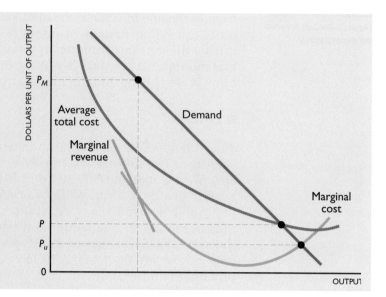

FIGURE 19.6

Regulation of Monopoly

The price established by a commission might be P, where the demand curve intersects the average total cost curve. (Costs here include what the commission regards as a fair profit per unit of output.) In the absence of regulation, the monopolist would set a price of P_M. For price to equal marginal cost, price would have to equal P_u.

power, transportation, and other industries. These industries are big as well as important; they account for about 10 percent of the national output. Thus we need to know how these commissions operate and make decisions on prices and other matters.

Regulatory commissions often set the price—or the maximum price—at the level at which it equals average total cost, including a "fair" rate of return on the firm's investment. In Figure 19.6, the price would be established by the commission at P, where the demand curve intersects the average total cost curve (which includes what the commission regards as a fair profit per unit of output). Needless to say, there has been considerable controversy over what constitutes a fair rate of return. Frequently, commissions have settled on 8 to 10 percent. In addition, there has been a good deal of controversy over what should be included in the company's investment on which the fair rate of return is to be earned. A company's assets can be valued at **historical cost** or at **reproduction cost**: at what the company paid for them or at what it would cost to replace them. If the price level does not change much, these two approaches yield much the same answer. But if prices are rising, as they have been during most of the past 40 years, replacement cost will be greater than historical cost, with the result that the company will be allowed higher profits and rates if replacement cost is used. Most commissions now use historical cost.

Historical cost
Reproduction cost

■ DOES REGULATION AFFECT PRICES?

The regulatory commissions and the principles they use have become extremely controversial. *Many observers feel that the commis-*

sions are lax and that they tend to be captured by the industries they are supposed to regulate. Regulated industries, recognizing the power of such commissions, invest considerable time and money in attempts to influence the commissions. The public, on the other hand, often has only a foggy idea of what the commissions are doing and of whether it is in the public interest. According to some critics like Ralph Nader, "Nobody seriously challenges the fact that the regulatory agencies have made an accommodation with the businesses they are supposed to regulate—and they've done so at the expense of the public." For these and other reasons, some economists believe that regulation has little effect on prices.

It is hard to isolate and measure the effects of regulation on the average level of prices. Some leading economists have conducted studies that suggest that regulation has made little or no difference in this regard. Nobel laureate George Stigler, with Claire Friedland, of the University of Chicago compared the levels of rates charged for electricity by regulated and unregulated electric power companies. They found that there was no significant difference between the average rates charged by the two sets of firms. Other economists challenge Stigler and Friedland's interpretation of their factual findings, and much more research on this topic is needed. Nonetheless, it seems fair to conclude that although the simple model of the regulatory process presented above would predict lower regulated prices, on the average, than unregulated prices (of the same item), the evidence in support of this prediction is much weaker than might be supposed.

Whether or not regulation has a significant effect on the *average* level of prices, it certainly has an effect on *particular* prices charged by regulated firms. In some cases, it has reduced the price of a product. There seems to be general agreement that the Federal Energy Regulatory Commission kept the price of natural gas (in interstate commerce) below what this price would have been during the 1970s in the absence of regulation. In other cases, it has increased the price of a product.

EFFICIENCY INCENTIVES

As we have stressed, competitive markets provide considerable incentives for a firm to increase its efficiency. Firms that are able to push their costs below those of their competitors reap higher profits than their competitors. As a simple illustration, suppose that firms A and B both have contracts to produce 100 airplanes and that the price they will get for each airplane is $25 million. Firm A's management, which is diligent, imaginative, and innovative, gets the cost per airplane down to $24 million, and thus makes a healthy profit of $100 million. Firm B's management,

Network effects and the case against Microsoft

Bill Gates, Microsoft founder

In late 1997 the U.S. Department of Justice began an antitrust suit against Microsoft. The government's goal was to stop alleged anticompetitive practices involving the tie-in of its Internet browser with Windows 95. Behind the suit was a widespread concern that because of so-called network effects, Microsoft could squeeze out other competitors' browsers and Internet applications.

A network effect, or externality, refers to an early standard, such as a computer operating system (for example, Windows 95) that greatly influences future standards because of the need for compatibility. There are at least three reasons for being concerned about network externalities. First, the product that becomes a network standard will not necessarily be the most capable, most efficient, or highest-quality product on the

market. For example, economists and technology experts have been debating for some time whether the QWERTY keyboard and the VHS (versus the now little used Betamax) video format are the most efficient.

Second, high switching costs can raise the barriers to entry for competitors, especially if new products cannot interconnect with those already in the market. This can make network monopolies quite stable and reduces the dominant firm's incentives to introduce innovative products and services.

Third, a network monopolist may have advantages in selling complementary goods that allow it to extend its dominance from one market to another. This was the essence of the case against Microsoft—that it was using its dominant position as the supplier of operating systems to become the dominant supplier of Internet browsers and applications.

As compelling as these concerns are, there was an impressive array of legal and economic minds that disagreed with the government's positions. A recurring theme of their counter-arguments was that technology almost always undermines network externalities. The monopoly by IBM of computer mainframes was wiped out by the advent of the PC. Government-regulated telephone monopolies found themselves scrambling for market share with the widespread use of cellular phones and fiber-optic wires. Therefore, these experts argued, Microsoft's monopoly in operating systems was bound to be short lived.

Moreover, some prominent economists hired by Microsoft argued that even though its Windows operating system was used by over 90 percent of the market, this did not represent a monopoly. In fact they estimated that the monopoly price for Windows 98 was between $900 and $2,000, instead of the much lower market price. Why couldn't Microsoft charge the monopoly price? Because users might have chosen to stay with the earlier Windows 95 version.

Finally, pro-Microsoft advocates argued that even if the company enjoyed a network monopoly, this did not violate the Sherman Antitrust Act (see Chapter 20). In fact under this act, technological monopolies are legal. It is actions to defend or extend the monopoly that break the law.

In the end the presiding Judge, Thomas Penfield Jackson, ruled against Microsoft, in a decision released on November 5, 1999. Judge Jackson conceded that the network effect was probably not that strong in this case. On the contrary, precisely because Microsoft feared that it might lose its commanding lead in the market, it engaged in anticompetitive practices. In the final paragraph of the 207-page document the judge summarizes this view:

> Most harmful of all is the message that Microsoft's actions have conveyed to every enterprise with the potential to innovate in the computer industry. Through its conduct towards Netscape, IBM, Compaq, Intel and others, Microsoft has demonstrated that it

which is lazy, unimaginative, and dull, lets the cost per airplane rise to $26 million, and thus loses $100 million. Clearly, firm A is rewarded for its good performance, while firm B is penalized for its poor performance.

■ NO INCENTIVE FOR EFFICIENCY

One of the primary purposes of regulators is to prevent a monopoly from earning excessive profits. The firm is allowed only a "fair" rate of return on its investment. One problem with this arrangement is that the firm is guaranteed this rate of return regardless of how well it performs. If the regulators decide that the Sleepy Hollow Electric and Gas Company should receive a 10 percent rate of return on its investment, this is the rate of return it will receive regardless of whether the Sleepy Hollow Electric and Gas Company is managed well or poorly. Why is this a problem? Because, unlike the competitive firms discussed in the previous paragraph, there is no incentive for the firm to increase its efficiency.

The available evidence indicates that if a firm is guaranteed a fixed amount of profit for a job (regardless of how efficiently it does this job), the firm will tend to be less efficient than if the amount of profit it receives is directly related to its efficiency. The Department of Defense has found that when it bought goods or services on a cost-plus-fixed-fee basis, these goods and services were not produced as cheaply as when it bought them in a competitive market. This is reasonable. It takes time, energy, and lots of trouble to make a firm more efficient. Why should a firm's managers bother to induce added efficiency if the firm's profits are the same regardless of how efficient it is?

THE DEREGULATION MOVEMENT

Deregulation

In the late 1970s and early 1980s, there was a dramatic movement toward **deregulation** in the United States. A variety of industries, including airlines, railroads, trucking, and financial institutions, were affected. In the case of the airlines, the seeds for deregulation were sown in the 1970s with the appointment of Alfred Kahn, a Cornell economist, as head of the Civil Aeronautics Board. During the late 1970s, airlines were allowed to institute discount fares, and entry restrictions were relaxed. Eventually, Congress passed legislation that phased out the board's powers. The power to regulate routes terminated at the end of 1981, and the power to regulate rates terminated at the end of 1982.

EXPLORING FURTHER

THE DEFENSE OF MONOPOLY POWER

Not all economists agree that monopoly power is a bad thing. On the contrary, some respected voices in the economics profession have been raised to praise monopoly power. In discussing the social problems due to monopoly earlier in this chapter, we assumed that the rate of technological change is independent of an industry's market structure. Some economists, like the late Joseph Schumpeter of Harvard University, have challenged this assumption. *They assert that the rate of technological change is likely to be higher in an imperfectly competitive industry (monopoly, oligopoly, and so on) than in a perfectly competitive industry.* Since the rate of technological change affects productivity and living standards, in their view a perfectly competitive economy is likely to be inferior in a dynamic sense to an economy containing many imperfectly competitive industries.

■ ARGUMENTS BY SCHUMPETER

But is this assertion true? This question has been debated at great length. On the one hand, Schumpeter argues that firms under perfect competition have fewer resources to devote to research and experimentation than do firms under imperfect competition. Because profits are at a relatively low level, it is difficult for firms under perfect competition to support large expenditures on research and development. Moreover, he argues that unless a firm has sufficient control over the market to reap the rewards from an innovation, introducing the innovation may not be worthwhile. If competitors can imitate the innovation very quickly, the innovator may be unable to make any money from it.

■ REJOINDERS TO SCHUMPETER

Defenders of perfect competition retort that there is likely to be less pressure for firms in imperfect markets to introduce new techniques and products, since such firms have fewer competitors. Moreover, established firms in imperfect markets are better able

Fining the telephone company

The Nynex Corporation, which provides telephone service in New York State, was fined a substantial amount in 1996 by the New York Public Service Commission. The fines will eventually be returned to customers. The commission found that complaints against the company had risen, that more repair appointments had been missed, and that the company had provided poorer services, as measured by the state agency, than in the previous year.

Eugene Zeltmann, public service commissioner, said he found it "exceedingly embarrassing" that Nynex "continues to provide the worst infrastructure-related basic service quality of any other telephone company across the nation."* The commission was debating whether to approve the planned alliance between Nynex and Bell Atlantic. It did, and Nynex became part of Bell Atlantic. Do you think that such a deal should have been allowed?

*New York Times, August 23, 1996.

to drive out new entrants who are uncommitted to present techniques and likely to be relatively quick to adopt new ones. (New entrants, unlike established producers, have no vested interest in maintaining the demand for existing products and the profitability of existing equipment.) Also, there are advantages in having a large number of independent decision-making units. There is less chance that an important technological advance will be blocked by the faulty judgment of a few people.

It is very difficult to obtain evidence to help settle the question if it is posed in this way, since perfect competition is a hypothetical construct that does not exist in the real world. However, it does seem unlikely that a perfectly competitive industry (if such an industry could be constructed) would be able in many areas of the economy to carry out the research and development required to promote a high rate of technological change. Moreover, if entry is free and rapid, firms in a perfectly competitive industry will have little motivation to innovate. Although the evidence is not at all clear-cut, at least this much can be granted the critics of perfect competition.

■ MONOPOLY POWER, BIG BUSINESS, AND TECHNOLOGICAL CHANGE

Some economists go much further than asserting that a certain amount of market imperfection will promote a more rapid rate of technological change. *They say that an industry composed of or dominated by a few large companies is the best market structure for promoting rapid technological change.* John Kenneth Galbraith has said that the "modern industry of a few large firms [is] an almost perfect instrument for inducing technical change."[6] And in some circles, it is accepted as an obvious fact that giant firms with their financial strength and well-equipped laboratories are absolutely necessary to maintain a rapid rate of technological change.

Suppose that, for a market of given size, we could replace the largest firms by a larger number of somewhat smaller firms, and thus reduce the extent to which the industry is dominated by the largest firms. Is there any evidence that this would decrease the rate of technological change, as is sometimes asserted? The evidence currently available does not indicate that such a decrease in industrial concentration would reduce the rate of technological change in most industries. Specifically, the available studies do not show that total research and development expenditures in most industries would decrease if the largest firms were replaced by somewhat smaller ones. Nor do they indicate that the research and development expenditures carried out by the largest firms are generally more productive (or more ambitious or more risky) than those carried out by somewhat smaller firms. Moreover, they do not suggest that greater concentration of an industry results in a faster diffusion of innovations. However, if innovations require a large amount of capital, these studies do suggest that the substitution of a larger number of smaller firms for a few large ones may lead to slower commercial introduction of the innovations.

Thus, *contrary to the allegations of Galbraith and others, there is little evidence that industrial giants are needed in most industries to ensure rapid technological change and rapid utilization of new techniques.* This does not mean that industries composed only of small firms would necessarily be optimal for the promotion and diffusion of new techniques. On the contrary, there seem to be considerable advantages in a diversity of firm sizes. Complementarities and interdependencies exist among large and small firms. There is often a division of labor. Smaller firms may focus on areas requiring sophistication and flexibility and may cater to specialized needs, whereas bigger firms may concentrate on areas requiring large production, marketing, or technical resources. However, in

[6]John Kenneth Galbraith, *American Capitalism* (Boston: Houghton Mifflin, 1952), p. 91.

most industries there is little evidence that firms considerably smaller than the biggest firms are not big enough for these purposes.

■ HOW MUCH MONOPOLY POWER IS OPTIMAL?

The discussion in previous sections makes it clear that the case against monopoly power is not open and shut. A certain amount of monopoly power is inevitable in practically all real-life situations, since perfect competition is a model that can only be approximated in real life. Moreover, a certain amount of monopoly power may be needed to promote desirable technological change. The difficult problem is to determine how much monopoly power is optimal under various circumstances (and how this power is to be measured). Some economists (like Galbraith) are convinced that a great deal of monopoly power is both inevitable and desirable. Others believe the opposite. And the economic arguments are not strong enough to resolve the differences of opinion. Much more will be said on this score in Chapter 20.

REVIEW AND PRACTICE

■ SUMMARY

1 A monopoly is a market with one and only one seller. Monopolies may occur because of patents, control over basic inputs, and government action, among other reasons.

2 If average costs reach their minimum at an output rate large enough to satisfy the entire market, perfect competition cannot be maintained; the public often insists that the industry (a natural monopoly) be regulated by the government.

3 Since the monopolist is the only seller of the product, the demand curve facing the monopolist is the market demand curve, which slopes downward (rather than being horizontal as in perfect competition).

4 The unregulated monopolist will maximize profit by choosing the output where marginal cost equals marginal revenue, where marginal revenue is defined as the addition to total revenue attributable to the addition of one unit to sales.

5 If monopolists cannot prevent losses from exceeding fixed costs, they, like perfect competitors, will discontinue production. In contrast to the case in perfect competition, the long-run equilibrium of a monopolistic industry may not be marked by the absence of economic profits.

6 The output of a monopoly tends to be smaller and the price tends to be higher than under perfect competition. Economists tend to believe that society would be better off if more resources were devoted to the production of the good than under monopoly. The competitive output often is regarded as best.

7 One way that society has attempted to reduce the harmful effects of monopoly is through public regulation. Commissions often set price at the level at which it equals average total cost, including a "fair" rate of return on the firm's investment. In some industries (like airlines, trucking, and railroads), the late 1970s and early 1980s saw a strong movement toward deregulation.

8 Because regulated firms may be guaranteed a particular rate of return (regardless of how well or poorly they perform), there may be little incentive for them to increase their efficiency.

＊9 In defense of monopoly power, some economists, including Joseph Schumpeter, have asserted that the rate of technological change is likely to be greater in an imperfectly competitive industry than under perfect competition.

＊10 Contrary to the allegations of John Kenneth Galbraith and others, there is little evidence that giant firms are needed to ensure rapid technological change in a great many sectors of the economy. The situation is much more complex than such statements indicate, and the contributions of smaller firms are much greater than is commonly recognized.

■ PROBLEMS AND QUESTIONS

1 If you are the president of a firm that has a monopoly on a certain product, would you choose an output level where demand for the product is price inelastic? Explain.

2 Suppose that the amount demanded for a monopolist's product at each of a variety of prices of the product is as shown below:

QUANTITY DEMANDED (PER YEAR)	PRICE (DOLLARS)
8	1,000
7	2,000
6	3,000
5	4,000
4	5,000
3	6,000
2	7,000
1	8,000

Plot the firm's marginal revenue curve.

3 Suppose that the monopolist in question 2 has fixed costs of $10,000 and an average variable cost of $4,000. The average variable cost is the same for outputs of 1 to 10 units per year. What output rate will the firm choose? What price will it set?

4 Plot the marginal cost curve of the firm in question 3. Where does this curve intersect the marginal revenue curve you drew in question 2?

5 Suppose that the firm in question 3 experiences a 50 percent increase in both its fixed and average variable costs. If the demand curve in question 2 remains valid, what effect will this cost increase have on the output rate and price that the firm will choose?

*The starred items refer to material covered in Exploring Further.

■ KEY TERMS

monopoly

patents

network effects

total revenue

marginal revenue

public regulation

historical cost

reproduction cost

deregulation

■ VIEWPOINT FOR ANALYSIS

On April 6, 1998, Gary S. Becker, professor at the University of Chicago and the 1992 Nobel laureate in economics, wrote in his regular column for *Business Week*: "Competitors that develop superior technologies are far better protectors of consumers than government officials and bureaucrats who march to the beat of political popularity."*

(a) Can you think of technologies that have destroyed monopolies?

(b) Can monopolies prevent new technologies from coming to market? How?

(c) What role can the government play in making sure that an existing monopoly does not prevent consumers from enjoying the benefits of a new technology?

*"Economic Viewpoint," *Business Week*, April 6, 1998, p. 26.

CHAPTER 20

Monopolistic Competition, Oligopoly, and Antitrust Policy

LEARNING OBJECTIVES

In this chapter, you should learn:

- The conditions that define monopolistic competition, and those which define oligopoly
- How prices and outputs under monopolistic competition compare with those under perfect competition and monopoly
- How oligopolies are organized
- How prices and outputs under oligopoly compare with those under perfect competition and monopoly
- The nature of the major antitrust laws and their effectiveness

The aircraft industry is dominated by two firms: Boeing and Airbus. The beer industry is dominated by a few firms, such as Anheuser-Busch, Miller, and Coors. The retail drug industry is composed of many firms, but it is not a perfectly competitive industry. How are price and output determined in these industries? One purpose of this chapter is to answer this question.

The industries encountered in the real world are seldom perfectly competitive or monopolistic. Although perfect competition and monopoly are very useful models that shed much valuable light on the behavior of markets, they are polar cases. Economists have developed other models that portray more realistically the behavior of many modern industries. The model of monopolistic competition helps to explain market behavior in industries like retail drugstores, whereas the model of oligopoly pertains to industries like aircraft and beer.

In this chapter we examine how resources are allocated and prices are set under monopolistic competition and oligopoly. The results are of considerable significance, both because they give us a better understanding of how a variety of markets work and because they provide valuable information on the social desirability of monopolistic competition and oligopoly.

MONOPOLISTIC COMPETITION AND OLIGOPOLY: THEIR MAJOR CHARACTERISTICS

**Monopolistic
competition**

To begin with, we must recall what monopolistic competition and oligopoly are. **Monopolistic competition** *occurs where there are many sellers (as in perfect competition) but where there is product differentiation. In other words, the firms' products are not the same.* It does not matter whether the differences among products are real or imagined. What is important is that the consumer regards the products as different.

Oligopoly

Oligopoly *occurs in markets where there are few sellers.* There are two types of oligopolies, one where all sellers produce an identical product and one where the sellers produce somewhat different products. Examples of the first type, ***pure oligopoly***, are the markets for steel, cement, tin cans, and petroleum. Examples of the second type, ***differentiated oligopoly***, are the markets for automobiles and machinery.

In contrast to the extremes of perfect competition and monopoly, monopolistic competition and oligopoly are intermediate cases that include elements of competition and of monopoly, and so are more realistic than the two extremes.

MONOPOLISTIC COMPETITION

**Product
differentiation**

The key feature of monopolistic competition is **product differentiation**. In contrast to perfect competition, where all firms sell an identical product, firms under monopolistic competition sell somewhat different products. Each producer differentiates its product from that of other producers. This is the case in many U.S. markets. In many parts of retail trade, producers can differentiate their product by altering the product's physical makeup, the services they offer, and other such variables. Other differences, which may be spurious, are based on brand name, image making, advertising claims, and so on. In this way, the producers gain some monopoly power, but usually it is small, because the products of other firms are very similar.

In perfect competition, the firms included in an industry are easy to identify because they all produce the same product. But if product differentiation exists, it is no longer easy to define an industry, since each firm produces a somewhat different product. Nevertheless, it is useful to group together firms that produce similar products and call them a ***product group***. We can formulate a product group called "toothpaste" or "toilet soap" or "chocolate bars." The process by which we combine firms into product groups is bound to be somewhat arbitrary, since there is no way to decide how close a pair of substitutes must be to belong to the same product group. But it is assumed that meaningful product groups can be established.

Besides product differentiation, other conditions must be met for an industry to qualify as a case of monopolistic competition. First, *there must be a large number of firms in the product group.* In other words, the product must be produced by perhaps 50 to 100 or more firms, and each firm's product must be a fairly close substitute for the products of the other firms in the product group. Second, *the number of firms in the product group must be large enough so that each firm expects its actions to go unheeded by its rivals and is unimpeded by possible retaliatory moves on their part.* If there is a large number of firms, this condition will normally be met. Third, *entry into the product group must be relatively easy, and there must be no collusion, such as price fixing or market sharing, among firms in the product group.* If there is a large number of firms, collusion generally is difficult, if not impossible.

PRICE AND OUTPUT UNDER MONOPOLISTIC COMPETITION

Under monopolistic competition, what determines how much output a firm will produce and what price it will charge? If each firm produces a somewhat different product, it follows that the demand curve facing each firm slopes downward to the right. That is, if the firm raises its price slightly it will lose some but by no means all of its customers to other firms. And if it lowers its price slightly, it will gain some but by no means all of its competitors' customers. This is in contrast to perfect competition, where the demand curve facing each firm is horizontal.

Figure 20.1 shows the short-run equilibrium of a monopolistically competitive firm. The firm in the short run will set its price at P_0 and its output rate at Q_0, since this combination of price and output will maximize its profits. We can be sure that this combination of price and output maximizes profit, because marginal cost equals marginal revenue at this output rate. In the situation shown in Figure 20.1, economic profits will be earned because price P_0 exceeds average total cost C_0 at this output rate.

What will the equilibrium price and output be in the long run? One condition for long-run equilibrium is that each firm be making no economic profits or losses, since entry or exit of firms will occur otherwise, and entry and exit are incompatible with long-run equilibrium. Another condition for long-run equilibrium is that each firm be maximizing its profits. At what price and output will both these conditions be fulfilled? Figure 20.2 shows that long-run equilibrium is at a price of P_1 and an output of Q_1. The zero economic profit condition is met at this combination of price and

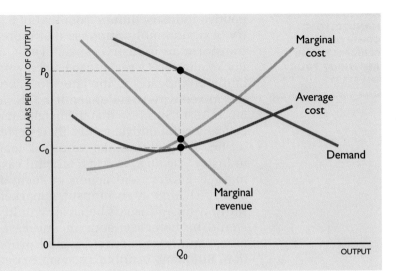

FIGURE 20.1

Short-Run Equilibrium: Monopolistic Competition

The firm will set its price at P_0 and its output rate at Q_0 since marginal cost equals marginal revenue at this output. It will earn a profit of $C_0 P_0$ per unit of output.

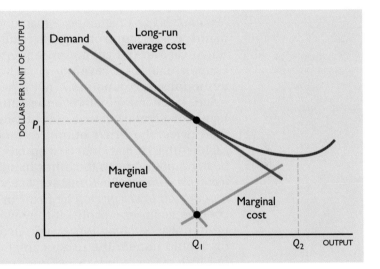

FIGURE 20.2

Long-Run Equilibrium: Monopolistic Competition

The long-run equilibrium is at a price of P_1 and an output of Q_1. There are zero profits, since long-run average cost equals price. Profits are being maximized, since marginal cost equals marginal revenue at this output.

output since the firm's average cost at this output equals the price P_1. And the profit-maximization condition is met, since the marginal revenue curve intersects the marginal cost curve at this output rate.[1]

■ COMPARISONS WITH PERFECT COMPETITION AND MONOPOLY

Market structure is important because it influences market behavior. We need to know how the behavior of a monopolistically com-

[1]For the classic work on monopolistic competition, see E. Chamberlin, *The Theory of Monopolistic Competition* (Cambridge, Mass.: Harvard University Press, 1933).

petitive industry differs from that of a perfectly competitive industry or a monopoly. Suppose that there exists a magician who can transform an industry's structure by a wave of a wand. (John D. Rockefeller was a real-life magician who transformed the structure of the oil industry in the late 1800s, but he seemed to favor mergers, mixed with some ungentlemanly tactics, over wands. See Case Study 19.1.) Suppose that the magician makes an industry monopolistically competitive, rather than perfectly competitive or monopolistic. What difference would it make in the behavior of the industry? Or, to take a less fanciful case, what difference would it make if government action or technological change resulted in such a change in an industry's market structure? It is difficult to say how the industry's behavior would be affected, because output would be heterogeneous in one case and homogeneous in the other, and its cost curves would probably vary with its organization. But many economists seem to believe that differences of the following kind can be expected.

1. *The firm under monopolistic competition is likely to produce less and charge a higher price than under perfect competition.* The demand curve confronting the monopolistic competitor slopes downward to the right. Consequently, as we saw in the previous chapter, marginal revenue must be less than price. Thus under monopolistic competition, marginal cost must also be less than price, since marginal revenue must equal marginal cost at the firm's profit-maximizing output rate. But if marginal cost is less than price, the firm's output rate must be smaller—and the price higher—than if marginal cost equals price, as is the case under perfect competition. On the other hand, *relative to monopoly, monopolistically competitive firms are likely to have lower profits, greater output, and lower price.* The firms in a product group might obtain positive economic profits if they were to collude and behave as a monopolist. Such an increase in profits resulting from the monopoly would benefit the producers. Consumers would be worse off because of the higher prices and smaller output of goods.

2. *A firm under monopolistic competition may be somewhat inefficient.* As shown in Figure 20.2, it produces a smaller-than-minimum-cost output. (It produces Q_1 units of output; the output where average cost is a minimum is Q_2 units of output.) Consequently, more firms exist than if average costs were minimized; this results in some overcrowding of the industry. Inefficiencies of this sort would not be expected under perfect competition. However, these apparent inefficiencies may not be socially undesirable if consumers value highly the product diversity occurring under monopolistic competition.

3. *Firms under monopolistic competition will offer a wider variety of styles, brands, and qualities than firms under perfect competition. Moreover, they will spend much more on advertising and other selling*

expenses than a perfectly competitive firm would. Whether this diversity is worth its cost is hard to say. Some economists are impressed by the apparent waste in monopolistic competition. They think it results in too many firms, too many brands, too much selling effort, and too much spurious product differentiation. But if the differences among products are real and are understood by consumers, the greater variety of alternatives available under monopolistic competition may be very valuable to consumers. The proper evaluation of the social advantages and disadvantages of product differentiation is harder than may appear at first sight.[2]

OLIGOPOLY

Oligopoly (domination by a few firms) is a common and important market structure in the United States; many industries, including steel, automobiles, oil, and electrical equipment, are oligopolistic. An example of an oligopolist is General Motors. *The key characteristic of oligopoly is interdependence, actual and perceived, among firms.* Each oligopolist formulates its policies with an eye to their effect on its rivals. Since an oligopoly contains a small number of firms, any change in one firm's price or output influences the sales and profits of its competitors. Moreover, since there are only a few firms, each must recognize that changes in its own policies are likely to result in changes in the policies of its rivals as well.

What factors are responsible for oligopoly? First, in some industries, *low production costs cannot be achieved unless a firm is producing an output equal to a substantial portion of the total available market,* with the consequence that the number of firms will tend to be rather small. Second, *there may be economies of scale in sales promotion* in certain industries, and this too may promote oligopoly. Third, entry into some industries may be blocked by *the requirement that a firm build and maintain a large, complicated, and expensive plant or have access to patents or scarce raw materials.* Only a few firms may be in a position to obtain all these prerequisites for membership in the club.

OLIGOPOLY MODELS

Unlike perfect competition, monopoly, and monopolistic competition, there is no single unified model of oligopoly behavior. Instead, *there are a number of models, each based on a somewhat*

---

[2]Before leaving the subject of monopolistic competition, it should be recognized that Professor Chamberlin's theory has been subjected to considerable criticism. As a case in point, the definition of the product group is ambiguous. See G. Stigler, *Five Lectures on Economic Problems* (London: Longmans Green, 1949).

different set of assumptions concerning the relationships among the firms that make up the oligopoly. Basically, no single model exists because economists have not yet been able to devise one that would cover all the relevant cases adequately.

THE THEORY OF GAMES

The rivalry among oligopolists has many of the characteristics of a game. As in a game, in oligopoly each firm must take account of its rivals' reactions to its own actions. For this reason, an oligopolistic firm cannot tell what effect a change in its output will have on the price of its product and on its profits unless it can guess how its rivals will respond to the change. To understand game theory, you have to know what a **game** is. It is a competitive situation where two or more persons pursue their own interests and no person can dictate the outcome. Poker is a game, and so is a situation in which two firms are engaged in competitive advertising campaigns. A game is described in terms of its players, rules, payoffs, and information conditions. These elements are common to all conflict situations.

Game

DEFINITIONS OF TERMS

More specifically, a ***player,*** whether a single person or an organization, is a decision-making unit. Each player has a certain amount of resources, and the ***rules of the game*** describe how these resources can be used. Thus the rules of poker indicate how bets can be made and which hands are better than others. A ***strategy*** is a complete specification of what a player will do under each contingency in the playing of the game. Thus a corporation president may tell subordinates how an advertising campaign should start and what should be done at subsequent times in response to various actions of competing firms. The game's outcome clearly depends on each player's strategies. A player's ***payoff*** varies from game to game. It is win, lose, or draw in checkers, and various sums of money in poker.

A SIMPLE TWO-PERSON GAME

For simplicity we will restrict our attention to *two-person games:* those with only two players. The relevant features of a two-person game can be shown by constructing a **payoff matrix**. To illustrate, consider the case of two big soap producers, Procter and Gamble

Payoff matrix

TABLE 20.1		POSSIBLE STRATEGIES FOR LEVER BROTHERS	
Payoff Matrix: Procter and Gamble and Lever Brothers	**POSSIBLE STRATEGIES FOR P & G**	**CONCENTRATE ON TV**	**CONCENTRATE ON MAGAZINES**
	Concentrate on TV	P & G's profit: $3 million Lever's profit: $2 million	P & G's profit $4 million Lever's profit: $3 million
	Concentrate on magazines	P & G's profit: $2 million Lever's profit: $3 million	P & G's profit: $3 million Lever's profit: $4 million

and Lever Brothers. Suppose that these two firms are about to stage rival advertising campaigns and that each firm has a choice of strategies. Procter and Gamble can choose to concentrate on either television ads or magazine ads; Lever Brothers has the same choice. Table 20.1 shows what will happen to the profits of each firm when each combination of strategies is chosen. If both firms concentrate on TV ads, Procter and Gamble gains $3 million and Lever Brothers gains $2 million. If Procter and Gamble concentrates on TV ads and Lever Brothers concentrates on magazine ads, Procter and Gamble gains $4 million and Lever Brothers gains $3 million. And so on.

■ PROCTER AND GAMBLE'S VIEWPOINT

Given the payoff matrix in Table 20.1, there is a definite optimal choice (called a ***dominant strategy***) for each firm. To see that this is the case, let's begin by looking at the situation from Procter and Gamble's point of view. If Lever Brothers concentrates on TV ads, Procter and Gamble will make more money ($3 million rather than $2 million) if it concentrates on TV rather than magazines. If Lever Brothers concentrates on magazines, Procter and Gamble will make more money ($4 million rather than $3 million) if it concentrates on TV rather than magazines. Thus, regardless of the strategy chosen by Lever Brothers, Procter and Gamble will do best to concentrate on TV.

■ LEVER BROTHERS' VIEWPOINT

Now let's look at the situation from the point of view of Lever Brothers. If Procter and Gamble concentrates on TV ads, Lever Brothers will make more money ($3 million rather than $2 million) if it concentrates on magazines rather than TV. If Procter and Gamble concentrates on magazines, Lever Brothers will make more money ($4 million rather than $3 million) if it concentrates on magazines rather than TV. Thus, regardless of the strategy chosen by Procter and Gamble, Lever Brothers will do best to concentrate on magazines.

■ THE SOLUTION OF THE GAME

At this point, the solution of this game is clear. *Procter and Gamble will concentrate on TV ads and Lever Brothers will concentrate on magazine ads.* This is the best that either firm can do.

COLLUSION AND CARTELS

■ HOW FIRMS COLLUDE

Collusion

Collusion occurs when firms get together and agree on price and output. Up to this point, we have assumed that oligopolists do not collude, but conditions in oligopolistic industries tend to promote collusion, since the number of firms is small and the firms recognize their interdependence. The advantages of collusion to the firms seem obvious: increased profits, decreased uncertainty, and a better opportunity to prevent entry.

Cartel

Not all collusion is disguised from the public or secret. In contrast to illicit collusion, a **cartel** is an open, formal collusive arrangement among firms. In many countries in Europe, cartels have been common and legally acceptable. In the United States, most collusive arrangements, whether secret or open cartels, were declared illegal by the Sherman Antitrust Act, which was passed in 1890.

However, this does not mean that such arrangements do not exist. Widespread collusion to fix prices occurred among U.S. electrical equipment manufacturers during the 1950s, and when the collusion was uncovered, a number of high executives were tried, convicted, and sent to jail (see Case Study 20.1). Moreover, collusion of this sort is not limited to a single industry or a single country. Some cartels, like that in quinine in the early 1960s, are international in scope.[3] A particularly famous international cartel is the Organization of Petroleum Exporting Countries (OPEC), which consists of 12 oil-producing countries, including Saudi Arabia and Iran.

[3]See "Collusion among Electrical Equipment Manufacturers" and "Quinine: An International Cartel," in E. Mansfield, ed., *Microeconomics: Selected Readings* (4th ed.; New York: Norton, 1982).

FIGURE 20.3

Price and Output of a Cartel

The marginal cost curve shows the marginal cost for the cartel as a whole. On the basis of the demand curve for the industry's product, the cartel can derive the marginal revenue curve. The output that maximizes the total profit of the cartel members is Q. The corresponding price is P.

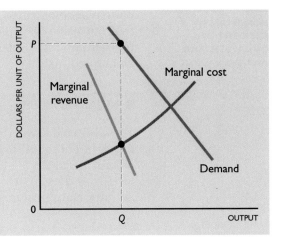

■ PRICE AND OUTPUT OF A CARTEL

If a cartel is established to set a uniform price for a particular product, what price will it charge? As a first step, the cartel must estimate the marginal cost curve for the cartel as a whole. Then it must find the output where its marginal cost equals its marginal revenue, since this output maximizes the total profit of the cartel members. In Figure 20.3, this output is Q. Thus if it maximizes cartel profits, the cartel will choose a price of P, which is the monopoly price. In short, *the cartel acts like a monopolist with a number of plants or divisions, each of which is a member firm.*

How will the cartel allocate sales among the member firms? If its aim is to maximize cartel profits, it will allocate sales to firms in such a way that the sum of the firms' costs is minimized. But this allocation is unlikely to occur in reality. The allocation process is a bargaining process, and firms with the most influence and the shrewdest negotiators are likely to receive the large sales quotas, even though this decreases the total profits of the cartel. Moreover, high-cost firms are likely to receive larger sales quotas than would be the case if total cartel profits were maximized, since they would be unwilling otherwise to stay in the cartel. In practice, it appears that cartels often divide markets geographically or in accord with a firm's level of sales in the past.

BARRIERS TO COLLUSION

The fact that oligopoly often can lead to collusion is not new. Back in 1776, Adam Smith warned that "people of the same trade seldom meet together even for merriment and diversion, but the conversation ends in a conspiracy against the public, or in some contrivance to raise prices." However, it must be borne in mind that collusive arrangements are often difficult to accomplish and to maintain for long. In particular, there are several important barriers to collusion.

■ LEGAL PROBLEMS

The antitrust laws, discussed in detail later in this chapter, forbid outright collusion and price fixing. This does not mean that firms do not break those laws; witness the electrical equipment manufacturers described in Case Study 20.1. But the antitrust laws are an important obstacle to collusion.

■ TECHNICAL PROBLEMS

Collusion is often difficult to achieve and maintain because an oligopoly contains an unwieldy number of firms, the product is quite heterogeneous, or the cost structures of the firms differ considerably. It is clear that a collusive agreement will be more difficult to achieve and maintain if there are a dozen oligopolists than if there are three or four. Moreover, if the products sold by the oligopolists differ substantially, it will probably be more difficult for them to find a common price strategy that will be acceptable to all. Similarly, if the firms' cost structures differ, it will be more difficult to get agreement, since the low-cost firms will be more inclined to cut price. For example, National Steel, after introducing low-cost continuous strip mills in the 1930s, became a price cutter in the steel industry.

■ CHEATING

There is a constant temptation for oligopolists to cheat on any collusive agreement. If other firms stick to the agreement, any firm that cheats—by cutting its price below that agreed to under the collusive arrangement—can take a lot of business away from the other firms and increase its profits substantially, at least in the short run. This temptation is particularly great when an industry's sales are depressed and its profits are low. Every firm is hungry for business, and it is difficult to resist. Moreover, one firm may be driven to cheating because it hears that another firm is doing so, with the eventual result that the collusive agreement is torn apart.

To illustrate the problems of maintaining a collusive agreement, let's return to the electrical equipment manufacturers described in Case Study 20.1. As the *Wall Street Journal* summed it up:

> One of the great ironies of the conspiracies was that no matter how hard the participants schemed, no matter how friendly their meetings

The electrical conspiracy

To illustrate how firms collude, consider electrical equipment manufacturers. During the 1950s, there was widespread collusion among about thirty firms selling turbine generators, switchgear, transformers, and other products with total sales of about $1.5 billion per year. Representatives of these firms got together and agreed on prices for many products. The available evidence indicates that both prices and profits tended to be increased by the collusive agreements, at least until the firms were prosecuted under the antitrust laws by the Department of Justice. The following statement by F. M. Scherer of Harvard University is a good description of some of the procedures used by these firms:

Some of the most elaborate procedures were devised to handle switchgear pricing. Each seller agreed to quote book prices in sales to private buyers, and meetings were held regularly to compare calculations for forthcoming job quotations. Sealed-bid competitions sponsored by government agencies posed a different set of problems, and new methods were worked out to handle them. Through protracted negotiation, each seller was assigned a specific share of all sealed-bid business, e.g., General Electric's share of the high voltage switchgear field was set at 40.3 percent in late 1958, and Allis-Chalmers' at 8.8 percent. Participants then coordinated their bidding so that each firm was lowest bidder in just enough transactions to gain its predetermined share of the market. In the power switching equipment line, this was achieved for a while by dividing the United States into four quadrants, assigning four sellers to each quadrant, and letting the sellers in a quadrant rotate their bids. A "phases of the moon" system was used to allocate low-bidding privileges in the high voltage switchgear field, with a new seller assuming low-bidding priority every two weeks. The designated bidder subtracted a specified percentage margin from the book price to capture orders during its phase, while others added various margins to the book price. The result was an ostensibly random pattern of quotations, conveying the impression of independent pricing behavior.*

General Electric, Westinghouse, and the other conspirators were found guilty of violating the antitrust laws. Some of the executives were sentenced to jail on criminal charges, and the firms had to pay large amounts to customers to make up for the overcharges. In particular, 1,800 triple damage suits against the firms resulted in payments estimated at between $400 million and $600 million.

*F. M. Scherer, *Industrial Market Structure and Economic Performance* (Boston: Houghton Mifflin, 1980), p. 160.

and communications might be, there was an innate tendency to compete. Someone was always violating the agreements to get more business and this continually called for new illegal plans. For example, price-cutting in sales of power switching equipment to government agencies was getting out of hand in late 1958. This led to the "quadrant" system of dividing markets.

As one executive of General Electric complained, "No one was living up to the agreement and we . . . were being made suckers. On every job someone would cut our throat; we lost confidence in the group." Given that these agreements were illegal, it is remarkable that such a complaint was uttered with a straight face.

PRICE LEADERSHIP

Price leader

In order to coordinate their behavior without outright collusion, some industries contain a **price leader**. It is quite common in oligopolistic industries for one or a few firms to set the price and for the rest to follow their lead. Two types of price leadership are the dominant firm model and the barometric firm model. *The **dominant firm** model applies to cases where the industry has a single large dominant firm and a number of small firms.* The dominant firm sets the price for the industry, but it lets the small firms sell all they want at that price. *The **barometric firm** model applies to cases where one firm usually is the first to make changes in price that are generally accepted by other firms in the industry.* The barometric firm may not be the largest or most powerful firm. Instead, it is a reasonably accurate interpreter of changes in basic cost and demand conditions in the industry as a whole. According to some authorities, barometric price leadership often occurs as a response to a period of violent price fluctuation in an industry, during which many firms suffer and greater stability is widely sought.

In the past, the steel industry was a good example of price leadership of the dominant firm variety. The largest firm in the industry, U.S. Steel, was formed in 1901 by the merger of a number of companies. Judge Elbert Gary, the first chairperson of the board of U.S. Steel, sought the cooperation of the smaller firms in the industry. He inaugurated a series of so-called Gary dinners, attended by all the major steel producers, from which were made declarations of industry policy on pricing and other matters. Since any formal pricing agreements would have been illegal, they made no such agreements. But, generally speaking, U.S. Steel set the pricing pattern and other firms followed. Moreover, this relationship continued long after Judge Gary had gone to his final reward. According to Walter Adams of Michigan State University, U.S. Steel typically set the pace, "and the other companies follow in lockstep—both in their sales to private customers and in their secret bids on government contracts."

Illustrating the attitude of other firms was the statement by the president of Bethlehem Steel to a congressional committee in 1939 that "in the main we . . . await the (price) schedules of the [U.S.] Steel Corporation." However, there was some secret price cutting, particularly during depressions. On at least one occasion,

U.S. Steel responded to such price cutting by announcing publicly that it would meet any price reduction it heard of. In this way, it attempted to discourage under-the-counter price cutting. In more recent times, U.S. Steel no longer seemed to be the price leader it once was. In 1962, it drew a great deal of criticism from President Kennedy for being the first steel firm to raise prices. Subsequently, smaller steel firms were often the first. Indeed, in 1968 the world was treated to the amusing spectacle of Bethlehem Steel announcing a price cut in order to counter some secret price cutting by the former price leader, U.S. Steel (which is now called USX Corporation).

NONPRICE COMPETITION

Oligopolists tend to compete more aggressively through advertising and product differentiation than through direct price reductions. In other words, when we observe the behavior of major oligopolies, we find that firms try hard to get business away from their rivals by outdoing them with better advertising campaigns and with improvements in the product; but it is less common for oligopolists to slug it out, toe to toe, with price reductions. This is an important characteristic of oligopoly. In contrast to the case of perfect competition, nonprice competition plays a central role in oligopoly. It is worthwhile, therefore, to note a few salient points about the advertising and product development strategies of oligopolists.

■ ADVERTISING

Advertising is a very big business. Tens of billions of dollars per year are spent on it in the United States. One important purpose of advertising is to convince the consumer that one firm's product is better than another's. Advertising expenditures often are larger in industries where there is less physical differentiation of the product than in industries where the product varies more. Thus the cigarette, liquor, and soap industries spend over 10 percent of their gross revenues (excluding excise taxes) on advertising, whereas the automobile industry spends less than 1 percent of its gross revenue on advertising.

The social desirability of much of this advertising is debatable, and much debated. While advertising can serve an important purpose by keeping the consumer better informed, some advertising is more misleading than informative. Unfortunately, it is difficult to make reliable estimates of the extent to which oligopolists may be overinvesting, from society's point of view, in advertising.

477

How Ford became number two and General Motors became number one

Bring this glamorous picture up to date and you replace the knight's charger with a new General Motors car...You substitute for the security of his armor the new Unisteel Turret Top Body by Fisher...Then beauty rides secure at its 1937 best!...For new Fisher glorifies the steel body with conspicuous new luxury and comfort, as well as with greater safety...The whole beautiful structure is fused into one integrally welded steel unit—with all its steel panels insulated against heat, cold and noise...You relax, at ease in mind and body, rewarded no more by your fellow passengers. You ride as you never rode before—in the new Unisteel Turret Top Body by Fisher—available only on General Motors cars.

THE **UNISTEEL** TURRET TOP BODY BY *Fisher*

An early GM advertisement

Henry Ford didn't invent the car, and he didn't invent the assembly line. But he brought the two together and gave the United States its first mass-produced car. Ford was an inventor and mechanic by trade, and no effort was spared to improve the car and the process by which it was built. The Tin Lizzie looked the same year after year, but Ford's mechanical genius made it run better each year than the last. His industrial genius made it cheaper to build and to buy. He paid the highest wages in industry, $5 a day, and he made a car his workers could afford to buy. It seemed as though he had devised the perfect competitive product: it never wore out, it kept getting cheaper, and it was never out of style.

The Model T wasn't the only car on the road. Americans were driving Pierce Arrows, Stutz Bearcats, and Duesenbergs, as well as the Chevrolets, Buicks, Oldsmobiles, and Cadillacs made by Ford's number one competitor, General Motors, headed by Alfred P. Sloan. Sloan once said, "The primary object of the corporation is to make money, not just to make motor cars. The core of the GM product policy lies in the concept of mass producing a full line of cars graded upward in quality and price." Sloan saw that even if GM could produce for less than Ford, it couldn't *increase* profits by *decreasing* prices. So to do battle with Ford's

black Model Ts, GM's massive research and development effort produced a brand for every pocketbook—Chevrolets, Pontiacs, Buicks, and Cadillacs—a color for every taste, and a wish list of options. Every year brought a new edition. GMs were old not when they wore out but when they went out of style.

Any business decision is a kind of gamble. Henry Ford bet that the United States wanted a car that would last forever, was cheap and easy to fix, and never went out of style. Alfred Sloan bet that there was something more attractive to U.S. drivers than a low price, that they were ready to have some fun with their cars, and that GM advertising could join their desires and GM's cars, at a profit to GM. Henry Ford knew cars, but Alfred Sloan knew the consumer, and he knew the twenties. By the time the Great Depression started in 1929, Henry Ford had yielded to reality and started varying his cars. But he had lost the 50 percent share of the market he had commanded and had to settle for second place.

▥ PRODUCT DEVELOPMENT

The development of new and improved products is also a very big business in the United States. In 1998, industry spent over $143 billion on research and development. In many industries, R & D is a central part of oligopolistic competition. For example, a spectacular case in the drug industry was the effect of American Cyanamid's Achromycin tetracycline, introduced in 1953, on sales of Aureomycin chlortetracycline, which had been marketed since late 1948. After an almost continuous upward trend in 1950 to 1953, Aureomycin sales dropped by nearly 40 percent during the first full year of the sale of Achromycin. Hardly a typical case, this nonetheless illustrates how one firm can take sales away from its rivals through new product development.

It is important to add, however, that much of industry's R & D is aimed at fairly minor improvements in products and processes. Moreover, a good deal of the engineering efforts of many important industries is aimed largely at style changes, not basic improvements in the product. A case in point is the automobile industry, which spends billions of dollars to produce the model changes that are familiar to car buyers throughout the land.

Perhaps the main reason why oligopolists would rather compete through advertising and product differentiation than through price is that a firm's rivals can easily and quickly match a price reduction, whereas they may find it difficult to match a clever advertising campaign or an attractive product improvement. Thus oligopolists tend to feel that they have a better chance of improving their long-run profits at the expense of their rivals in the arena of nonprice competition than by price cutting.

COMPARISON OF OLIGOPOLY WITH PERFECT COMPETITION

We have seen that economists have constructed a number of types of models of oligopoly behavior: game theoretic models, cartel models, price leadership models, and others. But there is no agreement that any of these models is an adequate general representation of oligopoly behavior. For this reason, it is difficult to estimate the effects of an oligopolistic market structure on price, output, and profits. Nonetheless, if a perfectly competitive industry were turned overnight into an oligopoly, it seems likely that certain changes would occur.

1. *Price would probably be higher than under perfect competition.* The difference between the oligopoly price and the perfectly competitive price will depend on the number of firms in the industry and the ease of entry. The larger the number of firms and the easier it is to enter the industry, the closer the oligopoly price will be to the perfectly competitive level.

2. If the demand curve is the same under oligopoly as under perfect competition, it also follows that *output will be less under oligopoly than under perfect competition.* However, it is not always reasonable to assume that the demand curve is the same in both cases, since the large expenditures for advertising and product differentiation incurred by some oligopolies may tend to shift the de-

mand curve to the right. Consequently in some cases both price and output may tend to be higher under oligopoly than under perfect competition.

3. *Oligopolistic industries tend to spend more on advertising, product differentiation, and style changes than perfectly competitive industries.* The use of some resources for these purposes is certainly worthwhile, since advertising provides buyers with information, and product differentiation allows greater freedom of choice. Whether oligopolies spend too much for these purposes is an open question. However, there is a widespread feeling among economists, based largely on empirical studies (and hunch), that in some oligopolistic industries such expenditures have been expanded beyond socially optimal levels.

4. One might expect on the basis of the models presented in this chapter that *the profits earned by oligopolists would be higher, on the average, than the profits earned by perfectly competitive firms.* This conclusion is supported by some statistical evidence. Joe Bain of the University of California found that firms in industries in which the biggest few firms had a large proportion of total sales tended to have higher rates of return than firms in industries in which the biggest few firms had a small proportion of total sales.[4]

THE ANTITRUST LAWS

National policies are too ambiguous and rich in contradictions to be summarized neatly and concisely. Consequently, it would be misleading to say that the United States has adopted a policy of promoting competition and controlling monopoly. To a large extent, it certainly is true that "competition is our fundamental national policy," as the Supreme Court said in 1963. But it is also true that we have adopted many measures to promote monopoly and to limit competition. On balance, however, we probably have gone further in promoting competition than other major industrialized countries, and the principal pieces of legislation designed to further this objective are the ***antitrust laws.***

---

[4]However, there has been much disagreement on this score. According to more recent evidence, a firm is likely to have higher than average profits if it has a relatively big share of the market, regardless of whether or not the industry as a whole is highly concentrated. For some relevant discussion, see L. Weiss, "The Concentration-Profits Relationship and Antitrust," in *Industrial Concentration, The New Learning*, eds. H. Goldschmid, H. J. Mann, and J. F. Weston (Boston: Little Brown, 1974); and H. Demsetz, "Industry Structure, Market Rivalry, and Public Policy," *Journal of Law and Economics*, April 1973.

An early cartoon opposing the trusts

THE SHERMAN ACT

In 1890, the first antitrust law, the Sherman Act, was passed by Congress. Although the common law had long outlawed monopolistic practices, it appeared to many Americans in the closing years of the nineteenth century that legislation was required to discourage monopoly and to preserve and encourage competition. The formation of trusts—monopolistic combines that colluded to raise prices and restrict output—brought the matter to a head. The heart of the Sherman Act lies in the following two sections:

> Section 1. Every contract, combination in the form of trust or otherwise, or conspiracy, in restraint of trade or commerce among the several states or with foreign nations, is hereby declared to be illegal. Every person who shall make any such contract or engage in any such combination or conspiracy, shall be deemed guilty of a misdemeanor....
> Section 2. Every person who shall monopolize, or attempt to monopolize or combine or conspire with any other person or persons to monopolize, any part of the trade or commerce among the several States, or with foreign nations shall be deemed guilty of a misdemeanor.

■ THE CLAYTON ACT

The first 20 years of experience with the Sherman Act were not very satisfying to its supporters. The ineffectiveness of the Sherman Act led in 1914 to passage by Congress of two additional laws: the Clayton Act and the Federal Trade Commission Act. The Clayton Act tried to be more specific than the Sherman Act in identifying certain practices that were illegal because they would

481

"substantially lessen competition or tend to create a monopoly." In particular, the Clayton Act outlawed unjustified price discrimination, a practice whereby one buyer is charged more than another buyer for the same product. It also outlawed the use of a *tying contract,* which makes the buyers purchase other items to get the product they want. Further, it outlawed mergers that substantially lessen competition; but since it did not prohibit one firm's purchase of a competitor's plant and equipment, it really could not stop mergers. In 1950, this loophole was closed by the Celler-Kefauver Anti-Merger Act.

■ THE FEDERAL TRADE COMMISSION ACT

The Federal Trade Commission Act was designed to prevent undesirable and unfair competitive practices. Specifically, it created a Federal Trade Commission to investigate unfair and predatory practices and to issue cease-and-desist orders. The act stated that "unfair methods of competition in commerce are hereby declared unlawful." However, the commission—composed of five commissioners, each appointed by the president for a term of seven years—was given the unenviable task of defining exactly what was "unfair." Eventually, the courts took away much of the commission's power; but in 1938, the commission acquired the function of outlawing untrue and deceptive advertising. Also, the commission has authority to carry out economic investigations of the structure and conduct of U.S. business.

THE ROLE OF THE COURTS

The antitrust laws, like any laws, are enforced in the courts. Typically, charges are brought against a firm or group of firms by the Antitrust Division of the Department of Justice, a trial is held, and a decision is reached by the judge. In key cases, appeals are made that eventually reach the Supreme Court. The real impact of the antitrust laws depends on how the courts interpret them. And the judicial interpretation of these laws has changed considerably over time.

   The first major set of antitrust cases took place in 1911 when the Standard Oil Company and the American Tobacco Company were forced to give up large shares of their holdings of other companies. In these cases, the Supreme Court put forth and used the

Rule of reason

famous **rule of reason**: that only unreasonable combinations in restraint of trade, not all trusts, required conviction under the Sherman Act. In 1920, the rule of reason was used by the Supreme Court in its finding that U.S. Steel had not violated the antitrust

The Supreme Court

laws even though it had tried to monopolize the industry, since the Court said it had not succeeded. Moreover, U.S. Steel's large size and its potential monopoly power were ruled beside the point since "the law does not make mere size an offense. It . . . requires overt acts."

During the 1920s and 1930s the courts, including the Supreme Court, interpreted the antitrust laws in such a way that they became as toothless as a new-born babe. Although Eastman Kodak and International Harvester controlled very substantial shares of their markets, the Court, using the rule of reason, found them innocent on the grounds that they had not built up their near-monopoly position through overt coercion or predatory practices. Moreover, the Court reiterated that mere size was not an offense, no matter how great the unexerted monopoly power might be.

In the late 1930s, this situation changed greatly, with the prosecution of the Aluminum Company of America (Alcoa). This case, decided in 1945 (but begun in 1937), reversed the decisions in the *U.S. Steel* and *International Harvester* cases. Alcoa had achieved its 90 percent share of the market by means that would have been considered "reasonable" in the earlier cases: keeping its price low enough to discourage entry, building capacity to take care of increases in the market, and so forth. Nonetheless, the Court decided that Alcoa, because it controlled practically all the industry's output, violated the antitrust laws. Thus to a considerable extent, *the Court used market structure rather than market conduct as a test of legality.*

THE ROLE OF THE JUSTICE DEPARTMENT

The impact of the antitrust laws is determined by the vigor with which the Antitrust Division of the Justice Department prosecutes cases. If the Antitrust Division prosecutes fewer cases, the laws are likely to have less effect. Like the judicial interpretation of the laws, the extent to which the Justice Department has prosecuted cases has varied from one period to another. Needless to say, the attitude of the political party in power had been an important determinant of how vigorously antitrust cases have been prosecuted. When the Sherman Act was first passed, it was of singularly little value. President Grover Cleveland's attorney general did not agree with the law and would not prosecute under it. "Trust-busting" was truly a neglected art until President Theodore Roosevelt devoted his formidable energies to it. In 1903, he established the Antitrust Division of the Justice Department. Moreover, his administration started the major cases that led to the *Standard Oil, American Tobacco,* and *U.S. Steel* decisions.

Subsequently, there was a long lull in the prosecution of antitrust cases, reflecting the Supreme Court's rule of reason doctrine and a strong conservative tide in the nation. The lull continued for about 25 years, until 1937, when there was a significant upsurge in activity on the antitrust front. Led by Thurman Arnold, the Antitrust Division entered one of the most vigorous periods of antitrust enforcement to date. Arnold went after the glass, cigarette, cement, and other industries; the most important case was that against Alcoa. The Antitrust Division attempted in this period to reopen cases that were hopeless under the rule of reason doctrine. With the change in the composition of the Supreme Court, Arnold's activism turned out to be effective.

THE EFFECTIVENESS OF ANTITRUST POLICY

How effective have the antitrust laws been? Obviously it is difficult to tell with any accuracy, since there is no way to carry out an experiment in which U.S. history is rewritten to show what would have happened if the antitrust laws had not been on the books. Many experts seem to feel that the antitrust laws have not been as effective as they might—or should—have been, largely because they do not have sufficient public support and there is no politically powerful pressure group pushing for their enforcement.

But this does not mean that the antitrust laws have had no effect. As Edward Mason of Harvard University has pointed out, their effectiveness is due "not so much to the contribution that particular judgments have made to the restoring of competition as it is to the fact that the consideration of whether or not a particular

The Justice Department

course of action may or may not be in violation of the antitrust acts is a persistent factor affecting business judgment, at least in large firms."[5] This same idea is summed up in the old saying that the ghost of Senator Sherman sits as an ex officio member of every firm's board of directors.

In 1982, two of the biggest antitrust cases in history were decided. According to one settlement, American Telephone and Telegraph Company divested itself of 22 companies that provide most of the nation's local telephone service and kept its Long Lines Division, Western Electric, and Bell Laboratories. According to the other settlement, a huge antitrust case against IBM Corporation, begun in 1969, was dropped by the government because it was "without merit." Although there is considerable skepticism in some quarters concerning the beneficial effects of the antitrust laws, these two cases show that they continue to play an important role in U.S. economic life.

In 1997 the U.S. Justice Department began another landmark antitrust case, this time against Microsoft (see Case Study 19.2). The government was concerned that Microsoft had used its prodigious market power and immense profits to stifle innovation and to harm both consumers and competitors, especially in the market for Internet browsers and applications. In November 1999, the presiding judge ruled against Microsoft. While the final antitrust judgments and actions against Microsoft may be years away, this

[5]Edward Mason, preface to Carl Kaysen and Donald Turner, *Antitrust Policy* (Cambridge, Mass.: Harvard University Press, 1959); reprinted in E. Mansfield, *Monopoly Power and Economic Performance* (4th ed.; New York: Norton, 1978).

case has already had major reverberations in the information technology sectors of the U.S. economy.

REVIEW AND PRACTICE

■ SUMMARY

1 Monopolistic competition occurs where there are many sellers whose products are somewhat different. The demand curve facing each firm slopes downward to the right. The conditions for long-run equilibrium are that each firm is maximizing profits and that economic profits are zero.

2 The firm under monopolistic competition is likely to produce less and charge a higher price than under perfect competition. Relative to pure monopoly, monopolistically competitive firms are likely to have lower profits, greater output, and lower prices. Firms under monopolistic competition will offer a wider variety of styles, brands, and qualities than will firms under perfect competition.

3 Oligopoly is characterized by a small number of firms and a great deal of interdependence, actual and perceived, among them. Oligopoly is a common market structure in the United States.

4 A game is a competitive situation where two or more persons (or organizations) pursue their own interests and none of them can dictate the outcome. Game theory is used to analyze oligopolistic markets.

5 Conditions in oligopolistic industries tend to promote collusion. A cartel is an open, formal, collusive arrangement. A profit-maximizing cartel will act like a monopolist with a number of plants or divisions, each of which is a member firm.

6 Price leadership is quite common in oligopolistic industries; one or a few firms apparently set the price and the rest follow their lead.

7 Relative to perfect competition, it seems likely that both price and profits will be higher under oligopoly. Moreover, oligopolistic industries will tend to spend more on advertising, product differentiation, and style changes than perfectly competitive industries.

8 In 1890, the Sherman Act was passed. It outlawed any contract, combination, or conspiracy in restraint of trade and made it illegal to monopolize or attempt to monopolize. In 1914, Congress passed the Clayton Act, and the Federal Trade Commission was created. The Celler-Kefauver Anti-Merger Act of 1950 was another antitrust development.

9 The real impact of the antitrust laws depends on the interpretation placed on these laws by the courts. Many observers seem to feel that the antitrust laws have not been as effective as they might—or should—have been, largely because they do not have sufficient public support. At the same time, many feel that the evidence, although incomplete and unclear, suggests that they have had a noteworthy effect on business behavior and markets. Three important recent cases involved AT&T, IBM, and Microsoft.

■ PROBLEMS AND QUESTIONS

1 Suppose that a cartel consists of four firms, each of which has a horizontal marginal cost curve. For each firm, marginal cost equals $4. Suppose that the marginal revenue curve for the cartel is $MR = 10 - 2Q$, where MR is marginal revenue (in dollars) and Q is the cartel's output per year (in thousands of units). What output rate will the cartel choose?

2 According to the Senate Subcommittee on Antitrust and Monopoly, "Some system of marketing quotas, whether overt or carefully hidden, must underlie any price-fixing agreement." Comment and evaluate.

3 "Perfect competition results in optimal efficiency and an optimal distribution of income. This is why the United States opts for a perfectly competitive economy." Comment and evaluate.

4 "The real impact of the antitrust laws depends on judicial interpretation." Comment and evaluate.

5 According to John Kenneth Galbraith, "The antitrust laws effectively protect the large business from social pressure or regulation by maintaining the myth that the market does the regulating instead." Do you agree? Why or why not?

■ KEY TERMS

monopolistic competition	collusion
oligopoly	cartel
product differentiation	price leader
game	rule of reason
payoff matrix	

■ VIEWPOINT FOR ANALYSIS

According to Douglas Greer of San Jose State University, "As a general rule, Anheuser-Busch serves as price leader for the [beer] industry. Aside from selected situations when [Anheuser-Busch] discounts . . . its aim is to set its prices as high as possible within the constraints of a growth objective. Of Anheuser-Busch's several brands, Budweiser, its biggest seller, is the key. Once the price of Bud has been set, the others fall into place depending on which rung of the price ladder they occupy (e.g., super-premium Michelob stands higher and popular-priced Busch sits lower). Most other brewers also key to Budweiser, usually matching Bud's prices for premiums and going somewhat above or below it for super premiums and populars."*

(a) If it is true that Anheuser-Busch is a price leader, does this mean that there is collusion among the beer producers? Why or why not?

(b) If a rival firm sets the price of its premium beer well below that of Budweiser, do you think that Anheuser-Busch will match the price cut? Why or why not?

(c) If Anheuser-Busch is a price leader, is it likely to be prosecuted for violation of the antitrust laws? Why or why not?

---

*L. Deutsch, ed., *Industry Studies* (Englewood Cliffs, N.J.: Prentice-Hall, 1993), p. 101.

CHAPTER 21

Pollution and the Environment

LEARNING OBJECTIVES

In this chapter, you should learn:

- What external diseconomies are and how they clarify the economic problem of pollution
- The distinction between private costs and social costs
- The relation of pollution to economic growth
- The goals and methods of public policy toward environmental quality

Chances are that you have heard of global warming, which became a major environmental issue in recent years. Many scientists and others fear that the burning of fossil fuels will increase the concentration of carbon dioxide and other "greenhouse" gases in the atmosphere, and thus warm the earth's surface. What would be the effects, and how should we respond to this potential change? One of the purposes of this chapter is to answer this question.

According to many scientists and social observers, one of the costs of economic growth is environmental pollution. For many years, people in the United States paid relatively little attention to the environment and what they were doing to it. But this attitude changed markedly in the last thirty years. The public became genuinely concerned about environmental problems. However, in the effort to clean up the environment, choices are not always clear, nor solutions easy.

OUR ENVIRONMENTAL PROBLEMS

■ WATER POLLUTION

To see what we mean by environmental pollution, let's begin with one of the most important parts of the environment: our water supplies. A broad range of human activities results in the discharge of large amounts of pollutants into streams, lakes, and the sea. Chemical wastes are released by industrial plants and mines, as well as by farms and homes when fertilizers, pesticides, and detergents run off into waterways. Oil is discharged into the waters by tankers, sewage systems, oil wells, and other sources. Organic compounds enter waterways from industrial plants and farms, as well as from municipal sewage plants; and animal wastes, as well as human wastes, contribute substantially to pollution.

Obviously, we cannot continue to increase the rate at which we dump wastes into our streams, rivers, and oceans. A river or ocean, like everything else, can bear only so much. The people of New Jersey know this well. In the summer of 1987, many New Jersey beaches were closed, when hundreds of dead dolphins, raw sewage, and even used syringes washed ashore. Of course, this is an extreme case, but many of our rivers, including the Hudson and the Ohio, are badly polluted. Water pollution is a nuisance and a threat.

■ AIR POLLUTION

If clean water is vital to our survival, so too is clean air. Yet the battle being waged against air pollution in most of our major cities has not been won. Particles of various kinds are spewed into the air by factories that utilize combustion processes, grind materials, or produce dust. Motor vehicles release lead compounds from gasoline and rubber particles worn from tires, and so help to create that unheavenly condition known as smog. Citizens of Los Angeles are particularly familiar with smog, but few major cities have escaped at least periodic air pollution. No precise measures have been developed to gauge the effects of air pollution on public health and enjoyment, but some rough estimates have suggested that perhaps 25 percent of all deaths from respiratory disease could be avoided by a 50 percent reduction in air pollution.

THE IMPORTANT ROLE OF EXTERNAL DISECONOMIES

**External
diseconomy**

The reason why our economic system has tolerated pollution of the environment lies largely in the concept of external diseconomies. An **external diseconomy** occurs when one person's (or firm's) use of a resource damages other people who cannot obtain proper compensation. When this occurs, a market economy is unlikely to function properly. The price system is based on the supposition that the full cost of using each resource is borne by the person or firm that uses it. If this is not the case and the user bears only part of the full costs, then the resource is not likely to be directed by the price system into the socially optimal use.

To understand why this is so, we begin by reviewing briefly how resources are allocated in a market economy. Resources are used in their socially most valuable way because they are allocated to the people and firms who find it worthwhile to bid most for them, assuming that prices reflect true social costs. Under these circumstances, a firm that maximizes its profits will produce the socially desirable output and use the socially desirable amounts of labor, capital, and other resources. Under these circumstances, there is no problem.

■ PRIVATE COST DOES NOT EQUAL SOCIAL COST

**Private costs
Social costs**

Suppose, however, that because of the presence of external diseconomies, people and firms do not pay the true social costs for resources. For example, suppose that some firms or people can use water and air for nothing, but that other firms or people incur costs as a consequence of this prior use. In this case, the **private costs** of using air and water differ from the **social costs**: *the price paid by the user of water and air is less than the true cost to society.* In a case like this, users of water and air are guided in their decisions by the private cost of water and air—by the prices they pay. Since they pay less than the true social costs, water and air are artificially cheap to them, so that they will use too much of these resources, from society's point of view.

Note that the divergence between private and social costs occurs if, and only if, the use of water or air by one firm or person imposes costs on other firms or persons. Thus, if a paper mill uses water and then treats it to restore its quality, there is no divergence between private and social costs. But when the paper mill dumps harmful wastes into streams and rivers (the cheap way to get rid of its by-products), the towns downstream that use the water must incur costs to restore its quality. The same is true of air pollution. If an electric power plant uses the atmosphere as a cheap and convenient place to dispose of wastes, people living and working nearby may incur costs as a result, since the incidence of respiratory and other diseases may increase. In such cases, there may be a divergence between private and social costs.

We said above that pollution-causing activities that result in external diseconomies represent a malfunctioning of the market system. At this point, the nature of this malfunctioning should be clear. *Firms and people dump too much waste material into the water and the atmosphere. The price system does not provide the proper signals because the polluters are induced to use our streams and atmosphere in this socially undesirable way by the artificially low price of disposing of wastes in this manner. Moreover, because the polluters do not pay the true cost of waste disposal, their products are artificially cheap, so that too much of them is produced.*

ECONOMIC GROWTH AND ENVIRONMENTAL POLLUTION

According to many authorities, economic growth—defined as increases in total economic output per capita—has been associated with increases in the level of environmental pollution. This is not very surprising, since practically all the things that are produced must eventually be thrown away in one form or another. Thus, as output per capita goes up, the level of pollution is likely to go up as well. For example, as we grow more affluent and increase the number of automobiles per capita, we also increase the amount of such air pollutants as nitrogen oxide and tetraethyl lead, both of which are emitted by automobiles.

But it is important to recognize that *pollution is not tied inextricably to national output.* Although increases in national output in the past have been associated with increases in pollution, there is no reason why this correlation must continue unchanged in the future. We can produce things that are heavy polluters of the environment—like electric power and automobiles—or we can produce things that do not pollute the environment nearly so much—like pianos and bicycles.

In recent decades, some people have suggested that we curtail our economic growth in order to reduce pollution. **Zero economic growth** is their goal. Very few economists seem to favor such a policy. Opponents of zero economic growth point out that more productive capacity would help produce the equipment required to reduce pollution. As we shall see, this equipment will not be cheap. Moreover, with proper public policies, we should be able to increase output without increasing pollution, if this is what our people want. In addition, as pointed out by the late Walter Heller of the University of Minnesota:

> Short of a believable threat of extinction, it is hard to believe that the public would accept the tight controls, lowered material living standards, and large income transfers required to create and manage a [no-growth] state. Whether the necessary shifts could be accomplished without vast unemployment and economic dislocation is another question. It may be that the shift to a no-growth state would throw the fragile ecology of our economic system so out of kilter as to threaten its breakdown. Like it or not, economic growth seems destined to continue.

Some people have also argued that technological change is the real villain responsible for pollution and that the rate of technological change should be slowed. Certainly, technological change has made people more interdependent and has brought about more and stronger external diseconomies. Technological change also results in ecological changes, some of which are harmful. For

Reserve mining: The price of cleaner water

Taconite tailings flowing from the Reserve Mining Company

Shortly after World War II, some farsighted entrepreneurs decided there was money to be made in a rock called taconite, found in abundance beside the famous Mesabi iron range in Minnesota. Taconite contains iron—not a lot of iron but enough to make a profit if you know how to crush it into sand-sized particles and separate the grains of iron from the rest of the rock. And that's what the Reserve Mining Company set out to do in the early 1950s. Since the refining process requires vast amounts of water, Reserve decided to mine the rock near Babbit, Minnesota, and transport it on its own railway to a processing plant 40 miles away, on the shores of the largest freshwater lake in the Americas, Lake Superior. The costs of the operation are the same as for most industries—rents, wages, capital costs, debt service—but in Reserve's case, there is a hidden cost as well.

For every ton of iron pellets Reserve manufactures, it also produces 2 tons of waste, taconite tailings, and for 15 years, Reserve was able to dump these tailings into Lake Superior at no cost to itself. Reserve's original idea was that the tailings could be dumped into a deep trough in the lake and that they would settle to a depth of 400 feet or more where they couldn't harm anybody or do any damage to the lake. But in fact no one really knew what was happening to those tailings or whether they posed any real hazard to the lake or to humans living around it. It was only a matter of time before Reserve's dumping practices came under fire. Environmentalists charged that Reserve was ruining Lake Superior. Reserve denied the charges but by late 1969 found itself involved in a court battle that would take seven years to resolve. One of the most hotly debated issues in the case was the discovery of asbestos-like fibers in the water supply of Duluth, Minnesota.

The court battle was resolved in 1977. Reserve was granted the necessary permits to begin construction of a new dumping facility. The cost of this new facility, by Reserve's calculations, was some $387 million. The costs of the new dumping site were absorbed in a number of ways: tax breaks, lower profits, higher prices. Today, there's little doubt that Lake Superior is a cleaner lake than it was before. Scientific analysis indicates that the asbestos levels have dropped by 90 percent.

example, detergents containing phosphate have induced water pollution by causing heavy overgrowths of algae.

But technological change is also a potential hero in the fight against pollution, because the creation of new technology is an important way to reduce the harmful side effects of existing techniques—assuming, of course, that we decide to use our scientists and engineers to this end. Contrary to some people's views, *pollu-*

tion is not the product of some mindless march of technology but of human action and inaction. There is no sense in blaming technology, when pollution is due basically to economic, social, and political choices and institutions.

Finally, it is frequently suggested that as our population increases we must expect more pollution. Many who advocate a policy of ***zero population growth*** advance the argument that it would help reduce the level of pollution. The available evidence indicates some relationship between a country's population and its pollution levels. But there are important differences in the amount of pollution generated by people in various countries. The average American is responsible for much more pollution than the average citizen of most other countries, because the average American is a much bigger user of electric power, detergents, pesticides, and other such products. It has been estimated that the United States, with less than one-twentieth of the world's population, produces about one-third of the wastes discharged into the air and water. Much more than economics is involved in the discussion of the optimal level of population. Although it is only one of a number of important factors, a country's population does affect the level of pollution, but as we shall see in subsequent sections, pollution can be reduced considerably even if population continues to grow.

PUBLIC POLICY TOWARD POLLUTION

Pollution is caused by defects in our institutions, not by malicious intent, greed, or corruption. In cases where waste disposal causes significant external diseconomies, economists generally agree that government intervention may be justifiable. But how can the government intervene? Perhaps the simplest way is

Direct regulation

through **direct regulation**: the issuance of certain enforceable rules for waste disposal. For example, the government can prohibit the burning of trash in furnaces or incinerators, or the dumping of certain materials in the ocean, and it can make any person or firm that violates these restrictions subject to a fine or perhaps even imprisonment. Also, the government can ban the use of chemicals like the harmful pesticide DDT or require that all automobiles meet certain regulations for the emission of air pollutants. Further, the government can establish quality standards for air and water.

Effluent fee

Another way the government can intervene is by establishing effluent fees. An **effluent fee** is a fee a polluter must pay to the government for discharging waste. In other words, a price is imposed on the disposal of waste into the environment; the more firms or individuals pollute, the more they must pay. The idea be-

Transferable emissions permits

Tax credits

hind the imposition of effluent fees is that they can bring the private costs of waste disposal closer to the true social costs. Faced with a closer approximation to the true social costs of their activities, polluters will reduce the extent to which they pollute the environment. Needless to say, many practical difficulties are involved in carrying out this seemingly simple scheme, but many economists believe that this can be a good way to deal with the pollution problem.

The government can also issue **transferable emissions permits**, each of which allows the holder of the permit to generate a certain amount of pollution. These permits, limited in number, are sold by the government to the highest bidders. The price of a permit is set by supply and demand. One advantage of transferable emissions permits is that the authorities can predict how much pollution there will be. After all, the total amount of pollution cannot exceed the amount authorized by the total number of permits issued. In contrast, if an effluent fee is adopted, it is difficult to predict how much pollution will result, since this depends on how polluters respond to the particular level of the effluent fee that is chosen. For this reason, transferable emissions permits are often preferred over effluent fees.

Still another way for the government to intervene is to establish **tax credits** for firms that introduce pollution-control equipment. There are, of course, many types of equipment that a plant can introduce to cut down on pollution—for example, scrubbers for catching poisonous gases, and electrostatic precipitators for decreasing dust and smoke. But such pollution-control equipment costs money, and firms are naturally reluctant to spend money on purposes where the private rate of return is so low. To reduce the burden, the government can allow firms to reduce their tax bill by a certain percentage of the amount they spend on pollution-control equipment. Tax incentives of this sort have been discussed widely in recent years, and some have been adopted.

POLLUTION-CONTROL PROGRAMS IN THE UNITED STATES

In recent decades, there has been considerable growth in government programs designed to control pollution. To take but one example, federal expenditures to reduce water pollution increased in the period from the mid-1950s to 1970 from about $1 million to $300 million annually. To curb water pollution, the federal government has for years operated a system of grants-in-aid to state, municipal, or regional agencies to help construct treatment plants, and grants are made for research on new treatment methods. In addition, the 1970 Water Quality Improvement Act authorized grants to demonstrate new methods and techniques and to estab-

The Kyoto environmental summit, emissions targets, and tradable permits

In December 1997 at the environmental summit in Kyoto, Japan, the world's 24 most-developed countries pledged to cut their greenhouse gas emissions by 2010. The reduction targets—which also give credit for planting trees that remove carbon dioxide from the atmosphere—are 7 percent below 1990 levels for the United States and 8 and 6 percent, respectively, for Europe and Japan.

These are aggressive targets, given that in the United States, before the Kyoto agreement, carbon emissions were projected to rise between 15 and 20 percent.

Proponents of the Kyoto accord pointed to three reasons why they believed it provided the formula for success. First, the agreement adopted differentiated targets, recognizing that each country must address climate change on the basis of its own national energy profile and circumstances. Second, the accord lets countries pursue their own paths to lower emissions. Third, the Kyoto agreement embraces market-based international mechanisms, including emissions trading.

Many economists believe that tradable emissions permits are an economically efficient way of reducing carbon emissions. For example, if one firm is able to reduce emissions cheaply while another finds it difficult to do so, the first will be able to sell permits to the second, thereby reducing the overall cost of achieving the environmental objective.

However, some economists believed that the Kyoto accord was not a formula for success. First and foremost, the treaty was unacceptable to developing countries, which are responsible for an increasing share of global emissions—about 45 percent by 2010. There is unlikely to be any generally acceptable principle for allocating emissions rights and targets between rich and poor countries, because of different resource endowments and levels of industrialization.

Second, many economists feel that the Kyoto accord should have included concrete actions to be taken by governments, especially a carbon tax. Without such actions, the concern is that not enough will be done to implement the Kyoto plan.

Only time will tell whether the Kyoto accord was a courageous first step or a missed opportunity. However, from an economics perspective, an accord such as Kyoto that is built on a market-based framework is more likely to succeed than one that is not.

lish programs to train people in water control management. (The federal government has also regulated the production and use of pesticides.) The states, as well as the federal government, have played an important role in water pollution control. They have set standards for allowable pollution levels, and many state governments have provided matching grants to help municipalities construct treatment plants.

In 1970, the federal government established a new agency, the Environmental Protection Agency (EPA). Working with state and local officials, this agency establishes standards for desirable air and water quality and devises rules for attaining these goals. The 1970 Clean Air Act directed the EPA to establish minimum ambient standards for air quality, and it set limits on the emission of carbon monoxide, hydrocarbons, and nitrous oxides from automobiles. But after a number of clashes between the EPA and the automakers, the EPA relaxed the deadlines by which these limits were supposed to be met. In 1972, amendments to the Water Pollution Act authorized the EPA to set up effluent standards for both privately and publicly owned plants. A stated goal of the amendments was to eliminate the discharge of pollutants into water by 1985, but, for reasons discussed in the next section, this goal was unrealistically stringent. In general, recent legislation has emphasized direct regulation, although there has been some use of transferable emissions permits. For example, in 1991 the Chicago Board of Trade voted to create a private market for rights to emit sulfur dioxide. The rights are issued to electric power companies by EPA as part of the nation's program to reduce acid rain.

Some people believe that public policy is moving too rapidly in this area; others believe that it is moving too slowly. It is not easy to determine how fast or how far we should go in attempting to reduce pollution. Those who will bear the costs of reducing pollution have an understandable tendency to emphasize (and perhaps inflate) the costs and discount the benefits of such projects. Those who are particularly interested in enjoying nature and outdoor recreation (like the Sierra Club) are understandably inclined to emphasize (and perhaps inflate) the benefits and discount the costs of such projects. Politics inevitably plays a major role in the outcome of such cases. The citizens of the United States must indicate, through the ballot box as well as the marketplace, how much they are willing to pay to reduce pollution.

HOW CLEAN SHOULD THE ENVIRONMENT BE?

One of the most fundamental questions about pollution control is: How clean do we want the air, water, and other parts of our environment to be? At first glance, it may seem that we should restore and maintain a pristine pure environment, but this is not a very sensible goal, since the costs of achieving it would be enormous. The Environmental Protection Agency has estimated that it would cost about $60 billion to remove 85 to 90 percent of water pollutants from industrial and municipal sources. This is hardly a trivial amount, but it is far less than the cost of achieving zero discharge of pollutants, which would be a truly staggering sum.

Fortunately, however, there is no reason to aim at so stringent a goal. *It seems obvious that, as pollution increases, various costs to society increase as well.* Some of these costs were described at the

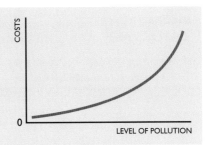

FIGURE 21.1

Costs to Society of Pollution

The costs to society of pollution increase with the level of pollution.

beginning of this chapter. For example, we pointed out that increases in air pollution result in increased deaths, and increases in water pollution reduce the recreational value of rivers and streams. Suppose that we could get accurate data on the cost to society of various levels of pollution. Of course, it is extremely difficult to get such data, but if we could, we could determine the relationship between the amount of these costs and the level of pollution. It would look like the hypothetical curve in Figure 21.1. The greater the level of pollution, the higher these costs will be.

But these costs are not the only ones that must be considered. *We must also take into account the costs of controlling pollution.* In other words, we must look at the costs to society of maintaining a certain level of environmental quality. These costs are not trivial, as we saw at the beginning of this section. To maintain a very low level of pollution, it is necessary to invest heavily in pollution-control equipment and to make other economic sacrifices.[1] If we could get accurate data on the cost to society of controlling pollution, we could find the relationship between the amount of these costs and the level of pollution. It would look like the hypothetical curve in Figure 21.2; the lower the level of pollution, the higher these costs will be.

■ A GOAL OF ZERO POLLUTION?

At this point, it should be obvious why we should not try to achieve a zero level of pollution. *The sensible goal for our society is to minimize the sum of the costs of pollution and the costs of controlling pollution.* In other words, we should construct a graph, as shown in

[1] It is important to recognize that the costs of pollution control extend far beyond the expense of constructing plants to treat water or control gas emissions. A serious pollution-control program can put firms out of business, put people out of work, and bring economic trouble to entire communities. Further, a pollution-control system can result in a redistribution of income. For example, automobiles, electric power, and other goods and services involving considerable pollution are likely to increase in price relative to other goods and services involving little pollution. To the extent that polluting goods and services play a bigger role in the budgets of the poor than of the rich, pollution controls hurt the poor and help the rich.

FIGURE 21.2

Costs to Society of Pollution Control

The more pollution is reduced, the higher the costs to society of pollution control are.

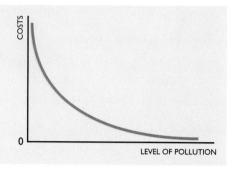

Figure 21.3, to indicate the relationship between the sum of these two types of costs and the level of pollution. Then we should choose the level of pollution at which the sum of these two types of costs is a minimum. Thus in Figure 21.3, we should aim for a pollution level of *A*. There is no point in trying for a lower level; such a reduction would cost more than it would be worth. For example, the cost of achieving a zero pollution level would be much more than it would be worth. Only when the pollution level exceeds *A* is the extra cost to society of the additional pollution greater than the cost of preventing it. For example, the cost of allowing pollution to increase from *A* to *B* is much greater than the cost of prevention.

It is easy to draw hypothetical curves but not so easy actually to measure these curves. Unfortunately, no one has a very clear idea of what the curves in Figure 21.3 really look like, although we can be sure that their general shapes are like those shown here. Thus no one really knows just how clean we should try to make the environment. Under these circumstances, expert opinion differs on the nature and extent of the programs that should be carried out. Moreover, as pointed out in a previous section, political considerations and pressures enter in. But one thing is certain: we will con-

FIGURE 21.3

Determining the Optimal Level of Pollution

The optimal level of pollution is at point *A*, since this is where the total costs are a minimum. Below point *A*, the cost to society of more pollution is less than the cost of preventing it. Above point *A*, the cost to society of more pollution is greater than the cost of preventing it.

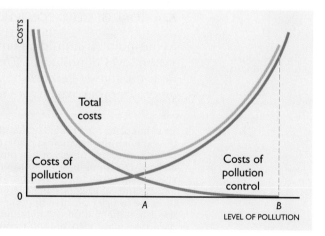

tinue to live with some pollution, and that, for the reasons just given, will be the rational thing to do.

■ RECENT DIRECTIONS OF ENVIRONMENTAL POLICY

In the late 1970s and early 1980s, policymakers became increasingly concerned that regulatory agencies like the EPA had been paying too little attention to the costs involved in reducing pollution. For example, a government study found that a relaxation of the EPA's 1977 standard for water-pollution control in the steel industry *with no change in its more stringent 1983 standard* would allow the industry savings in capital costs of $200 million. As President Carter's Council of Economic Advisers pointed out, "In making regulatory decisions on the speed of attaining standards, we should explicitly make a qualitative judgment about whether the gains from earlier attainment are worth the costs."

Going a step further, some experts, like Lester Lave and Gilbert Omenn of the Brookings Institution, have concluded from their studies that the Clean Air Act has not been very effective. In their view, "the application of pollution controls to existing plants and older cars has been limited, and costs have been excessive, largely because Congress has failed to confront [many of] the difficult issues."

During the 1980s, environmentalists and others charged that the Reagan administration was dismantling or at least emasculating the EPA. Anne Gorsuch resigned in 1983 as head of the EPA, as criticism of the agency continued to build. James Watt, former secretary of the interior, also angered environmentalists. Administration officials responded by claiming that they were trying to promote and restore balance between environmental objectives and economic growth.

The Bush administration seemed more interested in new environmental initiatives than the Reagan administration. In late 1990, major changes were made in the Clean Air Act. For example, the law called for tighter restrictions on the pollutants causing urban smog and on automobile exhausts (beginning in the 1994 model year), as well as new limits on coal-burning power plants that are aimed at reducing emissions of sulfur dioxide and nitrogen oxide, both regarded as causes of acid rain. Some economists estimated that compliance with the tougher standards could cost about $30 billion per year. Whether the benefits exceed the costs will not be known for many years.

The Clinton administration was more inclined to take action to reduce greenhouse gases than the Bush administration did, which in the words of President Clinton's Council of Economic Advisers, "adopted what was called a 'no regrets' policy; it was willing to take steps to reduce emissions only if those actions would be beneficial

Dolphin-safe tuna

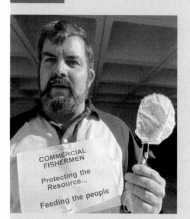

Person engaged in commercial fishing protesting government regulation

Sometimes U.S. environmental laws can, unintentionally, violate international treaties signed by the United States. This happened in the early 1990s when, under pressure from environmental groups, the United States passed the Marine Mammals Act. The act banned the import of tuna from Mexico because the methods used to catch tuna in the eastern Pacific by Mexican people engaged in fishing as an occupation were killing an estimated 130,000 dolphins a year. Mexico challenged the U.S. ban under the terms of the World Trade Organization (WTO). The United States helped found the WTO and has been a strong advocate of free trade. Thus, the Mexican challenge was an embarrassment for the United States. It also had the unfortunate result of pitting U.S. environmental groups against the WTO and poor commercial fishing Mexican people.

Free trade and environmental protection can sometimes seem to conflict when countries have different living standards and environmental priorities. When countries with stricter environmental standards try to impose them on countries with looser standards, they can run afoul of the multilateral trade agreements. The WTO and the agreements that form the foundation of the multilateral trading system do not permit discrimination against imports based on the methods of production, even if it means hurting the environment.

The basic reasoning is as follows: since each country's circumstances and priorities differ from those of other countries, every country will find something objectionable in other countries' production processes, and international trade will become more restrictive. Free trade principles aside, the Mexicans also questioned the fairness of threatening the jobs of 25,000 Mexicans engaged in commercial fishing to save marine mammals that were not endangered.

In the end, an agreement was worked out between the United States and Mexico, as well as with other countries that fished for tuna in the eastern Pacific. The number of dolphins killed in the process of catching tuna would be limited to 5,000, using a new type of net that would allow the dolphins to escape. The tuna catches would be monitored to be sure that they were "dolphin safe." The agreement satisfied U.S. environmental groups, saved Mexican jobs, and avoided a major trade confrontation between the United States and Mexico.

for other reasons. . . . In contrast, this administration sees cost-effective policies to reduce greenhouse gas emissions as appropriate 'insurance' against the threat of climate change."[2] During the Kyoto environmental summit in December 1997, the Clinton administration was able to incorporate some of its ideas about market-based solutions to reduce greenhouse gas emissions (see Case Study 21.2) into the agreement that was signed.

[2]*Economic Report of the President,* 1994, p. 184.

REVIEW AND PRACTICE

■ SUMMARY

1 One of the major social issues of the 2000s is environmental pollution. To a considerable extent, environmental pollution is an economic problem. Waste disposal and other pollution-causing activities result in external diseconomies.

2 Firms and individuals that pollute the water and air (and other facets of the environment) often pay less than the true social costs of disposing of their wastes in this way. Part of the true social costs is borne by other firms and individuals, who must pay to clean up the water or air or who must live with the consequences.

3 Because of the divergence of private from social costs, the market system does not result in an optimal allocation of resources. Firms and individuals create too much waste and dispose of it in excessively harmful ways. Because the polluters do not pay the full costs of waste disposal, their products are artificially cheap, with the result that they produce too much of these products.

4 The government can intervene in several ways to help remedy the breakdown of the market system in this area. One way is to issue regulations for waste disposal and other activities influencing the environment. Another is to establish effluent fees, charges a polluter must pay to the government for discharging wastes. Still another way is to issue transferable emissions permits.

5 It is extremely difficult to determine how clean the environment should be. The sensible goal for society is to permit the level of pollution that minimizes the sum of the costs of pollution and the costs of controlling pollution. However, no one has a very clear idea of what these costs are, and to a large extent the choices must be made through the political process.

■ PROBLEMS AND QUESTIONS

1 Suppose that the paper industry emits wastes into rivers and streams and that municipalities or firms downstream must treat the water to make it usable. Do the paper industry's private costs equal the social costs of producing paper? Why or why not?

2 Suppose that each ton of paper output results in pollution that costs municipalities and firms downstream $1 and that a law is passed that requires the paper industry to reimburse the municipalities and firms downstream for these costs. Prior to this law, the quantity of paper supplied at each price was:

PRICE OF PAPER (DOLLARS PER TON)	QUANTITY SUPPLIED (MILLION TONS)
1.00	10.0
2.00	15.0
2.50	17.5
3.00	20.0
4.00	25.0

After the law takes effect, what will be the quantity supplied at each price?

3 In question 2, which output—the one prevailing before the industry has to reimburse others or the one prevailing afterward—is socially more desirable? Why?

4 If the quantity of paper demanded at each price is as shown below, what will be the equilibrium output of paper before and after the paper industry has to reimburse the municipalities and firms downstream (as indicated in question 2)?

PRICE OF PAPER (DOLLARS PER TON)	QUANTITY DEMANDED (MILLION TONS)
1.00	30.0
2.00	25.0
3.00	20.0
3.50	17.5
4.00	15.0

5 Suppose that the social cost (in billions of dollars) due to pollution equals $5P$, where P is the level of pollution, and that the cost (in billions of dollars) of pollution control equals $10 - 2P$. What is the optimal level of pollution? Is this a typical case?

■ KEY TERMS

external diseconomy

private costs

social costs

direct regulation

effluent fee

transferable emissions permits

tax credits

■ VIEWPOINT FOR ANALYSIS

In 1993, Lester Brown, president of Worldwatch Institute, wrote that "The deterioration in living conditions for much of humanity during the eighties and early nineties will continue if economies are not modernized. . . . By far the most effective instrument to transform the economy quickly is tax policy, specifically the partial replacement of income taxes with environmental taxes."*

(a) Brown urged that the burning of fossil fuels be taxed. What did he hope to accomplish by this? Do you agree that such a tax would be worthwhile? Why or why not?

(b) What are the advantages of a tax on the burning of fossil fuels rather than direct regulations telling each firm, household, and government agency how much of such fuels they can burn? Aren't direct regulations a surer way of discouraging the burning of fossil fuels?

(c) Unless other countries join the United States in adopting such a tax, isn't it foolish for us to impose a tax on the burning of fossil fuels? Why or why not?

*L. Brown, "A New Era Unfolds," *Challenge*, May–June 1993, p. 46; reprinted in E. Mansfield, ed., *Leading Economic Controversies of 1997* (New York: Norton, 1997).

What Should Be Done about Global Warming?

Global warming has become one of the lively environmental issues of the 1990s. The main source of concern is the possibility that increasing concentrations of carbon dioxide and other greenhouse gases in the atmosphere, resulting from the burning of fossil fuels, will act like a blanket to insulate the planet and warm its surface. Although it is politically fashionable to call for bold environmental actions, there are great uncertainties about the extent of global warming and its economic impact which argue against hasty actions.

To begin with, climatologists believe that the average surface temperature of the earth will rise between 1 and 4 degrees Celsius over the next century. This will probably mean an increase in rainfall but could also result in hotter and drier climates in the U.S. grain belt. Rising temperatures will probably have the biggest impact on weather-dependent industries such as agriculture and forestry, and also on coastal activities. Not all the impacts would be negative. Warm-weather activities would be boosted, and the de-

Reduction of vehicle emissions is a commonly proposed solution to global warming.

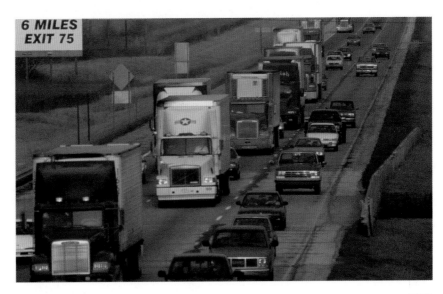

mand for space cooling would rise. However, the climate-sensitive sectors of the United States only account for about 15 percent of output. The rest of the economy would hardly be affected by a warmer climate. This is true for all the developed countries, where climactic changes would be likely to have a small impact—about 1 percent of output—over the next half-century. In contrast, small and poor countries, where agriculture alone can account for as much as one-third of GDP, are much more vulnerable.

There are many ways of responding to global warming, the first of which is prevention. The reduction of carbon dioxide emissions and reforestation (trees absorb carbon dioxide) are the most commonly proposed solutions. The former could have consequences for economic growth. A 10 to 20 percent reduction in greenhouse gases would have a negligible impact on economic growth, but a 60 percent cut in fossil fuel emission would have a dramatic effect, lowering world GDP by as much as 2 percent a year. While developed countries could absorb this, developing countries would be devastated by such a reduction in output.

Other elements of a response to global warming would include measures to simply adapt to warmer temperatures, as well as attempts at climatic engineering. However, well before any such actions are taken, more and better information will be needed on global warming and its economic impacts. Also, more research is needed on new technologies that could slow climate changes. Finally, any attempts to reduce emissions should use the market mechanism. For example, environmental taxes or fees are a more efficient way of reducing greenhouse gases than regulation because they allow the markets to minimize the costs of slowing global warming and strengthen the incentives to develop new technologies.

■ QUESTIONS

1 In 1990, President Bush's Council of Economic Advisers said that the use of transferable emissions permits would "provide a least-cost reduction in [greenhouse gas] emissions".* Is this true? Why?

2 Alan Manne of Stanford University and Richard Rickels of the Electric Power Research Institute have carried out a detailed study to estimate the economic costs of constraining carbon dioxide emissions. In particular, they looked at what would happen to world ouput if these emissions were stabilized at current levels, and then gradually reduced by 20 percent by the year 2020. The resulting loss in output for the United States alone would be about $1 trillion over the next century.† Do you think that we should begin such a program?

*Economic Report of the President, 1990, p. 218.

†A. Manne and R. Richels, "CO_2 Emission Limits: An Economic Cost Analysis for the USA," Energy Journal, no. 2 (April 1, 1990).

3 President Bush's Council of Economic Advisers also said that any strategy to limit aggregate emissions without worldwide participation would be likely to fail. Do you agree? If so, why?

4 Further, President Bush's Council of Economic Advisers said that any effective strategy must cover all greenhouse gases. Do you agree? Why?

5 In 1995, President Clinton's Council of Economic Advisers said that "Cost-effective greenhouse gas control policies must rely as much as possible on economic incentives, to motivate the response of the literally billions of people responsible for greenhouse gas–emitting activities."* Why are economic incentives so important?

*Economic Report of the President, 1995, p. 156.

PART FIVE

The Distribution of Income

CHAPTER 22

The Supply and Demand for Labor

LEARNING OBJECTIVES

In this chapter, you should learn:

- How the firm's demand curve for labor can be derived
- The nature of the market demand curve for labor
- How the equilibrium wage and quantity of labor are determined
- The role of labor unions in the U.S. economy
- How unions affect the wages earned by workers

The port of Philadelphia has been fighting hard against other ports like Wilmington, Delaware, and Miami, Florida, to maintain its dominant position as a destination for Chilean fruit. But union rules have made this fight very difficult. How are unions organized, and what determines their behavior? One purpose of this chapter is to answer this question.

Economists frequently classify inputs into three categories: labor, capital, and land. The disadvantage of this simple classification is that each category contains an enormous variety of inputs. Consider the services of labor, which include the work of a football star like Emmitt Smith, a salesman like Willy Loman, and a knight like Don Quixote. But this classification does have the important advantage of distinguishing between different types of inputs. In this chapter, we are concerned with the determinants of the price of labor. The next chapter will deal with the determinants of the prices of capital and land, as well as profits.

THE LABOR FORCE AND THE PRICE OF LABOR

At the outset it is important to note that, to the economist, labor includes a great deal more than the organized labor that belongs to trade unions. The secretary who works at General Motors, the young account executive at Merrill Lynch, the auto mechanic at your local garage, the professor who teaches molecular biology, all put forth labor. Moreover, as shown in Table 22.1, many more people work in the service industry and in retail trade than in manu-

TABLE 22.1

Employment on Nonagricultural Payrolls, by Major Industry, 1999

INDUSTRY	EMPLOYMENT (MILLIONS)
Mining	1
Construction	6
Manufacturing	18
Transportation and public utilities	6
Wholesale trade	7
Retail trade	22
Finance, insurance, and real estate	8
Services	39
Federal government	3
State and Local government	18
Total	128

Source: Economic Report of the President, 2000.

facturing. About two-thirds of the people employed are white-collar workers (such as salespeople, doctors, secretaries, or managers) and service workers (such as servers, bartenders, or cooks), whereas only about one-third are blue-collar workers (such as carpenters, mine workers, or laborers) and farm workers.

It is also worthwhile to preface our discussion with some data concerning how much people get paid. As shown in Table 22.2, average weekly earnings vary considerably from one industry to another. For example, in 1999, workers in manufacturing averaged

TABLE 22.2

Average Weekly Earnings, Selected Industries, 1960–99 (dollars)

YEAR	MANUFACTURING	CONSTRUCTION	RETAIL TRADE
1960	90	113	58
1965	108	138	67
1970	134	195	82
1975	190	265	108
1980	289	368	147
1985	386	464	175
1990	442	524	195
1995	515	587	221
1999	580	668	263

Source: U.S. Department of Labor.

about $580 a week, while construction workers averaged $668 a week, and workers in retail trade averaged $263 a week. Also, average weekly earnings vary considerably from one period to another. Table 22.2 shows that average weekly earnings in manufacturing in 1965 were only $108, as contrasted with $580 in 1999. In subsequent sections, we will investigate the reasons for these differences in wages, both among industries and over periods of time.

More broadly, we will be concerned in subsequent sections with the *price of labor,* which includes a great many forms of remuneration other than what we commonly regard as wages. As noted above, economists include as labor the services performed by professional people (such as lawyers, doctors, and professors) and self-employed businesspeople (such as electricians, mechanics, and barbers). Thus the amount such people receive per unit of time is included here as a particular sort of price of labor, even though these amounts are often called fees or salaries rather than wages.

Finally, it is important to distinguish between *money* wages and *real* wages. Whereas the money wage is the amount of money received per unit of time, the real wage is the amount of real goods and services that can be bought with the money wage. The real wage depends on the price level for goods and services as well as on the magnitude of the money wage. In recent years, the inflation we have experienced has meant that real wages have increased less than money wages; thus the increases in earnings in Table 22.2 exaggerate greatly the increase in real wages. In subsequent sections, since we will assume that product prices are held constant, our discussion will be in terms of real wages.

THE EQUILIBRIUM WAGE AND EMPLOYMENT UNDER PERFECT COMPETITION

■ THE FIRM'S DEMAND CURVE FOR LABOR

Let's begin by discussing the determinants of the price of labor under perfect competition. We assume that firms take the prices of their products, as well as the prices of all inputs, as given, and we assume that owners of inputs take input prices as given. Under these circumstances, what determines how much labor an individual firm will hire (at a specified wage rate)? Once we answer this question, we can derive a firm's demand curve for labor. A ***firm's demand curve for labor*** is the relationship between the price of labor and the amount of labor utilized by the firm. That is, it shows, for each price, the amount of labor that the firm will use.

TABLE 22.3

The Firm's
Demand for
Labor under
Perfect
Competition

NUMBER OF WORKERS PER DAY	TOTAL OUTPUT PER DAY	MARGINAL PRODUCT OF LABOR	VALUE OF MARGINAL PRODUCT (DOLLARS)
0	0		
		7	70
1	7		
		6	60
2	13		
		5	50
3	18		
		4	40
4	22		
		3	30
5	25		

■ THE PROFIT-MAXIMIZING QUANTITY OF LABOR

Let's assume that we know the firm's production function and that labor is the only variable input. Given the production function, we can determine the marginal product of labor when various quantities are used. (Recall that the marginal product of labor is the additional output resulting from an extra unit of labor.) The results of such a calculation are as shown in Table 22.3. If the price of the firm's product is $10, let's determine the value to the firm of each additional worker it hires per day.[1] According to Table 22.3, the firm achieves a daily output of 7 units when it hires the first worker, and since each unit is worth $10, this brings the firm's daily revenue up to $70. By hiring the second worker, the firm increases its daily output by 6 units, and since each unit is worth $10, the resulting increase in the firm's daily revenue is $60. Similarly, the increase in the firm's daily revenue from hiring the third worker is $50, the increase from hiring the fourth worker is $40, and so on.

How many workers should the firm hire per day if it wants to maximize profit? It should hire more workers as long as the extra workers result in at least as great an addition to revenue as they do

[1] For simplicity, we assume that the number of workers that the firm hires per day must be an integer, not a fraction. This assumption is innocuous and can easily be relaxed.

to costs. If the price of a worker is $50 per day, it is profitable for the firm to hire the first worker, since this adds $70 to the firm's daily revenue but only $50 to its daily costs. Also, it is profitable to hire the second worker, since this adds $60 to the firm's daily revenue but only $50 to its daily costs. The addition of the third worker does not reduce the firm's profits. But beyond three workers per day, it does not pay the firm to hire more labor. (The addition of a fourth worker adds $50 to the firm's daily costs but only $40 to its daily revenue.)

■ THE VALUE OF THE MARGINAL PRODUCT OF LABOR

Thus the optimal number of workers per day for this firm is three. Table 22.3 shows that this is the number of workers at which the value of the marginal product of labor is equal to the price of labor. What is the **value of the marginal product of labor**? It is the marginal product of labor multiplied by the product's price. In Table 22.3, the value of the marginal product of labor is $70 when between no and one worker is used per day. Why? Because the marginal product of labor is 7 units of output, and the price of a unit of output is $10. Thus this product, 7 times $10, equals $70.

Value of the marginal product of labor

To maximize profit, the value of the marginal product of labor must be set equal to the price of labor, because if the value of the marginal product is greater than labor's price, the firm can increase its profit by increasing the quantity of labor used, while if the value of the marginal product is less than labor's price, the firm can increase its profit by reducing the quantity of labor used. Thus *profits must be at a maximum when the value of the marginal product is equal to the price of labor.*

Given these results, it is a simple matter to derive the firm's demand curve for labor. Specifically, its demand curve must be the value-of-marginal-product schedule in the last column of Table 22.3. If the daily wage of a worker is between $51 and $60, the firm will demand two workers per day; if the daily wage of a worker is between $41 and $50, the firm will demand three workers per day; and so forth. Thus *the firm's demand curve for labor is its value-of-marginal-product curve,* which shows the value of labor's marginal product at each quantity of labor used. This curve is shown in Figure 22.1.[2]

---

[2]Strictly speaking, the firm's demand curve is the same as the curve showing the value of the input's marginal product only if this input is the only variable input. For a discussion of the more general case, see E. Mansfield, *Microeconomics: Theory and Applications* (10th ed., New York: Norton, 1997), Chap. 14.

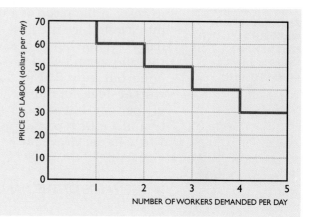

FIGURE 22.1

The Firm's Demand Curve for Labor under Perfect Competition

The firm's demand curve for labor is the firm's value-of-marginal-product curve, which shows the value of labor's marginal product at each quantity of labor used. The data for this figure come from Table 22.3.

THE MARKET DEMAND CURVE FOR LABOR

In previous sections, we were concerned with the demand curve of a single firm for labor. But many firms, not just one, are part of the labor market, and the price of labor depends on the demands of all of these firms. The situation is analogous to the price of a product, which depends on the demands of all consumers. *The* **market demand curve for labor** *shows the relationship between the price of labor and the total amount of labor demanded in the market. That is, it shows, for each price, the amount of labor that will be demanded in the entire market.* The market demand curve for labor, like any other input, is quite analogous to the market demand curve for a consumer good, which we discussed in detail in Chapter 17.

But there is at least one important difference. *The demand for labor and other inputs is a* **derived demand**, *since inputs are demanded to produce other things, not as an end in themselves.* This fact helps to explain why the price elasticity of demand is higher for some inputs than for others. In particular, the higher the price elasticity of demand for the product the input helps produce, the higher the price elasticity of demand for the input.

Market demand curve for labor

Derived demand

THE MARKET SUPPLY CURVE FOR LABOR

We have already seen that a product's price depends on its market supply curve as well as its market demand curve. This is equally true for labor. *The* **market supply curve for labor** *is the relationship between the price of labor and the total amount of labor supplied in the market.* When individuals supply labor, they are supplying

Market supply curve for labor

FIGURE 22.2

Backward-Bending Supply Curve for Labor

Beyond some point, increases in the price of labor may result in smaller amounts of labor's being supplied. The reason for a supply curve of this sort is that as the price of labor increases, the individuals supplying the labor become richer and want to increase their amount of leisure time.

Backward-bending supply curve

something they themselves can use, since the time that they do not work can be used for leisure activities. Because of this fact, the market supply curve for labor, unlike the supply curve for inputs supplied by business firms, may be **backward bending**, particularly for the economy as a whole. That is, *beyond some point, increases in price may result in smaller amounts of labor's being supplied.*

An example of a backward-bending supply curve is provided in Figure 22.2. What factors account for a curve like this? Basically, the reason is that as the price of labor increases, individuals supplying the labor become richer. And when they become richer, they want to increase their amount of leisure time, which means that they want to work less. Even though the amount of money per hour they give up by not working is greater than when the price of labor was lower, they nonetheless choose to increase their leisure time. This sort of tendency has shown up quite clearly in the last century. As wage rates have increased and living standards have risen, the average workweek has tended to decline.

Note that there is no contradiction between the assumption that the supply curve of labor or other inputs *to an individual firm* is horizontal under perfect competition and the fact that the *market* supply curve for the input may not be horizontal. For example, unskilled labor may be available to any firm in a particular area at a given wage rate in as great an amount as it could possibly use. But the total amount of unskilled labor supplied in this area may increase relatively little with increases in the wage rate. The situation is similar to the sale of products. As we saw in Chapter 18, any firm under perfect competition believes that it can sell all it wants at the existing price. Yet the total amount of the product sold in the entire market can ordinarily be increased only by lowering the price.

515

FIGURE 22.3

Equilibrium Price and Quantity of Labor

The equilibrium price of labor is *P*, and the equilibrium quantity of labor used is *Q*.

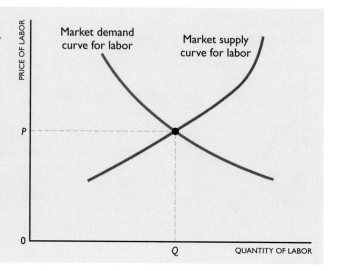

EQUILIBRIUM PRICE AND QUANTITY OF LABOR

Labor's price (or wage rate) is determined under perfect competition in essentially the same way that a product's price is determined: by supply and demand.

The price of labor will tend toward equilibrium at the level where the quantity of labor demanded equals the quantity of labor supplied. Thus, in Figure 22.3, the equilibrium price of labor is *P*. If the price were higher than *P*, the quantity supplied would exceed the quantity demanded and there would be downward pressure on the price. If the price were lower than *P*, the quantity supplied would fall short of the quantity demanded and there would be upward pressure on the price. By the same token, *the equilibrium amount of labor utilized is also given by the intersection of the market supply and demand curves.* In Figure 22.3, *Q* units of labor will be utilized in equilibrium in the entire market.

Graphs such as Figure 22.3 are useful, but it is important to look behind the geometry and to recognize the factors that lie behind the demand and supply curves for labor. Consider the market for surgeons and that for unskilled labor. As shown in Figure 22.4, the demand curve for the services of surgeons is to the right of the demand curve for unskilled labor (particularly at high wage rates). Why is this so? Because an hour of a surgeon's services is worth more to people than an hour of an unskilled laborer's services. In this sense, surgeons are more productive than unskilled laborers. Also, as shown in Figure 22.4, the supply curve for the services of surgeons is far to the left of the supply curve for unskilled labor. Why is this so? Because very few people are licensed surgeons, whereas practically everyone can do

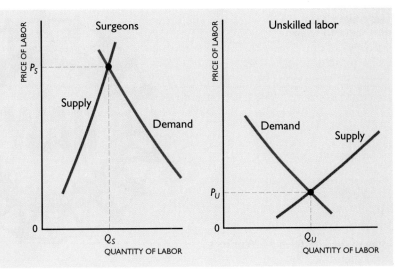

FIGURE 22.4

The Labor Market for Surgeons and Unskilled Labor

The wage for surgeons is higher than the wage for unskilled labor because the demand curve for surgeons is farther to the right and the supply curve for surgeons is farther to the left than the corresponding curves for unskilled labor.

unskilled labor. In other words, surgeons are much more scarce than unskilled laborers.

For these reasons, surgeons receive a much higher wage rate than unskilled laborers. As shown in Figure 22.4, the equilibrium price of labor for surgeons is much higher than that for unskilled labor. If unskilled laborers could quickly and easily turn themselves into competent surgeons, this difference in wage rates would be eliminated by competition, since unskilled workers would find it profitable to become surgeons. But unskilled workers lack the training and often the ability to become surgeons. Thus surgeons and unskilled labor are examples of ***noncompeting groups***. Wage differentials can be expected to persist among noncompeting groups because people cannot move from the low-paid to the high-paid jobs.

LABOR UNIONS

Over one-tenth of the nonfarm workers in the United States belong to a union, and the perfectly competitive model does not apply to these workers. The biggest unions are the National Education Association, the Teamsters, and the Food and Commercial Workers, each with 1.4 million members or more. Next come the Automobile, Aerospace, and Agricultural Implement Workers, the State, County, and Municipal Employees, and the United Auto Workers, each with over a million members.

The ***national unions*** are of great importance in the U.S. labor

Logo of the United Auto Workers

movement.[3] The supreme governing body of the national union is the convention, which is held every year or two. The delegates to the convention have the authority to set policy for the union. However, considerable power is exercised by the national union's officers.

A national union is composed of **_local unions_**, each in a given area or plant. Some local unions have only a few members, but others have thousands. The local union, with its own president and officers, often plays an important role in collective bargaining (which we will discuss later in this chapter). The extent to which the local unions maintain their autonomy varies from one national union to another. In industries where markets are localized (like construction and printing), the locals are more autonomous than in industries where markets are national (like steel, automobiles, and coal).

Finally, there is the AFL-CIO, a federation of national unions created by the merger of the American Federation of Labor and the Congress of Industrial Organizations in 1955. The AFL-CIO does not include all national unions. The United Mine Workers refused to join the AFL-CIO, and the Auto Workers left it in 1968. (The Teamsters were kicked out in the mid-1950s because of corruption, but in 1987 they were allowed to rejoin.) The AFL-CIO plays an important role in the U.S. labor movement, but because the national unions in the AFL-CIO have given up relatively little of their power to the federation, its authority is limited.

---

[3]Sometimes national unions are called international unions because some locals are outside the United States, for example, in Canada.

THE U.S. LABOR MOVEMENT

■ EARLY HISTORY OF U.S. LABOR UNIONS

To understand the nature and behavior of labor unions, let's look briefly at the history of the U.S. labor movement. Unions arose because workers recognized that acting together gave them more bargaining power than acting separately. They frequently felt that they were at the mercy of their employers, and they formed fraternal societies and unions to promote economic and social benefits for the members. However, until the 1930s unions in the United States were not very strong, partly because of employers' efforts to break them up and partly because the courts held that the unions' attempts to increase wages and influence working conditions were conspiracies in restraint of trade.

During the early 1930s, the tide began to turn. To a great extent, this was because of government encouragement of unions, in which the first important step was the Norris–La Guardia Act of 1932. This act made it much more difficult for courts to issue injunctions (cease-and-desist orders, to prevent striking or picketing) against unions, and it made *yellow-dog contracts*—agreements in which workers promised their employers not to join a union—unenforceable in federal courts. The next important step occurred in 1935, when Congress passed the Wagner Act, which made it an unfair labor practice for employers to refuse to bargain collectively with unions representing a majority of their workers or to interfere with their workers' right to organize. In addition, this act established the National Labor Relations Board to investigate unfair labor practices, to issue orders enforceable in federal courts, and to hold elections to determine which, if any, union would represent various groups of employees. The Wagner Act was a very important factor in encouraging the growth of labor unions in the United States—so important that it has often been called U.S. labor's Magna Carta.

The 1930s were years of spectacular union growth. Aided by the pro-union attitude of the Roosevelt administration, new legislation, and the energy of its leaders, total union membership rose from less than 3 million in 1933 to more than 10 million in 1941. World War II witnessed further growth in total union membership. Stimulated by the increase in total employment and the government's favorable attitude toward their growth, unions increased their membership from over 10 million in 1941 to almost 15 million—or about 36 percent of all nonfarm workers—in 1945. The government helped unions gain recognition in exchange for union cooperation in promoting war production. By the end of World War II, labor unions were conspicuous and powerful features of the economic landscape.

FIGURE 22.5

Structure of AFL-CIO

The AFL-CIO is organized
with the governing power
in the hands of a biennial
convention.

```
                        ┌──────────────────┐
                        │    Convention    │
                        └──────────────────┘
                                 │
                        ┌──────────────────┐
                        │ Executive Council│
                        └──────────────────┘
                                 │
                        ┌──────────────────┐
                        │     Officers     │
                        └──────────────────┘
        ┌────────────────────┼────────────────────┐
┌─────────────────┐ ┌─────────────────┐ ┌─────────────────┐
│  Committee on   │ │ International and│ │ Building trades │
│Political Education│ │ national unions │ │ and other depts │
└─────────────────┘ └─────────────────┘ └─────────────────┘
        ┌────────────────────┼────────────────────┐
┌─────────────────┐ ┌─────────────────┐ ┌─────────────────┐
│Directly affiliated│ │      Local      │ │ State and city  │
│  local unions   │ │     unions      │ │   federations   │
└─────────────────┘ └─────────────────┘ └─────────────────┘
```

THE STRUCTURE OF THE AFL-CIO

The AFL-CIO is organized along the lines indicated in Figure 22.5.
The constitution of the AFL-CIO puts supreme governing power in
the hands of a biennial convention. The national unions are represented at these conventions on the basis of their dues-paying membership. Between conventions, the AFL-CIO's business is directed
by its president (John Sweeney in 2000) and secretary-treasurer,
as well as by various committees and councils composed of representatives of various national unions or people elected at the
convention. The AFL-CIO contains seven trade and industrial departments, such as building trades, food and beverage trades, mar-
itime trades, and so forth. Also, as indicated by Figure 22.5, a few
local unions are not affiliated with a national union, but are directly affiliated with the AFL-CIO.

INTERNAL PROBLEMS IN LABOR UNIONS

As unions have grown older and more secure and powerful, there
has been more and more concern about the nature of their internal practices and leadership. After all, they are no longer the un-
derdogs that they were 80 years ago. They are huge organizations
with immense power. Both in this country and in Europe, observers have charged that unions are often far from democratic.
Members are frequently apathetic, for there is less interest in
union affairs now than in the early days when unions were fighting for survival, and the leadership of some unions has become en-

trenched and bureaucratic. Moreover, there are frequent charges that unions engage in racial and other forms of discrimination.

Another problem is *corruption within labor unions*. In the 1950s, a Senate committee (the McClellan Committee) conducted lengthy and revealing investigations that showed that the leaders of the Teamsters Union had misused union funds, had questionable relations with the underworld, and had "shamefully betrayed their own members." Other unions were also accused of corrupt practices. It is important, however, to avoid smearing the entire labor movement. Although racketeering and fraud unquestionably are problems, they tend to be localized in relatively few industries—particularly the building trades, trucking, longshoring, laundries, and hotels. Many responsible and honest leaders of the labor movement have tried hard to rid the labor movement of these unsavory practices.

■ POSTWAR LABOR LEGISLATION

After World War II, public sentiment turned somewhat against unions. Strikes and higher prices got under the skin of the consumer as well as the employer, and there began to be a lot of talk in Congress and elsewhere about the prewar Wagner Act having been too one-sided, giving too many advantages to labor in its contest with the employer. In 1947, despite bitter labor opposition, the Taft-Hartley Act was passed with the purpose of redressing the balance between labor and employers. The act established standards of conduct for unions as well as employers, defined unfair union practices, and stated that unions could be sued for acts of their agents. Also, the act outlawed the closed shop, which requires that firms hire only workers who are already union members, and stipulated that, unless the workers agree in writing, the **checkoff** is illegal. (The checkoff is a system in which the employer deducts union dues from each worker's pay and hands them over to the union.)

In addition, the act tried to increase protection against strikes in which the public's safety and health are involved. If the president decides that an actual or impending strike imperils the national health or safety, the president can appoint a fact-finding committee to investigate the situation. After receiving the committee's report, the president can tell the attorney general to obtain an injunction forbidding a strike for 80 days, during which the parties can continue to negotiate. A Federal Mediation Service was established to help the parties settle such negotiations. The act does not forbid a strike at the end of the 80 days if no agreement has been reached.

In response to the evidence of union corruption presented by the McClellan Committee, Congress passed the Landrum-Griffin Act in 1959. This act attempts to protect the rights of individual union members from abuse by union leaders. It contains a "bill of rights" for labor, guaranteeing that each member can participate in union elections, that elections be held by secret ballot, and that other steps be taken to protect the rights of the members. It also requires unions to file financial reports, forbids payments (beyond wages) by employers to union representatives, and prohibits loans exceeding $2,000 by unions to union officials.

HOW UNIONS INCREASE WAGES

Unions wield considerable power, and economists must include them in their analysis if they want their models of the labor market to be accurate. Let's begin to see how this is done by supposing that a union wants to increase the wage rate paid its members. How can it accomplish this objective? In other words, how can it alter the market supply curve for labor or the market demand curve for labor so that the price of labor—its wage—will increase?

1. *The union may try to shift the supply curve of labor to the left.* It may try to shift the supply curve, as shown in Figure 22.6, with the result that the price of labor will increase from P to P_1. How can the union cause this shift in the supply curve? Craft unions have frequently forced employers to hire only union members, and then restricted union membership by high initiation fees, reduction in new membership, and other devices. In addition, unions have favored legislation to reduce immigration, shorten working hours, and limit the labor supply in other ways.

FIGURE 22.6

Shift of Supply Curve for Labor

A union may try to shift the supply curve to the left by getting employers to hire only union members and then restricting union membership or by other methods.

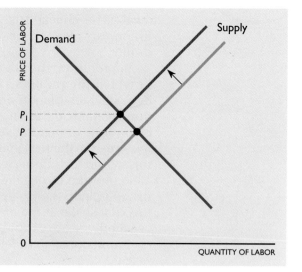

FIGURE 22.7

Direct Increase in Price of Labor

A union may try to get the employer to raise the wage from P to P_1 and let the higher wage reduce the opportunity for work. This is commonly done by strong industrial unions.

2. *The union may try to get the employers to pay a higher wage, while allowing some of the supply of labor forthcoming at this higher wage to find no opportunity for work.* In Figure 22.7, the union may try to exert presure on the employers to raise the price of labor from P to P_1. At P_1, not all of the available supply of labor can find jobs. The quantity of labor supplied is Q_2, while the amount of labor demanded is Q_1. The effect is the same as in Figure 22.6, but in this case the union does not limit the supply directly. It lets the higher wage reduce the opportunity for work. Strong industrial unions often behave in this fashion. Having organized practically all the relevant workers and controlling the labor supply, the union raises the wage to P_1. This is a common and important case.

3. *The union may try to shift the demand curve for labor upward and to the right.* If it can bring about the shift described in Figure 22.8, the price of labor will increase from P to P_2. To cause this shift in the demand for labor, the union may resort to **featherbedding**: it may try to restrict output per worker in order to increase the amount of labor required to do a certain job. (To cite but one case, the railroad unions have insisted on much unnecessary labor.) Unions also try to shift the demand curve by helping the employers compete against other industries or by encouraging Congress to pass legislation that protects the employers from foreign competition.

Featherbedding

COLLECTIVE BARGAINING

Collective bargaining

Collective bargaining is the process of negotiation between the union and management over wages and working conditions. Representatives of the union and management meet periodically to

523

FIGURE 22.8

Shift in Demand Curve for Labor

A union may try to shift the demand curve for labor to the right by featherbedding or other devices, and thus increase the wage from P to P_2.

work out an agreement or contract. Typically, each side asks at first for more than it expects to get, and compromises must be made to reach an agreement. The union representatives take the agreement to their members, who must vote to accept or reject it. If they reject it, they may vote to strike or to continue to negotiate.

Collective bargaining agreements vary greatly. Some pertain to only a single plant whereas others apply to an entire industry. However, an agreement generally contains the following elements: it specifies the extent and kind of recognition that management gives the union, the level of wage rates for particular jobs, the length of the workweek, the rate of overtime pay, the extent to which seniority will determine which workers will be first to be laid off, the nature and extent of management's prerogatives, and how grievances between workers and the employer will be handled.

Historically, industries and firms have extended recognition to unions by accepting one of three arrangements: the closed shop, the union shop, or the open shop. In a **closed shop**, workers must be union members before they can be hired. This gives the union more power than if there is a **union shop**, in which the employer can hire nonunion workers who must then become union members in a certain length of time after being hired. In an **open shop**, the employer can hire union or nonunion labor, and once employed, nonunion workers need not join the union. As we have seen, the closed shop was banned by the Taft-Hartley Act. The Taft-Hartley Act also says that the union shop is legal unless outlawed by state laws, and in about twenty states there are right-to-work laws that make the union shop illegal. Right-to-work laws are

Closed shop

Union shop

Open shop

The closing of the Herald Tribune

In 1965, New York City newspapers and their union employees were feeling the bite of computer technology. It took a linotype operator an hour to set 200 lines of newspaper type. A new machine called the teletypesetter could do the same work in as little as half an hour, and computerized typesetting equipment on the drawing board would be able to do it in 17 seconds. The new technology would increase productivity and save labor—and thus displace printers.

The International Typographical Union's Local Six ("Big Six") had the bargaining power to keep the new technology out or let it in. The union did not seek to stand in the way of progress; although automated and computerized typesetting machinery could cost the jobs of union printers, higher wages without the increased productivity of automation could force less profitable papers to merge or even close—and that would cost jobs too. Big Six wanted only to ensure that the new equipment would be operated by union members, so that the technology would not be used for union busting and its members and apprentices would be protected..

Six months of complicated maneuvering resulted in a contract without a strike. In addition to a pay raise, Big Six got what was in effect a veto over the introduction of automated equipment. The contract allowed the papers to use punch tape printing equipment, but set up a fund equal to 100 percent of the direct labor savings from the introduction of the new technology—a fund under the union's control and to be used to protect printers put out of work by the new equipment. The union had opened the door to automation, but it took most of what was saved and required the same wages and benefits from big, profitable papers as from unprofitable ones.

In less than a year, the new contract and the competitive New York newspaper business claimed their first victims. Profitable papers like the *New York Times* and the *Daily News* could afford to pay the price because they would save so much from automating. But three unprofitable papers, the *Herald Tribune,* the *Journal American,* and the *World Telegram,* merged into a new corporation, the World Journal Tribune Inc. Almost half the three papers' 4,700 employees lost their jobs, and about 400 Big Six printers were laid off.

April 25, 1966, was to have seen the first edition of the new *Herald Tribune* but was instead the first day of another strike. However, this strike was different. When Big Six had struck some papers in 1963, the others had shut down in solidarity. This time, the *Times,* the *News,* and the *Post* were on the stands as usual. And although Big Six had signed a contract with the World Journal Tribune by the end of May, the other unions had not, and the printers followed union tradition and refused to cross the picket lines. For 113 days the *Herald Tribune* presses were silent, and on August 16, John Hay Whitney, publisher of the *Herald Tribune,* announced its closing.

opposed by organized labor, which regards them as a threat to its security and effectiveness.

■ BASIC FORCES AT WORK

Collective bargaining is a power struggle. At each point in their negotiations, both the union and the employer must compare the costs (or benefits) of agreeing with the other party with the costs (or benefits) of continuing to disagree. The costs of disagreement are the costs of a strike, whereas the costs of agreement are the costs of settling on terms other than one's own. These costs are determined by basic market forces. For example, during periods when demand is great, employers are more likely to grant large wage increases because the costs of disagreement seem higher (a strike will prove more costly) than those of settlement. The outcome of the negotiations will depend on the relative strength of the parties. The strength of the employers depends on their ability to withstand a strike. The strength of the unions depends on their ability to keep out nonunion workers and to enlist the support of other unions, as well as on the size of their financial reserves.

RECENT TRENDS

The past twenty years have not been easy for organized labor. In the 1980s, many important unions cut back on their wage requests. In the automobile industry, U.S. firms found it difficult to compete with their Japanese rivals, and many experts attributed this partly to the very high wages in the U.S. auto industry. In the trucking industry, unionized firms found it increasingly difficult to compete with nonunion firms. More and more union members in industries like autos, trucking, steel, rubber, and the airlines began to worry about the effects of hefty wage increases on whether they would have jobs. The climate for collective bargaining was quite different than in earlier decades.

Labor negotiations in the auto industry in 1987 were a good illustration. An important issue in these negotiations was the reform in work rules. After seeing productivity increases of 20 percent or more at some plants that adopted Japanese-style manufacturing systems (which organized workers in teams), auto executives pressed for the reduction of rigid union job classifications and work rules. Some union officials agreed, but because work rules are set in local, not national, negotiations and because some union members have strongly resisted such changes, reform has not been easy.

Let's define a union concession as a wage reduction (or no

Why is Europe's unemployment rate so high?

Workers from several European countries demonstrate in Paris against job cuts.

In 1999, the U.S. unemployment rate was at a thirty-year low—just over 4 percent. The picture in western Europe was considerably less rosy—one in ten workers did not have a job. Unfortunately, the underlying causes of this high unemployment are mostly structural. In other words, high growth alone will not reduce the ranks of those without jobs. In fact, unemployment rates in most European countries rose for the better part of two decades.

Why has the experience of the U.S. and Europe been so different? A somewhat simplistic answer might be that European workers have been pricing themselves out of jobs. From 1970 to 1998, real (inflation-adjusted) labor costs in Europe rose by about 70 percent. In the United States, the rise was only 25 percent. However, during that same period, the U.S. economy created 70 percent more jobs, while employment in Europe increased by only 10 percent.

Thus, European workers and politicians seem to be less concerned about rising unemployment than about ensuring that those with jobs continued to receive large wage increases. Also, because of Europe's generous social welfare system, unemployed workers typically receive larger unemployment benefits for longer than their U.S. counterparts.

European labor laws, de facto, seem to be designed to protect "prime-age" workers (mostly male) in the 25 to 54 age bracket. In 1998, the proportion of men aged 25 to 54 employed (the employment ratio) in the United States was 89 percent. The equivalent share in Europe was only a little lower at 86 percent. For all other demographic groups, the European employment shares were lower in Europe than in the United States. For women aged 25 to 54, the employment ratio in Europe was 54 percent compared with 63 percent in the United States. For young workers, aged 15 to 24, the European ratio was 37 percent, against a U.S. ratio of 59 percent. For older workers, in the 55 to 64 age range, the difference was equally large: 37 percent in Europe versus 58 percent in the United States. Similarly, the proportion of the European unemployed who were without a job for over 12 months in 1998 was 49 percent, compared with a mere 9 percent in the United States.

Politically, the European trade-off between higher unemployment and preserving the higher wages of the prime-age workers does not seem to have created a political backlash. However, the economic cost has been heavy, with generous social welfare benefits' being financed with increasingly onerous tax burdens. Taxes in Europe are about 50 percent of GDP compared with 30 percent in the United States.

The current state of affairs in Europe's labor markets might be sustainable for another couple of decades, except for rapidly aging populations. Because of low birth rates, the working-age populations of many European countries will start declining in absolute terms in the next decade. This could produce a funding crisis for the social security systems in Europe, as fewer workers will be called on to fund the pensions of an ever-larger pool of retirees. One way out of such pension crisis could be reduced protection of the prime-age workers and increased incentives for the employment of women, the young, and the old. The resulting increase in the employment ratio could offset some of the adverse demographic effects of an aging population.

wage increase), a reduction in cost-of-living adjustments in pay, a relaxation of work rules, the adoption of a "two-tier" wage structure (where newly hired workers are paid at a lower rate than existing workers), or the substitution of profit sharing (and related) plans for a wage increase. In the late 1980s, a majority of workers in unions like the United Auto Workers, Steelworkers, Carpenters, Electrical Workers, and Food and Commercial Workers accepted concessions in their new contracts. In 1975 or 1980, such concessions were rare.

When the Clinton administration took office, organized labor hoped that it would have easier sledding. But in late 1993 Bill Clinton pushed through the North American Free Trade Agreement, which was anathema to many unions because they felt it would encourage U.S. firms to move factories (and jobs) to Mexico. Clearly, the unions have continued to find themselves under pressure. In 1997, the AFL-CIO announced that it would emphasize a campaign to reach out to working women. Whether this and other initiatives will increase union membership appreciably is hard to say.

REVIEW AND PRACTICE

■ SUMMARY

1 Assuming perfect competition, a firm will employ each type of labor in an amount such that its marginal product times the product's price equals its wage. In other words, the firm will employ enough labor so that the value of the marginal product of labor equals labor's price.

2 The firm's demand curve for labor, which shows for each price of labor the amount of labor the firm will use, is the firm's value-of-marginal-product curve (if labor is the only variable input). The market demand curve for labor shows the relationship between its price and the total amount of labor demanded in the market.

3 Labor's price depends on its market supply curve as well as on its market demand curve. Labor's market supply curve is the relationship between the price of labor and the total amount of labor supplied in the market. (Labor's market supply curve may be backward bending.)

4 An input's price is determined under perfect competition in essentially the same way that a product's price is determined: by supply and demand. The price of labor will tend in equilibrium to the level at which the quantity of labor demanded equals the quantity of labor supplied. By the same token, the equilibrium amount of labor utilized is also given by the intersection of the market supply and demand curves.

5 The AFL-CIO is a federation of national unions created by the merger in 1955 of the American Federation of Labor and the Congress of Industrial Organizations. It plays an important role in the U.S. labor movement, but because the national unions in the AFL-CIO have given up relatively little of their power to the federation, its authority is limited.

6 Unions can increase wages by shifting the supply curve of labor to the left, by shifting the demand curve for labor to the right, and by influencing the wage directly. Collective bargaining is the process of negotiation between union and management over wages and working conditions.

■ PROBLEMS AND QUESTIONS

I Suppose that a perfectly competitive firm's production function is as follows:

QUANTITY OF LABOR (YEARS)	OUTPUT PER YEAR (THOUSANDS OF UNITS)
0	0
I	3.0
2	5.0
3	6.8
4	8.0
5	9.0

The firm is a profit maximizer, and the labor market is competitive. Labor must be hired in integer numbers and for a year (no more, no less). If the firm hires 4 years of labor and if the price of a unit of the firm's product is $3, one can establish a range for what the annual wage prevailing in the labor market must be. What is the maximum amount it can be? What is the minimum amount? Why? Do these numbers seem realistic? Why or why not?

2 On the basis of the data in question 1, plot the marginal product of labor at various utilization rates of labor. Also, plot the value of labor's marginal product at each quantity of labor used.

3 "The unions should not be exempt from the antitrust laws." Comment and evaluate.

4 Describe the various ways that labor unions can influence the wage rate. Do you think that they attempt to maximize the wage rate? If not, what do you think their objectives are?

5 Suppose that you were the president of a small firm that hired nonunion labor. How would you go about estimating the marginal product of a certain worker or of certain types of workers? Would it be easy? If not, does this mean that the theory of wage determination is incorrect or useless?

■ KEY TERMS

value of the marginal product of labor	featherbedding
market demand curve for labor	collective bargaining
derived demand	closed shop
market supply curve for labor	union shop
backward-bending supply curve	open shop

■ VIEWPOINT FOR ANALYSIS

According to the *Philadelphia Inquirer*, June 26, 1993, "Ports as near as Chester and Wilmington and as far away as Miami and New Orleans are working like crazy to undermine Philadelphia's dominant position as the destination for Chilean fruit. . . . Antiquated union pacts still in force [in Philadelphia] require that up to five members of [the longshoremen's] union must be present on a gang unloading fruit, although only two (at most) are needed. . . . [If] things continue as they are on the Philadelphia docks, very soon the longshoremen here will have a lot of time off—without pay."*

(a) How can rival ports try to undermine Philadelphia's dominant position in this regard?

(b) Are these union contracts intended to shift the demand curve for longshoremen in Philadelphia? If so, why would the employers agree to such contracts?

(c) If you were president of the longshoremen's union in Philadelphia, would you support changes in these union contracts? If so, what sorts of changes would you support and why?

*Philadelphia Inquirer, June 26, 1993, p. A6.

CHAPTER 23

Interest, Rent, and Profit

LEARNING OBJECTIVES

In this chapter, you should learn:

- How the interest rate is determined and the economic functions it performs
- The nature and importance of the present value of future income
- The definition of rent
- The nature of profit and its function in a capitalistic economic system

The computer industry has had more than its share of heroic entrepreneurs, such as William Hewlett and David Packard. But no firm had a more colorful history than Apple Computer, which was founded by Steve Jobs and Steve Wozniak. What incentives did the price system dangle before these two entrepreneurs? One purpose of this chapter is to answer this question.

Not all income is received in the form of wages. The schoolteacher who has a savings account at the Bank of America receives income in the form of *interest*. The widow who rents out 100 acres of rich Iowa land to a farmer receives income in the form of *rent*. And people, like Jobs and Wozniak, who found and own a firm that develops a new type of computer receive income in the form of *profit*. All these types of income—interest, rent, and profit—are forms of property income. That is, they are incomes received by owners of property. In this chapter, we are concerned with the determinants of interest, rent, and profit. Also, we try to explain the social functions of each of these types of property income.

THE NATURE OF INTEREST

The English essayist Charles Lamb said, "The human species, according to the best theory I can form of it, is composed of two distinct races, the men who borrow and the men who lend." Whether or not such a cleavage exists, most of the human species, at one time or another, are borrowers or lenders of money. Thus, you almost certainly know that **interest** is a payment for the use of money, and that *the* **interest rate** *is the amount of money one must pay for the use of a dollar for a year*. If the interest rate is 8 percent, you must pay 8 cents for the use of a dollar for a year.

Interest rate

Everyone who borrows money pays interest. Consumers pay

531

interest on personal loans taken out to buy appliances, mortgages taken out to buy houses, and many other types of loans. Firms pay interest on bonds issued to purchase equipment and on short-term bank loans taken out to finance inventories. And governments pay interest on bonds issued to finance schools, highways, and other public projects.

Interest rates vary, depending on the nature of the borrower and the type of loan. One of the most important determinants of the rate of interest charged borrowers is the *riskiness* of the loan. If lenders have doubts about their chances of getting their money back, they will charge a higher interest rate than if they are sure of being repaid. Small, financially rickety firms have to pay higher interest rates than large blue-chip firms, and large, well-known firms have to pay higher interest rates than the federal government. Another factor that influences the interest rate is the *cost of bookkeeping and collection*. If a firm makes many small loans and must hound the borrowers to pay up, these costs are a great deal larger than if it makes one large loan. Consequently the interest rate that must be charged for such small loans is often considerably higher than for bigger loans.

Despite the diversity of interest rates encountered at any point in time in the real world, it is analytically useful to speak of the **pure rate of interest**, which is the interest rate on a riskless loan. The rate of interest on U.S. government bonds—which are about as safe as one can get in this world—comes close to being a pure rate of interest. Actual interest rates will vary from the pure rate, depending on the riskiness of the loan together with other factors, but the configuration of actual interest rates will tend to move up and down with the pure interest rate.

THE DETERMINATION OF THE INTEREST RATE

■ THE DEMAND FOR LOANABLE FUNDS

Demand curve for loanable funds

Since the interest rate is the price paid for the use of loanable funds, it, like any price, is determined by demand and supply. The **demand curve for loanable funds** shows the quantity of loanable funds demanded at each interest rate. The demand for loanable funds is a demand for what these funds will buy. Money is not wanted for its own sake, since it cannot build factories or equipment. Instead, it can provide command over resources—labor and equipment and materials—to do things like build factories or equipment.

As shown in Figure 23.1, the demand curve slopes downward to the right; this indicates that more loanable funds are demanded at a lower rate of interest than at a higher rate of interest. A very

FIGURE 23.1

Determination of the Equilibrium Rate of Interest

The interest rate is determined by the demand and supply of loanable funds, where the equilibrium level of the interest rate is *i*.

large demand for loanable funds stems from firms that want to borrow money to invest in capital goods like machine tools, buildings, and so forth. At a particular point in time a firm has available a variety of possible investments, each of which bears a certain rate of return, which indicates the investment's profitability or net productivity. At higher interest rates, a firm will find it profitable to borrow money for fewer of these projects than at lower interest rates.

Rate of return

To be more specific, *an asset's* **rate of return** *is the interest rate earned on the investment in the asset.* Suppose that a piece of equipment costs $10,000 and yields a permanent return to its owner of $1,500 per year.[1] (This return allows for the costs of maintaining the machine.) The rate of return on this piece of capital is 15 percent. Why? Because if an investment of $10,000 yields an indefinite annual return of $1,500, the interest rate earned on this investment is 15 percent.

If a firm maximizes profit, it will borrow to carry out investments where the rate of return, adjusted for risk, exceeds the interest rate. For example, it is profitable for a firm to pay 10 percent interest to carry out a project with a 12 percent rate of return, but it is not profitable to pay 15 percent interest for this purpose. (More will be said on this score in a subsequent section.) Consequently, the higher the interest rate, the smaller the amount that firms will be willing to borrow.

Large demands for loanable funds are also made by consumers and by the government. Consumers borrow money to buy

[1]It is unrealistic to assume that the yield continues indefinitely, but it makes it easier to understand the principle involved.

houses, cars, and many other items. The government borrows money to finance the building of schools, highways, housing, and many other types of public projects. As in the case of firms, the higher the interest rate, the smaller the amount that consumers and governments will be willing to borrow. Adding the demands of firms, consumers, and government together, we find the aggregate relationship at a given point in time between the pure interest rate and the amount of funds demanded—which is the demand curve for loanable funds. For the reasons given above, this demand curve looks the way a demand curve should: it is downward sloping to the right.

■ THE SUPPLY OF LOANABLE FUNDS

Supply curve for loanable funds

The **supply curve for loanable funds** is the relationship between the quantity of loanable funds supplied and the pure interest rate. The supply of loanable funds comes from households and

FIGURE 23.2

Effects on the Equilibrium Interest Rate of Shifts in the Demand and Supply Curves for Loanable Funds

If people become more willing to postpone consumption to future time periods, the supply curve will shift to the right, and the equilibrium interest rate will fall from i to i_0. If very profitable new investment opportunities are opened up, the demand curve will shift to the right, and the equilibrium interest rate will rise from i to i'_0.

firms that find the available rate of interest sufficiently attractive to get them to save. In addition, the banks play an extremely important role in influencing the supply of loanable funds. Indeed, banks can create or destroy loanable funds (but, as we have seen in Chapters 8 and 9, only within the limits set by the Federal Reserve, our central bank).

The equilibrium value of the pure interest rate is given by the intersection of the demand and supply curves. In Figure 23.1 the equilibrium rate of interest is i. Factors that shift the demand curve or supply curve for loanable funds tend to alter the interest rate. If people become more willing to postpone consumption to future time periods, the supply curve for loanable funds will shift to the right and the interest rate will decline. Or if inventions result in very profitable new investment possibilities, the demand curve will shift to the right and the interest rate will increase (see Figure 23.2).

However, this is only part of the story. Because of the government's influence on both the demand and supply sides of the market for loanable funds, the interest rate at any point in time is to a considerable extent a matter of public policy. A country's monetary policy can have a significant effect on the level of the interest rate. More specifically, when the Federal Reserve pursues a policy of easy money, this generally means that interest rates tend to fall in the short run, because the Fed is pushing the supply curve for loanable funds to the right. On the other hand, when the Federal Reserve pursues a policy of tight money, interest rates generally tend to rise in the short run, because the Fed is pushing the supply curve for loanable funds to the left (see Figure 23.3).

FIGURE 23.3

Effects on the Equilibrium Interest Rate of Federal Reserve Policies Influencing the Supply Curve for Loanable Funds

When the Federal Reserve pushes the supply curve to the right (from S to S_2), the equilibrium interest rate falls from i to i_2. When the Federal Reserve pushes the supply curve to the left (S to S_1), the equilibrium interest rate increases from i to i_1.

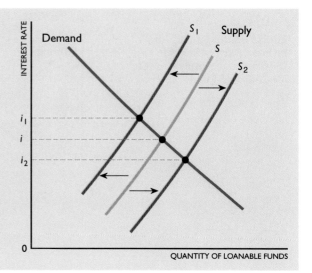

The government is also an important factor on the demand side of the market for loanable funds, because it is a big borrower. Between 1941 and 1945, it borrowed almost $200 billion to help finance World War II. During the 1980s and early 1990s, it borrowed huge amounts to finance the mammoth federal deficits. In 1999, total federal debt (excluding the debt of state and local governments) held by the public was about $3.2 trillion.

FUNCTIONS OF THE INTEREST RATE

Interest has often been a relatively unpopular and somewhat suspect form of income. Even the great Greek philosopher Aristotle, who was hardly noted for muddleheadedness, felt that money was "barren" and that it was improper to charge interest. In real life and in fiction, the moneylender is often the villain, almost never the hero. Yet *interest rates serve a very important function: they allocate the supply of loanable funds.*

At a given point in time, funds that can be used to construct new capital goods are scarce, and society faces the problem of allocating these scarce funds among alternative possible uses. One way to allocate the loanable funds is through freely fluctuating interest rates. When such funds are relatively scarce, the interest rate will rise, with the result that only projects with relatively high rates of return will be carried out since the others will not be profitable. On the other hand, when such funds are relatively plentiful, the interest rate will fall, and less productive projects will be carried out because they now become profitable.

■ CHOOSING THE MOST PRODUCTIVE PROJECTS

The advantage of using the interest rate to allocate funds is that only the most productive projects are funded. To see why, assume that all investments are riskless. *If firms can borrow all the money they want (at the prevailing interest rate) and if they maximize their profits, they will buy all capital goods and accept all investment opportunities where the rate of return on these capital goods or investment opportunities exceeds the interest rate at which the firms can borrow.*[2] The reason for this is clear enough. If one can borrow money at an interest cost that is less than the return on the borrowed money, clearly one can make money. Thus, if you borrow $1,000 at 3 percent per year interest and buy a $1,000 machine that has a rate of return of 4 percent per year, you receive a return of $40 per year and incur a cost of $30 per year. Since you make a profit of $10 per year, it obviously pays to buy this machine.

At a particular point in time, there are many possible capital goods that can be produced and investment projects that can be carried out. Their rates of return vary a great deal; some goods or projects have much higher rates of return than others. Suppose that we rank the capital goods or projects according to their rates of return, from highest to lowest. If only a few of the goods or projects can be accepted, only those at the top of the list will be chosen. But as more and more can be accepted, society and private investors must go further and further down the list, with the consequence that projects with lower and lower rates of return will be chosen. How many of these capital goods and investment projects will be carried out? As noted above, firms will continue to invest as long as the rate of return on these goods or projects exceeds the interest rate at which they can borrow. Thus it follows that *the most productive projects—all those with rates of return exceeding the interest rate—will be carried out.*

CAPITALIZATION OF ASSETS

In a capitalist economy, each asset has a market value. How can we determine what this value is? How much money is a particular asset worth? To keep things reasonably simple, suppose that you can get 5 percent on various investments open to you, for example, you can get 5 percent by investing your money in the stock of a local firm. That is, for every $1,000 you invest, you will receive a permanent return of $50 a year, and this is the highest return

---

[2]We assume here that the investment opportunities are independent in the sense that the rate of return from each opportunity is not influenced by whether some other opportunity is taken.

available. Now suppose that you have an opportunity to buy a piece of equipment that will yield you a permanent return of $1,000 per year. This piece of equipment is worth $1,000/.05 = $20,000 to you. Why? Because this is the amount you would have to pay for any other investment open to you that yields an equivalent amount, $1,000, per year. (If you must invest $1,000 for every $50 of annual yield, $20,000 must be invested to obtain an annual yield of $1,000.)

In general, if a particular asset yields a permanent amount, X dollars, each year, how much is this asset worth? In other words, how much should you be willing to pay for it? If you can get a return of $100 \times r$ percent per year from alternative investments, you would have to invest X/r dollars in order to get the same return as this particular asset yields. Consequently, this asset is worth

$$\frac{\$X}{r}.$$

Thus, if the rate of return on alternative investments had been 3 percent rather than 5 percent in the example above, the worth of the piece of equipment would have been $1,000/.03 = $33,333 (since $X = \$1,000$ and $r = .03$). This is the amount you would have to pay for any other investment open to you that yields an equivalent amount, $1,000, per year. To see this, note that if you must invest $1,000 for every $30 (not $50, as before) of annual yield, $33,333 (not $20,000, as before) must be invested to obtain an annual yield of $1,000.

Capitalization   This process of computing an asset's worth is called **capitalization**. Note one important point about an asset's capitalized value: Holding constant an asset's annual returns, the asset's worth is higher, the lower the rate of return available on other investments. Thus the piece of equipment discussed above was worth $33,333 when you could get a 3 percent return on alternative investments but worth only $20,000 when you could get a 5 percent return on alternative investments. This makes sense. After all, the lower the rate of return on alternative investments, the more you must invest in them in order to obtain annual earnings equivalent to those of the asset in question. Thus the more valuable is the asset in question.

This principle helps to explain why in securities markets bond prices fall when interest rates rise, and rise when interest rates fall. A **bond** is a piece of paper that states that the borrower will pay the lender a fixed amount of interest each year (and the principal when the bond comes due). Suppose that this annual interest is $100 and that the interest rate equals $100 \times r$ percent per year. Then, applying the results of the previous paragraphs, this bond will be worth 100/r dollars if the bond is due a great many years hence. Suppose the interest rate is 5 percent. Then it is worth $2,000. But if the interest rate rises to 10 percent, it will be worth only $1,000, and if the interest rate falls to 4 percent, it will be worth $2,500. Securities dealers make these sorts of calculations all the time, for they recognize that the value of the bond will fall when interest rates rise, and rise when interest rates fall.

THE PRESENT VALUE OF FUTURE INCOME

In the previous section, we determined the value of an asset that yields a perpetual stream of earnings. Now let's consider a case where an asset will provide you with a single lump sum at a certain time in the future. Suppose that you are the heir to an estate of $100,000, which you will receive in two years. How much is that estate worth now?

To answer this question, we must recognize the basic fact that *a dollar now is worth more than a dollar later.* Why? Because one can always invest money that is available now and obtain interest on it. If the interest rate is 6 percent, a dollar received now is equivalent to $1.06 received a year hence. Why? Because if you invest the dollar now, you'll get $1.06 in a year. Similarly, a dollar received now is equivalent to $(1.06)^2$ dollars two years hence. Why? Because if you invest the dollar now, you'll get $1.06 in a year and, if you reinvest this amount for another year at 6 percent, you'll get $(1.06)^2$ dollars.

Consequently, if the interest rate is 6 percent, the estate is worth $100,000/(1.06)^2$ dollars now. Since $(1.06)^2 = 1.1236$, the estate is worth

$$\frac{\$100,000}{1.1236} = \$89,000.$$

In general, if the interest rate is $100 \times r$ percent per year, a dollar received now is worth $1/(1 + r)^2$ dollars two years from now. Thus, whatever the value of the interest rate may be, the estate is worth

$$\frac{\$100,000}{(1 + r)^2}.$$

The principle that a dollar now is worth more than a dollar later is of fundamental importance. If you don't understand it, you don't understand a basic precept of the world of finance. Although

TABLE 23.1

Present Value of a Future Dollar

NUMBER OF YEARS HENCE (THAT DOLLAR IS RECEIVED)	INTEREST RATE (PERCENT)			
	4	6	8	10
	(CENTS)			
1	96.2	94.3	92.6	90.9
2	92.5	89.0	85.7	82.6
3	89.0	83.9	79.4	75.1
4	85.5	79.2	73.5	68.3
5	82.3	74.7	68.1	62.0
10	67.6	55.8	46.3	38.5
15	55.5	41.7	31.5	23.9
20	45.6	31.1	21.5	14.8

Present value

the example considered in previous paragraphs pertains only to a two-year period, this principle remains valid no matter how long the period of time we consider. Table 23.1 shows the **present value** of a dollar received at various dates in the future. Its present value declines with the length of time before the dollar is received (so long as the interest rate remains constant).

RENT: NATURE AND SIGNIFICANCE

Land

Besides interest, another type of property income is rent. To understand rent, one must understand what economists mean by land. **Land** is defined by economists as *any input that is fixed in supply, its limits established by nature.* Since certain types of minerals and natural resources are in relatively fixed supply, they are included in the economists' definition of land. Suppose that the supply of an input is completely fixed. Increases in its price will not increase its supply, and decreases in its price will not decrease its supply. Following the terminology of the classical economists of the nineteenth century, *the price of such an input is* **rent**. Note that rent means something quite different to an economist than to the man in the street, who considers rent the price of using an apartment or a car or some other object owned by someone else.

Rent

If the supply of an input is fixed, its supply curve is a vertical line, as shown in Figure 23.4. Thus the price of this input, its rent, is determined entirely by the demand curve for the input. If the demand curve is D_0, the rent is P_0; if the demand curve is D_1, the rent is P_1. Since the supply of the input is fixed, the price of the input can be lowered without influencing the amount supplied.

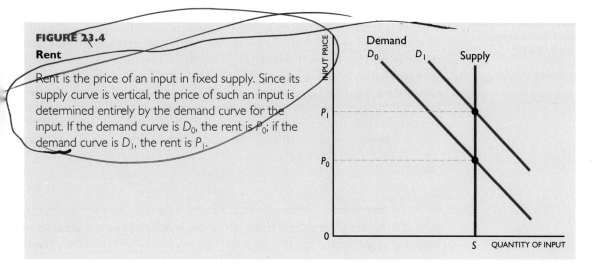

FIGURE 23.4

Rent

Rent is the price of an input in fixed supply. Since its supply curve is vertical, the price of such an input is determined entirely by the demand curve for the input. If the demand curve is D_0, the rent is P_0; if the demand curve is D_1, the rent is P_1.

Thus *a rent is a payment above the minimum necessary to attract this amount of the input.*[3]

Why is it important to know whether a certain payment for inputs is a rent? Because a reduction of the payment will not influence the availability and use of the inputs if the payment is a rent; if it is not a rent, a reduction of the payment is likely to change the allocation of resources. If the government imposes a tax on rents, there will be no effect on the supply of resources to the economy.

■ THE VIEWS OF HENRY GEORGE

In 1879, Henry George (1839–97) published a book, *Progress and Poverty,* in which he argued that rents should be taxed away by the government. In his view, owners of land were receiving substantial rents simply because their land happened to be well situated, not because they were doing anything productive. Since this rent was unearned income and since the supply of land would not be influenced by such a tax, George felt that it was justifiable to tax away such rent. Indeed, he argued that a tax of this sort should be the only tax imposed by the government.

Critics of George's views pointed out that land can be improved,

---

[3]In recent years, there has been a tendency among economists to extend the use of the word *rent* to encompass all payments to inputs above the minimum required to make these inputs available to the industry or to the economy. To a great extent these payments are costs to individual firms; the firms must make such payments to attract and keep these inputs, which are useful to other firms in the industry. But if the inputs have no use in other industries, these payments are not costs to the industry as a whole (or to the economy as a whole) because the inputs would be available to the industry whether or not these payments were made.

541

with the result that the supply is not completely price inelastic. Moreover, they argued that if land rents are unearned, so are many other kinds of income. In addition, they pointed out that it was unrealistic to expect such a tax to raise the needed revenue. George's single-tax movement gained a number of adherents in the last decades of the nineteenth century, and he even made an unsuccessful bid to become mayor of New York. Arguments in favor of a single tax continue to surface from time to time.

PROFIT

Profit

Besides interest and rent, another important type of property income is **profit**. The economist's concept of profit varies from the accountant's concept. According to accountants, profit is the amount of money the owner of a firm has left after paying wages, interest, and rent and after providing proper allowance for the depreciation of buildings and equipment. Economists reject this view; their position is that the opportunity costs of the labor, capital, and land contributed by the owner should also be deducted.

■ PROFIT STATISTICS

Available statistics concerning profits are based on the accountants' concept, not the economists'. Before taxes, corporation profits average about 5 to 10 percent of gross domestic product. Profits, expressed as a percentage of either net worth or sales, vary considerably from industry to industry and from firm to firm. (For example, the drug industry's profits in the postwar period have frequently been about 15 to 20 percent of net worth—considerably higher than in most other manufacturing industries.) Also, profits vary greatly from year to year and are much more erratic than wages. They fall more heavily in recessions and rise more rapidly in recoveries than wages do. Table 23.2 shows profit as a percentage of stockholders' equity in manufacturing in the United States in 1990 to 1999.

■ INNOVATION, UNCERTAINTY, AND MONOPOLY POWER

Why do profits, as economists define them, exist? Three important factors are innovation, uncertainty, and monopoly power. Suppose that an economy was composed of perfectly competitive industries, that entry was completely free, and that no changes in technology—no new processes, no new products, or other innovations—were permitted. Moreover, suppose that everyone could

TABLE 23.2

Annual Profit (after Taxes) as a Percentage of Stockholders' Equity, United States, 1990–99

YEAR	ALL MANUFACTURING CORPORATIONS	DURABLE GOODS INDUSTRIES	NONDURABLE GOODS INDUSTRIES
1990	10.6	7.9	13.1
1991	6.2	1.4	10.6
1992	2.1	−5.1	8.2
1993	8.0	5.7	10.0
1994	15.8	16.3	15.2
1995	16.0	15.4	16.6
1996	16.7	15.7	17.6
1997	16.7	16.3	17.1
1998	15.8	16.4	15.2
1999	17.1	17.3	16.7

Source: *Economic Report of the President*, 2000. The 1999 data is an average of the first three quarters.

predict the future with perfect accuracy. Under these conditions, there would be no profits or losses, because people would enter industries where profits exist, and thus reduce these profits eventually to zero, and would leave industries where losses exist, and thus reduce these negative profits eventually to zero. This sort of no-profit equilibrium has already been discussed in Chapter 18.

But in the real world, innovations of various kinds are made. For example, Du Pont introduces a new product like nylon, Henry Ford introduces the assembly line, or Marconi introduces the radio. The people who carry out these bold schemes are the **innovators**, those with vision and the daring to back it up. The innovators are not necessarily the inventors of new techniques or products, although in some cases the innovator and the inventor are the same. Often the innovator takes another's invention, adapts it, and introduces it to the market. According to economists like the late Joseph Schumpeter of Harvard, profits are the rewards earned by innovators. The profits derived from any single innovation eventually erode with competition and imitation, but other innovations replace them, with the result that profits from innovation continue to be made.

Innovators

In the real world, uncertainty also exists. Indeed, one of the real hazards in attempting to be an innovator is the **risk** involved. According to a theory set forth decades ago by the late Frank Knight of the University of Chicago, all economic profit is due to uncertainty. Profit is the reward for risk bearing. Assuming that people would like to avoid risk, they will prefer relatively stable, sure earnings to relatively unstable, uncertain earnings *if the average*

Risk

level of earnings is the same. Consequently, to induce people to take the risks involved in owning businesses in various industries, a profit—a premium for risk—must be paid to them.

Still another reason for the existence of profits is the fact that markets are not perfectly competitive. Under perfect competition, there will be a tendency in the long run for profits to disappear. But, as we have seen, this will not be the case if an industry is a monopoly or oligopoly. Instead, profits may well exist in the long run in such imperfectly competitive industries. Much of our economy is composed of imperfectly competitive industries. Monopoly profits are fundamentally the result of "contrived scarcities." Since a firm's demand curve is downward sloping if competition is imperfect, it pays the firm to take account of the fact that the more it produces, the smaller the price it will receive. That is, the firm realizes that it will spoil the market if it produces too much. Thus it pays firms to limit their output, and this contrived scarcity is responsible for the existence of the profits they make as a consequence.

THE FUNCTIONS OF PROFITS

To many people, profit seems to be "something for nothing." They do not recognize the innovative or risk-bearing functions of the owners of the firm, and consequently see no reason for the existence of profits. Other people, aware that profits arise because of imperfect competition, ignore the other functions of profit and regard it as entirely the ill-gotten gain of fat monopolists who smoke big cigars and sport a rapacious leer. But no group is more hostile to profits than the followers and disciples of Karl Marx. According to Marx, the difference between the amount the employers receive for their products and the amount they pay the laborers that produce them is "surplus value." And, according to Marx, this "surplus value," which includes what we would call profit, is a measure of, and a consequence of, the exploitation of labor by the owners of firms.

Marx's views and those of others who look on profits with suspicion and even distaste are rejected by most economists, who feel that profits play a legitimate and very important role in a capitalistic system. In such a system, consumers, suppliers of inputs, and firms try to advance their own interests. Workers try to maximize their earnings, capitalists look for the highest interest returns, landlords try to get the highest rents, and firm owners seek to maximize their profits. At first glance, this looks like a chaotic, dog-eat-dog situation, but, as we have seen, it actually turns out to be an orderly and efficient system—if competition is present.

The story of an Internet start-up

Homepage of Yahoo!, one of the most successful Internet-based companies

Over the past few years, there has been a remarkable boom in the creation of Internet-based companies. Some, including Amazon.com and e*Bay, have been spectacularly successful, turning their founders into billionaires (at least on paper) almost overnight. Many more have failed. However, it is the success stories that have encouraged others to assume the risks and to seek the rewards of starting up an Internet business.

To better understand this phenomenon, let's look at the story of a typical Internet start-up, as reported in the *Financial Times* on December 14, 1999.*

Until mid-1999, Pete Blackshaw, a 35-year-old Harvard M.B.A., was on the fast track at Procter and Gamble (P & G). He played a key role in Procter and Gamble's early efforts to develop a strategy for interactive marketing, and he represented the company in industrywide discussions on advertising and the Internet. In late 1999 Blackshaw left P & G and, along with a handful of friends and colleagues, founded a company called Planet Feedback.com. As Blackshaw described it, the new company offered an Internet-based service "aimed at transforming the way consumers relate to companies"—an electronic system that enabled cus-

tomers to channel complaints and comments on companies' products and services more effectively.

The technology of the Internet offers vast new opportunities for anyone with a good idea who is willing to bring it to market. The potential for a large payoff has encouraged many entrepreneurs, such as Pete Blackshaw, to give up lucrative careers to gamble on a future that, at least on the surface, looks quite risky.

However, the willingness of the Pete Blackshaws of this world to take risks is only half the story. New ventures need financing. One of the driving forces behind the Internet boom has been the willingness of venture capitalists to fund the start-up companies. From 1995 to 1999 venture capital investments rose from $6 billion to over $30 billion. According to Blackshaw, "The availability of venture capital is what compels us to leave large corporations and put our stake in the ground. A lot of smart money is looking for really good ideas out there." By the end of 1999, Blackshaw had been able to raise about $6 million in financing for the new company.

Time will tell whether Planet Feedback.com will succeed. However, without entrepreneurs, such as Blackshaw, who are willing to gamble their future and venture capitalists who are willing to finance them, the Internet boom would have fizzled out long ago.

*"Winning Ways: Ready Bucks and a Flair for Risk," *Financial Times,* December 14, 1999, p. 11.

■ PROFITS AND LOSSES: MAINSPRINGS OF A CAPITALISTIC SYSTEM

Profits and losses are principal movers of this system for several reasons.

1. *They are signals that indicate where resources are needed and where they are too abundant.* When there are economic profits in an industry, this is the signal for resources to flow into it; when economic losses exist in an industry, this is the signal for resources to leave it.

2. *Profits are very important incentives for innovation and for betting on the future.* For an entrepreneur like Joseph Wilson of Xerox, profits are the bait society dangles before him to get him to take the risks involved in marketing a new product, like xerography. If his judgment turns out to be faulty, losses—negative profits—are the penalties society imposes on him.

3. *Profits are society's reward for efficiency.* Firms that use inefficient techniques or produce an inappropriate amount or type of product are penalized by losses. Firms that are particularly alert, efficient, and adaptive receive profits. Further, profits enable firms to embark on new projects. Thus the profits that Xerox earned on xerography are currently being used to support its new ventures into other types of business machines.

The importance of profits in a free enterprise economy is clear enough. However, this does not mean that all profits are socially justified or that the system as a whole cannot be improved. Monopoly profits may not be socially justified, and a competitive system, despite its advantages, may produce some socially undesirable effects, such as an undesirable income distribution.

REVIEW AND PRACTICE

■ SUMMARY

1 Interest is a payment for the use of money. Interest rates vary a great deal, depending on the nature of the borrower and the type and riskiness of the loan. One very important function of interest rates is to allocate the supply of loanable funds.

2 The pure interest rate—the interest rate on riskless loans—is, like any price, determined by the interaction of supply and demand. However, because of the influence of the government on both the demand and supply sides of the market, it is clear that the pure interest rate is to a considerable extent a matter of public policy.

3 In a capitalist system, each asset has a market value that can be determined by capitalizing its earnings. Holding constant an asset's annual return, the asset's worth is higher, the lower the rate of return available on other investments.

4 Any asset has a rate of return, which indicates its net productivity. An asset's rate of return is the interest rate earned on the investment in the asset. If firms maximize profits, they must carry out all projects where the rate of return exceeds the interest rate at which they can borrow.*

5 Rent is the price obtained for inputs that are fixed in supply. Since the supply of the input is fixed, its price can be lowered without influencing the amount supplied. Thus, if the government imposes taxes on rents, there will be no effect on the supply of resources to the economy.

6 Another important type of property income is profit. Available statistics on profits are based on the accountants' concept, not the economists', with the result that they do not exclude the opportunity costs of the labor, capital, and land contributed by the owners of the firm. Profits play a very important and legitimate role in a free enterprise system.

7 Two of the important factors responsible for the existence of profits are innovation and uncertainty. Profits are the rewards earned by innovators and a payment for risk bearing. Still another reason for the existence of profits is monopoly power; because of contrived scarcity, profits are made by firms in imperfectly competitive markets.

■ PROBLEMS AND QUESTIONS

1 Suppose that the quantity of loanable funds demanded at each interest rate is as follows:

QUANTITY DEMANDED (BILLIONS OF DOLLARS)	INTEREST RATE (PERCENT)
50	4
40	6
30	8
20	10

Plot the demand curve for loanable funds on a graph. Describe the various kinds of borrowers that are on the demand side of the market for loanable funds.

Suppose that the quantity of loanable funds supplied at each interest rate is as follows:

QUANTITY SUPPLIED (BILLIONS OF DOLLARS)	INTEREST RATE (PERCENT)
20	4
25	6
30	8
35	10

Plot the supply curve for loanable funds on the same graph you used to plot the demand curve. What is the equilibrium rate of interest? If anti-usury laws do not permit interest rates to exceed 6 percent, what do you think will happen in this market?

2 Describe the social functions of the interest rate. Do you agree with Aristotle that it is improper to charge interest?

*In practice, firms often base their decisions on discounted cash flow rather than rates of return. The present discussion is necessarily simplified. For a more complete discussion, see Mansfield, *Microeconomics: Theory and Applications*, 10th ed.

3 Assume that you inherit $1,000, which will be paid to you in two years. If the interest rate is 8 percent, how much is this inheritance worth now? Why?

4 "The supply curve for iron ore is horizontal, so its price is a rent." Comment.

5 According to Table 23.2, profits in 1991 and 1992 were lower than in previous and subsequent years. Why? Also, profits during 1991–92 were lower in durable than nondurable goods industries. Why?

■ KEY TERMS

interest rate	land
demand curve for loanable funds	rent
rate of return	profit
supply curve for loanable funds	innovators
capitalization	risk
present value	

■ VIEWPOINT FOR ANALYSIS

John Smith, CEO of General Motors, said in a speech at Mackinac Island in 1993: "Like it or not, there is simply no affordable technology that would increase the fuel economy . . . to . . . 40 miles-per-gallon, which is what's now being advocated by some people in Washington, D.C. The customer's voice is the one we must listen to if we want to survive and thrive, and they are telling us—loud and clear—that they are not willing to pay the cost in terms of mass reduction, diminished performance, or price that would result from a 40 miles-per-gallon . . . standard."*

(a) Does the profit (or loss) of General Motors depend only on the customer's voice, or does it depend on the voice of the federal government as well? Explain.

(b) Profits and losses are the mainsprings of a capitalist economy. If it is unprofitable for the auto companies to increase fuel economy to 40 miles per gallon, should the government force them to do so? Why or why not?

(c) If it is unprofitable for General Motors to increase fuel economy to 40 miles per gallon, doesn't this mean that it is not economically worthwhile to achieve this increase? Why or why not?

*Vital Speeches, October 1, 1993, p. 763.

CHAPTER 24

Poverty, Income Inequality, and Discrimination

LEARNING OBJECTIVES

In this chapter, you should learn:

■ The extent of income inequality in the United States

■ How the tax structure affects the distribution of income in the United States

■ The nature of the Social Security program

■ The nature and limitations of the major antipoverty programs

■ The economic effects of discrimination

Political leaders, both Democrats and Republicans, have expressed concern over the nation's welfare programs. Before and after his election as president, Bill Clinton said that he wanted to change existing programs of the sort. For one thing, more emphasis would be put on training programs to help people get out of poverty. What causes poverty in a rich country like the United States, and what can be done about it? One purpose of this chapter is to examine this question.

HOW MUCH INEQUALITY OF INCOME?

Income inequality

We don't have to be very perceptive social observers to recognize that there is great **income inequality** in the United States. But our idea of what the distribution of income looks like depends on the sort of family and community we come from. A child brought up in Lake Forest, a wealthy suburb of Chicago, is unlikely to be as aware of the incidence of poverty as a child brought up on Chicago's poor South Side. For a preliminary glimpse of the extent of income inequality in the United States, scan Table 24.1, which shows the percentage of all households (which includes families and unrelated individuals living together) in the United States that were situated in various income classes in 1998. According to the table, the bottom fifth of the nation's households received an income of less than $16,116 in 1998. On the other hand, the top fifth of the nation's households received an income of $75,000 or more in 1998.

TABLE 24.1

Percentage Distribution of Households by Income, 1998

MONEY INCOME (DOLLARS)	PERCENTAGE OF ALL HOUSEHOLDS	PERCENTAGE OF TOTAL TOTAL INCOME RECEIVED
Under 16,116	20	4
16,116–30,408	20	9
30,408–48,337	20	15
48,337–75,000	20	23
75,000–132,199	15	28
132,199 and over	5	21
Total	100	100

Source: U.S. Census Bureau.

It may come as a surprise to some that so large a percentage of the nation's households made less than $16,116. The image of the affluent society projected in the Sunday supplements and on some television programs is strangely out of tune with these facts. Yet, to put these figures in world perspective, it should be recognized that Americans are very rich relative to other peoples. This fact is shown clearly by Table 24.2, which gives for various countries the level of income per person, which is the total income of each nation divided by its population. The United States is among the leaders in this table.

TABLE 24.2

Selected Countries Grouped by Approximate Level of Income per Capita[a]

I. Countries with income per capita exceeding $10,000

United States	France	Japan
Australia	Germany	Spain
Canada	Greece	Sweden
Denmark	Hong Kong	Switzerland

II. Countries with income per capita between $2,500 and $10,000

Brazil	Mexico	Turkey
Malaysia	Russia	Venezuela

III. Countries with income per capita less than $2,500

El Salvador	India	Iran
Haiti	Indonesia	Thailand

[a]All figures in 1999 dollars.
Source: Standard & Poor's DRI, *The World Outlook,* First Quarter, 2000.

Kevin Brown is one of the highest-paid baseball players.

WHY INEQUALITY?

Nonetheless, recognizing that our poor are better off than the bulk of the population in many other countries, the fact remains that there is substantial *income inequality* in this country. Why is this the case? On the basis of our discussion of labor and property incomes in previous chapters, this question is not hard to answer. One reason is that some people possess greater abilities than others. Since Kevin Brown and Mo Vaughn have extraordinary skill as baseball players, it is easy to understand why they make a lot of money. Another reason is differences in the amount of education and training people receive. Thus physicians or lawyers must receive a higher income than people in occupations requiring little or no training. (Otherwise it would not pay for people to undergo medical or legal training.) Still another reason is that some people own large amounts of property. Thus, because of a shrewd choice of ancestry, current members of the Ford, Rockefeller, and Mellon families get high incomes from inherited wealth. Still other reasons are that some people have managed to obtain monopoly power, and others have had an extraordinary string of good luck.

EFFECT OF THE TAX STRUCTURE ON INCOME INEQUALITY

So far we have looked at the distribution of before-tax income. But we must also consider the effect of the tax system on income inequality.

Progressive tax
Regressive tax

A tax is **progressive** if the rich pay a higher proportion of their income for the tax than do the poor. A tax is **regressive** if the rich pay a smaller proportion of their income for the tax than do the poor.

Needless to say, people who feel that the tax system should promote a redistribution of income from rich to poor favor progressive, not regressive, taxes. Besides the personal income tax, other progressive taxes are inheritance or estate taxes. (The federal government levies a gift tax to prevent wealthy people from circumventing the estate tax by giving their money away before death.) State governments also levy inheritance taxes (on persons who inherit money) and estate taxes (on the deceased's estate). All this is applauded by reformers who oppose accumulation and preservation of inherited wealth. But, as in the case of the personal income tax, the portion of an estate subject to taxes can be reduced through clever use of various loopholes, all quite legal. Thus the estate tax is not as progressive as it looks.

Not all taxes are progressive; examples of regressive taxes are not hard to find. General sales taxes of the sort used by most states and some cities are regressive, since high-income people pay a smaller percentage of their income in sales taxes than do low-income people. The Social Security and payroll tax is also regressive. It is difficult to tell whether the corporation income tax is progressive or regressive. At first glance, it seems progressive because the owners of corporations—the stockholders—tend to be wealthy people, and to the extent that the corporate income tax is paid from earnings that might otherwise be paid to the stockholders, one might conclude that it is progressive. But this ignores the possibility that the corporation may pass the tax on to the consumer by charging a higher price; in this case the tax may not be progressive.

INCOME INEQUALITY: THE PROS AND CONS

■ THE CASE AGAINST INCOME INEQUALITY

Many distinguished social philosophers have debated the merits and demerits of making the income distribution more equal. We cannot consider all the subtler points, but those who favor greater equality make four main arguments.

1. *They say that inequality of income lessens total consumer satisfaction, because an extra dollar given to a poor person provides him or her with more extra satisfaction than the loss of a dollar takes away from a rich person.* According to the British economist A. C. Pigou, "It is evident that any transference of income from a relatively rich man to a relatively poor man of similar temperament, since it en-

ables more intense wants to be satisfied at the expense of less intense wants, must increase the aggregate sum of satisfactions." A problem in this very appealing argument is its assumption that the rich man and the poor man have the same capacities to gain enjoyment from income. Most economists believe that there is no scientific way to make such comparisons. They deny that the satisfaction one person derives from an extra dollar of income can be measured against the satisfaction another person derives from an extra dollar. Although such comparisons may be drawn, they rest on ethical, not scientific, grounds.

2. *It is argued that income inequality is likely to result in unequal opportunities for young people to gain advanced education and training.* The children of the rich can get an education, while the children of the poor often cannot. The result is that some able and productive people may be denied an education simply because their parents are poor. This is a waste of resources.

3. *It is argued that income inequality is likely to lead to political inequality.* The rich may well influence legislation and political decisions more strongly than the poor, and there is likely to be one kind of justice for the rich and another kind for the poor.

4. The arguments for income equality have been carried a step forward by John Rawls, the Harvard philosopher. He says that, *if people were framing a constitution for society without knowing what their class position would be, they would opt for equality.* And he argues that "all social values . . . are to be distributed equally unless an unequal distribution . . . is to everyone's advantage"; that is, unless an unequal distribution is to the advantage of society's least-privileged group. Although Rawls's book, *A Theory of Justice*, has had considerable impact, many economists have pointed out that his prescription for society might not appeal to people who were willing to take risks. Suppose that you could establish a society that guaranteed every family $30,000 a year (no more, no less) or one where 99 percent of all families would receive $40,000 and 1 percent would receive $24,000. You might choose the latter kind of society because, although there is a small chance that you would do worse than in the egalitarian case, the chance of doing better seems worth this risk.

■ THE CASE FOR INCOME INEQUALITY

In general, people who favor income inequality make five arguments.

1. *They argue that income inequality is needed to give people an incentive to work and create.* After all, if everyone receives the same income, why bother to increase your production, to try to invent a new process, or to work overtime? Whatever you do, your income

will be the same. This is an important point, though it overlooks the fact that nonmonetary incentives like pride in a job well done can be as important as monetary incentives.

2. *Advocates of income inequality claim that it permits greater savings, and thus greater capital formation.* Although this seems reasonable, it is not hard to cite cases where countries with greater inequality of income invest less, not more, than countries with less inequality of income. Thus some Middle Eastern countries with great income inequality have not had relatively high investment rates.

3. *Advocates of income inequality say that the rich have been important patrons of new and high-quality products that benefit the entire society.* They argue that there are social advantages in having certain people with the wherewithal to pioneer in consumption and to support art and culture. In their view, a completely egalitarian society would be rather dull.

4. *Advocates of income inequality point out that, even if everyone received the same income, the poor would not be helped a great deal, because the wealthy are relatively few.* If the riches of the rich were transferred to the poor, each poor person would get only a little, because there are so many poor and so few rich.

5. According to Harvard's Robert Nozick and others, *one must look at the justice of the process leading to the distribution of income and wealth in order to determine whether a certain degree of income inequality is unfair.* For example, suppose that an entertainer carries out a series of shows that are very successful and that the entertainer makes a lot of money. The process by which the entertainer makes this money is entirely legitimate. (People voluntarily pay for the tickets to the shows—and enjoy every minute of them!) According to this view, the resulting inequality of income is not unfair.

THE TRADE-OFF BETWEEN EQUALITY AND EFFICIENCY

In trying to decide how much income inequality you favor, it is important to recognize that measures taken to reduce inequality are likely to decrease economic efficiency. In other words, *if we reduce inequality, we may well cut society's total output.* Why? Because, as pointed out in the previous section, people are likely to have less incentive to produce if their incomes are much the same regardless of how much they produce. This does not mean that all measures designed to reduce income inequality are bad. What it does mean is that if you want to reduce income inequality, you should be sensitive to the effects on output. In particular, you should try to find policies that will attain a given reduction in inequality at a minimum cost in terms of reduced output.

In view of the strong feelings of many advocates and opponents of reduced income inequality, it is not surprising that they sometimes make extreme statements about the nature of the trade-off between equality and efficiency. Some egalitarians deny that there is any trade-off at all. They claim that inequality can be reduced without any cut in output. Some opponents of reductions in income inequality assert that there will be a catastrophic fall in output if the existing income distribution is tampered with. Although far too little is known about the quantitative character of this trade-off, there seems to be general agreement among economists that the truth lies somewhere between these two extremes.

People vary considerably in their evaluation of how much society should pay (in terms of decreased total output) for a particular reduction in income inequality. The late Arthur Okun of the Brookings Institution suggested that to characterize your own feelings on this score, it is useful to view money as a liquid and to visualize a bucket that carries money from the rich to the poor. The bucket is leaky, so only part of what is taken from the rich can be given to the poor. If the leak is very small, a dollar taken from the rich may result in 99 cents going to the poor. Many people would accept a loss of this magnitude. If the leak is very large, a dollar taken from the rich may result in only 5 cents going to the poor. Few people would accept this big a loss. How big a loss would you accept? The larger the leak that you would find acceptable, the more willing you are to accept output losses in order to attain decreases in income inequality.

The argument between the advocates and opponents of reduced income inequality involves much more than economics. Whether you favor greater or less income inequality depends on your ethical and political beliefs. It is not a matter economics alone can settle. What economists can do is assess the degree of income inequality in a country and suggest ways to alter the gap between the haves and have-nots in accord with the dictates of the people or their leaders. In recent decades, economists in and out of government have devoted much effort to designing programs aimed at reducing poverty. To understand these programs, we must discuss what poverty is and who the poor are.

WHAT IS POVERTY?

Some people are fond of saying that everything is relative. Certainly this is true of poverty. Moreover, poverty is certainly subjective. Consider the average young executive making $80,000 a year. After a bad day at the office or a particularly expensive family shopping spree, the executive is likely to claim, to anyone who will listen, to be as poor as a church mouse.

There is no well-defined income level that can be used in all times and places as a touchstone to define poverty. Poverty is partly a matter of how one person's income stacks up against that of others. What most people in the United States today regard as stark poverty would have seemed like luxury to many Americans of 200 years ago—and would seem like luxury in parts of Asia and Africa today. Consequently, one must be careful not to define poverty in such a way that it cannot be eliminated, and then try to eliminate it. If poverty is defined as being in the bottom 10 percent of the income distribution, how can a war against poverty ever be won? Regardless of what measures are taken, there will always be a bottom 10 percent of the income distribution, unless all income inequality is eliminated (which is highly unlikely).

Poverty

Perhaps the most widely accepted definition of **poverty** in the United States today is the one developed by the Social Security Administration, which began by determining the cost of a *minimal nutritionally sound food plan* (given by the Department of Agriculture). Then, since low-income families spend about one-third of their incomes on food, this food cost was multiplied by 3 to obtain an income level that was used as a criterion for poverty. Families with less income were regarded as "living below the poverty level."

On the basis of such computations, a family of four needed an income of about $17,000 to make it barely over the Social Security Administration's poverty line in 1999. (Since farm families typically have lower food costs, the estimates for them are somewhat lower.) Although one could quarrel with this figure on various counts, most people probably would agree that families with income below this level are poor.[1]

■ LONG-TERM DECLINE IN THE INCIDENCE OF POVERTY

According to estimates made by the federal government, about 13 percent of the total population (or about 24 percent of households) in the United States was below the Social Security Administration's poverty line in 1999. In absolute terms, this means that around 35 million people were poor enough to fall below the criterion described above.

Fortunately, the incidence of poverty (measured by this criterion) generally has been declining in the United States. In 1947 about 30 percent, in 1960 about 20 percent, and in 1992 about 14 percent of the people were poor by this definition. This is what we would expect. As the average level of income rises, the proportion

---

[1]The basic figures come from the Department of Commerce's *Current Population Reports*, which explain in detail the way in which these figures are derived. The method described in the text is crude, but it provides results that are quite close to those of more complicated methods. Since 1969, the poverty line has been calculated on the basis of the Consumer Price Index, not the price of food.

of the population falling below the poverty line (which is defined by a relatively fixed dollar amount of income) will tend to decrease. Nonetheless, the fact that poverty is being eliminated in the United States does not mean that this process is going on as fast as it should. Many observers feel, as we shall see in subsequent sections, that poverty could and should be eradicated more rapidly.

■ CHARACTERISTICS OF THE POOR

Naturally, the poor are not confined to any particular demographic group, but some types of families are much more likely than others to be below the poverty line. In particular, *African Americans are much more likely to be poor than whites.* In 1995, 29 percent of African Americans were poor, whereas 11 percent of whites were poor. Also, *families headed by females are much more likely to be poor than families headed by males.* In addition, very large families (seven persons and over) are much more likely to be poor than others.

■ REASONS FOR POVERTY

To a considerable extent, the reasons why families are poor lie beyond the control of the families themselves. About one-third of poor adults have suffered a disability of some sort, the premature death of the family breadwinner, or family dissolution. Some have had to face a smaller demand for their occupation (because of technological or other change) or the decline of their industry or geographical area. Some have simply lived "too long": their savings have given out before their minds and bodies have. Another instrumental factor in making some families poor is discrimination of various kinds. The most obvious type is racial, but others exist as well: discrimination based on sex, religion, age, residence, education, and seniority. In addition, some people are poor because they have very limited ability or little or no motivation. These factors should not be overlooked.

There are important barriers which tend to separate the poor from the rest of society. As the University of Wisconsin's Robert Lampman pointed out:

> Barriers, once established, tend to be reinforced from the poverty side by the alienated themselves. The poor tend to be cut off from not only opportunity but even from information about opportunity. A poverty subculture develops which sustains attitudes and values that are hostile to escape from poverty. These barriers combine to make events nonrandom; e.g., unemployment is slanted away from those inside the feudalistic walls of collective bargaining, disability more commonly occurs in jobs reserved for those outside the barriers, the

subculture of poverty invites or is prone to self-realizing forecasts of disaster.

Judging from the available evidence, poverty often is self-perpetuating. Some families tend to be poor year after year, and their children tend to be poor. Because the families are poor, the children are poorly educated, poorly fed, and poorly cared for, and poverty is transmitted from one generation to the next. It is a vicious cycle.

SOCIAL INSURANCE

OLD-AGE INSURANCE

Social security

Until about seventy years ago, the federal government played little or no role in helping the poor. Private charity was available in limited amounts and state and local governments provided some help, but the general attitude was "sink or swim." Self-reliance and self-support were the watchwords. The Great Depression of the 1930s, which changed so many attitudes, also made a marked change in this area. In 1935, with the passage of the **Social Security Act**, the federal government established a social insurance system providing compulsory old-age insurance for both workers and self-employed people, as well as unemployment insurance. By 1998, about 44 million Americans were receiving about $31 billion per month in benefits from the resulting system of old-age and survivors' insurance.

Old-age insurance

Every wage earner covered under the Social Security Act pays a tax; the employer also pays a tax, which is equal to that paid by the employee. The amount that one can expect to receive each month in **old-age insurance** benefits depends on one's average monthly earnings. Also, the size of the benefits depends on the number of years one has worked. If you retire at 65, the monthly benefits are greater than if you retire at 62. These benefits are a retirement annuity. In other words, they are paid to the wage earner from the date of retirement to the time he or she dies. In addition, when a wage earner dies, Social Security provides payments to his or her spouse, to dependent parents, and to children until they are about 18 years of age (21 if they are in school). Further, payments are made to a wage earner (and dependents) if he or she is totally disabled and unable to work.

CONTROVERSIES OVER SOCIAL SECURITY

There are a number of controversial aspects of the Social Security program.

1. *The Social Security tax is regressive,* since those with very high annual earnings pay a smaller proportion of their income in Social Security taxes than do those with low annual earnings. For this and other reasons, many observers believe that the system is not as generous to the poor as it should be.

2. *Some people are disturbed that the Social Security system is not really an ordinary insurance system at all.* An ordinary insurance program must have assets that are sufficient to finance all the benefits promised to the people in the program. This is not the case for Social Security. But this does not mean that you won't receive your Social Security. What it does mean is that the Social Security system is a means of transferring income each year from the working young and middle-aged to the retired old people. It will be up to future Congresses to determine what these benefits will be. Only time will tell how much you will receive.

3. *Some people are disturbed that Social Security is mandatory.* Milton Friedman is concerned that the government interferes with an individual's freedom to plan for the future by forcing him or her to be a member of the Social Security system. (Workers might be able to obtain larger pensions by investing the money that they contribute to Social Security in investments of their own choosing.) Other observers retort that without a mandatory system, some workers would make inadequate provision for their old age and might become public charges.

4. *Some people are concerned that Social Security is an impediment to saving and capital formation.* Martin Feldstein, Harvard professor and former chairperson of President Reagan's Council of Economic Advisers, feels that Americans save relatively little because they depend on Social Security to take care of their old age. This, he believes, tends to depress capital formation in the United States, since savings can be used to build factories, expand old plants, and add in various ways to the nation's stock of capital. He favors a slowdown in the rate of growth of Social Security and more reliance on private pensions and personal savings.

▪ MEDICARE, UNEMPLOYMENT INSURANCE, AND OTHER PROGRAMS

Medicare

In 1965, Congress extended the Social Security program to include **Medicare**, a compulsory hospitalization insurance plan plus a voluntary insurance plan covering doctors' fees for people over 65. The hospitalization insurance pays for practically all the hospital costs of the first 90 days of each spell of illness, as well as some additional costs. The plan covers about 80 percent of doctors' fees after the first $100. This program is also an important factor in preventing and alleviating poverty. The incidence of illness is relatively high among the elderly; with the rapid rise in medical costs, it has become more difficult for them to afford decent care.

559

Job training programs and the war on poverty

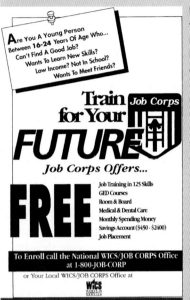

A Job Corps recruiting poster

The Affluent Society, the best-selling book by President Kennedy's friend, the economist John Kenneth Gal-braith, focused the president's attention on one of the United States's most serious problems: poverty. Galbraith pointed out that, although everybody recognized the need for investment in factories and equipment, society was neglecting the need for investment in people, in education and training. The concept of structural unemployment was discussed widely during the Kennedy administration. (Recall from Chapter 4 that structural unemployment occurs when new goods and new technologies call for new skills, and workers with old skills cannot find jobs.) Although the tax cut of 1964—as well as other federal measures that helped to lower unemployment to 3.8 percent in 1966—weakened some of the arguments regarding the importance of structural unemployment, plans were made for job training programs. These programs would be unlike those of the 1930s, when unemployment reflected a cyclical downturn rather than the poor job skills of the participants, and unlike Social Security and other programs designed to reduce the symptoms of poverty, these would be designed to reduce its causes.

President Johnson picked up the war on poverty that Kennedy had begun. Defense Secretary McNamara had observed high illiteracy rates among low-income military recruits and draftees and advocated training through the military as the answer. In 1967, the McNamara idea was developed into a program called the Job Corps, which was the key training program in the War on Poverty bill. Under the program, teenagers, mostly high school dropouts, would receive education and vocational training at Job Corps camps around the country. The effectiveness of the Job Corps proved controversial, although its supporters could point to many success stories. Twenty years later, conservatives in particular argued that the Job Corps' results were not worth the cost.

Besides instituting old-age, survivors', and medical insurance, the Social Security Act also encouraged the states to set up systems of **unemployment insurance**. Such systems now exist in all states and are financed by taxes on employers. Once an insured worker is unemployed, he or she can obtain benefits after a short waiting period, generally a week. In 1994, the average weekly benefit was about $180. In most states, there is a 26-week ceiling on the duration of benefits. Clearly, unemployment insurance is another important device to keep people from falling below the poverty line.

ANTIPOVERTY PROGRAMS

According to the eighteenth-century English poet and essayist Samuel Johnson, "A decent provision for the poor is the true test of civilization." There is general agreement that our social insurance programs, although useful in preventing and alleviating poverty, are not an adequate or complete antipoverty program. For one thing, they focus largely on the elderly, which means that they do not aid many poor people. They do not help the working poor; and even for the unemployed, they provide only limited help for a limited period of time.

Consequently, the government has started a number of additional programs specifically designed to help the poor, although many of them are aimed more at the symptoms of poverty than at its basic causes. There are programs that provide goods and services to the poor. The biggest of these programs is **Medicaid**, which pays for the health care of the poor. The *food programs*, which have distributed food to needy families, are also of major significance in this regard. The federal government has given stamps that can be used to buy food to local agencies, which have sold them (at less than the equivalent of market prices) or have given them to low-income families.

Medicaid

In 1996, a major change was enacted in the nation's welfare programs, which have provided the poor with cash payments. The most important single program of cash payments was the Aid to Families with Dependent Children. (In 1990, this program paid out more than $20 billion.) In 1996, this program was replaced by a system of block grants and much greater authority for the states. The states have considerable latitude in how they use their grants. Also, work requirements are established for most people seeking welfare or other benefits. States that do not meet these requirements may lose some of their federal grants.

■ THE NEGATIVE INCOME TAX

There has been widespread dissatisfaction with antipoverty—or welfare—programs. One suggestion that has received serious consideration is the negative income tax, an idea proposed by two Nobel laureates: Stanford University's Milton Friedman (an adviser to presidential candidate Barry Goldwater in 1964 and to President Nixon) and Yale's James Tobin (an adviser to President Kennedy).

Negative income tax

A **negative income tax** would work as follows. Just as families with reasonably high incomes *pay* taxes, families with low incomes would *receive* a payment. In other words, the poor would pay a *negative* income tax. Figure 24.1 illustrates how a negative income

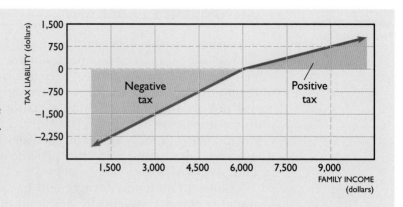

FIGURE 24.1

Example of Negative Income Tax

A family with more than $6,000 in income pays taxes. Thus a family with an income of $9,000 pays $750 in taxes. A family with an income less than $6,000 receives a payment. Thus a family with an income of $1,500 is paid $2,250.

tax might work; it shows the amount a family of four would pay, or receive, in taxes for incomes at various levels. According to Figure 24.1, $6,000 is the **break-even income**: the income at which a family of four neither pays nor receives income taxes. Above $6,000, a family pays taxes. Thus a family with an income of $9,000 pays $750 in taxes. Below $6,000 a family receives a payment. Thus a family with an income of $1,500 is paid $2,250.

However, many citizens remain skeptical about the negative income tax. For one thing, they are antagonistic to the idea of giving people an income without requiring any work in return. They also are unwilling to transfer large amounts from rich to poor. This amount would depend on how high the break-even income was set and on the negative tax rates. In the late 1960s, it was estimated that a negative income tax would have meant that those above the break-even income level would transfer about $25 billion to those below the break-even level. Despite the attractive features of a negative income tax, a transfer of this magnitude has proved unacceptable in many quarters.

Also, some economists regard the results of the experiments with a negative income tax in Seattle and Denver to have been disappointing. These experiments, carried out with a sample of households, seem to indicate that under a (generous) negative income tax people work significantly less, apparently because they are more willing to quit work and less willing to search hard for a new job.

THE PROBLEM OF DISCRIMINATION

■ RACIAL DISCRIMINATION

Discrimination

Poverty, **discrimination**, and race are closely intertwined. Despite recent improvements, the sad fact is that racial discrimina-

Is welfare reform working?

President Clinton signs the 1996 welfare reform bill.

In August 1996, the U.S. Congress passed a landmark welfare reform bill the goals of which were to end sixty years of federally guaranteed payments to low-income families and to encourage welfare recipients to enter the workforce. Specifically, the Aid to Families with Dependent Children (AFDC) program was replaced with the Temporary Assistance for Needy Families. The AFDC was launched, in the 1930s, primarily to help widows. However, with the increase in divorce rates and teen pregnancies, the program became a benefit for single mothers. Well before the passage of the welfare reform bill, there was growing concern that the AFDC program had created a large disincentive to work and had produced a large "permanent welfare underclass."

The Temporary Assistance for Needy Families offers payments in return for work. In the context of this program, work is defined quite flexibly to include everything from remedial classes to training to subsidized jobs in the private sector to workfare-style community jobs, paid for by state and local governments. The new welfare law also forces welfare recipients to find a job within two years and mandates that no one receives welfare payments for more than five years cumulatively over a lifetime. Welfare reform has also given state and local governments much more discretion over how to create new job opportunities for former welfare recipients and how to train these new entrants into the labor force.

Has welfare reform worked? Based on the huge drop in welfare rolls, the answer is a resounding yes. After hitting a peak of 14 million in 1993, welfare rolls were down 50 percent by the end of 1999. More than 80 percent of this drop occurred after the passage of the welfare reform bill in 1996. Also the share of unwed mothers who are employed rose from less than 50 percent in the mid-1990s to over 60 percent by the end of the 1990s.

However, it would be premature to conclude that the entire decline in welfare rolls was due to welfare reform. Strong economic growth in the late 1990s and the fall in the unemployment rate to a thirty-year low were major contributing factors. There is little doubt that the reforms passed in 1996 provided a strong incentive for former welfare recipients to participate in the economic boom. Unfortunately, the true test of welfare reform will only come during the next economic downturn when the unemployment rate rises and many families at the low end of the income scale fall on hard times again.

TABLE 24.3

Economic Characteristics of Whites and African Americans, United States 1998

	WHITE	AFRICAN AMERICAN
Median family income (dollars)	49,023	29,404
Percent of persons in poverty	8.0	23.4
Percent unemployed (males)	3.9	8.9
Percent unemployed (females)	3.9	9.0
Percent unemployed (male teenagers)	14.1	30.1

Source: Economic Report of the President, 2000.

tion occurs in many walks of life in many areas of the United States. Table 24.3 shows certain aspects of the relative position of the white and African American populations in the United States. The average income of African Americans is less than two-thirds that of whites. Over one-quarter of the African American population is below the poverty line, compared to only about one-ninth of the white population. The unemployment rate is much higher among African Americans than whites. Also, on the average, whites complete more years of schooling than African Americans, and a larger percentage of whites than of African Americans are college graduates.

There is considerable agreement that at least part of these economic differences is the result of discrimination. Nonwhites are often prevented from reaching certain occupational or managerial levels. For example, it is rare to find an African American in the higher reaches of management in many corporations. To a considerable extent they are cut off from job opportunities at higher levels by lack of education. But even at much lower levels, they are kept out of certain occupations by union policy (the building trades are a good example), and even when they do essentially the same kind of work as whites, there is sometimes a tendency to pay them less.

■ EFFECTS OF DISCRIMINATION

Some important effects of racial discrimination can be demonstrated by using the theory of wages. (The general point of this discussion holds true whether discrimination is on racial or other grounds.) The important thing to recognize at the outset is that nonwhite labor is not allowed to compete with white labor. This results in two different labor markets, one for whites and one for nonwhites. As shown in Figure 24.2, the demand curve for nonwhite labor is quite different from the demand curve for white labor; this reflects the fact that nonwhites are not allowed to enter many of the more productive occupations. Because of the difference in the demand (and supply) curves, the equilibrium wage for nonwhites P_N, is lower than for whites P_W.

How does this equilibrium differ from a situation of no discrimination? If nonwhites and whites competed in the same labor market, the total demand for labor—regardless of color—and the total supply of labor—regardless of color—would be as shown in panel B of Figure 24.2; the wage for all labor—regardless of color— would be P_T. A comparison of P_T with P_N shows that the wage rate of nonwhites would increase considerably. A comparison of P_T with P_W shows that the wage rates of whites would decrease slightly. The slight cut in white wages would be much smaller than the considerable increase in nonwhite wages, since the nation's total production (and income) would increase because nonwhites could be put to more productive use.

Thus the effect of discrimination is to exploit nonwhites, by reducing their wages relative to whites, and to lower the nation's total output. Fortunately, there is evidence that racial discrimination is lessening. In part because of changing attitudes among whites, the growing restiveness of nonwhites, and the coming of age of new leadership, the old patterns of segregation and discrimination are breaking down. For example, African Americans are now being recruited actively by many prestigious colleges, and they are being hired and promoted to responsible positions in firms where formerly they remained at a relatively menial level. Progress is slow, but it unquestionably exists.

FIGURE 24.2

Racial Discrimination

Under discrimination, the demand curve for white labor is quite different from that for nonwhite labor, and the supply curve of white labor is quite different from that of nonwhite labor, so that the equilibrium wage for nonwhites P_N is lower than for whites P_W. If there were no discrimination, the wage for all labor, nonwhite or white, would be P_T.

A. The case of discrimination

B. No discrimination

■ DISCRIMINATION AGAINST WOMEN

Needless to say, discrimination is not limited to nonwhites—African Americans, Hispanics, Asians, and Native Americans. There is some discrimination against older workers. Even more widespread is discrimination against women. Holding age and education constant, women earn much less than men. To some extent, this difference in earnings arises because women work shorter hours and often have less experience in their jobs than men. But even after adjusting for factors such as education, work experience during the year, and lifetime work experience, there remains a substantial differential between the earnings of men and women. To a considerable extent, this differential is probably the result of discrimination, the nature of which has been described by the Council of Economic Advisers:

> There is clearly prejudice against women engaging in particular activities. Some patients reject women doctors, some clients reject women lawyers, some customers reject automobile saleswomen, and some workers reject women bosses. Employers also may have formulated discriminatory attitudes about women, exaggerating the risk of job instability or client acceptance and therefore excluding women from on-the-job training which would advance their careers. In fact, even if employers do estimate correctly the average job turnover of women, women who are strongly committed to their jobs may suffer from "statistical discrimination" by being treated as though their own behavior resembled the average. The extent to which this type of discrimination occurs depends on how costly it is for employers to distinguish women who will have a strong job commitment from those who will not. Finally, because some occupations restrict the number of newcomers they take in and because women move in and out of the labor force more often, more women than men tend to fall into the newcomer category and to be thus excluded. For example, restrictive entry policies may have kept women out of the skilled crafts.
>
> On the other hand, some component of the earnings differential and of the occupation differential stems from differences in role orientation which start with differences in education and continue through marriage, where women generally are expected to assume primary responsibility for the home and subordinate their own outside work to their household responsibilities. It is not now possible to distinguish in a quantitative way between the discrimination which bars women from jobs solely because of their sex, and the role differentiation whereby women, either through choice or necessity, restrict their careers because of the demands of their homes. Some may label the latter as a pervasive social discrimination which starts in the cradle; nonetheless, it is useful to draw the distinction.

In various ways, the government has set out to discourage discrimination against women. The Equal Pay Act of 1963 requires employers to pay men and women equally for the same work, and

Equal pay for work of "comparable worth"

Women's earnings tend to be considerably lower than men's. A striking fact about female employment is that although women can be found in virtually all occupations, they predominate overwhelmingly in a few like nursing and secretarial work. In 1986, women constituted 94 percent of registered nurses, 98 percent of secretaries, and 85 percent of servers in the United States.

Some believe that these jobs are underpaid because they tend to be filled by women, and to eliminate what they regard as a major inequity, they argue for "equal pay for work of comparable worth." The idea is to

compare the worth of one occupation with that of another occupation and to press for equal wage rates for them if they are judged to be of equal worth. Thus, if a nurse does work that is of equal worth to that of an accountant, nurses should get the same wage as accountants.

To measure the worth of an occupation, many proponents of "comparable worth" propose the use of a job evaluation point system. In 1983, a federal court found the state of Washington guilty of discrimination because it paid male-dominated occupations more than "comparable" female-dominated occupations. To determine what occupations were comparable, every state job was evaluated in terms of "accountability," "knowledge and skills," "mental demands," and "working conditions." A committee decided how many points to give each occupation on each of these criteria, and two occupations were regarded of comparable worth if they got the same total number of points.

An enormous amount of controversy has engulfed this decision, which said that Washington should

raise women's wages and grant restitution for past injuries to them. Although higher courts reversed this decision, many politicians have supported the idea that an occupation's wage rate should be determined in this way by "comparable worth." In 1989, a law was enacted in Ontario, Canada, that says that employers must assess jobs in which at least 60 percent of the employees are women and use such a job evaluation system to see how much women should be paid.

Many economists are opposed to the use of such job evaluation systems to set wage rates. In their view, the proper determinants of wage rates are the supply and demand curves discussed in Chapter 22, which together set wage rates in competitive markets. To ignore these supply and demand curves is to run the risk that some occupations will have shortages while others will have too many people. Certainly, job evaluation systems of this sort may reduce economic efficiency. However, proponents of these job evaluation systems emphasize equity, not efficiency; in their view, these systems will promote equity.

Title VII of the Civil Rights Act of 1964 bars discrimination in hiring, firing, and other aspects of employment. In addition, a number of women have been appointed to high-ranking government jobs, including economists Juanita Kreps (who has been secretary of commerce), Marina Whitman (who has served as a member of the President's Council of Economic Advisers), Alice Rivlin (a former member of the Federal Reserve Board), Nancy Teeters (a former member of the Federal Reserve Board), and Janet Yeller (a former chair of the President's Council of Economic Advisers). All these measures undoubtedly will have a beneficial effect, but it

567

must be recognized that eliminating discrimination of this kind will require basic changes in the attitudes of both males and females. The problem of discrimination against women is likely to be with us for a long time.

REVIEW AND PRACTICE

■ SUMMARY

1 Many factors are responsible for existing income differentials. Some people are abler, better educated, or luckier than others. Some people have more property or more monopoly power than others.

2 Critics of income inequality argue that it lessens total consumer satisfaction because an extra dollar given to the poor provides them with more extra satisfaction than the loss of a dollar takes away from the rich. Also, they argue that income inequality leads to social and political inequality.

3 Defenders of income inequality point out that it is scientifically impossible to make interpersonal comparisons of utility and argue that income inequality is needed to provide incentives for people to work and create and that it permits greater capital formation.

4 There is no well-defined income level that can be used in all times and all places to determine poverty. Perhaps the most widely accepted definition of poverty in the United States today is the one developed by the Social Security Administration.

5 To a considerable extent, the reasons for their poverty lie beyond the control of the poor people. Some poor adults have suffered a disability of some sort, the premature death of the family breadwinner, or family dissolution. Most heads of poor families do not have jobs.

6 The government aids the poor by providing them with goods and services—food-stamp programs, for instance. Other programs, like Aid to Families with Dependent Children, have given them cash. When these programs are taken into account, the percentage of the population falling below the poverty line has been reduced considerably.

7 There is widespread dissatisfaction with existing antipoverty—or welfare—programs. They are judged to be inefficient, their costs have increased at an alarming rate, and they have provided little incentive for people to get off welfare. In 1996, a major change was made in the nation's welfare programs.

8 Despite recent improvements, the sad fact is that racial discrimination occurs in many walks of life in many areas of the United States. Nonwhites may be cut off from educational and job opportunities, and even when nonwhites do essentially the same kind of work as whites, there is sometimes a tendency to pay them less.

9 There is also much discrimination against women, which makes them less likely than men to enter better-paying occupations. Even after adjusting for factors such as education and work experience, women earn substantially less than men.

■ PROBLEMS AND QUESTIONS

1 In 1987, there seemed to be bipartisan agreement that Aid to Families with Dependent Children should be transformed into a vehicle for education, training, and work. In what sense is work the solution to dependency? Can training and job placement enable long-term welfare recipients to break out of poverty and dependency?

2 "The Social Security system is actuarially unsound. The amounts currently collected in Social Security taxes do not equal the amounts currently paid out in benefits. We cannot keep this up!" Comment and evaluate.

3 According to some economists, Social Security should be voluntary, not mandatory. Present the arguments on each side of this issue in as much detail as you can.

4 Do the official government statistics concerning poverty recognize that many people below the poverty line receive noncash benefits from the government? If not, does this mean that these statistics are useless? Explain.

5 People are classified as poor on the basis of their current money income. Should the following items also be taken into account?
(a) The assets of the person or family
(b) The existence of rich relatives of the person or family
(c) The person's or family's income over a period of years, not a single year

■ KEY TERMS

income inequality	old-age insurance
progressive tax	Medicare
regressive tax	Medicaid
poverty	negative income tax
Social Security	discrimination

■ VIEWPOINT FOR ANALYSIS

According to June O'Neil, former head of the Congressional Budget Office, the percent of African American families headed by a woman (no husband present) has increased from 22 percent in 1959 to 59 percent in 1990. In her view, "Experts cannot agree on why the female-headed family has increased so dramatically, but there is a growing consensus that growing up in [such a single-parent] family, dependent on welfare, is detrimental for children's chances to do well in school, work, and marriage. . . ."*

(a) Suppose that the welfare system is such that, if a family has a father present, it is ineligible for welfare payments. Would you favor such a system? Why or why not?

(b) Is the encouragement of the formation of such single-parent families the only criticism directed at existing government policies in this area? If not, what are other criticisms?

(c) Would a negative income tax encourage the formation of such single-parent families?

*Economic Times (New York: Conference Board, February 1993), p. 5.

The Biggest Investment You'll Probably Ever Make

The biggest investment you'll probably ever make is in a house. The ordinary procedure is for a house buyer to take out a mortgage, often from a savings and loan association or a bank. A mortgage is a loan; the house itself becomes security (or collateral) for the loan. If you fail to meet the mortgage payments, the lender can foreclose the mortgage, which means that the lender is entitled to take possession of the house.

To figure out how much your payments must be each month, the lender determines how much you must pay so that, when the mortgage terminates, you will have repaid the amount you borrowed and paid the stipulated interest on your debt. The size of the monthly mortgage payment depends on three things—(1) the amount you borrow, (2) how long the mortgage extends, and (3) the interest rate. The more that you borrow, the higher your monthly payment, holding all other things equal. And the higher the interest rate and the shorter the period of the mortgage, the higher your monthly payment.

To be more specific, look at the accompanying table, which shows the monthly payment per $1,000 borrowed. As you can see,

Monthly Mortgage Payments (per $1,000 borrowed)	INTEREST RATE (PERCENT)	LENGTH OF MORTGAGE (YEARS)			
		15	20	25	30
		(DOLLARS)			
	7	8.99	7.76	7.07	6.66
	7.5	9.28	8.06	7.39	7.00
	8	9.56	8.37	7.72	7.34
	8.5	9.85	8.68	8.06	7.69
	9	10.15	9.00	8.40	8.05
	9.5	10.45	9.33	8.74	8.41
	10	10.75	9.66	9.09	8.78

the monthly payment is $9.66 per $1,000 borrowed, if the mortgage extends for 20 years and the interest rate is 10 percent. Thus, if you take out a $60,000 mortgage (at 10 percent for 20 years), the monthly payment is 60 times $9.66, or $579.60.

As noted above, much of the monthly payment is used to repay part of the principal of the loan. The rest goes for interest on the portion of the loan that is not yet repaid. Over the lifetime of the mortgage, a very substantial amount is paid by the borrower for interest. If you take out a 20-year, $60,000 mortgage at an interest rate of 10 percent, you will pay $79,104 in interest over the life of the mortgage. And the higher the interest rate, the bigger the amount you will pay in interest. Thus, if the interest rate is 9.5 percent (rather than 10 percent), you will pay $74,352 (rather than $79,104) in interest over the life of a 20-year $60,000 mortgage. As you can see, *a difference of .5 percentage point in the interest rate increases the total interest payments by about $5,000!*

■ QUESTIONS

1 If the interest rate is 8 percent and if you take out a mortgage of $70,000 extending for 25 years, what is the monthly payment?

2 If the interest rate is 9 percent, and if you take out a mortgage of $70,000 extending for 25 years, what is the monthly payment?

3 Based on your answers to questions 1 and 2, how much does a 1 percentage point increase in the interest rate (from 8 to 9 percent) increase the total monthly payments over the life of the 25-year, $70,000 mortgage?

4 Suppose that you decide to sell a house for $80,000. The buyer, because of problems in raising cash, will pay you this amount a year after taking possession of the house. Are you really getting $80,000 for the house? Why or why not?

5 If the interest rate is 8 percent, how much are you getting for the house discussed in question 4?

PART SIX

Growth, Government, and International Economics

CHAPTER 25

Economic Growth

LEARNING OBJECTIVES

In this chapter, you should learn:

- What economic growth is and how it is measured
- The role of diminishing marginal returns in economic growth
- The effects of investment on economic growth
- The role of public policy in promoting economic growth

In 1994, Boeing was launching its new 777, a wide-bodied 350- to 400-passenger jet aircraft. To save time and money in the development process, Boeing used a new computer-aided design system. What is such a system, and how is it related to economic growth? One purpose of this chapter is to answer this question.

Turning from the aircraft industry to the population at large, the human condition has changed considerably during the past century, at least in the industrialized countries of the world. Rising living standards have brought a decline in poverty, though by no means its disappearance. How has this increase in per capita output been achieved? This question has fascinated economists for a long time. Although we still are far from completely understanding the process of economic growth, our knowledge has increased considerably through the efforts of economic researchers, here and abroad. In this chapter, we discuss the process of economic growth in industrialized countries.

WHAT IS ECONOMIC GROWTH?

Economic growth

There are two common measures of the rate of **economic growth**. The first is the rate of growth of a country's real gross domestic product, which tells us how rapidly the economy's total real output of goods and services is increasing. The second is the rate of growth of *per capita* real gross domestic product, which is a better measure of the rate of increase of a country's standard of living. We will use the second measure unless we state otherwise. Two aspects of the rate of growth of per capita real gross domestic product should be noted from the start.

1. *This measure is only a very crude approximation to the rate of increase of economic welfare.* For one thing, gross domestic product

575

does not include one good that people prize most highly: leisure. For another, gross domestic product does not value accurately new products and improvements in the quality of goods and services and does not allow properly either for noneconomic changes in the quality of life or for the costs of environmental pollution. Nor does gross domestic product take account of how the available output is distributed. Clearly, it makes a difference whether the bulk of the population gets a reasonable share of the output or a favored few get most of it.

2. *Small differences in the annual rate of economic growth can make very substantial differences in living standards a few decades hence.* For example, per capita GDP in the United States was about $33,000 in 1999. If it grows at 2 percent per year, it will be about $40,200 (1999 dollars) in the year 2009, whereas if it grows at 3 percent per year, it will be about $44,300 (1999 dollars) in the year 2009. Thus an increase of 1 percentage point in the growth rate means a $4,100—or 10 percent—increase in per capita GDP in the year 2009. Even an increase of one-quarter of 1 percentage point can make a considerable difference. If the growth rate increases from 1.75 to 2 percent per year, per capita GDP in the year 2009 will increase from $39,250 to $40,200.

ECONOMIC GROWTH AS A POLICY OBJECTIVE

Following World War II, governments throughout the world became much more involved in trying to stimulate economic growth. In the United States, the government was not much inclined to influence the growth rate before the war. Of course, the government did many things that had some effect on the rate of economic growth, and in a general sort of way was interested in promoting economic growth. But it was normally taken for granted that, left to its own devices, our economy would manage to grow at more or less the proper rate.

Whether the government should increase the rate of economic growth is, of course, a political decision; and your opinion of such a government policy will depend on many things, including your attitude toward present sacrifice for future material gain. As we shall see in subsequent sections, *a more rapid rate of growth can often be achieved only if consumers are willing to give up some consumption now so that they and their children can have more goods and services in the future.* To the extent that you believe that private decisions place too little weight on the future and too much weight on the present, you may be inclined to support a government policy designed to increase the growth rate. Otherwise you may not favor such a policy.

Thomas Malthus

THOMAS MALTHUS AND POPULATION GROWTH

A country's rate of economic growth depends, among other things, on how much the quantities of inputs of various kinds increase. To illuminate the nature of the growth process, we discuss the effect on the rate of economic growth of increasing each kind of input, holding the others constant. We begin by looking at the effects of changes in the quantity of labor. Economists have devoted a great deal of attention to the effects of population growth on the rate of economic growth. The classic work was done by Thomas Malthus (1776–1834), a British parson who devoted his life to academic research. The first professional economist, he taught at a college established by the East India Company to train its administrators— and was called "Pop" by his students behind his back. Whether "Pop" stood for population or not, Malthus' fame is based on his theories of **population growth**.

**Population
growth**

Malthus believed that the population tends to grow at a geometric rate. In his *Essay on the Principle of Population*, published in 1798, he pointed out the implications of such a constant rate of growth:

> If any person will take the trouble to make the calculation, he will see that if the necessities of life could be obtained without limit, and the number of people could be doubled every twenty-five years, the population which might have been produced from a single pair since the Christian era, would have been sufficient, not only to fill the earth quite full of people, so that four should stand in every square yard,

577

but to fill all the planets of our solar system in the same way, and not only them but all the planets revolving around the stars which are visible to the naked eye, supposing each of them . . . to have as many planets belong to it as our sun has.

In contrast to the human population, which tends to increase at a geometric rate, the supply of land can increase slowly if at all.[1] And land, particularly in Malthus's time, was the source of food. Consequently, it seemed to Malthus that the human population was in danger of outrunning its food supply: "Taking the whole earth," he wrote, ". . . and supposing the present population to be equal to a thousand millions, the human species would increase as the numbers 1, 2, 4, 8, 16, 32, 64, 128, 256, and subsistence as 1, 2, 3, 4, 5, 6, 7, 8, 9. In two centuries, the population would be to the means of subsistence as 256 to 9; in three centuries as 4096 to 13; and in two thousand years the difference would be incalculable."

■ A BLEAK PROSPECT

Certainly, Malthus's view of humanity's prospects was bleak; as he himself acknowledged, "the view has a melancholy hue." Gone is the optimism of Adam Smith. According to Malthus, the prospect for economic progress was very limited. Given the inexorable increase in human numbers, the standard of living will be kept at the minimum level required to keep body and soul together. If it exceeds this level, the population will increase and drive the standard of living back down. On the other hand, if the standard of living is less than this level, the population will decline because of starvation. Certainly, the long-term prospects were anything but bright. Thomas Carlyle, the famous historian and essayist, called economics "the dismal science." To a considerable extent, economics acquired this bad name through the efforts of Parson Malthus.

Malthus's theory can be interpreted in terms of the law of diminishing marginal returns (recall Chapter 15). Living in what was still largely an agricultural society, he emphasized the role of land and labor as resources and assumed a relatively fixed level of technology. Since land is fixed, increases in labor—due to population growth—will eventually cause the marginal product of labor to get smaller and smaller because of the law of diminishing marginal returns. (Recall from Chapter 22 that the marginal product of labor is the additional output resulting from an extra unit of labor.) In other words, because of this law, the marginal product of labor will behave as shown in Figure 25.1, with the result that continued

---

[1]Of course, it does not matter to Malthus's argument whether the population doubles every 25 years or every 40 years. The important thing is that it increases at a geometric rate.

FIGURE 25.1

Diminishing Marginal Returns and the Effect of Population Growth

According to Malthus, the labor force will tend to *P* because, if output per worker exceeds *A*, population will increase, and if output per worker is less than *A*, starvation will reduce the population.

growth of the labor force will ultimately bring economic decline—that is, a reduction in output per worker. This happens because, as the marginal product of labor falls with increases in the labor force, the average product of labor will eventually fall as well—and the average product of labor is another name for output per worker.

Of course, Malthus recognized that various devices could keep the population down: war, famine, and birth-control measures, among others. In fact, he tried to describe and evaluate the importance of various checks on population growth. For example, suppose that population tends to grow to the point where output per worker is at a subsistence level—just sufficient to keep body and soul together. If this is the case and if the subsistence level of output per worker is *A*, then the labor force will tend to equal *P* in Figure 25.1. Why? Because, as noted above, Malthus believed that if the standard of living rises appreciably above *A*, population will increase, and thus force it back toward *A*. On the other hand, if the standard of living falls below *A*, some of the population will starve, and thus push it back toward *A*.

■ EFFECTS OF POPULATION GROWTH

Was Malthus right? Among the developing countries of the world, his analysis seems very relevant today. During the past sixty years, the population of the developing countries has grown very rapidly, in part because of the decrease in death rates attributable to the transfer of medical advances from the industrialized countries to the developing countries. Between 1940 and 1970, the total population of Asia, Africa, and Oceania almost doubled. There has been a tendency for growing populations to push hard against food supplies in some of the countries of Africa, Latin America,

FIGURE 25.2

Shift over Time in the Marginal Product of Labor

Technological change has shifted the marginal-product-of-labor curve to the right.

and Asia; the Malthusian model can explain important elements of the situation.

However, Malthus's theory seems far less relevant or correct for the industrialized countries. In contrast to his model, population has not increased to the point where the standard of living has been pushed down to the subsistence level. On the contrary, the standard of living has increased dramatically in all the industrialized countries. The most important mistake Malthus made was to underestimate the extent and importance of technological change. Instead of remaining fixed, the marginal-product-of-labor curve in Figure 25.1 moved gradually to the right, as new methods and new products increased the efficiency of agriculture. In other words, the situation was as shown in Figure 25.2. Thus as population increased, the marginal product of labor did not go down. Instead, technological change prevented the productivity of extra agricultural workers from falling.

Among the industrialized nations, have countries with relatively high rates of growth of population had relatively low—or relatively high—rates of economic growth? In general, there seems to be little or no relationship between a nation's rate of population increase and its rate of economic growth. Figure 25.3 plots the rate of population increase against the rate of growth of output per person-year in 11 industrialized countries between 1913 and 1959. The results suggest that there is little or no relation between them, and the relationship that exists appears to be direct rather than inverse.

DAVID RICARDO AND CAPITAL FORMATION

A contemporary and good friend of Malthus who also contributed to the theory of economic growth was David Ricardo (1772–1823). Of all the titans of economics, he is probably the least known to the

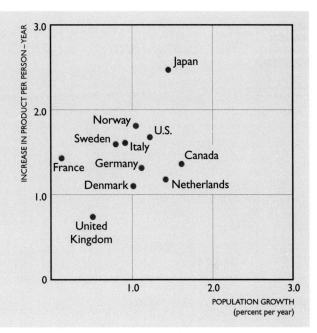

FIGURE 25.3

Relationship between Population Growth and Increases in National Product per Person-Year, 11 Industrialized Countries, 1913–59

In industrialized countries, there is little or no relationship between a country's rate of population growth and its rate of economic growth.

general public. Smith, Malthus, Marx, and Keynes are frequently encountered names. Ricardo is not, although he made many brilliant contributions to economic thought. An extremely successful stockbroker who retired at the age of 42 with a very large fortune, he devoted much of his time to highly theoretical analyses of the economic system and its workings. In contrast to Malthus, who was reviled for his pessimistic doctrines, Ricardo and his writings were widely admired in his own time. He was elected to England's House of Commons and was highly respected there.

■ RICARDO ON INCOME DISTRIBUTION

Ricardo was concerned in much of his work with the distribution of income. Unlike Adam Smith, who paid much less attention to the conflict among classes, Ricardo emphasized the struggle between the industrialists—a relatively new and rising class in his time—and the landowners—the old aristocracy that resisted the rise of the industrial class. This clash was reflected in the struggle in Britain around 1800 over the so-called Corn Laws (*corn* being a general term covering all types of grain). Because of the increase of population, the demand for grain increased in Britain, and so caused the price of grain to rise greatly. This meant higher profits for the landowners. But the industrialists complained bitterly about the increase in the price of food, because higher food prices meant that they had to pay higher wages. As the price of grain

CASE STUDY 25.1

The Club of Rome's "Limits to Growth" report

In 1974, an M.I.T.-based group produced a pessimistic analysis called the Club of Rome's "Limits to Growth" report. The report concluded that if the world's burgeoning population were to consume resources at the rate of the United States, many critical resources, minerals especially, would soon become very scarce and that with scarcity, prices would rise to unacceptable levels, and economic and industrial growth would slow down.

The notion was not new. Thomas Malthus in 1798 had considered that population growth, and hence consumption, would soon undermine growth—indeed, civilization itself—in Europe. In 1908, President Theodore Roosevelt worried about a diminishing supply of raw materials and gathered a commission to ponder the future of a United States without minerals and metals. More resources were quickly found. In 1944, there was another review, and 21 commodities were placed on the endangered list. By now, those commodities should have been exhausted. None has been. What has repeatedly pulled us back from the pessimists' brink of doom?

Copper has often been listed as a mineral due for future scarcity. It is subject to fluctuating prices. In peak-price years, there is a flurry of exploration, and new low-grade prophyries across the world are added to the tonnage in reserve. But in those peak-price years, before new mines have time to develop, another factor comes into play: It becomes cost-effective for users to find substitutes for copper, like aluminum or plastics. And once substitutes are found, copper consumption does not return to its original levels. The telecommunications industry is a recent example where massive substitution has taken place, as fiber optics have come to the fore in intracity communications.

So the Club of Rome doomsayers would seem to be discredited on two counts: Increased prices generate greater supplies through improved exploration and mining technology, and increased prices encourage substitution of other materials (and the recycling of scrap) to satisfy demand.

But aren't the planet's mineral resources finite? They are, although the geochemical cycle that creates minerals is virtually infinite. Not much gets off the planet, and we have hardly scratched the surface in our search for greater supplies. The costs of extraction from deep within the earth's crust or the ocean floor might look excessively expensive today, but they looked astronomical a century ago, and the relative cost of minerals has remained roughly constant; it has hardly increased even with diminishing returns. Basic raw materials, then, will not run out for centuries. Our growth will continue, less dependent on supplies than on our technological ability and the wisdom of our investment.

---

increased, merchants began to import cheap grain from abroad. But the landowners, who dominated Parliament, passed legislation, the Corn Laws, to keep cheap grain out of Britain. In effect the Corn Laws imposed a high tariff, or duty, on grain.

According to Ricardo's analysis, the landlords were bound to capture most of the benefits of economic progress, unless their control of the price of grain could be weakened. As national output increased and population expanded, poorer and poorer land had to be brought under cultivation to produce the extra food. As the cost of producing grain increased, its price would increase, and so would the rents of the landlords. The workers and the industrialists, on the other hand, would benefit little, if at all. As the price of grain increased, the workers would have to get higher wages—but only high enough to keep them at a subsistence level (since Ricardo agreed entirely with his friend Malthus on the population issue). Thus the workers would be no better off; neither would the industrialists, who would wind up with lower profits because of the increase in wage rates.

Ricardo felt that the Corn Laws should be repealed and that free trade in grain should be permitted. In a beautiful piece of theoretical analysis that is still reasonably fresh and convincing nearly two hundred years after its publication, he laid out the basic principles of international trade and pointed out the benefits to all countries that can be derived by specialization and free trade. For example, suppose that England is relatively more efficient at producing textiles, and France is relatively more efficient at producing wine. Then, on the basis of Ricardo's analysis, it can be shown that each country is likely to be better off by specializing in the product it is more efficient at producing—textiles in England, wine in France—and trading this product for the one the other country specializes in producing.

■ RICARDO'S VIEW OF CAPITAL FORMATION

Capital formation

Let's turn to the effect on economic growth of increases in physical capital, holding other inputs and technology fixed. Ricardo constructed some interesting theories concerning the effects of **capital formation**—that is, investment in plant and equipment—on economic growth. Other things held constant, a nation's output depends on the amount of plant and equipment that it has and operates. Moreover, one can draw a curve showing the marginal product of capital—the extra output that would result from an extra dollar's worth of capital—under various assumptions about the total amount of capital in existence. This curve will slope downward to the right, as shown in Figure 25.4, because of the law of

FIGURE 25.4
Marginal Product of Capital

This curve shows the marginal product of capital under various assumptions concerning the total amount of capital. For example, if there is $100 billion of capital, the marginal product of capital is $A, whereas if there is $150 billion of capital, the marginal product of capital is $B.

diminishing marginal returns. As more and more capital is accumulated, its marginal product eventually must decrease. For example, if $100 billion is the total investment in plant and equipment (or total capital), the extra output to be derived from an extra dollar of investment is worth $A; if the total investment is increased to $150 billion, however, the economy must resort to less-productive investments, and the extra output to be derived from an extra dollar of investment is only worth $B.

The curve in Figure 25.4 leads to the conclusion that investment in plant and equipment, although it will increase the growth rate up to some point, will eventually be unable to increase it further. As more and more is invested in new plant and equipment, less and less productive projects must be undertaken. Finally, when all the productive projects have been carried out, further investment in plant and equipment will be useless. At this point—$200 billion of total capital in Figure 25.4—further investment in plant and equipment will not increase output at all.

This kind of analysis led Ricardo to the pessimistic conclusion that the economy would experience decreases in the profitability of investment in plant and equipment, and the eventual termination of economic growth.

■ WAS RICARDO RIGHT?

Have we seen decreases in the profitability of investment in plant and equipment, and the eventual termination of economic growth? No. Ricardo, like Malthus, was led astray by underestimating the extent and impact of future changes in technology. Suppose that, because of the development of major new products and processes, lots of new opportunities for profitable investment arise. Obviously, the effect on the curve in Figure 25.4 is to shift it to the right, because there are more investment opportunities than before above a certain level of productivity. But if this curve shifts to the right, as shown in Figure 25.5, we may be able to avoid Ricardo's pessimistic conclusions.

To see how this can occur, note that if X in Figure 25.5 is the relevant curve in a particular year and if $100 billion is the total amount of capital, an extra dollar of investment in plant and equipment would have a marginal product of $C. A decade later, if Y is the relevant curve and if the total amount of capital has grown to $150 billion, the marginal product of an extra dollar of investment in plant and equipment is still $C. Thus there is no reduction in the productivity of investment opportunities despite the 50 percent increase in the total amount of capital. Because of technological change and other factors, productive and profitable new investment opportunities are opened up as fast as old ones are invested in.

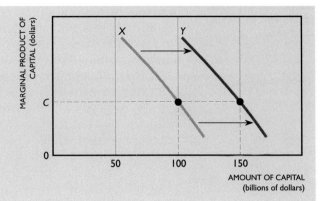

FIGURE 25.5

Effects of Technological Change on the Marginal Product of Capital

Technological change has shifted the marginal-product-of-capital curve to the right. (Actually, Ricardo's variable input was a combined dose of capital and labor.)

The history of the United States is quite consistent with this sort of shift in investment opportunities over time. Even though we have poured an enormous amount of money into new plant and equipment, we have not exhausted or reduced the productivity or profitability of investment opportunities. The rate of return on investment in new plant and equipment has not fallen. Instead, it has fluctuated around a fairly constant level during the past eighty years.

CAPITAL FORMATION AND ECONOMIC GROWTH

To see more clearly the role of investment in the process of economic growth, let's extend the model we discussed in Chapter 5. Suppose we ignore the government and consider only the private sector of the economy. Suppose that the full-employment, noninflationary GDP this year is $1,000 billion and that the consumption function is such that consumption expenditure is $900 billion if GDP is $1,000 billion. If intended investment this year is $100 billion, with the result that GDP is in fact $1,000 billion, *next year's full-employment GDP will increase because this year's investment will raise the nation's productive capacity.* In other words, this year's investment increases next year's full-employment GDP. The amount of the increase in full-employment GDP depends on the **capital-output ratio**, which is the number of dollars of investment (or extra capital goods) required to produce an extra dollar of output. For example, if the capital-output ratio is 2, $2 of investment is required to increase full-employment GDP by $1.

■ EFFECT OF INVESTMENT ON FULL-EMPLOYMENT GDP

Let's look more closely at the effect of investment on full-employment GDP. If the capital-output ratio is 2, full-employment GDP will increase by $50 billion as a consequence of the $100 billion of investment. Thus full-employment GDP next year is $1,050 billion. On the other hand, suppose that this year's investment is $200 billion rather than $100 billion and that the consumption function is such that consumption expenditure is $800 billion rather than $900 billion if GDP is $1,000 billion. What will full-employment GDP be next year? If the capital-output ratio is 2, it will be $1,100 billion. Why? Because the $200 billion in investment will increase full-employment GDP by $100 billion—from $1,000 billion to $1,100 billion.

Thus the full-employment GDP will be larger if investment is $200 billion than if it is $100 billion. Similarly, full-employment GDP will be larger if investment is $300 billion than if it is $200 billion. If the capital-output ratio is 2, full-employment GDP will be $1,150 billion next year if investment is $300 billion. Why? Because the $300 billion in investment will increase full-employment GDP by $150 billion—from $1,000 to $1,150 billion.

In general, the greater the percentage of GDP that the society devotes to investment this year, the greater will be the increase in its full-employment GDP. Thus *so long as the economy sustains noninflationary full employment and the capital-output ratio remains constant, the rate of growth of national output will be directly related to the percentage of GDP devoted to investment.*[2]

■ SOME EVIDENCE CONCERNING THE EFFECTS OF INVESTMENT

Certainly, this result seems sensible enough. If a country wants to increase its growth rate, it should produce more blast furnaces, machine tools, and plows, and fewer cosmetics, household furniture, and sports cars. But all this is theory. What do the facts suggest? Table 25.1 shows the rate of investment and the growth rate in six major industrialized nations in the 1990s. The investment rate was highest in Japan, but the growth rate was the lowest. The investment rate was lowest in the United States, but the growth rate was the highest. This does not negate the importance of investment; instead it suggests that there is no simple cause-and-effect relationship between growth and investment. There is growing evidence that the efficiency, or productivity, of capital is much higher in the United States, compared with Japan. This suggests

[2]It can be shown that the rate of growth of GDP equals s/b, where s is the proportion of GDP that is saved (and invested) and b is the capital-output ratio, assuming that both s and b are constant and that full employment is maintained. For example, if b is 2 and $s = 0.10$, GDP will grow at 5 percent per year, since $0.10/2 = 0.05$. This result is part of the so-called Harrod-Domar growth model developed by the late Sir Roy Harrod of Oxford and Evsey Domar of M.I.T. Although useful, this result must be employed with caution since it is based on highly simplified assumptions.

TABLE 25.1

Rate of Growth of Output and Investment as a Percentage of Output (1990–99)

NATION	ANNUAL AVERAGE	
	RATE OF GROWTH OF OUTPUT (PERCENT)	PERCENT OF OUTPUT INVESTED
France	1.6	19.6
Germany	1.7	22.4
Canada	2.3	18.5
Japan	1.3	29.1
United Kingdom	2.0	17.1
United States	3.2	15.0

Source: Standard & Poor's DRI, *World Outlook*, First Quarter, 2000

that the same amount of capital can deliver a lot more growth in the United States than in Japan.

THE ROLE OF HUMAN CAPITAL

Human capital

A country's rate of economic growth is influenced by the rate at which it invests in **human capital** as well as physical capital. It may seem odd to speak of *human* capital, but every society builds up a certain amount of human capital through investments in formal education, on-the-job training, and health programs. You often hear people talk about investing in their children's future by putting them through college. For the economy as a whole, the expenditure on education and public health can also be viewed—at least partly—as an investment, because consumption is sacrificed in the present in order to make possible a higher level of per capita output in the future.

The United States invests in human capital on a massive scale. In the late 1990s, it devoted between $600 billion and $700 billion annually to gross investment in formal education. In addition, $100 billion to $150 billion was spent each year on worker training, excluding informal efforts to improve skills and performance. These enormous and rapidly growing investments in human capital have unquestionably increased the productivity, versatility, and adaptability of our labor force. They have certainly made a major contribution to economic growth.

Income tends to rise with a person's education. Using this relationship to measure the influence of education on a person's productivity, some economists, notably University of Chicago's Nobel laureates Theodore Schultz and Gary Becker, have tried to estimate the profitability, both to society and to the person, of an investment in various levels of education. Becker has tried to estimate the rate of return from a person's investment in a college education. According to his estimates, the typical urban white male in 1950 received about a 10 percent return (after taxes) on his investment in tuition, room, books, and other college expenses (including the earnings he gave up by being in college rather than at work). This was a relatively high return—much higher, for example, than if the student simply put the equivalent amount of money in a savings bank or in government bonds.

During the 1970s and early 1980s, real private rates of return from investments in schooling were estimated to be 10 to 13 percent for secondary education and 8 to 10 percent for higher education. However, because it is so difficult to adjust for differences among people in ability and effort, these results should be viewed with caution.

THE ROLE OF TECHNOLOGICAL CHANGE

Technological change

A country's rate of economic growth depends on the rate of **technological change**, as well as on the extent to which quantities of inputs of various kinds increase. Indeed, the rate of technological change is perhaps the most important single determinant of a country's rate of economic growth. Recall from Chapters 1 and 11 that technology is knowledge concerning the industrial and agricultural arts. Thus technological change often takes the form of new methods of producing existing products; new designs that make it possible to produce goods with important new characteristics; and new techniques of organization, marketing, and management. Two examples of technological change are new ways of producing power (for example, atomic energy) and new fibers (for example, nylon).

We have already seen that technological change can shift the curves in both Figures 25.2 and 25.5, and thus ward off the law of diminishing marginal returns. But note that new knowledge by itself has little impact. *Unless knowledge is applied, it has little effect on the rate of economic growth.* A change in technology, when applied for the first time, is called an ***innovation***, and the firm that first applies it is called an ***innovator***. Innovation is a key stage in the process leading to the full evaluation and utilization of a new process or product. The innovator must be willing to take the risks involved in introducing a new and untried process, good, or service, and in many cases, these risks are high. Once a change in technology has been applied for the first time, the ***diffusion process***—the process by which the use of the innovation spreads from firm to firm and from use to use—begins. How rapidly an in-

Bill Gates of Microsoft—one of the world's most successful entrepreneurs

novation spreads depends heavily on its economic advantages over older methods or products. The more profitable the use of the innovation is, the more rapidly it will spread.

Joseph Schumpeter (1883–1950), Harvard's distinguished economist and social theorist, stressed the important role played by innovators in the process of economic growth. In Schumpeter's view, innovators are the mainspring of economic progress, the people with the foresight to see how new things can be brought into being and the courage and resourcefulness to surmount the obstacles to change. For this trouble, innovators receive profit, but this profit eventually is whittled down by competitors who imitate the innovators. The innovators push the curves in Figures 25.2 and 25.5 to the right, and once their innovations are assimilated by the economy, other innovators may shove these curves somewhat farther to the right. For example, one innovator introduces vacuum tubes, and a later innovator introduces semiconductors; one innovator introduces the steam locomotive, and a later innovator introduces the diesel locomotive. This process goes on and on, and is a main source of economic growth.

ENDOGENOUS TECHNOLOGICAL CHANGE

Recent economic theories stress that the rate and direction of technological change is influenced by economic factors, a fact long recognized by economists who have studied technology. In the jargon of economists, technological change is to some extent *endogenous,* which means that it is determined within (not outside) the overall economic system. While invention is an activity characterized by great uncertainty, it nonetheless shares most of the characteristics of other economic activities. In particular, the amount of resources devoted to inventing in a particular field depends heavily on how profitable the production of such inventions is.

Thus, the rate of technological change in a particular area is influenced by the same kinds of factors that determine the output of any good or service. On the one hand, there are demand factors which influence the level of profits from particular types of technological change. For example, if a prospective change in technology reduces the cost of a particular product, increases in the demand for the product are likely to increase the returns from effecting this technological change. Similarly, a growing shortage and a rising price of the inputs saved by the technological change are likely to increase the returns from effecting it. As an illustration, consider the history of English textile inventions. During the eighteenth century, there was an increase in the demand for yarn, due to decreases in the price of cloth and increased cloth output. This increase in demand, as well as shortages of spinners and increases in their wages, raised the returns to inventions that increased productivity in the spinning processes and directly stimulated the work leading to such major inventions as the water frame, the spinning jenny, and the spinning mule.

On the other hand, there are also supply factors which influence the cost of making particular kinds of technological change. Obviously, whether people try to solve a given problem depends on whether they think it can be solved and on how costly they think it will be to solve, as well as on the expected payoff if they are successful. The cost of making science-based technological changes depends on the number of scientists and engineers in relevant fields and on advances in basic science; for example, advances in physics clearly reduced the cost of effecting changes in technology in the field of atomic energy. In addition, the rate of technological change depends on the amount of effort devoted to making modest improvements that lean heavily on practical experience. Although there is often a tendency to focus attention on the major, spectacular inventions, it is by no means certain that technological change in many industries is due chiefly to these inventions, rather than to a succession of minor improvements; for example, it has been shown that technological change in shipbuilding has been largely the result of gradual evolution. In industries where this is a dominant source of technological change and where technological change is only loosely connected with scientific advance, one would expect the rate of technological change to depend on the number of people working in the industry and in positions to make improvements of this sort.

ENTREPRENEURSHIP AND THE SOCIAL ENVIRONMENT

Still another set of basic factors influencing a coutry's level of potential output and its rate of economic growth is its economic, social, political, and religious climate. It is difficult, if not impossible, to measure the effect of these factors, but there can be no doubt of their importance. Some societies despise material goods and emphasize the glories of the next world. Some societies are subject to such violent political upheavals that it is risky, if not foolish, to invest in the future. Some societies are governed so corruptly that economic growth is frustrated. And some societies look down on people engaged in industry, trade, or commerce. Obviously, such societies are less likely to experience rapid economic growth than others with a more favorable climate and conditions.

The relatively rapid economic growth of the United States was undoubtedly stimulated in part by the attitude of its people toward material gain. It is commonplace to note that the United States is a materialistic society, a society that esteems business success, that bestows prestige on the rich, that accepts the Protestant ethic (which, crudely stated, is that work is good), and that encourages individual initiative. The United States has been criticized over and over again for some of these traits, often by countries frantically trying to imitate its economic success. Somewhat less obvious is the fact that, because the United States is a young country whose people came from a variety of origins, it did not inherit many feudal components in the structure of society. This too was important in promoting economic growth.

The United States has also been characterized by great economic and political freedom, by institutions that have been flexible enough to adjust to change, and by a government that has encouraged competition in the marketplace. This has meant fewer barriers to new ideas. Also, the United States has for a long time enjoyed internal peace, order, and general respect for property rights. There have been no violent revolutions since the Civil War, and for many years we were protected from strife in other lands by two oceans—which then seemed much broader than they do now. All these factors undoubtedly contributed to rapid economic growth.

Entrepreneurs

The U.S. economy also seems to have been able to nurture a great many **entrepreneurs** and a vast horde of competent business executives. During the twentieth century, U.S. entrepreneurs were responsible for such basic innovations as the automobile

Computer-assisted design and manufacture at Boeing aircraft

In the 1960s and 1970s, the design and manufacture of a Boeing 727 or 747 were far from smooth processes. Drawings were hand-done, and passed from hand to hand with each requested improvement. And when designs got to the shop floor, often they did not quite fit. Parts had to be rejigged, shaved, and modified here and there. The manufacturing process was full of fits and starts—beautiful and safe in the end, but inefficient and expensive getting there.

In 1978 and 1979, work began on the Boeing 767 and 757. Sophisticated interactive computer graphics were developed for drafting the designs. Each part, each point on every surface, was built into a mathematical program and stored on computer to be manipulated for any slight change. A set of drawings could now be changed in a day, rather than a week, and with more accuracy than before. *Computer-assisted design (CAD)* had arrived in the aircraft industry. In the back rooms, productivity and growth increased.

The effect was felt on the assembly line too. Fewer modifications had to be made on the shop floor. Costs were reduced because the designs could be applied more accurately at lower tolerances. Airplane components fit together better. *Computer-assisted manufacturing (CAM)* controlled equipment precisely, and so turned out wingskins, spare assemblies, and dozens of delicate rivets for quality in flight.

It all took some time to go through the learning process, but Boeing now experiences less overtime in rework and fewer delays in start-up. For the newest generation of planes, such as the 777, productivity has been enhanced even more as computers have been more fully linked in design and manufacture. Technology will continue to increase growth in output per hour of labor.

assembly line, pioneered by Henry Ford (see Case Study 25.3). In many areas, the United States gained a technological lead over other countries, which was maintained for many years. In the past thirty years, according to many observers, our technological lead has been reduced considerably. This has caused concern among U.S. government officials and business executives.

The Ford assembly line

Ford's Highland Park factory, 1913

At the turn of the century, there were dozens of different models of automobiles. Made in tiny machine shops, they were all designed and made differently, some gas-driven, some steam-driven, some electric. With car prices at around $5,000, the embryonic industry was supported by the New England wealthy. In Michigan machine shops, however, there was another idea: getting a car on the road for $1,000.

By 1908, the first Model T rolled off Henry Ford's plant in Highland Park, Detroit. That year, Ford led the industry in the number of cars sold and turned a $3 million profit. Yet in a country of 89 million people, there were still fewer than 200,000 auto-mobiles. To sell more cars, there had to be further reduction in price. Ford and his friends figured out that a $600 car would tap this market. Between 1912 and 1914, the new Highland Park factory was completely reorganized. Before then, a worker spent half his day walking about to get small components for the assembly of the main component, which stayed in one place until assembly was complete. Ford's idea was to place the machine tools in such a way that the car parts could move past the equipment to complete subassembly; then these partially assembled parts would move past other lines of tools to final assembly. Stationary workers would help the line along.

To attain this goal, Ford had first to rationalize work tasks and routines. He invested in labor; his stunning $5 a day wage rate doubled the Michigan average overnight, and his workforce also stabilized overnight, from a terrible 60 percent turnover rate per month. A second requirement was a standard design: cars must come off the line as alike as pins at a pin factory. But above all, Ford had to risk a heavy investment in machine tools and the moving assembly plant. In 1914, the Highland Park factory represented $3.6 million in new plant and $2.8 million in machine tool equipment. Although these tools were complicated, they were called "farmer's tools," because they allowed even green farmhands to produce large quantities of high-quality work.

Output per worker shot up. Labor hours per engine dropped from 35 to 23; a person who made 35 magnetos in a day could now produce 95; and most radical of all, the endless chain-driven conveyor for chassis production meant that a chassis was turned out in 1.5 labor-hours, compared with 12.5 labor-hours before. Each worker had more equipment to use, and although the wage had doubled, output increased even more. Sales of the Model T rose from 78,000 to 500,000, and the price came down to $600 per car and then to $360 per car in 1916.

THE GAP BETWEEN ACTUAL AND POTENTIAL OUTPUT

Up to this point, our discussion of economic growth has centered on the factors that determine how rapidly a country's potential output grows—factors like technological change, increased education, investment in plant and equipment, and increases in the labor force. In other words, we have focused on the factors responsible for rightward shifts of the long-run aggregate supply curve. Although we have not paid much attention in this chapter to the gap between actual and potential output, this does not mean that increases in output per capita cannot be achieved by reducing this gap. Obviously, they can be.

However, only so much can be achieved by squeezing the slack out of the economy. For example, if there is a 7 percent unemployment rate, output per capita can be increased by perhaps 6 percent simply by reducing the unemployment rate to 5 percent. *But this is a one-shot* improvement. To get any further increase in output per capita, the country must increase its potential output. This doesn't mean that it isn't important to maintain a high level of employment in the economy. Of course it is, for reasons discussed at length in Chapter 4. But the point we are making is that once the economy gets to full employment, no further increase in output per capita can occur by this route. If a country wants further increases in output per capita over the long haul, it must influence the factors responsible for the rate of growth of potential output.

One of the most positive developments of the late 1990s and early 2000s was a significant increase in productivity growth in the United States. On the basis of this, economists estimate that, instead of growing at 2.5 percent, potential real GDP is increasing at a 3.5 percent rate. A 1 percentage point increase in trend growth over an extended period of time can have a huge impact on per capita income and standard of living. This "productivity miracle" is largely due to the ability of the United States to take advantage of the supply-side benefits of the twin technological revolutions of the PC and the Internet. Working in the United States's favor have been its flexible labor markets, relatively liberal immigration policies, vibrant venture capital markets, strong entrepreneurial culture, and open, competitive product markets.

REVIEW AND PRACTICE

▨ SUMMARY

❙ Economic growth is measured by the increase of per capita real gross domestic product, an index that does not measure accurately the growth of economic welfare but is often used as a first approximation.

2 One factor that may influence a country's rate of economic growth is the rate at which its population grows. In Malthus's view, population growth, unless checked in some way, ultimately meant economic decline, since output could not grow in proportion to the growth in population. The law of diminishing marginal returns ensured that beyond some point, holding the quantity of land constant, increases in labor would result in smaller and smaller increments of output. However, Malthus underestimated the extent and importance of technological change, which offsets the law of diminishing marginal returns.

3 Another factor that determines whether per capita output grows rapidly or slowly is the rate of expenditure on new plant and equipment. Without technological change, more and more of this sort of investment would result in increases in the amount of capital per dollar of output and decreases in the profitability of investment in plant and equipment, as Ricardo pointed out. But because of technological change, none of these things has occurred. According to the available evidence, a country's rate of economic growth seems directly related to its rate of investment in plant and equipment.

4 A factor with an important effect on a country's rate of economic growth is the rate at which it invests in human capital. The United States invests in human capital on a massive scale, and these enormous and rapidly growing investments have unquestionably increased the productivity, versatility, and adaptability of our labor force.

5 To a considerable extent, economic growth here and abroad has resulted from technological change. A change in technology, when applied for the first time, is called an innovation, and the firm that first applies it is called an innovator. Innovation is a key stage in the process leading to the full evaluation and utilization of a new process or product. Unless knowledge is used, it has little effect on the rate of economic growth.

6 Still another set of basic factors influencing the rate of economic growth is the economic, social, and political climate of the country. Some societies despise material goods, are subject to violent political upheavals, or are governed by corrupt groups. Such societies are unlikely to have a high rate of economic growth.

7 Finally, the rate of economic growth is also affected by the extent and behavior of the gap between actual and potential GDP. However, once a country gets to full employment, it cannot grow further by reducing this gap.

▓ PROBLEMS AND QUESTIONS

1 Suppose that a society produces only two goods, food and tractors, and that in 2001 and 2002 the maximum quantity of food that it can produce, given that it produces the following quantity of tractors, is as given below:

QUANTITY OF FOOD (MILLIONS OF TONS)	QUANTITY OF TRACTORS (THOUSANDS OF TRACTORS)
0	9
1	8
2	7
3	5
4	3
5	0

If this society produces 4,000 tractors and 3 million tons of food in 2001 and 5,000 tractors and 3 million tons of food in 2002 (its population remaining constant), has any economic growth occurred between 2001 and 2002? If so, to what is it due?

2 Suppose that the society in question 1 produces 6,000 tractors and 3 million tons of food in 2003 (its population remaining the same as in 2002). Has any economic growth occurred between 2002 and 2003? If so, is it due entirely to a shift in the production possibilities curve? How can you tell?

3 Suppose that a society produces only one commodity, wheat, and that it has the following aggregate production function:

HOURS OF LABOR (MILLIONS)	BUSHELS OF WHEAT (BILLIONS)
0	0
1	2
2	4
3	6
4	7
5	7

What is the marginal product of labor when between 1 and 2 million hours of labor are used? When between 2 and 3 million hours of labor are used? When between 4 and 5 million hours of labor are used? Do the results conform to the law of diminishing marginal returns? Why or why not?

4 Suppose that an advance in technology doubles the output that can be obtained from each amount of labor in question 3. Under these new conditions, what is the marginal product of labor when between 1 and 2 million hours of labor are used? When between 4 and 5 million hours of labor are used? Do the results conform to the law of diminishing marginal returns? Why or why not?

5 In question 3, suppose that the subsistence wage was 1,400 bushels of wheat. According to Malthus, what would have been the equilibrium labor force? What factors would push the labor force toward this level? What would be the effect of the technological advance in question 4 on the equilibrium labor force?

6 Some studies indicate that what matters most to people is their income relative to others around them rather than the absolute level of their income. Would this fact tend to reduce the importance of growth as a means of helping the poor? Explain.

7 "Ricardo's pessimistic view of the prospects for economic growth stemmed from his assumptions concerning the capital-output ratio. If he had recognized that it was not fixed, he would have been closer to correct." Comment and evaluate.

■ KEY TERMS

economic growth	human capital
population growth	technological change
capital formation	entrepreneurs

■ VIEWPOINT FOR ANALYSIS

In 1994, Linda Cohen of the University of California, Irvine, and Roger Noll of Stanford University wrote that:

> During the past decade government officials have sought new goals for their research dollars. The most important emerging theme in their programs is international competitiveness: the federal government should support R & D to increase American industrial productivity, thereby helping industry in global economic competition. We believe the new competitiveness rationale will not succeed in reinvigorating the national R & D effort. First, competitiveness is not a politically powerful substitute for the cold war in forging a durable, bipartisan coalition for supporting R & D at the generous levels typical of past decades. Second, the methods for implementing the new programs are shaped by political necessity and so are likely to undermine the economic performance of the programs.*

(a) Why should the government support R & D to increase U.S. industrial productivity?

(b) Do you agree that competitiveness is not a politically powerful substitute for the cold war in forging suport for R & D? Why or why not?

(c) If the methods for implementing the new programs are shaped by political necessity, do you agree that they are likely to undermine the economic performance of the programs? Why or why not?

*L. Cohen and R. Noll, "Privatizing Public Research," *Scientific American,* September 1994.

CHAPTER 26

Public Goods and the Role of the Government

LEARNING OBJECTIVES

In this chapter, you should learn:

- The nature and extent of the government's role in the economy
- The characteristics of a public good
- The nature and importance of externalities
- What determines the incidence of a tax
- The purposes of the tax system

During his first term as president, Bill Clinton talked about raising cigarette taxes by $2 a pack. What would be the effect of such a tax increase, and is the government justified in getting involved in this way in the nation's economy? One purpose of this chapter is to discuss this question.

To state that the United States is a mixed capitalist system, in which both government decisions and the price system play important roles, is hardly to provoke a controversy. But going a step beyond takes us into areas where viewpoints often diverge. The proper functions of government and the desirable size and nature of government expenditures and taxes are not matters on which all agree. Indeed, the question of how big government should be, and what its proper functions are, is hotly debated by conservatives and liberals throughout the land. In Chapters 6 through 14 we discussed the role of the government in stabilizing economic fluctuations. In this chapter we consider other roles for the government in the economy.

WHAT FUNCTIONS SHOULD THE GOVERNMENT PERFORM?

In Chapter 2 we discussed the limitations of the price system. Although it is generally agreed that there is a role for the government to redistribute income in favor of the poor, provide public goods, and offset the effects of external economies and diseconomies, there is considerable disagreement over how far the government should go in these areas, and what additional areas the government should be responsible for. Some people feel that "big government" is already a problem, that government is doing too much. Others believe that the public sector of the economy is being undernourished and that government should be allowed to do more. This is a fundamental question, and one that involves a great deal more than economics.

■ CONSERVATIVE VIEW

On the one hand, conservatives, such as Nobel laureate Milton Friedman, believe that the government's role should be limited severely. They feel that economic and political freedom is likely to be undermined by excessive reliance on the state. Moreover, they tend to be skeptical about the government's ability to solve the social and economic problems at hand. They feel that the prevailing faith in the government's power to make a substantial dent in these problems is unreasonable, and they call for more and better information concerning the sorts of tasks government can reasonably be expected to do—and do well. They point to the slowness of the government bureaucracy, the difficulty in controlling huge government organizations, the inefficiencies political considerations can breed, and the difficulties in telling whether government programs are successful or not. On the basis of these considerations, they argue that the government's role should be carefully circumscribed.

The flavor of the conservative position on this question is evident in the remarks of the late George Stigler, a Nobel laureate at the University of Chicago:

> I consider myself courageous, or at least obtuse, in arguing for a reduction in governmental controls over economic life. You are surely desirous of improving this world, and it assuredly needs an immense amount of improvement. No method of displaying one's public-spiritedness is more popular than to notice a problem and pass a law. It combines ease, the warmth of benevolence, and a suitable disrespect for a less enlightened era. What I propose is, for most people, much less attractive: close study of the comparative performance of public and private economy, and the dispassionate appraisal of special remedies that is involved in compassion for the community at large.

■ LIBERAL VIEW

To such remarks, liberals respond with very telling salvos of their own. Just as conservatives tend to be skeptical of the government's ability to solve important social and economic problems, so liberals tend to be skeptical about the price system's ability to solve these problems. They point to the important limitations of the

599

price system, and they assert that the government can do a great deal to overcome these limitations, by regulating private activity and by subsidizing and providing goods and services that the private sector produces too little of.

According to some distinguished liberals, like Harvard's John Kenneth Galbraith, the public sector of the economy has been starved of needed resources, while the private sector has catered to relatively unimportant wants. In his best-selling book, *The Affluent Society*, Galbraith argued that consumers are led by advertising and other promotional efforts to purchase more and more goods of marginal significance to them. On the other hand, in his opinion, the nation is suffering because too little is spent on government services like education, transportation, and urban renewal.[1]

Liberals tend to be less concerned than conservatives about the effects on personal freedom of greater governmental intervention in the economy. They point out that the price system also involves a form of coercion by awarding the available goods and services to those who can pay their equilibrium price. In their view, people who are awarded only a pittance by the price system are coerced into discomfort and malnutrition.

ESTABLISHING "RULES OF THE GAME"

Rules of the game

Although there is considerable disagreement over the proper role of the government, both conservatives and liberals agree that it must do certain things. The first of these is to establish the **rules of the game**—a legal, social, and competitive framework enabling the price system to function as it should.

■ MAINTAINING A LEGAL AND SOCIAL FRAMEWORK

Specifically, *the government must see to it that contracts are enforced, that private ownership is protected, and that fraud is prevented.* Clearly, these matters must be tended to if the price system is to work properly. Also, *the government must maintain order (through the establishment of police and other forces), establish a monetary system (so that money can be used to facilitate trade and exchange), and provide standards for the weight and quality of products.*

As an example of this sort of government intervention, consider the Pure Food and Drug Act. This act, originally passed in 1906 and subsequently amended in various ways, protects the con-

---

[1]J. K. Galbraith, *The Affluent Society* (3d rev. ed.; New York: New American Library, 1978). For a quite different viewpoint, see M. Friedman *Capitalism and Freedom,* (Chicago: University of Chicago Press, 1962).

sumer against improper and fraudulent activities on the part of producers of foods and drugs. It prohibits the merchandising of impure or falsely labeled food or drugs, and it forces producers to specify the quantity and quality of the contents on labels. These requirements strengthen the price system. Without them, the typical consumer would be unable to tell whether food or drugs are pure or properly labeled. Unless consumers can be sure that they are getting what they pay for, the basic logic underlying the price system breaks down. Similar regulations and legislation have been instituted in fields other than food and drugs, and for similar reasons.

■ MAINTAINING A COMPETITIVE FRAMEWORK

Besides establishing a legal and social framework that will enable the price system to do its job, *the government must also see to it that markets remain reasonably competitive.* Only if markets are competitive will prices reflect consumer desires properly. If, on the other hand, markets are dominated by a few sellers (or a few buyers), prices may be rigged by these sellers (or buyers) to promote their own interests. For example, if a single firm is the sole producer of aluminum, it is a safe bet that this firm will establish a higher price than if there were many aluminum producers competing among themselves. In Chapters 19 and 20, we studied the social problems due to monopoly.

REDISTRIBUTION OF INCOME

We have already noted the general agreement that governments should redistribute income in favor of the poor. In other words, *it is usually felt that help should be given to people who are ill, handicapped, old and infirm, disabled, or unable for other reasons to provide for themselves.* To some extent, the nation has decided that income—or at least a certain minimum income—should be divorced from productive services. Of course, this doesn't mean that people who are too lazy to work should be given a handout. It does mean that people who cannot provide for themselves should **Income redistribution** be helped. To implement this principle of **income redistribution**, various payments are made by the government to needy people, including the aged, the handicapped, the unemployed, and pensioners.

These welfare payments are to some extent a "depression baby," for they grew substantially during the Great Depression of the 1930s, when relief payments became a necessity. But they also represent a feeling shared by a large segment of the population

601

that human beings should be assured that, however the wheel of fortune spins and whatever number comes up, they will not starve and their children will not be deprived of a healthy environment and basic schooling. Of course, someone has to pay for this. Welfare payments allow the poor to take more from the nation's output than they produce. In general, the more affluent members of society contribute some of their claims on output to pay for these programs by paying taxes. By using its expenditures to help certain groups and by taxing other groups to pay for these programs, the government accomplishes each year, without revolt and without bayonets, a substantial redistribution of income. This is a crucial aspect of the government's role in our economy.

PROVIDING PUBLIC GOODS

As we have indicated, the government provides many public goods. Let's consider the nature of public goods in more detail.

▓ WHAT IS A PUBLIC GOOD?

Public good

One hallmark of a **public good** is that it can be consumed by one person without diminishing the amount that other people consume of it. Public goods tend to be relatively indivisible; they often come in such large units that they cannot be broken into pieces that can be bought or sold in ordinary markets. Also, *once such goods are produced, there is no way to bar certain citizens from consuming them.* Whether or not citizens contribute toward their cost, they benefit from them. This means that the price system cannot be used to handle the production and distribution of such goods.

An oft-cited example of a public good is a lighthouse. There might be general agreement that the cost of building a particular lighthouse would be more than justified by the benefits (saving lives, fewer shipwrecks, cheaper transportation). Nonetheless, no private firm or person might build and operate such a lighthouse because they might be unable to charge the ships using the lighthouse for the service.[2] Nor would any single user gain enough from the lighthouse to warrant constructing and operating it. Moreover, voluntary contributions are very unlikely to support such a lighthouse, because individual users are likely to feel that their contribution will not affect whether it is built and that they

---

[2]Under some circumstances, lighthouses have been able to charge users. For example, English lighthouses sometimes assessed the shipowners at the docks. Ordinarily only one ship was in sight of the lighthouse at a particular point in time. The light would not be shown if the ship (which was identified by its flag) had not paid.

will be able to use the lighthouse whether or not they contribute. Consequently, the lighthouse might be established and operated only if the government intervenes.

■ NATIONAL DEFENSE: A MAJOR EXAMPLE

National defense is another example of a public good. The benefits of expenditure on national defense extend to the entire nation. Extension of the benefits of national defense to an additional citizen does not mean that any other citizen gets less of these benefits. Also, there is no way of preventing citizens from benefiting from them, whether they contribute to their cost or not. Thus there is no way to use the price system to provide for national defense. Since it is a public good, national defense, if it is to reach an adequate level, must be provided by the government.

■ DECISION MAKING REGARDING PUBLIC GOODS

Essentially, deciding how much to produce of a public good is a political decision. The citizens of the United States elect officials who decide how much should be spent on national defense and how it should be spent. These elected representatives are responsive to special interest groups, as well as to the people as a whole. Many special interest groups lobby hard for the production of certain public goods. For example, an alliance of military and industrial groups presses for increased defense expenditures.

The tax system is used to pay for the production of public goods. In effect, the government says to each citizen, "contribute a certain amount of money to pay for the expenses incurred by the government." The amount particular citizens are assessed may depend on their income (as in the income tax), the value of all or specific types of their property (as in the property tax), the amount they spend on certain types of goods and services (as in the sales tax), or on still other criteria. In the 1990s, the tax system has often been the object of enormous controversy. Much more will be said about the tax system, and the controversies swirling around it, in a later section of this chapter.

EXTERNALITIES

Externalities

It is generally agreed that *the government should act in regard to* **externalities**; *it should encourage the production of goods and services that entail external economies and discourage the production of those that entail external diseconomies.* Take the pollution of air and water discussed in Chapter 21. When a firm or individual dumps wastes into the water or air, other firms or individuals often must pay all or part of the cost of putting the water or air back into a usable condition. Thus the disposal of these wastes entails external diseconomies. Unless the government prohibits certain kinds of pollution, enforces air and water quality standards, charges polluters in accord with the amount of waste they dump into the environment, or issues transferable emissions permits, there will be socially undesirable levels of pollution.

■ EFFECTS OF EXTERNAL DISECONOMIES

To see how such externalities affect the social desirability of the output of a competitive industry, consider Figure 26.1, where the industry's demand and supply curves are contained in the top left-hand panel. As shown there, the equilibrium output of the industry is Q_0. If the industry results in no external economies or diseconomies, this is likely to be the socially optimal output. But what if the industry results in external diseconomies, such as the pollution described above? Then the industry's supply curve does not fully reflect the true social costs of producing the product. The supply curve that reflects these social costs is S_1, which, as shown in the top right-hand panel of Figure 26.1, lies to the left of the in-

FIGURE 26.1

Effect of External Economies and Diseconomies on the Optimal Output of a Competitive Industry

The optimal output is Q_0 if neither external economies nor diseconomies are present. If there are external diseconomies, curve S_1 reflects the true social costs of producing the product, and Q_1 is the optimal output. If there are external economies, curve D_1 reflects the true social benefits of producing the product, and Q_2 is the optimal output.

dustry's supply curve. The optimal output of the good is Q_1, which is less than the competitive output Q_0.

What can the government do to correct this situation? There are many ways that it can intervene to reduce the industry's output from Q_0 to Q_1. For example, it can impose taxes on the industry. If these taxes are of the right type and amount, they will result in the desired reduction of output.

■ EFFECTS OF EXTERNAL ECONOMIES

What if the industry results in external economies? For example, what if the manufacture of one industrial product makes it cheaper to produce other products? Then the industry's demand curve underestimates the true social benefits of producing the product. The demand curve that reflects these social benefits correctly is D_1, which, as shown in the bottom panel of Figure 26.1, lies to the right of the industry's demand curve. The optimal output of the good is Q_2, which is greater than the competitive output Q_0.

As in the case where the industry results in external diseconomies, the government can intervene in various ways to change the industry's output. But in this case, the object is to increase, not decrease, its output. To accomplish this, the government can, among other things, grant subsidies to the industry. If they are of the right type and amount, they can be used to increase the industry's output from Q_0 to Q_2.

THE THEORY OF PUBLIC CHOICE

According to many economists interested in the theory of public choice, many factors induce the government to make decisions that are not efficient from an economic point of view. Just as the price system suffers from certain limitations, so the government has shortcomings as a mechanism for promoting economic welfare. These factors, discussed below, often result in expanded government expenditures.

■ SPECIAL INTEREST GROUPS

It is no secret that politicians try to stay in office. In some cases, they must decide whether to adopt a policy that benefits a small number of people, each of whom will gain a great deal, at the expense of a very large number of people, each of whom will lose very little. The small group of gainers (the *special interest group*) is likely to be well organized, well financed, and vocal. The large

The Tennessee Valley Authority

The TVA dam at Fort Loudoun

power to the depressed area. And the local utilities challenged the TVA all the way.

By 1954 the TVA was well established and requested funds from Congress to build a steam-driven electric plant. Congress rejected the proposal because it did not feel that the TVA should be expanded further into a federal power facility not exclusively hydroelectric, nor that it should be made into an even larger business.

Why is it proper for the government to provide for flood control, but not to build steam-driven electric power plants? The rationale for the government's providing a service is a breakdown of the free market, that is, the failure of the private sector to provide the proper quantity of certain goods and services. Flood control and navigation are clearly public goods, and insofar as electrification is a by-product of flood control, it is reasonable for the government to provide this service too. But the proposed steam-driven electrical generators could have been as easily provided by the private sector as by the government.

The Great Mississippi Flood of 1927 left 800,000 homeless and focused national attention on the federal government's responsibility for flood control. Such control had been considered for years on the Tennessee River. Senator George W. Norris of Nebraska campaigned for federal support for river control in the 1920s and 1930s, but his attempts were unsuccessful, largely because local utilities feared that by building dams, the federal government would be providing not only flood control but electric power as well.

The debate continued until 1933, when the Roosevelt administration created the Tennessee Valley Authority (TVA). The TVA was foremost a construction project that would create jobs in a depressed economy, but it was also created for regional development that would yield benefits for many years to come. In addition to its responsibility for flood control and for improving the navigability of the Tennessee's waters, the TVA built housing, worked on agricultural development, and provided electric

group of losers is likely to be unaware of its losses and more indifferent to the outcome of this decision, since each member of this group has little at stake. In a case of this sort, a politician will be inclined to adopt the policy favoring the special interest group. Why? Because the politician, by not adopting this policy, would lose the support of this group. On the other hand, by adopting this policy, the politician is unlikely to lose the support of the large group of people that are hurt by it because they are much more interested in other issues where they have more at stake.

There are many cases where politicians have adopted policies favoring special interest groups, even though the total gains to the special interest groups are less than the total losses to other segments of society. Whereas such policies are unsound economics, they have been regarded as good politics. One example is the enactment of tariffs and quotas that reduce domestic competition and result in consumers' paying higher prices. Also, government services that benefit special interest groups often are expanded, to the detriment of society at large.

■ BUREAUCRATIC INEFFICIENCY

Many observers contend that government agencies are less efficient than private firms. As we have seen in previous chapters, the price system establishes strong incentives for firms to minimize their costs. If firms can lower their costs, they can increase their profits, at least temporarily. Government officials, on the other hand, often have less incentive to reduce costs. Indeed, it is sometimes claimed that there is an incentive to increase costs, since an agency's power and influence is directly related to the size of its budget. Unfortunately, we do not have a great deal of evidence concerning whatever differences may exist between the efficiency of government agencies and of private firms, largely because of the difficulties in measuring the efficiency or inefficiency of government agencies. For example, how efficient is the Environmental Protection Agency? Because it is so difficult to measure the EPA's output and because it is so difficult to find a standard against which to measure its performance, this question is exceedingly difficult to answer.

One area where there has been evidence of inefficiency has been the development and production of new weapons by the Department of Defense and its contractors. There have been spectacular overruns in development and production costs. To some extent, such cost increases reflect the fact that new weapon systems tend to push the state of the art, so that problems must be expected. But in addition, the firms that develop and produce these weapon systems often submit unrealistically low bids to get a contract, knowing that they are likely to get approval for cost increases later on. According to some observers, like Merton J. Peck of Yale University and F. M. Scherer of Harvard University, these cost overruns have also been due to "inadequate attention to the efficient utilization of technical, production, and administrative manpower—areas in which major cost reductions are possible."

■ NONSELECTIVITY

Another point made by public-choice theorists is that when citizens vote for their elected officials, they vote for a "bundle" of political programs. For example, in a particular election, the two candidates may be John Brown, who favors increased defense spending, reduced capital gains taxes, and a tougher policy against drug use, and Jane Smith, who opposes all these things. If you favor increased defense spending and a tougher policy against drug use, but oppose reduced capital gains taxes, there is no way that you can elect a candidate who mirrors your preferences. All you can do is vote for the candidate whose bundle of programs is closest to your preferences.

In contrast, when citizens make choices in the marketplace, they are better able to pick a set of goods and services that is in accord with their preferences, since they do not have to buy items that they do not want. If you want a shirt and a tie, you can buy them without having to buy a pair of socks as well. Since citizens cannot be so selective with regard to goods and services in the public sector, public-choice theorists hold that the provision of such goods and services tends to be inefficient.

To conclude this brief section on the theory of public choice, it is important to recognize that no one is accusing government officials of being stupid, lazy, or corrupt. Some undoubtedly are, but this is true of business executives as well. The point is that the incentives faced by government officials and the nature of the political process result in decision making that can be suboptimal from an economic point of view. This helps to explain why the government, like the price system, can bungle the job of organizing the nation's economic activities. Neither is a panacea.

PRINCIPLES OF TAXATION

As we saw in Chapters 6 and 12, the government finances most of its expenditures through taxation. According to the English political philosopher Edmund Burke, "To tax and to please, no more than to love and to be wise, is not given to men." What constitutes a rational tax system? Are there any generally accepted principles to guide the nation in determining who should pay how much? The answer is that there are some principles most people accept, but they are so broad and general that they leave plenty of room for argument and compromise. Specifically, two general principles of taxation command widespread agreement.

■ BENEFIT PRINCIPLE

Benefit principle

The first principle, called the **benefit principle**, is that *people who receive more from a certain government service should pay more in taxes to support it.* Certainly few people would argue with this idea. However, it is frequently difficult, if not impossible, to apply.

For example, there is no good way to measure the amount of the benefits received by a particular taxpayer from many public services, such as police protection.

■ ABILITY-TO-PAY PRINCIPLE

**Ability-to-pay
principle**

The second principle is the **ability-to-pay principle**. It means that *people should be taxed so as to result in a socially desirable redistribution of income.* In practice, this has ordinarily meant that the wealthy have been asked to pay more than the poor. This idea, too, has generally commanded widespread assent—although this, of course, has not prevented the wealthy from trying to avoid its being applied to them.

■ APPLICATIONS OF THESE PRINCIPLES

It follows from these principles that if two people are in essentially the same circumstances (their income, purchases, utilization of public services are the same), then they should pay the same taxes. This is an important rule, innocuous though it may seem. It says that equals should be treated equally; *whether one is a Republican and the other is a Democrat, or whether one is a friend of the president and the other is his enemy, or whether one has purely salary income and the other has property income, they should be treated equally.* Certainly, this is a basic characteristic of an equitable tax system.

It is easy to relate most of the taxes in our tax structure to these principles. For example, the first principle, the benefit principle, is the basic rationale behind taxes on gasoline and license fees for vehicles and drivers. Those who use the roads are asked to pay for their construction and upkeep. Also, the property tax, levied primarily on real estate, is often supported on these grounds. It is argued that property owners receive important benefits—fire and police protection, for example—and that the extent of the benefits is related to the extent of their property.

The personal income tax is based squarely on the second principle: ability to pay. A person with a large income pays a higher proportion of income in personal income taxes than does a person with a smaller income. In 1998, if a couple's income (after deductions and exemptions) was $10,000, their federal income tax rebate was $3,756, whereas if their income was $50,000, their federal income tax payment was $4,815. Also, estate and inheritance taxes hit the very rich much harder than the middle class.

The principles cited above are useful and important, but they do not take us very far toward establishing a rational tax structure. They are too vague and leave too many questions unanswered. If I use about the same amount of public services as you do, but my income is twice yours, how much more should I pay in taxes? Twice as much? Three times as much? Half as much? These principles throw no real light on many of the detailed questions that must be answered by a real-life tax code.

THE PERSONAL INCOME TAX

The federal **personal income tax** brings in hundreds of billions of dollars a year. Yet many people are unaware of just how much they are contributing, because it is deducted from their wages each month or each week, so that they owe little extra when April 15 rolls around. (Indeed, they may even be due a refund.) This pay-as-you-go scheme reduces the pain, but of course it does not eliminate it; taxes are never painless.

■ THE TAX SCHEDULE

Obviously, how much a family has to pay in personal income taxes depends on the family's income. The tax schedule (as of 1998) is as shown in Table 26.1. The second column shows how much a couple would have to pay if their income were the amount shown in the first column. At an income of $30,000, their income tax would be $2,565; at an income of $50,000, their income tax would be $4,815. Clearly, the percentage of income owed in income tax increases as income increases, but this percentage does not increase indefinitely. Even if the couple made $500,000 in 1998, the percentage of income owed in income tax would not have exceeded 35 percent.

TABLE 26.1

Federal Personal Income Tax, Married Couple with Two Dependents, 1998

INCOME AFTER DEDUCTIONS AND PERSONAL EXEMPTIONS	PERSONAL INCOME TAX (DOLLARS)	MARGINAL TAX RATE (PERCENT)	AVERAGE TAX RATE (PERCENT)
10,000	−3,756	15	−37.6
20,000	−1,811	15	−9.1
35,000	2,565	15	7.3
50,000	4,815	15	9.6
75,000	10,371	28	13.8

■ THE MARGINAL TAX RATE

It is instructive to look further at how the "tax bite" increases with income. In particular, let's ask ourselves what proportion of an *extra* dollar of income the couple will have to pay in personal income taxes. In other words, what is the **marginal tax rate:** the tax on an extra dollar of income? The third column of Table 26.1 shows that the marginal tax rate was 15 percent if the couple's income was $10,000 or $30,000, 28 percent if it was $75,000. The top marginal tax rate in 1998 was 39.6 percent.

THE PROPERTY TAX AND THE SALES TAX

The **property tax** is the fiscal bulwark of our local governments. The way it works is simple enough. Most towns and cities estimate the amount they will spend in the next year or two, and then determine a property tax based on the assessed property values in the town or city. If there is $500 million in assessed property values in the town and the town needs to raise $5 million, the tax rate will be 1 percent of assessed property value. In other words, each property owner will have to pay 1 percent of the assessed value of his or her property. There are well-known problems in the administration of the property tax. First, assessed values of property often depart significantly from actual market values; the former are typically much lower than the latter. And the ratio of assessed to actual value is often lower among higher-priced pieces of property; thus wealthier people tend to get off easier. Second, there is widespread evasion of taxes on personal property: securities, bank accounts, and so on. Many people simply do not pay up. Third, the property tax is not very flexible; assessments and rates tend to change rather slowly.

The **sales tax,** of course, is a bulwark of state taxation. It provides a high yield with relatively low collection costs. Most of the states have some form of general sales tax, the rate being usually between 3 and 6 percent. If the rate is 4 percent, retailers add to the price of goods sold to consumers an amount equal to 4 percent of the consumer's bill. This extra amount is submitted to the state as the general sales tax. Some states exempt food purchases from this tax, and a few exempt medical supplies. Where they exist, these exemptions help reduce the impact of the sales tax on the poor, but in general the sales tax imposes a greater burden relative to income on the poor than on the rich, for the simple reason that the rich save a larger percentage of their income. Practically all a poor family's income may be subject to sales taxes; a great deal of a rich family's income may not be, because it is not spent on consumer goods, but is saved.

Proposition 13

Supporters celebrate the passage of Proposition 13.

The combination of inflation and a housing shortage led to a rapid increase in land values in California in the late 1970s. This in turn resulted in steadily increasing property taxes. Homes that sold for $600 after World War II were selling for $60,000 in the late 1970s, and it was not unusual for homeowners to be paying over $2,000 per year in property taxes. Many homeowners felt that the burden of local taxes was too much and that it was time to cut government expenditures. The taxpayers' revolt, led by Howard Jarvis, began with the collection of over a million signatures, more than enough to place Proposition 13 on the California state ballot. Proposition 13 would limit property taxes to 1 percent—a 60 percent rollback that would wipe out some $7 billion of local government funds. At the polls, Proposition 13 easily passed with 65 percent of the vote.

Subsequently, local government spending leveled out throughout the state, and local government services suffered. Public employees were laid off, and services such as summer school classes, library services, and garbage collection were curtailed. Some of the other consequences came as a surprise to voters. For example, of the $7 billion tax rollback, corporations got the lion's share.

Jarvis was back in 1980 with a new initiative: Proposition 9, which would have cut state income taxes by 50 percent. This time, however, Jarvis's opponents focused on equity issues. Amid widespread charges that Proposition 9 might simply let the rich get richer at the expense of the less well-to-do, Jarvis was defeated and the tax revolt fever began to cool down.

Who really pays the property tax or the sales tax? To what extent can these taxes be shifted to other people? The answer is not as straightforward as one might expect. For the property tax, the owner of unrented residential property swallows the tax, since there is no one else to shift it to. But the owner of rented property may attempt to pass along some of the tax to the tenant. In the case of a general sales tax, it is generally concluded that the consumer pays the tax. But if the tax is imposed on only a single commodity, the extent to which it can be shifted to the consumer depends on the demand and supply curves for the taxed commodity. The following section explains in some detail why this is the case.

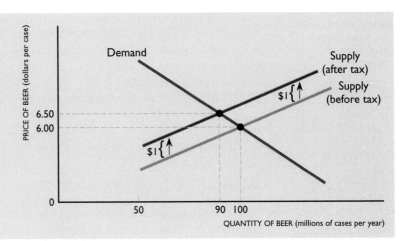

FIGURE 26.2

Effect of a $1 Tax on a Case of Beer

The tax shifts the supply curve upward by $1. Since the demand curve is unaffected, the equilibrium price of beer increases from $6.00 to $6.50 per case.

TAX INCIDENCE

Tax incidence

Who pays the tax is the **tax incidence**. Suppose that a sales or excise tax is imposed on a particular good, say, beer. In Figure 26.2, we show the demand and supply curves for beer before the imposition of the tax. With no tax, the equilibrium price of a case of beer is $6, and the equilibrium quantity is 100 million cases. If a tax of $1 is imposed on each case produced, what is the effect on the price of each case? Or to see it from the beer drinker's perspective, how much of the tax is passed on to the consumer in the form of a higher price?

Since the tax is collected from the sellers, *the supply curve is shifted upward by the amount of tax,* as shown in Figure 26.2. For example, if the pretax price had to be $5 a case to induce sellers to supply 80 million cases of beer, the posttax price would have to be $1 higher, or $6 a case, to induce the same supply. Similarly, if the pretax price had to be $6 a case to induce sellers to supply 100 million cases of beer, the posttax price would have to be $1 higher, or $7 a case, to induce the same supply. The reason why the sellers require $1 more per case to supply the pretax amount is that they must pay the tax of $1 per case to the government. To wind up with the same amount as before (after paying the tax), they require the extra $1 per case.

■ WHO PAYS THE TAX?

Figure 26.2 shows that after the tax is imposed, the equilibrium price of beer is $6.50, an increase of $.50 over its pretax level. Consequently, in this case half the tax is passed on to consumers, who pay $.50 per case more for beer. And half the tax is swallowed by the sellers, who receive (after they pay the tax) $.50 per case less for beer. But it is not always true that sellers pass half the tax on to consumers and absorb the rest themselves. On the contrary, in some cases, consumers may bear almost all the tax (and sellers practically none of it), whereas in other cases consumers may bear almost none of the tax (and sellers practically all of it). The result will depend on how sensitive the quantity demanded and the quantity supplied are to the price of the good.

■ SENSITIVITY OF DEMAND TO PRICE

In particular, holding the supply curve constant, *the less sensitive the quantity demanded is to the price of the good, the bigger the portion of the tax that is shifted to consumers.* To illustrate this, consider Figure 26.3, which shows the effect of a $1-per-case tax on beer in two markets, one (panel B) where the quantity demanded is much more sensitive to price than in the other (panel A). As is evident, the price increase to consumers resulting from the tax is much greater in the latter market (panel A) than in the former (panel B). And the amount of the tax that is absorbed by producers is much less in the latter market (panel A) than in the former (panel B).

FIGURE 26.3

Effect on Tax Incidence of the Sensitivity of the Quantity Demanded to Price

The supply curve is the same in panel A as in panel B. The quantity demanded is more sensitive to price in panel B than in panel A. Before the tax the equilibrium price is P_0 in both panels. After the tax the equilibrium price is P_1 in panel A and P_2 in panel B. The increase in price to the consumer is greater if the quantity demanded is less sensitive to price (panel A) than if it is more sensitive (panel B).

FIGURE 26.4

Effect on Tax Incidence of the Sensitivity of the Quantity Supplied to Price

The demand curve is the same in panel A as in panel B. The quantity supplied is more sensitive to price in panel A than in panel B. Before the tax the equilibrium price is P_3 in both panels. After the tax the equilibrium price is P_4 in panel A and P_5 in panel B. The increase in price to the consumer is greater if the quantity supplied is more sensitive to price (panel A) than if it is less sensitive (panel B).

■ SENSITIVITY OF SUPPLY TO PRICE

It can also be shown that, holding the demand curve constant, *the less sensitive the quantity supplied is to the price of the good, the bigger the portion of the tax that is absorbed by producers.* To illustrate this, consider Figure 26.4, which shows the effect of a $1-per-case tax on beer in two markets, one (panel A) where the quantity supplied is much more sensitive to price than in the other (panel B). As is evident, the price increase to consumers resulting from the tax is much greater in the former market (panel A) than in the latter (panel B). And the amount of the tax that is absorbed by producers is much less in the former market (panel A) than in the latter market (panel B).

■ EFFECT OF TAX ON QUANTITY

Finally, note that the tax reduces the equilibrium quantity consumed of the taxed good—beer in this instance. One reason why governments impose taxes on goods like cigarettes and liquor is that they are regarded (in some circles at least) as socially undesirable. Clearly, the more sensitive the quantity demanded and quantity supplied are to price, the larger the reduction in the equilibrium quantity. Thus, if the government imposes a tax of this sort to reduce the quantity consumed of the good, the effect will be greater if both the quantity demanded and the quantity supplied are relatively sensitive to price.

REVIEW AND PRACTICE

■ SUMMARY

1 To a considerable extent, the government's role in the economy has developed in response to the limitations of the price system. There is considerable agreement that the government should redistribute income in favor of the poor, provide public goods, and offset the effects of external economies and diseconomies. Also, it is generally felt that the government should establish a proper legal, social, and competitive framework for the price system.

2 Beyond this, however, there are wide differences of opinion on the proper role of government in economic affairs. Conservatives tend to be suspicious of "big government," whereas liberals are inclined to believe that the government should do more.

3 Basically, the amount that the government spends on various activities and services must be decided through a country's political processes. Voting by ballots must be substituted for voting by dollars.

4 Just as the price system suffers from limitations, so does the government. Special interest groups sometimes gain at the expense of society as a whole. Government agencies sometimes have little incentive to increase efficiency. Citizens find it difficult to be selective in their choice of goods and services in the public sector. In recent years, economists seem to have put more emphasis on these (and other) limitations of the public sector.

5 It is generally agreed that people who receive more in benefits from a certain government service should pay more in taxes to support it. It is also generally agreed that people should be taxed so that the result is a socially desirable redistribution of income and that equals should be treated equally. But these general principles, although useful, cannot throw light on many of the detailed questions a real-life tax code must answer.

6 The personal income tax is a very important source of federal revenue, the sales tax is an important source of state revenue, and the property tax is an important source of local revenue.

7 If a tax is imposed on a single commodity, the extent to which it can be shifted to the consumer depends on the demand and supply curves for the taxed commodity. If the quantity demanded is relatively insensitive to the price of the good or if the quantity supplied is relatively sensitive to the price, a large portion of the tax is shifted to consumers.

■ PROBLEMS AND QUESTIONS

1 "I believe the government should do only that which private citizens cannot do for themselves or which they cannot do so well for themselves." Interpret and comment. Indicate how one might determine in practice what the legitimate functions of government are, according to this proposition.

2 "The ideal public policy, from the viewpoint of the state, is one with identifiable beneficiaries, each of whom is helped appreciably, at the cost of many unidentifiable persons, none of whom is hurt much." Interpret and comment. Indicate how this proposition might be used to help predict government behavior.

3 Explain why national defense is a public good but a rifle is not a public good.

4 "I cannot get the amount of national defense I want and you, a different amount." Explain. Is this true of all public goods?

5 Suppose that the quantity supplied of gin at each of the following prices is as given on the next page:

PRICE OF GIN (DOLLARS PER QUART)	QUANTITY SUPPLIED (MILLIONS OF QUARTS)
4	5
5	6
6	7
7	8
8	9
9	10

Plot the supply curve on graph paper. Suppose that the government imposes a tax of $2 per quart on gin and that the tax is collected from the sellers. Plot the posttax supply curve on graph paper.

6 Under the circumstances described in question 5, suppose that the quantity of gin demanded is 7 million quarts, regardless of the price (so long as it is between $4 and $9 per quart). What will be the equilibrium price of gin before the tax and after it? How much of the tax is passed on to the consumer?

7 Under the circumstances described in question 5, suppose that the demand curve for gin is a horizontal line at $6 per quart. If this is the case, what will be the equilibrium price of gin before the tax and after it? How much of the tax is passed on to the consumer?

■ KEY TERMS

rules of the game

income redistribution

public good

externalities

benefit principle

ability-to-pay principle

tax incidence

■ VIEWPOINT FOR ANALYSIS

According to *Business Week,* March 22, 1993, "Raising cigarette taxes by $2 a pack would generate some $30 billion a year in federal revenue—even after allowing for a fall-off in consumption. . . . While $2 a pack may sound high, per-pack taxes total $3.68 in Denmark, $2.55 in Britain, and $2.11 in Germany. The knowledge of smoking's dangers has reduced consumption in the U.S., but every year the tobacco industry wins new customers—and the health industry some potential candidates for expensive and often fruitless care. Raising the financial disincentive could make Americans healthier. . . ."*

(a) Under what circumstances would a $2 increase in the cigarette tax raise the price per pack by $2? Under what circumstances would it have no effect on the price?

(b) If the supply curve for cigarettes is horizontal and if the arc price elasticity of demand for cigarettes is 0.3 (which is a reasonable estimate, according to existing studies), what would be the effect on cigarette consumption of a tax that doubled the price of a pack of cigarettes?

(c) Should the government try to discourage smoking in this way? Who would be the gainers? Who would be the losers? What position would you take on this issue?

Business Week, March 22, 1993, p. 102.

CHAPTER 27

International Trade

LEARNING OBJECTIVES

In this chapter, you should learn:

■ The definition of comparative advantage and its relation to international trade

■ What tariffs and quotas are

■ The impact of tariffs and quotas on international trade

■ The arguments for and against tariffs and quotas

McKinsey and Company, a leading consulting firm, published a report that concluded: "Given our finding that global competition leads to higher productivity, a specific step that can be taken to encourage global competition is to phase out the variety of different trade restrictions that are in effect in Europe, the U.S., and Japan." What are these trade restrictions, and why do many observers urge that they be phased out? One purpose of this chapter is to answer this question.

Practically all people realize that they are not islands unto themselves and that they benefit from living with, working with, and trading with other people. Exactly the same is true of countries. They too must interact with one another, and they too benefit from trade with one another. No country can be an island unto itself, not even the United States. To understand how the world economy functions, you must grasp the basic economic principles of international trade.

U.S. FOREIGN TRADE

Although small relative to our national product, U.S. foreign trade plays a very important role in our economic life. Many of our industries depend on other countries for markets or for such raw materials as coffee, tea, or tin. Our *exports*—the things we sell to other countries—amount to about 10 percent of our gross domestic product. In absolute terms, our exports (and imports) are bigger than those of any other nation. Without question, our way of life would have to change considerably if we could not trade with other countries.

SPECIALIZATION AND TRADE

Why do we trade with other countries? Do we, and our trading partners, benefit from this trade? And if so, what determines the sorts of goods we should export and import? These are very important questions, among the most fundamental in economics. The answers are not new. They have been well understood for considerably more than a century, from the work of such great economists as David Hume, David Ricardo, Adam Smith, and John Stuart Mill.

■ WHY DO INDIVIDUALS TRADE?

As a first step, it is useful to recognize that the benefits *countries* receive through trade are essentially the same as those *individuals* receive through trade. Consider the hypothetical case of John Barrister, a lawyer, with a wife and two children. The Barrister family, like practically all families, trades continually with other families and with business firms. Since Mr. Barrister is a lawyer, he trades his legal services for money which he and his wife use to buy the food, clothing, housing, and other goods and services his family wants. Why does the Barrister family do this? What advantages does it receive through trade? Why doesn't it attempt to be self-sufficient?

To see why the Barrister family is sensible indeed to opt for trade rather than self-sufficiency, let's compare the current situation—where Mr. Barrister specializes in the production of legal services and trades the money he receives for other goods and services—with the situation if the Barrister family attempted to be self-sufficient. In the latter case, the Barristers would have to provide their own transportation, telephone service, foodstuffs, clothing, and a host of other things. Mr. Barrister is a lawyer—a well-trained, valuable, productive member of the community. But if he were to try his hand at making automobiles—or even bicycles—it might be a total loss. If the Barrister family attempted to be self-sufficient, it might be unable to provide many of the goods it now enjoys.

■ WHY DO COUNTRIES TRADE?

Trade permits specialization, and specialization increases output. This is the advantage of trade, both for individuals and for countries. In our hypothetical case, it is obvious that because he can trade with other families and with firms, Mr. Barrister can specialize in doing what he is good at: law. Consequently, he can be more productive than if he were forced to be a jack-of-all-trades, as he

619

would have to be if he could not trade with others. The same principle holds for countries. Because the United States can trade with other countries, it can specialize in the goods and services it produces particularly well. Then it can trade them for goods that other countries are especially good at producing. Thus both we and our trading partners benefit.

Some countries have more and better resources of certain types than others. Saudi Arabia has oil, Canada has timber, Japan has skilled labor, and so on. *International differences in resource endowments and in the relative quantity of various types of human and nonhuman resources are important bases for specialization.* Consider countries with lots of fertile soil, little capital, and much unskilled labor. They are likely to find it advantageous to produce agricultural goods, whereas countries with poor soil, much capital, and highly skilled labor will probably do better to produce capital-intensive high-technology goods. We must recognize, however, that the bases for specialization do not remain fixed over time. Instead, as technology and the resource endowments of various countries change, the pattern of international specialization changes as well. For instance, the United States specialized more in raw materials and foodstuffs about a century ago than it does now.

ABSOLUTE ADVANTAGE

To clarify the benefits of trade, consider the following example. Suppose that the United States can produce 2 electronic computers or 5,000 cases of wine with 1 unit of resources. Suppose that France can produce 1 electronic computer or 10,000 cases of wine with 1 unit of resources. Given the production possibilities in each country, are there any advantages in trade between the countries? And if so, which commodity should each country export, and which commodity should each country import? Should France export wine and import computers, or should it import wine and export computers?

To answer these questions, assume that the United States is producing a certain number of computers and a certain amount of wine—and that France is producing a certain number of computers and a certain amount of wine. If the United States shifts 1 unit of its resources from producing wine to producing computers, it will increase its production of computers by 2 computers and reduce its production of wine by 5,000 cases of wine. If France shifts 1 unit of resources from the production of computers to the production of wine, it will increase its production of wine by 10,000 cases and reduce its production of computers by 1 computer.

TABLE 27.1

Case of Absolute Advantage

	INCREASE OR DECREASE IN OUTPUT OF:	
	COMPUTERS	WINE (THOUSANDS OF CASES)
Effect of United States's shifting 1 unit of resources from wine to computers	+2	−5
Effect of France's shifting 1 unit of resources from computers to wine	−1	+10
Net effect	+1	+5

Table 27.1 shows the *net* effect of this shift in the utilization of resources on *world* output of computers and of wine. World output of computers increases (by 1 computer) and world output of wine increases (by 5,000 cases) as a result of the redeployment of resources in each country. Thus *specialization increases world output.*

Moreover, if world output of each commodity is increased by shifting 1 unit of U.S. resources from wine to computers and shifting 1 unit of French resources from computers to wine, it follows that world output of each commodity will be increased further if each country shifts *more* of its resources in the same direction. This is because the amount of resources required to produce a unit of each good is assumed to be constant, regardless of how much is produced.

Thus in this situation, one country—the United States—should specialize in producing computers, and the other country—France—should specialize in producing wine. This will maximize world output of both wine and computers and permit a rise in both countries' standards of living. Complete specialization of this sort is somewhat unrealistic, since countries often produce some of both commodities, but this simple example illustrates the basic principles involved.

COMPARATIVE ADVANTAGE

The case just described is a very special one, since one country (France) has an absolute advantage over another (the United States) in the production of one good (wine), whereas the second country (the United States) has an absolute advantage over the first (France) in the production of another good (computers). What do we mean by the term "absolute advantage"? Country A has an **absolute advantage** over country B in the production of a good when country A can produce a unit of the good with fewer resources than can country B. Since the United States can produce a computer with fewer units of resources than France, it has an absolute advantage over France in the production of computers. Since France requires fewer resources than the United States to produce a given amount of wine, France has an absolute advantage over the United States in the production of wine.

But what if one country is more efficient in producing both goods? If the United States is more efficient in producing both computers and wine, is there still any benefit to be derived from specialization and trade? At first glance, you are probably inclined to answer no. But if this is your inclination, you should reconsider, because you are wrong.

A NUMERICAL EXAMPLE

To see why specialization and trade have advantages even when one country is more efficient than another at producing both goods, consider the following example. Suppose the United States can produce 2 electronic computers or 5,000 cases of wine with 1 unit of resources, and France can produce 1 electronic computer or 4,000 cases of wine with 1 unit of resources. In this case, the United States is a more efficient producer of both computers and wine. Nonetheless, as we shall see, world output of both goods will increase if the United States specializes in the production of computers and France specializes in the production of wine.

Table 27.2 demonstrates this conclusion. If 2 units of U.S. resources are shifted from wine to computer production, 4 additional computers and 10,000 fewer cases of wine are produced. If 3 units of French resources are shifted from computer to wine

TABLE 27.2

Case of Comparative Advantage

	INCREASE OR DECREASE IN OUTPUT OF:	
	COMPUTERS	WINE (THOUSANDS OF CASES)
Effect of United States's shifting 2 units of resources from wine to computers	+4	−10
Effect of France's shifting 3 units of resources from computers to wine	−3	+12
Net effect	+1	+2

production, 3 fewer computers and 12,000 additional cases of wine are produced. Thus the combined effect of this redeployment of resources in both countries is to increase world output of computers by 1 computer and to increase world output of wine by 2,000 cases. Even though the United States is more efficient than France in the production of both computers and wine, world output of both goods will be maximized if the United States specializes in computers and France specializes in wine.

Basically, this is because although the United States is more efficient than France in the production of both goods, it has a greater advantage in computers than in wine. It is twice as efficient as France in producing computers, but only 25 percent more efficient than France in producing wine. To derive these numbers, recall that 1 unit of resources will produce 2 computers in the United States, but only 1 computer in France. Thus the United States is twice as efficient in computers. On the other hand, 1 unit of resources will produce 5,000 cases of wine in the United States, but only 4,000 cases in France. Thus the United States is 25 percent more efficient in wine.

■ TRADE DEPENDS ON COMPARATIVE ADVANTAGE

**Comparative
advantage**

A country has a **comparative advantage** in those products where its efficiency relative to other nations is highest. Thus in this case the United States has a comparative advantage in the production of computers and a comparative disadvantage in the production of wine. So long as a country has a comparative advantage in the production of some commodities and a comparative disadvantage in the production of others, it can benefit from specialization and trade. A country will specialize in products in which it has a comparative advantage and import those in which it has a comparative disadvantage. The point is that *specialization and trade depend on comparative, not absolute, advantage.* One of the first economists to understand the full significance of this fact was David Ricardo, the English economist of the early nineteenth century.

THE TERMS OF TRADE

Terms of trade

The **terms of trade** are defined as the quantity of imported goods that a country can obtain in exchange for a unit of domestic goods. Thus, in our previous example, the terms of trade are measured by the ratio of the price of a computer to the price of a case of wine, since this ratio shows how many cases of French wine the United States can get in exchange for a U.S. computer. It is important to note that this ratio must be somewhere between 2,500:1 and 4,000:1. By diverting its own resources from computer production to wine production, the United States can exchange a computer for 2,500 cases of wine. Since this is possible, it will not pay the United States to trade a computer for less than 2,500 cases of wine. Similarly, since France can exchange a case of wine for 1/4,000 of a computer by diverting its own resources from wine to computers, it clearly will not be willing to trade a case of wine for less than 1/4,000 of a computer.

But where will the price ratio lie between 2,500:1 and 4,000:1? The answer depends on the *world supply and demand for the two products.* The stronger the demand for computers (relative to their supply) and the weaker the demand for wine (relative to its supply), the higher the price ratio. On the other hand, the weaker the demand for computers (relative to their supply) and the stronger the demand for wine (relative to its supply), the lower the price ratio.

▓ INCOMPLETE SPECIALIZATION

In our numerical example, the United States should specialize completely in computers, and France should specialize completely in wine. This result stems from the assumption that the cost of producing a computer or a case of wine is constant. If, on the other hand, the cost of producing each good increases with the amount produced, the result is likely to be incomplete specialization. In other words, although the United States will continue to specialize in computers and France will continue to specialize in wine, each country will also produce some of the other good as well. This is a more likely outcome, since specialization generally tends to be less than complete.

INTERNATIONAL TRADE AND INDIVIDUAL MARKETS

We have emphasized that countries can benefit by specializing in the production of goods for which they have a comparative advantage and trading these goods for others for which they have a comparative disadvantage.[1] But how do a country's producers know

[1]The principle of comparative advantage is useful in explaining and predicting the pattern of world trade, as well as in showing the benefits of trade. For example, consider the exports of Great Britain and the United States. Robert Stern of the University of Michigan compared British and U.S. exports of 39 industries. In 21 of the 24 industries where our labor productivity was more than three times that of the British, our exports exceeded British exports. In 11 of the 15 industries where our labor productivity was less than three times that of the British, our exports were less than British exports. Thus in 32 out of 39 industries, the principle of compara-

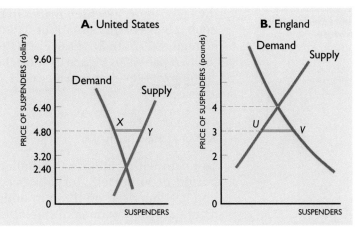

FIGURE 27.1

Determination of Quantity Imported and Exported under Free Trade

Under free trade, price will equal $4.80, or £3. The United States will export *XY* units, the English will import *UV* units, and *XY* = *UV*.

A. United States

B. England

whether they have a comparative advantage or disadvantage in the production of a given commodity? They do not call up the local university and ask the leading professor of economics (although that might not always be such a bad idea). Instead, as we shall see in this section, the market for the good provides the required signals.

To see how this works, let's consider a new (and rather whimsical) product: bulletproof suspenders. Suppose that the Mob, having run a scientific survey of mobsters and cops, finds that most of them wear their suspenders over their bulletproof vests. As a consequence, the Mob's shooters are instructed to render a victim immobile by shooting holes in the victim's suspenders (thus making his trousers fall down and trip him). Naturally, the producers of suspenders will soon find it profitable to produce a new bulletproof variety, an innovation that, it is hoped, will make a solid contribution to law and order. The new suspenders are demanded only in the United States and England, since the rest of the world wears belts. The demand curve in the United States is as shown in panel A of Figure 27.1, and the demand curve in England is as shown in panel B. Suppose further that this product can be manufactured in both the United States and England. The supply curve in the United States is as shown in panel A, and the supply curve in England is as shown in panel B.

Take a closer look at Figure 27.1. Note that prices in England are expressed in pounds (£) and prices in the United States are expressed in dollars ($). This is quite realistic. Each country has its

tive advantage, as interpreted by Stern, predicted correctly which country would export more. This is a high batting average, since labor is not the only input and labor productivity is an imperfect measure of true efficiency. Moreover, as we shall see in subsequent sections, countries raise barriers to foreign trade, and so prevent trade from taking place in accord with the principle of comparative advantage.

own currency, in which prices in that country are expressed. As of 2000, £1 was equal to about $1.60. In other words, you could exchange a £1 note for $1.60, or $1.60 for a £1 note. For this reason, the two panels of Figure 27.1 are lined up so that a price of $3.20 is at the same level as a price of £2, $4.80 is at the same level as £3, and so on.

▧ NO FOREIGN TRADE

To begin with, suppose that bulletproof suspenders cannot be exported or imported, perhaps because of a very high tariff (tax on imports) imposed on them in both the United States and England. (One can readily imagine members of both Congress and Parliament defending such a tariff on the grounds that a capacity to produce plenty of bulletproof suspenders is important for national defense.) If this happens, the price of bulletproof suspenders will be $2.40 in the United States and £4 in England. Why? Because, as shown in Figure 27.1, these are the prices at which each country's demand curve intersects its supply curve.

▧ FOREIGN TRADE PERMITTED

Next, suppose that international trade in this product is permitted, perhaps because both countries eliminate the tariff. Now what will happen? Since the price is lower in the United States than in England, people can make money by sending this product from the United States to England. After all, they can buy it for $2.40 in this country and sell it for £4 (=$6.40) in England. But they will not be able to do so indefinitely. As more and more suspenders are supplied by the United States for the English market, the price in the United States must go up (to induce producers to produce the additional output) and the price in England must go down (to induce consumers to buy the additional quantity).

When an equilibrium is reached, *the price in the United States must equal the price in England.* If this did not happen, there would be an advantage in increasing U.S. exports (if the price in England were higher) or in decreasing U.S. exports (if the price in the United States were higher). Thus only if the prices are equal can an equilibrium exist.

At what level will this price—which is common to both countries—tend to settle? Obviously, *the price must end up at the level where the amount of the good one country wants to export equals the amount the other country wants to import.* In other words, it must settle at $4.80, or £3 (since this is the price where $XY = UV$). Otherwise, the total amount demanded in both countries would not equal the total amount supplied in both countries. And any reader who has mastered the material in Chapter 2 knows that such a situation cannot be an equilibrium.

■ THE SIGNAL OF MARKET FORCES

At this point, we can see how market forces indicate whether a country has a comparative advantage or a comparative disadvantage in the production of a certain commodity. *If a country has a comparative advantage, it turns out—after the price of the good in various countries is equalized and total world output of the good equals total world demand for it—that the country exports the good under free trade and competition.* In Figure 27.1, it turns out that the United States is an exporter of bulletproof suspenders under free trade, because the demand and supply curves in the United States and England take the positions they do. The basic reason why the curves take these positions is that the United States has a comparative advantage in the production of this good. To put things in a nutshell, a country's producers can tell (under free trade) whether they have a comparative advantage in the production of a certain commodity by seeing whether it is profitable for them to export it. If they can make a profit, they have a comparative advantage.

TARIFFS AND QUOTAS

■ WHAT IS A TARIFF?

Tariff

Despite its advantages, not everyone benefits from free trade. On the contrary, the well-being of some firms and workers may be threatened by foreign competition, and they may press for a **tariff**, a tax the government imposes on imports. The purpose of a tariff is to cut down on imports in order to protect domestic industry and workers from foreign competition. A secondary reason for tariffs is to produce revenue for the government.

To see how a tariff works, consider the market for wristwatches. Suppose that the demand and supply curves for wristwatches in the United States are as shown in panel A of Figure 27.2 and that the demand and supply curves for wristwatches in Switzerland are as shown in panel B. Clearly, Switzerland has a comparative advantage in the production of wristwatches, and under free trade the price of a wristwatch would tend toward $10 in the United States and toward 14 Swiss francs in Switzerland. (Note that 1.4 Swiss francs are assumed to equal 1 dollar.) Under free trade, the United States would import 10 million wristwatches from Switzerland.

Now if the United States imposes a tariff of $10 on each wrist-

FIGURE 27.2

Effect of a Tariff on Swiss Watches

Under free trade, price would equal $10, or 14 Swiss francs. If a tariff of $10 is imposed on each watch imported from Switzerland, there will be a complete cessation of imports. Price in the United States will increase to $15, and price in Switzerland will fall to 10 Swiss francs.

A. United States

B. Switzerland

watch imported from Switzerland, the imports will completely cease. Any importers who buy watches in Switzerland at the price (when there is no foreign trade) of 10 Swiss francs—which equals about $7—must pay a tariff of $10; this makes their total cost about $17 per watch. But this is more than the price of a watch in the United States when there is no foreign trade (which is $15). Consequently, there is no money to be made by importing watches—unless Americans can be persuaded to pay more for a Swiss watch than for an identical U.S. watch.

■ THE SOCIAL COSTS OF TARIFFS

What is the effect of the tariff? The domestic watch industry receives a higher price—$15 rather than $10—than it would without a tariff. And the workers in the domestic watch industry may have more jobs and higher wages than without the tariff. The victim of the tariff is the U.S. consumer, who pays a higher price for wristwatches. Thus the domestic watch industry benefits at the expense of the rest of the nation. But does the general public lose more than the watch industry gains? In general, the answer is yes. The tariff reduces the welfare of the nation as a whole.

The tariff in Figure 27.2 is a ***prohibitive tariff,*** a tariff so high that it stops all imports of the good in question. Not all tariffs are prohibitive. (If they were, the government would receive no revenue at all from tariffs.) In many cases, the tariff is high enough to stop some but not all imports, and, as you would expect, the detrimental effect of a nonprohibitive tariff on living standards is less than that of a prohibitive tariff. But this does not mean that nonprohibitive tariffs are harmless. On the contrary, they can do lots of harm to domestic consumption and living standards.

WHAT IS A QUOTA?

Quotas

Besides tariffs, other barriers to free trade are **quotas**, which many countries impose on the amount of certain commodities that can be imported annually. The United States sets import quotas on sugar and has exerted pressure on foreigners to get them to limit the quantity of autos and textiles that they will export to us. To see how a quota affects trade, production, and prices, let's return to the market for wristwatches. Suppose the United States places a quota on the import of wristwatches; no more than 6 million wristwatches can be imported per year. Figure 27.3 shows the effect of the quota. Before it was imposed, the price of wristwatches was $10 (or 14 Swiss francs), and the United States imported 10 million wristwatches from Switzerland. The quota forces the United States to reduce its imports to 6 million.

What will be the effect on the U.S. price? The demand curve shows that if the price is $12, U.S. demand will exceed supply by 6 million watches; in other words, we will import 6 million watches. Thus once the quota is imposed, the price will rise to $12, since *this is the price that will reduce our imports to the amount of the quota.* A quota—like a tariff—increases the price of the good. (Note too that the price in Switzerland will fall to 12 Swiss francs. Thus the quota will reduce the price in Switzerland.)

THE SOCIAL COSTS OF QUOTAS

Both a quota and a tariff reduce trade, raise prices, protect domestic industry from foreign competition, and reduce the standard of living of the country as a whole. But most economists tend to regard quotas with even less enthusiasm than they do tariffs. Under

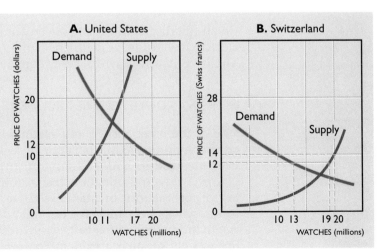

FIGURE 27.3

Effect of a Quota on Swiss Watches

Before the quota is imposed, the price is $10, or 14 Swiss francs. After a quota of 6 million watches is imposed, the price in the United States rises to $12, and the price in Switzerland falls to 12 Swiss francs.

many circumstances, a quota insulates local industry from foreign competition even more effectively than a tariff does. Foreigners, if their costs are low enough, can surmount a tariff barrier, but if a quota exists, there is no way they can exceed the quota. Moreover, a (nonprohibitive) tariff provides the government with some revenue, whereas quotas do not even do that. The windfall price increase from a quota accrues to the importer who is lucky enough or influential enough (or sufficiently generous with favors and bribes) to get an import license. (However, if the government auctions off the import licenses, it can obtain revenue from a quota.)

■ EXPORT SUBSIDIES AND OTHER NONTARIFF BARRIERS TO FREE TRADE

Finally, **export subsidies,** another means by which governments try to give their domestic industries an advantage in international competition, are also a major impediment to free trade. Such subsidies may take the form of outright cash disbursements, tax exemptions, preferential financing or insurance arrangements, or other preferential treatment for exports. Export subsidies and other such measures frequently lead to countermeasures. Thus to counter foreign export subsidies on goods sold here, the U.S. government has imposed tariff duties on such goods.

Other nontariff barriers to free trade include licensing requirements and unreasonable product quality standards. By granting few licenses (which are required in some countries to import goods) and by imposing unrealistically stringent product quality standards, governments discourage imports.

ARGUMENTS FOR TARIFFS AND QUOTAS

Given the disadvantages to society at large of tariffs and other barriers to free trade, why do governments continue to impose them? There are many reasons, some sensible, some irrational.

■ THE NATIONAL DEFENSE ARGUMENT

One of the most convincing arguments is the desirability of maintaining a domestic industry for purposes of *national defense.* Thus even if Sweden had a comparative advantage in producing airplanes, we would not allow free trade to put our domestic producers of aircraft out of business if we felt that a domestic aircraft industry was necessary for national defense. Although the Swedes are by no means unfriendly, we would not want to import our entire supply of such a critical commodity from a foreign country, where the supply might be shut off for reasons of international politics. (Recall the Arab oil embargo of the 1970s.)

This is a perfectly valid reason for protecting certain domestic industries, and many protective measures are defended on these grounds. To the extent that protective measures are in fact required for national defense, economists go along with them. The restrictions entail social costs (some of which were described in previous sections), but these costs may well be worth paying for enhanced national security. The trouble is that many barriers to free trade are defended on these grounds when in fact they protect domestic industries only tenuously connected with national security. Moreover, even if there is a legitimate case on defense grounds for protecting a domestic industry, subsidies are likely to be a more straightforward and efficient way to do so than tariffs or quotas.

■ OTHER ARGUMENTS FOR TARIFFS

Besides national defense, several other arguments for tariffs or quotas can make sense.

1. *Tariffs or other forms of protection can be justified to foster the growth or development of young industries.* Suppose that Japan has a comparative advantage in the production of a certain semiconductor, but Japan does not presently produce this item. It may take Japanese firms several years to become proficient in the relevant technology and to take advantage of the relevant economies of scale. While this industry is "growing up," Japan may impose a tariff on such semiconductors, and thus shield its young industry from competition it cannot yet handle. This "infant industry" argument for tariffs has a long history; Alexander Hamilton was one of its early exponents. Needless to say, it is *not* an argument for *permanent* tariffs, since infant industries are supposed to grow up—and the sooner the better. (Moreover, a subsidy for the industry would probably be better and easier to remove than a temporary tariff, according to many economists.)

2. *Tariffs sometimes may be imposed to protect domestic jobs and to reduce unemployment at home.* In the short run this policy may succeed, but we must recognize that other countries are likely to retaliate by enacting or increasing their own tariffs, so that such a policy may not work very well in the long run. Many economists believe that a more sensible way to reduce domestic unemployment is to use the tools of fiscal and monetary policies rather than tariffs. According to this view, if workers are laid off by industries that cannot compete with foreign producers, proper monetary and fiscal policies, together with retraining programs, should enable these workers to switch to other industries that can compete.

631

CASE STUDY 27.1

Restrictions on U.S. imports of Japanese autos

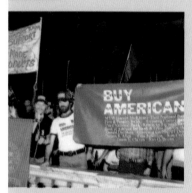

Workers rally to fight foreign competition

When the first Japanese cars arrived on the West Coast in the 1970s, no one saw them as a threat to U.S. jobs. Although they were cheaper and more fuel efficient than U.S.-made cars, most Americans couldn't be bothered; with gasoline at 30 cents a gallon, the difference in cost between a car that got 30 miles per gallon and one that got 10 was not very great, even for someone who drove a lot.

But all this changed with the Arab oil embargo of 1973. As gas prices climbed, Americans took another look at small foreign cars. With expensive U.S. labor and outmoded facilities on one side, and Japanese efficiency and management techniques on the other, Japan seemed to be winning the war in the showroom.

While imports may create as many jobs as they consume in the long run, in the short run many smokestack industry workers can be left permanently unemployed or underemployed. Worried U.S. workers wanted protection, and they found a strong advocate in Representative John Dingell, one of the leaders of an emerging protectionist movement in Congress. Dingell spoke with President Reagan and Trade Representative William Brock and warned that if voluntary restrictions on Japanese auto imports weren't adopted, Congress would impose mandatory ones. Faced with this choice, the Japanese agreed in negotiations to voluntary restrictions.

The restrictions worked. As the number of Japanese auto imports dropped between 1981 and 1982, domestic auto industry employment rose. But the cost of saving hundreds of *thousands* of U.S. jobs was restricted choice and higher prices for hundreds of *millions* of U.S. consumers. Hefty dealer markups were imposed on the scarcer but still-popular imports, and as sticker prices rose on Toyotas and Datsuns, General Motors, Ford, and Chrysler found that they could raise prices too.

The combined price paid by consumers for trade restrictions is very high; it has been estimated that each job protected from foreign competition with quotas or tariffs costs consumers about $160,000 in higher prices—more than enough to support the holder of that job. While trade restrictions may save jobs in the short run, they lock inefficiencies into the U.S. economy and merely delay needed efforts to divert people and assets into areas of the economy in which the United States has a competitive advantage—and which therefore offer long-term employment and profit possibilities.

---

3. *Tariffs sometimes may be imposed to prevent a country from being too dependent on only a few industries.* Consider a Latin American country that is a major producer of bananas. Under free trade, this country might produce bananas and little else, and so put its entire economy at the mercy of the banana market. If the price of bananas fell, the country's national income would decrease drastically. To promote industrial diversification, this country may establish tariffs to protect other industries, for example, certain types of light manufacturing. In a case like this, the tariff protects the country from having too many of its eggs—or bananas—in a single basket.

4. *Tariffs may sometimes improve a country's terms of trade, that*

NAFTA: "Jobs, jobs, jobs" or a "giant sucking sound"?

Opponents of NAFTA like Ross Perot feared the agreement would send U.S. jobs to Mexico.

In the autumn of 1993 as Congress was considering passage of the North American Free Trade Agreement (NAFTA), a fierce debate was raging over the impact of freer trade between the United States, Canada, and Mexico. Members of the Clinton administration claimed that NAFTA would generate a lot of new jobs. Opponents, such as Texas billionaire and one-time presidential candidate for the Reform Party Ross Perot, talked about the "giant sucking sound" of jobs and investment heading south of the border.

In the end Congress passed NAFTA and the claims on both sides of the debate proved to be egregiously exaggerated. In 1998 the Bank of Montreal (Canada), Harris Bank (United States), and Grupo Financiero Bancomer (Mexico) surveyed 361 companies in the three North American economies to assess the impact of NAFTA on employment. Between early 1994 and the end of 1997, 48 percent of these companies added jobs, 41 percent saw no increase in jobs, and only 11 percent had cut payrolls. More to the point, only 1 out of the 361 companies reported any NAFTA-related jobs losses.

Between 1998 and 2000 all three economies continued to grow rapidly, and in the United States the unemployment rate reached a thirty-year low. Moreover, after a brief dip during the Mexican financial crisis in 1995 and 1996, U.S. exports to Mexico rose to record levels. While NAFTA played only a small part in the U.S. boom, it is also clear that the NAFTA-related losses were minuscule. In other words, there were no sucking sounds.

What about the impact of NAFTA on Mexico? Some analysts have blamed the Mexican financial crisis on NAFTA. However, the crisis had little to do with NAFTA; it was triggered by unsustainable macroeconomic policies in 1994 (basically both fiscal and monetary policies were too stimulative) and political instability (two assassinations and an insurgency in Chiapas province). In fact NAFTA, along with a financial rescue package put together by the United States, helped Mexico to enjoy a rapid, export-led recovery.

NAFTA also helped to lock in economic reforms in Mexico. During earlier financial crises the typical response of the government was to raise tariff barriers and impose capital controls. During 1995 the Mexican government went to great pains to assure foreign investors that it would stay the course on economic reforms and keep its economy open to trade and capital flows. This was truly a paradigm shift. After the debt crisis of the early 1980s Mexico and other Latin American economies suffered through a "lost decade," and it took foreign investors nine years before they were willing to invest in the region again. After the 1995 Mexican crisis, international investors stayed away for only nine months.

NAFTA also inoculated Mexico against the Asian crisis in 1997 and the Brazilian crisis in 1999. During both of those episodes, Mexico's economy continued to grow.

In the final analysis, NAFTA probably has had a bigger positive impact on the Mexican economy than the U.S. economy. This is to be expected, since the former is one-twentieth the size of the latter. However, NAFTA, as all other free-trade agreements, has had a beneficial impact on the United States as well (for example, lower prices and greater efficiencies).

is, the ratio of its export prices to its import prices. The United States is a major importer of bananas. If we impose a tariff on bananas, and thus cut down on the domestic demand for them (because the tariff will increase their price), the reduction in our demand is likely to reduce the price of bananas abroad. Consequently, foreign producers of bananas will really pay part of the tariff. However, other countries may retaliate, and if all countries pursue such policies, few, if any, are likely to find themselves better off.

REVIEW AND PRACTICE

■ SUMMARY

1 International trade permits specialization, and specialization increases output. This is the advantage of trade, both for individuals and for countries.

2 Country A has an absolute advantage over country B in the production of a good when country A can produce a unit of the good with fewer resources than country B can. Trade can be mutually beneficial even if one country has an absolute advantage in the production of all goods.

3 Specialization and trade depend on comparative, not absolute, advantage. A country is said to have a comparative advantage in those products in which its efficiency relative to other countries is highest. Trade can be mutually beneficial if a country specializes in the products in which it has a comparative advantage and imports the products in which it has a comparative disadvantage.

4 If markets are relatively free and competitive, producers will automatically be led to produce in accord with comparative advantage. If a country has a comparative advantage in the production of a certain good, it will turn out—after the price of the good in various countries is equalized and total world output of the good equals total world demand—that this country is an exporter of the good under free trade.

5 A tariff is a tax imposed by the government on imports, to cut down on imports in order to protect domestic industry and workers from foreign competition. Tariffs benefit the protected industry at the expense of the general public, and, in general, a tariff costs the general public more than the protected industry (and its workers and suppliers) gains.

6 Quotas are another barrier to free trade. They too reduce trade, raise prices, protect domestic industry from foreign competition, and reduce the standard of living of the country as a whole.

7 Tariffs, quotas, and other barriers to free trade can sometimes be justified on the basis of national security and other noneconomic considerations. Moreover, tariffs and other forms of protection can sometimes be justified to protect infant industries, to prevent a country from being too dependent on only a few industries, and to carry out other national objectives.

■ PROBLEMS AND QUESTIONS

1 Suppose that the United States can produce 3 electronic computers or 3,000 cases of wine with 1 unit of resources, while France can produce 1 electronic computer or 2,000 cases of wine with 1 unit of resources. Will specialization increase world output?

2 Suppose that the United States has 100 units of resources while France has 50 units. On the basis of the data in question 1, draw the production possibilities curve in each country. (Recall Exploring Further in Chapter 1.) Without international trade, what will be the ratio of the price of an electronic computer to the price of a case of wine in each country?

3 Given the information in questions 1 and 2, how will firms in France and the United States know whether they should produce wine or electronic computers? Must the government instruct them on this score? Why or why not?

4 Under the circumstances described in questions 1 and 2, will each country specialize completely in the production of one or the other good? Why or why not? What factors result in incomplete specialization in the real world?

5 According to Hendrik Houthakker, "Our workers get high real income not because they are protected from foreign competition, but because they are highly productive, at least in certain industries." Do you agree? Why or why not?

6 According to Richard Cooper, "Technological innovation can undoubtedly strengthen the competitive position of a country in which the innovation takes place, whether it be one which enlarges exports or displaces imports." Give examples of this phenomenon, and discuss various ways that one might measure the effects of technological innovation on a country's competitive position.

7 "The principle of comparative advantage doesn't work. The United States exports electronic computers to Japan and imports electronic consumer goods like TV sets from Japan." Comment and evaluate.

8 Would you favor a high tariff on imported steel if you were (a) an automobile worker, (b) a steel worker, (c) an automobile buyer, and (d) a plastics worker? Explain your reasoning in each case.

■ KEY TERMS

absolute advantage	**tariff**
comparative advantage	**quotas**
terms of trade	

■ VIEWPOINT FOR ANALYSIS

On June 20, 1997 Sidney Weintraub of the Center for Strategic and International Studies in Washington, D.C., wrote in an op ed piece in The *Wall Street Journal:* "In the entire period of NAFTA's existence [a little over three years at the time this op ed piece appeared], the Department of Labor has certified some 125,000 people as being adversely affected by U.S. investment in, and imports from, Canada and Mexico. This number is about equal to the number of new jobs created in the U.S. every two weeks. About 10,000 of those who were certified took advantage of the benefits in the NAFTA legistlation."*

(a) What do the statistics imply about the impact of NAFTA, in particular, and trade, in general, on U.S. employment?

(b) What happened to the workers who did not apply for the compensation benefits available through the NAFTA legislation?

(c) What else can the government do to help those workers who have been displaced by imports from other countries?

*"In the Debate about NAFTA, Just the Facts Please," *Wall Street Journal,* June 20, 1997, p. A19.

CHAPTER 28

Exchange Rates and the Balance of Payments

LEARNING OBJECTIVES

In this chapter, you should learn:

- What exchange rates are
- The workings of the gold standard, fixed exchange rates, and flexible exchange rates
- The factors underlying recent problems in the international monetary system
- The arguments for and against trying to stabilize the value of the dollar (relative to other currencies)

The value of the dollar in terms of foreign currencies is highly variable. In 1985, a dollar was worth about 235 Japanese yen; in 2000, it was worth only about 110 Japanese yen. Why was this change of importance to U.S. tourists visiting Japan or to exporters or importers? One purpose of this chapter is to answer this question.

In addition, we must consider several other questions. What are exchange rates, and how are they determined? How are international business transactions carried out? Should there be fixed or flexible exchange rates? What problems have afflicted the international monetary system in recent years? These questions, which are both fundamental and timely, are taken up in this chapter.

INTERNATIONAL TRANSACTIONS AND EXCHANGE RATES

Suppose you want to buy a book from a Japanese publisher, and the book costs 1,650 yen. (The Japanese currency consists of yen, not dollars.) To buy the book, you must somehow get yen to pay the publisher, since this is the currency in which the publisher deals. Or, if the publisher agrees, you might pay in dollars, but the publisher would then have to exchange the dollars for yen, because its bills must be paid in yen. Whatever happens, either you or the publisher must somehow exchange dollars for yen, since international business transactions, unlike transactions within a country, involve two different currencies.

If you decide to exchange dollars for yen to pay the Japanese

Exchange rate

publisher, how can you make the exchange? The answer is simple. You can buy Japanese yen at a bank, just as you might buy lamb chops at a butcher shop. Just as the lamb chops have a price (expressed in dollars), so the Japanese yen have a price (expressed in dollars). The bank may tell you that each yen you buy will cost you $.009. This makes the **exchange rate** between dollars and yen .009 to 1, since it takes .009 dollars to purchase 1 yen.

In general, *the exchange rate is simply the number of units of one currency that exchanges for a unit of another currency.* The obvious question is: What determines the exchange rate? Why is the exchange rate between Japanese yen and U.S. dollars what it is? Why doesn't a yen exchange for 25 cents, rather than just under 1 cent? These basic questions will occupy us in the next several sections.

EXCHANGE RATES UNDER THE GOLD STANDARD

Gold standard

As a starter, let's see how exchange rates were determined under the **gold standard**, which prevailed before the 1930s. *If a country was on the gold standard, a unit of its currency was convertible into a certain amount of gold.* Before World War I the dollar was convertible into one-twentieth of an ounce of gold, and the British pound was convertible into one-quarter of an ounce of gold. Thus, since the pound exchanged for 5 times as much gold as the dollar, the pound exchanged for $5. The currency of any other country on the gold standard was convertible into a certain amount of gold in the same way; *to see how much its currency was worth in dollars, you divided the amount of gold a unit of its currency was worth by the amount of gold (one-twentieth of an ounce) a dollar was worth.*

Why did the exchange rate always equal the ratio between the amount of gold a foreign currency was worth and the amount of gold a dollar was worth? Why did the price of a British pound stay at $5 before World War I? To see why, suppose that the price (in dollars) of a pound rose above this ratio—above $5. Instead of exchanging their dollars directly for pounds, Americans would have done better to exchange them for gold and then exchange the gold for pounds. By this indirect process, Americans could have exchanged $5 for a pound, so they would have refused to buy pounds at a price above $5 per pound.

Similarly, if the price of a pound fell below $5, the British would have refused to sell pounds, since they could have obtained $5 by converting the pound into gold and the gold into dollars. Thus *because Americans would refuse to pay more than $5 and the British would refuse to accept less, the price of a pound had to remain at about $5. (In practice, the pound could be a few cents above or* *below $5, because it costs money to transport gold in order to carry out the conversion.)*

▓ BALANCE BETWEEN EXPORTS AND IMPORTS

But what ensured that this exchange rate, dictated by the gold content of currencies, would result in a rough equality of trade between countries? If £1 exchanged for $5, perhaps the British might find our goods so cheap that they would import a great deal from us, while we might find their goods so expensive that we would import little from them. Under these circumstances, the British would have to ship gold to us to pay for the excess of their imports from us over their exports to us, and eventually they could run out of gold. Could this happen? If not, why not? These questions occupied the attention of many early economists. The classic answers were given by David Hume, the Scottish philosopher, in the eighteenth century.

Hume pointed out that under the gold standard a mechanism ensured that trade would be brought into balance and that neither country would run out of gold. This mechanism worked as follows. If, as we assumed, the British bought more from us than we bought from them, they would have to send us gold to pay for the excess of their imports over their exports. As their gold stock declined, their price level would fall. (Recall the quantity theory of money discussed in Chapter 13.) As our gold stock increased, our price level would rise. Thus, because of our rising prices, the British would tend to import less from us; because of their falling prices, we would tend to import more from them. Consequently, the trade between the two countries would tend toward a better balance. Eventually when enough gold had left Britain and entered the United States, prices here would have increased enough and prices in Britain would have fallen enough to put imports and exports in balance.

THE FOREIGN EXCHANGE MARKET

Flexible exchange rates

The gold standard is long gone, and after many decades of fixed exchange rates (discussed in a later section), the major trading countries of the world began to experiment with **flexible exchange rates** in early 1973. Let's consider a situation where exchange rates are allowed to fluctuate freely, like the price of any commodity in a competitive market. In a case of this sort, exchange rates, like any price, are determined by supply and demand. There is a market for various types of foreign currency—Mexican pesos, British pounds, Japanese yen, and so on—just as there are markets for various types of meat.

FIGURE 28.1

Determination of the Exchange Rate between Dollars and Japanese Yen under Freely Fluctuating Exchange Rates

Under freely fluctuating exchange rates, the equilibrium price of a Japanese yen would be $.009 if the demand and supply curves for marks are as shown here.

In the case of the Japanese yen, the demand and supply curves may look like those shown in Figure 28.1. The demand curve shows the amount of Japanese yen that people with dollars will demand at various prices of a yen. The supply curve shows the amount of Japanese yen that people with yen will supply at various prices of a yen. Since the amount of Japanese currency supplied must equal the amount demanded in equilibrium, *the equilibrium price (in dollars) of a Japanese yen is given by the intersection of the demand and supply curves.* In Figure 28.1, this intersection is at $.009.

■ THE DEMAND AND SUPPLY SIDES OF THE MARKET

Let's look in more detail at the demand and supply sides of this market. On the *demand* side are people who want to import Japanese goods (like the book you want to buy) into the United States, people who want to travel in Japan (where they'll need Japanese money), people who want to build factories in Japan, and others with dollars who want Japanese currency. The people on the *supply* side are those who want to import U.S. goods into Japan, Japanese who want to travel in the United States (where they'll need U.S. money), people with yen who want to build factories in the United States, and others with yen who want U.S. currency.

When Americans demand more Japanese VCRs or cars (causing the demand curve to shift upward and to the right), the price (in dollars) of the Japanese yen will tend to increase. Thus, if the demand curve for yen shifts as shown in Figure 28.2, the result will be an increase in the equilibrium price (in dollars) of a yen from .009 to .011. Conversely, when the Japanese demand more U.S. cars or computers (resulting in a shift of the supply curve downward and to the right), the price (in dollars) of the Japanese yen will tend to decrease.

639

FIGURE 28.2

Effect of Shift in Demand Curve for Japanese Yen

Because of the demand curve's shift to the right, the equilibrium price of a Japanese yen increases from $.009 to $.011.

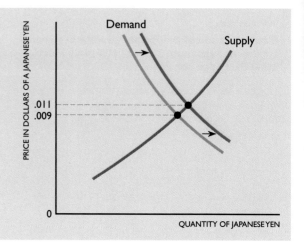

To see why an increase in Japanese demand for U.S. cars or computers shifts the supply curve downward and to the right, recall that the supply curve shows the amount of yen that will be supplied at each price of a yen. Thus a shift downward and to the right in the supply curve means that more yen will be supplied at a given price (in dollars) of the yen. Given the posited increase in Japanese demand for U.S. goods, such a shift in the supply curve would be expected.

■ APPRECIATION AND DEPRECIATION OF A CURRENCY

Appreciation
Depreciation

Two terms frequently encountered in discussions of the foreign exchange market are **appreciation** and **depreciation**. When country A's currency becomes more valuable relative to country B's currency, country A's currency is said to appreciate relative to that of country B, and country B's currency is said to depreciate relative to that of country A. In Figure 28.2, the yen appreciated relative to the dollar and the dollar depreciated relative to the yen. This use of terms makes sense. Since the number of dollars commanded by a yen increased, the yen became more valuable relative to the dollar and the dollar became less valuable relative to the yen.

Note that such a change in exchange rates would not have been possible under the gold standard. Unless a country changed the amount of gold that could be exchanged for a unit of its currency, exchange rates were fixed under the gold standard. Sometimes governments did change the amount of gold that could be exchanged for their currencies. For example, in 1933 the United States increased the price of gold from $21 an ounce to $35 an ounce. When a country increased the price of gold, this was called a ***devaluation of currency.***

■ DETERMINANTS OF EXCHANGE RATES

In a previous section, we saw that flexible exchange rates are determined by supply and demand. But what are some of the major factors determining the position of these supply and demand curves?

Relative price levels. In the long run, the exchange rate between any two currencies may be expected to reflect differences in the price levels in the two countries. To see why, suppose that Japan and the United States are the only exporters or importers of automobiles and that automobiles are the only product they export or import. If an automobile costs $16,000 in the United States and 2,400 yen in Japan, what must be the exchange rate between the dollar and the yen? Clearly, a yen must be worth .0066 dollar, because otherwise the two countries' automobiles would not be competitive in the world market. If a yen were set equal to .009 dollar, this would mean that a Japanese automobile would cost $21,818 (that is, 2,400,000 times $.0066), which is far more than what a U.S. automobile would cost. Thus foreign buyers would obtain their automobiles in the United States.

Based on this theory, one would expect that *if the rate of inflation in country A is higher than in country B, country A's currency is likely to depreciate relative to country B's.* Suppose that costs double in the United States but increase by only 25 percent in Japan. After this burst of inflation, an automobile costs $32,000 (that is, 2 times $16,000) in the United States and 3,000,000 yen (that is 1.25 times 2,400,000 yen) in Japan. Thus, the new value of the yen must be .0107 dollar, rather than the old value of .0066 dollar. (Why .0107 dollar? Because this is the exchange rate that makes the new cost of an automobile in the United States, $32,000, equivalent to the new cost of an automobile in Japan, 3,000,000 yen.) Because the rate of inflation is higher in the United States than in Japan, the dollar depreciates relative to the yen.

Relative rates of growth. Although relative price levels may play an important role in the long run, other factors tend to exert more influence on exchange rates in the short run. In particular, *if one country's rate of economic growth is higher than the rest of the world, its currency is likely to depreciate.* If a country's economy is booming, this tends to increase its imports. If there is a boom in the United States, Americans will tend to import a great deal from other countries. If a country's imports tend to grow faster than its exports, its demand for foreign currency will tend to grow more rapidly than the amount of foreign currency that is supplied to it. Consequently, its currency is likely to depreciate.

641

Relative interest rate levels. If the rate of interest in Japan is higher than in the United States, banks, multinational corporations, and other investors in the United States will sell dollars and buy yen in order to invest in the high-yielding Japanese securities. Also, Japanese investors (and others) will be less likely to find U.S. securities attractive. Thus the yen will tend to appreciate relative to the dollar, since the demand curve for yen will shift to the right and the supply curve for yen will shift to the left. In general, *an increase in a country's interest rates leads to an appreciation of its currency, and a decrease in its interest rates leads to a depreciation of its currency.* In the short run, interest rate differentials can have a major impact on exchange rates, since there is a huge amount of funds that is moved from country to country in response to differentials in interest rates.

■ THE ADJUSTMENT MECHANISM UNDER FLEXIBLE EXCHANGE RATES

Under flexible exchange rates, what ensures a balance in the exports and imports between countries? The situation differs from that described by David Hume, since Hume assumed the existence of the gold standard. Under flexible exchange rates, the balance is achieved through changes in exchange rates. Suppose that for some reason, Britain is importing far more from us than we are from Britain. This will mean that the British, needing dollars to buy our goods, will be willing to supply pounds more cheaply. In other words, the supply curve for British pounds will shift downward and to the right, as shown in Figure 28.3. This will cause the price of a pound to decline from P_1 dollars to P_2 dollars. Or, from Britain's point of view, the price (in pounds) of a dollar will have been bid up by the swollen demand for imports from the United States.

FIGURE 28.3

Adjustment Mechanism

If Britain imports more from us than we do from Britain, the supply curve for British pounds will shift downward and to the right; this will result in a decline of the price of the pound from P_1 to P_2 dollars. If Britain tries to maintain the price at P_1 dollars, the British government will have to exchange dollars for $(Q_S - Q_D)$ pounds.

Because of the increase in the price (in pounds) of a dollar, our goods will become more expensive in Britain. Thus the British will tend to reduce their imports of our goods. At the same time, since the price (in dollars) of a pound has decreased, British goods will become cheaper in the United States, and this will stimulate us to import more from Britain. Consequently, as our currency appreciates in terms of theirs—or, to put it another way, as theirs depreciates in terms of ours—the British are induced to import less and export more. Thus there is an automatic mechanism (just as there was under the gold standard) to bring trade between countries into balance.

FIXED EXCHANGE RATES

**Fixed exchange
rates**

Although many economists believed that exchange rates should be allowed to fluctuate, very few exchange rates really did so in the period from the end of World War II up to 1973. Instead, there were mostly **fixed exchange rates** by government action and international agreement. Although they may have varied slightly about the fixed level, the extent to which they were allowed to vary was small. Every now and then, governments changed the exchange rates, for reasons discussed below, but for long periods of time, they remained fixed.

If exchange rates remain fixed, the amount demanded of a foreign currency may not equal the amount supplied. Consider the situation in Figure 28.4. If A is the demand curve for Japanese yen, the equilibrium price of a yen is $.007. But suppose the fixed exchange rate between dollars and yen is .006 to 1; that is, each yen

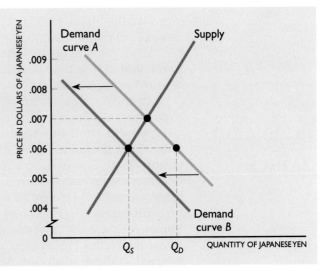

FIGURE 28.4

Fixed Exchange Rate

The equilibrium price of a Japanese yen is $.007, if A is the demand curve. If $.006 is the fixed exchange rate, the U.S. government may try to shift the demand curve for yen from A to B to bring the equilibrium exchange rate into equality with the fixed exchange rate.

exchanges for $.006. Unless the government intervenes, more Japanese yen will be demanded at a price of $.006 per yen than will be offered. Specifically, the difference between the quantity demanded and the quantity supplied will be $Q_D - Q_S$. Unless the government steps in, a black market for Japanese yen may develop, and the real price may increase toward $.007 per yen.

■ TYPES OF GOVERNMENT INTERVENTION

To maintain exchange rates at their fixed levels, governments can intervene in a variety of ways. For example, they may reduce the demand for foreign currencies by reducing defense expenditures abroad, by limiting the amount that their citizens can travel abroad, and by curbing imports from other countries. Thus, in the case depicted in Figure 28.4, the U.S. government might adopt some or all of these measures to shift the demand curve for Japanese yen downward and to the left. If the demand curve can be pushed from A to B, the equilibrium price of a Japanese yen can be reduced to $.006, the fixed exchange rate. For the time being, there will no longer be any mismatch between the quantity of yen demanded and the quantity supplied.

When exchange rates are fixed, mismatches of this sort cannot be eliminated entirely and permanently. To deal with such temporary mismatches, governments enter the market and buy and sell their currencies in order to maintain fixed exchange rates. Take the case of post–World War II Britain. At times the amount of British pounds supplied exceeded the amount demanded. Then the British government bought up the excess at the fixed exchange rate. At other times, when the quantity demanded exceeded the amount supplied, the British government supplied the pounds desired at the fixed exchange rate. As long as the equilibrium exchange rate was close to (sometimes above and sometimes below) the fixed exchange rate, the amount of its currency the government sold at one time equaled, more or less, the amount it bought at another time.

But in some cases governments have tried to maintain a fixed exchange rate far from the equilibrium exchange rate. The British government tried during the 1960s to maintain the price (in dollars) of the pound at $2.80, even though the equilibrium price was about $2.40. The situation was as shown in Figure 28.5. Since the quantity of British pounds supplied exceeded the quantity demanded at the price of $2.80, the British government had to buy the difference. That is, it had to buy $(Q_S - Q_D)$ pounds with dollars. Moreover, it had to keep on exchanging dollars for pounds in these quantities for as long as the demand and supply curves remained in these positions. Such a situation could not go on indefi-

FIGURE 28.5

Balance-of-Payments Deficit

Because the British pound is overvalued at $2.80, the quantity of pounds demanded (Q_D) is less than the quantity supplied (Q_S). The shortfall—($Q_S - Q_D$) pounds—is the balance-of-payments deficit.

nitely, since the British government eventually had to run out of dollars. How long it could go on depended on how big Britain's reserves of gold and foreign currency were.

BALANCE-OF-PAYMENTS DEFICITS AND SURPLUSES

Under a system of fixed exchange rates, economists and financial analysts look at whether a country has a balance-of-payments deficit or surplus to see whether its currency is above or below its equilibrium value. What is a balance-of-payments deficit? What is a balance-of-payments surplus? It is important that both these terms be understood.

■ BALANCE-OF-PAYMENTS DEFICIT

Balance-of-payments deficit

If a country's currency is *overvalued* (that is, if its fixed price exceeds the equilibrium price), the quantity supplied of its currency will exceed the quantity demanded. This is a **balance-of-payments deficit**. Let's return to the case where the price of the British pound was set at $2.80. Under these circumstances, the quantity supplied of pounds exceeds the quantity demanded by ($Q_S - Q_D$) pounds, as shown in Figure 28.5. This amount—($Q_S - Q_D$) pounds—is Britain's balance-of-payments deficit (see Figure 28.5). As pointed out in the previous section, it is the number of pounds that Britain's central bank, the Bank of England, must purchase. To pay for these pounds, the Bank of England must give up some of its *reserves* of foreign currencies or gold.

In a situation of this sort, there may be a run on the overvalued currency. Suppose that speculators become convinced that the country with the balance-of-payments deficit cannot maintain the

645

artificially high price of its currency much longer because its reserves are running low. Because they will suffer losses if they hold
onto a currency that is devalued, the speculators are likely to sell
the overvalued currency (in Figure 28.5, the British pound) in very
large amounts, and thus cause an even bigger balance-of-payments
deficit for the country with the overvalued currency. Faced with
the exhaustion of its reserves, the country is likely to be forced to
allow the price of its currency to fall.

■ BALANCE-OF-PAYMENTS SURPLUS

**Balance-of-
payments surplus**

If a country's currency is *undervalued* (that is, if its price is less
than the equilibrium price), the quantity demanded of its currency
will exceed the quantity supplied. This is a **balance-of-payments
surplus**. What if the price of the Japanese yen was set at $.006,
even though its equilibrium price was about $.007? As shown in
Figure 28.6, the quantity of yen demanded exceeds the quantity
supplied by $(Q'_D - Q'_S)$ yen under these circumstances. This
amount—$(Q'_D - Q'_S)$ yen—is Japan's balance-of-payments surplus
(see Figure 28.6). Japan can keep the price of the yen at $.006 only
if it provides these $(Q'_D - Q'_S)$ yen in exchange for foreign currencies and gold. By doing so, it increases its reserves.

Whereas a country with an overvalued currency is likely to be
forced by the reduction in its reserves to reduce the price of its
currency, a country with an undervalued currency is unlikely to be
forced by the increase in its reserves to increase the price of its
currency. And a country with an undervalued currency often is reluctant to increase the price of its currency, because of political
pressures by its exporters (and their workers), who point out

FIGURE 28.6

Balance-of-Payments Surplus

Because the Japanese yen is undervalued
at $.006, the quantity of yen demanded
(Q'_D) is greater than the quantity supplied
(Q'_S). The surplus—$(Q'_D - Q'_S)$ yen—
is the balance-of-payments surplus.

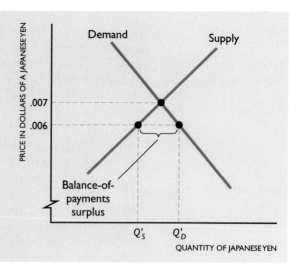

that such a revaluation would make the country's goods more expensive in foreign markets and thus would reduce its exports. Consequently, when exchange rates were fixed, countries with undervalued currencies were less likely to adjust their exchange rates than countries with overvalued currencies.

■ MEASURING DEFICITS AND SURPLUSES

If we are given the demand and supply curves for a country's currency, it is a simple matter to determine the deficit or surplus in its balance of payments. All we have to do is subtract the quantity demanded of the currency from the quantity supplied. However, since we do not observe these demand and supply curves in the real world, this method of determining the deficit or surplus, while fine in principle, is not practical. The available data show only the total amount of the country's currency bought and the total amount of the country's currency sold. Since each unit of the country's currency that is bought must also be sold, it is evident that the total amount bought must equal the total amount sold. Given that this is the case, how can one identify and measure a balance-of-payments deficit or surplus?

The answer lies in the transactions of the country's central bank. If the central bank's purchases or sales of currency make up for the difference between the quantity demanded and the quantity supplied, it will purchase currency if there is a balance-of-payments deficit and sell currency if there is a balance-of-payments surplus. The amount it purchases or sells measures the size of the deficit or surplus. In other words, the official transactions of this country's government with other governments are used to measure the deficit or surplus. Roughly speaking, this is how a balance-of-payments deficit or surplus was traditionally measured. However, beginning in May 1976, the U.S. government stopped publishing figures on the deficit or surplus in our balance of payments. Under the current regime of flexible exchange rates, changes in demand and supply for foreign exchange generally show up as changes in exchange rates, rather than in the transactions of the central bank. Thus figures regarding the deficit or surplus in our balance of payments have lost much of their previous meaning.

EXCHANGE RATES: PRE–WORLD WAR II EXPERIENCE

Now that we are familiar with a balance-of-payments deficit and surplus, we can begin to see how various types of exchange rates have worked out. What has been our experience with the gold standard? With fixed exchange rates? With flexible exchange rates?

During the latter part of the nineteenth century, the gold standard seemed to work very well, but serious trouble developed after World War I. During the war, practically all the warring countries went off the gold standard to keep people from hoarding gold or from sending it to neutral countries. After the war, some countries tried to reestablish the old rates of exchange. Because the wartime and postwar rates of inflation were greater in some countries than in others, under the old exchange rates the goods of some countries were underpriced and those of other countries were overpriced. According to the doctrines of David Hume, this imbalance should have been remedied by increases in the general price level in countries where goods were underpriced and by reductions in the general price level in countries where goods were overpriced. But wages and prices proved to be inflexible, and, as one would expect, it proved especially difficult to adjust them downward. When the adjustment mechanism failed to work quickly enough, the gold standard was abandoned.

During the 1930s, governments tried various schemes. This was the time of the Great Depression, and governments were trying frantically to reduce unemployment. Sometimes a government allowed the exchange rate to be flexible for a while, and, when it found what seemed to be an equilibrium level, fixed the exchange rate there. Sometimes a government depreciated the value of its own currency relative to those of other countries in an attempt to increase employment by making its goods cheap to other countries. When one country adopted such policies, however, others retaliated; this caused a reduction in international trade and lending, but little or no benefit for the country that started the fracas.

THE GOLD-EXCHANGE STANDARD

In 1944, the Allied governments (in World War II) sent representatives to Bretton Woods, New Hampshire, to work out a more effective system for the postwar era. It was generally agreed that competitive devaluations, such as occurred in the 1930s, should be avoided. Out of the Bretton Woods conference came the ***International Monetary Fund (IMF),*** which was set up to maintain a stable system of fixed exchange rates and to ensure that when exchange rates had to be changed because of significant trade imbalances, disruption was minimized.

The system developed during the postwar period was generally labeled the ***gold-exchange standard,*** as opposed to the gold standard. Under this system, the dollar—which had by this time taken the place of the British pound as the world's key currency—was convertible (for official monetary purposes) into gold at a fixed price. And since other currencies could be converted into dollars

The abandonment of the gold standard

Franklin D. Roosevelt

During the forty years before World War I, world trade prospered under a system of exchange rates such that currencies were pegged to gold and fixed relative to one another. During World War I, however, as countries expanded their money supplies rapidly to pay for the war effort, every country experienced sharp inflation and different relative rates of inflation. The previous fixed exchange rates could not have been honored, so the payment of gold for currency was suspended for the war's duration.

Although relative rates of inflation had changed radically during the war, in 1925 the United Kingdom decided to fix the pound to gold at the prewar level. The primary reason was to preserve the value of bonds and other fixed income securities, which had lost value during the wartime inflation. Wealthy and influential bondholders pressured the government to reverse the inflation, and pegging the price of the pound to gold was the first step in trying to reestablish the prewar price level.

Countries that had undervalued currencies, such as France and the United States, prospered during the 1920s. France in particular had "export-led" growth, and it accumulated vast reserves of foreign exchange and gold. The British economy, however, stagnated for the six years that it was on the gold standard at the prewar rate. The United Kingdom found itself importing too much and could not compete against foreign producers because its own goods were much higher priced than foreign goods. Only by either devaluing the pound or forcing wages down could the United Kingdom compete. If it failed to do either, it would constantly be sending out more pounds than it was collecting in foreign currencies. Foreigners would then ex-

change those pounds for gold, and so drain gold from the country.

Sterling weakened in July 1930, and despite efforts to arrange foreign financing to defend the pound and a hike in the U.K. discount rate, gold withdrawals accelerated by September. On September 21, Britain abandoned the gold standard. The pound fell from $4.86 to $3.25 within a few days but recovered to about $3.50.

Pressure shifted to the dollar as the French withdrew gold from the United States. The United States raised its discount rate from 1.5 to 3.5 percent in October 1930, and this was not offset by open market operations. Bank failures spread. The U.S. money supply, commodity prices, security prices, imports, and (to a lesser extent) industrial production declined faster after the British devaluation than before. The United States lost gold throughout 1932, and the early-1933 banking crises worsened the outflow.

On March 4, President Roosevelt closed the banks and let the dollar float. The dollar fell vis-à-vis the pound, and it was not until 1936 that a stabilization of the dollar, the pound, and the franc was worked out.

at fixed exchange rates, other currencies were convertible indirectly into gold at a fixed price.

During the early postwar period, the gold-exchange standard worked reasonably well. However, it was not too long before problems began to develop. As noted in a previous section, when exchange rates are fixed, a U.S. balance-of-payments deficit is evidence of pressure on the dollar in foreign exchange markets. During the period from 1950 to 1972 (the last full year when exchange rates were fixed), the United States showed a chronic deficit in its balance of payments. This chronic deficit caused considerable uneasiness and concern, both here and abroad.

In March 1973, representatives of the major trading countries met in Paris to establish a system of fluctuating exchange rates, and thus abandoned the Bretton Woods system of fixed exchange rates. This was a major break with the past, and one that was greeted with considerable apprehension as well as hope. However, the major trading countries did not go so far as to establish completely flexible exchange rates. Instead, the float was to be managed. Central banks would step in to buy and sell their currency. Thus the United States agreed that "when necessary and desirable" it would support the value of the dollar. Also, some European countries decided to maintain fixed exchange rates among their own currencies but to float jointly against other currencies.

FIXED VERSUS FLEXIBLE EXCHANGE RATES

Why, until 1973, did most countries fix their exchange rates rather than allow them to fluctuate? One important reason was the feeling that flexible exchange rates might vary so erratically that it might be difficult to carry out normal trade. Thus U.S. exporters of machine tools to Britain might not know what British pounds would be worth six months from now, when they would collect a debt in pounds. According to the proponents of fixed exchange rates, fluctuating rates would increase uncertainties for people and firms engaged in international trade and thus reduce the volume of such trade. Moreover, they argued, the harmful effects of speculation over exchange rates would increase if exchange rates were flexible, because speculators could push a currency's exchange rate up or down and destabilize the exchange market. They argued further that flexible exchange rates might promote more rapid inflation, because countries would be less affected by balance-of-payments discipline.

Many economists disagreed, feeling that flexible exchange rates would work better. They asked why flexible prices are used and trusted in other areas of the economy but not in connection with foreign exchange. They pointed out that a country would have more autonomy in formulating its fiscal and monetary policies if exchange rates were flexible, and they claimed that speculation regarding exchange rates would not be destabilizing. But until 1973, the advocates of flexible exchange rates persuaded few of the world's central bankers and policymakers.

Are currency speculators to blame for the volatility in international financial markets?

These protestors were forced into debt by the Mexican peso crisis.

Recently one Western head of state described currency speculation as the "AIDS of our economies." His comments echoed a growing sentiment among some policymakers and analysts that currency speculators are to blame for the volatility in financial markets. While the temptation to find scapegoats may prove irresistible, the reasons behind the financial markets' turmoil in recent years are far more complex than is suggested by such simplistic characterizations.

During the 1990s there were a surprisingly large number of international financial crises, including two attacks on the European Exchange Rate Mechanism (ERM) in 1992 and 1993, two runs on the dollar in 1994 and 1995, the Mexican peso devaluation in late 1994, the Asian crisis in 1997, the Russian crisis in 1998, and the Brazilian crisis in 1999. To gain some perspective on the causes of this market turmoil, it is helpful to begin by looking at the size of the world financial markets. The daily turnover in the foreign exchange markets alone is $1.5 trillion, which is about 20 percent of total annual world exports and about 4 percent of total annual world GDP. The total foreign exchange reserves held by the central banks of all the IMF member countries is slightly less than $1 trillion (less than the turnover in

one 24-hour period). Thus, central bank efforts to go against these markets are doomed to fail. The best monetary authorities can hope to achieve is to surprise the markets from time to time and inflict losses on a few traders.

The power of the central banks has steadily eroded as the volume in the foreign exchange markets has risen rapidly, increasing fivefold over the past decade. The exponential growth in these markets has been driven by a number of factors including financial deregulation and the removal of capital controls, the increased use of new technologies to link the 24-hour global markets, financial innovations (for example, derivatives), and increased cross-border diversification.

While speculators are everyone's favorite scapegoat, the truth of the matter is that there are many thousands of traders with large positions in the market. No single trader or group of traders can effectively dominate the market for any length of time. Most are driven by market fundamentals or prevailing market psychology. Also, while it is tempting to think of speculative attacks on currencies as a recent phenomenon, such attacks were a regular feature of the Bretton Woods system, especially during its final years.

FIGURE 28.7

Value of the U.S. Dollar in Terms of Major Foreign Currencies, 1967–99 (March 1973 = 100)

Source: Board of Governors of the Federal Reserve System.

HOW WELL HAVE FLOATING EXCHANGE RATES WORKED?

Since 1973, exchange rates have been flexible, not fixed. However, there has been some intervention by central banks to keep the movement of exchange rates within broad bounds, but this intervention generally has not been very great. The result has been considerable volatility in exchange rates. The exchange rate between the dollar and the Japanese yen has sometimes varied by 2 percent or more from one day to the next and by 15 percent or more over a period of several months. As shown in Figure 28.7, the value of the dollar (in terms of other major currencies) has gyrated substantially during the past twenty years.

Unquestionably, the variations in exchange rates, some of which are erratic and without fundamental economic significance, have made international transactions more difficult. Thus Renault, the French auto manufacturer, is reported to have hesitated to launch an export drive into the U.S. market because of the erratic behavior of the dollar-franc exchange rate.

During the 1970s, the value of the dollar fell considerably, as shown in Figure 28.7. Between September 1977 and March 1978, and again between June and October 1978, the value of the dollar fell by about 10 percent, in part because of our unfavorable balance of trade (because we pursued a more expansionary policy than our major trading partners) and because interest rates were higher abroad than here.[1]

---

[1]A country is said to have a *favorable* balance of merchandise trade if its exports of merchandise are more than its imports of merchandise, and an *unfavorable* balance of merchandise trade if its exports of merchandise are less than its imports of merchandise.

The rise and fall of the Bretton Woods system

In July 1944, in Bretton Woods, New Hampshire, representatives of 44 countries met for 22 days to create a blueprint for a new world economic order. To ensure stability, the Bretton Woods agreements outlined a new system of international cooperation. The linchpin of the system was the U.S. dollar and its convertibility to gold.

Bretton Woods provided a framework for the rebuilding of Europe. And the United States played the key role in financing Europe's recovery. The Marshall Plan, created in 1947, gave millions of dollars to Europe. This flow of dollars and goods was soon supplemented by loans and private investments from the United States. The U.S. economy reaped immediate benefits from Europe's rebuilding. As fast as the dollars were pumped overseas, they flowed back here to pay for U.S. machinery and goods. In the decade fol-

lowing the war, Europe imported billions of dollars' worth of products from the United States. But by the mid-1950s, European economies were no longer so dependent on U.S. goods.

By the 1960s, our payments abroad for imports, investments, and foreign aid had far exceeded our receipts. Whereas there had been an international shortage of dollars during the previous decade, now the world faced a dollar glut. This overwhelming supply of dollars piled up in the vaults of foreign central banks. These banks began to redeem dollars for U.S. gold. Between 1964 and 1966, U.S. gold reserves dropped by 2 billion dollars.

The United States pressured foreign central banks to retain their dollars. The government also tried to restrict the amount of money invested or spent overseas but to little avail. None of these moves could halt the

growing dollar glut or convince currency speculators that the dollar would not be devalued. Speculators dumped billions' worth of dollars on the foreign exchange markets. By the time Richard Nixon assumed the presidency, the system carefully crafted at Bretton Woods was on the verge of collapse. Finally, in March 1973 the major developed economies abandoned the Bretton Woods system of fixed exchange rates.

Fifty-five years after the historic conference, economists and politicians still applaud the goals and the accomplishments of Bretton Woods. It was an historic undertaking to set up rules and procedures to promote world trade that would benefit all countries. Many of the institutions and policies are still in service. But not the exchange rate system. It fell victim to the chronic U.S. balance-of-payments deficit.

During the early 1980s, the dollar staged a spectacular rebound. Between 1980 and 1985, its value rose by about 60 percent. In large part, this was due to the fact that inflation in the United States seemed to have moderated, real interest rates here were higher than in other countries (partly the result of huge government borrowing to finance its deficits), and the rates of return from investments here seemed relatively high. This marked appreciation of the dollar hurt U.S. exporters, since their goods became very expensive to foreigners, but it helped to keep a lid on inflation, since imported goods were relatively cheap, and many U.S. firms could not raise their own prices very much without losing business to imported goods.

In the late 1980s, the dollar took a dive; it lost practically all the value it had gained in the early 1980s. In part, this was due to lower interest rates in the United States and to the feelings of speculators that the dollar was overvalued. Also, according to many

The Euro: Europe's new currency

The euro was launched in 1999, with currency to begin circulation in 2002.

On January 1, 1999 the new European currency—the euro—was launched. The preparations for the introduction of the new currency took the better part of a decade. Even the launch itself is being phased in. Between January 1999 and January 2002, the euro is only being used for electronic transactions and official settlements. The new bills and coins will begin circulation on January 1, 2002. And the local currencies (German marks, French francs, Italian lire, and so on) will be phased out by June 30, 2002.

The key design features of the European Monetary Union (EMU) were laid out in a treaty signed in the port city of Maastricht in the Netherlands, in December of 1991. The Maastricht Treaty set out a series of stringent preconditions for countries that wanted to join the EMU. These included government deficit and national debt targets that were 3 percent and 60 percent of GDP, respectively. The goal of these preconditions was to rein in profligate governments, such as those in Bel-

gium and Italy. However, the architects of EMU also wanted to reassure countries with strong currencies, such as Germany, that the new currency would be based on solid foundations.

By the spring of 1997, all but one European Union member (Greece) qualified to join EMU. However, three of the remaining 14 (Great Britain, Denmark, and Sweden) opted out of the first round of countries joining the monetary union. This left 11 countries (France, Germany, Italy, the Netherlands, Spain, Portugal, Ireland, Belgium, Luxembourg, Austria, and Finland) as the first-round members.

The Maastricht Treaty also established a new European Central Bank (ECB) which now sets monetary policy (primarily short-term interest rates) for all 11 EMU members.

How successful has the euro been? The launch of the euro went off very smoothly, thanks to the years of preparation. However, almost

immediately, the euro began to lose value against other major currencies, falling by 20 percent relative to the U.S. dollar in a little over a year. Some of this weakness was due to an initial lack of confidence in the new currency and the ECB. The currency also suffered because of poor economic fundamentals (especially weak growth) in the European economies during the launch year, 1999.

In some respects, EMU has been very successful. To begin with, it has improved the fiscal balances across Europe. More recently, member countries have pledged to keep their budget deficits even smaller than called for in the Maastricht criteria, to preclude a return to profligacy.

Second, the advent of the euro has spurred a wave of merger and acquisition activity in Europe, which will, hopefully, improve the competitiveness of many European industries. Finally, EMU has also given birth to a truly pan-European corporate bond market, which now rivals that of the United States.

However, there are also concerns about how well suited EMU is to the existing structure of the European economies. For example, in 1999 and 2000 some economies at the periphery of Europe (Ireland, Spain, Portugal, and Finland) were growing much faster than the economies at the core (Germany and France). Interest rates in the peripheral countries should have risen substantially, so as to cool these economies down. At the same time, interest rates in the core countries should have risen much less, if at all. However, thanks to EMU, short-term interest rates across the member countries are identical; in other words most of Europe now has a "one size fits all" monetary policy. In the end, the ECB decided to raise interest rates only a little, thus running the risk that the smaller peripheral countries would overheat.

A related problem concerns asymmetric shocks. For example, what if a crisis in emerging markets hits Germany and Italy much harder than France? What should the European Central Bank do? In fact the ECB faced exactly this type of dilemma in early 1999. In a world of multiple, flexible exchange rates, the adjustment process would include the depreciation of the exchange rates in Germany and Italy. However, this ad-justment mechanism is no longer available to the 11 members of the EMU.

How do the regions of the United States—which also have a single currency—cope with asymmetric shocks? Consider a rise in oil prices that would hurt Massachusetts but boost the economy of Texas. The United States has two other adjustment mechanisms that help to equilibrate the impact of such asymmetric shocks. First, it has a well-developed system of federal fiscal transfers. As Massachusetts goes into a recession, residents there pay less taxes and receive more unemployment compensation and other federal benefits. The reverse is true in booming Texas. Thus, there is a transfer of funds from Texas to Massachusetts, cooling down the former and helping to boost the latter. Such a system of transfers does not exist in Europe. Second, as people lose jobs in Massachusetts, they often will move to other states (for example, Texas) where there are better job opportunities. This type of labor market flexibility also does not exist in Europe. Many economists are concerned that the next time Europe is hit by an asymmetric shock, the impact will be even higher unemployment (see Case Study 22.2) in the hardest hit countries. This could create severe social and political tensions within EMU.

The launch of the euro was unquestionably successful. However, the new currency has yet to be put to the test.

economists, it was partly because a number of governments sold dollars and bought other currencies in order to bring down the dollar's value. In other words, there was some coordination of major governments' policies to try to reduce the value of the dollar. During the early 1990s, the dollar moved within a much narrower band relative to other currencies, compared to the 1980s. However, thanks in large part to the emerging markets crisis, the dollar staged a minirally in the late 1990s. However, the strength of the dollar contributed to a deterioration of the U.S. trade deficit to record levels. In time, this will put downward pressure on the dollar, in the same way that it did in the late 1980s.

SHOULD THE VALUE OF THE DOLLAR BE STABILIZED?

According to some economists, like John Williamson of the Institute for International Economics, governments should do more to stabilize the value of the dollar. They argue that governments should buy and sell currencies so as to keep exchange rates within certain *target zones,* as well as coordinate monetary and fiscal policies. Under the Louvre accord of 1987, the biggest countries tried to stabilize their currencies within certain ranges that were agreed on, but these ranges were not published as formal targets. In late 1987, when the U.S. government objected to the policies of some of the other countries, it ignored this accord and permitted the dollar to drop.

Other economists, like Harvard's Martin Feldstein, feel that it would be a mistake to try to stabilize the value of the dollar. In their view, attempts of this sort would mean that monetary and fiscal policies would have to be diverted from their proper roles, thus sacrificing the traditional goals of price stability and high employment. And if the value of the dollar were stabilized, it "would mean harmful distortions in the balance of trade and in the international flow of capital."[2]

Although flexible exchange rates have been in operation for almost 30 years, the truth is that a clear assessment of their success—or lack of it—is hard to make because we don't know what would have occurred if some other system of exchange rates had been adopted. Clearly, flexible rates have not lived up to the claims of some of their proponents, but neither have they been as disastrous as some of their opponents claimed. So far, they've enabled us to muddle through, although not without substantial problems.

REVIEW AND PRACTICE

■ SUMMARY

1 An important difference between international business transactions and business transactions within a country is that international business transactions involve more than one currency. The exchange rate is the number of units of one currency that exchanges for a unit of another currency.

2 Under a system of flexible exchange rates, the market for foreign exchange functions like any other free market, where the exchange rate is determined by supply and demand. Under such a system, exchange rates tend to move in a way that removes imbalances among countries in exports and imports. The price of a country's currency tends to fall (rise) if its inflation rate and growth rate are relatively high (low) or if its interest rate is relatively low (high).

3 Until 1973, when exchange rates became more flexible, most exchange rates were fixed by government action and international agreement; exchange rates were allowed to vary slightly, but only slightly, about the official rate.

4 If exchange rates are fixed, the amount of a foreign currency demanded may not equal the amount supplied. To maintain exchange rates at the official levels, governments enter the market and buy and sell their currencies as needed. They also intervene by curbing imports, limiting foreign travel, and other measures.

5 Under a system of fixed exchange rates, a country will have a balance-of-payments deficit if its currency is overvalued and a balance-of-payments surplus if its currency is undervalued. A balance-of-payments deficit is the difference between the quantity supplied

[2]M. Feldstein, "The Case against Trying to Stabilize the Dollar," *American Economic Review*, May 1989.

and the quantity demanded of the currency. A balance-of-payments surplus is the difference between the quantity demanded and quantity supplied of the currency.

6 In recent years, variations in exchange rates, some of which were erratic and without fundamental economic significance, have made international transactions more difficult. Although there is no indication that flexible exchange rates will be forsaken, some observers feel that central banks should intervene to a greater extent to influence exchange rates.

■ PROBLEMS AND QUESTIONS

1 Suppose that the quantity of Japanese yen demanded at each price (in dollars) of a yen is as follows:

QUANTITY DEMANDED (BILLIONS OF YEN)	PRICE OF A YEN (IN DOLLARS)
20	.007
15	.008
10	.009
5	.01

Plot this demand curve on a graph. What sorts of groups, organizations, and individuals are part of the demand side of this market?

2 Suppose that the quantity of Japanese yen supplied at each price (in dollars) of a yen is as follows:

QUANTITY SUPPLIED (BILLIONS OF YEN)	PRICE OF A YEN (IN DOLLARS)
8	.007
9	.008
10	.009
11	.01

Plot this supply curve on the same graph as the demand curve in question 1. What sorts of groups, organizations, and individuals are part of the supply side of this market?

3 On the basis of the information in questions 1 and 2, what is the equilibrium value of the exchange rate if it is completely flexible? Why? Is the exchange rate between the U.S. dollar and the Japanese yen completely flexible at present?

4 Suppose that the exchange rate is fixed and that the price (in dollars) of a yen is set at $.008. On the basis of the data in questions 1 and 2, will the quantity of yen demanded equal the quantity supplied? What sorts of government actions will have to be taken?

5 During the 1950s and 1960s, the British government reacted to deficits in its balance of payments by adopting deflationary monetary and fiscal policies (temporarily at least). Was this sensible? Why or why not?

6 Under what circumstances would you be willing to invest $10,000 (if you had $10,000) in (a) El Salvador, (b) Poland, (c) Japan, and (d) India? What interest rate would you expect? What guarantees would you expect? Why?

7 "Under flexible exchange rates, reserves play a much less important role than under fixed exchange rates." What does this mean? Do you agree? Why or why not?

8 Country X has been confronted with a balance-of-payments deficit. Explain how it can eliminate this deficit by (a) changing its exchange rate, (b) changing its price level, and (c) adopting controls.

■ KEY TERMS

exchange rate	depreciation
gold standard	fixed exchange rates
flexible exchange rates	balance-of-payments deficit
appreciation	balance-of-payments surplus

■ VIEWPOINT FOR ANALYSIS

On December 15, 1999, in an op ed piece in the *Financial Times*, Connie Mack, U.S. senator from Florida and chairwoman of the Joint Economic Committee, wrote: "The world economy is becoming a single market. As such, the existence of more than 150 different national currencies makes less and less economic sense. The instability caused by having so many currencies is one of the reasons there is growing interest in official dollarization, whereby emerging market countries abolish their own currencies and adopt the U.S. dollar as legal tender."*

(a) What are the advantages of dollarization?

(b) What do countries give up when they adopt the dollar as legal tender?

(c) Under what circumstances would the advantages of dollarization outweigh the disadvantages?

---

*"Time to Reap the Dollar's Rewards," *Financial Times*, December 16, 1999, p. 15.

Globalization: Should We Fear It or Embrace It?

When the World Trade Organization (WTO) planned a ministerial meeting in Seattle for late November of 1999 to discuss further liberalization of world trade, no one could have guessed that the WTO and the Seattle meeting would become lightning rods for a vast array of groups opposed to globalization. Alternately called the "Debacle in Seattle" and the "Carnival against Capitalism," the demonstrations around the WTO meeting (which at one point turned violent) were planned by 500-odd organizations that ranged from the AFL-CIO to the Sierra Club to Raging Grannies. Participants carried placards that read "WTO Kills People—Kill the WTO," "WTO Breeds Greed, "and "Free Trade = Dead Sea Turtles."

What is it about globalization that triggers such strong reactions?

Globalization refers to the closer integration of the world economy through the flows of good, services, capital, and labor across borders. This is not a new phenomenon. In the late nineteenth century, the world economy, by some measures, was as integrated as it is today. Both trade and capital flows, as a share of GDP, were close to where they are at the beginning of the twenty-first century.

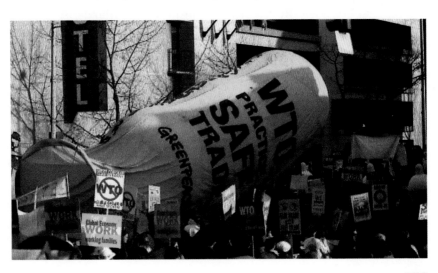

Protests led to riots in Seattle during the WTO Conference in November 1999.

This earlier incarnation of globalization was propelled by the advent of the steamship and the telegraph.

Unfortunately, two world wars and the Great Depression brought about a damaging reversal of global integration. It has taken the past fifty years for trade and capital flows to regain their pre–World War I prominence in the global economic landscape. This time around, the driving forces have been the twin revolutions in telecommunications and information technology, along with a concerted effort by governments (through organizations such as the WTO) to reduce barriers to trade. In some respects, globalization is more widespread now than it was a hundred years ago. More countries are participating today, including a large number of emerging markets. Also, globalization has spread beyond goods to services, information technology, retail trade, and even public utilities.

Proponents of globalization argue that by enabling a greater international division of labor and a more efficient allocation of savings, the integration of product and capital markets raises productivity and average living standards. Likewise, broader access to foreign products allows consumers to enjoy a wider range of goods and services at lower cost. Indeed, the past fifty years have been the most economically dynamic and prosperous in human history. International trade has been one of the engines of this wealth creation. Since the 1950s, world trade has grown about three times as fast as output. In the past couple of decades, foreign direct investment has grown at an even faster pace.

One compelling way to see the wealth-creating power of globalization is to compare the development, over the past fifty years of West Germany, South Korea, and Taiwan, on the one hand, and East Germany, North Korea, and China on the other. At the end of World War II, each pair of countries had similar living standards. By the 1980s the living standards in the former, more-globalized countries were three to five times higher than in the latter, more economically isolated, group. This huge disparity was an important factor behind the collapse of Communism and the eventual reintegration of both China and East Germany into the global economy. Since the late 1980s, many emerging markets have joined the globalization bandwagon by unilaterally opening up their economies to trade and investments. It is ironic that while demonstrators (mostly from developed countries) marched in Seattle, delegates from many emerging markets (including China) were applying to join the WTO.

Opponents of globalization raise a number of concerns that merit discussion. The first and most visceral is that globalization destroys jobs. However, trade and globalization create more jobs than they destroy (see Case Study 27.2). In fact, globalization creates better (higher productivity) jobs precisely because the free flows of goods and capital improve the allocation of resources and economic efficiency. During the rapid globalization of the 1990s the United States was successful in creating tens of millions of high quality jobs. Many of these were in the software and financial service industries, which are among the most global and least-protected sectors of the U.S. eonomy.

A related concern is that globalization worsens the distribution of income through the destruction of low-skilled jobs in industrialized economies, as those jobs migrate to emerging markets. It is true that in the last twenty years the income disparity between workers with only a high school education and those with (at least) a college degree has widened dramatically. However, this has much more to do with the revolution in information technology than with globalization. Recent studies show that the impact of technology on jobs is three times more powerful than the combined impacts of trade and immigration. The solution to this concern is not to slow globalization but to invest more in education and skills training.

Some opponents of globalization worry that the distribution of income worldwide has also become more unequal. This concern is justified, however, not because globalization has gone too far but because it has not gone far enough. The fastest-growing countries in the last two decades—mostly in Asia—are also the ones that have become the most globalized. The laggards are the countries that have been less integrated into the world economy.

Similarly, those against globalization are concerned that multinational corporations are exploiting low-cost workers in emerging markets. This concern is misguided on two counts. First, multinationals usually employ high-skilled workers, providing them with training and better job opportunities. Second, the lowest-cost workers are usually in the rural areas of emerging markets, where subsistence farming and child labor are the norm. For these people, the choice is not between a good job and a bad job (or working and going to school in the case of children) but between any work and starvation. Here again, the solution to this problem is not to slow globalization but to accelerate it so that these countries can become wealthier and can afford to improve the lives of all their people (through better education, better health care, and so on). In the last twenty years the levels of poverty in both China and India have fallen dramatically as both countries have embraced more open and export oriented development strategies.

Environmentalists opposed to globalization are afraid that emerging markets have lower environmental standards than industrialized countries and, therefore, trade with these countries will worsen the global environment and kill off dolphins (Case Study 21.3), turtles, and various endangered species. There are many problems with this line of thinking, as well intentioned as it may be. First, many emerging markets do put rising living standards before environmental concerns and resent having the environmental standards of industrialized countries imposed on them. There is nothing inherently wrong with this. Why should emerging markets not have the opportunity to industrialize (and pollute) as the United States and Europe did 100 years ago? Second, greater prosperity is the best way to improve both working conditions and environmental conditions. As countries develop and the basic needs of people for food, shelter, and health are met, environmental awareness also improves.

In the end globalization turns out to be one of the most effective ways to improve living standards worldwide. The challenge is not to slow or to stop this process but to help those that have been left behind and to make sure that the gains from globalization are distributed more evenly.

■ QUESTIONS

1 What groups benefit from globalization?

2 What groups are hurt by it?

3 How can the beneficiaries compensate the losers?

Glossary

absolute advantage the ability of one country to produce a commodity more cheaply than another country

adaptive expectations a situation where people change their forecasts of the variable in question to conform to its current level

aggregate demand curve a curve, sloping downward to the right, that shows the level of real national output that will be demanded at various economywide price levels

aggregate production function the relationship between the amount used of each of the inputs available in the economy and the resulting amount of potential output, that is, the most output that existing technology permits the economy to produce from various quantities of all available inputs

aggregate supply curve a curve, sloping upward to the right, that shows the level of real national output that will be supplied at various economywide price levels

alternative cost the value of what certain resources could have produced had they been used in the best alternative way; also called **opportunity cost**

American Federation of Labor–Congress of Industrial Organizations (AFL-CIO) a federation of national labor unions formed in 1955 by the merger between the American Federation of Labor (originally a federation of unions organized along craft lines) and the Congress of Industrial Organizations (originally a federation of unions organized along industrial lines)

antitrust laws legislation (such as the Sherman Act, the Clayton Act, and the Federal Trade Commission Act) intended to promote competition and control monopoly

appreciation of currency an increase in the value of one currency relative to another

automatic stabilizers structural features of the economy that tend by themselves to stabilize national output, without the help of legislation or government policy measures

average fixed cost the firm's total fixed cost divided by its output

average product of an input total output divided by the amount of input used to produce this amount of output

average product of labor total output per unit of labor

average propensity to consume the fraction of disposable income that is spent on consumption; equal to personal consumption expenditure divided by disposable income

average total cost the firm's total cost divided by its output;

equal to average fixed cost plus average variable cost

average variable cost the firm's total variable cost divided by its output

backward-bending supply curve for labor a supply curve for labor inputs showing that beyond some point, increases in price may result in the supply of smaller amounts of labor

balance-of-payments deficit the difference between the quantity supplied and the quantity demanded of a currency when the currency is overvalued (that is, priced above its equilibrium price)

balance-of-payments surplus the difference between the quantity demanded and the quantity supplied of a currency when the currency is undervalued (that is, priced below its equilibrium price)

balanced budget a budget in which tax revenues equal government expenditures

barometric firm in an oligopolistic industry, any single firm that is the first to make changes in prices, which are then generally accepted by other firms

base year a year chosen as a reference point for comparison with some later or earlier year

budget a statement of the government's expenditures and tax revenues for a fiscal year

budget deficit the amount by which tax revenues fall short of government expenditures

budget surplus the amount by which tax revenues exceed government expenditures

business cycle the cyclical fluctuations in national output over time

$C + I + G + (X - M_f)$ **line** a curve showing total intended spending (the sum of intended consumption expenditure, investment expenditure, government expenditure, and net exports) at various levels of gross domestic product

capital resources (such as factory buildings, equipment, raw materials, and inventories) that are created within the economic system for the purpose of producing other goods

capital consumption allowance the value of the capital (that is, the plant, equipment, and structures) that is worn out in a year; also called **depreciation**

capital formation investment in plant and equipment

capital goods output consisting of plant and equipment that are used to make other goods

capital-output ratio the ratio of the total capital stock to annual national output

capitalism an economic system characterized by private ownership of the tools of production, freedom of choice and of enterprise whereby consumers and firms can pursue their own self-interest, competition for sales among producers and resource owners, and reliance on the free market

capitalization of assets a method of computing the value of an asset by calculating the present value of the expected future income this asset will produce

cartel an open formal collusive arrangement among firms

central bank a government-established agency that controls the supply of money and supervises the country's commercial banks; the central bank of the United States is the Federal Reserve

checkoff a system whereby an

employer deducts union dues from each worker's pay and hands them over to the union

closed shop a situation where firms can hire only workers who are already union members

collective bargaining a process of negotiation between union and management over wages and working conditions

collusion a covert arrangement whereby firms agree on price and output levels in order to decrease competition and increase profits

commercial banks financial institutions that hold demand and other checkable deposits and permit checks to be written on them, and lend money to firms and individuals

comparative advantage the law that states that a country should produce and export goods which it can produce at *relatively* lower costs than other countries

compensation of employees the wages and salaries paid by firms and government agencies to the suppliers of labor, including supplementary payments for employee benefits (such as payments into public and private pension and welfare funds)

complements commodities that tend to be consumed together, that is, commodities with a negative cross elasticity of demand such that a decrease in the price of one will result in an increase in the quantity demanded of the other

constant dollar amounts amounts measured in base-year dollars (that is, according to the purchasing power of the dollar in some earlier year), in order to express value in a way that corrects for changes in the price level

constant returns to scale a long-run situation where, if the firm increases the amount of all inputs by the same proportion, output increases by the same proportion as each of the inputs

consumer an individual or household that purchases the goods and services produced by the economic system

consumer goods output consisting of items that consumers purchase, such as clothing, food, and drink

Consumer Price Index a measure of U.S. inflation, calculated by the Bureau of Labor Statistics, originally intended to measure changes in the prices of goods and services purchased by urban wage earners and clerical workers; expanded in 1978 to cover all urban consumers

consumption function the relationship between consumption spending and disposable income, that is, the amount of consumption expenditure that will occur at various levels of disposable income

corporate profits the net income of corporations (corporate profits before income taxes), including dividends received by the stockholders, retained earnings, and the amount paid by corporations as income taxes

corporation a fictitious legal person separate and distinct from the stockholders who own it, governed by a board of directors elected by the stockholders

cost function the relationship between cost and a firm's level of output, that is, what a firm's costs will be at various levels of output

Council of Economic Advisers a group established by the Employment Act of 1946, whose function is to help the president formulate and assess the economic policies of the government

craft union a labor union that

665

includes workers in a particular craft (such as machinists or carpenters)

creeping inflation an increase in the general price level of a few percent per year that gradually erodes the value of money

cross elasticity of demand the percentage change in the quantity demanded of one commodity resulting from a 1 percent change in the price of another commodity; may be either positive or negative

crowding-out effect the tendency for an increase in public sector expenditure to result in a cut in private-sector expenditure

crude quantity theory of money and prices the theory that if the velocity of circulation of money remains constant and real gross domestic product remains fixed at its full-employment level, it follows from the equation of exchange $(MV = PQ)$ that the price level will be proportional to the money supply

cyclical unemployment joblessness that occurs because of business fluctuations

decreasing returns to scale a long-run situation where, if the firm increases the amount of all inputs by the same proportion, output increases by a smaller proportion than each of the inputs

deflating the conversion of values expressed in current dollars into values expressed in constant dollars, in order to correct for changes in the price level

demand curve for loanable funds a curve showing the quantity of loanable funds that will be demanded at each interest rate

demand curve for money a curve representing the quantity of money that will be demanded at various interest rates (holding constant real GDP and the price level)

demand deposits checking accounts; bank deposits subject to payment on demand

demand-side inflation an increase in the general price level that occurs because of rightward shifts of the aggregate demand curve. There is too much aggregate spending, too much money chasing too few goods

depreciation the value of the capital (that is, plant, equipment, and structures) that is worn out in a year; also called **capital consumption allowance**

depreciation of currency a decrease in the value of one currency relative to another

depression a period when national output is well below its potential (full-employment) level; a severe recession

derived demand demand for labor and other inputs not as ends in themselves but as means to produce other things

devaluation of currency under the gold standard, a decrease in the value of a currency as a consequence of an increase in the price of gold

differentiated oligopoly a market structure (such as those for automobiles and machinery) where there are only a few sellers of somewhat different products

diffusion process the process by which the use of an innovation spreads from firm to firm and from use to use

direct regulation government issue of enforceable rules concerning the conduct of firms

discount rate the interest rate the Federal Reserve charges for loans to commercial banks

discretionary policy policy that

is formulated at the discretion of the policymakers (in contrast to rigid policy rules or feedback policy rules)

disposable income the total amount of income people receive after taxes

dominant firm in an oligopolistic industry, a single large firm that sets the price for the industry but lets the small firms sell all they want at that price

easy monetary policy a monetary policy that increases the money supply and reduces interest rates

economic profits the excess of a firm's profits over what it could make in other industries

economic resources resources that are scarce and thus command a nonzero price

economics the study of how resources are allocated among alternative uses to satisfy human wants

economies of scale efficiencies that result from carrying out a process (such as production or sales) on a large scale

effluent fee a fee that a polluter must pay to the government for discharging waste

emerging markets (economies) economies that are either in the early stages of development or in a state of economic transition (the former Commuist bloc countries); also known as developing economies

equation of exchange a way of restating the definition of the velocity of circulation of money, such that the amount received for the final goods and services during a period equals the amount spent on those final goods and services during the same period (that is, $MV = PQ$)

equilibrium a situation in which there is no tendency for change

equilibrium level of gross domestic product the value of national output at which the flow of income generated by this level of output results in a level of spending precisely sufficient to buy this level of output

equilibrium price a price that shows no tendency for change, because it is the price at which the quantity demanded equals the quantity supplied; the price toward which the actual price of a good always tends to move

exchange rate the number of units of one currency that can purchase a unit of another currency

excise tax a tax imposed on each unit sold of a particular product, such as cigarettes or liquor

expansion the phase in the business cycle after the trough during which national output rises

explicit cost the cost of resources for which there is an explicit payment

exports the goods and services that a country sells to other countries

external diseconomy a situation that occurs when consumption or production by one person or firm results in uncompensated costs to another person or firm

external economy a situation that occurs when consumption or production by one person or firm results in uncompensated benefits to another person or firm

externalities external economies and diseconomies

featherbedding a practice whereby a union restricts output per worker in order to increase the amount of labor required to do a certain job

Federal Open Market Committee (FOMC) a group, composed of the seven members of the Federal Reserve Board plus five presidents of Federal Reserve Banks, which makes decisions concerning the purchase and sale of government securities, in order to control bank reserves and the money supply

Federal Reserve Board the Board of Governors of the Federal Reserve System, composed of seven members appointed by the president for 14-year terms, whose function is to promote the nation's economic welfare by supervising the operations of the U.S. money and banking system

Federal Reserve System a system established by Congress in 1913 that includes commercial banks, the 12 Federal Reserve Banks, and the Board of Governors of the Federal Reserve System

feedback policy rule a rule allowing the behavior of the variable governed by the policy rule to change, depending on future circumstances

final goods and services goods and services that are destined for the ultimate user (such as flour purchased for family consumption)

firm an organization that produces a good or service for sale in an attempt to make a profit

firm's demand curve for labor a curve showing the relationship between the price of labor and the amount of labor demanded by a firm, that is, the amount of labor that will be demanded by a firm at various wage rates

firm's supply curve a curve, usually sloping upward to the right, showing the quantity of output a firm will produce at each price

fiscal policy the policy of the government regarding taxes and government expenditures to stabilize the economy

fixed input a resource used in the production process (such as plant and equipment) whose quantity cannot be changed during the particular period under consideration

food programs federal antipoverty programs that distribute food to the poor, either directly from surpluses produced by farm programs or indirectly via stamps that can be exchanged for food

45-degree line a line that contains all points where the amount on the horizontal axis equals the amount on the vertical axis

fractional-reserve banking the practice whereby banks hold less cash than the amount they owe their depositors

free resources resources (such as air) that are so abundant that they can be obtained without charge

frictional unemployment temporary joblessness, such as that occurring among people who have quit jobs, people looking for their first job, and seasonal workers

full employment the minimum level of joblessness that the economy could achieve without undesirably high inflation, recognizing that there will always be some frictional and structural unemployment

game a competitive situation where two or more players pursue their own interests, no player can dictate the outcome, and all players are mutually aware

gold-exchange standard an exchange rate system developed after World War II, under which the dollar was directly convertible into gold at a fixed price, and other currencies, since they could be converted into dollars at fixed exchange rates, were thus indirectly convertible into gold at a fixed price

gold standard a method of exchange rate determination prevailing until the 1930s, under which currencies were convertible into a certain amount of gold

government purchases federal, state, and local government spending on final goods and services, excluding transfer payments

gross domestic product (GDP) the value of the total amount of final goods and services produced by the economy during a period of time; measured either by the expenditure on the final goods and services or by the income generated by the output

gross private domestic investment all additions to a country's stock of private investment goods, that is, all investment spending, including purchases of tools, equipment, and machinery, all construction expenditures, and the change in total inventories

historical cost of assets what a firm actually paid for its assets

implicit contracts agreements between workers and firms that are not found in any formal, written contracts

implicit cost the cost (for which there is no explicit payment) of the resources that are provided by the owners of a firm, measured by what these resources could bring if they were used in their best alternative employment

imports the goods and services that a country buys from other countries

income elasticity of demand the percentage change in the quantity demanded of a commodity resulting from a 1 percent increase in total money income (all prices being held constant)

income tax a federal, state, or local tax imposed on personal income and corporate profits

incomes policy a policy to control inflation that sets some targets for wages and prices in the economy as a whole, gives particular firms and industries detailed guides for making wage and price decisions, and provides some inducements for firms and unions to follow these guidelines

increasing returns to scale a long-run situation where if a firm increases the amount of all inputs by the same proportion, output increases by a larger proportion than each of the inputs

indirect business taxes taxes (such as general sales taxes, excise taxes, and customs duties) that are imposed not directly on the business itself but on its products or services, and hence are treated by firms as costs of production

individual demand curve a curve showing the relationship between individual consumer demand for a good and its price, that is, how much of a good an individual consumer will demand at various prices

industrial union a labor union that includes all the workers in a particular plant or industry (such as autos or steel)

inflation an increase in the general level of prices economywide

inflationary gap a positive gap between actual and potential output

innovation the first commercial application of a new technology

innovator a firm that is first to apply a new technology

input any resource used in the production process

interest the payment of money by borrowers to suppliers of money capital

interest rate the annual amount that a borrower must pay for the use of a dollar for a year

intermediate good a good that is not sold to the ultimate user but is used as an input in producing final goods and services (such as flour to be used in manufacturing bread)

Keynesians economists who share many of the beliefs of John Maynard Keynes. His principal tenet was that a capitalist system does not automatically tend toward a full-employment equilibrium (due in part to the rigidity of wages). Keynesians tend to believe that a free-enterprise economy has weak self-regulating mechanisms that should be supplemented by activist fiscal (and other) policies.

labor human effort, both physical and mental, used to produce goods and services

labor force the number of people employed plus the number of those unemployed (actively looking for work and willing to take a job if one were offered)

labor productivity the amount of output divided by the number of units of labor employed

Laffer curve a curve representing the relationship between the amount of income tax revenue collected by the government and the marginal tax rate, that is, how much revenue will be collected at various marginal tax rates

land natural resources, including minerals as well as plots of ground, used to produce goods and services

law of diminishing marginal returns the principle that if equal increments of a given input are added (the quantities of other inputs being held constant), the resulting increments of product obtained from the extra unit of input (the marginal product) will begin to decrease beyond some point

law of diminishing marginal utility the principle that if a person consumes additional units of a given commodity (the consumption of other commodities being held constant), the resulting increments of utility derived from the extra unit of the commodity (the marginal utility) will begin to decrease beyond some point

law of increasing costs the principle that as more and more of a good is produced, the production of each additional unit of the good is likely to entail a larger and larger opportunity cost

legal reserve requirements regulations, imposed by the Federal Reserve System in order to control the money supply, requiring banks (and other institutions) to hold a certain fraction of deposits as cash reserves

liabilities the debts of a firm

loanable funds funds (including those supplied by households and firms that find the rate of interest high enough to get them to save) that are available for borrowing by consumers, businesses, and government

long run the period of time during which all a firm's inputs are variable, that is, during which the firm could completely change the resources used in the production process

long-run average cost function the minimum average cost of producing various output levels when any desired type or scale of plant can be built

M1 narrowly defined money supply, which includes coins, currency, demand deposits, and other checkable deposits

M2 broadly defined money supply, which includes savings deposits, small time deposits, money market mutual fund balances, and money market deposit accounts, as well as the components of the narrowly defined money supply, M1 (coins, currency, demand deposits, and other checkable deposits)

marginal cost the addition to total cost resulting from the addition of the last unit of output

marginal product of an input the addition to total output that results from the addition of an extra unit of input (the quantities of all other inputs being held constant)

marginal product of labor the additional output resulting from the addition of an extra unit of labor

marginal propensity to consume the fraction of an extra dollar of disposable income that is spent on consumption

marginal propensity to save the fraction of an extra dollar of disposable income that is saved

marginal revenue the addition to total revenue that results from the addition of one unit to the quantity sold

marginal tax rate the proportion of an extra dollar of income that must be paid in taxes

marginal utility the additional satisfaction derived from consuming an additional unit of a commodity

market a group of firms and individuals that are in touch with each other in order to buy or sell some good or service

market demand curve a curve, usually sloping downward to the right, showing the relationship between a product's price and the quantity demanded of the product

market demand curve for labor a curve showing the relationship between the price of labor and the total amount of labor demanded in the market

market structure the type or organization of a market, determined by the number and size of buyers and sellers in the market, the ease with which new firms can enter, the extent of product differentiation, and other factors

market supply curve a curve, usually sloping upward to the right, showing the relationship between a product's price and the quantity supplied of the product

market supply curve for labor a curve showing the relationship between the price of labor and the total amount of labor supplied in the market

Medicaid a federal program that pays for the health care of the poor

Medicare a compulsory hospitalization program plus a voluntary insurance plan for doctors' fees for people over 65, included in the Social Security program

menu cost a cost incurred when a firm changes its price

model a theory composed of assumptions that simplify and abstract from reality, from which conclusions or predictions about the real world are deduced

monetarists economists generally sharing the belief that business cycle fluctuations are due largely to changes in the money supply. Many monetarists think that a free-enterprise economy has effective self-regulating mechanisms that activist fiscal and monetary policies tend to disrupt. Some monetarists, like Milton Friedman, advocate a rule for stable growth in the money supply of 3 to 5 percent per year.

monetary base the reserves of commercial banks plus currency outside the banks

monetary policy the exercise of the central bank's control over the quantity of money and the level of interest rates in order to promote the objectives of national economic policy

money anything that serves as a medium of exchange and a standard and store of value; the unit in which the prices of goods and services are measured

money income income measured in current dollars (actual money amounts)

monopolistic competition a market structure in which there are many sellers of somewhat differentiated products, entry is easy, and there is no collusion among sellers. Retailing seems to have many of the characteristics of monopolistic competition

monopoly a market structure (such as those for public utilities) in which there is only one seller of a product

national debt the amount owed by the government. To cover the difference between expenditures and tax revenues, the government sells bonds, notes, and other forms of IOUs

natural monopoly an industry in which the average costs of producing the product reach a minimum at an output rate large enough to satisfy the entire market, so that competition among firms cannot be sustained and one firm becomes a monopolist

near-money assets (such as government bonds) that can be converted into cash, though not quite as easily as time and savings accounts

negative income tax a system whereby families with incomes below a certain break-even level would receive, rather than make, a government income tax payment

net exports the amount spent by foreigners on a country's goods and services (exports) minus the amount a country spends on foreign goods and services (imports)

network effects or **externalities** situations where the value of a product to one user increases with the number of other users

new classical macroeconomists a group, led by Robert Lucas, that believes that the government cannot use monetary and fiscal policies to close recessionary and inflationary gaps because, if firms and individuals formulate their expectations rationally, they will tend to frustrate the government's attempts to use activist stabilization policies

new Keynesians a group that believes, like the Keynesians, that prices and wages tend to be rigid in the short run (but in contrast to the Keynesians, has developed theories to explain why such wage and price stickiness can be expected)

nominal expressed in current dollars (actual money amounts)

normative economics economic propositions about what ought to be, or about what a person, organization, or country ought to do

old-age insurance benefits paid under the Social Security program to retired workers

oligopoly a market structure (such as those for autos and steel) in which there are only a few sellers of products that can be either identical or differentiated

open market operations the purchase and sale of U.S. government securities on the open market by the Federal Reserve in order to control the quantity of bank reserves

open shop a situation where a firm can hire both union and nonunion workers, with no requirement that nonunion workers ever join a union

opportunity cost the value of what certain resources could have produced had they been used in the best alternative way; also called **alternative cost**

overvaluation of currency the setting of a currency's price above the equilibrium price

parity the principle that farmers should be able to exchange a given quantity of farm output for the same quantity of nonfarm goods and services they would have been able to purchase at some point in the past; in effect, the principle that farm prices should increase at the same rate as the prices of the goods and services that farmers buy

partnership a form of business organization whereby two or more people agree to own and conduct a business, with each party contributing some proportion of the capital and/or labor and receiving some proportion of the profit or loss

peak the point in the business cycle where national output is highest relative to its potential (full-employment) level

perfect competition a market structure in which there are many sellers of identical products, no one seller or buyer has control over the price, entry is easy, and resources can switch readily from one use to another. Many agricultural markets have many of the characteristics of perfect competition.

personal consumption expenditures the spending by households on durable goods, nondurable goods, and services

Phillips curve a curve representing the relationship between the rate of increase in the price level and the level of unemployment

positive economics descriptive statements, propositions, and predictions about the economic world that are generally testable by an appeal to the facts

potential gross domestic product the total amount of goods and services that could have been produced had the economy been operating at full capacity or full employment

precautionary demand for money the demand for money because of uncertainty about the timing and size of future disbursements and receipts

price discrimination the practice whereby one buyer is charged more than another buyer for the same product

price elastic the demand for a good if its price elasticity of demand is greater than 1

price elasticity of demand the percentage change in quantity demanded resulting from a 1 percent change in price; by convention, always expressed as a positive number

price elasticity of supply the percentage change in quantity supplied resulting from a 1 percent change in price

price index the ratio of the value of a set of goods and services in current dollars to the value of the same set of goods and services in constant dollars

price inelastic the demand for a good if its price elasticity of demand is less than 1

price leader in an oligopolistic industry, a firm that sets a price that other firms are willing to follow

price supports price floors imposed by the government on a certain good

price system a system under which every good and service has a price and which in a purely capitalistic economy carries out the basic functions of an economic system (determining what goods and services will be produced, how the output will be produced, how much of it each person will receive, and what the country's growth of per capita income will be)

private cost the price paid by the individual user for the use of a resource

product differentiation the process by which producers create real or apparent differences between products that perform the same general function

product group a group of firms that produce similar products that are fairly close substitutes for one another

product market a market where products are bought and sold

production function the rela-tionship between the quantities of various inputs used per period of time and the maximum quantity of output that can be produced per period of time, that is, the most output that existing technology permits the firm to produce from various quantities of inputs

production possibilities curve a curve showing the combinations of amounts of various goods that a society can produce with given (fixed) amounts of resources

profit the difference between a firm's revenue and its costs

progressive tax a tax whereby the rich pay a larger proportion of their income for the tax than do the poor

prohibitive tariff a tariff so high that it prevents imports of a good

property tax a tax imposed on real estate and/or other property

proprietors' income the net income of unincorporated businesses (proprietorships and partnerships)

proprietorship a firm owned by a single individual

prosperity a period when national output is close to its potential (full-employment) level

public goods goods and services which can be consumed by one person without diminishing the amount of them that others can consume and which there is no way to prevent citizens from consuming, whether they pay for them or not

public sector the government sector of the economy

pure oligopoly a market structure (like those for steel, cement, tin cans, and petroleum) in which there are only a few sellers of an identical product

pure rate of interest the interest rate on a riskless loan

quota a limit imposed on the amount of a commodity that can be imported annually

rate of return the annual profit per dollar invested that businesses can obtain by building new structures, adding new equipment, or increasing their inventories; the interest rate earned on the investment in a particular asset

rational expectations expectations that are correct on the average (forecasting errors are random); the forecaster makes the best possible use of whatever information is available

real expressed in constant dollars

real business cycle models theories asserting that business fluctuations are due predominantly to shifts in the aggregate supply curve resulting from new technology, good or bad weather, and so on

real income income measured in constant dollars (that is, the amount of goods and services that can be bought with the income)

recession the phase in the business cycle after the peak, during which national output falls

recessionary gap a negative gap between actual and potential output

regressive tax a tax whereby the rich pay a smaller proportion of their income for the tax than do the poor

rent in the context of Chapter 23, the return derived from an input that is fixed in supply

reproduction cost of assets what the firm would have to pay to replace its assets

resource market a market where resources are bought and sold

resources inputs used to produce goods and services

retained earnings the total amount of profit that the stockholders of a corporation have reinvested in the business, rather than withdrawing as dividends

rigid policy rule a rule specifying completely the behavior of the variable governed by the policy rule (for example, Milton Friedman's suggestion that the money supply be set so that it grows at a fixed, agreed-on rate)

rule of reason the principle that not all trusts but only unreasonable combinations in restraint of trade require conviction under the antitrust laws

runaway inflation a very rapid increase in the general price level that wipes out practically all the value of money

sales tax a tax imposed on the goods consumers buy (with the exception, in some states, of food and medical care)

saving the process by which people give up a claim on present consumption goods in order to receive consumption goods in the future

saving function the relationship between total saving and disposable income, that is, the total amount of saving that will occur at various levels of disposable income

Say's law the principle that the production of a certain amount of goods and services results in the generation of an amount of income precisely sufficient to buy that output

short run in the context of Chapters 15 to 20, the period during which at least one of a firm's inputs (generally its plant and equipment) is fixed

Social Security a program that imposes taxes on wage earners and employers and provides old-age, survivors', disability, and medical benefits to workers covered under the Social Security Act

stagflation a simultaneous combination of high unemployment and high inflation

structural deficit the difference between government expenditures and tax revenues that would result if gross domestic product were at its potential, not its actual, level

structural unemployment joblessness that occurs when new goods or new technologies call for new skills, and workers with older skills cannot find jobs

substitutes commodities with a positive cross elasticity of demand (a decrease in the price of one commodity will result in a decrease in the quantity demanded of the other commodity)

supply curve for loanable funds a curve showing the relationship between the quantity of loanable funds supplied and the pure interest rate

supply-side economics a set of propositions concerned with influencing the aggregate supply curve through the use of financial incentives such as tax cuts

supply-side inflation inflation resulting from leftward shifts of the aggregate supply curve

tariff a tax imposed by the government on imported goods (designed to cut down on imports and thus protect domestic industry and workers from foreign competition)

tax avoidance legal steps taken by taxpayers to reduce their tax bill

tax evasion misreporting of income or other illegal steps taken by taxpayers to reduce their tax bills

technological change new methods of producing existing products, new designs that make it possible to produce new products, and new techniques of organization, marketing, and management

technology society's pool of knowledge concerning how goods and services can be produced from a given amount of resources

terms of trade the ratio of an index of export prices to an index of import prices

tight monetary policy a monetary policy that restrains or reduces the money supply and raises interest rates

total cost the sum of a firm's total fixed cost and total variable cost

total fixed cost a firm's total expenditure on fixed inputs per period of time

total revenue a firm's total dollar sales volume

total variable cost a firm's total expenditure on variable inputs per period of time

transactions demand for money the holding of money in cash or in checking accounts in order to pay for final goods and services

transferable emissions permit each permit allows the holder of the permit to generate a certain amount of pollution. These permits, limited in number, are sold by the government to the highest bidders at a price set by supply and demand.

transfer payments payments made by the government or private business to individuals who do not contribute to the production of goods and services in exchange for them

trough the point in the business cycle where national output is lowest relative to its potential (full-employment) level

tying contract the practice whereby buyers must purchase other items in order to get the product they want

undervaluation of currency the setting of a currency's price below the equilibrium price

unemployment according to the definition of the Bureau of Labor Statistics, joblessness among people who are actively looking for work and would take a job if one were offered

unemployment rate the number of people who are unemployed divided by the number of people in the labor force

union shop a situation where firms can hire nonunion workers who must then become union members within a certain length of time after being hired

unitary elasticity a price elasticity of demand equal to 1

utility a number representing the level of satisfaction that a consumer derives from a particular good or group of goods

value-added the amount of value added by a firm or industry to the total worth of a product

value of the marginal product of labor the marginal product of labor (the additional output resulting from the addition of an extra unit of labor) multiplied by the product's price

variable input a resource used in the production process (such as labor or raw material) whose quantity can be changed during the particular period under consideration

velocity of circulation of money rate at which the money supply is used to make transactions for final goods and services, that is, the average number of times per year that a dollar is used to buy the final goods and services produced. It equals nominal GDP divided by the money supply

wage and price controls limits imposed by the government on the amount by which wages and prices can rise, in order to reduce the inflation rate at a given unemployment rate

wage-price spiral a series of steps whereby higher wage demands by workers prompt firms to raise their prices to consumers; this in turn raises the general cost of living and prompts workers to make yet higher wage demands

wage rate the price of labor

Photo Credits

International Business Machines Corporation (4, 254); Bettmann/ Corbis (5, 30, 49, 101, 154, 206, 234, 278, 344, 433, 525, 527, 612, 649); Reuters NewMedia Inc./Corbis (7); Macgill Adams/Wilderness Alaska (19); Burlington Industries (24); Honda of America (25, 77); Warder Collection (26, 63, 99, 103, 105, 158, 176, 577); Sotheby's (52); U.S. Department of Agriculture (55); U.S. Department of Commerce (73); Bob Rowan, Progressive Image/Corbis (76); U.S. Navy, Department of Defense (80); Educational Film Center (109, 478); Philip James Corwin/Corbis (123); Photo Researchers, Inc. (133); U.S. Office of Management and Budget (153); Dwight D. Eisenhower Library (156); The Picture Group (172, 200, 374, 534, 632); AP/Wide World Photos (178, 236, 304, 459, 500, 592, 633, 651); U.S. Department of Treasury (183); Bill Ross/Corbis (188); Robert Maass/Corbis (193); The Bank of America (195); The Federal Reserve Board (203, 222); Magnum Photos (226); National Aeronautics and Space Administration (250); Pete Carmichael/The Image Bank (256); Jose Pelaez/The Stock Market, Inc. (258); James Marshall/Corbis (280); The Nasdaq Stock Market, Inc. (309); Internal Revenue Service (319); Ronald Reagan Library (322); Todd Haimann/Corbis (280); Joseph Sohm, Chromosohm Inc./Corbis (342); Philip Gould/Corbis (349); Todd Gipstein/Corbis (355); American Petroleum Institute (377, 481); State Historical Society of Wisconsin (404); Ric Ergenbright/Corbis (407); Wolfgang Kaehler/ Corbis (434); BP America, Inc. (451); Judy Griesedieck/Corbis (456); Richard Smith/Corbis (475); Supreme Court of the United States (483); U.S. Department of Justice (485); Minnesota Department of Natural Resources (492); Robert Visser/Greenpeace (495); Patrick Bennett/Corbis (503); United Auto Workers (518); Yahoo! Inc. (545); Los Angeles Dodgers, Inc. (551); Women in Community Service, Inc. (560); The White House (563); Jay Bruff (567); Pictor (571); Microsoft (589); The Henry Ford Museum (593); Tennessee Valley Authority (606); European Monetary Institute/European Central Bank (654); Keith Wood/Greenpeace (659).

Index